Steve Fallon

Hong Kong
& Macau

The Top Five

1 Star Ferry
Cross Victoria Harbour on one of these old workhorses (p291)

2 Temple Street Night Market
Nosh, live opera, fortune tellers and lots of cheap clothes (p94)

3 Tian Tan Buddha
Lantau's massive religious icon, especially from the Ngong Ping 360 cable car (p133)

4 The Peak Tram
The hair-raising funicular that will whisk you to the Peak (p302)

5 Lan Kwai Fong
Central's throbbing nightlife heart, where Chinese tourists watch you watch them watch you (p71)

Contents

Introducing Hong Kong	5
City Life	7
Arts	23
Food	33
History	49
Sights	63
Walking Tours	139
Eating	149
Entertainment	197
Activities	215
Shopping	227
Sleeping	249
Excursions	275
Transport	287
Directory	307
Macau	327
Language	379
Index	389
Map Section	403

Published by Lonely Planet Publications Pty Ltd
ABN 36 005 607 983

Australia Head Office, Locked Bag 1, Footscray,
Victoria 3011, ☎ 03 8379 8000, fax 03 8379 8111,
talk2us@lonelyplanet.com.au

USA 150 Linden St, Oakland, CA 94607,
☎ 510 893 8555, toll free 800 275 8555,
fax 510 893 8572, info@lonelyplanet.com

UK 72–82 Rosebery Ave, Clerkenwell, London,
EC1R 4RW, ☎ 020 7841 9000, fax 020 7841 9001,
go@lonelyplanet.co.uk

© Lonely Planet 2006
Photographs © Greg Elms and as listed (p386) 2005

Printed by SNP Security Printing Pte Ltd, Singapore

The Author

Steve Fallon

A native of Boston, Massachusetts, Steve graduated from Georgetown University with a Bachelor of Science in modern languages, including Chinese. After he had worked for several years for an American daily newspaper and earned a Master's Degree in journalism, his fascination with the 'new' Asia led him to Hong Kong, where he lived for over a dozen years, working for a variety of media and running his own travel bookshop. Steve lived in Budapest for 2½ years before moving to London in 1994, and returns to his 'hometown' of Hong Kong almost annually. He has written or contributed to more than two dozen Lonely Planet titles, including *China* and *Best of Hong Kong*.

PHOTOGRAPHER
Greg Elms

Greg completed a Bachelor of Arts in Photography at the Royal Melbourne Institute of Technology, then embarked on a travel odyssey across Australia, Southeast Asia, India, Africa, Europe and the Middle East. He has been photographer for numerous award-winning books, and has worked for magazines, ad agencies, designers and, of course, book publishers such as Lonely Planet.

STEVE'S TOP HONG KONG DAY

A tip-top night usually demands a tiptoe morning, but I need to hammer myself awake today. What better way than by having early dim sum at City Hall Maxim's Palace (p152)? Two hours (and as many Extra-Strength Tylenols) later, the tide is high and I'm not holding on; time to jump on the MTR and then the KCR West Rail for Yuen Long and the Mai Po Nature Reserve (p112). After communing with feathered friends – almost a species for every day of the year – I've half a mind to check out the new Hong Kong Wetland Park (p111). Instead I remain on the move, with the Light Rail taking me to Tuen Mun and the ferry bound for Tung Ching on Lantau. Before I know it, I'm on the Ngong Ping 360 cable car (p133), climbing upward for Ngong Ping village and the Tian Tan Buddha statue (p133). After devotions and devouring (at the vegetarian canteen, p195), I follow the Lantau Trail (p220) westward for a couple of kilometres (just to say I've done it); bus 1 (or 2 or 4, for that matter) on the Keung Shan Rd takes me to Mui Wo (p132). As luck would have it, there's an inter-island ferry at the pier waiting to take me to Cheung Chau and a seafood meal at one of the Praya St restaurants (p192). I'll catch a late-evening ferry back to Central and check out what's on at the Hong Kong Fringe Club (p152) before walking down memory lane at the Cavern (p211) in Lan Kwai Fong.

Introducing Hong Kong

It's mass-produced and handmade, frightfully old and as new as tomorrow. It's kitschy and tasteful, sometimes raunchy, often prissy. It's crowded and deafening, it's peaceful and deserted. It's all of these things and much, much more. It's Hong Kong – a place that simply shouldn't be but is.

Hong Kong is, for certain, like no other place on earth and, despite all the changes, setbacks and even triumphs since China resumed sovereignty in 1997, it remains a vibrant and exciting city in which to live and visit. Almost 7 million people call a territory of just over 1100 sq km home, but are squeezed on to only about 10% of the available land space. That means 14 million elbows and an equal number of buttocks all seeking standing or sitting room and all the problems that such scrambling brings with it – smog, odour, clutter and clatter.

Hong Kong means many different things to as many different people. For some it's the view from the Peak by day or Hong Kong Island's skyline by night as the spectacular lights of its immense towers dance in unison. For others it's a morning of dim sum, with dozens of bite-sized savouries to sample, or a Chinese banquet at night, with fewer but much more substantial dishes. And some people – hikers, birders, climbers or just lovers of the great outdoors – say nothing beats the Hong Kong countryside for its beauty, facilities and accessibility.

That's because Hong Kong has something to suit every taste and interest. Shoppers will trip over themselves trying to reach the huge malls of Central, Admiralty and Kowloon, the street-fashion factory outlets in Causeway Bay and Tsim Sha Tsui and the warehouse outlets of Ap Lei Chau. Fans of modern architecture will appreciate Hong Kong's arresting Central district; world-class museums abound for those who wish to dig deeper into local history and culture. Travellers with a sense of romance and adventure will jump aboard a tram or the Star Ferry simply for the journey.

Hong Kong has a surprising number of natural retreats, and for those who yearn to breathe free (or freer), sandy beaches and secluded but well-marked walks await. Much of Lantau Island, a short ferry ride away, is designated parkland. The New Territories cuts a huge swathe to the north and, while it is becoming increasingly urbanised, it still

LOWDOWN

Population 6.89 million

Time zone GMT + 8 hours

3-star double room From $700 to $1000

Coffee at a café bar From $20

Pint of beer From $35 ($25 at happy hour)

MTR ticket From $4 to $26 ($3.80 to $23.10 with an Octopus Card)

MTR stations 53 on seven lines

7 minutes Length of time it takes to cross Victoria Harbour on the Star Ferry from Central to Tsim Sha Tsui

45% Percentage increase in the number of visitors to Hong Kong from the mainland in 2004

No-nos Going topless, dispensing white flowers, betting on the number '4'

offers dramatic scenery, challenging hikes and one of the region's most important wetlands for birds.

Gastronomes will be spoiled for choice in the city's eclectic eateries, and not just when selecting Chinese and other Asian dishes; Hong Kong today is a veritable atlas of world food. Hong Kong's bars, pubs and clubs colour the spectrum, from the alternative and the chic to the oh-so-refined.

Within easy striking distance of Hong Kong is Macau, a charming, somewhat less commercial 'Special Autonomous Region' just an hour away by ferry that returned to Chinese rule in 1999 after some 450 years under Portuguese rule. The Portuguese legacy combined with things Chinese has created a unique 'Macanese' culture, and the pastel-coloured Catholic churches and civic buildings, narrow streets, traditional shops and splendid Portuguese and Macanese food give Macau more of a Mediterranean than southern Chinese feel. Today Macau brims not just with atmosphere but sights as well, and a host of unique museums make the territory much more than just a charming diversion from Hong Kong. What's more, the plethora of new casinos has turned what was once a sleepy backwater into the entertainment centre of the South China coast.

The two 'Special Economic Zones' just over the border in the mainland – the 'anything goes' cowboy town of Shenzhen and leafy Zhuhai, with just about anything you would want available – may not be world-class destinations on their own, but they offer an interesting contrast to their southern neighbours. Visiting them also gives travellers a glimpse at the direction in which China is heading in the early 21st century.

Hong Kong remains every bit the 'moveable feast' that Paris was to Hemingway. Arrive here with your eyes and ears open, your taste buds and olfactory senses primed, and your fingers at the ready in order to see and hear, taste, smell and touch the essence of Hong Kong and its Pearl River delta neighbours.

ESSENTIAL HONG KONG

- Chi Lin Nunnery (p98)
- Graham St Market (p157)
- Hong Kong Heritage Museum (p119)
- Lantau (p129)
- Mai Po Nature Reserve (p112)

City Life

Hong Kong Today   8

City Calendar   10

Culture   12
  Identity 12
  Lifestyle 14
  Fashion 16
  Sport 17
  Media 17
  Language 18

Economy & Costs   18

Government & Politics   19

Environment   20
  The Land 20
  Green Hong Kong 20
  Pollution Problems 21
  Urban Planning & Development 22

City Life

HONG KONG TODAY

'Hong Kong is like no other place in the world, where the East collides head on with the West' was a sentence we wrote some years back in an article that dealt with the territory as an exotic destination and the statement continues to be true today. Superlatives and clichés are – and always have been – acceptable to people in this, the world's largest Cantonese city.

As Hong Kong commences its 10th year of autonomy or self-government or whatever the 'one country, two systems' principle is actually supposed to mean (even China can not explain that one coherently), the territory is not without its problems and concerns. While some of them hail from outside its boundaries there are others that are very much self-inflicted.

The first concern, according to an opinion poll conducted by *HK Magazine,* is that of democracy – too little, of course (unless you belong to one of the pro-Beijing parties). It can often feel that the 'good fight' is being fought by such capable souls as the benign Martin Lee, the indefatigable Emily Lau, earnest Christine Loh and loopy Leung (Long Hair) Kwok-hung, who likes to wear Che Guevara T-shirts during Legislative Council sessions, but what is the point when the chief executive is not even elected by the people of Hong Kong but handpicked by the central government in Beijing?

The second biggest worry for Hong Kong people is pollution, especially of the air, and indignant fingers point to the mainland (particularly Shenzhen) for causing the mess. But a reality check reveals that half of the coal-powered plants in the Pearl River delta are financed and/or owned by Hong Kong companies as are many of the factories in Guangdong province.

Other concerns are health and poverty – almost 17% of the 3.5 million-strong workforce earns less than $6000 or US$780 a month – and that perennial Hong Kong worry: the cosy relationship between government and big business. In the latest illustration, a lucrative residential, office and retail development project in Pok Fu Lam called Cyberport was handed over to a single developer without open tender. Critics are very concerned that the government will go the same route with the ambitious cultural district planned for the 40-hectare reclaimed area of West Kowloon.

But these were not the only matters on people's minds. Several other issues – from the sublime to the truly subnormal – were keeping Hong Kong people awake at night – a not insignificant irritant for a population that stays up later than everyone else except for the Portuguese, Taiwan people and Koreans, with some 66% not getting to bed before midnight.

First up in what was assumed to be a minor hassle for the Agriculture, Fisheries & Conservation Department (AFCD) in November 2003 – netting an escaped pet crocodile in the Shan Pui River that runs through Yuen Long – turned out to be a migraine of mammoth proportions when the wily reptile eluded AFCD experts, a croc wrestler from Down Under and teams from the mainland for seven not-so-snappy months. In June 2004 a local fisherman finally brought 'Pui Pui' under control (the Hong Kong papers seemed to see a message in that – local people solving local problems) and the toothed one was packed off to the Kadoorie Farm & Botanic Garden. The government sent the fisherman a note of thanks and some new nets. He said he wanted cash instead.

Next in January 2005, colonies of red fire ants *(Solenopsis invicta)* were found at several sites in Hong Kong, including the new Hong Kong Wetland Park and the planned West Kowloon Cultural District, and a panic of SARS proportions broke out. It's true that red fire ants, originally from South America, are aggressive, inflict a painful sting and can wipe out indigenous species. But they can be kept under control and very much are as far away as the USA (where the city of Marshall, Texas, fetes them with an annual Fire Ant Festival) and as close as Guangdong province. And for those who would point a blaming finger at the Latinos, ecologists point out that the barren rock that Hong Kong once was has been hosting such 'invaders' since the beginning of time.

Shanghai Street, Tsim Sha Tsui (p89)

Finally in April 2005 the Food & Environmental Hygiene Department issued a report based on analyses of 750 dim sum indicating that Hong Kong's favourite food was high in fat and salt, low in calcium and fibre and could be bad for health. The reaction was swift and predictable, with the government criticised for its paternalistic and meddlesome ways. Still, Har Gau Lite® could be the way of the future and you saw it – and the registered trademark – here first.

TOP FIVE BOOKS ON HONG KONG CULTURE & STYLE

- *Ancestral Images* by Hugh D R Baker (1979) – long out of print but often available on Amazon and at second-hand bookshops, this is the first of a three-volume set, including *More Ancestral Images* (1980) and *Ancestral Images Again* (1981), which looks at every imaginative aspect of traditional rural Hong Kong culture by topic.
- *Culture Shock! Hong Kong: A Guide to Customs and Etiquette* by Betty Wei Pei-ti & Elizabeth Li (2003) – this expanded edition of a classic is an excellent introduction to Hong Kong culture and modus operandi for living or doing business with people here.
- *The Hong Kong Collection: Memorabilia of a Colonial Era* by Nigel Cameron & Patrick Hase (1998) – photographic essay on 200 objects (flags, swords, trophies, regimental regalia etc) unique to Hong Kong that have now vanished into the ether.
- *Hong Kong Style* by Peter Moss (1999) – this is an excellent and richly illustrated introduction to Hong Kong's approach to design and lifestyle and does not limit itself to things Chinese.
- Images of Asia from Oxford University Press (various) – this delightful series includes several thin volumes on topics relating to Hong Kong and Cantonese culture, including *Temples of the Empress of Heaven; Chinese New Year; The Cheongsam;* and *South China Village Culture.*

CITY CALENDAR

No matter what the time of year, you're almost certain to find some colourful festival or event occurring in Hong Kong. For the most part exact dates vary from year to year, so if you want to time your visit to coincide with a particular event, check the website of the Hong Kong Tourism Board (www.discoverhongkong.com). For tourist high and low seasons in Hong Kong see p250.

Many Chinese red-letter days, both public holidays and privately observed affairs, go back hundreds, even thousands, of years, and the true origins of some are often lost in the mists of time. Most – but not all – are celebrated in both Hong Kong and Macau. For festivals and events specific to Macau, see p377. For dates of Hong Kong's public holidays, see p314.

JANUARY
CHINESE NEW YEAR
Southern China's most important public holiday takes place in late January/early February (see the boxed text, opposite) and is welcomed in by a huge international parade at Tamar (now the PLA Central Barracks) site along the waterfront between Central and Wan Chai.

HONG KONG CITY FRINGE FESTIVAL
www.hkfringe.com.hk
The Fringe Club sponsors three weeks of eclectic performances both local and from overseas between late January and early February.

WORLD BOUTIQUE HONG KONG
www.worldboutiquehk.com
Organised by the Hong Kong Trade Development Council (HKTDC), this fair/event showcases collections from both established and up-and-coming fashion designers as well as brands from around the world.

FEBRUARY
HONG KONG ARTS FESTIVAL
www.hk.artsfestival.org
Hong Kong's most important cultural event is a month-long extravaganza of music, performing arts and exhibitions by hundreds of local and international artists.

HONG KONG MARATHON
www.hkmarathon.com
This major sporting event dating back to 1997 also includes a half-marathon and 10km race and attracts 30,000 participants.

SPRING LANTERN FESTIVAL
A colourful lantern festival on the 15th day of the first moon (mid- to late February) marking the end of the New Year period and the day for lovers.

MARCH
HONG KONG ARTWALK
www.hongkongartwalk.com; adult/student $400/75
Some 40 galleries in Central, Soho and Sheung Wan throw open their doors on a weekday (usually Wednesday) from 6pm to midnight to expose their art, offer viewers snacks and drinks supplied by the area's restaurants and raise money for charity.

HONG KONG RUGBY WORLD CUP SEVENS
www.hksevens.com.hk
Hong Kong's premier sporting event, this seven-a-side tournament is held over three days at Hong Kong Stadium and attracts teams and spectators from all over the world.

MAN HONG KONG INTERNATIONAL LITERARY FESTIVAL
www.festival.org.hk
This 10-day festival celebrates all things bookish and attracts novelists, short story writers, poets and so on from around the region and the world.

APRIL
CHING MING
A family celebration held early in the month, this is the time when people visit and clean the graves of ancestors.

HONG KONG INTERNATIONAL FILM FESTIVAL
www.hkiff.org.hk
This is a two-week extravaganza with screenings of more than 240 films from around the world.

BIRTHDAY OF TIN HAU

A festival in late April/early May in honour of the patroness of fisherfolk and one of the territory's most popular goddesses; in Macau it is known as the A-Ma Festival.

CHEUNG CHAU BUN FESTIVAL

www.cheungchau.org

Taking place around late April/early May, this is an unusual festival that is observed uniquely on Cheung Chau (p128).

MAY

BIRTHDAY OF LORD BUDDHA

A public holiday during which Buddha's statue is taken from monasteries and temples and ceremoniously bathed in scented water.

JUNE

DRAGON BOAT FESTIVAL

This festival, also known as Tuen Ng (Double Fifth) as it falls on the fifth day of the fifth moon, commemorates the death of the 3rd-century BC poet-statesman who hurled himself into a river to protest against a corrupt government. Dragon boat races are held throughout the territory and in Macau, but the most famous are at Stanley.

AUGUST

HONG KONG INTERNATIONAL ARTS CARNIVAL

www.hkiac.gov.hk

This unusual festival promotes performances by and for children and focuses on the Hong Kong Cultural Centre in Tsim Sha Tsui.

HUNGRY GHOSTS FESTIVAL

Celebrated on the first day of the seventh moon (sometime between August and September), when the gates of hell are opened and 'hungry ghosts' (restless spirits) are freed for two weeks to walk the earth. On the 14th day, paper 'hell' money and votives in the shape of cars, houses and clothing are burned for the ghosts and food is offered.

MAIDENS' FESTIVAL

A minor holiday, also known as Seven Sisters Day, that's held on the seventh day of the seventh moon and reserved for girls and young lovers.

KUNG HEI FAT CHOI (AND HAPPY NEW YEAR TOO)!

The Lunar New Year is the most important holiday of the Chinese year. Expect colourful decorations but not much public merrymaking; for the most part, this is a family festival, though there is a parade on the first day, a fantastic fireworks display over Victoria Harbour on the second evening, and one of the largest horse races is held at Sha Tin on day three.

Chinese New Year, which mainlanders call the Spring Festival, begins on the first new moon after the sun enters Aquarius (ie any time between 21 January and 19 February) and ends, at least officially, 15 days later. In Hong Kong it is a three-day public holiday.

The build-up to the holiday – the end of the month known as the 'Bitter Moon' since it's the coldest part of the year in Hong Kong – is very busy as family members clean house, get haircuts and cook, all of which are activities prohibited during the holiday. Debts and feuds are settled, and employees get a one-month New Year bonus.

You'll see many symbols in Hong Kong at this time of year, all of which have special meaning for people here. Chinese use a lot of indirect speak, and 'punning' is very important in the use of symbols. A picture of a boy holding a gàm-yéw (goldfish) and a hàw-fàa (lotus flower) is wishing you 'abundant gold and harmony' since that's what the words can also mean when said in a different tone. Symbols of bats (fùk) are everywhere since the word also means 'good luck'. The peach and plum blossoms decorating restaurants and public spaces symbolise both the arrival of spring and 'immortality', while the golden fruit of the kumquat tree is associated with good fortune. The red and gold banners you'll see in doorways are wishing all and sundry 'prosperity', 'peace' or just 'spring'.

Punning also carries over into foods eaten during the Lunar New Year holidays. Faat-choy (sea moss) and hò-sí (dried oysters) is a popular dish as the names of the key ingredients can also mean 'prosperity' and 'good business'. Lots of fish, chicken (gài), which also means 'luck', and prawns (hàa, or 'laughter') is served as are noodles for 'longevity'.

Of course, much of the symbolism and well-wishing has to do with wealth and prosperity. Indeed, 'gùng-háy faat-chòy', the most common New Year greeting in southern China, literally means 'respectful wishes, get rich'. The lài-sí packet is very important. It's a small red and gold envelope in which new bills (usually $10 or $20) are enclosed and given as gifts by married people to children and singles.

The first day of Chinese New Year will fall on 29 January in 2006, 18 February in 2007, and 7 February in 2008.

SEPTEMBER
MID-AUTUMN FESTIVAL
A colourful festival held on the 15th night of the eighth moon (sometime in September or October) marking an uprising against the Mongols in the 14th century when plans for a revolution were passed around in little round 'moon' cakes, which are still eaten on this day.

OCTOBER
CHEUNG YEUNG
Celebrated on the ninth day of the ninth month (mid- to late October), and based on a Han dynasty story, where an oracle advised a man to take his family to a high place to escape a plague. Many people still head for the hills on this day and also visit the graves of ancestors.

HONG KONG YOUTH ARTS FESTIVAL
www.hkyaf.com
Young talent perform at various cultural venues around town.

DECEMBER
OMEGA HONG KONG OPEN GOLF CHAMPIONSHIPS
www.omegahongkongopen.com
Hong Kong's premier golfing event is held at the Hong Kong Golf Club at Fanling.

CULTURE
IDENTITY
The population of Hong Kong is 6.89 million, with an annual growth rate of less than 1%. Once a very young society, Hong Kong is ageing rapidly; the median age rose from 30 in 1989 to just below 40 in 2005.

The vast majority, around 95%, of Hong Kong's population is ethnic Chinese, most of whom can trace their origins to Guangdong province in southern China. About 60% of Hong Kong Chinese were actually born in the territory, with the other 35% born in China.

Hong Kong has a large community of foreigners, but this figure is deceiving since many 'foreign passport holders' are actually Hong Kong Chinese. In any case, of the 523,880 people so described, the three largest groups are Filipinos at 132,770, Indonesians

THE GODS & GODDESSES OF SOUTH CHINA

Chinese religion is polytheistic, meaning it worships many deities. Virtually every household has its house, kitchen and/or door god; trades and businesses have their own deities too. Pawnshop owners pray to Kwan Yu for example, while students worship Man Cheung.

The following are profiles of some of the most important deities:

Kwan Yu A real-life Han dynasty soldier born in the 2nd century AD and sometimes referred to as Kwan Tai, Kwan Yu (Guanyu in Mandarin) is the red-cheeked god of war worshipped not just for his prowess in battle but for his righteousness, integrity and loyalty. He is the patron of soldiers, restaurateurs, the police force and members of secret societies, including the Triads.

Kwun Yam Kwun Yam (Guanyin in Mandarin) is the Buddhist equivalent of Tin Hau (see below). As the goddess of mercy she radiates tenderness and compassion for the unhappy lot of us mortals. In Macau her name is spelled Kun Iam.

Man Cheung This civil deity (Wen Chang in Mandarin) was a Chinese statesman and scholar of the 3rd century BC. Today he is worshipped as the god of literature and is represented holding a writing brush. He shares the Man Mo Temple (p74) in Sheung Wan with Kwan Yu.

Tin Hau The queen of heaven, whose duties include protecting seafarers, Tin Hau (Tianhou in Mandarin) is arguably the most popular god in Hong Kong and in Macau, where she also goes under the name A-Ma. There are almost 60 temples dedicated to her in Hong Kong alone.

Tou Tei Known as Toudei in Mandarin, Tou Tei is the earth god who rules over anything and everything from a one-room flat or shop to a section of a village or town. Shrines to Tou Tei are usually small and inconspicuous but always a delight.

DOS & DON'TS

There aren't many unusual rules of etiquette to follow in Hong Kong; in general, common sense will take you as far as you'll need to go. But on matters of identity, appearance, gift-giving and the big neighbour to the north, local people might see things a little differently than you do. For pointers on how to conduct yourself at the table, see p37.

- Clothing – beyond the besuited realm of business, smart casual dress is acceptable even at swish restaurants, but save your bikini for the beach and keep your thongs/flip-flops in the hotel.
- Colours – these are often symbolic to the Chinese. Red symbolises good luck, virtue and wealth (though writing in red can convey anger or unfriendliness). White symbolises death so think twice before giving white flowers.
- Face – think status and respect (both receiving and showing): keep your cool, be polite and order a glass of vintage Champagne at the Pen or Mandarin. That'll show 'em.
- Gifts – if you want to give flowers, chocolates or wine as a gift to someone, they may appear reluctant for fear of seeming greedy but insist and they'll give in. Don't be surprised if they don't open a gift-wrapped present in front of you, though; to do so would be impolite. Cash is the preferred wedding gift and is given in the form of *lai-si* (p11).
- Name Cards – Hong Kong is name-card crazy and in business circles it is a must. People simply won't take you seriously unless you have one (be sure to offer it with both hands). Bilingual cards can usually be printed within 24 hours; try printers along Man Wa Lane in Sheung Wan or ask your hotel to direct you. Expect to pay about $200 for 100 cards.

at 95,460 and Americans at 31,130, closely followed by Canadians at 29,260 and Thais at 28,820. Britons and Australians fall well behind the rest at only 19,900 and 19,600 respectively.

It's difficult to generalise about a city and a society of almost 7 million people, but the most common preconceptions about Hong Kong people in the past were that they were racist and greedy and, in the case of service staff, discourteous to the point of rudeness.

The word *gwái-ló*, meaning 'ghost person' (*gwái-páw* is used for Caucasian women, *hàak-gwái* for a 'black ghost'), was used regularly and often contemptuously. And although Caucasians have 'possessed' this word and use it jocularly among themselves, it was – and remains – a deeply pejorative word in Hong Kong; ask any Chinese.

The rudeness seems to have almost disappeared entirely. Some people say it's because the economic crisis of 1998 and subsequent global downturn in 2001 and 2002 had Hong Kong people eating humble pie for the first time in decades. Others say that when many Hong Kong Chinese people awoke on 1 July 1997 they realised something for the first time: they were different from their cousins on the mainland. Chinese, yes, through and through, but somehow different...

All this is not to make excuses for the colonial government or to suggest many people would like to see its return. Hong Kong is Chinese, and an essential part of China. Everyone has known that since 1841; it just took a while to settle the matter. But it is now Chinese with an international flavour. This was thanks, to some degree, to 156 years under the *yìng-gok-yàn* (British).

The dominant religions in Hong Kong are Buddhism and Taoism, entwined with elements of Confucianism, ancient animist beliefs and ancestor worship. The number of active Buddhists in Hong Kong is estimated at around 700,000, though the figure probably includes a good number of Taoists as well.

On a daily level the Chinese are much less concerned with the high-minded philosophies and asceticism of Buddha, Confucius or Laozi (the founder of Taoism), and visits to temples, monasteries and shrines, which number some 600 in Hong Kong, are usually made to ask the gods' blessings or favours for specific things: a relative's health, the birth of a son, the success of a business, or even a lucky day at the racetrack.

Many other faiths are practised in Hong Kong apart from traditional Chinese ones. There are an estimated 536,000 Christians, about 55% of whom are Protestant and 45% Catholic. Hong Kong is also home to approximately 70,000 Muslims (more than half of whom are ethnic Chinese), 15,000 Hindus and 8000 Sikhs. The Jewish community, which can trace its roots back to the time of the British arrival, numbers about 1500. For a list of churches, temples and mosques, see p320.

LIFESTYLE

For its size, Hong Kong is a very safe city and most people will feel quite at home here. It is safe to walk around just about anywhere in the territory after dark, though it's best to stick to well-lit areas. Tourist districts like Tsim Sha Tsui are heavily patrolled by the police.

People work very hard in Hong Kong – the 5½-day workweek is still the norm for many – and they make great use of what little free time their schedules allow. Favourite pursuits include dining together (be it yum cha, a 12-course banquet or a huge bowl of *wàn-tàn-mín* at a food stall with friends), gambling at the Mark Six lottery, the football pools or (and most importantly) a day of fluttering at the races in Sha Tin or Happy Valley or watching or participating in organised sport – from cricket and tennis to football and rugby (p216).

It is highly unlikely that you will see the inside of a Hong Kong Chinese person's home; it's a rare privilege even for long-term expatriate residents to be invited over by friends. It's not that people here are inhospitable – just the opposite in fact – but flats here are very small (tiny by some standards) and most people prefer to entertain guests outside at restaurants.

Chinese meals out are social and very noisy, very raucous events. Westerners drink together to relax and let off steam; Chinese people eat. Although lots of Hong Kong Chinese drink alcohol (and some of them problematically), for the vast majority of the population a night spent in a pub or a bar carousing with friends doesn't even place.

In a restaurant a group of people typically sit at a round table and order dishes (at least one per person) from which everyone partakes. Ordering a dish just for yourself – as some

VERY SUPERSTITIOUS

While Hong Kong may appear as Western as a Big Mac on the surface, many old Chinese traditions persist. Whether people still believe in all of them or just go through the motions to please parents, neighbours or coworkers is hard to say. But Hong Kong Chinese are too astute to leave something as important as joss, or 'luck', to chance.

Feng Shui

Literally 'wind water', feng shui (or geomancy in English) aims to balance the elements of nature to create a harmonious environment. It's been in practice since the 12th century, and continues to influence the design of buildings, highways, parks, tunnels and grave sites. To guard against evil spirits, who can move only in straight lines, doors are often positioned at an angle. For similar reasons, beds cannot face doorways. Ideally, homes and businesses should have a view of calm water (even a goldfish tank helps). Corporate heads shouldn't have offices that face westward, otherwise profits will go in the same direction as the setting sun.

Fortune Telling

There are any number of props and implements that Chinese use to predict the future but the most common method of divination in Hong Kong are the chim, or 'fortune sticks' found at Buddhist and Taoist temples that must be shaken out of a box onto the ground and then read by a fortune-teller. Palm-readers usually examine both the lines and features of the hand (left for men, right for women) but may also examine your facial features. Apparently there are eight basic shapes, but 48 recognised eye patterns that reveal character and fortune.

Numerology

In Cantonese the word for 'three' sounds similar to 'life', 'nine' like 'eternity' and the ever-popular number 'eight' like 'prosperity'. Lowest on the list is 'four', which shares the same pronunciation with the word for 'death'. As a result the right number can make or break a business and each year the government draws in millions of dollars for charity by auctioning off automobile licence plates that feature lucky numbers. The Bank of China Tower was officially opened on 8 August 1988 (8/8/88), a rare union of the prosperous numbers. August is always a busy month for weddings.

Zodiac

As in the Western system of astrology, the Chinese zodiac has 12 signs, but their representations are all animals. Your sign is based on the year of your birth (according to the lunar calendar). Being born or married in a particular year is believed to determine one's fortune, so parents often plan for their children's sign. The year of the dragon sees the biggest jump in the birth rate, closely followed by the year of the tiger. A girl born in the year of the pig could have trouble later in life.

people still do in Chinese restaurants in Europe – would be unthinkable here; everyone wants a piece (literally) of the action. And it's also not unusual for one person at the table to take command and order on everyone's behalf. That's usually the host.

If you are attending a formal affair or have been issued a rare invitation to eat at someone's home, it's best to wait for some signal from the host before digging in. If you are the guest, you will most likely be invited to take the first taste. Often your host will serve it to you, placing a piece of meat, chicken or fish in your bowl. If a whole fish is served, you might be offered the head as the cheeks are considered the tastiest part. It's alright to decline; someone else will gladly devour the delicacy.

And if you've been invited out by a friend or contact, don't ever try to pay (or even help to pay) the bill. Accept that 'no' graciously, say 'thank you' and never ever force the issue. For a guest to pay for their host would make the latter lose face – and big time.

Hong Kong is a highly educated society by Asian standards, with a literacy rate of just under 94%. The education system is based on the British model. Primary education is free and compulsory for nine years (generally from ages six to 15). At secondary level, students begin to specialise; some go on to university or college preparatory programs, while others select vocational education combined with apprenticeships.

An ongoing debate in Hong Kong concerns the medium of instruction at secondary level. While primary school classes are taught almost exclusively in Cantonese (with the exception of international schools), about a quarter of HK's 405 secondary schools use English, with the rest – about 293 schools in total – teaching in the vernacular.

The official reason has always been that the schools considered English a useful language for success in life, with the goal being the creation of a biliterate (written Chinese and English) and trilingual (Cantonese, Mandarin and English) society. Most parents, however, sent their children to so-called Anglo-Chinese schools in order for them to secure a place at Hong Kong University, where lectures are given in English. When the post-handover government insisted that government-assisted schools make the switch to tuition in Cantonese, all hell broke loose. Eventually a compromise was reached and those schools fulfilling certain requirements (some 112 of them) were allowed to teach in English. The independent and mostly self-funding English Schools Foundation, which runs 19 English-language institutions, including five secondary schools, receives a government grant.

At the tertiary level, education is competitive but, with the opening of so many new universities (p323) in the past two decades, not as fierce as it once was. Just over 20% of the eligible age group now has the chance to secure a university placement in degree or non-degree courses – more than double the figure in 1990. The most prestigious tertiary institution in the territory and the most difficult of Hong Kong's eight universities to enter is Hong Kong University. To be accepted into the Faculty of Medicine there is a sure sign that the successful applicant will go far in life.

That's not to say Western medicine has taken over in Hong Kong. Chinese herbal medicine remains very popular and seems to work best for the relief of common colds, flu and for chronic conditions that resist Western medicine, such as migraine headaches, asthma and chronic backache. The pills on sale in herbal medicine shops are generally broad-spectrum, while a prescription remedy will usually require that you take home bags full of specific herbs and cook them into a thick, vile-smelling broth.

It is a widely held belief in China that overwork and sex wears down the body and that such 'exercise' will result in a short life. To counter the wear and tear, some Chinese practice *jeun-bó* (the consumption of tonic food and herbs). This can include, for example, drinking raw snake's blood or bear's bile, or eating deer antlers, all of which are claimed to improve vision, strength and sexual potency. Similarly, the long life of the tortoise can be absorbed through a soup made from its flesh.

Like herbal medicine, Chinese acupuncture tends to be more helpful in treating long-term complaints than acute conditions and emergencies. The exact mechanism by which acupuncture works is not fully understood. The Chinese talk of energy channels or meridians, which connect the needle insertion point to the particular organ, gland or joint being treated. The acupuncture point is sometimes quite far from the area of the body being treated, and knowing just where to insert the needle is crucial. Acupuncturists have identified more than 2000 insertion points, but only about 150 are commonly used.

FASHION

Not so long ago, the strength of the Hong Kong fashion industry lay in its ability to duplicate designs. Indeed, for many travellers a shopping trip to Hong Kong meant amassing *faux* but authentic-looking Chanel purses, Louis Vuitton bags and Cartier wrist watches.

With the crackdown by the Hong Kong government on such activities and a maturing of the market, the industry has taken on a much more creative role, finding a new voice in everything from haute couture and casual wear to hip street fashion.

The fashion industry here includes: established designers who, for the most part, are couturiers and create one-off made-to-measure outfits; younger 'name' designers who have popular collections and sell both in Hong Kong and for export; and local brands, covering the spectrum from evening and party wear to casual and street wear.

Of the established designers a few names stand out, including the New York–based Vivienne Tam, who was trained in Hong Kong, and Walter Ma, often cited as the voice of Hong Kong fashion, whose women's wear is both sophisticated and adventurous. Barney Cheng's designs are very luxurious, often embellished with beads and sequins, and he sews for the stars. Other names to watch out for include Lu Lu Cheung, especially her Terra Rosalis line, with subtle, Japanese-influenced pieces; Cecilia Yau and her gowns; Johanna Ho, whose low-key outfits are characterised by elegant straight lines and stylish but classic design; and Dorian Ho, the current darling of the designer fashion pack whose D'Orient line is classic but modern. Blanc de Chine does mostly tailored outfits, which are quietly elegant, very exclusive and distinctively Oriental. Blue de Chine is their junior line.

Among the younger designers, Benjamin Lau produces innovative but very wearable pieces noted for their fine cutting. His Madame Benjie line of contemporary ready-to-wear for young women is one of the few in Hong Kong not influenced by trends. The signature pieces of one of the most amusing designers in the game, Pacino Wan, are T-shirts with

Cheongsam for sale, Li Yuen Street East (p71), Central

kooky stencilling and denim jackets and skirts. Ruby Li is another young designer producing fun to wear pieces for the young and trendy; Virginia Lai concentrates on evening wear in her Virginia L line. Lu Lu Cheung's assistant designer, Otto Tang, with his cotton uppers, leather pants and torn fishnet stockings, is a name to watch. Grace Choi makes great use of embroidery and beads in her styles.

Arguably the most exciting aspect of the Hong Kong fashion industry at the moment is the meteoric rise in recent years of local brands. In the late 1980s and early '90s, established smart casual brands such as Esprit, Michel Renés and Giordano made room for much more edgy lines: Kitterick, set up by three Hong Kong Polytechnic students in 1988, their Indu-Homme line and the D-mop house's Blues Heroes. Young people flocked to 'micro malls' such as Island Beverley in Causeway Bay and the Rise Commercial Centre in Tsim Sha Tsui (p232).

Today some of the more popular brands are the i.t group (www.izzue.com), with a hip casual-wear line and its 5cm line of easy coordinates and trendy street-wear, and Fait a Main, women's contemporary lines designed by John Cheng distributed by Lane Crawford. Henry Lau's Spy, with

THE WARDROBE OF SUZIE WONG

Neon-coloured Indian saris are beautiful things when fastidiously wrapped and tucked, and Japanese kimonos can be like bright cocoons from which a chrysalis coyly peaks. And what's so wrong with a sarong with a palm tree and blue lagoon as backdrop?

But there's nothing quite like a cheongsam, the close-fitting sheath that is as Chinese as a bowl of won ton noodle soup. It lifts where it should and never pulls where it shouldn't. And those thigh-high side slits – well, they're enough to give any man apoplexy. It's sensuous but never lewd; it reveals without showing too much.

Reach into any Hong Kong Chinese woman's closet and you're bound to find at least one cheongsam (*qípáo* in Mandarin), the closest thing Hong Kong has to national dress. It's there for formal occasions like Chinese New Year gatherings, work (restaurant receptionists and nightclub hostesses wear them), school (cotton cheongsams are still the uniform at several colleges and secondary schools) or for the 'big day'. Modern Hong Kong brides may take their vows in white, but when they're slipping off for the honeymoon, they put on a red cheongsam.

It's difficult to imagine that this bedazzling dress started life as a man's garment. During the Qing dynasty, the Manchus ordered Han Chinese to emulate their way of dress – elite men wore a loose 'long robe' (*chèung-pò*) with a 'riding jacket' (*mǎa-kwáa*) while women wore trousers under a long garment. By the 1920s, modern women in Shanghai had taken to wearing the androgynous changpao, which released them from layers of confining clothing. From this outfit evolved the cheongsam.

The 'bourgeois' cheongsam dropped out of favour in China when the Communists came to power in 1949 and was banned outright during the Cultural Revolution, but the 1950s and '60s was the outfit's heyday. This was the era of Suzie Wong (the cheongsam is sometimes called a 'Suzie Wong dress') and, although hemlines rose and dropped, collars stiffened and more darts were added to give it a tighter fit, the cheongsam has remained essentially the same: elegant, sexy and very Chinese.

three branches, is funky and provocative, while Moiselle, with some 50 shops in the territory, stocks embroidered and beaded tops, dresses and footwear. Shanghai Tang has modern off-the-rack designs with traditional Chinese motifs, often dyed in vibrant colours. G2000 is into the executive look. Its U2 brand is a leader in casual and weekend wear.

SPORT

Sir Murray MacLehose, Hong Kong governor from 1971 to 1982 and a keen walker, is credited with opening up large tracts of Hong Kong's countryside to hikers and trekkers; hiking is today one of the most popular outdoor activities in Hong Kong (p219). Many of Hong Kong's beaches opened during Sir Murray's term and local Chinese, apathetic to swimming and other water sports just a generation ago, now take to the water like ducks. Windsurfing and wakeboarding are also popular; indeed, Hong Kong's only Olympic gold medallist so far is a windsurfer from Cheung Chau.

Organised sport is equally popular in Hong Kong, notably horse racing, football, rugby and cricket and there are local championships and cups in each sport. For details, see p216.

MEDIA

A total of 52 daily (or almost daily) newspapers and upwards of 800 periodicals are published in the well-read territory of Hong Kong. The vast majority of the publications are in Chinese, with the largest-selling dailies being the sensationalist *Oriental Daily News* and the government's gadfly, the *Apple Daily,* which is usually not allowed to send journalists over the border. *Ta Kung Pao, Wen Wei Pao* and *Hong Kong Commercial Daily* all toe the government line and are pro-Beijing. According to independent surveys, the most trusted newspapers are *Ming Pao,* Hong Kong's newspaper of record, and the business-orientated *Hong Kong Economic Journal.*

Two English language dailies, the *South China Morning Post* and the *Hong Kong Standard,* compete for the expatriate and Westernised Chinese markets, though there is also an English-language version of *China Daily* on sale here. For details see p319. For information on other Hong Kong media see p321 and p322.

LANGUAGE

The Official Languages Ordinance of 1974 names Hong Kong's two official languages as English and Cantonese. Cantonese, a southern Chinese dialect (or language, depending on your definition), is spoken in Guangdong and Guangxi provinces on the mainland as well as in Hong Kong and Macau. Cantonese preserves many archaic features of spoken Chinese that date back to the Tang dynasty, which is why Tang and Sung dynasty poetry scan and sound better in Cantonese than in Mandarin.

While Cantonese is used in Hong Kong in everyday life by the vast majority of the population, English remains the *lingua franca* of commerce, banking and international trade and is still used in the law courts. There has been a noticeable decline in the level of English-speaking proficiency in the territory, however, due to emigration and the switch by many secondary schools, which previously (and in theory) taught all their lessons in English, to Chinese vernacular education. In general, most Hong Kong Chinese – even those who have attended school taught in English – cannot hold a candle to their cousins in Singapore, who often speak English almost as a first language.

On the other hand, the ability to speak Mandarin is on the increase here due to the political realities. For a Cantonese native speaker, Mandarin is far easier to learn than English. It's not uncommon these days to hear Cantonese and Mandarin being spoken in a sort of fusion-confusion.

For more on what to say and how to say it in Cantonese, see the Language chapter (p380), where you'll also find shorter sections in Mandarin and Portuguese. Lonely Planet also publishes the more comprehensive *Cantonese* and *Mandarin* phrasebooks.

ECONOMY & COSTS

Although Hong Kong presents its much vaunted laissez faire economic policies as a capitalist's dream, considerable sections of the economy, including transport and power generation, are dominated by a handful of cartels and monopolistic franchises. Nonetheless, Hong Kong's economy is by far the freest in Asia, enjoying low taxes, a modern and efficient port and airport, excellent worldwide communications and strict anticorruption laws.

Hong Kong has moved from labour- to capital-intensive industries in recent decades. Telecommunications, banking, insurance, tourism and retail sales have pushed manufacturing into the background, and almost all manual labour is now performed across the border in southern China. Service industries employ about 85% of Hong Kong's workforce and make up more than 88% of its GDP. The shift from manufacturing to services has not been without problems. The change may have seen a dramatic increase in wages, but there has not been a corresponding expansion of the welfare state.

Hong Kong has a very small agricultural base. Only 2% of the total land area is under cultivation and just under 19,000 people – a mere 0.5% of the workforce – is engaged in agriculture or fishing. Most food is imported from the mainland.

Indeed, Hong Kong depends on imports for virtually all its requirements; it buys half of its water supplies from the mainland. China is by far Hong Kong's largest trading partner, accounting for more than 40% of

HOW MUCH?

Hong Kong is a relatively pricey destination. You survive on, say, $250 a day, but it will require a good deal of self-discipline. Better to budget something along the lines of $400 for midrange options. Accommodation is the biggest expense, followed by drinking at Hong Kong's bars.

Bowl of won ton noodles $10 to $25

Cup of coffee from $20

Laundry (5kg) $45 to $50

Litre of bottled water $8 to $12

Litre of petrol $12.10 to $12.70

MTR fare (Central to Tsim Sha Tsui) $9; $7.90 with Octopus card

Pint of beer from $35 (happy hour from $25)

Copy of South China Morning Post $7

Souvenir T-shirt $35 to $100

Star Ferry fare (Central to Tsim Sha Tsui) 1st/2nd class $2.20/1.70

the territory's total imports and exports. Japan, Taiwan, the USA, Singapore, South Korea and the European Union follow.

The early 21st century was a trying time for the Hong Kong economy overall. Hong Kong maintained an average GDP growth of 5% through the 1990s and peaked at 10% in 2000, but fell to just 0.6% in 2001. Four years later a surge in trade with China and a 45% increase of visitors from the mainland saw consumer prices rise (and deflation disappear) for the first time in almost six years. Unemployment fell to a two-year low of 6.7%, and the economy grew by 8% in 2004. In terms of purchasing power, Hong Kong's annual per capita GDP of US$34,200 is by far the highest in Asia (Japan's is US$29,400) and ranks ninth worldwide. By comparison China's amounts to just $5600.

Hong Kong people get to keep most of their earnings. The maximum personal income tax is 16%, company profits tax is 17.5% and there are no capital gains or transfer taxes. A 60% slump in property values after 1997 forced the government to halt land sales in order to save the market in 2003, thereby slashing government income and raising concerns about the narrowness of the tax base. But values have now climbed back up by 30%. Generous personal tax allowances mean only a little more than 40% of the working population of 3.54 million pays any salaries tax at all and a mere 0.3% pays the full 16%.

Hong Kong has traditionally suffered from a labour shortage. Most of the menial work (domestic, construction etc) is performed by imported labour, chiefly from Southeast Asia. The labour shortage is most acute in the hi-tech and financial fields, prompting the government to consider further relaxing restrictions on importing talent from the mainland, a move deeply unpopular with Hong Kong's working class.

GOVERNMENT & POLITICS

The government of the Hong Kong Special Administrative Region (SAR) is a complicated hybrid of a quasi-presidential system glued awkwardly onto a quasi-parliamentary model. It is not what could be called a democratic system, although democratic elements exist within its structure.

The executive branch of government is led by the chief executive, Donald Tsang, who was selected to replace Shanghai business tycoon Tung Chee Hwa, who resigned in March 2005. He was uncontested and elected by an 800-member election committee dominated by pro-Beijing forces in June two weeks after the nomination period closed.

The chief executive selects members (currently numbering 21) of the Executive Council, which serves effectively as the cabinet and advises on policy matters. The top three policy secretaries are the chief secretary for the administration of government, the financial secretary and the secretary for justice. Council members are usually civil servants or from the private sector.

The unicameral, 60-seat Legislative Council is responsible for passing legislation proposed by the Executive Council. It also approves public expenditure and, in theory, monitors the administration. Council members are elected for four-year terms.

In the September 2004 election, the pro-democracy bloc, including the Association for Democracy and People's Livelihood, the Democratic Party and the Frontier Party, won almost two-thirds of the popular vote, but due to the rules of appointment they took only 25 seats (ie 40% of the total). This is because only half of the 60 council seats are returned through direct election, with the other 30 chosen by narrowly defined, occupationally based 'functional constituencies'. With a few exceptions, 'corporate voting' is the rule, enfranchising only a few powerful and conservative members of each functional constituency.

The judiciary is headed by the chief justice and is, according to the Basic Law, independent of the executive and the legislative branches. The highest court in the land is the Court of Final Appeal, which has the power of final adjudication.

The 18 District Boards, created in 1982 and restructured in 1997, are meant to give Hong Kong residents a degree of control in their local areas. These boards consist of government officials and elected representatives, but they have little power.

Although the stated aim of the Basic Law is 'full democracy', it supplies no definition for this. In April 2004, China's legislators ruled out universal suffrage in Hong Kong's

2007 election of its chief executive as well as for its 2008 Legislative Council election, citing concern that such reforms could undermine political stability and economic development. Changes to the system can only be made with the agreement of the chief executive and a two-thirds majority of the legislature. With the democratic camp in the minority in the Legislative Council, many are pessimistic about the prospects of installing genuine democracy in Hong Kong.

ENVIRONMENT

THE LAND

Hong Kong measures 1103 sq km and is divided into four major areas: Hong Kong Island, Kowloon, the New Territories and the Outlying Islands.

Hong Kong Island covers 81 sq km, or just over 7% of the total land area. It lies on the southern side of Victoria Harbour, and contains the main business district, Central. Kowloon is a peninsula on the northern side of the harbour. The southern tip, an area called Tsim Sha Tsui (pronounced jìm-sàa-jéui), is a major tourist area. Kowloon only includes the land south of Boundary St, but land reclamation and encroachment into the New Territories gives it an area of about 47 sq km, or just over 4% of the total. The New Territories occupies 747 sq km, or more than 68% of Hong Kong's land area, and spreads out like a fan between Kowloon and the border with mainland China. What was once the territory's rural hinterland has become in large part a network of 'New Towns'. The Outlying Islands refers to the territory's 234 islands, but does not include Hong Kong Island or Stonecutters Island, which is off the western shore of the Kowloon Peninsula and has been absorbed by land reclamation. Officially, they are part of the New Territories and their 228 sq km make up just over 20% of Hong Kong's total land area.

Almost half the population lives in the New Territories, followed by Kowloon (30.1%), Hong Kong Island (19.7%) and the Outlying Islands (2%). A tiny percentage (0.1%, or under 7000 people) live at sea. The overall population density is 6300 people per sq km, with Kwun Tong in New Kowloon the most densely populated place on earth, with 50,820 people per sq km.

GREEN HONG KONG

When you finally reach it, Hong Kong's countryside is very lush and, although only 12% of the land area is forested, some 415 sq km (or 38% of the territory's total landmass) has been designated as protected country parks. These 23 parks – for the most part in the New Territories and Outlying Islands, but encompassing the slopes of Hong Kong Island too –

City skyline, Central (p68)

A STERILE HYBRID

Hong Kong can look and feel like an artificial place – concrete jungles sprouting on reclaimed land, parks and gardens landscaped within an inch of their lives – so what better symbol for the SAR than the *Bauhinia blakeana*, a sterile tree with purple blossoms unique to the territory?

French priests apparently discovered the tree near the seashore in Central in the late 19th century. As no identical one had been found anywhere else in the world, it was declared a new species of bauhinia (of which there are 250 to 300) and named after Sir Henry Blake, governor of Hong Kong from 1898 to 1904.

The *Bauhinia blakeana*, also known as the Hong Kong Orchid Tree, has spreading branches and broad, heart-shaped leaves. Its delicately scented flowers have five magenta-coloured petals and white stamens; it blossoms from early November to March. The tree does not produce seeds and can only be propagated by air-layering, cutting or grafting. Thus all *Bauhinia blakeana* today are direct descendants of that single tree discovered by the priests.

comprise uplands, woodlands, coastlines, marshes and all of Hong Kong's 17 freshwater reservoirs. In addition, there are 15 'special areas' (eg Tai Po Kau Nature Reserve) as well as four protected marine parks and one marine reserve.

Hong Kong counts an estimated 3100 species of indigenous and introduced plants, trees and flowers, including Hong Kong's own flower, the bauhinia *(Bauhinia blakeana;* see the boxed text, above). Hong Kong's beaches and coastal areas are also home to a wide variety of plant life, including creeping beach vitex *(Vitex trifolia),* rattlebox *(Croatalaria retusa),* beach naupaka *(Scaevola sericea)* and screw pine *(Pandanus tectorius).*

One of the largest natural habitats for wildlife in Hong Kong is the Mai Po Marsh (p112). There are also sanctuaries in the wetland areas of Tin Shui Wai (Hong Kong Wetland Park) and Kam Tin.

Wooded areas throughout the territory are habitats for warblers, flycatchers, robins, bulbuls and tits. Occasionally you'll see sulphur-crested cockatoos, even on Hong Kong Island, and flocks of domestic budgerigars (parakeets) – domestic pets that have managed to fly the coop.

The areas around some of Hong Kong's reservoirs shelter a large number of aggressive long-tailed macaques and rhesus monkeys, both of which are non-native species. Common smaller mammals include woodland and house shrews and bats. Occasionally spotted are leopard cats, Chinese porcupines, masked palm civets, ferret badgers, wild boar and barking deer. An interesting (but rare) creature is the Chinese pangolin, a scaly mammal resembling an armadillo that rolls itself up into an impenetrable ball when threatened.

Frogs, lizards and snakes – including the red-necked keelback, which has not one but *two* sets of fangs – can be seen in the New Territories and the Outlying Islands. Hong Kong is also home to an incredible variety of insects. There are some 200 species of butterflies and moths alone, including the giant silkworm moth with a wingspan of over 20cm. One 'favourite' arachnid is the enormous woodland spider, the female of which can sometimes be seen trapping and feeding on small birds.

Hong Kong waters are rich in sea life, including sharks (three-quarters of Hong Kong's 40-odd gazetted beaches are equipped with shark nets) and dolphins, including Chinese white dolphins (see the boxed text, p133) and finless porpoises. Endangered green turtles call on Sham Wan beach on Lamma to lay eggs (see the boxed text, p126), and there are some 80 species of stony coral. One of Hong Kong's few remaining colonies of horseshoe crab lives in Tung Chung Bay, where the first part of the proposed Pearl River delta bridge (p341) will be built.

POLLUTION PROBLEMS

Pollution has been and remains a problem in Hong Kong, but it wasn't until 1989, with the formation of the Environmental Protection Department, that government authorities acted decisively to clean up the mess. The EPD has had to deal with decades of serious environmental abuse and – almost as serious – a population that until recently didn't know (or care) about the implications of littering and pollution.

The EPD was set up as an advisory and regulatory body to deal with the 17,500 tonnes of domestic, industrial and construction waste produced in Hong Kong each day. Three large landfills in the New Territories now absorb all of Hong Kong's daily 9440 tonnes of municipal waste (though they will be full in eight to 12 years). This, as well as the increased use of private garbage collectors and more recycling, which amounted to more than 40% of total municipal waste in 2003, appears to be having some effect.

Another of Hong Kong's most serious problems is air pollution, responsible for up to 15,600 premature deaths a year. Ceaseless construction, a high proportion of diesel vehicles and industrial pollution from Shenzhen have made for dangerous levels of particulate matter and nitrogen dioxide, especially in Central, Causeway Bay, Mong Kok and Tung Chung. Case numbers of asthma and bronchial infection have soared in recent years, and doctors blame it on poor air quality; in September 2004 Hong Kong air pollution reached a record high of 200, putting Hong Kong's air quality in the severest classification. An hourly update of Hong Kong's air pollution index can be found on the EPD's website (www.info .gov.hk/epd).

The Hong Kong and Guangdong provincial governments have signed a joint intent to reduce regional emissions of breathable suspended particulates, nitrogen oxides, sulphur dioxide and volatile organic compounds by more than half by 2010. The switch from diesel fuel to LPG by Hong Kong's taxis and newly registered minibuses has reduced the first two by 13% and 23% respectively in four years, but Hong Kong's ever-growing fleet of buses continues to run overwhelmingly on diesel. According to the Hong Kong Observatory, it was impossible to see across Victoria Harbour 18% of the time during daylight hours – or one day out of six – in 2004.

Water pollution has been one of Hong Kong's most serious ecological problems over the years. Victoria Harbour remains in a pitiful state, suffering from the effects of years of industrial and sewage pollution, though a disposal system called the Harbour Area Treatment Scheme has been collecting up to 70% of the sewage entering the harbour and the *E.coli* count (the bacteria that can indicate the presence of sewage) has stabilised. Farms in the New Territories have been given grants to install their own sewage disposal systems and are fined heavily for dumping untreated industrial or animal waste into freshwater rivers or streams. A great deal of damage has already been done, but the percentage of rivers in the 'good' and 'excellent' categories increased from 34% in 1986 to 76% in 2003.

The quality of the water at Hong Kong's 41 gazetted beaches must be rated 'good' or 'fair' to allow public use, but many beaches here fall below the World Health Organization's levels for safe swimming due to pollution. Since 1998 water has been tested at each beach every two weeks during the swimming season (April to October) and judgements made based upon the level of *E. coli* present in the sample. The list of beaches deemed safe enough for swimming (an average 34 in 2004) is printed in the newspapers and on the EPD's website.

An especially annoying form of pollution in Hong Kong is the noise created by traffic, industry and commerce. Laws governing the use of construction machinery appear strict on paper, but there's often a way around things. General construction is allowed to continue between the hours of 7pm and 7am as long as builders secure a permit.

URBAN PLANNING & DEVELOPMENT

Hong Kong has been expanding through land reclamation since 1851, and landfill has increased the total surface area of the territory some 6% since 1887. In recent years reclamation has continued apace in Victoria Harbour, prompting fears among many that Hong Kong's most scenic (and valuable) spot will soon disappear under hardcore. (The harbour is already about half the size it was in the mid-19th century.)

Hong Kong's Court of Final Appeal forced the government to rethink plans for a 26-hectare landfill in January 2004. But despite a mass outcry and protests organised by the Society for Protection of the Harbour (www.friendsoftheharbour.org), two reclamation projects near Central are going ahead and at full tilt. Watch this (and that) space.

For an idea of how Hong Kong will look in the near and distant future, visit Hong Kong Planning & Infrastructure Exhibition Gallery (p70) near City Hall in Central.

Arts ■

Architecture 24
Traditional Chinese &
Colonial Architecture 24
Contemporary Architecture 25

Cinema 25

Painting 27
Contemporary Art 27

Sculpture 29

Music 29
Classical 29
Traditional Chinese 29
Cantopop 29

Theatre 30
Chinese Opera 31

Literature 31

Arts

The epithet 'cultural desert' can no longer be used to describe Hong Kong. There are both philharmonic and Chinese orchestras, Chinese and modern dance troupes, a ballet company, several theatre groups and numerous art schools and organisations. Government funds also allow local venues to bring in top international performers, and the number of international arts festivals hosted here seems to grow each year. Local street-opera troupes occasionally pop up around the city. Both local and mainland Chinese opera troupes can also sometimes be seen in more formal settings.

There are two art forms enjoying something of a renaissance in Hong Kong: fine arts (especially painting) and literature. The former is due to the influx of contemporary work – a lot of it derivative but some of it very good indeed – from the mainland, the new-found maturity inherent in much local painting and the increased interest in the annual Hong Kong ArtWalk (see the boxed text, p28) event. Home-grown literature in English, which has been quietly simmering away for the past decade or so, has been recently brought to the boil by the annual – and very successful – Man Hong Kong International Literary Festival (p31).

ARCHITECTURE

Over the years Hong Kong has played host to everything from Tao temples and Qing dynasty forts to Victorian churches and Edwardian hotels. But Hong Kong's ceaseless cycle of deconstruction and rebuilding means that few structures have survived the wrecking ball. Needless to say, enthusiasts of modern architecture will have a field day.

TRADITIONAL CHINESE & COLONIAL ARCHITECTURE

About the only examples of pre-colonial Chinese architecture left in urban Hong Kong are Tin Hau temples dating from the early to mid-19th century, including those at Tin Hau near Causeway Bay, Stanley, Aberdeen and Yau Ma Tei. Museums in Chai Wan and Tsuen Wan have preserved a few Hakka village structures that predate the arrival of the British. For anything more substantial, however, you have to go to the New Territories or the Outlying Islands, where walled villages, fortresses and even a 15th-century pagoda (p145) can be seen.

Colonial architecture is also in short supply. Most of what is left is on Hong Kong Island, especially in Central, such as the Legislative Council building (formerly the Supreme Court; p71), built in 1912, and Government House (p70), residence of all British governors from 1855 to 1997. In Sheung Wan there is Western Market (p75), built in 1906, and in the Mid-Levels the Edwardian-style Old Pathological Institute, now the Hong Kong Museum of Medical Sciences (p76) dating from 1905. The Old Stanley Police Station (1859; p86) and nearby Murray House (1848; p86) are important colonial structures in the southern part of Hong Kong Island.

The interesting **Hong Kong Antiquities & Monuments Office** (Map pp420–1; ☎ 2721 2326; www

> **TOP FIVE**
> **CONTROVERSIAL BUILDINGS**
>
> - **Bank of China Tower** (p69) – stunning geometric building by IM Pei – pity about the feng shui, which geomancers say is awful
> - **Hongkong & Shanghai Bank building** (p70) – Norman Foster's award-winning but very expensive 'robot' (apparently that's what it looks like to some)
> - **Hong Kong Cultural Centre** (p90) – is it a petrol station or a public toilet? The debate continues...
> - **Jardine House** (p71) – one too many orifices – and thus its comparison to at least one body part
> - **Two International Finance Centre** (p72) – Hong Kong's tallest building (by far) proves that size does matter

Contemporary architecture (below), Central

.amo.gov.hk; 136 Nathan Rd, Tsim Sha Tsui; ☺ 9am-5pm Mon-Sat), housed in a British schoolhouse that dates from 1902, has information and exhibits on current preservation efforts. For further information, an excellent source book is *Colonial Hong Kong: A Guide* by Stephen Vines.

CONTEMPORARY ARCHITECTURE

Hong Kong Island's skyline is becoming increasingly attractive – it was always dramatic – and its beauty is further enhanced by the Victoria Harbour in the forefront and the Peak in the background.

Hong Kong's verticality was born out of necessity – the scarcity of land and the sloping terrain have always put property at a premium in this densely populated place. Some buildings, such as Central Plaza (p78) and Two International Finance Centre (p72), have seized height at all costs; others are smaller but revel in elaborate detail, such as the Hongkong & Shanghai Bank building (p70). A privileged few, such as the Hong Kong Convention & Exhibition Centre (p79), have even been able to make the audacious move to go horizontal.

It's not unfair to say that truly inspired modern architecture only reached Hong Kong when Sir Norman Foster's award-winning Hongkong & Shanghai Bank building opened in Central in 1985. For the first time the territory was seeing what modern architecture can and should be: innovative, functional and startlingly beautiful. And since then, things have only got better.

For more on Hong Kong's contemporary architecture, pick up a copy of the illustrated vest-pocket guide *Skylines Hong Kong* by Peter Moss or the more specialist *Hong Kong: A Guide to Recent Architecture* by Andrew Yeoh and Juanita Cheung.

CINEMA

While painting and literature are enjoying a new lease of life in early 21st century Hong Kong, the art of film-making is moribund. Once the 'Hollywood of the Far East', churning out 245 films in 1994 alone and coming in third behind Hollywood and Mumbai, Hong Kong produced only 60 films in 2004, ranking 10th (even behind the Philippines). What's more, up to half of all local films produced here go directly into video format, to be pirated and sold as DVDs in the markets of Mong Kok and Shenzhen. Imports now account for between 55% and 60% of the Hong Kong film market.

25

Modern Hong Kong cinema arrived with the films of Bruce Lee, who first appeared in *The Big Boss* (1971), and the emergence of kung fu as a film genre. The 'chop sockey' trend continued through the 1970s and into the early '80s, when bullet-riddled action films took over.

Two directors of this period stand out. King Hu directed several stylish Mandarin kung fu films in the early 1970s, and the films of today still take his work as a reference point for action design. Michael Hui, along with his brother Sam, produced many popular social comedies, including *Private Eyes* (1976) and *The Pilferers' Progress* (1977; directed by John Woo). In terms of actors, Jackie Chan was making his mark during this period, with kung fu movies such as *Snake in the Eagle's Shadow* (1978) and *Drunken Master* (1978) – both directed by Yuen Wo Ping – but he later moved on to police-related stories such as *The Protector* in 1985 and the highly popular *Police Story* series.

Overall, however, it was an uphill battle for the local product at this time, with market share declining in the face of foreign competition. The upturn came in the mid-1980s, with John Woo's *A Better Tomorrow* series. Also prominent were the historical action films by Tsui Hark, including the *Once Upon a Time in China* (1991) featuring great action design and a stirring score.

The new wave of Hong Kong films in the 1990s attracted fans worldwide, particularly John Woo's blood-soaked epics *Hard Boiled* (1992) and *The Killer* (1989). Woo was courted by Hollywood and achieved international success directing films such as *Face/Off* (1997) and *Mission Impossible 2* (2000).

Jackie Chan, whose blend of kung fu and self-effacing comedy is beloved the world over, is one of several local stars to make it in Hollywood. He starred in *Crime Story* (1993), Stanley Tong's better-than-average action flick *Rumble in the Bronx* (1996) and teamed up with Owen Wilson in *Shanghai Noon* (2000) and *Shanghai Knights* (2003). Lamma native Chow Yun Fat featured in *The Replacement Killers* (1998) and *Anna & the King* (1999). Jet Li, star of *Lethal Weapon 4* (1998) and *Romeo Must Die* (2000), is another Hong Kong boy who has made a splash overseas. Wong Kar Wai, director of the cult favourite *Chungking Express* (1994), received the Palme d'Or at the Cannes Film Festival in 1997 for his film *Happy Together*.

Wong's sublime *In the Mood For Love* (2000) raised Hong Kong film to a new level and earned its star, Tony Leung, the Best Actor award at Cannes. Its follow-up, also starring Leung, was the beautifully shot but confusing and overly indulgent *2046* (2004), the title of which refers to a hotel room number and not sometime in the mid-21st century.

Memorable recent films include Yau Ching's *Ho Yuk (Let's Love Hong Kong;* 2002), the story of three alienated women pursuing or being pursued or not being pursued by each other; *Infernal Affairs* (2002) and its two follow-ups by Andrew Lau Wai-Keung and Alan

TOP FIVE HONG KONG FILMS

- *A Better Tomorrow* (1986) – John Woo's fast-packed gangster film, which examines loyalty and brotherhood among a couple of high-flying Triad buddies and a brother who is a policeman, set the standard for Hong Kong cinema for a decade. The 20-minute 'bullet ballet' finale is memorable.
- *Chungking Express* (1994) – a New Wave cop flick that isn't a cop flick, director Wong Kar Wai creates two separate (but connected) stories about cops dealing with love and relationships – the first with a drug-smuggling femme fatale in a blond wig and the second (Tony Leung) with a Jean Seberg–like Faye Wong. Powerful (and, at times, very funny) stuff.
- *In the Mood for Love* (2000) – Wong Kar Wai's triumphant (and exceedingly stylish) tale of infidelity and obsession stars Maggie Cheung and Tong Leung as two neighbours in 1960s Hong Kong who discover their spouses are having an affair together. Ab-fab fashion and styling.
- *Made in Hong Kong* (1997) – Fruit Chan's low budget film that went on to win a number of awards is the story of a moody young gang member whose life is turned upside down when he finds the suicide note of a young girl. It's a pretty bleak take on Hong Kong youth post-1997.
- *Once Upon a Time in China* (1991) – the ultimate kung fu film, Tsui Hark's first in a series of five follows hero Wong Fei Hung as he battles corrupt government officials, violent local gangsters and evil foreign entrepreneurs in order to protect his martial arts school and the people around him in 19th-century China.

Mak Siu-Fai, in which lonely cop Leung attempts to re-enter civilian life after 10 years undercover in a Triad gang; and *It Had to Be You* (2005) by Andrew Loo Wang-Hin and Maurice Li Ming-Man, a screwball comedy in which restaurant co-workers spar, plot against and then fall in love with one another. Other directors to watch out for include Peter Chan Ho-sun who made *He's a Woman, She's a Man* (1994), *Comrades, Almost a Love Story* (1996) and *The Love Letter* (1999); Chan Muk Sing (the *Gen-Y Cops* series); and Stanley Kwan who made *Full Moon in New York* (1989).

Hong Kong has been the setting of many Western-made films, including: *Love is a Many-Splendored Thing* (1955), starring William Holden, and Jennifer Jones as his Eurasian doctor paramour, with great shots on and from Victoria Peak; *The World of Suzie Wong* (1960), with Holden again and Nancy Kwan as the pouting bar girl from Wan Chai; *Enter the Dragon* (1973), Bruce Lee's first Western-made kung fu vehicle; *The Man with the Golden Gun* (1974), with Roger Moore as James Bond and filmed partly in a Tsim Sha Tsui topless bar; *Year of the Dragon* (1985), with Micky Rourke; and *Tai-Pan* (1986), the less-than-successful film version of James Clavell's doorstop novel (don't miss the bogus typhoon footage). Other foreign films shot partly or in full here include *Double Impact* (1991), *Mortal Kombat* (1995), *Rush Hour 2* (2001), with great shots of the harbour, and *Tomb Raider: The Cradle of Life* (2003), in which Laura Croft parachutes from Two International Finance Centre. An excellent source for spotting familiar locations is the HKTB's two-part freebie *Hong Kong Movie Odyssey Guide.*

Excellence in Hong Kong films is recognised each April with the presentation of the Hong Kong Film Awards, the territory's own 'Oscars'. The annual two-week Hong Kong International Film Festival, held in April and now in its third decade, brings in more than 240 films from 40 countries.

PAINTING

Painting in Hong Kong falls into three broad categories: classical Chinese, Western and modern local. Local artists dedicated to preserving such classical Chinese disciplines as calligraphy and Chinese landscape painting have usually spent years studying in China, and their work tends to reflect current trends in classical painting there. While Hong Kong does not have a great deal of home-grown Western art, the Hong Kong Museum of Art in Tsim Sha Tsui has both a permanent collection and temporary exhibits from abroad. Hong Kong modern art has gone through many phases – from the dynamic to the moribund – since it first arrived on the scene after WWII.

CONTEMPORARY ART

Contemporary Hong Kong art differs enormously from that produced in mainland China, and for good reason. Those artists coming of age in Hong Kong after WWII were largely (though not entirely) the offspring of refugees, distanced from the memories of economic deprivation, war and hunger. They were the products of a cultural fusion and sought new ways to reflect a culture that blended two worlds – the East and the West.

In general, Chinese are interested in traditional forms and painting processes – not necessarily composition and colour. Brush strokes and the utensils used to produce them are of vital importance and interest. In traditional Chinese art, change for the sake of change was never the philosophy or the trend; Chinese artists would compare their work with that of the master and judge it accordingly.

The influential Lingnan School of Painting, founded by the watercolourist Chao Shao-an (1905–98) in the 1930s and moved to Hong Kong in 1948, attempted to redress the situation. It combined traditional Chinese, Japanese and Western artistic traditions to produce a unique and rather decorative style, and basically dominated what art market there was in Hong Kong for the next two decades. An important figure of this time was Luis Chan (1905–95), the first Hong Kong Chinese artist to paint in the Western style.

WWII brought great changes not only to China but to Hong Kong, and the post-war generation of artists was characterised by an intense search for identity – Hong Kong rather than Chinese. It also set the stage for the golden age of modern Hong Kong art to come.

The late 1950s and early '60s saw the formation of several avant-garde groups, including the influential Modern Literature and Art Association, which counted Lui Shou-kwan (1919–75), Irene Chou (1924–) and Wucius Wong (1936–) among its members. Very structural, but at the same time inspired, the association spawned a whole generation of new talent obsessed with romanticism and naturalism. The Circle Art Group, founded in 1963 by Hon Chee Fun (1922–), was influenced by Abstract Expressionism and characterised by its spontaneous brush work. Two other important names of this period were contemporaries Gaylord Chan (1925–) and Ha Bik-Chuen (1925–).

Like young artists in urban centres everywhere, Hong Kong painters today are concerned with finding their orientation in a great metropolis through personal statement. They are overwhelmingly unfussed with orthodox Chinese culture and older generations' attempt to amalgamate East and West. To their mind the latter is now over and done with; judging from their work, they are now looking for something that is uniquely Hong Kong. Among those painters to watch out for are Victor Lai (1961–), a figurative artist much influenced by Francis Bacon and the German Expressionists, David Chan (1950–), who studied under Lui Shou-kwan and experiments with calligraphy and graphics; Wilson Shieh (1970–), who uses traditional Chinese *gùng-bàt* (fine-brush) painting techniques and forms to examine contemporary themes; Francis Yu (1963–), one of Hong Kong's most important oil painters, who combines Western and Chinese elements (especially

A GALLERY OF GALLERIES

In addition to the half-dozen commercial galleries below, all of which take part in the annual Hong Kong ArtWalk (p10) mega-event held in early March, nonprofit exhibition spaces on the cutting edge are **Para/Site Artspace** (Map pp408–9; ☎ 2517 4620; www.para-site.org.hk; 4 Po Yan St, Sheung Wan; ☯ noon-7pm Wed-Sun), one of the most important artists' cooperatives in Hong Kong; **Shanghai Street Artspace** (Map p423; ☎ 2770 2157; www.shout-art .org; 404 Shanghai St, Yau Ma Tei; ☯ 11am-2pm & 3-8pm Tue-Sun), a project of the Hong Kong Arts Development Council, with video assemblages, photography, computer art and mixed media; and the **Cattle Depot Artists Village** (Map pp418–19; ☎ 2104 3322, 2573 1869; 63 Ma Tau Kok Rd, To Kwa Wan; ☯ 2-8pm Tue-Sun), a one-time slaughterhouse in far-flung To Kwa Wan in east Kowloon that is home to a colony of local artists who live, work and exhibit here. You might also try the **Hong Kong Visual Arts Centre** (p80) in Hong Kong Park.

For more galleries than you'll know what to do with, check out the Hong Kong Gallery Guide website (www .hongkonggalleries.com).

- **Grotto Fine Art** (Map p412; ☎ 2121 2270; www.grottofineart.com; 2nd fl, 31C-D Wyndham St, Central; ☯ 11am-7pm Mon-Sat) This small but exquisite gallery represents predominantly Hong Kong artists whose work cover everything from painting and sculpture to mixed media.
- **Hanart TZ Gallery** (Map pp408–9; ☎ 2526 9019; www.hanart.com; Room 202, 2nd fl, Henley Bldg, 5 Queen's Rd Central; ☯ 10am-6.30pm Mon-Fri, 10am-6pm Sat) Hanart is *la crème de la crème* of art galleries in Hong Kong and was instrumental in establishing the reputation of many of the artists discussed in the Contemporary Art section of this chapter.
- **John Batten Gallery** (Map p412; ☎ 2854 1018; www.johnbattengallery.com; Ground fl, 64 Peel St, Soho; ☯ 1-7pm Tue-Sat, 2-5pm Sun) This gallery is charged with the enthusiasm and vision of its director, who is the Hong Kong ArtWalk organiser. He shows Asian painting (especially from the Philippines) and photography that is of consistently good quality.
- **Plum Blossoms** (Map p412; ☎ 2521 2189; www.plumblossoms.com; Ground fl, Shop 6, Chinachem Hollywood Centre, 1-13 Hollywood Rd, Central; ☯ 10am-6.30pm Mon-Sat) The shop where Rudolf Nureyev used to buy his baubles (and other celebrities continue to do so) is one of the most exquisite and well-established in Hong Kong. It promotes Asian (especially Chinese) contemporary artists.
- **Schoeni Art Gallery** (Map p412; ☎ 2869 8802; www.schoeni.com.hk; 21-31 Old Bailey St, Soho; ☯ 10.30am-6.30pm Mon-Sat); **Central branch** (Map p412; ☎ 2542 3143; 27 Hollywood Rd; ☯ 10.30am-6.30pm Mon-Sat) This Swiss-owned gallery, which has been a feature on Hollywood Rd for almost a quarter-century, specialises in Neorealist and Postmodern mainland Chinese art.
- **Sin Sin Fine Art** (Map p412; ☎ 2858 5072; www.sinsincom.hk; Ground fl, 1 Prince's Tce, Soho; ☯ 10.30am-7.30pm Tue-Sat, 2-7pm Sun) This eclectic gallery owned and run by a local fashion designer shows predominantly Hong Kong, mainland Chinese and Southeast Asian art.

characters) in his work; and Cheng Chi-fai (1971–), who uses oils to capture uniquely Hong Kong landscapes and city scenes.

The best place to view the works of modern Hong Kong painters is the Contemporary Hong Kong Art Gallery in the Hong Kong Museum of Art (p90) in Tsim Sha Tsui. Commercial galleries that specialise in local art are Grotto Fine Art (see the boxed text, opposite) and Hanart TZ Gallery (see the boxed text, opposite).

The best sources for up-to-date information on contemporary Hong Kong and other Asian art are the bimonthly **Asian Art News** (www.asianartnews.com) and the **Asia Art Archive** (Map pp408–9; ☎ 2815 1112; www.aaa.org.hk; 2nd fl, 208 Wah Koon Building, 181-191 Hollywood Rd, Sheung Wan; ⏰ 10am-6pm Mon-Sat).

SCULPTURE

Hong Kong's most celebrated sculptor of recent years was Antonio Mak, who died tragically at the age of 43 in 1994. Working primarily in bronze, Mak focused on the human figure as well as on animals important in Chinese legend and mythology (eg horses and tigers) and was greatly influenced by Rodin. His work employs much visual 'punning'; for example, in his *Mak's Bible from Happy Valley*, a racing horse is portrayed with a wing-like book made of lead across its back. The word 'book' in Cantonese has the same sound as 'to lose (at gambling)'. The painter Ha Bik-Chuen (opposite) has also worked extensively in mixed media and bronze.

Salisbury Gardens (p90), leading to the entrance of the Hong Kong Museum of Art in Tsim Sha Tsui, is lined with modern sculptures by contemporary Hong Kong sculptors. Dotted among the greenery of Kowloon Park (p91) is Sculpture Walk, with 30 marble, bronze and other weather-resistant works by both local and overseas artists, including a bronze by Mak called *Torso* and one by Britain's late Sir Eduardo Paolozzi (1924–2005) called *Concept of Newton*.

The quarterly **World Sculpture News** (www.worldsculpturenews.com) is a good start for those interested in contemporary Hong Kong and other Asian sculptors.

MUSIC
CLASSICAL

Western classical music is very popular among Hong Kong Chinese. The territory boasts the Hong Kong Philharmonic Orchestra and Hong Kong Sinfonietta as well as chamber orchestras, while the Hong Kong Chinese Orchestra often combines Western orchestration with traditional Chinese instruments. Overseas performers of world repute frequently make it to Hong Kong, and the number of foreign performances soars during the territory's most important cultural event, the Hong Kong Arts Festival (p10), in February/March each year.

TRADITIONAL CHINESE

You won't hear much traditional Chinese music on the streets of Hong Kong, except perhaps the sound of the doleful *dì-dáa,* a clarinet-like instrument played in a funeral procession; the hollow-sounding *gú* (drums) and crashing *làw* (gongs) and *bạt* (cymbals) at temple ceremonies and lion dances; or the *yi-wú,* a fiddle with 'two strings' favoured by beggars for its plaintive sound. The best place to hear this kind of music in full orchestration is by attending a concert given by the **Hong Kong Chinese Orchestra** (www.hkco.org) or a Chinese opera (p31).

CANTOPOP

Hong Kong's home-grown popular music scene is dominated by 'Cantopop' – original compositions that often blend Western rock or pop with traditional Chinese melodies and lyrics. Rarely radical, the songs invariably deal with such teenage concerns such as unrequited love and loneliness; to many they sound like the American pop songs of the 1950s. The music is slick and eminently singable – thus the explosion of karaoke bars throughout the territory. Attending a Cantopop concert is to see the city at its sweetest and most over the top, with screaming crows, silly dancing, Day-Glo wigs and enough floral tributes to set up a flower market.

Cantopop scaled new heights from the mid-1980s to mid-1990s and turned singers like Anita Mui, Leslie Cheung, Alan Tam, Priscilla Chan and Danny Chan into household names in Hong Kong and among Chinese communities around the world. The peak of this Cantopop golden age came with the advent of the so-called Four Kings: thespian/singer Andy Lau, Mr Nice Guy Jacky Cheung, dancer-turned-crooner Aaron Kwok and teen heart-throb Leon Lai.

It never quite reached that altitude again. Subsequent arrivals such as Beijing waif Faye Wong, Sammi Cheung, Kelly Chen and proto-hunk Nicholas Tse took their turns on the throne for a time. But today most stars are a packaged phenomenon; witness the industry's attempt to create 'Four New Kings' out of Leo Ku, Edmond Leung, Hacken Lee and Andy Hui and the female duo Twins who perform to a backing tape. Stars from the mainland and Taiwan – singer/songwriter Jay Chou is one example – are competing with local stars and gaining new fans here, and the strongest influences on local music are now coming from Japan and Korea.

The most unexpected 'talents' to emerge on the Hong Kong Cantopop scene in 2004 was one William Hung, a entrant in the American Idol competition whose geeky cover of Ricky Martin's 'She Bangs' earned the notoriety of nerdiness. Oddly for a place where the underdog remains very much unsung, where a popular aphorism (and warning) is 'Money talks, bullshit walks', when the Hong Kong–born Berkeley student returned to the territory with his tail between his legs, he was not only feted but contracted to do two albums and as many films.

THEATRE

Nearly all theatre in Hong Kong is Western in form, if not content. Most productions are staged in Cantonese, and a large number are new plays by Hong Kong writers. The plays often provide an insightful and sometimes humorous look at contemporary Hong Kong life and society. The independent **Hong Kong Repertory Theatre** (www.hkrep.com), formed in 1977, tends to stage larger-scale productions of both original works on Chinese themes or translated Western plays. More experimental troupes are the **Hong Kong Players** (www.hongkongplayers .com) and the multimedia **Zuni Icosahedron** (www.zuni.org.hk).

English-language theatre in Hong Kong is for the most part the domain of expatriate amateurs, and plays are more often than not scripted by local writers. Among the more popular venues are the Fringe Club theatres (p214) in Central. The Hong Kong Cultural Centre (p212), the Hong Kong Academy for the Performing Arts (p212), Hong Kong City Hall (p212) and the Shouson Theatre at the nearby Hong Kong Arts Centre (p212) all host foreign productions, ranging from your overblown Western musicals to minimalist Japanese theatre.

Chinese opera display, Hong Kong Museum of History (p92)

THE LION BOPS TONIGHT

The lion dance is one Chinese tradition that lives on in Hong Kong. Dancers and martial artists take position under an elaborately painted costume of a mythical Chinese lion. To the accompaniment of banging cymbals and, if in a remote location like one of the Outlying Islands, sometimes exploding firecrackers (which are illegal in Hong Kong), the lion leaps its way around the crowd, giving the dancers a chance to demonstrate their acrobatic skills. The lion's mouth and eyes open and close and a beard hangs down from the lion's lower jaw; the longer the beard, the more venerable the school that performs the dance. As it wends its way through the streets, the lion is sometimes rewarded with a lettuce hanging on a string outside a shop or restaurant, which it must reach up and grab between its jaws. Lion dances are most commonly seen during the Lunar New Year in late January or February.

CHINESE OPERA

Chinese opera (kek), a mixture of singing, dialogue, mime, acrobatics and dancing, is a world away from its Western counterpart, but the themes are pretty much the same: mortal heroes battle overwhelmingly powerful supernatural foes; legendary spirits defend the world against evil; lovers seek escape from domineering and disapproving parents.

Most foreigners will find that Chinese opera performances take some getting used to. Both male and female performers sing in an almost reedy falsetto designed to pierce through crowd noise, and the instrumental accompaniment often takes the form of drumming, gonging and other nonmelodic punctuation. Performances can last five to six hours, and the audience makes an evening of it – eating, chatting among themselves and changing seats when bored.

There are three types of Chinese opera performed in Hong Kong. Peking opera (gingkek) is a highly refined style that uses almost no scenery but a variety of traditional props. This is where you'll find the most acrobatics and swordplay. Cantonese opera (yuet-kek) is more a 'music hall' style, usually with a 'boy meets girl' theme, and often incorporating modern and foreign references. The most traditional is Chiu Chow opera (chiu-kek). It is staged almost as it was during the Ming dynasty, with stories from the legends and folklore of the Chiu Chow (Chaozhou in Mandarin), an ethnic group from the easternmost region of Guangdong province.

Costumes, props and body language reveal much of the meaning in Chinese opera. Check out the enlightening display on the subject at the Hong Kong Heritage Museum (p119), where the HKTB (p310) offers a Chinese opera appreciation course every Saturday from 2.30pm to 3.45pm.

The best time to see Cantonese opera is during the Hong Kong Arts Festival in February/March; outdoor performances are also staged in Victoria Park on Hong Kong Island during the Mid-Autumn Festival. At other times, you stumble upon a performance at the Temple Street night market (p246) in Yau Ma Tei, but the most reliable venue for opera performances year round is the Sunbeam Theatre (p214) in North Point.

LITERATURE

Until recently about the only English-language writer that Hong Kong could claim as its very own was the late Austin Coates (1922–97), who set two of his books – the autobiographical *Myself a Mandarin* and a novel called *The Road* – in the territory and also wrote a fictionalised account of the life of the celebrated 18th-century Macanese 'taipan' Martha Merop (p376). But, as the Man Hong Kong International Literary Festival, which launched in 2001, and the advent of the Hong Kong–based Dimsum (www.dimsum.com.hk) literary review both indicate, there has been a veritable explosion in home-grown literary activity and local interest in recent years.

Anyone who wants a 'taster' of Hong Kong literature since WWII should pick up a copy of the seminal *City Voices: Hong Kong Writing in English 1945 to the Present* (editors Xu Xi and Mike Ingham; 2003), which is a collection of novel excerpts, short stories, poems, essays and memoirs with ties to Hong Kong. *Hong Kong: Somewhere Between Heaven and Earth* (editor Barbara-Sue White; 1996) is a not-dissimilar anthology on Hong Kong but is more

31

HONG KONG IN PRINT

- *Chinese Walls* by Sussy Chako (1994) – a harrowing (and courageous) account of incest, infidelity and despair in a dysfunctional Chinese family living in Kowloon by the Chinese-Indonesian author now known as Xu Xi.
- *Dynasty* by Robert Elegant (1977) – a favourite and a rollicking good read, this novel describes the life and times of a young Englishwoman who marries into a family not unlike the Ho Tungs, a powerful Eurasian family dating back to the early colonial period.
- *Fragrant Harbour* by John Lanchester (2002) – this rather unconvincing door-stopper manages to record 70 years of Hong Kong history (from the 1930s) through the eyes of four characters whose lives intertwine. It's full of obscure facts like Hong Kong's toilets are flushed with seawater.
- *Gweilo: Memories of a Hong Kong Childhood* by Martin Booth (2004) – this much acclaimed memoir by the late British novelist and biographer captures the spirit and ethos of the Hong Kong of the 1950s but even newcomers to Hong Kong will wonder how a prepubescent boy – even an especially precocious one – managed to have many of the adventures he claimed to have had or witnessed so many pivotal events first hand.
- *Hong Kong Belongers* by Simon Barnes (1999) – this is a tortuous, mostly unbelievable story of an irritating young expat journalist – 'Alan Fairs is going back to Hong Kong… a land of laughter and tears… the land of his youth' – who lives on a fictitious island not unlike Lamma.
- *The Honourable Schoolboy Spy* by John Le Carré (1977) – the master of the thriller's most celebrated novel is a story of espionage and intrigue as seen through the eyes of one George Smiley, acting head of the British Secret Service in the Hong Kong of the early 1970s.
- *An Insular Possession* by Timothy Mo (1987) – this hefty book follows the careers of two young Americans who are determined to expose the corruption of British opium traders in China by leaving their trading company and starting a newspaper. The First Opium War lands them in pre-colonial Hong Kong.
- *Kowloon Tong* by Paul Theroux (1997) – this rather annoying novel focuses on an expatriate family's insecurities on the eve of the handover. Nothing like what was predicted here ever happened, of course.
- *Love is a Many-Splendored Thing* by Han Suyin (1952) – this novel, set in Hong Kong shortly after the end of the Chinese revolution and proclamation of the People's Republic of China, is based on a love affair the author had with a British foreign correspondent.
- *Myself a Mandarin* by Austin Coates (1968) – this positively charming work was based on Coates' work as a special magistrate dealing in traditional Chinese law in the New Territories during the 1950s. It's full of revelations about rural Hong Kong Chinese and their culture.
- *Overleaf Hong Kong* by Xu Xi (2005) – this fine collection of a dozen short stories and essays focuses largely on identity and *wàa-kiǜ* (*huaqiao* in Mandarin), or 'overseas Chinese'.
- *The Road* by Austin Coates (1959) – Coates' first book is a riveting tale of the colonial government's attempt to build a highway across Great Island (which sounds suspiciously like Lantau), and the effect it has on the government, the builders and the islanders.
- *Tai-Pan* by James Clavell (1966) – almost as thick as the Yellow Pages, *Tai-Pan* is a rather unrealistic tale of Western traders in Hong Kong's early days, but it's an easy read. The sequel to *Tai-Pan*, also set in Hong Kong, is another epic called *Noble House* (1981) about a fictitious *hàwng* (trading house).
- *The Monkey King* by Timothy Mo (1988) – Mo's first novel, set in 1950s Hong Kong, is the often hilarious account of one Wallace Nolasco, a Macanese who marries into a wickedly dysfunctional Cantonese merchant's family.
- *The Train to Lo Wu* by Jess Row (2005) – this perceptive and very subtly written collection of short stories by a former teacher at Chinese University explores the theme of alienation and feelings of being outside a place or community.
- *Triad* by Derek Lambert (1991) – British police superintendent, who has lost his son to drugs, takes on the Chinese underworld of Hong Kong and a very attractive missionary trying to convert the godfather. Gripping (though violent) police yarn.
- *The World of Suzie Wong* by Richard Mason (1957) – arguably the most famous – if not the best – novel set in Hong Kong this is the story of a Wan Chai–based prostitute with a heart of gold and the British artist who loves her.

historical than literary, with excerpts from such figures as Queen Victoria and the French novelist Jules Verne and reaching back as far as the Song dynasty (AD 960–1279). *Hong Kong Collage* (editor Martha PY Cheung; 1998) is a collection of stories and other writings by contemporary Chinese writers, most of whom were born and/or raised in Hong Kong.

Given its dramatic setting, its unique mixture of Chinese and Western cultures and its sensitive position at China's back door, Hong Kong has been the setting of legions of fictional books – from thrillers to romances (see the boxed text, above).

Food

History & Culture — 34

Cantonese Cuisine — 35

How Hong Kong People Eat — 35
Dim Sum 36
Etiquette 37

Staples & Specialities — 37
Eggs 37
Fish & Shellfish 38
Meat & Poultry 38
Noodles 39
Rice 39
Soup 40
Tofu 40
Vegetables 41
Dessert 41

Regional Variations — 41
Chiu Chow 41
Northern 42
Shanghainese 42
Sichuan 42

Vegetarians & Vegans — 43

Asian & International Food — 43

Drinks — 44
Nonalcoholic Drinks 44
Alcoholic Drinks 44

Menu Decoder — 45

Food

If the pursuit of wealth is the engine that drives Hong Kong, its fuel is food. Noodles are slurped, seafood savoured and dishes praised for their presentation, freshness or texture – as well as taste, of course. A Hong Kong housewife selects a fish for her family's dinner as a gem-cutter chooses a rough diamond; certain chefs enjoy celebrity status and are followed from restaurant to restaurant by gourmets as groupies pursue rock stars. Food – and the business of eating it – is taken *very* seriously in Hong Kong.

Depending on the district, it can be especially hard to find a good-quality, reasonably priced restaurant that has a menu in English. If you don't read or speak Cantonese, the problem can be alleviated by eating in a dim sum restaurant, where dishes are usually wheeled around on trolleys; just choose and point.

For pronunciation guidelines that will help you get the most out of the Cantonese Romanisations used throughout this book, see p380.

HISTORY & CULTURE

The story of Hong Kong cuisine begins with the collision of two empires. Before that seismic event, Hong Kong was a backwater in every sense. It had long been inhabited by humble fisherfolk, farmers and a lesser

Dim sum, City Hall Maxim's Palace (p152), Central

breed of pirate who had eked out a living for centuries all but unnoticed. In the 16th century, across the mouth of the Pearl River, the Portuguese established themselves in what is now Macau, and whatever attention the world focused on the region went there. But then came the First Opium War (p54) and the world turned its eyes to Hong Kong.

This did not bring good dining instantly. The British brought their own provisions, and in this far corner of the world continued to eat their gammon and sausage, pies and kippers, and wash it all down with milky tea and warm beer. The Chinese who flowed in with the British brought their culinary traditions, for the most part Cantonese ones. There was no immediate Promethean spark in the Hong Kong kitchen, but there began a slow building of the foundation of Hong Kong's culinary culture.

It was fortunate, for diners, that the Crown Colony had come to rely on the mainland city of Guangzhou (then Canton) for its survival, as it provided food, labour, building materials, water, cooks and inspiration. For mainland cooks, pay was better in Hong Kong; as a result the best cooks in China who went to Guangzhou ended up in Hong Kong. For many decades after the war, Hong Kong was the 'real' Guangzhou because there was the money (and the acumen) to strive for the best, the most exotic, the new. There were other Chinese people in Hong Kong, such as the Hakka, but their culinary contribution would have to wait to be noticed.

With the declaration of the People's Republic of China in 1949, floods of immigrants, including many chefs and cooks, came to Hong Kong from all over the mainland. From

Shanghai, Sichuan, Hunan and Beijing (Peking) they came, looking for safety, jobs and a new life. Though they might never see their homelands again, they could at least nourish themselves on the memories, keeping their birthplaces alive in the hearth and on the table.

CANTONESE CUISINE

Originating in Guangdong province from where most Hong Kong Chinese people can trace their roots, Cantonese food is by far the most popular cuisine in Hong Kong. And when it's done well (as it so often is here), it is the best of the lot. The flavours are more subtle than in other Chinese cooking styles, the sauces are rarely strong. It was from Guangdong, too, that the main bulk of Chinese emigrants went abroad. Consequently Cantonese cuisine established itself as 'Chinese cuisine' in the Western world.

Cantonese cuisine has the largest collection of specialised dishes in all of China and is characterised by elaborate preparation and the use of an infinite variety of ingredients. Subtle flavours are combined with a light touch of soy sauce and ginger, enhancing the freshness of the ingredients. Flavours are delicate and well balanced – neither salty nor oily – and are obtained through cooking techniques such as quick stir-frying and steaming.

The Cantonese are almost religious about the importance of fresh ingredients. It is common to see tanks in seafood restaurants full of finned and shelled creatures enjoying their final moments on terra *in*firma. Housewives still prefer a live chicken or pigeon plucked from (and plucked in, come to think of it) a market for the evening meal, though the cost of fresh poultry makes the supermarket variety more popular.

The love of food and the increase in foreign travel by local people means there's a lot more experimentation with food these days. Macadamia nuts find their way into scallop dishes, and you're just as likely to find sautéed cod slices with pine seeds and fresh fruit as you are traditional steamed grouper on a menu.

Seasonal foods still play a big role in what's on offer at restaurants. Hotpots of pork tripe and other innards can be found in winter, dried scallops with sea moss at Chinese New Year, and winter-melon soup in August.

Expensive dishes – some of which are truly tasty, others that carry with them something of a 'face' status – include abalone, shark's fin and bird's nest. Pigeon is a tasty Cantonese speciality served in various ways but most commonly roasted, chopped finely and eaten with lettuce and hoisin sauce (see the boxed text, p40).

There aren't many dishes or sauces unique to Hong Kong per se; even oyster sauce, which is so strongly associated with the territory, is originally from Guangzhou. There is, however, Hong Kong style – the territory's way of preparing a dish – and it's often an improvement on the original. Hong Kong chefs pride themselves on innovation: experimenting, improvising and creating. They will instantly seize upon a new ingredient and find ways to use it. For example, asparagus is a vegetable little known in the rest of China, but Hong Kong chefs serve it every day, combining it with baby abalone and olive oil or with caviar and preserved eggs. XO sauce only appeared on the territory's menus for the first time in the late 1980s.

Very high heat is an important factor in Hong Kong cooking. In most parts of China the clay pot is used for slow cooking, but in Hong Kong it is placed over a blast of high heat to quickly infuse flavours into the dish. And even more importantly, Hong Kong chefs hew to the concept of *wok chi* (*wok-hay* in Cantonese). The term refers to what could be called a hot wind that roars off a super-heated wok. This can only be achieved with a powerful fire burner that covers the entire underside of the wok, not just the small ring of fire found on the common cooker. This produces a fire so hot that home kitchens cannot use it. This cooking technique sears and carbonises the outer surfaces of foods and seals in flavour.

HOW HONG KONG PEOPLE EAT

In a world where food is paramount, it should come as no surprise that Hong Kong people eat up to five times a day: breakfast, lunch, afternoon tea, dinner and a late-night snack. Afternoon tea and a late-night snack are not considered meals, though; that's just filling up space. A proper meal must comprise rice and other dishes as garnishes.

SNACKING ON STREET-SAVVY SAVOURIES

Hong Kong people love to snack – favouring the savoury over the sweet in most cases. Apart from dim sum, the more traditional Chinese snacks eaten in Hong Kong are various seafood titbits, often served on a bamboo skewer. Squid or fish balls barbecued on a stick are examples. Fish-ball soup served in a styrofoam cup is a modern variation of a traditional snack. A winter snack that has to be smelt to be believed is *chau dau-fu* (stinky beancurd), which is fermented tofu deep-fried in oil.

For the most part, you buy these Cantonese munchies from pushcarts that tend to gather late at night in strategic locations, such as at ferry piers and outside cinemas. But a government crackdown on unsanitary and unsafe public catering – the portable stoves use pressurised gas canisters – has seen a drop in their numbers in recent years.

In Hong Kong, workers may breakfast at home or in a small restaurant specialising in breakfast foods such as *jùk*, a rice porridge also known as congee, which is either eaten plain or with a multitude of savoury garnishes and condiments. Secretaries and other office workers may grab a bowl of soup noodles and bring it to the work place, happily slurping away at their desks. At the weekend and on holidays everyone goes out for dim sum for breakfast, brunch or even lunch.

Lunch in the built-up areas during the week will often be a set lunch consisting of one or two dishes at a fixed price. However, lunch can also be a bowl of soup noodles with shrimp won tons or a plate of rice with roast pork, duck or goose. It may be something more elaborate at one of the hotel dining rooms or even a buffet.

Afternoon tea in Hong Kong is especially popular on weekends at the good hotels. This can be an elaborate affair, a traditional English high tea, or dim sum. It may be at the office and comprise little more than tea and biscuits or a steamed bun. At home a housewife may invite her neighbour over for tea and melon seeds or sesame crisps. Labourers will stop for just a few minutes to pour a cup of tea and eat a custard tart before going back to work.

Dinner is a big event every day, especially dinner in a restaurant. The majority of Hong Kong people live in very small flats with handkerchief-sized kitchens; dining out with friends and family solves the problem of space. This is one reason Hong Kong's restaurants are always so noisy; this is where people come to catch up on all the gossip, make plans, tell jokes and just enjoy life.

Dishes at a Chinese meal are always served together. Tables, which are always round in Chinese restaurants, are often equipped with a turntable – a lazy Susan – on which the food is placed. It's not unusual for dishes to be served with tiny saucers filled with various sauces, with *si-yàu* (soy sauce), *gaai-laat* (hot mustard) and *laat-jiù jeung* (chilli sauce) the most common ones. Feel free to stand up and lean over the table to dip if the sauce is on the other side.

Often you'll see several small bottles on the table, usually containing soy sauce and vinegar. The vinegar is usually a dark colour and is easily confused with soy sauce, so taste some first before pouring. Sauces aren't dumped on food – instead the food is dipped into a separate dish. Staff will usually let you know which sauce goes with which dish.

DIM SUM

Dim sum *(dím sàm)* is a uniquely Cantonese 'meal', eaten as breakfast, brunch or lunch. The term literally means 'to touch the heart', but 'snack' is more accurate. The act of eating dim sum is usually referred to as yum cha *(yám chàa)*, meaning 'to drink tea' as the beverage is always consumed in copious amounts with dim sum.

Eating dim sum is a social occasion and something you should do in a group. You can eat dim sum alone or as a couple, of course, but it consists of many separate dishes, which are meant to be shared; you can't simply order a plate with a variety of dim sum items. Having several people to share with means you can try many different dishes.

Dim sum delicacies are normally steamed in small bamboo baskets. Typically, each basket contains three or four identical pieces; you pay by the number of baskets you order. The baskets are stacked up on pushcarts and rolled around the dining room.

You don't need a menu (though these exist, but almost always in Chinese only); just stop the waiter and choose something from the cart. It will be marked down on a bill left on the table. Don't try to order everything at once. Each cart has a different selection, so take your time and order as they come. It's said that there are about 1000 different dim sum dishes.

Dim sum restaurants are normally brightly lit and very large and noisy – it's rather like eating in an aircraft hangar. Nevertheless, it can get very crowded, especially at lunch time.

ETIQUETTE

The Chinese are, by and large, casual about etiquette at the table, and they don't expect foreigners to understand all of their dining customs. But there are a few unique ways of doing things here that are useful to know.

The Chinese think nothing of sticking their chopsticks into a communal dish, which is one reason why hepatitis is still a problem in China and, less so, in Hong Kong and Macau. Better restaurants provide separate serving chopsticks or even spoons with each dish; if so, use them. Leaving chopsticks sticking vertically into the bowl – as unlikely as that sounds – is a bad omen as they resemble incense sticks in a bowl of ashes, a sign of death. And never, ever, flip a fish over to reach the flesh on the bottom. The next fishing boat you pass will capsize. Just use your chopsticks to break off pieces through the bones.

If you absolutely can't manage chopsticks, don't be afraid to ask for a fork; nearly all Chinese restaurants have them. It's better to swallow a little humble pie than miss out on all those treats set before you.

At a Chinese meal, everyone gets an individual bowl of rice or a small soup bowl. It's quite acceptable to hold the bowl close to your lips and shovel the contents into your mouth with chopsticks. An alternative is to hold a spoon in one hand and use the chopsticks to push the food onto the spoon. Then use the spoon as you normally would.

If the food contains bones, just put them directly on the tablecloth beside your plate or bowl. And you needn't use a napkin to hide what you're doing; except at very upmarket restaurants most Hong Kong people just spit them on the table.

Chinese make great use of toothpicks – foreign residents of Hong Kong sometimes call them 'Chinese dessert' – after a meal and even occasionally between courses. The polite way to use them is to cover your mouth with one hand while using the toothpick with the other.

Beer, soft drinks or even wine or brandy *may* be served with the meal, but tea most definitely will; for details see p44. When your waiter or host pours your tea, thank them by tapping your middle and index fingers lightly on the table. When the teapot is empty and you want a refill of hot water, signal the waiter by taking the lid off the pot and resting it on the handle.

Toasts in Hong Kong are not usually accompanied by long-winded speeches as the can be in the West, but are usually limited to the words *yúm sing* (roughly, 'down the hatch').

STAPLES & SPECIALITIES

What are the staples and specialities of a people who are not only willing but eager to eat anything and everything so long as it has 'its back to the sky' (as they say in Cantonese) – including such 'delicacies' as pig's tongue, 'snow frog' (toad's ovaries), snake and bamboo pith? Here you'll find the foods from every region of China and every other part of the world for that matter. The best we can do is tell you what you will find most of in Hong Kong, and advise you to keep an eye out for more.

EGGS

Eggs – all kinds – are consumed with relish in Hong Kong. Chicken, duck and goose eggs, fish, prawn and crab roe – Hong Kong people are overjoyed with ova.

A taste sensation are 1000-year-old eggs, which are actually just a month or two old, and are called *pày dáan* (preserved egg) in Cantonese. They are duck eggs soaked in a lime solution, which turns the egg white a translucent green and the yolk a greyish green. These are usually served as a starter or as a condiment to accompany another dish.

Salted duck eggs, called *hàam-ngaap dáan*, are soaked in a saline solution for about 40 days. This process crystallises the yolk and turns it bright orange. Unlike preserved eggs, these must be cooked. They may be broken into a dish of stir-fried tofu or fried rice, or hard-boiled and chopped up into a bowl of congee. Hard-boiled *hàam-ngaap dáan* make a tasty, though filling, breakfast on their own. You can recognise salted eggs at the market because they are wrapped in what looks like cow manure but is actually just packed earth.

FISH & SHELLFISH

Cantonese love freshly and simply prepared seafood and fish – and with China's long coastline and many rivers and lakes, it is no wonder that fish has always been important to their diet. In Chinese, the word for fish is *yéw,* which can also mean 'plenty' or 'abundance'. So the final dish at a formal dinner banquet is traditionally a whole fish, signifying to the guests that although many courses have already been consumed, there is plenty more to eat if they so desire.

When the fish, crab, prawn or lobster is plucked from the sea (or river or pond), it must be cooked immediately. It is vital to capture the freshness of the fish in the wok – a maxim held by chefs in every Chinese kitchen around the world. In fact Cantonese chefs have an insistence bordering on obsession for freshness, so it is common to see fish tanks in many restaurants in Hong Kong.

MEAT & POULTRY

The people of Hong Kong consume more protein per capita than any other group in the world. Of course some of that is tofu, but this is far and away the most carnivorous city in China. Pork is the premier meat, as it is anywhere in China, but chicken – often bought live at the market then plucked – duck and beef are also relished and served braised, steamed or fried. One of the favourite ways of preparing certain meats, especially pork, is

FRUIT

Along with peaches, pears and apples from North America and Europe, Hong Kong imports an enormous variety of fruits from Australia, South Africa and Southeast Asia, including some really exotic ones. Special fruits to look out for include those listed here.

carambola – bright yellow fruit also known as star fruit, which is exactly what it looks like when sliced horizontally

custard apple – the size of an apple, this fruit has a bumpy green-grey skin and a sweet, custardlike taste

durian – a large fruit shaped like a rugby ball that has tough spikes and looks impenetrable. After breaking it open with a big knife and peeling off the skin, you'll encounter the next obstacle, a powerful odour that many can't abide. The creamy fruit is actually delicious – it tastes of garlic custard with alcohol mixed in – and is even used to make ice cream in Thailand and Malaysia. The season is April to June.

hami melon – a large oval melon with the cantaloupe-like skin, this sugary fruit comes from China's Xinjiang province and is sold only in summer

jackfruit – this large segmented fruit is fine stuff when ripe, but tastes a bit like American chewing gum

longan – the skin of this fruit, whose name means 'dragon eye' in Chinese, is brown, and the clear fruit crunchy, but otherwise the taste is similar to that of a lychee. Its season is from June to early August.

lychee – a red, pulpy fruit with white flesh, which has a single seed; the smaller the seed the better the fruit (available in June)

mango – the variety sold in Hong Kong are the yellow-skinned fruits from the Philippines

mangosteen – beneath the thick, smooth purple skin of this fruit is white flesh that has a delicious sour-sweet flavour

pomelo – similar to a large grapefruit but sweeter and drier

rambutan – distantly related to the lychee, with a similar taste, rambutans have hairy red skin that makes them look like tiny suns. The season is from May to October.

barbecuing it; you'll also see *chàa siù* (roast pork) and *siù ngaap* (roast duck) hanging from hooks in restaurant windows, the fat dripping into pans below. Lamb and mutton are unknown outside northern Chinese restaurants. Southern Chinese cannot stand the smell.

NOODLES

Noodles are thought to have originated in northern China during the Han dynasty (206 BC to AD 220) when the Chinese developed techniques for the large-scale grinding of flour. Not only were noodles nutritious, cheap and versatile, they were portable and could be stored for long periods. Legend credits Marco Polo with having brought noodles to Italy in 1295, where it developed into pasta.

Durian for sale, Graham St Market (p157), Central

Chinese like to eat noodles at all times, but especially at birthdays and the New Year since the shape symbolises longevity. That's why it's bad luck to break noodles before cooking them. You just may be shortening more than you think.

Various regions of China (and other parts of Asia too) claim different types of noodles as their own, but Hong Kong people don't care. They eat them all. Thin, translucent strands made from mung bean starch are called *fán-sì* (cellophane noodles or bean threads). They are used most often in Southeast Asian dishes, and are usually cooked in soups or deep-fried. *Háw-fán* are wide, white, flat, slippery rice noodles, and are usually pan fried.

The Cantonese word for noodle is *mín*, and *cháau mín* (fried noodles) are arguably the most popular dish here. There are many variations, but most often the thin noodles are fried crisp. The story goes that in the 19th century a certain Chinese cook was employed by the railroad. When frying noodles one day for the boss, the lazy fellow fell asleep and when he awoke the noodles were burnt to a crisp. As he had no more noodles he served them to the boss and hoped for the best. But the boss, never having had 'chow mein' before, pronounced them delicious and demanded that they be served every day.

Won ton are not exactly noodles, more noodle packets and not dissimilar to ravioli. Ranging in size from that of a watch face to bigger than a golf ball, they are filled with minced prawns, pork or vegetables and can be fried, steamed or added to soup.

Restaurant windows fogged from the steam of vats bubbling with won ton noodle soup or congee are great places to sample Hong Kong's indigenous 'fast food'. Noodles come in a variety of colours, textures and cooking styles. Yellow balls of twinelike noodles are most common with won ton in soup, sometimes with a few pieces of green vegetable thrown in for extra crunch. If you think won ton noodles have the slight taste of ammonia, that's because alkali and duck egg are sometimes added when mixing the dough for the noodles.

RICE

Rice is deeply, er, ingrained in Chinese culinary tradition and an inseparable part of virtually every meal. The Chinese don't ask 'Have you had your dinner/lunch yet?' but 'Have you eaten rice yet?'. It's that central to the equation.

The Chinese revere rice not only as their staff of life but also for its aesthetic value. Its mellow aroma is not unlike bread. Its texture when properly prepared – soft yet offering some resistance, the grains detached – sets off the textures of the foods that surround it, their shimmering colours the more vivid for the rice's stark whiteness. Flavours are brought into better focus by its simplicity. Rice is the unifier of the table, bringing all the dishes into harmony.

SAUCES & FLAVOURINGS

Chinese cooking employs certain spices and flavourings that are not major players in a Western kitchen: star anise (a clovelike spice that yields a strong liquorice flavour and is used to enhance soups and stews); five-spice powder (ground star anise blended with fennel or anise seed, cloves, cinnamon and Sichuan peppercorns that is used to flavour barbecued meats and stews); and sesame oil (added to marinades or at the last moment of cooking to flavour certain dishes).

Sauces, both cooked with meat or fish or used for dipping, that are central to Chinese cooking include those below.

black bean sauce – fermented black beans (a type of soya bean) combined with soy sauce, ginger, rice wine, sugar and oil

hoisin sauce – sweet, slightly piquant brown paste made from soya beans, red beans, sugar, garlic, vinegar, chilli, sesame oil and flour (essential with Peking duck)

oyster sauce – thick dark sauce made from oysters, water, salt, soy sauce and cornstarch and often served over vegetables

soy sauce – the quintessential Chinese condiment and cooking ingredient made through a fermentation process involving soya beans and wheat flour or barley. There is a wide range of soy sauces available, all of which can be divided into light and dark soy. Light soy is used in things like soup, when the cook wants a delicate flavour of soy but not the colour, and as a condiment. Dark soy contains caramel and is richer and thicker. It's used in marinades and sometimes as a condiment.

XO sauce – very popular, newfangled condiment made from crushed conpoy (dried scallops), chilli, garlic and oil

Rice comes in lots of different preparations – as congee, the rice porridge that is favoured and flavoured at breakfast, or fried with tiny shrimps, pork or vegetables and eaten at lunch or as a snack. Glutinous rice dumplings are made from sticky rice, to which pork, chicken or prawns have been added, wrapped in lotus leaves and steamed. But plain steamed white rice – neutral yet fragrant – is what you should order at dinner. It's the canvas on which to paint your own culinary masterpiece.

Congee

Hong Kong is famous for its *jùk*. Unless you're prepared to accept rice powder as a rapid-cooking substitute (and *we* are not), it demands standing and stirring for a couple of hours until the grains have engorged and exploded into a porridge-like consistency; few people have the time or inclination for that amount of work. You can eat congee plain with *yàu-jaa-gwái* (devils' tails), dough rolled and fried in hot oil, or dressed for the fair with salted pork, fish balls, condiments, toasted garlic and/or bean sprouts. It's comfort food at its best (and, by the way, an excellent hangover cure or easer).

SOUP

In Hong Kong, a balanced meal simply must have a soup. Traditionally it was the beverage component of the meal, and nowadays it shares that role with other liquids. It is also one of the chief means by which the Chinese maintain their health. Soup is the main vehicle for the delivery of medicinal and balance-enhancing properties of foods. It gives you heat in winter and keeps you cool in summer. Traditionally it's one of the last courses served at a banquet.

TOFU

The pressed curd of the soya bean is sometimes called 'poor man's meat'. Tofu contains all the essential amino acids, is low in calories and devoid of cholesterol. It is mainly used for its texture – there is not much taste to it – and it goes well with many other ingredients. You can do absolutely anything with tofu: deep-fry, sauté, steam, bake, simmer, broil or purée it. It comes in three textures: soft, which is added to soups or steamed dishes where cooking time is brief; semisoft, which is used in stir-fry dishes; and firm, used for stuffing and deep-frying.

Other tofu products include tofu skin, which is the skin that forms when the soya beans are being boiled. It is used to add texture to stir-fry dishes and to wrap up meat and fish. You will also find marinated tofu sold in jars, the taste of which can be extremely strong, but not as strong as *chau dau-fu* (see the boxed text, p36).

VEGETABLES

Cantonese people are mad for vegetables, especially greens, and consume great quantities of *choy-sàm* (rape or flowering cabbage), *tùng-choy* (water spinach), *bak choi* (Chinese white cabbage), *baak-choy* (spinach), *sài-làan-fàa* (broccoli), *sàang-choy* (lettuce) and *gaai-láan* (Chinese broccoli). Other popular vegetables include bamboo shoots, bean sprouts, bitter melon (gourd), eggplant, long beans, mushrooms (black, tree ear and straw varieties), roots (such as lotus, taro) and water chestnuts.

DESSERT

Dessert (at least as Westerners know it) is not a big-ticket item at Chinese meals. Hong Kong Chinese will traditionally end a meal with *tàwng séui* (sweet soup) – made of red beans, almonds or black sesame – or, more commonly, fresh fruit, usually oranges as they symbolise wealth. At dim sum you may find warm egg-custard tarts, steamed buns with sweet red-bean paste, coconut snowballs (sweet rice-flour balls dressed with coconut slices), and various other sweets made with sesame seeds. You will never be served fortune cookies at the end of a meal at a Hong Kong Chinese restaurant. These are a foreign invention.

REGIONAL VARIATIONS

China can be divided into many geographical areas, and each area has a distinct style of cooking. Not surprisingly, the ingredients used in the food tend to reflect the agricultural produce available in that region. Northern China, for example, is suited to growing wheat, so noodles, dumplings and other gluten-based preparations are common. In the south, where the climate is warm and wet, rice is the staple. The Sichuan area, where spices grow well, is famous for its fiery hot dishes. Coastal areas, needless to say, excel in their preparations of seafood.

It is not only geography that determines the ingredients used – tradition and culture play a part as well. The Cantonese, the most adventurous among the Chinese when it comes to food, are known for their willingness to eat virtually anything. Consequently, animals with physical and/or sexual prowess (real or imagined) are widely sought after. Snake meat, for example, is considered good for the health, especially in winter, and the more venomous the serpent, the greater its reputation as a revitaliser. Older women drink snake blood because they believe it cures or alleviates arthritis. Some men are convinced the blood is an aphrodisiac, so it's often mixed with Chinese wine and drunk.

The most popular Chinese cuisines in Hong Kong after home-grown Cantonese are Chiu Chow, northern (ie the food of Beijing and Mongolia), Shanghainese and Sichuan. All of these cuisines are widely available here though sometimes there's something of an overlap. For example, many restaurants that bill themselves as northern will include dishes from Sichuan and vice versa.

CHIU CHOW

The Chiu Chow (or Chaozhou in Mandarin) people hail from the area around the seaport of Shantou (formerly Swatow) in northeast Guangdong province. Although part of that province, Chiu Chow cuisine is distinctive enough to be identified as a regional form of cooking on its own. Birds' nests gathered on the cliffs of Southeast Asia are a speciality. These are, in fact, nests made from the saliva of swiftlets, which contains semidigested seaweed. Other Chiu Chow dishes reflect a love of seafood, including *yèw-chi-tàwng* (shark's-fin soup).

Chiu Chow cuisine puts even more emphasis on accompanying sauces than Cantonese cooking does. Sauces can be on the sweet side, and they often use orange, tangerine or sweet bean as flavouring agents. There is a wonderful garlic and vinegar dip for the famous *chiù-jàu lô-séui ngáap* (Chiu Chow soyed goose) and a jam made from kumquats goes with *tìm-sèwn hùng-siù hàa/hâai kàu* (deep-fried shrimp/crab balls). A distinctive sauce known as *jìn jiù* is made from a skilful blend of spices including wild peppercorn, pepper and chillies, and is an integral component of many Chiu Chow dishes. Duck and goose, cooked in an aromatic sauce that is used again and again and known as *lô séui* (old water), are also popular.

Other Chiu Chow specialities include *chiù-jàu yì-mìn* (pan-fried egg noodles served over chives) and *chiù-jàu yéw tàwng* (aromatic fish soup). And no Chiu Chow meal is complete without thimble-size cups of strong and bitter *tit-gwùn-yàm* (iron Buddha tea), a fermented oolong, at the finish.

NORTHERN

This cuisine hails from the wheat basket in the chilly north-central provinces of China. Thus steamed bread, noodles and dumplings, especially *gáau-jí* and *wòk-tip* (pan-stickers), figure more frequently than rice. Lamb and mutton, seldom seen in the south, appear on menus thanks to the region's nomadic populations.

The food of north China can be identified by the extensive use of oils, such as sesame oil and chilli oil, coupled with such ingredients as vinegar, garlic, spring onions, bean pastes and dark soy sauce.

The most famous speciality of northern Chinese cuisine is *bàk-gìng hàau ngáap* (Peking duck), served with pancakes, hoisin sauce and shreds of spring onion. Another Mongolian-influenced favourite is *dáa-bìn-lo* ('hotpot' or 'steamboat'), in which raw meat, tofu, vegetables and noodles are dipped into bubbling broth at the table by diners and cooked to taste. Hotpot is usually eaten in winter.

Fuu-gwai-gài or *hàt-yì-gài* (beggar's chicken), another popular northern dish, was supposedly created by a pauper who stole a chook but had no pot to cook it in. Instead, he plucked it, covered it with clay and put it on the fire – and yet another dish rose from the flames, phoenix-like, to join the panoply of 'culinary immortals by accident'. Nowadays, the whole, partially deboned chicken is stuffed with pork, Chinese pickled cabbage, onions, mushrooms, ginger and other seasonings, wrapped in lotus leaves, sealed in wet clay or pastry and baked for several hours in hot ash.

SHANGHAINESE

The cuisine of the Shanghai area contains more oil and is generally richer, sweeter and more strongly flavoured than other Chinese styles of cooking. Stewing, frying and braising are the principal cooking techniques here. Seafood, preserved vegetables, pickles and salted meats are widely used. A speciality are the dishes of cold meats served with various sauces.

Shanghai winters are cold; as in northern China, bread, thick noodles and a wide range of dumplings are staples. During the hot and humid summers, people prefer cooling foods, such as dishes prepared with tofu, fish, prawns and mushrooms.

There are a large number of Shanghainese restaurants in Hong Kong – the cuisine seems to have enjoyed something of a renaissance in recent years – so you won't have to look far for a good one.

SICHUAN

The west-central provinces of Sichuan and Hunan are known for their spicy food but, in reality, the heat is nothing compared with that of, say, Thai or even Indian cuisine. Chillies are widely used in this style of cooking, along with aniseed, coriander, fennel seed, garlic, peppercorns, broad-bean paste and vinegar. Dishes are simmered to give the chilli peppers time to work into the food. Not all dishes are hot.

Sichuan food aims for a perfect blend of five key flavours: sweet, sour, salt, pepper and, of course, hot; a good example is *sèwn-laat tàwng* (hot-and-sour soup). The food is highly fragrant, and the contrast in textures interesting – a result of intricate cooking methods. Stir-fried dishes, for instance, are deep-fried, then returned to the wok and cooked to the point where juices are almost entirely reduced. The results are chewy yet tender, dry yet flavoursome.

The Sichuan speciality *jèung chàa ngáap* (camphor-smoked duck) is a serious contender to Peking duck as China's top fowl dish. The bird is seasoned with ginger, orange peel, cinnamon, peppercorns and coriander, then marinated in Chinese rice wine. After an initial steaming, the duck is smoked over a charcoal fire sprinkled with chips of camphorwood and red tea leaves. It is served with fluffy white steamed buns.

Protein-rich tofu in all its forms is another of Sichuan's treasures. *Màa-pàw dau-fu* (grandmother's tofu), in which minced pork, chilli, soy sauce, rice wine, peppercorn and spring onion have been added to the beancurd, is a Sichuan dish eaten throughout China.

VEGETARIANS & VEGANS

Chinese vegetarian food has undergone a renaissance in recent years and it is consumed by devout Buddhists and the health-conscious alike. Out of Buddhist piety many Hong Kong people will become vegetarians on the first and 15th day of the lunar month.

Chinese chefs are masters at adding variety to vegetarian cooking and creating 'mock meat' dishes. Dishes formed to resemble (and taste like) spareribs or chicken are made from layered pieces of dried beancurd or fashioned from mashed taro root.

Large monasteries, including Po Lin (p195) on Lantau, often have vegetarian restaurants, though you will also find many restaurants in Kowloon and on Hong Kong Island. For the most part they are Cantonese or Shanghainese and strictly vegetarian as they are owned and operated by Buddhists.

You don't have to go to a vegetarian restaurant to find meatless dishes, though. Vegetarian congee is available in most noodle shops, and dim sum houses serve a number of vegetarian treats, including *chùng-yàu-béng* (onion cakes) and *fuu-pày-géwn* (crispy tofu roll).

Western vegetarian food is reasonably hard to come by here if you want anything more complex than a salad, though there are options in Central and on Lamma island. Some Indian restaurants are exclusively vegetarian, but most in Hong Kong offer a combined menu.

Meal at Kubrick Bookshop Café (p184), Yau Ma Tei

ASIAN & INTERNATIONAL FOOD

Hong Kong's surfeit of Thai eateries offers the diner a lot of choice, especially in Kowloon Tong. Vietnamese and Indonesian/Malaysian are other Southeast Asian favourites; the best places to look for these cuisines are Causeway Bay and Tsim Sha Tsui.

Korean barbecue restaurants, where you cook à table and share up to a dozen small dishes of crisp vegetables and spicy *kimchi* (hot pickled cabbage), can be found everywhere, but especially in Sheung Wan and Wan Chai. Japanese restaurants are usually pricey unless you go to chains such as Genki Sushi, where sushi is served on a conveyor belt.

One option you shouldn't overlook is Hong Kong's subcontinental restaurants; Chungking Mansions in Tsim Sha Tsui has a vast array of Indian 'messes' (simple, usually unlicensed restaurants) serving basic but authentic Indian and Pakistani cuisine.

With Hong Kong people travelling much more widely and frequently these days, they've been much more adventurous with Western cuisines. Nowadays you'll find everything from French and Italian to Russian and Argentine on offer here.

DRINKS
NONALCOHOLIC DRINKS
Coffee
The last few years have seen a miniature explosion of cafés (see the individual entries in the Eating chapter, p150) – both big chain coffee shops and independents – in Hong Kong. In general, they are expensive but serve a wide range of coffees. Local people enjoy *dung/bìng gaa-fè* (ice coffee), a soft drink that can also be bought everywhere in cans.

Juices
Corner sundry shops and stalls in Hong Kong sell a whole range of made-on-the-spot fruit juices that cost from $6 a glass, but avoid the ones where the blenders (liquidisers) are already full and just spun around a couple of times for each customer. Orange, carrot, star fruit and sugar-cane juices are the best. A very central place to try is a market stall called Golden Fruit Juice (Map p412; ☎ 2869 9610; Ground fl, 32 Pottinger St, Central).

Soft Drinks
Fleecy is a cold and sweet drink that contains some sort of lumpy mixture, usually red or green mung beans, pineapple or some other fruit, and black grass jelly. Condensed milk or ice cream is usually part of the mixture. You can sample these drinks at Chinese fast-food outlets throughout Hong Kong.

Tea
In Chinese restaurants, tea is either offered free of charge or costs a couple of dollars for a large pot that is refilled indefinitely.

There are three main types: green (or unfermented) tea *(lùk chàa)*; black tea *(hùng chàa,* or 'red tea' in Chinese), which is fermented and includes the ever-popular *bó-láy (pǔěr* in Mandarin) and oolong tea *(wù-lúng chàa),* which is semifermented. In between are countless scented variations, such as *hèung-pín* (jasmine), which is a blend of black tea and flower petals, and compressed teas.

Chinese tea is never served with milk or sugar.

ALCOHOLIC DRINKS
Beer
Lager is by far and away the most popular alcoholic beverage in Hong Kong, and there's a wide choice of the amber nectar in supermarkets, convenience stores and bars. The Hong Kong market is dominated by two beers brewed under licence here: Carlsberg (Denmark) and San Miguel (Philippines). Tsingtao, China's slightly fruity export beer, is sold everywhere.

At the same time, the Aberdeen-based Hong Kong Beer Company (☎ 2580 2390; edwardiu@ hkbeer.com.hk) makes a German-style lager microbrew called Hong Kong Beer, as well as several beers for local bars, including: Aldrich Bay Pale Ale, not unlike an English-style India Pale Ale (IPA); Too Soo Brew, a medium-bodied lager; and Rickshaw Porter Ale, an Irish-style dry stout.

Brandy & Spirits
Cognac was the tipple of choice among Hong Kong's wealthier drinkers until relatively recently, when younger people decided it was elitist and old-fashioned and began to develop a preference for wines and other spirits. Hong Kong is now the third-biggest market in Asia for French wines and spirits, but half of that is re-exported, mostly to the mainland. Supermarkets, department stores, restaurants and bars usually have a decent selection of spirits and wines.

Wine

Though the Chinese tend to refer to all their own alcohol as 'wine' in English, the majority are spirits distilled from grains like rice, sorghum or millet. Most are potent, colourless and extremely volatile. They are available in supermarkets, restaurants and a few bars.

The best known, and most expensive, Chinese 'wine' is *mao tai*, distilled from millet. Another one is *gò·lèung* (*gāoliáng* in Mandarin), which is made from sorghum.

MENU DECODER

See p380 for pronunciation guidelines.

Useful Words & Phrases

Where would you go for (a) ...?	*láy wuí heui bin·dǫ ...*	你會去邊度…？
banquet	*sik dǫai chàan*	食大餐
cheap meal	*sik pèng·yé*	食平嘢
local specialities	*dǫy·fàwng siú·sik*	地方小食
yum cha	*yám·chàa*	飲茶
Can you recommend a ...?	*yáu màt hó ... gaai·xiu*	有乜好…介紹？
bar	*jáu·bàa*	酒吧
canteen	*faai·chàan·tèng*	快餐廳
cooked food stall	*suk·sik·dawng*	熟食檔
restaurant	*chàa·làu*	茶樓
snack shop	*lìng·sik·dim*	零食店
tea house	*chàa·gún*	茶館
I'd like ..., please.	*ng·gòy ngáw yiu ...*	唔該我要…
a menu (in English)	*(yìng·màn) choy·dàan*	(英文)菜單
a table for (five)	*(ńg wái) ge tóy*	(五位）嘅檯
the set lunch	*to·chàan*	套餐
the bill	*màai·dàan*	埋單
a fork	*chàa*	叉
a knife	*dò*	刀
a spoon	*gàng*	羹
I'd like a local speciality.	*ngáw séung sik dǫy·fàwng fùng·mǫy choy*	我想食地方風味菜
What would you recommend?	*yáu màt·yé hó gaai·siu*	有乜嘢好介紹？
I'm (a) vegetarian.	*ngáw hai sik jàai ge*	我係食齋嘅

Fish & Shellfish

bǫak·cheuk·hàa·	白蝦	steamed fresh prawns
chìng jìng yèw	清蒸魚	whole steamed fish, usually grouper, served with spring onion, ginger and soy sauce
jìn hò béng	煎蠔餅	oyster omelette
jiù yìm yàu·yéw	煎蠔餅	squid dry-fried with salt and pepper in a wok
say yàp lùng hàa	煎蠔餅	lobster in black bean sauce
siù yéw chi	煎蠔餅	braised shark's fin
tìm sèwn yéw	煎蠔餅	sweet-and-sour fish, usually yellow croaker
yéw dáan	煎蠔餅	fish balls, usually made from pike

Meat & Poultry

chàa siù	叉燒	roast pork
hò yàu ngàu yuk	蠔油牛肉	sliced beef with oyster sauce
hùng siù jèw sáu	紅燒豬手	red simmered pork knuckle
hùng siù pàai guàt	紅燒排骨	braised pork spareribs
jaa jí gài	炸子雞	crispy-skin chicken
jèung chàa ngáap	樟茶鴨	camphor-smoked duck
jui gài	醉雞	'drunken chicken'; poached chicken that has been marinated in broth and rice wine and served cold as an appetiser
lìng mùng gài	檸檬雞	lemon chicken
muì choi kau yuk	霉菜扣肉	twice-cooked pork with pickled cabbage
sì jiù cháau pàai gwàt	豉椒炒排骨	beef spareribs in black bean sauce
siù ngáap	燒鴨	roast duck
siù ngáw	燒鵝	roast goose
siù yéw jèw	燒乳豬	roast suckling pig
tìm sèwn pàai gwàt	甜酸排骨	sweet-and-sour pork spareribs
yìm guk gài	鹽焗雞	salt-baked Hakka-style chicken

Rice & Noodle Dishes

chàa·siù faan	叉燒飯	barbecued pork with rice
cháau·faan	炒飯	fried rice
cháau·mìn	炒麵	fried noodles
fán·sì	粉絲	cellophane noodles or bean threads
gài jùk	雞粥	chicken congee
gòn siù yì·mìn	乾燒伊麵	dry-fried noodles
hàam·yéw cháau·faan	鹹魚炒飯	fried rice with salted fish
háw·fàn	河粉	wide, white, flat rice noodles that are usually pan fried
hói·nàam gài	海南雞	Hainanese steamed chicken served with chicken-flavoured rice
sìng·jàu cháau·mìn	星州炒麵	Singapore noodles; rice noodles stir-fried with curry powder
sìn·hàa hàa wàn·tàn	鮮蝦餛飩	won tons made with prawns
wàn·tàn mìn	餛飩麵	won ton noodle soup
yáu·jaa·gwái	油炸鬼	'devils' tails'; dough rolled and fried in hot oil
yèung·jàu cháau·mìn	揚州炒麵	Cantonese-style fried rice
yèw daan	魚蛋	fish balls
yéw pín jùk	魚片粥	congee with sliced fish

Sauces

gaai laat	芥辣	hot mustard
hò yàu	蠔油	oyster sauce
laat jiù jeung	辣椒醬	chilli sauce
sì yàu	豉油	soy sauce

Soups

baak·choy tàwng	白菜湯	Chinese cabbage soup
dáan fàa·tàwng	蛋花湯	'egg flower' (or drop) soup; light stock into which a raw egg is dropped
dùng·gwàa tàwng	冬瓜湯	winter-melon soup
hàai yuk sùk mái gàng	蟹肉粟米羹	crab and sweet corn soup

wàn·tàn tàwng	餛飩湯	won ton soup
yèw·chi tàwng	魚翅湯	shark's-fin soup
yin wàw gàng	燕窩羹	bird's-nest soup

Vegetarian Dishes

chìng dàn bàk gù tòng	清燉北菇湯	black mushroom soup
chùn géwn	春卷	vegetarian spring rolls
gài ló máy	雞滷味	mock chicken, barbecued pork or roast duck
gàm gù sún jìm	金菇筍尖	braised bamboo shoots and black mushrooms
law hon jàai yì mìn	羅漢齋伊麵	fried noodles with braised vegetables
law hon jàai	羅漢齋	braised mixed vegetables
yè choi gún	耶菜卷	cabbage rolls

Cantonese Dishes

baak cheuk hàa	白灼蝦	poached fresh prawns served with dipping sauces
chìng cháau gàai láan	清炒芥蘭	stir-fried Chinese broccoli
chìng jìng sek bàan yéw	清蒸石班魚	steamed grouper with soy sauce
gèung chùng guk háai	薑蔥焗蟹	baked crab with ginger and spring onions
háai yuk pàa dau miù	蟹肉扒豆苗	sautéed pea shoots with crab meat
háai yuk sùk mái gàng	蟹肉栗米羹	crab and sweet corn soup
hò yàu choi sàm	蠔油菜心	choisum with oyster sauce
hò yàu ngàu yuk	蠔油牛肉	stir-fried sliced beef with oyster sauce
jiù yìm pàai gwàt	椒鹽排骨	deep-fried spareribs served with coarse salt and pepper
sài làan fàa daai jí	西蘭花帶子	stir-fried broccoli with scallops
sè gàng	蛇羹	snake soup
sị jiù sìn yáu	豉椒鮮魷	stir-fried cuttlefish with black bean and chilli sauce
siù yéw gaap	燒乳鴿	roast pigeon

DIM SUM

chàa siù bàau	叉燒包	steamed barbecued pork buns
chéung fán	腸粉	steamed rice flour rolls with shrimp, beef or pork
chìng cháau sì choi	清炒時菜	fried green vegetable of the day
chiù·jàu fán gwáw	潮州粉果	steamed dumpling with pork, peanuts and coriander
chùn géwn	春卷	fried spring rolls
fán gwáw	粉果	steamed dumplings with shrimp and bamboo shoots
fu pày géwn	腐皮卷	crispy beancurd rolls
fung jáau	鳳爪	fried chicken feet
hàa gáau	蝦餃	steamed shrimp dumplings
law mai gài	糯米雞	sticky rice wrapped in lotus leaf
pàai gwàt	排骨	small braised spareribs with black beans
sàan jùk ngàu yuk	山竹牛肉	steamed minced beef balls
siù máai	燒賣	steamed pork and shrimp dumplings

Chiu Chow Dishes

bàk gù sài làan fàa	北菇西蘭花	stewed broccoli with black mushrooms
bìng fàa gwùn yin	冰花官燕	cold sweet bird's-nest soup served as a dessert
chèng jiù ngàu yuk sì	青椒牛肉絲	fried shredded beef with green pepper
chiù·jàu ló séui ngáw	潮州滷水鵝	Chiu Chow soyed goose
chiù·jàu yéw tòng	潮州魚湯	aromatic fish soup

chiù·jàu yì mịn	潮州伊麵	pan-fried egg noodles served with chives
dung jîng hạai	凍蒸蟹	cold steamed crab
fòng yéw gàam lgam	方魚甘藍	fried kale with dried fish
jeung hèung ngáap	醬香鴨	deep-fried spiced duck
jìn jeui gài	煎醉雞	diced chicken fried in a light sauce
sẹk láu gài	石榴　雞	steamed egg-white pouches filled with minced chicken
tịm·sèwn hụng·siù hàa/hại kàu	甜酸紅燒蝦／蟹球	prawn (crab) balls with sweet, sticky dipping sauce

Northern Dishes

bàk gù pạa géwn baak choi	北菇扒卷白菜	Tianjin cabbage and black mushrooms
bàk·gịng fûng jàu làai mịn	北京封州拉麵	noodles fried with shredded pork and bean sprouts
bàk·gịng tịn ngáap	北京填鴨	Peking duck
chòng bàau yèung yụk	蔥爆羊肉	sliced lamb with onions on sizzling platter
chòng yáu béng	蔥油餅	pan-fried spring onion cakes
dáa bìn lọ	打邊爐	Chinese hotpot or steamboat
fu gwai gài/hạt yì gài	富貴雞／乞丐雞	'beggar's chicken'; partially deboned chicken stuffed with pork, Chinese pickled cabbage, onions, mushrooms, ginger and other seasonings, wrapped in lotus leaves, sealed in wet clay or pastry and baked for several hours in hot ash
gòn cháau ngạu yụk sì	乾炒牛肉絲	dried shredded beef with chilli sauce
sàam sìn tòng	三鮮湯	clear soup with chicken, prawn and abalone

Shanghainese Dishes

chùng pạy hạai	重皮蟹	hairy crabs (an autumn dish)
chùng séw wọng yéw	松鼠黃魚	sweet-and-sour yellow croaker fish
fáw téui siù choi	火腿燒菜	Shanghai cabbage with ham
hụng siù jèw sáu	紅燒豬手	simmered pigs knuckle
jaa jí gài	炸子雞	deep-fried chicken
jeui gài	醉雞	drunken chicken
lùng jéng hàa jạn	龍井蝦仁	shrimps with 'dragon-well' tea leaves
m hèung ngạu yụk	五香牛肉	cold spiced beef
sẹung·hói chò cháau	上海粗炒	fried Shanghai-style (thick) noodles with pork and cabbage
siú lụng bàau	小籠包	steamed minced pork dumplings

Sichuan Dishes

cheui páy wọng yèw pín	脆皮黃魚片	fried fish in sweet-and-sour sauce
ching jiu ngau yok si	青椒牛肉絲	sautéed shredded beef and green pepper
daam daam mịn	擔擔麵	noodles in savoury sauce
gòn jìn say gwai dáu	乾煎四季豆	pan-fried spicy string beans
gòng baau gài dìng	宮爆雞丁	sautéed diced chicken and peanuts in sweet chilli sauce
jèung chạa hàau ngáap	樟茶烤鴨	duck smoked in camphor wood
máa ngái séung sẹw	螞蟻上樹	'ants climbing trees'; cellophane noodles braised with seasoned minced pork
mạa pạw dạu fụ	麻婆豆腐	stewed beancurd with minced pork and chilli
say·chèwn mịng hàa	四川明蝦	Sichuan chilli prawns
sèwn lạat tòng	酸辣湯	hot-and-sour soup with shredded pork (and sometimes congealed pig's blood)
wuị gwàw yụk	回鍋肉	slices of braised pork with chillies
yèw hèung ké jí	魚香茄子	sautéed eggplant in a savoury, spicy sauce

History ∎

The Recent Past 50
Post-1997 Hong Kong 50
The Rise & Fall of Tung 51

From the Beginning 52
Early Inhabitants 52
The Five Great Clans 52
An Imperial Outpost 53
Arrival of the 'Outer Barbarians' 54
Opium & War 54
British Hong Kong 55
Growing Pains 56
A Sleepy Backwater 56
The Road to Boomtown 57
A Society in Transition 58
The 1997 Question 58
'One Country, Two Systems' 59
Tiananmen & Its Aftermath 60
Democracy & the Last Governor 60

History

THE RECENT PAST

Strictly speaking, the story of Hong Kong as it exists today – a Special Administrative Region (SAR) of the People's Republic of China – begins only on 1 July 1997, when the mainland resumed control of the territory after more than a century and a half of British rule.

Though it might sound glib, the only reasonable answer to the question 'What has changed since the handover?' is 'Everything and nothing'. Indeed, Chinese people (though not necessarily *Hong Kong* Chinese people) now rule the roost but, as in the colonial days, the Legislative Council remains essentially toothless and ultimate power rests with the chief executive as it did with the British governor. The clamour to be heard may be louder and better organised but the government's response is just as mealy-mouthed as it was under the British. And while mainland Chinese still sit across the table, it's no longer a negotiating table but a dining one; visitors from across the border now account for more than 50% of tourism, and revenue from this has been instrumental in helping Hong Kong's economy get back on its feet.

POST-1997 HONG KONG

While the predicted political storm failed to appear immediately after the handover, other slip-ups and disasters – economic recession, a plague and an ill-fated launch for the new airport – helped to sandbag the new Hong Kong SAR in its early years.

The financial crisis that had rocked other parts of Asia began to be felt in Hong Kong at the end of 1997. A strain of deadly avian flu, which many people feared would become a worldwide epidemic, saw Hong Kong slaughtering some 1.4 million chickens. Then came the 'Chek Lap Kok-up' of 1998, when the much-trumpeted new airport opened to a litany of disasters. Hong Kong was making world headlines again – but for all the wrong reasons.

The credibility of the SAR administration was severely damaged in 1999 when the government challenged a high court ruling allowing residency rights for the China-born offspring of parents who became Hong Kong citizens after 1997. The ruling was based on certain clauses of the Basic Law – Hong Kong's mini-constitution – that made 1.6 million people from the mainland eligible for right of abode in the territory. The SAR administration appealed to the standing committee of the National People's Congress (NPC), China's rubber-stamp parliament, to 'reinterpret' these clauses. The NPC complied, and ruled according to what the law drafters 'meant' but had somehow failed to write into law. Once again many people felt that the government was acting in its own – and not their – interest.

Meanwhile, chief executive Tung Chee Hwa's popularity declined rapidly. He was increasingly seen as Beijing's lackey, often dictatorial and aloof but strangely weak and indecisive in times of crisis. One example of the latter was his handling of Falun Gong, a spiritual movement that had emerged in China in 1992. Although the Basic Law guaranteed religious freedom in the SAR – and word was that Beijing had given Tung carte blanche to make his own decision – the chief executive waffled and in early 2001 followed the mainland's lead and branded Falun Gong a 'vicious cult', a move that would limit the group's activities in Hong Kong.

4000–1500 BC	AD 25–220
Small groups of Neolithic hunter-gatherers and fisherfolk settle coastal areas	Chinese imperial rule extends to what is now Hong Kong during the Han dynasty

THE RISE & FALL OF TUNG

Despite his standing in the polls, Tung was returned for a second five-year term in March 2002 and moved to reform the executive branch, instituting a cabinet-like system within which secretaries would be held accountable for their portfolios.

Hopes were raised but then dashed as the government became mired in controversy. In July 2002 the Hong Kong Stock Exchange proposed to delist stocks that traded under $0.50, and created a market panic that wiped $11 million off the market in an hour. Then, in March 2003, the government's failure to contain the Severe Acute Respiratory Syndrome (SARS) epidemic (below) at an early stage provoked a torrent of blame. And those were just two in a litany of such fiascos.

In July 2003 the government was set to legislate a national security bill called Article 23, which Beijing had added to Hong Kong's Basic Law in the aftermath of the Tiananmen student movement of 1989. The bill dealt with acts 'endangering public security' such as treason, subversion and sedition and was deeply unpopular with Hong Kong people. On July 1 – Hong Kong Establishment Day and a public holiday – 500,000 people took to the streets to voice their opposition to the bill. The government deleted certain clauses in the bill and, two months later, delayed its passage indefinitely.

At the end of the following year the government was forced to scrap the sale of a public-housing property fund worth a cool US$2.7 billion just hours before it was due to list when a court sided with an elderly tenant's challenge to the sale. It was a major blow to investors – something not lost on the leadership in Beijing. The following day Chinese President Hu Jintao called on Tung to 'reflect on the past' and 'learn from his mistakes', a severe scolding by Chinese political standards. Even more humiliating for Tung, Hu made the comments while visiting that economic miracle Macau on the fifth anniversary of its return to Chinese sovereignty.

In March 2005 Tung was appointed to the Chinese People's Political Consultative Conference, China's top advisory body, which many people saw as an upstairs demotion. It came as no great surprise then when just two days later Tung announced his resignation as chief executive, citing overwork as the reason. His interim replacement was the bow tie–wearing chief secretary Sir Donald Tsang, who straddled both Hong Kong's regimes as financial secretary from 1995 to 2001 and had been knighted under Chris Patten in 1997. Tsang was elected uncontested in June 2005 two weeks after the nomination period closed.

SARS IN THE SAR

The outbreak of Severe Acute Respiratory Syndrome (SARS) in March 2003 was devastating for Hong Kong. The virus, which causes a deadly type of atypical pneumonia, was brought to Hong Kong from the mainland and, by the time it was over, 299 Hong Kong people had died and another 1755 had become infected (the figures were 349 and 5328 respectively in mainland China).

Hong Kong was brought to a standstill during this period, with schools and local activities shut down and many expatriates fleeing the territory. Local people stayed indoors and wore face masks when outside; exhaled or projected droplets and close contact spread the virus and those who contracted the virus first seemed to be the most contagious. Strict hygiene protocols were put into place, such as thorough cleaning in common areas and routine temperature checks (both of which continue to this day), and finally the crisis came to an end. The washing of hands has increased dramatically, public areas are noticeably cleaner, and spitting – always frowned upon here – now carries a staggeringly high fine.

12th–16th centuries	1276
Hong Kong's Five Clans settle in what is now the New Territories	Mongol ships defeat imperial fleet in the Pearl River; Song dynasty emperor drowns in Hong Kong

FROM THE BEGINNING

While it is true that the story of Hong Kong as it exists today only starts in 1997, like so much else in this part of the world, there is much more to it than that. A lot was going on in these parts before the handover and even before that wintry morning in 1841 when a contingent of British marines clambered ashore and planted the Union flag on the western part of Hong Kong Island, claiming it for the Crown.

EARLY INHABITANTS

Hong Kong has supported human life since at least the late Stone Age. Archaeological finds – tools, pottery and other artefacts – suggest that as far back as the Neolithic period (c 4000–1500 BC) nomadic gatherers, hunters and fisherfolk lived along the coast, constantly shifting their settlements from bay to bay. They appear to have enjoyed a relatively nutritious diet of iron-rich vegetables, small mammals, shellfish and fish harvested far offshore.

Finds uncovered at almost 100 archaeological sites in the territory, including a rich burial ground discovered on the island of Ma Wan in 1997 and three hoards on the west coast of the Tuen Mun peninsula, suggest that the inhabitants of these settlements were warlike. The remnants of Bronze Age habitations (c 1500–220 BC) unearthed on Lamma and Lantau islands and at some 20 other sites – as well as the eight geometric rock carvings that can still be viewed at various locations along Hong Kong's coastline – also indicate that these early peoples practised some form of ancient religion based on cosmology.

THE FIVE GREAT CLANS

Just when the area that is now Hong Kong became an integral part of the Chinese empire is difficult to say. Salvage anthropologists believe that the aboriginal population, the Yue, a people possibly of Malay stock who migrated from Southeast Asia, were interacting in some way with dynastic China by the time of the Qin dynasty (221–207 BC). What is certain, however, is that by the time of the Eastern Han dynasty (AD 25–220), Chinese imperial rule had been extended over the region. The discovery of a number of Han coins on Lantau and Kau Sai Chau islands and at several important digs, including the tomb of a senior Han warrior at Lei Cheng Uk in central Kowloon and So Kwun Wat southeast of Tuen Mun, testifies to this.

The first of Hong Kong's mighty 'Five Clans', Han Chinese whose descendants hold political and economic clout to this day, began settling in walled villages in the fertile plains and valleys of what are now the New Territories around the 12th century AD. The first and most powerful of the arrivals were the Tang, who initially settled around Kam Tin. The once-moated hamlet of Kat Hing Wai (*wài* means 'protective wall', *tìn* means 'field'), which is probably the most visited of the remaining traditional walled villages in the New Territories, formed part of this cluster.

The Tang were followed by the Hau, who spread around present-day Sheung Shui, and the Pang from central Jiangsu province, who settled in what is now the area around Fanling. These three clans were followed by the Liu in the 15th century and the Man a century later.

The Cantonese-speaking newcomers called themselves Punti, the English transliteration of *bún-day,* meaning 'indigenous' or 'local' – something they clearly were not. They looked down on the original inhabitants, many of whom had been shunted off the land and had moved onto the sea to live on boats. It is thought that today's fisher people called the Tanka, or 'egg people' (a derogatory term used in Cantonese for boat dwellers) emerged from this

1582	Mid-18th century
Jesuit priests arrived in southern China and impress imperial court with their scientific knowledge	Arrival of Hakka groups from northeastern China

Lei Cheng Uk Han Tomb Museum (p96), New Kowloon

persecuted group. The Tanka in turn feuded with the Hoklo boat people, a rival fishing community originating from the coastal regions of present-day Fujian province, which has retained its own language.

AN IMPERIAL OUTPOST

Clinging to the southern edge of the Chinese province of Canton (now Guangdong), the peninsula and islands that became the territory of Hong Kong counted only as a remote pocket in a neglected corner of the Chinese empire. Among the scattered communities of farmers and fisherfolk were pirates who hid from the authorities among the rocky islands that afforded easy access to the nearby Pearl River.

Hong Kong's first recorded encounter with imperial China was in the 13th century, and it was as brief as it was tragic. In 1276 a group of loyal retainers of the Song dynasty (AD 960–1279) smuggled the boy emperor, Duan Zong, south to the remote fringes of the empire after the Song capital, Hangzhou, had fallen to the Mongol hordes sweeping China. Nine-year-old Duan Zong drowned when Mongol ships defeated the tattered remnants of the imperial fleet in a battle on the Pearl River.

The Punti flourished until the struggle that saw the moribund Ming dynasty (1368–1644) overthrown. The victorious Qing (1644–1911), angered by the resistance put up by southerners loyal to the *ancien régime* and determined to solve the endemic problem of piracy, in the 1660s ordered a forced evacuation inland of all the inhabitants of Guangdong's coastal San On district, including Hong Kong. All crops and properties were destroyed, and the resulting famine reduced a thriving coastal population of almost 20,000 to little more than 2000.

These turbulent times saw the birth of the Triads (p94). Originally founded as patriotic secret societies dedicated to overthrowing the Qing dynasty and restoring the Ming, they would degenerate over the centuries into Hong Kong's own version of the Mafia. Today's Triads still recite an oath of allegiance to the Ming, but their loyalty is to the dollar rather than the vanquished Son of Heaven.

1757	1840
The *cohong* (local merchants' guild) awarded the monopoly on China's trade with foreigners in Guangdong	Start of First Opium War, lasting two years

More than four generations passed before the population was able to recover to its mid-17th-century levels, boosted in part by the influx of the Hakka (Cantonese for 'guest people'). These hardy migrants from northeastern China were resented by the southerners for their aggressiveness, studiousness and self-sufficiency. Most are now assimilated into the Cantonese-speaking mainstream of Hong Kong, but some retain their own language, songs and folklore. Hakka women can be recognised in the New Territories by their distinctive bamboo hats with wide brims and black cloth fringes.

ARRIVAL OF THE 'OUTER BARBARIANS'

Regular trade between China and Europe began in 1557 when Portuguese navigators were granted permission to set up a base within a walled enclave in Macau, 65km west of Hong Kong. Jesuit priests arrived in 1582, and their scientific and technical knowledge so impressed the imperial court that a few of the clerics were permitted to live in Peking (now Beijing).

For centuries, the Pearl River estuary had been an important trading artery centred on the port of Canton (now Guangzhou). Arab traders had entered – and sacked – the settlement as early as the 8th century AD. Guangzhou was 2500km south of Peking, and the Cantonese view that the 'mountains are high and the emperor is far away' was not disputed in the imperial capital. The Ming emperors regarded their subjects to the south as no less than witches and sorcerers, their language unintelligible and their culinary predilections downright disgusting. It was therefore fitting that the Cantonese should trade with the 'outer barbarians', or foreign traders.

Dutch traders came in the wake of the Portuguese and were in turn followed by the French. British ships had begun arriving as early as 1685 from the East India Company concessions along the coast of India, and by 1714 the company had established 'factories', offices and warehouses with 'factors' (or managers), in Guangzhou to trade for tea, silk and porcelain. By the end of the 18th century, the flags of more than a dozen nations, including Britain, would be flying over the buildings along 13 Factories St.

In 1757 an imperial edict awarded the *cohong,* a local merchants' guild, the monopoly on China's trade with foreigners. Numerous restrictions were placed on European traders: it was illegal for them to learn the Chinese language or to deal with anyone except merchants of the *cohong*; they could not enter Guangzhou proper but were restricted to Shamian Island in the Pearl River; they were allowed to remain only for the trading season (November to May); and they had to leave their wives and families behind in Macau.

OPIUM & WAR

While Europe had developed a voracious demand for Chinese products, especially tea, the Chinese were largely self-sufficient, for the most part shunning foreign manufactured goods. The foreigners' ensuing trade deficit was soon reversed, however, after the British discovered a commodity that the Chinese did want: opium. In 1773 they unloaded 1000 chests of the narcotic from Bengal at Guangzhou, each containing almost 70kg of Indian opium.

Addiction swept China like wildfire, and sales of what the Chinese called 'foreign mud' skyrocketed. The British, with a virtually inexhaustible supply of the drug from the poppy fields of India, developed the trade aggressively, and opium formed the basis of most of their transactions with China by the start of the 19th century.

Alarmed by the drain of silver out of the country to pay for the opium and the spread of addiction, Emperor Chia Ch'ing (Jiaqing; r 1796–1820) issued an edict in 1799 banning the trade in opium in China, while his son and successor, Tao Kuang (Dao Guang; r 1820–50), banned the drug from Whampoa (now Huangpo) and Macau in 1820. But in Guangzhou

1842	1856
Treaty of Nanking cedes Hong Kong Island in perpetuity to Great Britain	Second Opium War, lasting until 1860

the *cohong* and corrupt officials helped ensure that the trade continued, and fortunes were amassed on both sides. Imports of the drug increased further after 1834, when the British East India Company lost its monopoly on China trade and other firms rushed in, delivering some 40,000 chests of opium to China each year, some from as far away as Turkey and the Levant.

This was all supposed to change in June 1839 with the arrival of Lin Zexu, governor of Hunan and a mandarin of great integrity, with orders from Beijing to stamp out the opium trade once and for all. It took Lin a week to surround the British garrison in Guangzhou, cut off their food supplies and demand the surrender of all opium in their possession. The British held out for six weeks until they were ordered by the chief superintendent of trade, Captain Charles Elliot, to turn over more than 20,000 chests of the drug. Lin then had the shipment – some 2.3 million catties (or almost half a tonne) – publicly burned in the city of Taiping.

Elliott suspended all trade with China while he awaited instructions from London. The foreign secretary, Lord Palmerston, goaded by prominent Scottish merchants William Jardine and James Matheson, ordered the Royal Navy in Guangzhou to force a settlement in Sino-British commercial relations. An expeditionary force of 4000 men under Rear Admiral George Elliot, a cousin of Charles, was sent to extract reparations and secure favourable trade arrangements from the Chinese government.

What would become known as the First Opium War (or First Anglo-Chinese War) began in June 1840. British forces besieged Guangzhou before sailing north and occupying or blockading a number of ports and cities along the Yangtze River and the coast as far as Shanghai. To the emperor's great alarm, the force threatened Beijing, and he sent his envoy (and Lin's successor) Qi Shan to negotiate with the Elliots. In exchange for the British withdrawal from northern China, Qi agreed to the Convention of Chuenpi (now Chuanbi), which ceded Hong Kong Island to Britain.

Though neither side, in fact, actually accepted the terms of the convention, a couple of subsequent events would see Hong Kong's fate signed and sealed. In January 1841 a naval landing party hoisted the British flag at Possession Point (now Possession St) on Hong Kong Island. The following month Captain Elliot attacked the Bogue Fort in Humen, took control of the Pearl River and laid siege to Guangzhou, withdrawing only after having extracted concessions from merchants there. Six months later a powerful British force led by Elliot's successor, Sir Henry Pottinger, sailed north and seized Amoy (Xiamen), Ningpo (Ningbo), Shanghai and other ports. With the strategic city of Nanking (Nanjing) under immediate threat, the Chinese were forced to accept Britain's terms.

The Treaty of Nanking abolished the monopoly system of trade, opened five 'treaty ports' to British residents and foreign trade, exempted British nationals from all Chinese laws and, most important of all (in hindsight if not at the time), ceded the island of Hong Kong to the British 'in perpetuity'. The treaty, signed in August 1842, set the scope and character of the unequal relationship between China and Western nations for the next half-century.

BRITISH HONG KONG

'Albert is so amused at my having got the island of Hong Kong', wrote Queen Victoria to King Leopold of Belgium in 1841. While the queen's consort may have seen the funny side of her owning an apparently useless lump of rock off the southern coast of China, Lord Palmerston was less than amused. 'A barren island with hardly a house upon it!' he raged in a letter to Captain Elliot, the man responsible for the deal. '[It] will never be a mart for trade.'

Even in the early 1840s Hong Kong was not quite the backwater portrayed by the foreign secretary. At the time, Hong Kong contained about 20 villages and hamlets, with a population

1865	1888
Hongkong & Shanghai Bank founded	Peak Tram opens

of some 3650 on land and another 2000 living on fishing boats. While 80% of the terrain was too mountainous to farm and lacked water, it did offer one distinct advantage for the British trading fleet: a deep, well-sheltered harbour.

The place was familiar to British sailors, who had been using the fine harbour to anchor vessels carrying opium since the 1820s and knew of a waterfall on the island's southern shore as a source of fresh water. They called the island Hong Kong, after the Cantonese name *hèung-gáwng,* or 'fragrant harbour'.

As Captain Elliot saw it, from here the British Empire and its merchants could conduct all their trade with China and establish a permanent outpost, under British sovereignty, in the Far East. But the British merchants in Guangzhou and the Royal Navy sided with Lord Palmerston; a small barren island with nary a house on it was not the type of sweeping concession that a British victory was supposed to achieve. Nonetheless, Hong Kong formally became a British possession on 26 June 1843, and its first governor, Sir Henry Pottinger, lost no time in declaring that the island would soon be awash in the riches of commerce. It would – but not in his lifetime.

GROWING PAINS

What would later be called the Second Opium War (or Second Anglo-Chinese War) broke out in October 1856 when Chinese soldiers boarded the British merchant schooner *Arrow* to search for pirates. French troops supported the British in this war, while Russia and the USA lent naval support. The first stage of the war was brought to an end two years later by the Treaty of Tientsin (Tianjin), which gave foreigners the right to diplomatic representation in Beijing.

Despite warnings from the Chinese, the British tried to capitalise on this agreement in 1859 by sending a flotilla carrying the first British envoy and minister plenipotentiary up the Pei Ho River to Beijing. The Chinese fired on the armada, which sustained heavy losses. Using this as a pretext, a combined British and French force invaded China and marched on Beijing. The victorious British forced the Chinese to the Convention of Peking in 1860, which ratified the Treaty of Tientsin and ceded the Kowloon Peninsula and Stonecutters Island to Britain. Britain was now in complete control of Victoria Harbour and its approaches.

Within 40 years Hong Kong's population had almost tripled and the British army felt it needed more land to protect the colony. When the Qing dynasty was at its nadir, fending off concessionary demands from France, Germany and Russia and losing a war with Japan (1894–95), in which the Chinese were forced to cede Formosa (Taiwan), Hong Kong made its move.

The government petitioned China for a land extension and in June 1898 the Second Convention of Peking presented Britain with a larger-than-expected slice of territory running north to the Shumchun (Shenzhen) River, and 235 islands, increasing the colony's size by 90%. But instead of annexing the 'New Territories', the British agreed to sign a 99-year lease, beginning on 1 July 1898 and ending at midnight on 30 June 1997.

A SLEEPY BACKWATER

While the *háwng* – Hong Kong's major trading houses, including Jardine, Matheson and Swire – prospered from their trade with China, the colony hardly thrived in its first few decades. Fever, bubonic plague and typhoons threatened life and property, and at first the colony attracted a fair number of criminals and vice merchants. Opium dens, gambling clubs and brothels proliferated; just a year after Britain took possession, an estimated 450 prostitutes worked out of two dozen whorehouses. Australian 'actresses' were based in Lyndhurst Tce – *baak fàa gàai,* or 'White Flower Street', in Chinese.

1898	1900
Second Convention of Peking leases the New Territories to Hong Kong for 99 years	Population jumps to 265,000 from 33,000 in 1850

Gradually, however, Hong Kong began to shape itself into a more substantial community. The territory's population leapt from 33,000 in 1850 to 265,000 in 1900. Gas and electrical power companies were set up, ferries, trams, the Kowloon-Canton Railway and the new-fangled High Level Tramway (later known as the Peak Tram) provided a decent transport network, and land was reclaimed. The waterfront Praya in Victoria (now Central) was flanked by handsome new buildings, the hill sides had been planted with trees, colonials flocked to the races at Happy Valley and the prestigious Hong Kong Club opened. More than a few visitors were as impressed with the colony's social life as they were its development. Nonetheless, from the late 19th century right up to WWII, Hong Kong lived in the shadow of the treaty port of Shanghai, which had become Asia's premier trade and financial centre – not to mention its style capital.

Hong Kong also became a beacon for China's regular outflow of refugees. One of the earliest waves was sparked by the Chinese Revolution of 1911, which ousted the decaying Qing dynasty and ushered in several decades of strife, rampaging warlords and famine. The civil war in China kept the numbers of refugees entering the colony high, but the stream became a flood after Japan invaded China in 1937. As many as 750,000 mainland Chinese sought shelter in Hong Kong over the next three years.

Hong Kong's status as a British colony would only offer the refugees a temporary haven, however. The day after its attack on the US naval base at Pearl Harbor on 7 December 1941, Japan's military machine swept down from Guangzhou and into Hong Kong. After just over two weeks of fierce but futile resistance, British forces surrendered on Christmas Day, beginning nearly four years of Japanese occupation.

Conditions were harsh, with indiscriminate massacres of mostly Chinese civilians; Western civilians were incarcerated at Stanley Prison on Hong Kong Island. Many Hong Kong Chinese fled to Macau, administered by neutral Portugal. In the latter years of the war Japan actually started deporting people from Hong Kong in a bid to ease the severe food shortages there. The population, numbering about 1.6 million in 1941, was reduced to some 610,000 by the end of the war.

THE ROAD TO BOOMTOWN

After Japan's withdrawal from Hong Kong, and subsequent surrender in August 1945, the colony looked set to resume its hibernation. But events both at home and on the mainland forced the colony in a new direction.

Just before WWII Hong Kong had begun to shift from entrepôt trade servicing China to home-grown manufacturing. The turmoil on the mainland, leading to the defeat of the Nationalists by the victorious Communists in 1949, unleashed a torrent of refugees – both rich and poor – into Hong Kong. By 1947 the population had once again reached the level it had been at the start of the war and, by the end of 1950, it had reached 2.3 million.

When Beijing sided with North Korea that year and went to war against the forces of the USA and the UN, the UN embargo on all trade with China (1951) threatened to strangle the colony economically. But on a paltry, war-torn foundation, local and foreign businesses built a huge manufacturing (notably textiles and garments) and financial services centre that transformed Hong Kong into one of the world's great economic miracles.

Much of Hong Kong's success depended on the enormous pool of cheap labour from China. Working conditions in those early years of economic revolution were often Dickensian: 16-hour days, unsafe working conditions, low wages and child labour were all common. Refugee workers endured, and some even earned their way out of poverty into prosperity. The Hong Kong government, under international pressure, eventually began to establish and enforce labour standards, and the situation gradually improved.

Despite the improvements trouble flared up in the 1950s and '60s due to social discontent and poor working conditions. Feuding between Communist and Nationalist supporters in

1910	1937
Kowloon-Canton Railway completed	Japan invades China; 750,000 mainland Chinese flee to Hong Kong over the next three years

Hong Kong led to riots in 1957 and again in 1962. Further riots in 1966, ostensibly over a 10-cent fare increase on the Star Ferry, demonstrated the frustration many local people had with the colonial government.

When the Communists came to power in China in 1949, many people were sure that Hong Kong would be overrun. Even without force, the Chinese could simply have ripped down the fence on the border and sent the masses to settle on Hong Kong territory. In 1962 China actually staged what looked like a trial run for this, sending 70,000 people across the frontier in a couple of weeks. But though the Chinese continued to denounce the 'unequal treaties', they recognised Hong Kong's importance to the national economy.

In 1967, at the height of the so-called Cultural Revolution, when the ultra leftist Red Guards were in de facto control in China, Hong Kong's stability again looked precarious. Riots rocked the colony, bringing with them a wave of bombings, looting and arson attacks. A militia of 300 armed Chinese crossed the border, killing five policemen and penetrating 3km into the New Territories before pulling back.

Property values in Hong Kong plunged, as did China's foreign exchange earnings, as trade and tourism ground to a halt. However the bulk of the population – and, importantly, the Hong Kong police – stood firm with the colonial authorities. By the end of the 1960s China, largely due to the intervention of Premier Chou Enlai, had come to its senses and order had been restored.

A SOCIETY IN TRANSITION

After what had been 'a testing time for the people of Hong Kong', as the annual *Hong Kong Yearbook* summed it up at the end of 1967, Hong Kong got on with the business of making money, which included improving the territory's infrastructure. In 1972 the Cross-Harbour Tunnel between Causeway Bay and Hung Hom opened, ending the reliance on ferry transport between Hong Kong Island and Kowloon. The following year the expansion of the first 'New Town' – Sha Tin – was completed, paving the way for better housing for millions of Hong Kong people. The first line of the colony's own underground railway, the Mass Transit Railway (MTR), opened in 1979.

Although Hong Kong's stock market had collapsed in 1973, its economy resumed its upward trend later in the decade. At the same time many of Hong Kong's neighbours, including Taiwan, South Korea and Singapore, began to mimic the colony's success. Just as their cheap labour was threatening to undermine the competitive edge of Hong Kong manufacturers, China began to emerge from its self-imposed isolation. Deng Xiaoping, who took control of China in the confusion after Mao Zedong's death in 1976, opened up the country to tourism and foreign investment in 1978.

Deng's 'Open Door' policy, designed to pull China into the 20th century, revived Hong Kong's role as the gateway to the mainland. Local and foreign investment in China grew and trade in Hong Kong skyrocketed as it became the trans-shipment point for China's exports and, later on, imports. Underpinning the boom was the drive to rake in as much profit as possible ahead of 1997, when Hong Kong's once and future master would again take over.

THE 1997 QUESTION

In reality, few people gave much thought to Hong Kong's future until the late 1970s, when the British and Chinese governments met for the first time to decide what would happen in (and after) 1997. Britain was legally bound to hand back only the New Territories – not Hong Kong Island and Kowloon, which had been ceded to it forever. However, with nearly half of Hong Kong's population living in the New Territories by that time, it would have been an untenable division.

1945	1949
Japan surrenders to the Allies; Hong Kong returns to British rule	Communist forces are victorious in China; refugees flood into Hong Kong

It was Deng Xiaoping who decided that the time was ripe to recover Hong Kong, forcing the British to the negotiating table. In December 1984, after more than two years of closed-door wrangling, the two parties announced that the UK had agreed to hand back the entire colony just after midnight on 30 June 1997. The decision laid to rest political jitters and commercial concerns that had seen the Hong Kong dollar collapse – and subsequently be pegged to the US dollar – in 1983, but there was considerable resentment that the fate of 5.5 million people had been decided without their input and that Whitehall had chosen not to provide Hong Kong people with full British passports and the right of abode in the UK.

Despite soothing words from China, Britain and the Hong Kong government, over the next 13 years the population of Hong Kong suffered considerable anxiety at the possible political and economic consequences of the handover. Tens of thousands of people immigrated to Canada, the USA, Australia, the UK and New Zealand, or at least managed to secure a foreign passport and right of abode there.

'ONE COUNTRY, TWO SYSTEMS'

Under the agreement signed by China and Britain, which is enshrined in a document known as *The Sino-British Joint Declaration on the Question of Hong Kong*, the 'British-administered territory' of Hong Kong would disappear and be reborn as a Special Administrative Region (SAR) of China. The joint declaration affirmed that Hong Kong would retain its prehandover social, economic and legal systems for the 50 years following the handover in 1997. This meant the Hong Kong SAR would be permitted to continue with its current capitalist system, while across the border the Chinese would remain with the system that it labelled socialist. The Chinese catch phrase for this was 'One Country, Two Systems'.

In 1988 the details of this rather unorthodox system of government were spelled out in *The Basic Law for Hong Kong*, the SAR's future constitution. The Basic Law, ratified by the National People's Congress (NPC) in Beijing in 1990, confirmed that Hong Kong people would govern Hong Kong. It preserved Hong Kong's English common law judicial system and guaranteed the right of property and ownership. It also included the rights of assembly, free speech, association, travel and movement, correspondence, choice of occupation, academic research, religious belief and the right to strike. The SAR would enjoy a high degree of autonomy with the exception of foreign affairs and matters of defence.

As guarantees of individual freedoms and respect for human rights are written into China's own constitution, few Hong Kong Chinese held much faith in the Basic Law. The guarantees were seen as empty promises and quite a few felt the Basic Law provided Beijing with the means to interfere in Hong Kong's internal affairs to preserve public order, public morals and national security. Hong Kong's fledgling democratic movement denounced the Joint Declaration as the new 'unequal treaty' and the Basic Law as a 'basic flaw'.

Although Hong Kong under the British had never been more than a benignly ruled oligarchy, Whitehall had nevertheless promised to introduce democratic reforms prior to the handover. But it soon became apparent that British and Chinese definitions of democracy differed considerably. Beijing made it abundantly clear that it would not allow Hong Kong to establish its own democratically elected government. The chief executive was to be chosen by a Beijing-appointed panel of delegates; the people of Hong Kong would elect some lower officials. In the face of opposition from Beijing, planned elections for 1988 were postponed until 1991 after a rigged referendum was interpreted to demonstrate acceptance of a 'slower pace of democracy'.

1979	1983
First line of the Mass Transit Railway (MTR) opens	Hong Kong dollar collapses and is pegged to the US dollar

TIANANMEN & ITS AFTERMATH

The concern of many Hong Kong people over their future turned to out-and-out fear on 4 June 1989, when Chinese troops used tanks and machine guns to mow down pro-democracy demonstrators in Beijing's Tiananmen Square. The massacre of students and their supporters horrified Hong Kong people, many of whom had donated funds and goods to the demonstrators. Up to one million Hong Kong people – one in six of the population – braved a typhoon to march in sorrow and anger. As the Chinese authorities spread out to hunt down activists, an underground smuggling operation, code-named Yellow Bird, was set up in Hong Kong to spirit them to safety overseas.

The Tiananmen massacre, still marked annually on the evening of 4 June with a candle-light vigil in Hong Kong Island's Victoria Park, was a watershed for Hong Kong. Sino-British relations deteriorated, the stock market fell 22% in one day and a great deal of capital left the territory for destinations overseas.

The Hong Kong government sought to rebuild confidence by announcing plans for a new airport and shipping port; with an estimated price tag of $160 billion, this was the world's most expensive infrastructure project of the day. But China had already signalled its intentions loudly and clearly.

Hong Kong–based Chinese officials who had spoken out against the Tiananmen killings were yanked from their posts or sought asylum in the USA and Europe. Local Hong Kong people with money and skills made a mad dash to emigrate to any country that would take them. During the worst period more than 1000 people were leaving each week, especially for Canada and Australia.

Tiananmen had strengthened the resolve of those people who either could not or would not leave, giving rise to the territory's first official political parties. In a bid to restore credibility, the government introduced a Bill of Rights in 1990, and the following year bestowed on Hong Kong citizens the right to choose 18 of the 60 members of the Legislative Council (Legco), which until then had been essentially a rubber-stamp body chosen by the government and special-interest groups.

DEMOCRACY & THE LAST GOVERNOR

Hong Kong was never as politically apathetic as was generally thought in the 1970s and '80s. The word 'party' may have been anathema to the refugees who had fled from the Communists or Nationalists in the 1930s and '40s, but not necessarily to their sons and daughters.

Born and bred in the territory, these first-generation Hong Kong youths were entering universities and colleges by the 1970s and becoming politically active. Like student activists everywhere, they were passionate and idealistic, agitating successfully for Chinese to be recognised as an official language alongside English. They opposed colonialism, expressed pride in their Chinese heritage and railed against the benign dictatorship of the Hong Kong colonial government. But their numbers were split between those who supported China – and the Chinese Communist Party – at all costs and those who had reservations or even mistrusted it.

The first to consider themselves 'Hong Kong people' rather than refugees from China, this generation formed the pressure groups emerging in the 1980s to debate Hong Kong's future. By the end of the decade they were coalescing into nascent political parties and preparing for the 1991 Legco elections.

The first party to emerge was the United Democratic Party, led by outspoken democrats Martin Lee and Szeto Wah. The pair, initially courted by China for their anticolonial positions and appointed to the committee that drafted the Basic Law, subsequently infuriated

1989	1990
Tiananmen massacre propels dissidents to Hong Kong	The Basic Law for Hong Kong ratified; Bill of Rights introduced

Hong Kong and Chinese flags, Golden Bauhinia (p78), Wan Chai

Beijing by publicly burning copies of the proto-constitution in protest over the Tiananmen massacre. Predictably, China denounced them as subversives.

Sino-British relations worsened with the arrival in 1992 of Chris Patten, Hong Kong's 28th – and last – British governor. Patten lost no time in putting the British plans for limited democracy back on track and even widened their scope.

His legislative reforms were not particularly radical – he lowered the voting age from 21 to 18 and broadened the franchise for the indirectly elected segment of Hong Kong's complicated electoral system. Even so, Hong Kong people were largely sceptical at first, with many wondering why Britain had chosen to wait until such a late date to start experiments in democracy.

China reacted badly, first levelling daily verbal attacks at the governor, then threatening the post-1997 careers of any prodemocracy politicians or officials. When these tactics failed, China targeted Hong Kong's economy. Negotiations on certain business contracts straddling 1997 suddenly came to a halt, and Beijing scared off foreign investors by boycotting all talks on the new airport program.

Sensing that it had alienated even its supporters in Hong Kong, China backed down and in 1994 gave its blessing to the new airport at Chek Lap Kok. It remained hostile to direct elections, however, and vowed to disband the democratically elected legislature after 1997.

In August 1994 China adopted a resolution to abolish the terms of office of Hong Kong's three tiers of elected bodies – the legislature, the municipal councils and the district boards. A Provisional Legislative Council was elected by Beijing, which included pro-Beijing councillors that had been defeated by democratic ones in the sitting Legco. The rival chamber met over the border in Shenzhen, as it had no authority in Hong Kong until the transfer of power three years later. This provisional body served until May 1998, when a new Legislative Council was elected partially by the people of Hong Kong, partially by business constituencies and partially by power brokers in Beijing.

As for the executive branch of power, no one was fooled by the pseudo election, choreographed by China in 1996, to select Hong Kong's first postcolonial leader. But Tung Chee

1997	1998
Hong Kong returns to Chinese sovereignty; Tung Chee Hwa named chief executive; avian flu breaks out in Hong Kong	Hong Kong International Airport opens at Chek Lap Kok; Southeast Asian financial crisis continues to affect Hong Kong's economy

Hwa (1937–), the Shanghai-born shipping magnate destined to become the SAR's first chief executive, won approval by retaining Patten's right-hand woman, Anson Chan, as his chief secretary and Donald Tsang as financial secretary.

China agreed to a low-key entry into Hong Kong, and People's Liberation Army (PLA) troops were trucked straight to their barracks in Stanley, Kowloon Tong and Bonham Rd in the Mid-Levels. On the night of 30 June 1997 the handover celebrations held in the purpose-built extension of the Hong Kong Convention & Exhibition Centre in Wan Chai were watched by millions of people around the world. Prince Charles was stoic and Chris Patten shed a tear while Chinese Premier Jiang Zemin beamed. 'Now we are masters of our own house', intoned the new chief executive and, with barely a rustle, the curtain fell on a century and a half of British-ruled Hong Kong.

2003	2005
Outbreaks of Severe Acute Respiratory Viral Pneumonia (SARS) kill just under 300 people	Tung Chee Hwa resigns as chief executive and is replaced by financial secretary Donald Tsang, who is elected to the post three months later

Itineraries 66
Organised Tours 66

Hong Kong Island 68

Central 68
Sheung Wan 73
Western Districts 75
The Mid-Levels 75
The Peak 76
Admiralty & Wan Chai 77
Causeway Bay 80
Happy Valley 82
Island East 83
Island South 84

Kowloon 88

Tsim Sha Tsui 89
Tsim Sha Tsui East & Hung Hom 92
Yau Ma Tei 93
Mong Kok 95
New Kowloon 96

New Territories 108

Tsuen Wan 108
Tai Mo Shan 110
Tuen Mun 110
Yuen Long 111
Mai Po Marsh 112
Kam Tin 113
Fanling & Sheung Shui 114
Tai Po 115
Plover Cove 116
Tai Po Kau 117
University 117
Sha Tin 118
Sai Kung Peninsula 120
Tap Mun Chau 121
Tung Ping Chau 123
Clearwater Bay Peninsula 123

Outlying Islands 124

Lamma 125
Cheung Chau 127
Lantau 129
Peng Chau 135
Ma Wan 136
Tsing Yi 136
Tung Lung Chau 137
Po Toi 138

Sights

Sights

Although the Hong Kong Special Administrative Region (SAR) is divided politically into 18 districts of varying sizes, these political divisions are not of much interest or use to the traveller. For visitors, the territory can be divided into four main areas – Hong Kong Island, Kowloon, the New Territories and the Outlying Islands. Each of these include a number of neighbourhoods.

This chapter begins in Central on the northern side of Hong Kong Island. As its name implies, this district is where much of what happens (or is decided) in Hong Kong takes place; come here for business, sightseeing, umpteen transport options, and entertainment in the Lan Kwai Fong and Soho nightlife districts. Contiguous to Central to the west is more traditional Sheung Wan, which manages to retain the feel of pre-war Hong Kong in parts, and rising above Central are the Mid-Levels residential area and the Peak, home to the rich, the famous and the indefatigable Peak Tram. To the east of Central are Admiralty, not much more than a cluster of office towers, hotels and shopping centres these days but still an important transport hub; Wan Chai, a seedy red-light district during the Vietnam War but now a popular entertainment area; and Causeway Bay, the most popular shopping district on Hong Kong Island.

Just south of Causeway Bay is Happy Valley, celebrated for its racecourse. Further east along the coast are the various districts of Island East – Quarry Bay, Sai Wan Ho, Shau Kei Wan and Chai Wan – offering shopping centres in spades, some worthwhile venues for wining and dining, and a surprising number of excellent museums. Island South is made up of tranquil Shek O, which has become something of an activities centre; Stanley, with its fashionable restaurants, cafés and famous market; Repulse Bay and Deep Water Bay, where

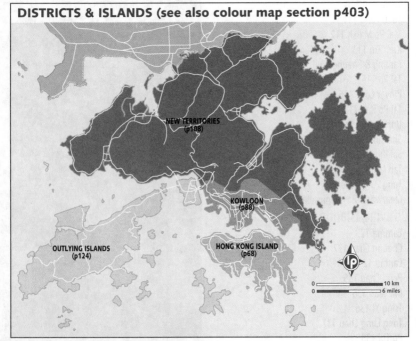

DISTRICTS & ISLANDS (see also colour map section p403)

NEW TERRITORIES (p108)

KOWLOON (p88)

OUTLYING ISLANDS (p124)

HONG KONG ISLAND (p68)

0   10 km
0   6 miles

Aberdeen (p87)

you'll find the two most popular beaches on the island; and Aberdeen, Hong Kong's original settlement, where you can ride in a sampan (motorised launch) around the harbour or visit nearby Ocean Park, Hong Kong's home-grown amusement and theme park.

North of Hong Kong Island and across Victoria Harbour is Kowloon, with its epicentre the shopping and entertainment district of Tsim Sha Tsui. To the east is the reclaimed area of Tsim Sha Tsui East, awash with top-end hotels and world-class museums, and Hung Hom, from where rail journeys to and from mainland China and the New Territories begin and end. To the north of Tsim Sha Tsui are the working-class areas of Yau Ma Tei, where you'll stumble across pawnshops, outdoor markets, Chinese pharmacies, mahjong parlours and other retailers plying their time-honoured trades, and Mong Kok, a somewhat seedy district of street markets and brothels. Beyond are the districts of so-called New Kowloon – Sham Shui Po, Kowloon Tong, Kowloon City, Wong Tai Sin and Diamond Hill – which contain everything from the cheapest computers in town to the largest temple complex in Hong Kong.

The New Territories, once Hong Kong's country playground, is today a mixed bag of housing estates and some surprisingly unspoiled rural areas and country parks. We've divided it into the New Towns of Tsuen Wan, Tuen Mun, Fanling, Sheung Shui, Tai Po and Sha Tin, all of which are worth a visit for their temples, monasteries and/or museums hidden somewhere below all the skyscrapers, and its more tranquil areas: the Hakka walled villages of Kam Tin; Tai Mo Shan, Hong Kong's highest peak; Mai Po Marsh, an important wetland for wildlife; Tai Po Kau, with its thickly forested nature reserve; and the idyllic Sai Kung Peninsula and the remote islands of Tap Mun Chau and Tung Ping Chau, which can be reached easily from points in the New Territories.

The Hong Kong archipelago counts hundreds of islands, but the vast majority are uninhabited, inaccessible or both. Among the so-called Outlying Islands that can be reached easily on a day trip from Hong Kong Island (or, at the weekend and on public holidays, Kowloon) are: Cheung Chau, with its traditional village and fishing fleet; Lamma, celebrated for its restaurants and easy country walks; Lantau, the largest island of all, with excellent beaches and country trails; little Peng Chau, laid-back and something of a shopping mecca; Ma Wan and Tsing Yi, the 'anchors' for the two colossal bridges linking Lantau with the New Territories; Tung Lung Chau, with the remains of a 300-year-old fort; and Po Toi, a haven for seafood-lovers.

In this chapter, the Transport boxed texts provide quick reference for the location of Mass Transit Rail (MTR), Kowloon-Canton Railway (KCR), Light Rail and bus stations, ferry piers, tram stops etc in each district. For more detailed information on how to get to, from and around Hong Kong Island, Kowloon, the New Territories and the Outlying Islands, including routes, schedules and fares, see p288. For suggestions on the best maps and plans, see p316.

ITINERARIES

One Day

Catch a tram up to the **Peak** (p76) for a good view of the city and stretch your legs on a summit circuit before lunching at the **Peak Lookout** (p163). Back down at sea level, stroll through **Hong Kong Park** (p79) and visit the **Flagstaff House Museum of Tea Ware** (p80) before continuing on to **Pacific Place** (p241) in Admiralty for a spot of shopping. Carry on to **Wan Chai** (p202) for a sundowner or two and a meal at **R66** (p167) for the views.

Two Days

If you've got an extra day in Hong Kong, take the Star Ferry to **Tsim Sha Tsui** (p89) and visit the **Hong Kong Museum of Art** (p90), **Hong Kong Space Museum & Theatre** (p90) or **Hong Kong Museum of History** (p92), have yum cha at **Wan Loong Court** (p181) in the Kowloon Hotel, then do some shopping along **Nathan Road** (p91), until you're ready for afternoon tea at the **Peninsula Hong Kong** (p261). Also worthwhile is a wander up to **Yau Ma Tei** (p93), for the **Temple Street night market** (p94), where the open-air Cantonese opera entertainment and street food is a treat.

Three Days

On your third day, wander around **Central** (p68) and **Sheung Wan** (p73), poking your head into traditional shops before lunching and visiting a few galleries in **Soho** (p71). Take a tram to **Wan Chai** (p77) for a night of Chinese opera or some theatre at the **Hong Kong Arts Centre** (p212), and strut your stuff at a Wan Chai bar before dining late at the **369 Shanghai Restaurant** (p164).

One Week

If you have one week you can see many of the sights listed in the Hong Kong Island and Kowloon sections, visit one of the Outlying Islands, make it to the New Territories and even get to Macau. Choose **Lantau** (p129) for the **Tian Tan Buddha** (p133), the fabulous walks and the beaches, or **Lamma** (p125) for its seafood restaurants. In the New Territories, **Kam Tin** (p113) and surrounds, the **Sai Kung Peninsula** (p120) and **Mai Po Marsh** (p112) are all sure bets. Take a day trip to **Macau** (p328) and spend the night there if time allows.

ORGANISED TOURS

Tourism is one of Hong Kong's main money-spinners, so it's not surprising that there is a mind-boggling number of tours available to just about anywhere in the territory. If you only have a short time in Hong Kong or don't want to deal with public transport, an organised tour may suit you. Some tours are standard excursions covering major sights on Hong Kong Island such as the Peak and Hollywood Rd, while other tours take you on harbour cruises, out to the islands or through the New Territories.

For walking and outdoor-adventure tours in Hong Kong, see p140. For tours to Macau, see p342.

Air

If you hanker to see Hong Kong from on high – and hang the expense – **Heliservices** (☎ 2802 0200, 2488 1659; www.heliservices .com.hk) has chartered Aerospatiale Squir-

rels for up to five passengers available for $2888/5000 for each 15-/30-minute period. They depart from rooftop helipads atop the Peninsula Hong Kong annexe. **Heli Hong Kong** (☎ 2108 9899; www.helihongkong.com) charges just $800 per person for a 12-minute flight over Hong Kong. A half-hour flight in a six-seater Eurocopter costs $5000; count on $10,000 for an hour's flight over and around most of the territory. Heli Hong Kong flights depart from the **West Kowloon Heliport** (Map pp420–1) just south of where Austin Rd West and Nga Cheung Rd meet in Tsim Sha Tsui (Kowloon MTR).

Boat

The **Hong Kong Tourism Board** (HKTB; p323) offers a one-hour free ride on the *Duk Ling*, a traditional Chinese junk complete with red triangular sails, every Thursday at 2pm and 4pm. The junk departs from Tsim Sha Tsui Public Pier and no prebooking is necessary.

The easiest way to see the full extent of Victoria Harbour from sea level is to join a circular **Star Ferry Harbour Tour** (☎ 2118 6201, 2118 6202; www.starferry.com.hk/harbour tour), of which there are a number of different options. A single daytime round trip, departing from the Star Ferry pier in Tsim Sha Tsui hourly between 2.05pm and 5.05pm daily, costs $35/32 for adults/concessions (children aged three to 12 and seniors over 65). A full-/half-day hopping pass, available from 11.05am to 7.05pm/5.05pm respectively, costs $80/60 for adults and $72/54 for concessions. At night, a two-hour round trip (at 7.05pm and 9.05pm) is $115/104 for adults/concessions. A single night ride taken between 6.05pm and 11.05pm costs $80/72 and a hopping pass $150/135. There are also departures from the piers at Central, Wan Chai and Hung Hon; see the website for details.

Many agents, including **Gray Line** (☎ 2368 7111; www.grayline.com.hk), **Splendid Tours & Travel** (☎ 2316 2151; www.splendidtours.com) and **Hong Kong Dragon Cruise** (☎ 2131 8181; www.nwft.com.hk), run by New World First Travel, have tours of Victoria and Aberdeen Harbours, but the company with the longest experience in these is **Watertours** (Map pp420–1; ☎ 2926 3868; www.watertour shk.com; Shop 5C, Ground fl, Star House, 3 Salisbury Rd, Tsim Sha Tsui; 🕙 9am-9pm). Some eight different tours of the harbour and the Outlying Islands, as well as dinner and cocktail cruises, are available. Prices range from $220 ($130 for children aged two to 12) for the Morning Harbour & Noon Day Gun Firing Cruise, to $670 ($620 for children) for the Top of Town & Night Cruise. If you want to take in the enormity of the Tsing Ma Bridge, Watertours' Afternoon Western Shoreline Cruise (adult/child $220/130) can take you there.

For the Outlying Islands, **HKKF Travel** (☎ 2533 5339, 2533 5315; info@hkkf.com.hk) has a five-hour Outlying Islands Escapade ($320) that takes in Cheung Chau and Lamma. Departure is from pier 4 at the Outlying Islands ferry terminal in Central.

Bus

For first-time visitors to Hong Kong trying to get their bearings, **Splendid Tours & Travel** (☎ 2316 2151; www.splendidtours.com) has some interesting 'orientation' tours of Hong Kong Island, Kowloon and the New Territories. The tours last four to five hours and

HONG KONG'S TOP 10 FREEBIES

- the spectacle from the public viewing gallery viewing deck at the **Bank of China** (p69)
- **Chi Lin Nunnery** (p98), where peace and serenity doesn't cost a cent
- **Flagstaff House Museum of Tea Ware** (p80), where you'll find neither bull nor bill
- Hong Kong's long-distance **hiking trails** (p219), especially the MacLehose Trail
- Wednesday is 'admission free' day at six **Hong Kong museums**: Hong Kong Heritage Museum (p119), Hong Kong Museum of Art (p90), Hong Kong Museum of Coastal Defence (p84), Hong Kong Museum of History (p92), Hong Kong Science Museum (p93) and Hong Kong Space Museum, excluding Space Theatre (p90)
- **Hong Kong Zoological & Botanical Gardens** (p70) for free walks and gratis squawks
- **Kadoorie Farm & Botanic Garden** (p110), where the butterflies (and cows and dragonflies) are free
- **Lantau Link Visitors Centre** (p137), where 'wow' cachet is cash-free
- **Tian Tan Buddha** (p133) for a cost-free superlative
- Victoria Harbour and Hong Kong Island's skyline from the **Avenue of the Stars** (p93) and the **Tsim Sha Tsui East Promenade** (p93), with stars at your feet and over your head.

Sights

ORGANISED TOURS

cost $280/190 per adult/child aged three to 12 years. Another tour company to try is the old stalwart **Gray Line** (☎ 2368 7111; www .grayline.com.hk), which has a five-hour tour ($295/190) taking in Man Mo Temple, Victoria Peak, Aberdeen and Repulse Bay.

Some of the most popular surface tours of the New Territories are offered (or subcontracted) by the **Hong Kong Tourism Board** (p323). The ever-popular Land Between Tour takes in the Yuen Yuen Institute temple complex in Tsuen Wan and Tai Mo Shan lookout, as well as several other sights. The full-day tour (adult/child under 16 or senior over 60 $395/345) takes 6½ hours and includes lunch; the half-day tour ($295/245) is five hours, without lunch. The five-hour Heritage Tour ($295/245), which does not include lunch, takes in such New Territories sights as Man Mo Temple in Tai Po, the Tang Chung Ling Ancestral Hall in Leung Yeuk Tau village and the walled settlement of Lo Wai. Contact the **HKTB tours reservation hotline** (☎ 2368 7112; 🕙 7am-9pm) for information and bookings.

Walking

For tailor-made, personal walking tours of both urban and rural Hong Kong, contact **Walk Hong Kong** (☎ 9187 8641, 9359 9071; www.walkhongkong.com), which is run by a couple of long-term expatriates.

An unusual way of touring Hong Kong with a 'guide' is on offer from an outfit called **Walk the Talk** (☎ 2380 7756; www.walkthetalk.hk). It's effectively an audioguide that uses your mobile phone. For $150 (or $88 if you don't need a Hong Kong SIM card), you get guided tours of Central, Tsim Sha Tsui and Macau. Each is made up of 15 to 20 segments that last two to three minutes each and contain history and stories as well as suggestions on where to eat, shop and visit the loo. You can buy Walk the Talk tour packages, which include a pocket-size map, access code and/or SIM card, from any HKTB information centre.

HONG KONG ISLAND

Although Hong Kong Island makes up just over 7% of the territory's total land area (and its population about 22% of the whole), its importance as the historical, political and economic centre of Hong Kong far outweighs its size. For a start, it was here that the original settlement, Victoria, was founded.

Most of the major businesses, government offices, a good many top-end hotels and restaurants, nightlife areas and exclusive residential neighbourhoods are on Hong Kong Island. It is where you'll find the ex-governor's mansion, the stock exchange, the Legislative Council and High Court, the territory's premier shopping districts, the original horseracing track and a host of other places that define Hong Kong's character. Not surprisingly, many of Hong Kong's top sights are also on the island.

The commercial heart of Hong Kong, Central, pumps away on the northern side of the island, where banks and businesses and a jungle of high-rise apartment blocks and hotels are bunched together. Though a few old monuments have been preserved here, it remains a metropolis overwhelmed by a dazzling modernity. One of the best ways to see the northern side of the island is to jump on one of the green double-decker trams that trundle between Kennedy Town in the west and Shau Kei Wan in the east.

The southern side of Hong Kong Island has a totally different character to that of the north. The coast is dotted with fine beaches – including those at Big Wave Bay, Deep Water Bay, Shek O, Stanley and Repulse Bay – where the water is clean enough to swim.

CENTRAL
Eating p151; Sleeping p253

All visitors to Hong Kong inevitably pass through Central – sightseeing, taking care of errands such as changing money or buying plane tickets, en route to the bars and restaurants of Lan Kwai Fong and Soho, or boarding or getting off the Airport Express to/from Hong Kong International Airport at Chek Lap Kok.

As Hong Kong's business centre, Central has some impressive architectural treasures (p24) that can be quite magnificent, especially at night when some 18 skyscrapers put on a lightshow. Though Hong Kong has always been less than sentimental about its past (see the boxed text, p87), there's an eclectic assortment of historical civic buildings and churches in the district. Parks, gardens and other green 'lungs' help to round out the picture.

The district was originally named Victoria after the British sovereign who had ascended to the throne just two years before a naval landing party hoisted the British flag at Possession Point west of here in 1841. But as the 'capital' of the territory, it has been called Central at least since WWII.

Orientation

Though very much open to interpretation, Central's limits are Garden Rd to the east, somewhere between the disused Central Market and Wing On Centre to the west, Caine Rd and the Hong Kong Zoological & Botanical Gardens to the south, and the harbour to the north.

Central's main thoroughfares going west to east are Connaught Rd Central, Des Voeux Rd Central and Queen's Rd Central. Important streets running (roughly) south (ie uphill) from the harbour are Garden Rd, Ice House St, Pedder St and Pottinger St.

The best way to view Central is from a Star Ferry as it crosses the harbour from Kowloon. Conveniently, the best place from which to start exploring the district

TRANSPORT

MTR Central station (Map pp408–9) on Central and Tsuen Wan lines.

Airport Express Hong Kong station below IFC Mall (Map pp408–9).

Bus Central bus terminus below Exchange Square (Map pp408–9) for bus 6 and bus 260 to Stanley and Repulse Bay, bus 15 to the Peak on Hong Kong Island, bus 101 to Hung Hom in Kowloon, and bus 960 to Tuen Mun in the New Territories; Edinburgh Pl (Map pp408–9) for bus 15C to Peak Tram (lower terminus).

Tram Along Des Voeux Rd Central (Map pp408–9).

Star Ferry Pier (Map pp408–9) at Edinburgh Pl for ferries to Tsim Sha Tsui, Tsim Sha Tsui East and Hung Hom in Kowloon.

Central Escalator Lower terminus at Central Market (Map pp408–9) to the Mid-Levels.

Peak Tram Lower terminus at 33 Garden Rd (Map pp408–9) to the Peak.

Outlying Islands Ferry Ferries (Map pp408–9) to Discovery Bay (pier 3), Lamma (pier 4), Cheung Chau (pier 5), Lantau and Peng Chau (pier 6).

---

is the **Star Ferry pier** (Map pp408–9), from where the floating green workhorses (see the boxed text, p291) carry passengers to and from Tsim Sha Tsui.

BANK OF CHINA BUILDINGS
Map pp408-9
Central MTR
To the east of the HSBC building is the old **Bank of China (BOC) building** (2A Des Voeux Rd Central), built in 1950, which now houses the bank's Central branch and, on the top three (13th to 15th) floors, the exclusive China Club, which evokes the atmosphere of old Shanghai. The BOC is now headquartered in the awesome **Bank of China Tower** (1 Garden Rd) to the southeast, designed by Chinese-born American architect IM Pei and completed in 1990.

The 70-storey Bank of China Tower is Hong Kong's third-tallest structure after Two International Finance Centre in Central and Central Plaza in Wan Chai. The asymmetry of the building is puzzling at first glance but is really a simple geometric exercise. Rising from the ground like a cube, it is successively reduced, quarter by

quarter, until the south-facing side is left to rise upward on its own.

Many local Hong Kong Chinese see the building as a huge violation of the principles of feng shui. For example, the bank's four triangular prisms are negative symbols in the geomancer's rule book; being the opposite to circles, these triangles contradict what circles suggest – money, prosperity, perfection. The **public viewing gallery** (☉ 8am-6pm Mon-Fri) on the 43rd floor offers panoramic views of Hong Kong.

CENTRAL DISTRICT POLICE STATION
Map p412
10 Hollywood Rd; bus 26
Part of this compound of four-storey buildings dates back to 1864, though other blocks were added in 1910 and 1925. The police moved out in late 2004 and, at the time of writing, the government was considering putting the buildings and the valuable chunk of land on which they sit up for commercial tender, despite a public outcry against the move.

EXCHANGE SQUARE Map pp408-9
8 Connaught Pl; Central MTR
West of Jardine House, this complex of three elevated office towers is home to the Hong Kong Stock Exchange and a number of businesses and offices. Access is via a network of overhead pedestrian walkways stretching west to Sheung Wan and linked to many of the buildings on the other side of Connaught Rd. The ground level of the 52-storey Towers I and II is given over to the Central bus and minibus terminus; Tower III is 32 levels high. The stock exchange is located at the main entrance to Towers I and II. Guided tours of the stock exchange are possible but are generally intended for people involved in the financial field and must be requested by fax five days in advance (☎ 2522 1122; fax 2868 4084).

FORMER FRENCH MISSION BUILDING
Map pp408-9
1 Battery Path; Central MTR
The **Court of Final Appeal**, the highest judicial body in Hong Kong, is now housed in the neoclassical former French Mission building, a charming structure built by an American trading firm in 1868. It served as the Russian Consulate in Hong Kong until 1915 when the French Overseas Mission

bought it and added a chapel and a dome. The building was the headquarters of the provisional colonial government after WWII. Tree-lined Battery Path links Ice House St with Garden Rd. Just before the mission building is pretty **Cheung Kong Garden**, which developers were required to lay out when they built the 70-storey Cheung Kong Centre to the south.

GOVERNMENT HOUSE Map pp408-9
☎ 2530 2003; Upper Albert Rd; Central MTR

Parts of this erstwhile official residence of the governor of Hong Kong, opposite the northern end of the Zoological & Botanical Gardens, date back to 1855 when Governor Sir John Bowring was in residence. Other features, including the dominant central tower linking the two original buildings, were added in 1942 by the Japanese, who used it as military headquarters during the occupation of Hong Kong in WWII. Hong Kong's first chief executive, Tung Chee Hwa, refused to occupy Government House after taking up his position in 1997, claiming the feng shui wasn't satisfactory, and his successor, Donald Tsang, has followed suit.

Government House is open to the public three or four times a year, notably one Sunday in March, when the azaleas in the mansion gardens are in full bloom.

HONG KONG CITY HALL Map pp408-9
☎ 2921 2840; 1 Edinburgh Pl; Central MTR

Southwest of Star Ferry pier, City Hall was built in 1962 and is still a major cultural venue in Hong Kong, with concert and recital halls, a theatre and exhibition galleries. It is currently undergoing a major face-lift. Within the so-called Lower Block but entered to the east of City Hall's main entrance, the **Hong Kong Planning & Infrastructure Exhibition Gallery** (☎ 3102 1242; www.info.gov .hk/infrastructuregallery; 3 Edinburgh Pl; admission free; ☼ 10am-6pm Wed-Mon) may not sound like a crowd-pleaser but it will awaken the Meccano builder in more than a few visitors. The exhibition follows an 18.5m 'walk' past recent, ongoing and future civil engineering, urban renewal and environment improvement projects.

HONG KONG ZOOLOGICAL & BOTANICAL GARDENS Map pp408-9
☎ 2530 0154; www.lcsd.gov.hk/en/ls_park.php; Albany Rd; admission free; ☼ terrace gardens

6am-10pm, zoo & aviaries 6am-7pm, greenhouses 9am-4.30pm; bus 3B, 12 or 40M

Established in 1871 as the Botanic Garden, these 5.6-hectare gardens are a pleasant collection of fountains, sculptures, greenhouses, a playground, a zoo and some fabulous aviaries. Along with exotic trees, plants and shrubs, some 160 species of bird are in residence here – including non-native sulphur-crested cockatoos, which are attractive but damage the local vegetation. The zoo is surprisingly comprehensive, with more than 70 mammals and 40 reptiles, and is also one of the world's leading centres for the captive breeding of endangered species (there are 16 different species of endangered animal being bred here).

The gardens are divided by Albany Rd, with the plants and aviaries in the area to the east, close to Garden Rd, and most of the animals to the west. The animal displays are mostly primates (lemurs, gibbons, macaques, orang-utans etc); other residents include a jaguar and radiated tortoises.

The Hong Kong Zoological & Botanical Gardens are at the top (ie southern) end of Garden Rd. It's an easy walk from Central, but you can also take bus 3B or 12 from the stop in front of Jardine House on Connaught Rd Central or bus 40M from the Central bus terminus below Exchange Square. The bus takes you along Upper Albert Rd and Caine Rd on the northern boundary of the gardens. Get off in front of Caritas House, at 2 Caine Rd, and follow the path across the street and up the hill to the gardens.

HONGKONG & SHANGHAI BANK BUILDING Map pp408-9
1 Queen's Rd Central; Central MTR

Fittingly, the statue of Sir Thomas Jackson in Statue Square is gazing at the stunning headquarters of what is now HSBC (formerly the Hongkong & Shanghai Bank), designed by British architect Sir Norman Foster in 1985. The two bronze lions guarding the bank's main entrance were designed by British sculptor WW Wagstaff to mark the opening of the bank's previous headquarters in 1935; the lions are known as Stephen – to the left as you face them – and Stitt, after two bank employees of the time. The Japanese used the lions as target practice during the occupation; you can still see bullet holes on Stitt.

The Hongkong & Shanghai Bank Building is a masterpiece of precision, sophistication and innovation. And why not? It was the world's most expensive building (it cost upward of US$1 billion) when it opened in 1985. The building reflects architect Sir Norman's wish to create areas of public and private space and to break the mould of previous bank architecture. The ground floor is public space, which people can traverse without entering the building; from there, escalators rise to the main banking hall. The building is inviting to enter – not guarded or off limits. Hong Kong Chinese, irreverent as always, call the 52-storey glass and aluminium structure the 'Robot Building'.

It's worth taking the **escalator** (9am-4.30pm Mon-Fri, 9am-12.30pm Sat) to the 3rd floor to gaze at the cathedral-like atrium and the natural light filtering through.

JARDINE HOUSE Map pp408-9
1 Connaught Pl; Central MTR
A short distance southeast of Star Ferry pier, this 52-storey silver monolith punctured with 1750 porthole-like windows was Hong Kong's first true 'skyscraper' when it opened as the Connaught Centre in 1973.

Lan Kwai Fong (above), Central

Hong Kong Chinese like giving nicknames to things – and people, be they friend or foe – and the centre has been dubbed the 'House of 1000 Arseholes'.

LAN KWAI FONG & SOHO Map p412
Central MTR
South of Queen's Rd Central and up hilly D'Aguilar or Wyndham Sts is Lan Kwai Fong, a narrow, L-shaped pedestrian way that is Hong Kong Island's chief entertainment district and popular with expats and Hong Kong Chinese alike. In recent years it has become one of the first ports of call for mainland tour groups, but they're here to gawp – not to party. The bars are generally nothing to get excited about – standing out for little more than their similarity – but it's a fun place to do a little pub-crawling, especially at happy hour. Lan Kwai Fong has more pubs and bars than restaurants; for the latter head west to Soho (from 'South Of HOllywood Rd'), which is *above* Hollywood Rd.

LEGISLATIVE COUNCIL BUILDING
Map pp408-9
8 Jackson Rd; Central MTR
The colonnaded and domed neoclassical building on the east side of Statue Square was once the old Supreme Court. Built in 1912 of granite quarried on Stonecutters Island, it has served as the seat of the Legislative Council (Legco) since 1985. Standing atop the pediment is a blindfolded statue of Themis, the Greek goddess of justice and natural law. During WWII it was a headquarters of the Gendarmerie, the Japanese version of the Gestapo, and many people were executed here. Across Jackson Rd to the east is **Chater Garden**, which was a cricket pitch until 1975.

LI YUEN STREET EAST & WEST
Maps pp408-9 & p412
 10am-7pm; Central MTR
These two narrow and crowded alleyways linking Des Voeux Rd Central with Queen's Rd Central are called 'the lanes' by Hong Kong residents and were traditionally the place to go for fabric and piece goods. Most vendors have now moved to Western Market (p75) in Sheung Wan, and today you'll find the usual mishmash of cheap clothing, handbags, backpacks and costume jewellery.

LOWER ALBERT ROAD & ICE HOUSE STREET Maps pp408-9 & p412
Central MTR

Lower Albert Rd, where the massive SAR Government Headquarters (Map pp408–9; 18 Lower Albert Rd) is located, has many interesting buildings. The attractive off-white stucco and red-brick structure at the top of the road is the Dairy Farm Building (Map p412), built for the Dairy Farm Ice & Cold Storage Company in 1898 and renovated in 1913.

Today it houses the Fringe Club (p214), the excellent M at the Fringe restaurant (p154) and the illustrious Foreign Correspondents' Club of Hong Kong (☎ 2521 1511; www.fcchk.org), where we've spent many a pleasant evening disgracing ourselves and making some of the best friends we've ever had. Towering above the Dairy Farm Building on the opposite side of the road is the Bishop's House (Map p412), built in 1851 and the official residence of the Anglican Bishop of Victoria.

From the Dairy Farm Building, Ice House St doglegs into Queen's Rd Central. Just before it turns north, a wide flight of stone steps leads down to Duddell St (Map pp408–9). The four wrought-iron China Gas lamps at the top and bottom of the steps were placed here in the 1870s and are listed monuments.

MARKETS Map pp408-9
Central MTR

Zoo-like Central Market (cnr Queen's Rd Central & Queen Victoria St) was shut down during the SARS epidemic in 2003. Though it has yet to reopen (and probably will not), the three-storey building marks the start of the 800m-long Central Escalator (see the boxed text, p140), which transports pedestrians through Central and Soho and as far as Conduit Rd in the Mid-Levels.

If you want to have a close look at the exotic produce that Hong Kong prides itself in selling and consuming, head uphill to the Graham St Market (p157). The squeamish should stay away; fish are cut lengthwise, but above the heart so that it continues to beat and pump blood around the body, keeping it fresher than fresh.

ONE & TWO INTERNATIONAL FINANCE CENTRE Map pp408-9
1 Harbour View St; Hong Kong MTR

These two tapering, pearl-coloured colossi sit atop the International Finance Centre (IFC) Mall and Hong Kong station, terminus of the Airport Express and the Tung Chung MTR lines. Both were partly designed by Cesar Pelli, the man responsible for Canary Wharf in London. One IFC, which opened in 1999, is a 'mere' 38 levels tall. At 88 storeys, Two IFC, topped out in mid-2003, is Hong Kong's tallest (though not prettiest) building. Given the local penchant for bestowing nicknames on everything, Two IFC has been christened 'Sir YK Pao's Erection', a reference to the owner of the development company that built the tower.

You can't get to the top of Two IFC but you can get pretty high up by visiting the Hong Kong Monetary Authority Information Centre (☎ 2878 1111; wwwhkma.gov.hk; 55th fl, Two IFC, 8 Finance St; admission free; ☽ 10am-6pm Mon-Fri, 10am-1pm Sat), which contains exhibition areas related to the Hong Kong currency, fiscal policy and banking history and a research library. There are guided tours at 10.30am and 11am Monday to Saturday, with additional departures at 2.30pm and 3pm on weekdays.

ST JOHN'S CATHEDRAL Map pp408-9
☎ 2523 4157; www.stjohnscathedral.org.hk; 4-8 Garden Rd; admission free; ☽ 7am-6pm; Central MTR

Consecrated in 1849, this Anglican cathedral is one of the very few colonial structures still standing in Central. Criticised for blighting the colony's landscape when it was first erected, St John's is now lost in the forest of skyscrapers that make up Central. The tower was added in 1850 and the chancel extended in 1873.

Services have been held here continuously since the cathedral opened, except in 1944, when the Japanese Imperial Army used it as a social club. The cathedral suffered heavy damage during WWII and after the war the front doors were remade using timber salvaged from HMS Tamar, a British warship that used to guard the entrance to Victoria Harbour, and the beautiful stained-glass East Window was replaced. You walk on sacred ground in more ways than one at St John's: it is the only piece of freehold land in Hong Kong. There's usually a free organ concert at 1.15pm on Wednesdays. Enter from Battery Path.

STATUE SQUARE Map pp408-9
Central MTR

Statue Square, due south of Star Ferry pier, is divided roughly in half by Chater Rd. In

MAID IN HONG KONG

A large number of households in Hong Kong have an amah, either a live-in maid who cooks, cleans, minds the children and/or feeds the dog, or someone who comes in once or twice a week. In the old days amahs were usually Chinese spinsters who wore starched white tunics and black trousers, put their hair in a long plait and had a mouthful of gold fillings. Their employers became their families. Today, however, that kind of amah is virtually extinct, and the work is now done by foreigners – young women (and increasingly men) from the Philippines, Indonesia, Nepal, Thailand and Sri Lanka on two-year renewable FDH ('foreign domestic helper') work visas.

Filipinos are by far the largest group, accounting for some 65% of the territory's 240,000 foreign domestic workers. While the Indonesians descend on Victoria Park and the Nepalese prefer Tsim Sha Tsui on their one day off (usually Sunday), Filipino amahs take over the pavements and public squares of Central. They come in their thousands to share food, gossip, play cards, read the Bible and do one another's hair and nails. You can't miss them around Statue Square, Exchange Square and the plaza below the HSBC building.

Though it doesn't seem very attractive, for young Filipinos a contract to work in Hong Kong is a dream come true, an escape from the dust and poverty of the provincial Philippines, even if the minimum monthly salary is only $3320 (but more than twice what they would earn in Singapore or Malaysia). But such 'freedom' doesn't come without a heavy price. According to Hong Kong–based **Asian Migrant Centre** (www.asian-migrants.org), as much as 25% of foreign domestic helpers in Hong Kong suffer physical and/or sexual abuse from their employers. If you'd like to learn more, read *Maid to Order in Hong Kong: Stories of Filipina Workers* by Nicole Constable based on interviews the author conducted with amahs throughout Hong Kong.

the northern part, which can be accessed via a pedestrian underpass from the pier, is the **Cenotaph** (Greek for 'empty tomb'; 1923), a memorial to Hong Kong residents killed during the two world wars. Due west is the venerable **Mandarin Oriental** (p254), which opened in 1963 and is consistently voted the best hotel in the world, and to the east the **Hong Kong Club Building** (1 Jackson Rd), which houses a prestigious club of that name that was still not accepting Chinese members until well after WWII. The original club building, a magnificent four-storey colonial structure, was torn down in 1981 despite public outcry, and was replaced with the modern bow-fronted monstrosity there now.

On the south side of Chater Rd, Statue Square has a collection of fountains and covered outside seating areas; it is best known in Hong Kong as the meeting place of choice for tens of thousands of Filipino migrant workers on the weekend, especially Sunday, when it becomes a cacophony of Tagalog, Vizayan and Ilocano (see the boxed text, above).

The square derives its name from the various effigies of British royalty on display here that were spirited away by the Japanese during the occupation. Only one statue actually remains, a bronze likeness of Sir Thomas Jackson, a particularly successful Victorian chief manager of the Hongkong & Shanghai Bank, which was founded in 1865.

SHEUNG WAN

Eating p161

West of Central, Sheung Wan once had something of a feel of old Shanghai about it. But much of that has disappeared under the jackhammer, and many of the old 'ladder streets' (steep inclined streets with steps) once lined with stalls and street vendors have been cleared away to make room for more buildings or the MTR. Nevertheless, traditional shops and businesses cling on and the area is worth exploring.

Hollywood Road (Map p412), which got its name from all the holly bushes that once thrived here, is an interesting street to explore. The eastern end is lined with upmarket antique and carpet shops and trendy eateries. However, once you head west of Aberdeen St or so, the scene changes: you'll soon be passing traditional wreath and coffin makers, as well as several funeral shops with hell money (fake money burned as an offering to the spirits of the departed) and paper votives in the shape of cars, mobile telephones and computers to help the dearly departed communicate and get around on the other side.

Orientation

The limits of Sheung Wan are difficult to define, but basically the district stretches from the Sheung Wan MTR station in the east to King George V Memorial Park and

Eastern St in the west. The harbour – or, rather, Connaught Rd West – is the northern border while Hollywood Rd is the southern limit.

CAT STREET Map pp408-9
🕒 9am-6pm; bus 26

Southwest of Sheung Wan MTR station and just north of (and parallel to) Hollywood Rd is **Upper Lascar Row**, the official name of 'Cat Street', a pedestrians-only lane lined with antique and curio shops and stalls selling found objects, cheap jewellery, ornaments, carvings and newly minted ancient coins. It's a fun place to trawl through for a trinket or two but expect more rough than diamonds. There are proper shops on three floors of the **Cat Street Galleries** (Casey Bldg, 38 Lok Ku Rd; 🕒 10am or 11am-6pm Mon-Sat), a small shopping centre entered from Upper Lascar Row.

MAN MO TEMPLE Map pp408-9
☎ 2540 0350; 124-126 Hollywood Rd; admission free; 🕒 8am-6pm; bus 26

This busy 18th-century temple is one of the oldest and most famous in Hong Kong. Man Mo (literally 'civil' and 'martial'), is dedicated to two deities. The civil deity is a Chinese statesman of the 3rd century BC called Man Cheung, who is worshipped as the god of literature and is represented holding a writing brush. The military deity is Kwan Yu (or Kwan Tai), a Han-dynasty soldier born in the 2nd century AD and now venerated as the red-cheeked god of war; he is holding a sword. Kwan Yu's popularity in Hong Kong probably has more to do with his additional status as the patron god of restaurants, pawnshops, the police force and secret societies such as the Triads (see the boxed text, p94).

Outside the main entrance are four gilt plaques on poles that are carried at procession time. Two plaques describe the gods being worshipped inside while others request silence and respect within the temple grounds and warn menstruating women to keep out of the main hall. Inside the temple are two 19th-century sedan chairs shaped like houses, which are used to carry the two gods at festival time. The coils suspended from the roof are incense cones burned as offerings by worshippers. Off to the side are fortune-tellers ready and willing to tell you of your (undoubtedly excellent) fate.

TRANSPORT

MTR Sheung Wan station (Map pp408–9) on Central line.

Bus Des Voeux Rd Central (Map pp408–9) for buses 5, 5A and 10 and Hollywood Rd for bus 26 (Map p412) to Central, Admiralty & Wan Chai.

Tram Along Des Voeux Rd Central and Des Voeux Rd West (Map pp408–9).

Macau Ferry Terminal (Map pp408–9) at Shun Tak Centre.

MAN WA LANE Map pp408-9
Sheung Wan MTR

Just a block east of the Sheung Wan MTR station, this narrow alley is a good introduction to traditional Sheung Wan. Stalls here specialise in name 'chops', a stone (or wood or jade) seal that has a name carved in Chinese on the base. When dipped in pasty red Chinese ink, the name chop can be used as a stamp or even a 'signature'. The merchant will create a harmonious (and auspicious) Chinese name for you.

POSSESSION STREET Map pp408-9
Bus 26

A short distance west of Cat St, next to **Hollywood Road Park** and before Hollywood Rd meets Queen's Rd West, is Possession St. This is thought to be where Commodore Gordon Bremmer and a contingent of British marines planted the Union flag on 26 January 1841 and claimed Hong Kong Island for the Crown (though no plaque marks the spot). Queen's Rd runs in such a serpentine fashion as it heads eastward because it once formed the shoreline of Hong Kong Island's northern coast, and this part of it was called Possession Point.

TAI PING SHAN TEMPLES Map pp408-9
Bus 26

Tai Ping Shan, a tiny neighbourhood in Sheung Wan and one of the first areas to be settled by Chinese after the founding of the colony, has several small temples clustered around where Tai Ping Shan St meets Pound Lane. **Kwun Yam Temple** (34 Tai Ping Shan St) honours the ever-popular goddess of mercy – the Buddhist equivalent of Tin Hau. Further to the northwest, the recently renovated **Pak Sing Ancestral Hall** (42 Tai Ping Shan St) was originally a storeroom for bodies awaiting burial in China. It contains the ancestral tablets of some 3000 departed souls.

WESTERN MARKET Map pp408-9
☎ 2815 3586; 323 Des Voeux Rd Central & New Market St; ◷ 9am-7pm; Sheung Wan MTR
When the textile vendors were driven out of the lanes linking Queen's and Des Voeux Rds Central in the early 1990s, they were moved to this renovated old market built in 1906 with its distinctive four corner towers. You'll find knick-knacks, jewellery and toys on the ground floor, piece goods on the 1st, and an unusual Chinese restaurant called the Grand Stage (p162) on the 2nd floor.

WESTERN DISTRICTS
Beyond Sheung Wan are the districts of Sai Ying Pun and Shek Tong Tsui, which are often lumped together as 'Western' by English speakers, and Kennedy Town, a working-class Chinese district at the end of the tramline.

Kennedy Town's maritime connections can still be felt the closer you get to the Praya (officially Kennedy Town New Praya) – from the Portuguese word *praia* meaning 'beach' or 'coast', which was commonly used in Hong Kong in the days when Portuguese merchants were a force to be reckoned with on the high seas.

The area wedged between the Mid-Levels and Sheung Wan doesn't have an official name as such but is usually called Pok Fu Lam after the main thoroughfare running through it. It's a district of middle-class housing blocks, colleges and Hong Kong's most prestigious university.

HONG KONG UNIVERSITY Map pp406-7
☎ 2859 2111; www.hku.hk; Pok Fu Lam Rd; bus 23
Established in 1911, HKU is the oldest and most competitive to get into of Hong

Kong's eight universities. What is unimaginatively called the Main Building, completed in the Edwardian style in 1912, is a declared monument. Several other early-20th-century buildings on the campus, including the Hung Hing Ying (1919) and Tang Chi Ngong Buildings (1929), are also protected.

The University Museum & Art Gallery (☎ 2241 5513; www.hku.hk/hkumag; Fung Ping Shan Bldg, 94 Bonham Rd; admission free; ◷ 9.30am-6pm Mon-Sat, 1.30-5.30pm Sun), to the left of the university's Main Building and opposite the start of Hing Hon Rd, houses collections of ceramics and bronzes, plus a lesser number of paintings and carvings. The bronzes are in three groups: Shang and Zhou dynasty ritual vessels; decorative mirrors from the Warring States period to the Tang, Song, Ming and Qing dynasties; and almost 1000 small Nestorian crosses from the Yuan dynasty, the largest such collection in the world. (The Nestorians formed a Christian sect that arose in Syria, were branded heretics and moved into China during the 13th and 14th centuries.)

THE MID-LEVELS
Eating p161; Sleeping p253
The Mid-Levels, halfway up the Peak (both literally and figuratively), is solidly residential and home to Chinese middle-class families and the lion's share of expats. As such, it has relatively little to offer tourists in the way of sights, though there are a few gems – particularly houses of worship – hidden within the forest of marble-clad apartment blocks. Check out the Roman Catholic Cathedral of the Immaculate Conception (Map pp408–9; ☎ 2523 0384; 16 Caine Rd), built in 1888 and financed largely by the Portuguese faithful from Macau; the Jamia Mosque (Map pp408–9; ☎ 2526 0786; 30 Shelley St), erected in 1849 and also called the Lascar Mosque; and the Ohel Leah Synagogue. In recent years, the dining and entertainment area of Soho, which straddles the borders of Central and the Mid-Levels, and the Central Escalator (see the boxed text, p140) have brought new life to this district.

Orientation
Another district with rather elastic boundaries, the Mid-Levels stretches roughly from Hong Kong University and Pok Fu Lam in the west to Kennedy Rd in the east. Caine

---

TRANSPORT

Bus Bonham Rd (Map pp408–9) for bus 3B to Jardine House in Central, bus 23, 40 or 40M to Admiralty, and bus 103 to Gloucester Rd in Causeway Bay.

Green Minibus Bonham Rd (Map pp408–9) for bus 8 to Man Kwong St near Star Ferry pier (Map pp408–9).

Sights

HONG KONG ISLAND

TRANSPORT

Bus Hollywood Rd (Map p412) for bus 26 to Central; Robinson Rd (Map pp408–9) for bus 3B to Jardine House in Central, and bus 23 to Admiralty.

Green Minibus Caine Rd and Ladder St (Map pp408–9) for bus 8 or bus 22 to Central.

Central Escalator Caine Rd (museum), Robinson Rd (synagogue).

Rd is the northern boundary and the Peak the southern one. But the Mid-Levels are as much a state of mind as a physical area, and some people regard the middle-class residential areas further east to be the Mid-Levels as well.

HONG KONG MUSEUM OF MEDICAL SCIENCES Map pp408–9

☎ 2549 5123; www.hkmms.org.hk; 2 Caine Lane; adult/child, student or senior over 60 $10/5; free after 2pm Tue; 10am-5pm Tue & Thu-Sat, 10am-7pm Wed, 1-5pm Sun; bus 3B

This small museum houses medical implements and accoutrements (including an old dentistry chair, an autopsy table, herbal medicine vials and chests to name a few) and offers a rundown on how Hong Kong coped with the 1984 bubonic plague, but is less interesting for its exhibits than for its architecture. It is housed in what was once the Pathological Institute, a breezy Edwardian-style brick-and-tile structure built in 1905 and fronted by palms and bauhinia trees. The exhibits comparing Chinese and Western approaches to medicine are unusual and instructive.

OHEL LEAH SYNAGOGUE Map pp408–9

☎ 2589 2621, 2857 6095; 70 Robinson Rd; admission free; 10.30am-7pm Mon-Thu (by appointment only); bus 3B or 23

This renovated Moorish Romantic temple, completed in 1902 when that style of architecture was all the rage in Europe, is named after Leah Gubbay Sassoon, matriarch of a wealthy (and philanthropic) Sephardic Jewish family that traces its roots back to the beginning of the colony. Be sure to bring some sort of ID if you plan to visit the sumptuous interior.

THE PEAK

Eating p163

On your first clear day in Hong Kong, make tracks for the Peak, the highest point on the island. Not only is the view one of the most spectacular cityscapes in the world, it's also a good way to put Hong Kong and its layout into perspective. Repeat the trip up on a clear night; the views of illuminated Central below and Tsim Sha Tsui across the harbour in Kowloon are superb.

The Peak has been *the* place to live in Hong Kong ever since the British arrived. Taipans (company bosses) built summer houses here to escape the heat and humidity – it's usually about 5°C cooler up here than lower down – and the Peak Hotel, 'removed high above the dust and noise of the town', offered the traveller 'those few days of quiet rest so necessary after a long sea voyage'. Or so a guidebook from 1911 called *Hong-kong and Its Vicinity* maintained…

Orientation

When people refer to the Peak, they generally mean the plateau at an elevation of 370m with the seven-level Peak Tower, the huge titanium anvil rising above the Peak Tram terminus and containing themed venues, shops and restaurants, and the adjacent Peak Galleria, an overblown four-storey shopping centre with some 60 shops and restaurants. They don't mean the summit itself.

Half the fun of going up to the Peak is riding the **Peak Tram** (p302). In 1885 everyone thought Phineas Kyrie and William Kerfoot Hughes were mad when they announced their intention to build a tramway to the top, but it opened three years later, silencing the scoffers and wiping out the sedan-chair trade in one fell swoop. Since then, what was originally called the High Level Tramway has never had an accident (comforting if you have doubts about the strength of the cable) and suspended its services only during WWII and the rainstorms of 1966, which washed half the track down the hillside.

The Peak can also be reached directly by bus from Central, Admiralty, Wan Chai and Causeway Bay, and by green minibus from Central.

LOVER'S ROCK Map pp414-15

Off Bowen Rd; green minibus 24A

A kilometre or so northeast of the Police Museum is what the Chinese call *Yan Yuen*

Sek, a phallus-shaped boulder on a bluff at the end of a track above Bowen Rd. This is a favourite pilgrimage site for childless women and those who think their lovers, husbands or sons could use the help of prayer and a joss stick or two. It's especially busy during the Maidens' Festival held on the seventh day of the seventh moon (mid-August). The easiest way to reach here is to take green minibus 24A from the Admiralty bus station. Get off at the terminus (Shiu Fai Tce) and walk up the path behind the housing complex.

PEAK GALLERIA Map pp408-9
118 Peak Rd; Peak Tram
Both the Peak Tower and the neighbouring Peak Galleria are designed to withstand winds of up to 270km/h, theoretically more than the maximum velocity of a No 10 typhoon. You can reach the Peak Galleria's viewing deck, which is larger than the one in the Peak Tower, by taking the escalator to level 3. Inside the centre you'll find a number of expensive restaurants and retail shops, from art galleries to duty-free stores.

PEAK TOWER Map pp408-9
128 Peak Rd; Peak Tram
The Peak Tower, with its attractions, shops and restaurants, is a good place to bring the kids. **Ripley's Believe It or Not Odditorium** (☎ 2849 0698; adult/child $90/50; ☼ 10am-10pm) on level 3 is similar to the branches of this chain seen around the world, with some 450 exhibits in a dozen galleries of the weird and not-so-wonderful (mannequins of women weighing tonnes, stuffed five-legged calves, skulls with crowbars embedded in them etc). On level 4 there's an outpost of **Madame Tussaud's** (☎ 2849 6966; adult/child $95/55;

☼ 10am-10pm), with eerie (and scary) wax likenesses of international stars as well as local celebrities such as Jackie Chan, Andy Lau, Michelle Yeoh and Kelly Chen.

There is an open-air viewing terrace with coin-operated binoculars on level 5 of the Peak Tower.

POLICE MUSEUM Map pp406-7
☎ 2849 7019; 27 Coombe Rd; admission free; ☼ 2-5pm Tue, 9am-5pm Wed-Sun; bus 15 or 15B
Housed in a former police station, this seldom-visited museum in neighbouring Wan Chai Gap, an attractive residential area en route to the Peak, deals with the history of the Hong Kong Police Force, which was formed in 1844 and dropped its 'royal' tag in 1997. The museum houses the intriguing Triad Societies Gallery and the very well-supplied Narcotics Gallery.

VICTORIA PEAK Map pp408-9
Some 500m to the northwest of the Peak Tram terminus up steep Mt Austin Rd, Victoria Peak (552m) is the highest point on Hong Kong Island. The old governor's mountain lodge near the summit was burned to the ground by the Japanese during WWII, but the gardens remain and are open to the public.

You can walk around Victoria Peak without exhausting yourself. Harlech Rd on the south side and Lugard Rd on the northern slope together form a 3.5km loop that takes about an hour to walk. If you feel like a longer walk, you can continue for a further 2km along Peak Rd to Pok Fu Lam Reservoir Rd, which leaves Peak Rd near the car park exit. This goes past the reservoir to the main Pok Fu Lam Rd, where you can get bus 7 to Aberdeen or back to Central.

Another good walk leads down to **Hong Kong University** (p75). First walk to the west side of Victoria Peak by taking either Lugard or Harlech Rds. After reaching Hatton Rd, follow it down. The descent is steep, but the path is clear.

For information on the 50km-long **Hong Kong Trail**, which starts on the Peak, see p220.

ADMIRALTY & WAN CHAI
Eating p164; Sleeping p254
To the east of Central is Admiralty, a district you might not even notice were it not for the dominating **Pacific Place** (Map pp408–9)

TRANSPORT

Peak Tram Upper terminus (Map pp408–9) in Peak Tower (entrance level 4, exit level 3).

Bus Bus 15 to Central bus terminus below Exchange Square (Map pp408–9), bus 15B to Wan Chai and Causeway Bay (Map pp414–15) via Police Museum Caine Rd and Ladder St, and bus 515 (Fri-Sun) to North Point.

Green Minibus Bus 1 to Edinburgh Pl (southeast of City Hall) in Central and bus 24A to Admiralty.

shopping centre and several modern buildings of note, including the blindingly gold **Far East Finance Centre** (Map pp408–9; 16 Harcourt Rd), which is known locally as 'Amah's Tooth' in reference to the traditional Chinese maids' preference for gold fillings and caps.

East of Admiralty is Hong Kong Island's most famous district: Wan Chai, or 'Little Bay'. If you choose to believe some of the tourist brochures, Wan Chai is still inseparably linked with the name of Suzie Wong – not bad considering that the book dates back to 1957 and the movie to 1960. Although Wan Chai had a reputation during the Vietnam War as an anything-goes redlight district, today it is mainly a centre for shopping, business and more upscale entertainment. If you want to see how far Wan Chai has come since then, check out the fortress-like **Hong Kong Convention & Exhibition Centre** (opposite) and two of Hong Kong's most important cultural centres, the **Academy for the Performing Arts** (below) and the **Hong Kong Arts Centre** (opposite), standing side by side to the southwest of the convention centre.

It's a different world south and southeast of this 'new' Wan Chai. Sandwiched between Johnston Rd and Queen's Rd East (Map pp414–15) are row after row of narrow streets harbouring all sorts of traditional shops, markets and workshops.

Orientation

Admiralty is a small district, bordered by Cotton Tree Dr in the west and Arsenal St in the north. Hong Kong Park effectively cuts it off from the Mid-Levels and the Peak to the south, and Harcourt Rd is its barrier to the harbour in the north. Wan Chai carries on from Admiralty in the west to Canal Rd and Causeway Bay in the east; its three main roads are Jaffe, Lockhart and Hennessy Rds. The harbour is the limit to the north, and to the south it's Queen's Rd East.

ACADEMY FOR
THE PERFORMING ARTS Map pp414-15
☎ 2584 8500; www.hkapa.edu; 1 Gloucester Rd, Wan Chai; Admiralty MTR
With its striking triangular atrium and an exterior Meccano-like frame that is a work of art in itself, the academy building (1985) is a Wan Chai landmark and an important venue for music, dance and scholarship.

TRANSPORT
MTR Admiralty station (Map pp408–9) on Central and Tsuen Wan lines and Wan Chai station (Map pp414–15) on Central line.

Bus Admiralty bus terminus below Queensway Plaza and Admiralty MTR station (Map pp408–9) for buses 6 and 6A to Stanley and Repulse Bay, bus 15 to the Peak, bus 12A to Macdonnell and Bowen Rds, bus 101 to Hung Hom and Kowloon City in Kowloon, and bus 960 to Tuen Mun in the New Territories; Wan Chai ferry pier bus terminus (Map pp414–15) for bus 40M to the Mid-Levels; Harbour Rd in Wan Chai (Map pp414–15) for bus 18 to Connaught Rd Central, Gloucester Rd in Wan Chai for bus 307 to Tai Po in the New Territories.

Tram East along Queensway, Johnston Rd and Hennessy Rd (Map pp414–15) to Causeway Bay; west to Central and Sheung Wan.

Star Ferry Wan Chai ferry pier (Map pp414–15) to Hung Hom and Tsim Sha Tsui in Kowloon.

CENTRAL PLAZA Map pp414-15
18 Harbour Rd, Wan Chai; bus 18
At just under 374m, Central Plaza, which was completed in 1992, is just 3m shorter than the newer Two IFC. The glass skin of the tower has three different colours – gold, silver and terracotta – and the overall impression is rather garish.

Central Plaza functions as one of the world's biggest clocks. There's method to the madness of those four lines of light shining through the glass pyramid at the top of the building between 6pm and midnight. The bottom level indicates the hour: red is 6pm; white 7pm; purple 8pm; yellow 9pm; pink 10pm; green 11pm. When all four lights are the same colour, it's right on the hour. When the top light is different from the bottom ones, it's 15 minutes past the hour. If the top two and bottom two are different, it's half-past the hour. If the top three match, it's 45 minutes past the hour. So, what time is it now?

GOLDEN BAUHINIA Map pp414-15
Golden Bauhinia Sq, 1 Expo Dr, Wan Chai; bus 18
A 6m-tall statue, including pedestal, of Hong Kong's symbol, called the Forever Blooming Bauhinia, stands on the waterfront promenade just in front of the Hong Kong Convention & Exhibition Centre to mark

the return of Hong Kong to Chinese sovereignty in 1997 and the establishment of the Hong Kong SAR. The flag-raising ceremony, held daily at 7.50am and conducted by the Hong Kong Police, has become a 'must see' for visiting tourist groups from the mainland. There's a pipe band on the 1st, 11th and 21st of each month at 7.45am. From the Wan Chai MTR station, leave via exit A5.

HONG KONG ARTS CENTRE
Map pp414-15

☎ 2582 0200; www.hkac.org.hk; 2 Harbour Rd, Wan Chai; Admiralty MTR

Due east of the Academy for the Performing Arts is the Hong Kong Arts Centre. Along with theatres, including the important Agnès B Cinema (p213), you'll also find here the Pao Sui Loong & Pao Yue Kong Galleries (☎ 2824 5330; admission free; ☺ 10am-6pm during exhibitions). Extending over floors four and five, there's room to host retrospectives and group shows in all visual media. The curatorial vision is lively without being too provocative.

HONG KONG CONVENTION & EXHIBITION CENTRE Map pp414-15

☎ 2582 8888; www.hkcec.com; 1 Expo Dr, Wan Chai; bus 18

Due north of the Wan Chai MTR station, the Hong Kong Convention & Exhibition Centre, which was built in 1988 and extended onto a man-made island in the harbour for the handover in 1997, has been variously compared with a bird's wing, a banana leaf and a lotus petal. For more information, see p25.

HONG KONG DESIGN CENTRE
Map pp408-9

☎ 2522 8688; www.hkdesigncentre.org; 28 Kennedy Rd, the Mid-Levels; admission free; ☺ 9am-6pm (variable); bus 12A

The design centre, just opposite the Hong Kong Visual Arts Centre, is housed in one of the most graceful colonial buildings in the territory. Built in 1896, it served as a bank, the offices of the Japanese Residents Association of Hong Kong before WWII and a school until it was renovated and given to the Hong Kong Federation of Designers. Even if it does not have any exhibitions open to the public, the exterior and public areas are worth a look.

HONG KONG PARK Map pp408-9

☎ 2521 5041; www.lcsd.gov.hk/en/ls_park.php; 19 Cotton Tree Dr, Admiralty; admission free; ☺ park 6am-11pm, conservatory & aviary 9am-5pm; Admiralty MTR

Deliberately designed to look anything but natural, Hong Kong Park is one of the most unusual parks in the world, emphasising artificial creations such as its fountain plaza, conservatory, artificial waterfall, indoor games hall, playground, t'ai chi garden, viewing tower, museum and arts centre. For all its artifice, the 8-hectare park is beautiful in its own weird way and, with a wall of skyscrapers on one side and mountains on the other, makes for some dramatic photographs.

The best feature of the park is the Edward Youde Aviary, named after a much-loved governor (1982–87) and China scholar who

Edward Youde Aviary (above), Hong Kong Park, Admiralty

died suddenly while in office. Home to more than 600 birds representing some 90 different species, the aviary is a huge and very natural-feeling place. Visitors walk along a wooden bridge suspended some 10m above the ground and at eye level with the tree branches, where most of the birds are to be found. The **Forsgate Conservatory** on the slope overlooking the park is the largest in Southeast Asia.

At the park's northernmost tip is the **Flagstaff House Museum of Tea Ware** (☎ 2869 0690; www.lcsd.gov.hk/en/cs_mus_lcsd.php; 10 Cotton Tree Dr; admission free; ⌚ 10am-5pm Wed-Mon). Built in 1846 as the home of the commander of the British forces, it is the oldest colonial building in Hong Kong still standing in its original spot. The museum, a branch of the Hong Kong Museum of Art, houses a collection of antique Chinese tea ware: bowls, teaspoons, brewing trays, sniffing cups (used particularly for enjoying the fragrance of the finest oolong from Taiwan) and, of course, teapots made of porcelain or purple clay from Yixing.

The **KS Lo Gallery** (☎ 2869 0690; 10 Cotton Tree Dr; admission free; ⌚ 10am-5pm Wed-Mon), in a small building just southeast of the museum, contains rare Chinese ceramics and stone seals collected by the gallery's eponymous benefactor.

The **Hong Kong Visual Arts Centre** (☎ 2521 3008; 7A Kennedy Rd; admission free; ⌚ 10am-9pm Wed-Mon), housed in the Cassels Block of the former Victoria Barracks, within Hong Kong Park at its eastern edge, since 1992, supports local sculptors, printmakers and potters, and stages temporary exhibitions.

Hong Kong Park is an easy walk from either Central or the Admiralty MTR station. You can also take bus 3B, 12M, 23, 23B, 40 or 103 and alight at the first stop on Cotton Tree Dr. Bus 12A runs between Chater Rd in Central and Kennedy Rd.

HOPEWELL CENTRE Map pp414-15
183 Queen's Rd East, Wan Chai; bus 6 or 6A

This 64-storey cylinder, built as the headquarters of Hong Kong property and construction magnate Gordon Wu, wins no beauty contests, but it was the tallest building in Asia for almost a decade until 1989. It is located on a slope so steep that the rear entrance is on the 17th floor. The centre's revolving restaurant, **R66** (p167) is reached via two bubble-shaped external elevators.

HUNG SHING TEMPLE Map pp414-15
☎ 2527 0804; 129-131 Queen's Rd East, Wan Chai; ⌚ 8am-6pm; bus 6 or 6A

Nestled in a leafy nook on the southern side of Queen's Rd East, this narrow and dark temple (which is also called Tai Wong Temple) is built atop huge boulders in honour of a Tang dynasty official who was well known for his virtue (important) and ability to make predictions of great value to traders (ultra-important).

OLD WAN CHAI POST OFFICE
Map pp414-15
Cnr Queen's Rd East & Wan Chai Gap Rd, Wan Chai; bus 6 or 6A

A short distance to the east of Wan Chai Market is this important colonial-style building erected in 1913 and now serving as a resource centre operated by the **Environmental Protection Department** (☎ 2893 2856; ⌚ 10am-5pm Mon & Tue, Thu-Sat, 10am-1pm Wed, 1-5pm Sun).

WAN CHAI MARKET Map pp414-15
264 Queen's Rd East, Wan Chai; ⌚ 6am-8pm; bus 6 or 6A

Wan Chai's covered market was built in the geometric Bauhaus style in 1937. It has yet to be listed and may be torn down for yet another block of flats, so have a look before it is too late.

CAUSEWAY BAY
Eating p169; Sleeping p256

Causeway Bay, which is Tung Lo Wan (Copper Gong Bay) in Cantonese, was the site of a British settlement in the 1840s and was once an area of godowns (a Hong Kong 'business' or 'pidgin English' word for warehouses) and a well-protected harbour for fisherfolk and boatpeople.

The new Causeway Bay, one of Hong Kong's top shopping and nightlife areas, was built up from swampland and the bottom of the harbour. Jardine Matheson, one of Hong Kong's largest *hâwng* (major trading houses or companies), set up shop here, which explains why many of the streets in the district bear its name: Jardine's Bazaar, Jardine's Crescent and Yee Wo St (the name for Jardine Matheson in Cantonese).

Causeway Bay is primarily for shopping, especially trendy clothing (p16), and, to a lesser degree, dining out. The biggest and best shopping centre is in **Times Square** (p243), an enormous block with offices, four floors of restaurants and 10 retail levels.

Orientation

Causeway Bay is a relatively small but densely packed district. Canal Rd is its border to the west and Victoria Park is the eastern limit. From north to south it runs from the harbour and the typhoon shelter to Leighton Rd. Tin Hau, the site of Hong Kong Island's most famous temple erected in honour of the queen of heaven, is at the southeastern edge of Victoria Park.

CAUSEWAY BAY TYPHOON SHELTER

Map pp414-15
Causeway Bay MTR
Not so long ago the waterfront in Causeway Bay used to be a mass of junks and sampans huddling in the typhoon shelter for protection, but these days it's nearly all yachts. The land jutting out to the west is Kellett Island, which has been a misnomer ever since a causeway connected it to the mainland in 1956, and further land reclamation turned it into a peninsula. It is home to the **Royal Hong Kong Yacht Club** (☎ 2832 2817; Hung Hing Rd), which retains its 'Royal' moniker in English (only).

CENTRAL LIBRARY Map pp414-15

☎ 2921 0503; www.hkpl.gov.hk; 66 Causeway Rd; ⏱ 10am-9pm Thu-Tue, 1-9pm Wed, 10am-7pm some public holidays; tram
This architectural monstrosity, a 12-storey neoclassical-postmodern building with Ionic columns, a Roman pediment and sandy-yellow tiles, is both a research and lending library and contains some 1.2 million volumes (p316). It also has some 24 public-access computer terminals where you can check emails and surf the web.

NOONDAY GUN Map pp414-15

221 Gloucester Rd; Causeway Bay MTR
Noel Coward made the so-called Noonday Gun famous with his satirical song *Mad Dogs and Englishmen* (1924), about colonials who braved the fierce heat of the midday sun while the local people sensibly remained indoors: 'In Hong Kong/they strike a gong/ And fire off a noonday gun/To reprimand each inmate/Who's in late'. Apparently when Coward was invited to pull the lanyard, he was late and it didn't go off until 12.03pm.

TRANSPORT

MTR Causeway Bay and Tin Hau stations (Map pp414–15) on Central line.

Bus Yee Wo St (Map pp414–15) for buses 5, 5B and 26 to Admiralty and Central, bus 112 to Hung Hom and Sham Shui Po in Kowloon, and bus 170 to Tai Wai and Sha Tin in the New Territories; Leighton Rd (Map pp414–15) for bus 63 to Stanley and Repulse Bay; Gloucester Rd (Map pp414–15) for bus 106 to Hung Hom and Wong Tai Sin in Kowloon.

Green Minibus Bus 40 from Tang Lung St and Yee Wo St (Map pp414–15) to Stanley.

Tram Along Hennessy Rd and Yee Wo St (Map pp414–15) to Central and Shau Kei Wan; along Percival St (Map pp414–15) to Happy Valley.

Built in 1901 by Hotchkiss of Portsmouth this recoil-mounted 3lb cannon is one of the few vestiges of the colonial past in Causeway Bay and is its best-known landmark. The original six-pounder was lost during WWII; its replacement was deemed too noisy and was exchanged for the current gun in 1961. The gun stands in a small garden opposite the Excelsior Hotel on Gloucester Rd – the first plot of land to be sold by public auction in Hong Kong (1841) – and is fired at noon every day. Eight bells are then sounded, signalling the end of the forenoon watch. The gun also welcomes in the New Year at midnight on 31 December.

Exactly how this tradition got started remains a mystery. Some people say that Jardine Matheson fired the gun without permission to bid farewell to a departing managing director or to welcome one of its incoming ships. The authorities were so enraged by the company's insolence that, as punishment, Jardine's was ordered to fire the gun every day. A more prosaic explanation is that, as at many ports around the world (including London), a gun was fired at noon daily so that ships' clocks – crucial for establishing longitude and east–west distances at sea – could be set accurately.

The Noonday Gun is accessible via a tunnel through the basement car park in the World Trade Centre, just west of the Excelsior Hotel. From the taxi rank in front of the hotel, look west for the door marked 'Car Park Shroff, Marina Club & Noon Gun'. It's open from 7am to midnight daily.

Noonday Gun (p81), Causeway Bay

TIN HAU TEMPLE Map pp414-15

☎ 2721 2326; 10 Tin Hau Temple Rd; ⏱ 7am-6pm; Tin Hau MTR

Southeast of Victoria Park, Hong Kong Island's most famous Tin Hau temple is relatively small and dwarfed by surrounding high-rises. Before reclamation, this temple dedicated to the patroness of seafarers stood on the waterfront. It has been a place of worship for three centuries, though the current structure is only about 200 years old. The temple bell dates from 1747, and the central shrine contains an effigy of Tin Hau with a blackened face.

VICTORIA PARK Map pp414-15

☎ 2570 6186; www.lcsd.gov.hk/en/ls_park.php; Causeway Rd; Causeway Bay & Tin Hau MTR

At 17 hectares, the biggest patch of public greenery on Hong Kong Island, Victoria Park is a popular place to escape to. The best time to stroll around is in the morning during the week, when it becomes a forest of people practising the slow-motion choreography of t'ai chi. At the weekend they are joined by Indonesian amahs, who prefer it to Central (see the boxed text, p73).

Between April and November you can take a dip in the **swimming pool** (☎ 2570 4682; adult/child 3-13 & senior over 60 $19/9; ⏱ 6.30am-10pm with 1hr closure at noon & 5pm Apr-Oct). The park becomes a

flower market a few days before the Chinese New Year and is the site of the Hong Kong Flower Show in March. It's also worth a visit during the **Mid-Autumn Festival** (p12), when people turn out en masse carrying lanterns.

HAPPY VALLEY

Eating p173

Happy Valley – called *Páau-máa-dáy* (Horse Running Place) in Cantonese – has been a popular residential area for expats since the early days of British settlement, though, having built their houses on what turned out to be swampland, early residents had to contend with severe bouts of malaria. There are some interesting cemeteries to the west and southwest of Wong Nai Chung Rd. They are divided into Protestant, Roman Catholic, Muslim, Parsee and Hindu sections, and date back to the founding of Hong Kong as a colony. The district's most important drawcard, however, is the Happy Valley Racecourse.

Orientation

Happy Valley is essentially the racetrack in the centre of circular Wong Nai Chung Rd and the residential areas to the east and south, where the main streets are Shan Kwong Rd, Sing Woo Rd and Blue Pool Rd.

HAPPY VALLEY RACECOURSE
Map pp414-15

☎ 2895 1523, 2966 8111; www.happyvalleyrace course.com; 2 Sports Rd; tram

Although Hong Kong residents can also play the Mark Six lottery and bet on football fixtures, horseracing, worth more than US$1 billion annually, remains the most popular form of gambling. The first horse races were held in 1846 at Happy Valley and became an annual event. Now meetings are held both here and at the newer and larger (but less atmospheric) **Sha Tin Racecourse** (p119) in the New Territories. For details on placing bets, see p216.

If you know nothing about horse racing but would like to attend, consider joining the Come Horseracing Tour available through **Gray Line** or **Splendid Tours & Travel** (p67) during the racing season. The tour ($490, except at nine special and cup meetings when it is $540 to $790) includes admission to the Visitors' Box of the Hong Kong Jockey Club Members' Enclosures and buffet lunch. Tours scheduled at night last about 5½ hours, while daytime tours are about seven hours long.

Racing buffs can wallow in the history of the place at the **Hong Kong Racing Museum** (☎ 2966 8065; www.hkjc.com/english /museum/mu02_index.htm; 2nd fl, Happy Valley Stand, Wong Nai Chung Rd; admission free; ☉ 10am-5pm Tue-Sun, 10am-12.30pm on racing days), with eight galleries and a cinema showcasing celebrated trainers, jockeys and horseflesh, and key races over the past 150 years. The most important event in the history of the Happy Valley Racecourse – individual winnings notwithstanding – was the huge fire in 1918 that killed hundreds of people. Many of the victims were buried in the cemeteries surrounding the track.

TRANSPORT

MTR Causeway Bay station (Map pp414–15; exit A) on Central line, a 15-minute walk south.

Bus Wong Nai Chung Rd for bus 1 to Exchange Square in Central, bus 5A to Des Voeux Rd Central, and bus 19 to North Point.

Tram Along Wong Nai Chung Rd (Map pp414–15) to Causeway Bay, Central, Kennedy Town, and Shau Kei Wan.

ISLAND EAST

Eating p173; Sleeping p259

Eastern is a large district that is primarily residential, with some of Hong Kong Island's largest housing estates (eg Tai Koo Shing in Quarry Bay). As elsewhere on the island, however, office towers stand cheek by jowl with residential areas. There are not as many restaurants and nightspots in this area as there are in Central, Wan Chai and Causeway Bay to lure you onto the MTR's Central line, but the shopping is good and there are a handful of top-class museums.

Orientation

The Eastern District runs from Causeway Bay to Siu Sai Wan, at the eastern end of Hong Kong Island's north coast. Major settlements are North Point, Quarry Bay, Sai Wan Ho, Shau Kei Wan and Chai Wan. The MTR is the quickest way to reach any of these destinations, but the tram, which goes as far as Shau Kei Wan, is much more enjoyable. Count on about half an hour from Causeway Bay to the end of the line.

North Point & Quarry Bay

North Point, settled largely by Shanghainese after WWII, is a somewhat down-at-heel district with a couple of interesting markets, and the **Sunbeam Theatre** (p214), one of the best places to see and hear Chinese opera. Tong Chong St opposite the Quarry Bay MTR station has had a face-lift in recent years and is something of a restaurant and nightlife strip. The main attraction at Quarry Bay is **Cityplaza** (p242).

Sai Wan Ho
HONG KONG FILM ARCHIVE
Map pp406-7

☎ 2739 2139, bookings 2734 9009, 2119 7383; www.filmarchive.gov.hk; 50 Lei King Rd; admission free; ☉ main foyer 10am-8pm, box office noon-8pm Mon-Wed & Fri-Sun, resource centre 10am-7pm Mon Wed & Fri, 10am-5pm Sat, 1-5pm Sun; Sai Wan Ho MTR

The archive, which opened in 2001, is well worth a visit, even if you know nothing about Hong Kong films and film-making. It preserves, catalogues, studies and documents Hong Kong films – there are more than 400 in the vaults – and related material

TRANSPORT

MTR Central line with stations at North Point, Quarry Bay, Tai Koo Shing, Sai Wan Ho, Shau Kei Wan and Chai Wan (Map pp406–7); North Point and Quarry Bay also on Tseung Kwan O line.

Bus North Point (Map pp406–7) for buses 2 and 10 to Admiralty and Central, bus 515 (Fri-Sun) to the Peak, bus 63 (Mon-Sat) or 65 (Sun) to Stanley and Repulse Bay, bus 106 to Hung Hom, bus 110 to Tsim Sha Tsui in Kowloon, and bus 680 to Sha Tin in the New Territories; Shau Kei Wan (Map pp406–7) for bus 2 to Quarry Bay and bus 720 to Central.

Tram Along King's Rd, Kornhill Rd and Shau Kei Wan Rd.

Ferry North Point pier (Map pp406–7) to Hung Hom, Kowloon City and Kwun Tong; Sai Wan Ho pier (Map pp406–7) to Tung Lung Chau and Joss House Bay.

such as magazines, posters, records and scripts; there's a small exhibition hall with themed exhibits (opening hours vary), including videos with subtitles, and a 127-seat cinema (☎ 2734 9009) that shows Hong Kong and other films here throughout the year for $30 to $50.

To reach the film archive from the Sai Wan Ho MTR station, follow exit A, walk north on Tai On St and west on Lei King Rd.

Shau Kei Wan
HONG KONG MUSEUM OF COASTAL DEFENCE Map pp406-7
☎ 2569 1500; www.lcsd.gov.hk/en/cs_mus_lcsd .php; 175 Tung Hei Rd; adult/concession $10/5, admission free Wed; ☺ 10am-5pm Fri-Wed; Shau Kei Wan MTR

This museum doesn't exactly sound like a crowd pleaser but the displays it contains are as much about peace as war. Part of the fun is just to enjoy the museum's location. It has been built into the Lei Yue Mun Fort (1887), which took quite a beating during WWII, and has sweeping views down to the Lei Yue Mun Channel and southeastern Kowloon.

Exhibitions in the old redoubt, which you reach by escalator from street level, cover Hong Kong's coastal defence over six centuries – from the Ming and Qing dynasties, through the colonial years and Japanese

invasion, to the resumption of Chinese sovereignty. There's a historical trail through the casemates, tunnels and observation posts almost down to the coast.

To reach the museum take the MTR to Shau Kei Wan station and follow exit B2. From here follow the museum signs on busy Tung Hei Rd for about 15 minutes. Bus 84, which is accessible via exit A3 and runs between Shau Kei Wan and Siu Sai Wan, stops along Tung Hei Rd outside the museum.

Chai Wan
LAW UK FOLK MUSEUM Map pp406-7
☎ 2896 7006; www.lcsd.gov.hk/en/cs_mus_lcsd.php; 14 Kut Shing St; admission free; ☺ 10am-1pm & 2-6pm Mon-Wed, Fri & Sat, 1-6pm Sun; Chai Wan MTR

This small museum, a branch of the Hong Kong Museum of History dating from 1990, is housed in two restored Hakka village houses that have been standing in Chai Wan (Firewood Bay), a district of nondescript office buildings, warehouses and workers flats, for more than two centuries. The quiet courtyard and surrounding bamboo groves are peaceful and evocative, and the displays – furniture, household items and farming implements – simple but charming.

To reach the museum from the Chai Wan MTR station, follow exit B and walk for five minutes to the west.

ISLAND SOUTH
Eating p174

Though largely residential, the Southern District, which encompasses everything from Big Wave Bay and Shek O in the east to Aberdeen and Ap Lei Chau in the west, is full of attractions. At times it can feel like Hong Kong Island's backyard playground – from the beaches of Repulse Bay and Deep Water Bay and the outdoor activities available at Shek O, to Stanley Market, the shoppers' paradise, and Ocean Park, the large amusement and theme park near Aberdeen.

Orientation
Shek O lies halfway down a long peninsula in the southeast of Hong Kong Island; Stanley village is at the start of the next peninsula over, but you'll have to travel a bit further south to reach the best beach on Stanley

Peninsula. Further west along the southern coast is Repulse Bay, with its ever-heaving beach, Kwun Yam shrine, lucky bridge and posh shopping complex, and then Deep Water Bay, a much more serene beach and one of the best places in Hong Kong for wakeboarding (see p224). Aberdeen is at the western edge of the southern coast. From here, buses return to the northern side of the island either through the Aberdeen Tunnel or Pok Fu Lam Rd along the west coast.

Buses, and to a lesser extent green minibuses, are the best form of transport for getting to and around the southern part of Hong Kong Island. Though some go via the Aberdeen Tunnel, many buses (eg bus 6 to Stanley and Repulse Bay) climb over the hills separating the north and south sides of the island. It's a scenic, winding ride; for the outbound trip, make sure you sit on the upper deck on the right-hand side.

Shek O

Sometimes referred to as the 'last real village on Hong Kong Island', Shek O (Map pp406–7), has one of the best beaches on the island. And because it is not as accessible as the beaches to the west, it's usually less crowded. And it's only a 20-minute bus ride from Shau Kei Wan.

ACTIVITIES
Bus 9 or 309 (Sun only)
Shek O has all sorts of activities to keep you busy, amused and out of trouble. In the village itself, along with lovely **Shek O**

Beach, there's **miniature golf** ($13; 9am-6pm Apr-Sep, 9am-5.30pm Oct-Mar) and from **Dragon's Back**, the 280m-high ridge to the west of the village, there's both paragliding and abseiling. Walking is possible around Shek O Beach, though the terrain is steep and the underbrush quite thick in spots. You can also take advantage of several bicycle rental shops (bicycles from $15 a day) including **Tung Lok Barbecue Store** (2809 4692; 11am-8pm Mon-Fri, 11am-11pm Sat & Sun Apr-Sep, 10am-11pm Sat & Sun Oct) in the centre of the village.

BIG WAVE BAY Map pp406–7
Bus 9 or 309 (Sun only)
This fine and often deserted beach is located 2km to the north of Shek O. To get to Big Wave Bay follow the road north out of town, travel past the 18-hole **Shek O Golf & Country Club** (2809 2117; Shek O Rd), then turn east at the roundabout and keep going until the road ends.

One of eight prehistoric rock carvings (see p52) discovered in Hong Kong is located on the headland above Big Wave Bay.

Stanley

About 15km from Central as the crow flies, Stanley (Map p411) had an indigenous population of about 2000 when the British took control of the territory in 1841, making it one of the largest settlements on the island at the time. A prison was built near the village in 1937 – just in time for the Japanese to intern the builders. Stanley Prison is a

---

TRANSPORT

Bus Shek O: bus 9 to Shau Kei Wan MTR station (exit A3) and bus 309 (Sun and holidays only) to Wan Chai and Central bus terminus below Exchange Square (Map pp408–9); Stanley: bus 6, 6A, 6X or 260 (express via Aberdeen Tunnel) to Central, bus 14 to Shau Kei Wan and Sai Wan Ho via Tai Tam Tuk reservoir, and buses 73 and 973 to Repulse Bay and Aberdeen; Repulse Bay: buses 6, 6A, 6X and 260 to Central bus terminus and Aberdeen, and bus 973 to Aberdeen; Deep Water Bay: bus 6A or 260 to Central, and buses 73 and 973 to Aberdeen, Repulse Bay and Stanley; Aberdeen: bus 70 to Central, bus 37A, 37B or 70 to Admiralty, and bus 73 or 973 to Ocean Park, Repulse Bay and Stanley; Ocean Park: buses 73 and 973 to Aberdeen, Repulse Bay and Stanley, bus 6A, 6X, 70 or 260 (express via Aberdeen Tunnel) to Central, and bus 973 to Tsim Sha Tsui in Kowloon.

Minibus Repulse Bay to Edinburgh Place at Star Ferry pier in Central.

Green Minibus Stanley: bus 40 (24 hours) to Times Square, Tang Lung St and Yee Woo St (Map pp414–15) in Causeway Bay, and bus 16M to Chai Wan MTR station; Ocean Park: bus 6 to Star Ferry pier in Central.

Ferry Stanley: public pier to Aberdeen and Po Toi; Aberdeen: Aberdeen Promenade ferry pier to Yung Shue Wan, Pak Kok Tsuen, Sok Kwu Wan and Man Tat Wan on Lamma.

maximum security facility today. Hong Kong's contingent of British troops was housed in Stanley Fort at the southern end of the peninsula until 1995. It is now used by China's People's Liberation Army (PLA). There's a beach to the northeast of town that never gets as crowded as the one at Repulse Bay. The most important dragon-boat races are held at Stanley during the **Dragon Boat Festival** (Tuen Ng; p11) in early June.

HONG KONG CORRECTIONAL SERVICES MUSEUM Map p411

☎ 2147 3199; 45 Tung Tau Wan Rd; admission free; ⏱ 10am-5pm Tue-Sun; bus 6, 6A, 6X or 260

With Stanley Prison so close by, it's only natural that there should be a museum devoted to the subject here. The museum, about 500m southeast of Stanley Village Rd, has nine galleries that trace the history of jails, prisons and other forms of incarceration in Hong Kong. The mock cells, gallows and flogging stands will convince most of the error of their ways.

MURRAY HOUSE Map p411

Stanley Bay; bus 6, 6A, 6X or 260

At the start of the Chung Hom Kok Peninsula across the bay from Stanley Main St, the waterfront promenade lined with bars and restaurants, stands this three-storey colonnaded affair. Built in 1848 as officers' quarters, it took pride of place in Central, on the spot where the Bank of China Tower now stands, for almost 150 years until 1982. It was re-erected here and opened in 2001 after, well, a slight glitch (see the boxed text, opposite).

OLD STANLEY POLICE STATION Map p411

88 Stanley Village Rd; bus 6, 6A, 6X or 260

The most interesting building in the village itself is this two-storey structure built in 1859. It now contains a Wellcome supermarket.

ST STEPHEN'S BEACH & MILITARY CEMETERY Off Map p411

Bus 6A or 14

St Stephen's Beach, which has a café, showers and changing rooms, is south of the village. In summer you can hire windsurfing boards and kayaks from the water sports centre

(p224). To reach the beach, walk south along Wong Ma Kok Rd. Turn west (ie right) when you get to a small road (Wong Ma Kok Path) leading down to a jetty.

At the end of the road, turn south and walk past the boathouse to the beach. Bus 14 or 6A will take you close to the intersection with the small road.

Opposite the bus stop is **Stanley Military Cemetery** for armed forces personnel and their families. The oldest graves date back to 1843.

STANLEY MARKET Map p411

Stanley Village Rd; ⏱ 9am-6pm; bus 6, 6A, 6X or 260

No big bargains or big stings, just reasonably priced casual clothes (plenty of large sizes), bric-a-brac, toys and formulaic art, all in a nicely confusing maze of alleys running down to Stanley Bay. It's best to go during the week; at the weekend the market is bursting at the seams with both tourists and locals alike.

TEMPLES & SHRINES Map p411

Bus 6, 6A, 6X or 260

At the western end of Stanley Main St, past a tiny **Tai Wong shrine** and through the modern shopping complex called Stanley Plaza, is a **Tin Hau temple** (119 Stanley Main St; ⏱ 7am-6pm), built in 1767 and said to be the oldest building in Hong Kong. It has undergone a complete renovation since then, however, and is now a concrete pile (though the interior is traditional). A sign explains that the tiger skin hanging on the wall came from an animal that 'weighed 240 pounds, was 73 inches long, and three feet high [and] shot by an Indian policeman, Mr Rur Singh, in front of Stanley Police Station in the year 1942'.

Behind the Tin Hau temple is huge Ma Hang Estate. If you follow the path that passes by the side of the temple and continue up the hill, you'll reach **Kwun Yam Temple** (⏱ 7am-6pm).

Repulse Bay

The long beach with tawny sand at Repulse Bay – Chin Shui Wan (Shallow Water Bay) in Cantonese – is the most popular one on Hong Kong Island. Packed at the weekend and even during the week in summer, it's a good place if you like people-watching. The beach has showers and changing rooms and shade trees at the road side, but the water is pretty murky. Lifeguards keep extended hours here: from 9am to 6pm daily from March to November (8am to 7pm on Saturday and Sunday from June to August). Middle Bay and South Bay, about 10 and 30 minutes to the south respectively, have beaches that are usually much less crowded.

Repulse Bay is home to some of Hong Kong's richest residents, and the hills around the beach are strewn with luxury apartment blocks. This includes the pink, blue and yellow wavy number with a giant square hole in the middle called the Repulse Bay. This design feature was apparently added on the advice of a feng shui expert.

KWUN YAM SHRINE Map pp406-7
Repulse Bay Beach; bus 6, 6A, 6X or 260

Towards the southeast end of Repulse Bay Beach is an unusual shrine to Kwun Yam. The surrounding area has an amazing assembly of deities and figures – goldfish, rams, the money god and other southern Chinese icons, as well as statues of the goddess of mercy and Tin Hau. Most of the statues were funded by local personalities and businesspeople during the 1970s. In front of the shrine to the left as you face the sea is **Longevity Bridge**; crossing it is supposed to add three days to your life.

THE REPULSE BAY Map pp406-7
109 Repulse Bay Rd; bus 6, 6A, 6X or 260

The Repulse Bay, a copy of the wonderful old colonial Repulse Bay Hotel, built in 1922 and bulldozed 60 years later, contains a small shopping mall and several eateries, including the **Verandah Restaurant** (p175).

Deep Water Bay

A quiet little inlet with a beach flanked by shade trees, Deep Water Bay (Map pp406–7) is located a few kilometres northwest of Repulse Bay; lifeguards keep the same schedule as those at Repulse Bay Beach and in winter – ie December to February – they are on duty daily from 8am to 5pm. There are a few decent places to eat and have a drink, and barbecue pits at the southern end of the beach. If you want a dip in the water, this spot is usually less crowded than Repulse Bay. Opposite the beach is the nine-hole **Deep Water Bay Golf Club** (p218). Deep Water Bay Beach is a centre for wakeboarding (p224).

Aberdeen

For many years Aberdeen (Map p411) – Heung Gong Tsai (Little Fragrant Harbour) in Cantonese – was one of Hong Kong's top tourist attractions because of the large number of people (up to 6000, in fact) who

---

DON'T KNOW MUCH ABOUT HISTORY

Hong Kong does not have a stellar track record when it comes to preserving old buildings. Though things have improved over the past decade or so, traditionally if a structure sat on a 'valuable' piece of land (ie virtually every square centimetre of the built-up areas) or got in the way of progress (ie money) it was given a kiss on the derrière by the wrecker's ball and brought down, living on in old photographs and the memories of a dwindling population.

It came as no surprise, then, when the colonial government announced in 1982 that Murray House, Hong Kong's oldest colonial building, was going to have to make room for the new Bank of China Tower. But because Murray House had a Grade 1 classification, even the government couldn't just smash it to pieces as they had the old Hong Kong Club and the Central Post Office. Instead, the building would be dismantled and its more than 4000 pieces numbered and stored for 'safekeeping' and erection elsewhere. Time passed and when heritage societies demanded to know its whereabouts, the government admitted it had misplaced some of the pieces.

Scene and time change… It's the mid-1990s and – hurrah! hurrah! – the government has found the missing pieces stored in crates in Tai Tam. But there's a big problem. The limestone blocks and pillars had been wrapped in plastic sheeting and the numbers written or etched into their sides had spontaneously erased due to moisture building up on the soft stone. To its credit, the government rolled up its sleeves and it took its workers 3½ years to put this colossal puzzle back together again. And when they'd finished in early 2001, six columns were left over that they didn't know what to do with.

As you approach Murray House, which now contains a small exhibition area on the ground floor that looks at the history of the buildings and restaurants on the 1st, you'll see these idle Ionic columns standing rather forlornly off to the left along the waterfront promenade. Note, too, some of the numbers still visible on the building blocks to the right of the entrance.

lived and worked on the junks and other traditional sailing craft moored in the harbour and in the Aberdeen Typhoon Shelter off Aberdeen Praya Rd to the west. Over the years the number of boats has dwindled as more and more of these boatpeople have moved into high-rises or abandoned fishing as a profession.

AP LEI CHAU Maps pp406-7 & p411
Ap Lei Chau ferry
On the southern side of the harbour is Ap Lei Chau (Duck's Tongue Island), one of the most densely populated places in the world. It used to be a centre for building junks, but now it's covered with housing estates, including a huge one called South Horizons. There's not much to see there, but Ap Lei Chau is famous for its factory outlets and a walk across the bridge to the island affords good views. From Aberdeen Promenade you can get a boat across to Ap Lei Chau (adult/child under 12 $1.80/1).

OCEAN PARK Map pp406-7
☎ 2552 0291; www.oceanpark.co.hk;
Ocean Park Rd; adult/child 3-11 $185/93;
☼ 9.30am-8pm; bus 73 or 973
Ocean Park, southeast of Aberdeen town centre, is a fully fledged amusement and educational theme park, complete with a celebrated roller coaster called the Dragon, the Abyss 'turbo drop' and other stomach-turning rides. It is also something of a marine park, with a Pacific Pier housing sea lions and seals, daily dolphin and killer-whale shows, and aquariums. The Atoll Reef is particularly impressive, with over 2000 fish representing 200 species in residence. The walk-through Shark Aquarium has hundreds of different sharks on view and scores of rays. Bird-watchers are also catered for, with aviaries, a flamingo pond and the Amazing Birds Theatre, where our fine feathered friends put on regular aerial shows.

The park is divided into two sections. The main entrance is on the lowland side, where there are gardens and the Hong Kong Jockey Club Giant Panda Habitat, home to An An and Jia Jia. It is linked to the main section on the headland, where most of the attractions are found, by a scenic (and hair-raising) cable car. The headland section affords beautiful views of the South China Sea and at the rear entrance, where a giant escalator will bring you down to Tai Shue Wan and Shum Wan Rd, is the Middle

Kingdom, a sort of Chinese cultural village with temples, pagodas and traditional street scenes.

As well as the transport options listed on p85, Ocean Park has Citybus package tickets that include transportation and one-day admission to Ocean Park (adult/child $209/105) from Star Ferry pier and Admiralty (bus 629) daily, and from Hung Hom train station (bus 630) on Saturday and Sunday. Buses leave every 10 to 20 minutes from 9am or 9.30am to 3pm; the last buses return at 5.30pm.

SAMPAN TOURS
Aberdeen Promenade; bus 70 or 70M
Sampan tours can easily be arranged along Aberdeen Promenade, which runs south and parallel to Aberdeen Praya Rd. You can have your choice of private operators, which generally mill around the eastern end of the promenade, or licensed operators registered with the HKTB, such as the **Aberdeen Sampan Company** (Map p411; ☎ 2873 0310, 2873 0649; Aberdeen Praya Rd). The private sampans usually charge $50 per person for a 30-minute ride (about $80 to Sok Kwu Wan and $100 to Yung Shue Wan on Lamma), though you should easily be able to bargain this down if there are several of you.

TEMPLES Map p411
Aberdeen Main Rd; bus 70 or 70M
If you've got time to spare, a short walk through Aberdeen will bring you to a renovated **Tin Hau temple** (182 Aberdeen Main Rd; ☼ 8am-5pm). Built in 1851, it's a sleepy spot, but it remains an active house of worship. Close to the harbour is a **Hung Shing shrine** (cnr Aberdeen Main Rd & Old Main St), a chaotic collection of altars and smoking, ovenlike incense pots.

KOWLOON

The name 'Kowloon' is thought to have originated when the last emperor of the Song dynasty passed through the area during his flight from the Mongols in the late 13th century (p53). He is said to have counted eight peaks on the peninsula and concluded that there must therefore be eight dragons there. But the young emperor was reminded that with he himself present, there were actually nine dragons. Kowloon is thus derived from the Cantonese words *gáu,* meaning 'nine', and *lùng,* meaning 'dragon'.

Kowloon proper, the area ceded 'in perpetuity' to Britain by the Convention of Peking in 1860, extends north from the waterfront as far as Boundary St in Mong Kok. It covers about 12 sq km, but land reclamation and encroachment into the New Territories – the so-called New Kowloon – over the past 150-odd years has more than quadrupled its size to almost 47 sq km or just over 4% of the total landmass.

Kowloon's most important area, Tsim Sha Tsui, has none of the slickness or sophistication of Hong Kong Island's Central, except within the confines of its top-end hotels. The territory's historical and financial 'capital' lies on Hong Kong Island; Kowloon is the hinterland, a riot of commerce and tourism set against a backdrop of crumbling tenement blocks. Leave the glittering shopping centres and hotels behind and you begin to see where Hong Kong and China converge, culturally at least. East doesn't really meet West in Kowloon – it swallows it up.

In general, Kowloon is unexciting architecturally. Height restrictions for buildings, due to the proximity of the old Kai Tak International Airport in southeastern Kowloon, gave it a much lower skyline than that of northern Hong Kong Island though that's all changing – and fast. The waterfront Hong Kong Cultural Centre in Tsim Sha Tsui was a bold (and early) stab at turning Hong Kong into something more than a territory obsessed with wealth. The Peninsula Hotel is housed in one of Hong Kong's greatest colonial buildings and, at night, the promenade running east and northeast along Victoria Harbour from Star Ferry pier offers a technicolour backdrop of Central and Wan Chai. And there are some green spaces, such as Kowloon Park. What's more, Kowloon (and in particular Tsim Sha Tsui) has the lion's share of Hong Kong's most important museums.

TSIM SHA TSUI

Eating p176; Sleeping p260

Tsim Sha Tsui (roughly pronounced 'jìm-sàa-jéui' and meaning 'Sharp Sandy Point') is Hong Kong's tourist ghetto, and in the days of Kai Tak airport this is what most travellers saw as they first stepped off the bus from the airport. Countless clothing and shoe shops, restaurants, pubs, sleazy bars, camera and electronics stores, and hotels are somehow crammed into an area not much bigger than a square kilometre. Around Ashley, Hankow and Lock Rds is a warren of shops, restaurants and bars. It's a fun area to wander around, particularly in the evening. Nightlife areas include Knutsford Tce and, most recently, Minden Ave.

Orientation

The hotel and shopping district of Tsim Sha Tsui ('Tsimsy' to locals) lies at the very tip of the Kowloon Peninsula to the south of Austin Rd. (The area between Austin Rd and Jordan Rd is usually called Jordan by Hong Kong residents, but it can still be considered Tsim Sha Tsui here.) Chatham Rd South separates it from the hotels and shops of Tsim Sha Tsui East and the transport hub of Hung Hom. Tsim Sha Tsui's western and southern boundaries – Victoria Harbour – are lined with top-end hotels, shopping centres and cultural venues.

FORMER KCR CLOCK TOWER

Map pp420–1

Tsim Sha Tsui Public Pier; Star Ferry
Immediately east of Star Ferry pier, this 44m-high clock tower (1915) was once part of the southern terminus of the Kowloon-Canton Railway (KCR). Operations moved to

TRANSPORT

MTR Tsim Sha Tsui station (Map pp420–1) on Tsuen Wan line.

KCR East Tsim Sha Tsui station (Map pp420–1), terminus of the KCR East Rail.

Bus Star Ferry pier (Map pp420–1) for buses 2, 6 and 6A to Mong Kok, Yau Ma Tei and Sham Shui Po, and bus 5C to Hung Hom station and Kowloon City; Canton Rd (Map pp420–1) for bus 973 to Pok Fu Lam, Aberdeen, Repulse Bay and Stanley; Nathan Rd (Map pp420–1) for bus 271 to Tai Po and bus 281A to Sha Tin; Nathan Rd for bus 260X to Tuen Mun.

Green Minibus Hankow Rd (Map pp420–1) for buses 6 and 8 to Hung Hom station.

Star Ferry Pier (Map pp420–1) at western end of Salisbury Rd.

Outlying Islands Ferries Star Ferry pier (Map pp420–1) to Lantau and Cheung Chau (weekends).

Macau Ferries China ferry terminal (Map pp420–1) on Canton Rd.

the modern train station at Hung Hom to the northeast in late 1975. The station was demolished in 1978, though you can see a scale model of what it looked like if you visit the **Hong Kong Railway Museum** (p115) in Tai Po in the New Territories.

HONG KONG CULTURAL CENTRE

Map pp420-1

☎ 2734 2009; www.lcsd.gov.hk/CE/Cultural Service/HKCC/index_e.htm; 10 Salisbury Rd; ☻ 9am-11pm; Star Ferry

The odd, wavelike building clad in pink ceramic tiles behind the clock tower and opposite Star House is the Hong Kong Cultural Centre, one of Hong Kong's most distinctive – if not loved – landmarks. It opened in 1989 and was compared with everything from a cheaply tiled public toilet to a road-side petrol station.

Its controversial design notwithstanding, the centre is a world-class venue, with a 2085-seat concert hall, a Grand Theatre that seats 1750, a studio theatre for up to 535, rehearsal studios and an impressive foyer. The concert hall even has a Rieger Orgelbau pipe organ (with 8000 pipes and 93 stops), one of the largest in the world. On the building's south side is the beginning of a viewing platform from where you can admire Victoria Harbour and the skyline of Central and gain access to the **Tsim Sha Tsui East Promenade** (p93) and **Avenue of the Stars** (p93). Guided tours (adult/concession $10/5) lasting 30 to 45 minutes depart on certain afternoons each week; telephone ahead to book.

HONG KONG MUSEUM OF ART

Map pp420-1

☎ 7221 0116; www.lcsd.gov.hk/hkma; 10 Salisbury Rd; adult/child, student or senior over 60 $10/5, admission free Wed; ☻ 10am-6pm Fri-Wed; Star Ferry

To the southeast of the Hong Kong Cultural Centre, the Hong Kong Museum of Art has seven galleries, spread over six floors, exhibiting Chinese antiquities, Chinese fine art, historical pictures and contemporary Hong Kong art, and hosting temporary international exhibitions.

The seventh gallery houses the Xubaizhi collection of painting and calligraphy. Visitors will find the **Historical Pictures Gallery**, with its 18th- and 19th-century Western-style paintings of Macau, Hong Kong and

Guangzhou, and the **Contemporary Hong Kong Art Gallery** especially interesting. Audio guides are available for $10, and there are free English-language tours at 11am and 4pm Sunday to Wednesday and Friday, and at 3pm, 4pm and 5pm on Saturday.

When your feet get tired, take a seat in the hallway and enjoy the harbour views. Or head for the **Museum Café** (☎ 2370 3860; ☻ 10am-8pm Mon-Wed, 10am-10pm Fri-Sun). The **Museum Bookshop** (☎ 2732 2088; ☻ 10am-6.30pm Mon-Sat, 11am-6.30pm Sun) sells a wide range of books, prints and cards. **Salisbury Gardens**, which leads to the museum entrance, is lined with sculptures by contemporary Hong Kong sculptors. To reach the museum from the Tsim Sha Tsui MTR station, take exit E and walk south down Nathan Rd.

HONG KONG OBSERVATORY

Map pp420-1

☎ 2926 8200; www.hko.gov.hk; 134A Nathan Rd; Tsim Sha Tsui & Jordan MTR

What was until 1997 called the Royal Observatory is housed in a two-storey colonial structure east of Kowloon Park on the other side of Nathan Rd. It was built in 1883 and declared a historic monument exactly a century later. It continues to monitor Hong Kong's weather and sends up those frightening signals when a typhoon is heading for the territory (see the boxed text, p309). The observatory is *not* open to the public.

HONG KONG SPACE MUSEUM & THEATRE Map pp420-1

☎ 2721 0226; www.lcsd.gov.hk/CE/Museum/Space /index.htm; 10 Salisbury Rd; adult/concession $10/5, admission free Wed; ☻ 1-9pm Mon & Wed-Fri, 10am-9pm Sat, Sun & public holidays; Star Ferry

Just east of the Hong Kong Cultural Centre, this golf-ball-shaped building consists of the Hall of Space Science, the Hall of Astronomy and the large Space Theatre, one of the largest planetariums in the world. Exhibits include a lump of moon rock, rocket-ship models and NASA's 1962 *Mercury* space capsule.

The Space Theatre screens 'sky shows' and IMAX films on a massive screen; lasting about 40 minutes, they are mostly in Cantonese, but translations by headphones are available. The first show is at 1.30pm weekdays (12.20pm Saturday, 11.10am Sunday), the last at 8.30pm. Tickets are $32/16 for adults/concessions, and $24/12 in the front stalls; children under three are not allowed entry. Advance bookings can be made by phone up to one hour before show time.

KOWLOON MOSQUE & ISLAMIC CENTRE Map pp420-1
☎ 2724 0095; 105 Nathan Rd; ☺ 5am-10pm; Tsim Sha Tsui MTR

North of the intersection of Nathan and Haiphong Rds, the Kowloon Mosque & Islamic Centre is the largest Islamic house of worship in Hong Kong. The present building, with its dome and carved marble, was completed in 1984 to serve the territory's 70,000-odd Muslims, more than half of whom are Chinese, and can accommodate 2000 worshippers. It occupies the site of a mosque built in 1896 for Muslim Indian troops.

Muslims are welcome to attend services but non-Muslims should ask permission to enter. Remember to remove your shoes.

KOWLOON PARK Map pp420-1
☎ 2724 3344; www.lcsd.gov.hk/en/ls_park.php; 22 Austin Rd; ☺ 6am-midnight; Tsim Sha Tsui & Jordan MTR

Built on the site of a barracks for Indian soldiers in the colonial army, Kowloon Park is an oasis of greenery and a refreshing escape from the hustle and bustle of Tsim Sha Tsui. Pathways and walls crisscross the grass, birds hop around in cages, and towers and ancient banyan trees dot the landscape.

There's an aviary (☺ 6.30am-6.45pm Mar-Oct, 6.30am-5.45pm Nov-Feb) and a Chinese Garden and Sculpture Walk, featuring works by local artists. Kung Fu Corner, a display of traditional Chinese martial arts, takes place here from 2.30pm to 4.30pm on Sunday. The renovated Kowloon Park Swimming Complex (☎ 2724 3577; adult/child 3-13 or senior over 60 $19/9; ☺ 6.30am-10pm with 1hr close at noon & 5pm Apr-Oct, indoor 6.30am-9.30pm with 1hr close at noon & 5pm Nov-Mar) is complete with four pools and waterfalls. Visit on a weekday; on weekends there are so many bathers it's difficult to find the water.

NATHAN ROAD Map pp420-1
Tsim Sha Tsui MTR

Kowloon's main thoroughfare was named after Sir Matthew Nathan, governor of Hong Kong from 1904 to 1907. As Kow-

loon was very sparsely populated at the time and such a wide boulevard thought unnecessarily extravagant, it was dubbed 'Nathan's Folly'. There are banyans lining the road at the northern end near Austin Rd, but the trees that once lined the rest of the street and can be seen in not-so-old photographs were removed in 1976 when the MTR's first line was being built.

The southern end of Nathan Rd is known as the Golden Mile, reflecting both the price of property in this high-rent area and the retailers' success. Though lacking any tourist sights as such, the lower end of this boulevard is a sight in itself. Ramshackle blocks stacked with seedy guesthouses awkwardly rub shoulders with top-end hotels; touts sell fake Rolex watches; tailors ply their trade on street corners; and the pavements are chock-a-block with consumers scurrying from one shop to another. Anyone who chooses to stay at Chungking Mansions (p262), Mirador Mansion (p263) or Golden Crown Guest House (p264) will have this frenetic scene at their very doorstep.

Afternoon tea, Peninsula Hong Kong (p92), Tsim Sha Tsui

OCEAN TERMINAL Map pp420-1

☎ 2118 8668; www.harbourcity.com.hk; Salisbury Rd; ⏰ 11.30am-9pm; Star Ferry

To the north of the clock tower is **Star House** (3 Salisbury Rd), a frayed-looking retail and office complex. At its western end is the entrance to Ocean Terminal, the long building jutting into the harbour. It is part of the massive Harbour City shopping complex that stretches for half a kilometre north along Canton Rd and offers priceless views of Tsim Sha Tsui's western waterfront.

The stunning blue-and-white colonial structure on the hill above where Canton and Salisbury Rds meet is the former **Marine Police Headquarters**, built in 1884. Part of its grounds is now being developed.

PENINSULA HONG KONG Map pp420-1

☎ 2920 2888; www.peninsula.com; cnr Salisbury & Nathan Rds; Tsim Sha Tsui MTR

More than a Hong Kong landmark, the Peninsula, in the thronelike building opposite the Hong Kong Space Museum, is one of the world's great hotels (p261). Though it was being called 'the finest hotel east of Suez' just a few years after opening in 1928, the Peninsula was in fact one of several prestigious hostelries across Asia where everybody who was anybody stayed, lining up with (but not behind) the likes of the Raffles in Singapore, the Peace (then the Cathay) in Shanghai and the Strand in Rangoon (now Yangon).

Taking **afternoon tea** ($180 to $220; ⏰ 2-7pm) at the Peninsula is one of the best experiences in town – dress neatly and be prepared to queue for a table.

TSIM SHA TSUI EAST & HUNG HOM

Eating p183; Sleeping p266

The large triangular chunk of land east and northeast of Tsim Sha Tsui proper, built entirely on reclaimed land, is a cluster of shopping centres, hotels, theatres, restaurants and nightclubs. There are none of the old, crumbling buildings of 'real' Tsim Sha Tsui here – and like most reclaimed areas, it has that soulless, artificial feel that will take decades to remove. But two of Hong Kong's most important museums are here, and it offers an excellent vantage point from which to admire the harbour and Hong Kong Island's cityscape.

Among the features of Hung Hom, the contiguous district to the northeast, are the massive KCR East Rail station, on Wan Rd; the 12,500-seat **Hong Kong Coliseum** (☎ 2355 7234; 9 Cheong Wan Rd), which hosts concerts and sporting events; the **Hong Kong Polytechnic University** (☎ 2766 5100; Hong Chong Rd), opposite the station; and one of the strangest shopping venues in the territory, the **Wonderful World of Whampoa** (Map pp418–19; ☎ 2128 7710; www.whampoaworld.com; 18 Tak Fung St; ⏰ 10am-10pm), a full-scale concrete model of a luxury cruise liner. While presumably not very seaworthy, the 'ship' – 100m long and four decks tall – is impressive and works very well for what it was intended to be: a shopping centre with retail outlets, restaurants, a cinema and a playground on the top deck.

Orientation

Tsim Sha Tsui East is defined by Chatham Rd South to the west and Salisbury Rd to the south. The limit to the east is Hong Chong Rd, backed by the Hong Kong Coliseum and Hung Hom train station. To the north it ends at Cheong Wan Rd.

Hung Hom is further to the north and northeast and divided by the Hung Hom Bypass into two parts: the station and coliseum on the west side and residential Hung Hom to the east.

HONG KONG MUSEUM OF HISTORY

Map pp420-1

☎ 2724 9042; www.hk.history.museum; 100 Chatham Rd South; adult/child, student or senior over 60 $10/5, admission free Wed; ⏰ 10am-6pm Mon & Wed-Sat, 10am-7pm Sun & public holidays; Tsim Sha Tsui MTR

Hong Kong's newest museum, which opened its permanent exhibition in 2001, focuses on the territory's archaeology, natural history, ethnography and local history. It is well worth a visit not only to learn more about the subject but to understand how Hong Kong presents its history to itself and the world.

'The Hong Kong Story' takes visitors on a fascinating walk through the territory's past via eight galleries, starting with the natural environment and prehistoric Hong Kong – about 6000 years ago, give or take a year – and ending with the territory's return to China in 1997. Along the way you'll encounter replicas of village dwellings; traditional Chinese costumes and beds; a re-creation of an entire arcaded street in Central from 1881, including an old Chinese medicine shop; a tram from 1913; and film footage of WWII, including recent interviews with Chinese and foreigners taken prisoner by the Japanese.

Free guided tours of the museum are available in English at 10.30am and 2.30pm on Saturday and Sunday. Use exit B2 if walking from the Tsim Sha Tsui MTR station.

HONG KONG SCIENCE MUSEUM
Map pp420-1

☎ 2732 3232; www.lcsd.gov.hk/CE/Museum/Science; 2 Science Museum Rd; adult/concession $25/12.50, admission free Wed; ⏰ 1-9pm Mon-Wed & Fri, 10am-9pm Sat, Sun & public holidays; Tsim Sha Tsui MTR

The Hong Kong Science Museum is a four-level complex with more than 500 displays on computers, energy, physics, robotics, telecommunications, health and the like. Two-thirds of the exhibits are 'hands on'. Though some of them are beginning to look a little dated after 15 years or so, all the buttons to push and robot arms to operate will keep young (and some older) visitors entertained. Use exit B2 of the Tsim Sha Tsui MTR station.

TSIM SHA TSUI EAST PROMENADE
Map pp420-1
Star Ferry, Tsim Sha Tsui East ferry

Along with the Peak, this amazing waterfront walkway offers some of the best views in Hong Kong. It's a lovely place to stroll during the day, and at night the view of Central lit up in neon is mesmerising. Along

the first part of the promenade the new **Avenue of the Stars** pays homage to the Hong Kong film industry and its stars, with handprints, sculptures and information boards. This is the best place to watch the nightly Symphony of the Stars, a spectacular sound-and-light show involving some 20 buildings on the Hong Kong Island skyline from 8pm to 8.20pm.

The promenade officially starts at the New World Centre shopping centre and runs parallel to Salisbury Rd almost to the Hong Kong Coliseum and Hung Hom train station, but you can walk along the water all the way from Star Ferry pier in order to gain access to it. It gets especially crowded during the Chinese New Year fireworks displays in late January/early February and in June during the **Dragon Boat Festival** (p11).

YAU MA TEI
Eating p184; Sleeping p267

Immediately to the north of Tsim Sha Tsui is Yau Ma Tei, pronounced '*yàu-màa-dáy*' and meaning 'Place of Sesame Plants'. Today the only plants you'll find in this heavily urbanised neighbourhood are in the window boxes of *tàwng-láu*, the crumbling six-storey tenements that don't have lifts and more often than not have illegal huts on the roof. Yau Ma Tei's narrow byways are good places to check out Hong Kong's more traditional urban society. There are many interesting walks to take along the streets running east to west between Kansu St and Jordan Rd (Map pp420–1), including **Nanking Street** (mahjong shops and parlours), **Ning Po Street** (paper kites and votives, such as houses, mobile phones and hell money, to

TRANSPORT

MTR Jordan MTR station (Map pp420–1) on Tsuen Wan line, Yau Ma Tei MTR station (Map p417) on the Tsuen Wan and Kwun Tong line, and Kowloon MTR on the Tung Chung and Airport Express lines.

Bus Nathan Rd (Map pp420–1) for buses 2, 6 and 6A to Tsim Sha Tsui, bus 9 to Star Ferry pier, bus 203 to Tsim Sha Tsui East, bus 102 to Hung Hom, North Point and Quarry Bay, bus 104 to Wan Chai and Central; bus 60X to Tuen Mun, and bus 81 to Sha Tin.

Airport Express Kowloon station (Map pp420–1).

burn for the dead) and **Saigon Street** (herbalist shops, old-style tailors, pawnshops). On **Shanghai Street** you'll find Chinese bridal and trousseau shops. See p143 for a self-guided walk of this area.

Orientation

Yau Ma Tei is practically indistinguishable from its neighbours to the north (Mong Kok) and south (Tsim Sha Tsui). Indeed, the official designation of the district they form is Yau Tsim Mong. Yau Ma Tei starts at Jordan Rd and reaches north to somewhere between Waterloo Rd and Argyle St. King's Park and Gascoigne Rd are its borders to the east. To the west it reaches Yau Ma Tei Typhoon Shelter in Victoria Harbour, the West Kowloon reclamation site and the Kowloon station of the Tung Chung MTR and Airport Express lines.

JADE MARKET Maps pp420-1 & p423
Kansu & Battery Sts; ☺ 10am-5pm;
Yau Ma Tei MTR
The Jade Market, near the Gascoigne Rd overpass just west of Nathan Rd and split into two parts by the loop formed by

Battery St, has some 400 stalls selling all varieties and grades of jade from inside two covered markets. Unless you really know your nephrite from your jadeite, it's probably not wise to buy any expensive pieces here.

You can reach the market easily on foot from either the Jordan (exit A) or Yau Ma Tei (exit C) MTR stations. Bus 9 from the Star Ferry bus station will drop you off at the Kowloon Central Post Office at 405 Nathan Rd, which is just around the corner from the market.

TEMPLE STREET NIGHT MARKET
Map p423
☺ 4pm-midnight; Jordan, Yau Ma Tei MTR
Temple St, which extends from Man Ming Lane in the north to Nanking St in the south and is cut in two by the Tin Hau temple complex, is the liveliest night market in Hong Kong, and is *the* place to go for cheap clothes, *daai-pàai-dawng* (open-air street stall) food, watches, pirated CDs, fake labels, footwear, cookware and everyday items. Any marked prices should be considered mere suggestions – this is definitely a place to bargain.

THE TRIADS

Hong Kong's Triads, which continue to run the territory's drug, prostitution, gambling and loan-sharking rackets despite the change of government, weren't always the gangster operations they are today. They were founded as secret and patriotic societies that opposed the corrupt and brutal Qing (Manchu) dynasty and aided the revolution that brought down that moribund dynasty in 1911. The fact that these organisations had adopted Kwan Tai (or Kwan Yu), the god of war and upholder of righteousness, integrity and loyalty as their patron, lent them further respectability.

Unfortunately, the Triads descended into crime and illicit activities during the civil war on the mainland, and came in droves to Hong Kong after the Communists came to power in 1949. Today they are the Chinese equivalent of the Mafia. Sporting such names as 14K, Bamboo Union, Water Room and Peace Victory Brotherhood, the Triads have been increasingly successful at recruiting disaffected teenagers in Hong Kong's high-rise housing estates. The Hong Kong police estimate that there are just under 60 societies in the territory, though only about a third are active, with an estimated 100,000 members.

The Triad armoury is a hellish array of weapons ranging from meat cleavers and machetes to pistols and petrol bombs. If people default on a loan, Triad members encourage repayment by attacking them with large knives in the middle of the street.

Membership in a Triad is illegal in Hong Kong; indeed, it's an offence even to claim to be a member. Yet the Triads seem to be growing and have been trying to use wealth to muscle into legitimate businesses.

The Communists smashed the Triad-controlled drug racket in Shanghai after the 1949 revolution. The Triads have long memories and, before the handover, many Hong Kong–based hoods moved their operations to ethnic Chinese communities in such countries as Thailand, the Philippines, Australia, Canada and the USA. Since 1997, however, many Triads have moved back into Hong Kong and have even expanded their operations into the mainland, establishing links with corrupt government cadres and high-ranking soldiers in the People's Liberation Army.

The definitive work on the subject is *Triad Societies in Hong Kong* by WP Morgan, a former sub-inspector in the Royal Hong Kong Police. It's available in bookshops throughout the territory.

You'll also find a surfeit of fortune-tellers and herbalists and, occasionally, some free, open-air Cantonese opera performances here.

For street food, head for **Woo Sung St** (Map pp420–1), running parallel to the east, or to the section of Temple St north of the temple. You can get anything from a simple bowl of noodles to a full meal. There are also a few seafood and hotpot restaurants in the area.

The market officially opens in the afternoon, but most hawkers set up at about 6pm and leave by midnight. The market is at its best from about 7pm to 10pm, when it's clogged with stalls and people. If you want to carry on, visit the colourful **wholesale fruit market** (cnr Shek Lung & Reclamation Sts; ☽ midnight-dawn), which is always a hive of activity.

To reach Temple St market, take exit C2 from the Jordan MTR station and walk along Bowring St or exit C from the Yau Ma Tei MTR station and follow Man Ming Lane.

TIN HAU TEMPLE Map p423

☎ 2332 9240; cnr Public Square St & Nathan Rd; ☽ 8am-6pm; Yau Ma Tei MTR
A couple of blocks northeast of the Jade Market, this decent-sized temple is dedicated to Tin Hau, the goddess of seafarers. The temple complex also houses an altar dedicated to Shing Wong, the god of the city, and to To Tei, the earth god. You'll find a row of fortune-tellers through the last doorway on the right from the main entrance facing Public Square St; signs indicate which ones speak English. An incense spiral that lasts 10 days will set you back a mere $130.

The **Yau Ma Tei Police Station** (627 Canton Rd), a short distance to the east along Public Square St, was built in 1922 and is a listed building.

MONG KOK

Eating p184; Sleeping p267
Mong Kok (Prosperous Point) is one of Hong Kong's most congested working-class residential areas, as well as one of its busiest shopping districts.

This is where locals come to buy everyday items such as jeans, tennis shoes, computer accessories and kitchen supplies. Take a look at Fife St, which has an amazing collection of stalls selling old vinyl, books,

TRANSPORT

MTR Mong Kok and Prince Edward MTR stations (Map p423) on Tsuen Wan and Kwun Tong lines.

KCR Mong Kok station (Map p423) on the KCR East Rail.

Bus Nathan Rd (Map p423) for buses 2, 6 and 6A to Tsim Sha Tsui, bus 21 to Lai Chi Kok, bus 203 to Tsim Sha Tsui East, bus 102 to Hung Hom, North Point and Quarry Bay, bus 104 to Wan Chai and Central, and bus 81 to Sha Tin; Argyle St (Map p423) for bus 60X to Tuen Mun.

ceramics, machinery and music scores. Mong Kok is also a good place to buy backpacks, hiking boots and sporting goods (p247). Two blocks southeast of the Mong Kok MTR station (exit D3) is the **Tung Choi St market** (see the boxed text, p246), which runs from Argyle St in the north to Dundas St in the south.

The streets west of Nathan Rd reveal Hong Kong's seamier side, for this is where you'll find some of the city's seediest brothels. Mostly run by Triads, these places are often veritable prisons for young women. The Hong Kong police routinely raid these places, but a look at the rows of pastel-coloured neon strip lights on so many blocks is an indication that it's 'business as usual' despite the change in landlords.

Orientation

Mong Kok starts somewhere between Waterloo Rd and Argyle St to the south and ends at Boundary St in the north – strictly speaking, anything beyond that is the New Territories. The limit to the east is Waterloo Rd as it heads northward to Kowloon Tong and to the west the district of Tai Kok Tsui.

YUEN PO STREET BIRD GARDEN & FLOWER MARKET Map p423

☎ 2382 1785; Flower Market Rd; ☽ 7am-8pm; Prince Edward MTR
This market is a wonderful place to visit, if only to marvel at how the Hong Kong Chinese (especially men) fuss and fawn over their feathered friends. The Chinese have long favoured songbirds as pets; you often see local men walking around airing their birds and feeding them tasty

Bird cage, Yuen Po Street Bird Garden (p95), Mong Kok

creepy-crawlies with chopsticks. Some birds are also considered harbingers of good fortune, which is why you'll see some people carrying them to the racetrack.

There are hundreds of birds for sale from some 70 stalls here, along with elaborate cages carved from teak and bamboo. Adjacent to the bird garden is the flower market on Flower Market Rd, which keeps theoretically the same hours but only gets busy after 10am, especially on Sunday.

To get to the bird garden and flower market, from the Prince Edward MTR station, come out of exit B1 and walk east along Prince Edward Rd West for about 10 minutes.

NEW KOWLOON
Eating p185

The southernmost 35 sq km or so of the New Territories is officially called New Kowloon. Since Boundary St just above Mong Kok technically marks the division between Kowloon and the New Territories, these places – strictly speaking – belong to the latter. But they look and feel and consider themselves to be part of Kowloon and are thus considered so. 'New Kowloon' is an official designation, however, and never used by people in the street.

Orientation

New Kowloon encompasses as many as 20 different neighbourhoods, but only half a dozen are of much interest to travellers. From west to east they are Sham Shui Po, Kowloon

Tong, Kowloon City, Wong Tai Sin and Diamond Hill. The majority (and the places of interest described in this section) are within easy reach of an MTR station.

Sham Shui Po

A residential area of high-rises, Sham Shui Po (Map pp418–19) is famous for its market and computer emporiums (p248). North of (and easily accessible from) the district is Lei Cheng Uk Han Tomb, an important archaeological find.

APLIU STREET MARKET Map pp418-19
Apliu St, btwn Nam Cheong & Kweilin Sts; ⊙ noon-midnight; Sham Shui Po MTR

From the Sham Shui Po MTR station follow exit A1 and you'll soon fall right into this flea market, which features everything from clothing to antique clocks and coins, but specialises in second-hand electronic goods – radios, mobile phones, stereo systems, amplifiers and spare parts. The market spills over into Pei Ho St.

DRAGON CENTRE Map pp418-19
☎ 2307 9264; 37K Yen Chow St; ⊙ 10am-midnight; Sham Shui Po MTR

The Dragon Centre is a working-class shopping centre with a branch of the Sincere department store chain and a Wellcome. Take exit C1 from the Sham Shui Po MTR station if going there directly; an external escalator at the end of Ki Lung St will take you from street level to the 1st floor.

At nine levels, the Dragon Centre towers above the surrounding apartment blocks. There's a food court on level 8 ($20 to $35 buys a meal of soup, egg, pork and rice). On the same level, there's the Skyrink ice-skating rink (p224).

The attractive Sham Shui Po Police Station (37A Yen Chow St), just south of the Dragon Centre on the corner with Lai Chi Kok Rd and opposite Tai Nan St, was built in 1925.

LEI CHENG UK HAN TOMB MUSEUM
Map pp418-19

☎ 2386 2863; www.lcsd.gov.hk/CE/Museum /History/en/lcuht.php; 41 Tonkin St; admission free; ⊙ 10am-1pm & 2-6pm Mon-Wed, Fri & Sat, 1-6pm Sun & public holidays; Cheung Sha Wan MTR

This burial vault dating from the Eastern Han dynasty (AD 25–220) was discovered in 1955 when workers were levelling the

TRANSPORT

MTR Sham Shui Po MTR station (Map pp418–19) on Tsuen Wan line; Kowloon Tong MTR station (Map pp418–19) on Kwun Tong line; Lok Fu MTR station (Map pp418–19) on Kwun Tong line for Kowloon City; Wong Tai Sin and Diamond Hill MTR stations (Map pp418–19) on Kwun Tong line; Yau Tong MTR station (Map pp404–5) on Kwun Tong and Tseung Kwan O lines for Lei Yue Mun.

KCR Kowloon Tong station (Map pp418–19) on the KCR East Rail.

Bus Sham Shui Po: Yen Chow St (Map pp418–19) for buses 6 and 6A to Star Ferry pier; Kweilin St for bus 2 to Star Ferry pier; Kowloon Tong: Waterloo Rd (Map p423) for bus 182 to Wan Chai, Admiralty and Central, and bus 170 to Causeway Bay; Tat Chee Ave (Map pp418–19) for buses 2C and 203 to Tsim Sha Tsui; Kowloon City: Ma Tau Chung Rd (Map pp418–19) for buses 5 and 26 to Tsim Sha Tsui, and buses 101 and 111 to Wan Chai, Admiralty and Central; Prince Edward Rd for bus 11 to Diamond Hill; Wong Tai Sin: Tung Tau Tsuen Rd for bus 5 to Mong Kok and Tsim Sha Tsui; San Po Kong Rd for bus 111 to Wan Chai, Admiralty and Central; Diamond Hill: Choi Hung Rd for bus 9 to Mong Kok, Yau Ma Tei and Tsim Sha Tsui; Hollywood Plaza for bus 92 to Sai Kung; Lei Yue Mun: Yau Tong Centre for bus 14C to Kwun Tong MTR station (Map pp404–5).

hillside for a housing estate. It is one of Hong Kong's earliest surviving historical monuments and, believe it or not, was once on the coast.

The tomb consists of four barrel-vaulted brick chambers in the form of a cross and set around a domed central chamber; many of the bricks contained moulded patterns of fish, dragons and the like. It's encased in a concrete shell for protection and you can only peek through a plastic window; it's a bit of a journey for an anticlimactic peek through Perspex. The museum also contains some 58 pottery and bronze pieces taken from the tomb.

To reach the tomb, take bus 2 from the Star Ferry or bus 2A from Nathan Rd in Mong Kok; both stop in front of the museum. The nearest MTR station is Cheung Sha Wan; take exit A3 and walk 10 minutes to the northeast along Tonkin St.

Kowloon Tong

A posh residential area northeast of Mong Kok, Kowloon Tong (Map pp418–19) is home to colleges and universities, and both the **Hong Kong Baptist University** (Map pp418–19; ☎ 3411 7400), Hong Kong's most generously endowed seat of higher learning, and **City University of Hong Kong** (Map pp418–19; ☎ 2788 7654) are in the neighbourhood. You'll also find bridal shops and salons here with names like Cité du Louvre, where brides-to-be can buy their finery, have their photos done and even attend the ceremony itself, and (appropriately enough) a slew of knock-up shops – 'no-tells', as one wag called them, with revolving beds, velvet

flock wallpaper and heart-shaped Jacuzzis. They're very popular for 'matinées' and rented by the hour.

FESTIVAL WALK SHOPPING CENTRE
Map pp418-19

☎ 2844 2222; 80-88 Tat Chee Ave; ⏱ 10.30am-10pm; Kowloon Tong MTR, KCR
Kowloon Tong can claim Festival Walk, the territory's most luxurious shopping complex, and, in typical Hong Kong fashion, the centre boasts a fair few superlatives itself. Festival Walk has the largest cinema, bookshop and ice-skating rink (p224) in the territory. From the Kowloon Tong MTR station, take exit C2.

Kowloon City

Just west of what was once Kai Tak International Airport, the rather low-rent neighbourhood of Kowloon City (Map pp418–19) has two drawing cards: a wonderful park that was once the infamous Kowloon Walled City, and a string of authentic and excellent-value Thai restaurants (p186). The airport, which sits on a prime chunk of land, is now all but abandoned, except for a popular driving range (p219), and awaits development.

KOWLOON WALLED CITY PARK
Map pp418-19

☎ 2716 9962, 2762 2084; www.lcsd.gov.hk/en /ls_park.php; Tung Tau Tsuen, Tung Tsing, Carpenter & Junction Rds; ⏱ 6.30am-11pm; bus 1
The walls that enclose this beautiful park were once the perimeter of a notorious

village that technically remained part of China throughout British rule, as it was never included in the 1898 lease of the New Territories. The enclave was known for its vice, prostitution, gambling and – yikes, Yanks! – illegal dentists. In 1984 the Hong Kong government acquired the area, rehoused the residents elsewhere and built pavilions and ponds filled with turtles and goldfish and planted exquisite trees and shrubs, including a long hedge coaxed into the form of a dragon. The park opened in 1996. Close to the Carpenter Rd entrance of the park is the renovated Yamen building, once an almshouse. It contains displays on the history of the walled city, with a scale model of the village in the mid-19th century. At the park's north side are the remnants of the original South and East Gates.

To reach the park, take bus 1 from the Star Ferry bus station and alight at Tung Tau Tsuen Rd opposite the park. The closest MTR station is Lok Fu (exit B), from where you can board minibus 39M or walk for 15 minutes along Junction and Tung Tau Tsuen Rds.

Wong Tai Sin

The district of Wong Tai Sin to the north of Kowloon City is known for two things: its enormous and faceless housing estate and one of the most active temples in the territory.

SIK SIK YUEN WONG TAI SIN TEMPLE
Off Map pp418-19

☎ 2854 4333; Lung Cheung Rd; $2 donation requested; ☼ 7am-6pm; Wong Tai Sin MTR
This large Taoist temple complex adjacent to the Wong Tai Sin housing estate, was built in 1973 and is dedicated to the god of that name, who began his life as a humble shepherd in Zhejiang province. When he was 15 an immortal taught Wong Tai Sin how to make a herbal potion that could cure all illnesses. He is thus worshipped both by the sick and those trying to avoid illness. He is also a favourite god of businesspeople. The image of the god in the main temple was brought to Hong Kong from Guangdong province in 1915 and was initially installed in a temple in Wan Chai, where it remained until being moved to the present site in 1921.

Like many Chinese temples, this one is an explosion of colourful pillars, roofs, lattice work, flowers and shrubs. If you come in the early evening – Friday evening is the busiest time – you'll see hordes of businessmen and secretaries praying and divining the future with *chìm*, bamboo 'fortune sticks' that are shaken out of a box on to the ground and then read by a fortune-teller (they're available for free to the left of the main temple).

Behind the main temple and to the right are the **Good Wish Gardens** ($2 donation requested; ☼ 9am-4pm), replete with colourful pavilions (the hexagonal **Unicorn Hall**, with carved doors and windows, is the most beautiful), zigzag bridges, waterfalls and carp ponds.

Below the main temple and to the left as you enter the complex is an arcade filled with dozens of booths operated by fortune-tellers, some of whom speak English.

The busiest times at the temple are around Chinese New Year, Wong Tai Sin's birthday (23rd day of the eighth month – usually in September) and at weekends. Getting to the temple is easy. From the Wong Tai Sin MTR station, take exit B2 and then follow the signs or crowds (or both).

Diamond Hill

Spread out below the peak of the same name, the residential district of Diamond Hill is due east of Wong Tai Sin, and contains one of Hong Kong's most beautiful houses of worship.

CHI LIN NUNNERY Off Map pp418-19

☎ 2354 1604; 5 Chi Lin Dr; admission free; ☼ nunnery 9am-5pm, garden 6.30am-7pm; Diamond Hill MTR
This large Buddhist complex, originally dating from the 1930s, was rebuilt completely of wood in the style of the Tang dynasty in 1998. It is a serene place, with lotus ponds, immaculate bonsai tea plants and bougainvillea and silent nuns delivering offerings of fruit and rice to Buddha and arhats (Buddhist disciple freed from the cycle of birth and death) or chanting behind intricately carved screens. The design is intended to demonstrate the harmony of humans with nature and is pretty convincing – until you look up at the looming neighbourhood high-rises behind the complex.

(Continued on page 107)

1 *The Repulse Bay (p87), Repulse Bay* 2 *Postwar apartments on Shanghai Street, Kowloon (p88)* 3 *Hong Kong Design Centre (p79), the Mid-Levels* 4 *Historical wrought-iron China Gas lamps (p72), Duddell Street, Central*

1 *Exchange Square (p69), Central*
2 *The Bank of China Tower (p69), Central* **3** *Port hole windows of Jardine House (p71), Central* **4** *Hong Kong Cultural Centre (p90), Tsim Sha Tsui*

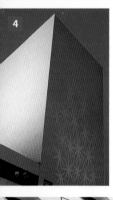

1 *Po Lin Vegetarian Restaurant (p195), Po Lin Monastery, Lantau* **2** *Goldfish at the Tung Choi St market (p246), Mong Kok* **3** *Incense coils burned as offerings at Man Mo Temple (p74), Sheung Wan* **4** *A dragon – a popular dashboard ornament*

1 *Hung Shing Temple (p80), Wan Chai* **2** *Shrine dedicated to the door god, one of South China's many gods (p12)* **3** *Kwan Tai temple (p135), Tai O, Lantau* **4** *Incense, hell money and other temple offerings (p73), Sheung Wan*

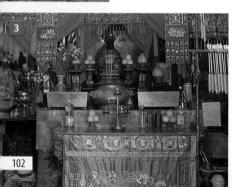

1 *Diners at Temple Street night market (p94), Yau Ma Tei*
2 *Curios, knick-knacks and memorabilia for sale, Cat Street (p74), Sheung Wan* **3** *Custard apples, Graham St Market (p157), Central*
4 *Flower market (p95), Mong Kok*

1 *Chinese tea (p44)* 2 *Religious statues for sale, Curio Alley (p244), Tsim Sha Tsui* 3 *Watches (p233) for sale* 4 *Times Square shopping mall (p243), Causeway Bay*

1 *Drop (p208), a hip club, Central* **2** *Posing in front of a poser, Central (p68)* **3** *Weighing medicinal herbs, Shanghai Street, Kowloon (p88)* **4** *Wellington Street, Central (p68)*

1 *Playing Chinese Chess, Kowloon Park (p91)* 2 *Avenue of the Stars (p93), Tsim Sha Tsui* 3 *School kids, Wan Chai (p77)* 4 *Linva Tailor (p236), Central*

(Continued from page 98)

You enter the complex through the Sam Mun, a series of 'three gates' representing the Buddhist precepts of compassion, wisdom and 'skilful means'. The first courtyard, which contains the delightful Lotus Pond Garden, gives way to the Hall of Celestial Kings, with a large statue of the seated Buddha surrounded by the deities of the four cardinal points. Behind that is the main hall containing a statue of the Sakyamuni Buddha flanked by two standing disciples and two seated Bodhisattvas (Buddhist holy people). Below the complex is a café selling vegetarian snacks and dim sum for $10 to $20.

To reach the nunnery from the Diamond Hill MTR station, take exit C2, walk through the Hollywood Plaza shopping centre and turn east (left) on to Fung Tak Rd. The nunnery is a five-minute walk away.

Lei Yue Mun

Southeast of the old Kai Tak airport is the residential neighbourhood of Kwun Tong (Map pp404–5 and Map pp418–19), and a bit further southeast is the rapidly modernising fishing village of Lei Yue Mun (Map pp404–5). *Láy-yèw* means 'carp' and *mùn* is 'gate'; the 'carp gate' refers to the channel separating southeast Kowloon from Hong Kong Island, which is the narrowest entrance to Victoria Harbour. Across the water on the island and looming on the hillside is 19th-century **Lei Yue Mun Fort** (Map pp406–7), which now contains the **Hong Kong Museum of Coastal Defence** (p84).

SAM KA TSUEN TYPHOON SHELTER
Yau Tong MTR
The 'village' of Lei Yue Mun is one of Hong Kong's prime seafood venues; there are some two dozen fish restaurants along Lei Yue Mun Praya Rd overlooking the typhoon shelter here. It's a colourful and lively place to dine by the water at night and is always busy. To get here from the Yau Tong MTR station, use exit A2 and follow Cha Kwo Ling Rd and Shung Shun St south for 15 minutes or catch green minibus 24M from outside the station. Bus 14C links the Yau Tong Centre halfway down the hill with the Kwun Tong MTR station.

SUPER SIZE HONG KONG

'Hong Kong spins superlatives as furiously as it does garments', we once wrote in the introduction of a series of articles for an Asia-based travel magazine. And while the former is history, with all the mills and factories having moved across the border with the mainland long ago, the latter is as true as it was almost 20 years ago when the articles first appeared. So true, in fact, that a few years ago the tourism people produced a 50-page brochure listing the biggest, brightest and bestest that Hong Kong had to offer.

A lot of the superlatives rest on their buts, however (if you catch the drift). Hong Kong *can* boast the world's tallest Buddha statue – as long as they string the words 'outdoor', 'seated' and 'bronze' in front of the claim. Actor, stuntman and all-round Mr Nice Guy, Jackie Chan, is 'the most popular star in the world' with the minor proviso of 'on his Internet site'. Hong Kong is without a doubt 'the world's leading exporter of garments, imitation jewellery, travel goods, handbags umbrellas, artificial flowers, toys and clocks'. Problem is, none of the stuff is made here. The boast begins: 'Using the competitive manufacturing base in mainland China...'. And Ting Kau Bridge? Well, at 1177m long, it is apparently ranked as *one* of the world's longest and largest three-towered, cable-stayed bridges. How many of those are there?

From the substandard to the ridiculous, did you know that Hong Kong:

- consumes more oranges than any other place on earth
- has the largest Australian Chamber of Commerce outside Australia
- boasts the world's largest floating restaurant
- claims the biggest Japanese-style nightclub
- holds the world record price for the auction of a blue and white porcelain vase from the Ming dynasty
- has the world's only museum located in the grounds of a public housing estate
- claims the world's largest neon advertising sign
- has the world's tallest soft drinks plant
- can claim the largest hotel mural in the world
- motorists own 1% of all the Rolls Royces ever produced?

You didn't? Well, now you do.

NEW TERRITORIES

The New Territories was so named because the area was leased to Britain in 1898, almost half a century after Hong Kong Island and four decades after Kowloon were ceded to the crown. For many years the area was Hong Kong's rural hinterland; however, since WWII, when some 80% of the land was under cultivation, many parts of the 'NT' – as the area is known locally – have become increasingly urbanised. In the past two decades the speed at which this development has taken place has been nothing short of heart-stopping.

Many Hong Kong residents make the New Territories their getaway for the weekend, and the eastern section, notably Sai Kung Peninsula in the northeast and the area around Clearwater Bay further south, has some of Hong Kong's most beautiful scenery and hiking trails. Life in these more rural parts of Hong Kong is more redolent of times past – simpler, slower, often more friendly.

The New Territories is large, comprising just 747 sq km, or almost 68% of Hong Kong's land area. Strictly speaking, everything north of Boundary St in Kowloon, up to the border with mainland China, is the New Territories. The northernmost part of the New Territories, within 1km of the Chinese frontier, is a 'closed border area' that is fenced and well marked with signs. It marks the boundary of the Hong Kong SAR with the Shenzhen Special Economic Zone (SEZ).

Some 3.5 million people, up from less than half a million in 1970, call the New Territories home – about half the total population of Hong Kong. Most of them live in 'New Towns'. Since its inception in the 1950s, the New Towns program has consumed more than half of the Hong Kong government's budget, with much of the funding spent on land reclamation, sewage, roads and other infrastructure projects.

In the past, the biggest impediment to growth in the New Territories was a lack of good transportation. Nowadays, getting to the New Territories has never been easier, particularly to the New Towns and areas of interest listed here. The KCR West Rail (Map pp404–5), which opened in late 2003, is now transporting passengers from Kowloon to the western New Territories as far as Tuen Mun. The MTR (Map pp404–5) goes to Tsuen Wan (on the Tsuen Wan line) in the west and Tseung Kwan O in the east, from where you can catch buses and minibuses to explore other parts of the New Territories. Travel to the northern New Territories is simple, fast and cheap with the KCR East Rail (Map pp404–5), which connects Tsim Sha Tsui, Hung Hom and Kowloon Tong with Sha Tin, Tai Po, Sheung Shui and the Chinese border at Lo Wu. There are also a number of buses linking Hong Kong Island and Kowloon with the New Territories.

Once in the New Territories, buses – run for the most part by the **Kowloon Motor Bus Co** (KMB; ☎ 2745 4466; www.kmb.com.hk) – and green minibuses – which run on just under 200 routes – are the main ways to get around. Catching a taxi is easy – at least to and from the New Towns; there are more than 2840 cabs cruising the streets and country roads of the New Territories. Ferries and *kaidos* (small, open-sea ferries) serve the more remote areas and a few large communities on the coast.

In the far west of the New Territories, the way to go is the KCR's Light Rail (Map pp404–5), a modern, street-level tram system that connects Tuen Mun with Yuen Long and stops at several interesting places along the way.

The HKTB has a handy information sheet with a map detailing the major bus routes in the New Territories. For more obscure or complex routes, check the KMB's website.

TSUEN WAN

Eating p186; Sleeping p270

Among the easiest destinations in the New Territories to reach, Tsuen Wan (Map p424), or 'Shallow Bay', is an industrial and residential New Town northwest of Kowloon, with some 290,000 inhabitants. It's nothing special, but it does have a fine (though small) museum and some of the most colourful and active temple and monastic complexes in Hong Kong. **Chung On St**, south of the Tsuen Wan MTR station, is famed for its jewellery and goldsmith shops. **Tak Wah Park** (☯ 6.30am-11pm) in the centre of town has ancient trees, footbridges over ponds and ornamental stone mountains.

Orientation

The MTR station is on Sau Lau Kok Rd with the Luk Yeung Galleria shopping centre above it. The main bus station is opposite the MTR on Castle Peak Rd (exit A2), but buses and green minibuses pick up and disgorge passengers throughout the New Town. The Sam Tung Uk Museum is within easy walking distance of the MTR station, though to reach the temples and monasteries in the hills to the north you should take a minibus. Tsuen Wan is the last station on the Tsuen Wan MTR line. If you're really in a hurry to get there or back, change to the Tung Chung MTR line at Lai King, which has fewer stops.

CHUK LAM SIM MONASTERY Map p424

☎ 2490 3392; Fu Yung Shan Rd; ◷ 8am-5pm; green minibus 85

Chuk Lam Sim Yuen (Bamboo Forest Monastery) is one of the most impressive temple complexes in Hong Kong. The temple was completed in 1932 when an aged monk was told by Tou Tei, the earth god, to build it. Ascend the flight of steps to the first temple, walk to the back and enter the second. This second temple contains three of the largest golden Buddhas in the territory (though mere shadows of the big one on Lantau Island, p133). Flanking the trio on either side is an equally impressive line-up of 12 Bodhisattvas, or Buddhists seeking enlightenment. The third temple contains another large image of Lord Gautama.

TRANSPORT

MTR Tsuen Wan MTR station (Map p424) on Tsuen Wan line.

KCR Tsuen Wan West station (Map pp404–5).

Bus Bus station (Map p424) for bus 60M to Tuen Mun town centre, bus 59M to Tuen Mun ferry pier, and bus 68M to Yuen Long; MTR station for bus A31 to airport, bus E31 to Tung Chung, and buses 234A and 234B to Sham Tseng (ferry to Ma Wan); Castle Peak Rd (Map p424) for bus 53 to Tuen Mun and Yuen Long; Sha Tsui Rd (Map p424) for bus 930 to Wan Chai, Admiralty and Central; Tai Ho Rd (Map p424) for bus 43X to Sam Tung Uk Rd; Tai Ho Rd North for bus 51 to Tai Mo Shan, MacLehose Trail and Kam Tin.

Green Minibus Shiu Wo St (Map p424) for bus 85 to Chuk Lam Sim Monastery, bus 81 to Yuen Yuen Institute and Western Monastery, and bus 82 to Shing Mun Reservoir and Pineapple Dam.

Chuk Lam Sim Monastery is northeast of Tsuen Wan MTR station. To reach it, take green minibus 85 from Shiu Wo St, which is two blocks due south of the MTR station (exit B1).

SAM TUNG UK MUSEUM Map p424

☎ 2411 2001; 2 Kwu Uk Lane; admission free; ◷ 9am-5pm Wed-Mon; Tsuen Wan MTR

This imaginative and well-tended museum is housed in a restored late-18th-century Hakka walled village, whose former residents, the Chan clan, were only resettled in 1980. Within the complex are a dozen three-beamed houses containing traditional Hakka furnishings, kitchenware, wedding items and agricultural implements, most of which came from two 17th-century Hakka villages in Bao'an county in Guangdong province. There are also special exhibits on such topics as rice farming in the New Territories. Behind the restored assembly and ancestral halls is the old village school, with interactive displays and videos on such topics as Hakka women, traditional crafts and traditional food.

At the Tsuen Wan MTR station, take exit E and walk five minutes southeast along Sai Lau Kok Rd to Kwu Uk Lane and the museum.

WESTERN MONASTERY Map p424

☎ 2411 5111; Lo Wai Rd; ◷ 8.30am-5.30pm; green minibus 81

A short distance down from the Yuen Yuen Institute, the Buddhist Western Monastery feels positively comatose compared with what's going on up the hill, but it has its charms nonetheless. The focal point of the monastery is a tall pagoda, on the 1st floor of which are five Buddhas sitting on a golden lotus. Depending on what time of day you visit, you may hear monks chanting mantras from down on the ground level.

YUEN YUEN INSTITUTE Off Map p424

☎ 2492 2220; Lo Wai Rd; ◷ 8.30am-5pm; green minibus 81

The Yuen Yuen Institute, a colourful temple complex for worshipping Taoist, Confucian and Buddhist deities in the hills northeast of Tsuen Wan, is very much on the tourist trail but well worth a visit nonetheless. The main building is a (vague) replica of the Temple of Heaven in Beijing. On the upper ground floor are three Taoist immortals seated in a quiet hall; walk down to the lower level to watch as crowds of the faithful pray and burn offerings to the 60 incarnations of Taoist saints lining the walls. This place is packed out at Chinese New Year.

To reach both the Institute and the Western Monastery, take minibus 81 from Shiu Wo St, two blocks due south of Tsuen Wan MTR station (exit B1). Bus 43X from along Tai Ho Rd, further south of the MTR station (exit D), will drop you off on Sam Tung Uk Rd. The monastery is several hundred metres and the institute is just up the hill.

TAI MO SHAN

Sleeping p270

Hong Kong's tallest mountain is not Victoria Peak but Tai Mo Shan (Map pp404–5), the 'big misty mountain' that, at 957m, is nearly twice as high as that relative molehill (552m) on Hong Kong Island. Climbing Tai Mo Shan is not difficult, and the views from the top are impressive when the weather is clear. There are numerous hiking trails on and around it, but you'll need to bring your own food and water. The Countryside Series *North-East & Central New Territories* map is the one you want for this area (p316). If you don't want to go it alone, contact any of the outfits listed on p219. The **Tai Mo Shan Country Park Visitor Centre** (☎ 2498 9326; ⏰ 9.30am-4.30pm Sat, Sun & holidays) is at the junction of Route Twisk (the name is derived from 'Tsuen Wan into Shek Kong') and Tai Mo Shan Rd, which is crossed by the MacLehose Trail.

To reach Tai Mo Shan from the Tsuen Wan MTR station, catch bus 51 on Tai Ho Rd North, alighting at the junction of Route Twisk and Tai Mo Shan Rd in Tsuen Kam Au. Follow Tai Mo Rd, which forms part of stage No 9 of the MacLehose Trail, east to the summit. On the right-hand side, about 45 minutes from the bus stop, a fork in the road leads south along a concrete path to the **Sze Lok Yuen Hostel** (p270).

For information on accessing stages of the MacLehose Trail and the Wilson Trail near Tai Mo Shan, see p220.

NG TUNG CHAI WATERFALL & KADOORIE FARM & BOTANIC GARDEN

Map pp404-5

☎ 2488 1317; www.kfbg.org.hk; Lam Kam Rd; admission free; ⏰ 9.30am-5pm; bus 64K

The area around the Ng Tung Chai Waterfall is scenic and worth a detour. It is near the village of Ng Tung Chai, which is several kilometres north of Tai Mo Shan and just south of Lam Kam Rd. There is actually a series of falls and streams here reached by taking the path leading to Ng Tung Chai and the Lam Kam Rd from the radio station on the summit of Tai Mo Shan.

Southwest of Ng Tung Chai is the Kadoorie Farm & Botanic Garden, a conservation and teaching centre where farmers receive practical training in crop and livestock management. The gardens are especially lovely, with many indigenous birds, animals, insects and plants in residence.

You can reach Kadoorie Farm most easily on bus 64K from Yuen Long (Tai Tong Rd) or Tai Po Market KCR East Rail station and get off on Lam Kam Rd near the sign for Ng Tung Chai village. If you walk from Tai Mo Shan to the village of Ng Tung Chai, you can catch green minibus 25K to Tai Po Market KCR East Rail station as well.

TUEN MUN

Eating p187

The largest and most important New Town in the western New Territories Tuen Mun (Map pp404–5; population 550,000) is now linked with other centres in Kowloon and the New Territories by the KCR West Rail. If you're travelling to Tuen Mun from Tsuen Wan or points in Kowloon or Hong Kong Island by bus, sit on the upper deck on the left side for spectacular views of the Tsing Ma Bridge linking Kowloon with Lantau Island.

In recent years a number of important archaeological discoveries have been made here, notably to the north and west of Tuen Mun town (see p52).

Orientation

As always in New Towns, the centre of Tuen Mun is dominated by commercial developments and shopping centres. Most buses stop at the station just west of the town hall, where you'll also find the Town Centre station of the Light Rail. The KCR's West Rail

---

TRANSPORT

Bus Bus 64K to Yuen Long and Tai Po Market.

Green Minibus Bus 25K to Tai Po Market.

TRANSPORT

KCR Tuen Mun and Tin Shui Wai West Rail stations (Map pp404–5).

Light Rail Tuen Mun and Town Centre to Ferry Pier Terminus line 507, to Tin Shui Wai (Map pp404–5) line 751; Town Centre to Yuen Long (Map pp404–5) line 614; Tin Shui Wai to Wetland Park lines 705 and 706.

Bus Bus station for bus 60M to Tsuen Wan, and bus 60X to Mong Kok and Yau Ma Tei; Castle Peak Rd for bus 53 to Tsuen Wan; Tuen Mun Rd for bus 260X to Tsim Sha Tsui, bus 63X to Nathan Rd in Yau Ma Tei and Tsim Sha Tsui, and bus 960 to Wan Chai, Admiralty and Central; Tuen Mun ferry pier for bus 59M to Tsuen Wan.

Ferry Tuen Mun ferry pier for boats to airport, Tung Chung and Tai O on Lantau.

interchanges at the Tuen Mun Light Rail station. Ferries to the airport, Tung Chung and Tai O on Lantau depart from the pier to the southwest of the town centre, which is also served by the Light Rail (p301).

CHING CHUNG TEMPLE Map pp404-5

☎ 2462 1507; Tsing Chung Koon Rd; ☻ 6am-6pm; Light Rail line 505

Ching Chung Koon (Green Pine Temple) is a huge Taoist complex northwest of Tuen Mun town centre. The main temple, which is on the left at the far end of the complex past rows of bonsai trees, bamboo and ossuaries, is dedicated to Lu Sun Young, one of the eight immortals of Taoism who lived in the 8th century. Flanking a statue of him are two of his disciples and outside the entrance to the main temple are pavilions containing a bell and a drum to call the faithful to pray or to rest.

Ching Chung Temple is directly opposite the Light Rail station of that name. To reach it from the Tuen Mun or Town Centre stations, catch line 505.

HONG KONG WETLAND PARK

Map pp404-5

☎ 3152 2666; www.afcd.gov.hk/others/wetland park; Wetland Park Rd, Tin Shui Wai; admission $30; ☻ 9.30am-4.30pm Mon & Wed-Sat, 10.30am-5.30pm Sun & holidays; Light Rail line 705 or 706

This 60-hectare ecological park, under construction in Tin Shui Wai north of Tuen Mun, focuses on the wetland ecosystems and biodiversity of the northwest New Territories. Eventually it will have trails, viewing platforms and bird hides as well as three major exhibition galleries, a theatre, classrooms and a resource centre – a kind of high-tech **Mai Po Marsh** (p112). At the time of writing, only a handful of the exhibits were open to the public, but they help to illustrate how ambitious and far-reaching the project is.

To reach the Hong Kong Wetland Park, take the KCR West Rail to Tin Shui Wai and board Light Rail line 705 or 706, alighting at the Wetland Park stop. The park can also be reached directly from Hong Kong Island: from the Admiralty MTR bus station on bus 967 or from Moreton Terrace in Causeway Bay on bus 969.

MIU FAT MONASTERY Map pp404-5

☎ 2461 8567; 18 Castle Peak Rd; ☻ 9am-5pm; Light Rail line 751

Miu Fat Monastery in Lam Tei, due north of Tuen Mun town centre, is one of the most well-kept and attractive Buddhist complexes in the territory. Guarding the entrance to the main temple are two stone lions and two stone elephants, and there are attractive gardens outside. This is an active monastery that preserves more of a traditional character than many smaller temples; you'll see Buddhist nuns in droves wearing brown robes.

On the ground floor there's a golden likeness of Buddha in a glass case; on the 2nd floor are three larger statues of Lord Gautama. The 1st floor is a vegetarian restaurant serving set meals and open to all (p187).

Miu Fat Monastery is easily reached by taking Light Rail line 751 from the Tuen Mun or Town Centre stops to Lam Tei station. The complex is on the opposite side of Castle Peak Rd; cross over the walkway and walk north 150m. Bus 63X from the Mong Kok MTR station and the Star Ferry in Tsim Sha Tsui also stops in front of the monastery.

YUEN LONG

There's nothing special at Yuen Long (Map pp404–5; Yuen Long KCR West Rail), which currently counts some 449,000 inhabitants, but it's the last stop on the Light Rail, an important transport hub and a gateway to the

Mai Po Marsh (see the following section). To the west of Yuen Long is the **Ping Shan Heritage Trail** (p145) one of the best spots to spend a tranquil hour or two in the western New Territories.

MAI PO MARSH

If you're a bird fancier, Mai Po Marsh, a fragile ecosystem (see the boxed text, below) in the northwestern New Territories, is one of the best places in Hong Kong to meet up with thousands of your feathered friends. For more detailed information about this and other areas, contact the Hong Kong Bird Watching Society (p217).

Orientation

Mai Po Marsh comprises some 1500 hectares of wetlands. It abuts Deep Bay, south of the border with the mainland. The part open to visitors, the Mai Po Nature Reserve, is in the centre.

MAI PO NATURE RESERVE Map pp404-5

☎ 2526 4473; San Tin, Yuen Long; admission $100 (plus $100 deposit); ⏰ 9am-6pm; bus 76K

The 270-hectare nature reserve includes the **Mai Po Visitor Centre** (☎ 2471 8272; ⏰ 9am-1pm & 2-5pm Thu-Tue) at the northeastern end, where you must register; the **Mai Po Education Centre** (☎ 2471 6306) to the south,

TRANSPORT

Bus Bus 76K to Yuen Long (On Tat Square station), and Fanling and Sheung Shui KCR East Rail stations.

Minibus Bus 17 to Sheung Shui.

with displays on the history and ecology of the wetland and Deep Bay; floating boardwalks and trails through the mangroves and mud flats; and a dozen hides (towers or huts from where you can watch birds up close without being observed). Disconcertingly, the cityscape of Shenzhen looms to the north.

Visitors are advised to bring binoculars (they may be available for rent at the visitor centre for $20) and cameras, and to wear comfortable walking shoes or boots but not bright clothing. It is best to visit at high tide (minimum 2m), when birds in their tens of thousands – mostly ducks, gulls, cormorants and kingfishers, but many rare species as well – flock to the area. Ring the **weather hotline** (☎ 187 8066) or the **Hong Kong Observatory** (☎ 2926 8200; www.hko.gov.hk /tide/etide_main.htm) for tidal times.

Foreign visitors (but not Hong Kong residents) can visit the nature reserve unaccompanied but numbers are limited so call in advance to book a time. Pay the $100 entrance fee and $100 deposit at the visitor

A WETLAND FOR HONG KONG

Bordering Deep Bay in the northwest New Territories, Mai Po Marsh is a protected network of mud flats, *gày-wài* (shallow shrimp ponds), reed beds and dwarf mangroves, offering a rich habitat of up to 340 species of migratory and resident birds, more than a third of them rarely seen elsewhere in the territory. The area attracts birds in every season but especially winter, when an average 54,000 migratory waterfowl, including such endangered species as the Dalmatian pelican, black-faced spoonbill, spotted and imperial eagle and black vulture, pass through the marshes. In the centre is the Mai Po Nature Reserve, jointly managed by the World Wide Fund for Nature Hong Kong and the government's Agriculture, Fisheries & Conservation Department.

Despite its protected status, the marsh's future is precarious. The water quality in Deep Bay is among the worst in the Hong Kong coastal area. The Environmental Protection Department (EPD) has found that levels of dissolved oxygen (DO) in the water have been declining since 1988. As a result, the numbers of crabs and mudskippers, on which the birds feed in winter, have declined. If the lower links of the food chain are seriously imperilled, the birds that depend on Mai Po as a stopping ground during migration could disappear, taking with them endangered mammals such as the leopard cat and otter.

Deep Bay neighbours the city of Shenzhen in mainland China, which is pumping out a rapidly increasing amount of sewage, about half of which is untreated. The only long-term solution to this environmental threat is for Shenzhen to build more sewage-treatment facilities but, as the population of the city expands faster than its infrastructure, this will take time.

Meanwhile, the only hope in the short term is that Hong Kong's increasingly wet summers will flush out and dilute many of the pollutants, helping to raise the number of crabs and mudskippers.

centre; the latter (presumably to ensure that you get out alive) will be returned when you leave the reserve.

The **World Wide Fund for Nature Hong Kong** (WWFHK; Map pp408–9; ☎ 2526 4473; www.wwf.org.hk; 1 Tramway Path), adjacent to the entrance of the Peak Tram in Central, can arrange guided visits to the marsh; ring between 9am and 5pm on weekdays to book. Three-hour tours ($70) leave the visitor centre at 9am, 9.30am, 10am, 2pm, 2.30pm and 3pm on Saturday, Sunday and public holidays, but are only conducted in English when there are a minimum of 10 visitors.

Bus 76K, which runs between Yuen Long and the Fanling and Sheung Shui KCR East Rail stations, will drop you off at Mai Po Lo Wai, a village along the main road just east of the marsh. The WWFHK car park is about a 20-minute walk from there. Red minibus 17 from San Fat St in Sheung Shui also goes to the car park. Alternatively, a taxi from Sheung Shui will cost $60.

KAM TIN

The area around Kam Tin (Fertile Field; Map pp404–5) is where the Tangs, the first of Hong Kong's mighty Five Clans, settled in the 12th century AD and where they eventually built their walled villages (p52).

Walled villages, which usually had moats, are a reminder that Hong Kong's early settlers were constantly menaced by marauding pirates, bandits and imperial soldiers. They remain one of the most popular destinations for visitors to the New Territories.

Orientation

Kam Tin contains two fortified villages: Kat Hing Wai and Shui Tau Tsuen. Most tourists go to Kat Hing Wai, as it is just off Kam Tin Rd, the main thoroughfare, and easily accessible. Shui Tau Tsuen is larger and less touristy, but don't expect to find remnants of ancient China. For details on Ping Kong, a seldom-visited walled village to the northeast, see p114.

KAT HING WAI Map pp404-5
Bus 64K

This tiny village is 500 years old and was walled in some time during the early Ming dynasty (1368–1644). It contains just one main street, off which a host of dark and narrow alleyways lead. There are quite a few new buildings and retiled older ones in the village. A small temple stands at the end of the street.

Visitors are asked to make a donation when they enter the village; put the money in the coin slot by the entrance. You can take photographs of the old Hakka women in their traditional black trousers, tunics and distinctive bamboo hats with black cloth fringes, but they'll expect you to pay (from about $10).

Kat Hing is just south of Kam Tin Rd. If travelling from Yuen Long, get off at the first bus stop, cross the road and walk east for 10 minutes.

SHUI TAU TSUEN Map pp404-5
Bus 64K

This 17th-century village, 15 minutes' walk north of Kam Tin Rd and signposted, is famous for its prow-shaped roofs decorated with dragons and fish along the ridges. Tiny traditional houses huddle inside Shui Tau Tsuen's walls.

The **Tang Kwong U Ancestral Hall** (🕙 9am-1pm, 2-5pm Wed, Sat & Sun) and, just north of it, the **Tang Ching Lok Ancestral Hall** (🕙 9am-1pm, 2-5pm Wed, Sat & Sun) in the middle of the village, were built in the early 19th century for ancestor worship. The ancestors' names are listed on the altar in the inner hall and on the long boards down the side. The sculpted fish, on the roof of the entrance hall, symbolise luck; in Cantonese, the word for 'fish' (*yéw*) sounds similar to the word for 'plenty' or 'surplus'. Between these two buildings is the small **Hung Shing Temple**. South of them is Shui Tau Tsuen's most impressive sight, the renovated **Yi Tai Study Hall** (🕙 9am-1pm & 2-5pm Wed, Sat & Sun), built in the first half of the 19th century and named after the gods of literature and martial arts. The **Tin Hau temple** on the outskirts of the village to the north was built in 1722 and contains an iron bell weighing 106kg.

TRANSPORT

Bus Kam Tin Rd for bus 64K to Yuen Long and Tai Po Market KCR East Rail station, bus 77K to Yuen Long, Sheung Shui and Fanling, bus 54 to Yuen Long and Shek Kong, and bus 51 to Tsuen Wan (via Route Twisk).

Green Minibus Shui Tau Tsuen bus 601 to Yuen Long.

There's been a lot of building in and around Shui Tau Tsuen in recent years – massive Tsing Long Hwy and the KCR West Rail extension straddle it to the west – and the old sits rather uncomfortably with the new. But the further north you walk beyond the village, the calmer and more tranquil it gets.

To reach Shui Tau Tsuen, which is signposted from Kam Tin Rd, walk north, go under the subway below the Kam Tin Bypass, pass Kam Tai Rd and cross over the river to Chi Ho Rd. Go over the small bridge spanning a stream, turn right and then left to enter the village from the east. The first thing you'll pass is the Yi Tai Study Hall.

FANLING & SHEUNG SHUI

What were two lazy country villages just a few short years ago, Fanling and Sheung Shui now form one of the largest New Town conurbations in the New Territories, with some 300,000 inhabitants. Get a feel for what they were once like by walking around the Luen Wo Hu district at the northern end of Fanling. Major sights are thin on the ground here, but there's an important Taoist temple within easy walking distance and, a short bus ride away, a seldom-visited walled village and the especially **Lung Yeuk Tau Heritage Trail** (p146). The posh 18-hole **Hong Kong Golf Course** (p218) at Fanling will be a draw for some.

Orientation

Fanling and Sheung Shui are in the north-central New Territories, much closer to the mainland (5km) than they are to Tsim Sha Tsui (20km). They are linked by San Wan Rd, along which the bulk of buses and green minibuses serving the two New Towns travel. The KCR West Rail stops in both Fanling and Sheung Shui.

FUNG YING SIN TEMPLE Map pp404-5
☎ 2669 9186; 66 Pak Wo Rd, Fanling;
⏰ 9am-5pm; Fanling KCR East Rail

The main attraction in the area is this huge Taoist temple complex opposite the Fanling KCR East Rail station and connected by an overhead walkway and subway. It has wonderful exterior murals of Taoist immortals and the Chinese zodiac, an orchard terrace, herbal clinic and a **vegetarian restaurant** (ground & 1st fls, Bldg A7; ⏰ 11am-4.30pm). Most important are the dozen ancestral halls behind the main temple, where the ashes of the departed are deposited in what might be described as miniature tombs, complete with photographs.

MARKETS Map pp404-5
Wo Mun & Luen On Sts, Fanling; Chi Cheong Rds, Sheung Shui; ⏰ 6am-8pm; bus 77K

These two lively markets frequented by Hakka people are worth a look, particularly early (ie before 10am). Sheung Shui market is 250m north of the KCR East Rail station. To reach the Fanling market in the old district of Luen Wo Hui, walk north along Sha Tau Kok Rd for about 1.5km or catch bus 77K from the Fanling KCR East Rail station. This bus carries on to the market in Sheung Shui.

PING KONG Map pp404-5
Bus 77K

This sleepy walled village in the hills south of Sheung Shui is seldom visited by outsiders. Like other walled villages still inhabited in Hong Kong, it is a mix of old and new, and has a lovely little **Tin Hau temple** in the centre. You can also go exploring around the farming area behind the village compound.

To get to Ping Kong from Sheung Shui, catch green minibus 58K from the huge minibus station south of the Sheung Shui Landmark North shopping centre on San Wan Rd. The centre is a short walk northwest of Sheung Shui KCR East Rail station. Alternatively, bus 77K between Yuen Long and the Sheung Shui and Fanling KCR East Rail stations travels along Fan Kam Rd. Alight at the North District Hospital stop and walk southeast along Ping Kong Rd to the village.

A taxi from the Sheung Shui KCR East Rail station to Ping Kong will cost $20.

TRANSPORT

KCR Fanling and Sheung Shui East Rail stations (Map pp404–5).

Bus KCR East Rail stations, Pak Wo Rd in Fanling and Choi Yun Rd in Sheung Shui for bus 76K to Yuen Long and Mai Po Marsh; KCR East Rail stations, Jockey Club Rd in Fanling and Po Shek Wu Rd in Sheung Shui for bus 77K to Ping Kong, Kam Tin and Yuen Long.

Green Minibus San Wan Rd in Sheung Shui for bus 58K to Ping Kong.

TAI PO

Eating p187

Another large residential and industrial New Town that has grown astronomically in just over a generation, the small market town of Tai Po (Map p424) counted a total of 25,000 people in 1974; today the population tops 320,000. It makes an excellent springboard for excursions into Plover Cove Country Park and Pat Sin Leng Country Park. **Four Lanes Square**, where four pedestrian streets converge in the centre of town, is a popular shopping area. The **Old Tai Po District Office** (Wan Tau Kok Lane) was built in 1907 and is one of the oldest examples of Western architecture in the New Territories.

Bicycles can be rented in season from several stalls around Tai Po Market KCR East Rail station, but try to arrive early – they often run out during the busiest times. There are a number of bicycle shops lining Kwong Fuk Rd northwest of the KCR station.

One cycling route not to miss is the ride to **Plover Cove Reservoir** (p117) on the northeast side of Tolo Harbour, or to the Chinese University of Hong Kong in Ma Liu Shui on the southwest side of the harbour. Allow at least half a day for either trip. There is an inland route to the university, but the coastal route linking the university with Tai Mei Tuk has the best views. Another option is to follow Ting Kok Rd east to the fishing village **San Mun Tsai** (Map pp404–5).

Orientation

Tai Po lies north and south of the Lam Tsuen River, at the westernmost point of Tolo Harbour. It counts two KCR East Rail stations – Tai Wo to the northwest and Tai Po Market to the southeast. Buses and green minibuses arrive and depart at the station on On Chee Rd, north of the Lam Tsuen River, on Heung Sze Wui St, close to the market and railway museum, and from Tai Po Market KCR station.

HONG KONG RAILWAY MUSEUM

Map p424

☎ 2653 3455; 13 Shung Tak St; admission free; ☼ 9am-5pm Wed-Mon; Tai Wo KCR East Rail

The museum is housed in the former Tai Po Market train station, built in 1913 in traditional Chinese style, and spills into the outside garden. Exhibits, including a

TRANSPORT

KCR Tai Wo and Tai Po Market KCR East Rail stations (Map p424).

Bus On Chee Rd bus station and Tai Po Market KCR East Rail station (Map p424) for bus 74K to San Mun Tsai; Tai Po Market KCR for bus 64K to Lam Kam Rd, Fong Ma Po, Tai Mo Shan, Kam Tin and Yuen Long; On Chee Rd station for bus 271 to Yau Ma Tei and Tsim Sha Tsui, bus 73X to Tsuen Wan, bus 74X to Diamond Hill and Kwun Tong MTR station; and bus 71K between Tai Wo and Tai Po Market KCR East Rail stations.

Green Minibus Tai Po Market KCR station and Heung Sze Wui St (Map p424) for bus 20K to San Mun Tsai; Tsing Yuen St for bus 25K to Ng Tung Chai (Tai Mo Shan); On Cheung Rd for overnight bus 501S to Sheung Shui KCR East Rail and Lam Tin MTR stations.

narrow-gauge steam locomotive dating back to 1911, detail the history of the development of rail transport in the territory. There is also much attention paid to the opening of the Kowloon-Canton Railway in 1910 and its original terminus in Tsim Sha Tsui, which moved to Hung Hong in 1975.

You can get to the museum most easily by alighting at Tai Wo KCR East Rail station, walking south through the Tai Wo Shopping Centre and housing estate and crossing the Lam Tsuen River via Tai Wo Bridge (the small one with the Chinese roof) leading from Po Nga Rd. The museum is just southeast.

LAM TSUEN WISHING TREE

Map pp404-5

Lam Kam Rd, Fong Ma Po; bus 64K

Until a short time ago Tai Po was the springboard for this large banyan, laden with coloured streamers of paper tied to oranges, in the village of Fong Ma Po to the southwest. The idea was to write your wish on a piece of paper, tie it to the citrus fruit and then throw it as high as you could up into the tree. If your fruit lodged in the branches, you were in luck – and the higher it went, the more chance there was of your wish coming true. But things got, er, out of hand just once too often and in February 2005, a week after the end of Chinese New Year, a large branch of the tree came crashing to the ground, dashing most punters' wishes once and for all.

There's been talk of anointing another tree nearby as a kind of arboreal oracle and taking down the old one; time will tell. In the meanwhile, there's a small **Tin Hau temple**, replete with fortune-tellers to take up the slack.

To reach the tree or trees (or none of the above), catch bus 64K from the Tai Po Market KCR East Rail station and alight at Fong Ma Po.

TAI PO MARKET Map p424
Fu Shin St; ⏱ 6am-8pm; Tai Wo KCR East Rail
Not to be confused with the KCR East Rail station of that name, this street-long outdoor wet market is a stone's throw from the Hong Kong Railway Museum and is one of the busiest and most interesting markets in the New Territories. Towards the northern end of the same street, the double-hall **Man Mo Temple** (⏱ 8am-6pm) is a major centre of worship for the Tai Po area. It was founded in the late 19th century and, like the Man Mo Temple found in Sheung Wan (p74), it is dedicated to the gods of literature and of war.

PLOVER COVE

The area around Plover Cove Reservoir is good hiking and cycling country and well worth at least a full day's exploring. It may be worthwhile getting a copy of Universal Publications' *Tseung Kwan O, Sai Kung, Clearwater Bay* or else the Countryside Series map *North-East & Central New Territories* (p316).

Bicycles can be rented at Tai Mei Tuk at several locations, including **Wong Kei** (☎ 2662 5200) and **Lung Kee Bikes** (☎ 2662 5266), both on Ting Kok Rd in Lung Mei Village, open 9.30am to 6pm and charging $20 a day. A bicycle track along the coast runs from Tai Mei Tuk to Chinese University at Ma Liu Shui. Ting Kok Rd in Lung Mei Village is also where you'll find a row of popular restaurants (p187). Rowboats are available for hire from **Sang Lee Boat Rental** (☎ 2498 9326; small/big boat per hr $20/50, per 6hr $120/250; ⏱ 9.30am-6pm) on the picture-postcard bay south of the main parking lot on Tai Mei Tuk Rd, where buses and minibuses terminate. Adjacent to the car park is the **Tai Mei Tuk Fish Farm** (p218), where you can try your luck angling for some freshwater fish.

TRANSPORT

Bus Bus 75K to Tai Po Market KCR East Rail station (Map p424) in Tai Po, and bus 74K to Sam Mun Tsai.

Green Minibus Bus 20C to Tai Po Market KCR station and Heung Sze Wui St (Map p424) in Tai Po, bus 20K to Sam Mun Tsai.

The **Plover Cove Country Park Visitor Centre** (Map pp404–5; ☎ 2498 9326; ⏱ 9.30am-4.30pm Sat, Sun & public holidays), a short distance further east from the car park on Ting Kok Rd, is where the **Pat Sin Leng Nature Trail** (see below) to Bride's Pool starts.

Orientation
The village of Tai Mei Tuk, the springboard for most of the activities in the Plover Cove area, is about 6km northeast of Tai Po Market KCR East Rail station and easily accessible by bus and green minibus.

PAT SIN LENG NATURE TRAIL
Map pp404-5
Bus 75K
This excellent (and easy) 4.4km-long trail, which should take from two to 2½ hours, leads from the Plover Cove Country Park Visitor Centre at Tai Mei Tuk and heads northeast for 4km to Bride's Pool; there are signboards numbered 1 to 22 so there is little danger of getting lost. The elevation gain is only 300m, the scenery is excellent and the two waterfalls at Bride's Pool are delightful, but the place gets packed at the weekend. You can either return to Tai Mei Tuk via Bride's Pool Rd on foot or catch green minibus 20C which stops at Tai Mei Tuk before carrying on to Tai Po Market KCR station. On Sunday and public holidays only, bus 275R links Bride's Pool with Tai Po. If you carry on north from Bride's Pool to Luk Keng on Starling Inlet, you can catch green minibus 56K, which will take you to Fanling KCR station. Those looking for a more strenuous hike can join stage No 9 of the **Wilson Trail** (p222) at Tai Mei Tuk on the Plover Cove Reservoir and head west into the steep Pat Sin Leng range of hills (named after the 'Eight Immortals' of Taoism) to Wong Leng Shan (639m). The trail then carries on westward to Hok Tau Reservoir and Hok Tau Wai (12km, four hours).

PLOVER COVE RESERVOIR Map pp404-5
Bus 75K

Plover Cove Reservoir was completed in 1968 and holds 230 million cubic metres of water; before then Hong Kong suffered from critical water shortages and rationing was not uncommon. Even after the reservoir opened, water sometimes had to be rationed; taps were turned on for only eight hours a day through the dry winter of 1980/81. The reservoir was built in a very unusual way. Rather than build a dam across a river, of which Hong Kong has very few, a barrier was erected across the mouth of a great bay. The sea water was siphoned out and fresh water – mostly piped in from the mainland – was pumped in.

TAI PO KAU

South of Tai Po is the small settlement of Tai Po Kau, which most visitors wouldn't give a second thought to were it not for the wonderful nature reserve here.

Orientation

Tai Po Kau Nature Reserve lies south of Tai Po, less than a kilometre inland from Tolo Harbour. The main entrance and the information centre are at the village of Tsung Tsai Yuen in the northernmost part of the reserve along Tai Po Rd.

TAI PO KAU NATURE RESERVE
Map pp404-5
Tai Po Rd; bus 70 or 72

The Tai Po Kau Nature Reserve is a thickly forested 460-hectare 'special area' and is Hong Kong's most extensive woodlands. It is home to many species of butterflies, amphibians, birds, dragonflies and trees, and is a superb place in which to enjoy a quiet walk. The reserve is crisscrossed with four main tracks ranging in length from 3km (red trail) to 10km (yellow trail), and a short nature trail of less than 1km. If possible,

---

TRANSPORT

Bus Po Heung St in Tai Po (Map p424) for bus 70 to Yau Ma Tei and Jordan Rd, bus 72 to Sham Shui Po, Lai Chi Kok and Sha Tin, and bus 72A to Chinese University and Tai Wai KCR East Rail station.

---

avoid the reserve on Sunday and public holidays, when the crowds descend upon the place en masse.

The reserve is supposed to emphasise conservation and education rather than recreation, and about 1km northwest of the reserve entrance and down steep Hung Lam Drive is the **Tai Po Kau Interactive Nature Centre** and the much-touted, over-priced **Museum of Ethnology** (☎ 2657 6657; www.taipokau.org; 2 Hung Lam Dr; adult/child under 12 or senior over 60 $25/15; ⊗ 10.30am-6.30pm Sat & Sun). In the same complex is the delightful **Little Egret Restaurant** (p188).

Tai Po Kau Nature Reserve is well served by buses. Alternatively, a taxi from Tai Po Market KCR East Rail station will cost $20 and from the University KCR East Rail station about $38.

UNIVERSITY

The **Chinese University of Hong Kong** (Map pp404-5; ☎ 2609 6000; www.cuhk.edu.hk), established in 1963, is in Ma Liu Shui and served by University KCR East Rail station. It is situated on a beautiful campus and its art museum is well worth a visit.

Orientation

Ma Liu Shui and the Chinese University of Hong Kong are southeast of Tai Po and Tai Po Kau, overlooking Tolo Harbour. The University KCR East Rail station is southeast of the three campuses (Chung Chi Campus, New Asia Campus and United Campus). Ferries from Ma Liu Shui ferry pier, opposite the university on the eastern side of Tolo Hwy and about 500m northeast of University station, serve the Sai Kung Peninsula (p120) and Tap Mun Chau (p121) twice daily (p292). A taxi from the station to the pier will cost $12.50.

CHINESE UNIVERSITY OF HONG KONG ART MUSEUM Map pp404-5
☎ 2609 7416; www.cuhk.edu.hk/ics/amm; Sir Run Run Shaw Hall, Central Ave; admission free; ⊗ 10am-4.45pm Mon-Sat, 12.30-5.30pm Sun; **University KCR East Rail**

The Chinese University of Hong Kong Art Museum is divided into two sections. The four-floor East Wing Galleries house a permanent collection of Chinese paintings,

TRANSPORT

KCR University station.

Bus Bus 72A to Tai Po Market KCR East Rail station (Map p424) in Tai Po.

Ferry To Sai Kung Peninsula, Tap Mun Chau and Tung Ping Chau.

calligraphy, ceramics and other decorative arts, including 2000-year-old bronze seals and a large collection of jade flower carvings. The West Wing Galleries stage five to six special exhibitions each year.

A shuttle bus from University station travels through the campus to the administration building at the top of the hill; for the museum, get off at the second stop. The bus runs every 20 to 30 minutes daily and is free except on Sunday ($5) from September to May. From June to August, it costs $1 on weekdays and $5 at the weekend.

SHA TIN

Eating p188; Sleeping p270

Sha Tin (Sandy Field; Map p425) is an enormous New Town (population 637,000) built mostly on land that was once a mud flat and produced some of the best rice in imperial China. Sha Tin retains some traditional Chinese houses, giving parts of it an historical feel absent in most of the other New Towns. Hong Kong Chinese flock to Sha Tin on the weekends to place their bets at the nearby racecourse or to shop at Sha Tin's **New Town Plaza** (Map p425; ☎ 2699 5992; www.newtownplaza.com; 18 Sha Tin Centre St; ☻ 10am-11pm), one of the biggest shopping centres in the New Territories. For visitors, the drawcards are the temples and one of the best museums in Hong Kong. You can rent bicycles from several kiosks in Sha Tin Park, south of New Town Plaza shopping centre, including **Power Three Company** (Map p425; ☎ 9225 8204; Kiosk No 3; per hr Mon-Fri $10, per hr/day Sat & Sun $15/40; ☻ 9am-7pm).

Orientation

Sha Tin lies in a narrow valley on both banks of a channel of the Shing Mun River. Fo Tan, where the racecourse is located, is to the north and northeast, and Tai Wai,

where you'll find the Hong Kong Heritage Museum, is to the south. Though once separate villages, they are now extensions of the Sha Tin conurbation. Sha Tin KCR East Rail station is west (and connected to) New Town Plaza in central Sha Tin. Buses arrive at and depart from the KCR East Rail station, the bus station below New Town Plaza and the one at City One Plaza on Ngan Shing St on the opposite side of the channel.

10,000 BUDDHAS MONASTERY

Map pp404-5

☎ 2691 1067; admission free; ☻ 9am-5pm; **Sha Tin KCR East Rail**

If you're big on Buddhas, head for this monastery, which sits on the top of Po Fook Hill about 500m northwest of Sha Tin KCR East Rail station. Built in the 1950s, the complex actually contains more than 10,000 Buddhas – some 12,800 miniature statues line the walls of the main temple. Dozens of life-sized golden statues of Buddha's followers flank the steep steps leading to the monastery complex. There is also a nine-storey pagoda.

To reach the monastery, take exit B at Sha Tin KCR station and walk down the ramp, passing a series of traditional houses at Pai Tau village on the left. Take the left onto Pai Tau St, and turn right onto Sheung Wo Che St. At the end of this road, a series of signs in English will direct you to the left along a concrete path and through bamboo groves to the first of some 400 steps leading up to the monastery.

AMAH ROCK Map pp404-5

This boulder southwest of Sha Tin may look like just a rock, but it's an oddly shaped one and, like many local landmarks in Hong Kong, it carries a legend. It seems that for many years a fisherman's wife would stand on this spot in the hills above **Lion Rock Country Park**, watching for her husband to return from the sea while carrying her baby on her back. One day he didn't come back – she waited and waited. The gods apparently took pity on her and transported her to heaven on a lightning bolt, leaving her form in stone. The name of the rock in Cantonese is **Mong Fu Shek**, or 'Gazing out for Husband Stone'. It's a popular place of pilgrimage for girls and young lovers during the Maiden's Festival on the seventh day of the seventh moon (mid-August).

As you take the KCR south from Sha Tin to Kowloon, Amah Rock is visible to the east (ie on the left-hand side) up on the hillside after Tai Wai KCR East Rail station, but before the train enters the tunnel.

CHE KUNG TEMPLE Map p425

☎ 2691 1733; Che Kung Miu Rd; admission free; ⏰ 7am-6pm; Che Kung Temple MOS Rail

This large Taoist temple complex, built in 1993, is on the opposite bank of the Shing Mun River channel in Tai Wai. It's dedicated to Che Kung, a Song-dynasty general credited with ridding Sha Tin of the plague; you'll see an enormous and quite powerful statue of the good general in the main temple to the left as you enter the complex. The main courtyard, flanked by eight statues of Taoist immortals, is always a hive of activity.

To reach the temple, take the KCR East Rail to Tai Wai station and change to the Ma On Shan Rail extension, alighting at Che Kung Temple station. The temple is just west.

HONG KONG HERITAGE MUSEUM

Map p425

☎ 2180 8188; www.heritagemuseum.gov.hk; 1 Man Lam Rd; adult/concession $10/5, admission free Wed; ⏰ 10am-6pm Mon & Wed-Sat, 10am-7pm Sun; Sha Tin KCR East Rail

Located southwest of Sha Tin town centre, this exceptional museum is housed in a three-storey, purpose-built structure that is reminiscent of an ancestral hall. It has both rich permanent collections and innovative temporary exhibits in a dozen galleries.

The ground floor contains a book and gift shop, the wonderful Children's Discovery Gallery, with eight learning and play zones (including 'Life in a Village', 'Shrimp Harvesting',

---

TRANSPORT

KCR Sha Tin (Map p425), Tai Wai (Map pp404–5), Fo Tan (Map pp404–5) and Racecourse (Map pp404–5) East Rail stations.

MOS Che Kung Temple (Map pp404–5) station.

Bus City One Plaza Sha Tin bus station (Map p425) for bus 182 to Wan Chai, Admiralty and Central; Sha Tin KCR East Rail bus station (Map p425) for bus 170 to Causeway Bay and Aberdeen, and bus 263 to Tuen Mun; New Town Plaza station (Map p425) for bus 80K to Tai Wai, bus 48X to Tsuen Wan, bus 72 to Tai Po, and bus 299 to Sai Kung.

'Mai Po Marsh') for kids aged four to 10, a Hong Kong Toy Story hands-on area for tots and an Orientation Theatre with a 12-minute introductory video in English on the hour. There's also a lovely teahouse (⏰ 10am-6pm).

Along with five thematic (ie temporary) galleries, the 1st floor contains the best of the museum's permanent collections: the New Territories Heritage Hall, with mock-ups of traditional shops, a Hakka fishing village and history of the New Towns; the Cantonese Opera Heritage Hall, where you can watch old operas on video with English subtitles, 'virtually' make yourself up as a Cantonese opera character on computer or just enjoy the costumes and sets; and the Chao Shao-an Gallery, devoted to the work of the eponymous water-colourist (1905–98) and founder of the Lingnan School of painting (p27).

The 2nd floor contains another thematic gallery and the TT Tsui Gallery of Chinese Art, an Aladdin's cave of fine ceramics, pottery, bronze, jade and lacquerware, stone carvings, and furniture. You may be interested in some of the gifts various Chinese provinces presented to China for the reunification, which are on display in the hallways.

To reach the Hong Kong Heritage Museum, take the KCR East Rail to Sha Tin station and walk south along Tai Po Rd. If coming from the Che Kung Temple, walk east along Che Kung Miu Rd, go under the subway and cross the footbridge over the channel. The museum is 200m to the east.

SHA TIN RACECOURSE Map pp404-5

☎ 2966 8111; www.sha-tin.com; Penfold Park; admission on race days public stands $10, members enclosures $50; Racecourse or Fo Tan KCR East Rail

Northeast of Sha Tin town centre is Hong Kong's second racecourse, which opened in 1978 and can accommodate up to 80,000 punters. In general, races are held on Saturday afternoon, and sometimes on Sunday and public holidays, from September to June; a list of race meetings is available from the HKTB or the racecourse website.

Bets are easily placed at one of the numerous computerised betting terminals run by the Hong Kong Jockey Club (p216). There is a worthwhile horseracing tour available for the interested but uninitiated; see p83.

The KCR Racecourse station, just west of the track, opens on race days only. Otherwise, get off at Fo Tan station and walk north along Lok King St, and its extension Lok Shun Path, for about 1.5km.

SAI KUNG PENINSULA

Eating p188; Sleeping p271

The Sai Kung Peninsula is the garden spot of the New Territories. It is also one of the last areas left in Hong Kong – the Outlying Islands notwithstanding – reserved for outdoor activities, and 60% of the peninsula is one huge 7500-hectare country park, divided into Sai Kung East and Sai Kung West. Though strictly speaking not on the peninsula, the 28,880-hectare **Ma On Shan Country Park** (Map pp404–5) is contiguous with it and access is from Sai Kung Town. The hiking is excellent in Sai Kung – the **MacLehose Trail** (p220) runs right across it – there's sailing galore and some of the best beaches in the territory are here.

A good website devoted exclusively to the area is the Sai Kung District Council's **Travel in Sai Kung** (www.travelinsaikung.org.hk).

Orientation

The Sai Kung Peninsula is in the northeastern New Territories. It is washed by Tolo Harbour to the north, Mirs Bay to the east, and Port Shelter to the south. On the southern end of the peninsula is High Island Reservoir, once a sea channel and now Hong Kong's second-largest source of fresh water.

Sai Kung Town

Originally a fishing village, Sai Kung Town (Map p425) is now more of a leafy suburb for people working in Kowloon and on Hong Kong Island, but it still has some of the feeling of a port. Fishing boats put in an occasional appearance, and down on the waterfront there's a string of seafood restaurants that draw customers from all around the territory.

TRANSPORT

Bus Sai Kung Town (Map p425) for bus 299 to Sha Tin KCR East Rail, bus 92 to Diamond Hill and Choi Hung, bus 96R (Sun and public holidays) to Wong Shek, Hebe Haven and Choi Hung and Diamond Hill MTR stations, bus 792M to Tseung Kwan O and Tiu Keng Leng MTR stations, and bus 94 to Wong Shek.

Green Minibus Sai Kung Town (Map p425) for buses 1A, 1M and 1S (12.30am-6.10am) to Hebe Haven and Choi Hung MTR station.

If travelling to Sai Kung from Choi Hung in Kowloon, the minibus (1A, 1M or 1S) is faster than bus 92, which also goes to the Diamond Hill MTR station. Bus 299 from Sha Tin takes you to Sai Kung via Ma On Shan and passes some lovely bays and isolated villages on the way.

ACTIVITIES

Sai Kung Town is an excellent springboard for hikes into the surrounding countryside. A *kaido* trip to one or more of the little offshore islands and their secluded beaches is also recommended (see the boxed text, p122). Windsurfing equipment can be hired from the **Windsurfing Centre** (☎ 2792 5605; ☽ 11am-6pm Mon-Fri, 10am-6pm Sat & Sun) at Sha Ha, just north of Sai Kung Town. Bus 94, heading for the pier at **Wong Shek** and the springboard for **Tap Mun Chau**, will drop you off. Or you can walk there from town in about 15 minutes.

Hebe Haven

The very small bay of Hebe Haven (Map pp404–5), which Cantonese speakers call Pak Sha Wan (White Sand Bay), is home to the **Hebe Haven Yacht Club** (☎ 2719 9682, 2719 3673; www.hhyc.org.hk), which has a large fleet of yachts and other pleasure craft all but choking Marina Cove.

To swim at Trio Beach, opposite the marina, catch a sampan from Hebe Haven to the long, narrow peninsula called Ma Lam Wat; along the way you'll pass a small Tin Hau temple on a spit of land jutting out to the south. The beach is excellent and the sampan trip should only cost a few dollars. You can also walk to the peninsula from Sai Kung Town; it's about 4km.

LIONS NATURE EDUCATION CENTRE

Map pp404-5

☎ 2792 2234; Pak Kong; http://parks.afcd.gov.hk /newparks/chi/education/lnec/eng/index.htm; admission free; ☽ 9.30am-5pm Wed-Mon; bus 92

This new 34-hectare attraction, 2km northwest of Hebe Haven and just off Hiram's Highway, is Hong Kong's first nature education centre and comprises everything from an arboretum, a medicinal plants garden and an insectarium to a mineral and rocks corner and a shell house. We love the Dragonfly Pond, which attracts up to a quarter of the more than 100 dragonfly species

Local sampan (p296)

found in Hong Kong. You can reach the centre on bus 92 from Diamond Hill MTR and Choi Hung, bus 96R on Sunday and holidays from Diamond Hill to Wong Shek Pier and green minibus 1A from Choi Hung.

Pak Tam Chung

Sai Kung Peninsula's easternmost point accessible by bus (No 94), Pak Tam Chung (Map pp404–5) is the start of the **MacLehose Trail** (p220).

SAI KUNG COUNTRY PARK VISITOR CENTRE Map pp404-5

☎ 2792 7365; Tai Mong Tsai Rd; ☺ 9.30am-4.30pm Wed-Mon; bus 94

While you're in Pak Tam Chung, visit the Sai Kung Country Park Visitor Centre, which is to the south of the village, just by the road from Sai Kung. It has excellent maps, photographs and displays of the area's geology, fauna and flora as well as its traditional villages and Hoi Ha Wan Marine Park.

SHEUNG YIU FOLK MUSEUM

Map pp404-5

☎ 2792 6365; Pak Tam Chung Nature Trail; admission free; ☺ 9am-4pm Wed-Mon; bus 94

This museum is a leisurely 20-minute walk from Pak Tam Chung south along the 1km-long **Pak Tam Chung Nature Trail.** The museum is part of a restored Hakka village typical of those found here in the 19th century. The village was founded about 150 years ago by the Wong clan, which built a kiln to make bricks. In the whitewashed dwellings, pigpens and cattle sheds, all surrounded by a high wall and watchtower to guard against raids by pirates, are farm implements, objects of daily use, furnishings and Hakka clothing.

Hoi Ha, Wong Shek, Chek Keng & Tai Long

There are several rewarding hikes at the northern end of the Sai Kung Peninsula, but the logistics can be a bit tricky. Be sure to take along a copy of the *Sai Kung & Clearwater Bay* Countryside Series map or Universal Publications' *Tseung Kwan O, Sai Kung, Clearwater Bay* (p316).

HOI HA WAN MARINE PARK

Map pp404-5

☎ 2957 8757; Hoi Ha; green minibus 7

A rewarding 6km walk in the area starts from the village of Hoi Ha (literally 'Under the Sea'), on the coast of Hoi Ha Bay, now part of the Hoi Ha Wan Marine Park, a 260-hectare protected area blocked off by concrete booms from the Tolo Channel and closed to fishing vessels. It's one of the few places in Hong Kong waters where coral still grows in abundance and a favourite with divers. You can visit anytime, but 1½-hour tours of the marine park are available in English at 10.30am and 2.15pm on Saturday, Sunday and public holidays. Be aware that you must register with the **Agriculture, Fisheries & Conservation Department** (AFCD; ☎ 2957 8757) in advance, however.

Green minibus 7 makes the run from Sai Kung daily, with the first departure at 8.45am and the last at 6.45pm. A taxi from there will cost $100.

TAP MUN CHAU

Eating p190

Tap Mun Chau (Map pp404–5), which translates as 'Grass Island', is very isolated and retains an old-world fishing village atmosphere. If you have the time (count on a full day), it's definitely worth the trip, and you will be rewarded with a feeling that's hard

Sights

NEW TERRITORIES

to come by in Hong Kong: isolation. The sailing is particularly scenic from Wong Shek, as the boat cruises through the narrow Tai Tan Hoi Hap – more reminiscent of a fjord in Norway than a harbour in Hong Kong.

Tap Mun Chau doesn't have accommodation, but you may get away with pitching a tent. There's only one restaurant on the island (p190), but there are shops selling snacks and drinks. For ferry routes, schedules and fares for Tap Mun Chau, see p292.

Orientation

Tap Mun Chau is found off the northeast coast of the New Territories, where the Tolo Channel empties into Mirs Bay, which is Tai

---

TRANSPORT

Ferry Tap Mun ferry pier (Map pp404–5) to Wong Shek and Chek Keng on the Sai Kung Peninsula, and Ma Liu Shui near University KCR East Rail station.

Pang Wan in Cantonese. Only Tung Ping Chau to the northeast in Mirs Bay is more remote.

SIGHTS & ACTIVITIES

As you approach the pier at Tap Mun village, you'll see fishing boats bobbing about in the small bay and, to the south, people working on fish-breeding rafts. Tap Mun village is noted for its **Tin Hau temple**

ISLAND HOPPING IN SAI KUNG

You can make any number of easy boat trips from Sai Kung Town, exploring the mosaic of islands that dot the harbour. It's a delightful way to spend a few hours or even an entire day. Most *kaidos* (small, open-sea ferries) leave from the pier on the waterfront, just in front of Hoi Pong Square.

The easiest (and cheapest) way to go is to jump aboard a 'scheduled' *kaido* (ie one that goes according to demand and when full) bound for the small island of **Yim Tin Tsai** ($10, 15 minutes).

On the way, the boat weaves through a number of small islands. The first island to the east of Sai Kung Town is **Yeung Chau** (Sheep Island). You'll be able to spot a horseshoe-shaped burial plot up on the slope; for reasons dictated by feng shui, the Chinese like to position graves with decent views of the sea. Southeast of Yeung Chau, **Pak Sha Chau** (White Sand Island) has a popular beach on its northern shore.

Just beyond Pak Sha Chau is the northern tip of the much larger **Kiu Tsui Chau** (Sharp Island), arguably the most popular island destination. Kiu Tsui Chau has several fine, sandy beaches: Kiu Tsui and, connected to it by a sand spit, Kiu Tau on the western shore and Hap Mun on the island's southern tip. Both can be reached by *kaido* ($10) directly from Sai Kung Town.

Yim Tin Tsai (Little Salt Field) is so called because the original fisherfolk who lived here augmented their income by salt-panning. A few minutes' walk from the jetty up a small flight of steps to the left is St Joseph's Chapel, the focal point of the island. This is Yim Tin Tsai's only house of worship, which is most unusual in an area of Hong Kong where temples devoted to Tin Hau proliferate. Apparently the villagers, who all belong to the same clan, converted to Catholicism 150 years ago after St Peter appeared on the island to chase away pirates who had been harassing them.

Yim Tin Tsai is connected to the much larger island of **Kau Sai Chau** by a narrow spit of land that becomes submerged at high tide. Kau Sai Chau is the site of the 36-hole **Jockey Club Kau Sai Chau Public Golf Course** (p218), a public link that can be reached by the course's direct ferry from Sai Kung (adult/child or senior $50/30 return), which departs every 20 minutes daily from 6.40am to 9pm; the last boat back is at 10pm. Boats dock in Sai Kung Town at the long pier opposite the new Sai Kung Waterfront Park. The 19th-century Hung Shing Temple at the southern tip of Kau Sai Chau won a Unesco restoration award in 2000.

Beyond Kau Sai Chau is **Leung Shuen Wan** (High Island), a long trip from Sai Kung Town, and the **High Island Reservoir**, which was built in 1978 by damming what was once a large bay with dolooses (huge cement barriers shaped like jacks); sea water was then siphoned out and fresh water pumped in. You can see one example of a doloose, weighing 25 tonnes, on display on the pier in Sai Kung Town (Map p425).

If you want to be out on the water for a longer period or to have greater flexibility as to where you go, you can hire your own boat. Finding a *kaido* for such a trip is no problem at all; you won't be on the pier for long before being approached by a bevy of enthusiastic *kaido* owners trawling for fares. Explain to the *kaido* owner where you want to go, how long you want to spend there and which way you wish to return. They don't speak much English, but if you point to the islands on Map pp404–5 in this book, they may get the picture. The usual price for this kind of trip is about $100 on weekdays, more at the weekend.

(Map pp404–5), which was built during the reign of Emperor Kang Xi of the Qing dynasty in the late 17th or early 18th century and is northeast from where the boat docks. The Tin Hau birthday festival in late April/early May (p11) is big here, although most of the participants come from elsewhere in Hong Kong. Part of the temple is devoted to the god of war, Kwan Tai (or Kwan Yu).

Other attractions here include an easy (and signposted) walk northward to **Mau Ping Shan** (125m), the island's highest point, a windy pebble **beach** on the southeastern shore and an odd stone formation called **Balanced Rock**, a couple of hundred metres south of the beach.

TUNG PING CHAU

A remote, crescent-shaped island, Tung Ping Chau (Map pp404–5) is part of **Plover Cove Country Park** (☎ 2498 9326; ⊕ 9.30am-4.30pm Sat, Sun & public holidays). The island and the waters around it, which teem with sea life (especially corals), form Hong Kong's fourth marine park.

At one time the island, which is called Tung Ping Chau (East Peace Island) to distinguish it from Peng Chau (same pronunciation in Cantonese) near Lantau, supported a population of 3000, but now it is virtually deserted. There are a couple of tiny settlements on the northeastern side, including Sha Tau, where you'll find a food stall.

Tung Ping Chau is just 12km from the mainland's Daya Bay nuclear power station and has Hong Kong's only radiation shelter, at Tai Tong just north of the pier.

For ferry routes, schedules and fares for Tung Ping Chau, see p292.

Orientation

Tung Ping Chau, sitting in splendid isolation in Mirs Bay in the far northeast of the New Territories, is as remote as it gets in Hong Kong. The distance from Ma Liu Shui to the southwest, from where the ferry serving the island departs, is 25km.

TRANSPORT

Ferry Tung Ping Chau ferry pier (Map pp404–5) to Wong Shek and Chek Keng on the Sai Kung Peninsula, and Ma Liu Shui near University KCR East Rail station.

SIGHTS & ACTIVITIES

Tung Ping Chau's highest point is only about 40m, but it has unusual rock layers in its cliffs, which glitter after the rain. The island has some sandy beaches on its east coast that are good for swimming. The longest one, to the northeast, is **Cheung Sha Wan**. There is a small **Tin Hau temple** on the southwestern coast of the island, and some small **caves** dotting the cliffs. A good 6km **walking trail** encircles the whole island.

CLEARWATER BAY PENINSULA

Clearwater Bay Peninsula is a wonderfully untamed and rough-contoured backdrop to urban Hong Kong – at least on its eastern shore. It is wedged in by Junk Bay (Tseung Kwan O) to the west and Clearwater Bay (Tsing Sui Wan) sitting to the east; Joss House Bay (Tai Miu Wan) lies to the south. Junk Bay is now the site of Tseung Kwan O, a New Town built on reclaimed land with a growing population of 325,000 and a sixth MTR line, but the eastern coastline remains fairly unscarred and offers some exceptional walks, fine beaches and one of the most important temples dedicated to Tin Hau on the South China coast.

Orientation

Clearwater Bay Peninsula is on the southeastern edge of the New Territories. The country park is divided into two parts: a long and narrow finger-shaped section stretching from Joss House Bay in the south almost to Port Shelter and a half-moon-shaped section to the east between Lung Ha Wan and Clearwater Bay.

BEACHES Map pp404-5

Bus 91 passes **Silverstrand Beach** (Ngan Sin Wan) north of Hang Hau before reaching Tai Au Mun; if you wish you can get off at Silverstrand and go for a dip. If you're heading for Lung Ha Wan, get off the bus at Tai Au Mun village and start walking. From Sai Kung, take bus 92 to where Hiram's Hwy and Clearwater Bay Rd meet and change there to bus 91.

From Tai Au Mun, Tai Au Mun Rd leads south to two fine, sandy beaches: **Clearwater Bay First Beach** and, a bit further southwest, **Clearwater Bay Second Beach**. In summer, try to go during the week, as both beaches can get very crowded on the weekend.

HONG KONG FOR CHILDREN, FROM A TO Z

There's a stack of things for kids to do and see in Hong Kong:

- **Avenue of the Stars** (p93) and its evening lightshow on Hong Kong Island's skyline and the frenzy that is Victoria Harbour
- **Beaches** (p218), especially ones with rocks to climb like Cheung Sha on Lantau
- **Cityplaza**, with its wonderful musical fountain and Ice Palace skating rink (p224)
- **Disneyland** (p131), Hong Kong's extravagant new amusement park
- **Escalator excitement** of going up and going down the world's longest moving staircase (see the boxed text, p140)
- **Ferries** (p291), especially the venerable old Star Ferry
- **Goldfish Market** (p143) for fun and/or good luck
- **Hong Kong Heritage Museum's** (p119) interactive display paradise and virtual Chinese opera makeup
- **Island-hopping** between Cheung Chau, Peng Chau and Lantau on the inter-island ferry (p292)
- **Junk and sampan trips**, especially in Aberdeen Harbour (p88)
- **Kowloon Park's** (p91) aviary, swimming-pool complex and Kung Fu Corner
- **Lantau Island** (p129) and its beaches, steep bus rides and big Buddha
- **MTR** and other forms of fun public transport, especially Hong Kong's trams
- **Noonday Gun** (p81) for the big noon boom
- **Ocean Park** (p88) and its Dragon roller coaster, killer whales and cable-car ride
- **Peak Tram** (p302) as it climbs Victoria Peak at a slant
- **Queen's Rd Central** (p68) and its malls galore for underage shopaholics
- **Repulse Bay** (p86) beach and Buddhist statues
- **Space Museum & Theatre** (p90) for big-screen entertainment
- **Tsim Sha Tsui East Promenade** (p93) with its nightly light show
- **Under** Tsing Yi Bridge looking up at the Lantau Link Visitors Centre (p136)
- **Victoria Park** (p82) for flowers and t'ai chi
- **Wong Tai Sin Temple** (p98) for pagodas, pungent incense and pick-up-sticks
- **XTC on Ice** (p158) and its sublime ice cream
- **Yuen Po Street Bird Garden** (p95) to confab with the birds
- **Zoological & Botanical Gardens** (p70) for feather and frond overload.

CLEARWATER BAY COUNTRY PARK
Map pp404-5

The heart of the country park is **Tai Au Mun**, from where trails head off in various directions, though the **Clearwater Bay Country Park Visitor Centre** (☎ 2719 0032; ◷ 9.30am-4.30pm Wed-Mon) is to the southeast in Tai Hang Tun. You can take the small road (Lung Ha Wan Rd) north from Tai Au Mun to the beach at **Lung Ha Wan** (Lobster Bay) and return via the 2.3km **Lung Ha Wan Country Trail**.

TAI MIU TEMPLE Map pp404-5
☎ 2519 9155; ◷ 8am-5pm

Further south along Tai Au Mun Rd is this ancient temple dedicated to Tin Hau. It is said to have been first built in the 13th century by two brothers from Fujian in gratitude to the goddess for having spared their lives during a storm at sea. It is particularly busy during the Tin Hau birthday festival in late April/early May (p11) and has been renovated in recent years.

Just behind the temple is a **Song-dynasty rock carving** dating from 1274 and recording both the visit of a superintendent of the Salt Administration and the history of two temples in Joss House Bay. It is the oldest inscription extant in Hong Kong.

From Tai Miu, hikers can follow the 6.6km-long **High Junk Peak Country Trail** up to **Tin Ha Shan** (273m) and then continue on to **High Junk Peak** (Tiu Yu Yung; 344m) before heading eastward back to Tai Au Mun.

TRANSPORT

Bus Bus 91 to Diamond Hill and Choi Hung MTR stations.

Green Minibus Bus 103M to Tseung Kwan O MTR station, bus 103 to Kwun Tong ferry pier, and bus 16 to Po Lam MTR station.

OUTLYING ISLANDS

In addition to Hong Kong Island, the territory of Hong Kong consists of another 234 islands. Together these 'Outlying Islands', as they are called here, make up about 20% of the territory's total land area but can claim only about 2% of its total population.

Hong Kong's islands vary greatly in size, appearance and character. While there are many that are little more than uninhabited rocks poking out of the South China Sea, Lantau is almost twice the size of Hong Kong Island.

Because they are so sparsely populated, the Outlying Islands are the territory's escape routes and its playgrounds. Among the magnets that attract local day-trippers and foreign visitors alike are country parks with hundreds of kilometres of hiking trails, fresher air and examples of some of the last remnants of traditional village life in Hong Kong.

From the tranquil lanes of Cheung Chau and Peng Chau to the monasteries of Lantau and the waterfront seafood restaurants of Lamma, Hong Kong's islands offer a world of peace and quiet along with a host of sights and activities. The islands are a colourful encyclopaedia of animal and plant life – a boon for nature lovers. What's more, some of Hong Kong's best beaches punctuate the rocky coasts.

The islands listed here are all easily accessible from Hong Kong Island daily, and Cheung Chau and Lantau can be reached from Kowloon at the weekend as well. For details on routes, schedule and fares, see p292. Because the tiny islands of Tap Mun Chau and Tung Ping Chau are best reached from the New Territories, they are both covered on p121 and p123.

LAMMA

Eating p190; Sleeping p271

At 13.6 sq km, the territory's third-largest island after Lantau and Hong Kong Island, Lamma (Map p426) is home to an estimated 5000 fisherfolk, farmers and foreigners, and the hills above the main village, Yung Shue Wan, are strewn with small homes and apartment blocks. Known mainly for the seafood restaurants at Sok Kwu Wan, the island's 'second' village, Lamma also has some good beaches, excellent hiking and lively pubs.

Perhaps the most interesting way for visitors to see a good portion of the island is to follow the 4km-long 'Family Trail' that runs between Yung Shue Wan and Sok Kwu Wan. This takes a little over an hour, and you can return to Central by ferry from there. Those with extra time should carry on to Tung O Wan, an idyllic bay some 30

www.lonelyplanet.com

TRANSPORT

Ferry Yung Shue Wan pier (Map p426) to pier 4 of Outlying Islands ferry terminal in Central, Pak Kok Tsuen (Lamma) and Aberdeen; Sok Kwu Wan pier (Map p426) to pier 4 of Outlying Islands ferry terminal in Central, Man Tat Wan (Lamma) and Aberdeen.

minutes further south at the bottom of a steep hill, and perhaps return to Sok Kwu Wan via Mo Tat Wan.

Orientation

Lamma is the closest inhabited island to Hong Kong Island; its northernmost tip is only 3km across the East Lamma Channel from Ap Lei Chau in Aberdeen. There are two main settlements on the island: Yung Shue Wan to the northwest and Sok Kwu Wan on the east coast of the island.

Information

There's a **HSBC branch** (☎ 2982 0787; 19 Main St) and a **post office** (3 Main St) in Yung Shue Wan. Bicycles are available for rent from **Hoi Nam Gift & Bicycle Shop** (☎ 2982 0128, 9364 4941; Ground fl, 37 Sha Po Old Village; per hr/day $15/50; ☺ 11am-7pm) in Yung Shue Wan on the main path to Sok Kwu Wan.

HUNG SHING YEH BEACH Map p426
Yung Shue Wan ferry

About a 25-minute walk southeast from the Yung Shue Wan ferry pier, Hung Shing Yeh Beach is the most popular beach on Lamma. But arrive early in the morning or on a weekday and you'll probably find it deserted. The beach is protected by a shark net and has toilets, showers and changing rooms, but the view of the power station across the bay takes some getting used to. There are a few restaurants and drinks stands nearby – the latter open at the weekend only, except in summer – as well as the **Concerto Inn** (p191), a hotel that also serves so-so Western food. Make sure you visit **Herboland** (Map p426; ☎ 9094 6206, 9414 2866; www.herboland.com.hk; Hung Shing Yeh Beach; ☺ 9am-6pm), a little organic farm at the end of the beach that sells its own herbs and herb products, including snacks and some 40 types of herbal tea.

LO SO SHING BEACH Map p426
Yung Shue Wan ferry

If you continue south from Hung Shing Yeh Beach, the path climbs steeply until it reaches a **Chinese-style pavilion** near the top of the hill. From this vantage point, it becomes obvious that the island is mostly hilly grassland and large boulders, though more and more trees are being planted. You will pass a second pavilion offering splendid views out to sea; from here a path leads from the Family Trail down to Lo So Shing Beach, the most beautiful on Lamma. The beach is not very big, but it has a nice cover of shade trees at the back for a break from the sun.

MO TAT WAN Map p426

The clean and relatively uncrowded beach at Mo Tat Wan is a mere 20-minute walk east of Sok Kwu Wan along a coastal path. Mo Tat Wan is OK for swimming but has no lifeguards. You can also reach here by *kaido* from Aberdeen, which continues on to Sok Kwu Wan.

SHAM WAN Map p426

Sham Wan (Deep Bay) is another beautiful bay to the southwest that can be reached from Tung O Wan by clambering over the hills. A trail on the left about 200m up the hill from Tung O leads south to a small and sandy beach. Don't come here from June to October, when Hong Kong's endangered green turtles nest (see the boxed text, below).

SOK KWU WAN Map p426
Sok Kwu Wan ferry

If you continue on the Family Trail you'll encounter another pavilion on a ridge, this time looking down onto Sok Kwu Wan (Picnic Bay), with its many fine restaurants, and fishing boats and rafts bobbing in the bay. Although still a small settlement, Sok Kwu Wan supports at least a dozen waterfront seafood restaurants that are popular with boaters. The small harbour at Sok Kwu Wan is filled with rafts from which cages are suspended and fish farmed. If entering Sok Kwu Wan from the south (ie from the Family Trail linking it with Yung Shue Wan), you'll pass three so-called '**kamikaze caves**', grottoes measuring 10m wide and 30m deep and built by the occupying Japanese forces to house motorboats wired with explosives to disrupt Allied shipping during WWII. They were never used. Further on and near the entrance to Sok Kwu Wan is a totally renovated **Tin Hau temple** dating back to 1826.

TUNG O WAN Map p426

A detour to this small and secluded bay, with a long stretch of sandy beach, while walking to Sok Kwu Wan from Yung Shue Wan or from Sok Kwu Wan itself is highly recommended. Just before the Tin Hau temple at the entrance to Sok Kwu Wan, follow the signposted path to the right southward, up and over the hill to the tiny village of **Tung O**. The walk takes about 30 minutes, over a rugged landscape, and

---

GREEN TURTLES & EGGS

Sham Wan has traditionally been the one beach in the whole of Hong Kong where endangered green turtles *(Chelonia mydas)*, one of three species of sea turtle found in Hong Kong waters, still struggle onto the sand to lay their eggs from early June to the end of August.

Female green turtles, which can grow to a metre in length and weigh 140kg, take between 20 and 30 years to reach sexual maturity and always head back to the same beach where they were born to lay their eggs, which takes place every two to six years. Fearing that Sham Wan would catch the eye of housing-estate developers and that the turtles would swim away forever, the area was declared a Site of Special Scientific Interest and closed. It is patrolled by the Agriculture, Fisheries & Conservation Department (AFCD) from June to October. Some eight turtles are known to have nested here since 1997 and some are now being tracked by satellite.

As well as developers, a major hurdle faced by the long-suffering turtles is the appetite of Lamma locals for their eggs. In 1994 three turtles laid about 200 eggs, which were promptly harvested and consumed by villagers. Several years later villagers sold eggs to Japanese tourists for $100 each. There is now a $50,000 fine levied on anyone caught on the beach during the nesting season. Anyone taking, possessing or attempting to sell one of the eggs faces a fine of $100,000 and one year in prison.

Gwài-dáan, or 'turtle egg', by the way, is one of the rudest things you can call a Cantonese-speaking person.

the first half is a fairly strenuous climb up steps and along a path. Don't do this walk at night unless it's a full moon, as there are only a few street lights at the start in Sok Kwu Wan.

If coming from Mo Tat Wan, take the trail immediately to the west of the pavilion above the beach and follow the signposted path up the hill and through bamboo groves and fields. It takes about 25 minutes to reach the sleepy village of **Yung Shue Ha** (Under the Banyan Tree) on the fringes of the bay. All of the Chinese who live there are from the same clan and have the surname of Chow. A member of this clan, Chow Yun Fat, the bullet-proof star of many John Woo films, was born and raised in Tung O.

The beach at Tung O Wan is a secluded and unspoiled stretch of sand, punctuated by chunks of driftwood and other flotsam.

YUNG SHUE WAN Map p426
Yung Shue Wan ferry

Though it's the larger of the island's two main villages, Yung Shue Wan (Banyan Tree Bay) remains a small place, with little more than a main street following the curve of the bay. Plastic was the big industry here at one time, but now restaurants, bars and other tourism-related businesses are the main employers. There is a small **Tin Hau temple** dating from the late 19th century at the southern end of Yung Shue Wan.

CHEUNG CHAU

Eating p192; Sleeping p272

Once a refuge for pirates, Cheung Chau (Long Island; Map p428) now supports a population of some 30,000 people on less than 2.5 sq km of territory. Many residents are commuters, but relatively few foreigners live here nowadays.

Archaeological evidence, including a 3000-year-old rock carving uncovered just below the Warwick Hotel (p272), suggests that Cheung Chau, like Lamma and Lantau, was inhabited at least as early as the Neolithic period. The island had a thriving fishing community at the time, and the early inhabitants – Hakka and Cantonese settlers – supplemented their income with smuggling and piracy.

When Canton (present-day Guangzhou) and Macau opened up to the West in the 16th century, Cheung Chau was a perfect

TRANSPORT

Ferry Cheung Chau ferry pier (Map p428) to pier 5 of Outlying Islands ferry terminal in Central, Lantau (Chi Ma Wan and Mui Wo), Peng Chau, and Tsim Sha Tsui Star Ferry pier (weekend only).

spot from which to prey on passing ships. The infamous and powerful 18th-century pirate Cheung Po Tsai is said to have had his base here, and you can still visit the cave where he supposedly stashed his booty at the southwestern tip of the island.

Fishing and aquaculture are important industries for a large number of the island's inhabitants, some of whom still live on junks and sampans anchored in the harbour. Bring your camera for some of the best shots of traditional maritime life on the south China coast.

Cheung Chau boasts several interesting temples, the most important being Pak Tai Temple, which hosts the annual Bun Festival, *the* red-letter day on Cheung Chau (see the boxed text, p128). The island has a few worthwhile beaches, and there are some relatively easy walks, including the one described on p147.

Orientation

Cheung Chau is a bone-shaped island lying 10km southwest of Hong Kong Island and just off the Chi Ma Wan Peninsula on southeastern Lantau. Cheung Chau village, where the ferry docks, is the only real settlement on the island.

Information

There is a **HSBC** (☎ 2981 1127; 116 Praya St) branch southeast of the cargo pier, and an **ATM** (19A Pak She Praya Rd) north of the ferry pier. The **post office** (2A Tai Hing Tai St) is in the market complex. There is no transport on Cheung Chau, but you can rent bicycles from a **kiosk** (☎ 2981 0227) at the northern end of Praya St for $10/30 per hour/day and two-seat pedal bikes for $30/80.

BEACHES Map p428
Cheung Chau ferry

Tung Wan Beach, Cheung Chau's longest and most popular (though not its prettiest) beach lies at the end of Tung Wan Rd, due

GOING FOR THE BUNS

The annual **Cheung Chau Bun Festival** (*Tàai-pìng chìng jiu* in Cantonese; www.cheungchau.org), which honours the god Pak Tai and is unique to the island, takes place over eight days in late April or early May, traditionally starting on the sixth day of the fourth moon. It is a Taoist festival, and there are four days of religious observances.

The festival is renowned for its bun towers, bamboo scaffolding up to 20m high that are covered with sacred rolls. If you visit Cheung Chau a week or so before the festival, you'll see the towers being built in front of Pak Tai Temple.

In the past, hundreds of people would scramble up the towers at midnight on the designated day to grab one of the buns for good luck. The higher the bun, the greater the luck, so everyone tried to reach the top. In 1978 a tower collapsed under the weight of the climbers, injuring two dozen people. Now everyone must remain on terra firma and the buns are handed out.

Sunday, the third day of the festival, features a procession of floats, stilt walkers and people dressed as characters from Chinese legends and opera. Most interesting are the colourfully dressed 'floating children', who are carried through the streets on long poles, cleverly wired to metal supports hidden under their clothing. The supports include footrests and a padded seat.

Offerings are made to the spirits of all the fish and livestock killed and consumed over the previous year. A priest reads out a decree calling on the villagers to abstain from killing any animals during the four-day festival, and no meat is consumed.

east of the ferry pier. The best part of Tung Wan is the far southern end, which is a great area for windsurfing. Just south of Tung Wan Beach, Kwun Yam Wan Beach is known to English speakers as **Afternoon Beach** and is a great spot for windsurfing.

Windsurfing has always been an extremely popular pastime on Cheung Chau, and Hong Kong's only Olympic gold medal winner to date, Lee Lai-shan, who took the top prize in windsurfing at the 1996 Olympics in Atlanta, grew up here. At the northern end of Afternoon Beach, the **Cheung Chau Windsurfing Water Sports Centre** (☎ 2981 8316; 1 Hak Pai Rd; ☷ 10am-7pm) rents sailboards for between $60 and $120 per hour, as well as single/double kayaks for $50/80. Jet skis and water-skiing cost $600 per hour, banana boats $250/450 per half-/full hour. There are also windsurfing courses available for $550. The best time for windsurfing here is between October and December.

At the southeastern end of Afternoon Beach a footpath leads uphill past a **Kwun Yam temple**, which is dedicated to the goddess of mercy. Continue up the footpath and look for the sign to the Fa Peng Knoll. The concrete footpath takes you past quiet, tree-shrouded villas.

From the knoll you can walk down to signposted Don Bosco Rd; it leads due south to rocky **Nam Tam Wan** (also known as Morning Beach), where swimming is possible. If you ignore Don Bosco Rd and continue walking west you'll come to the intersection of Peak and Kwun Yam Wan

Rds. Kwun Yam Wan Rd and its extension, School Rd, will take you back to Cheung Chau village.

Peak Rd is the main route to the island's cemetery in the southwestern part of the island; you'll pass several pavilions along the way built for coffin bearers making the hilly climb. Once at the cemetery it's worth dropping down to **Pak Tso Wan** (Italian Beach), a sandy, isolated spot that is good for swimming. At this point Peak Rd West becomes Tsan Tuen Rd, which continues north to Sai Wan.

CHEUNG CHAU TYPHOON SHELTER
Map p428
Cheung Chau ferry
Only the typhoon shelter at Aberdeen (p87) is larger than this one. Chartering a sampan for half an hour costs between $50 and $80, depending on the day, the season and the demand. Most sampans congregate around the cargo pier, but virtually any small boat you see in the harbour can be hired as a water taxi. Just wave and two or three will come forward. Be sure to agree on the fare first.

CHEUNG CHAU VILLAGE Map p428
Cheung Chau ferry
The island's main settlement lies along the narrow strip of land connecting the headlands to the north and the south. The waterfront is a bustling place and the maze of streets and alleyways that make up the village are filled with tumble-down shops

selling everything from plastic buckets to hell money as well as old Chinese-style houses. The streets close to the waterfront are pungent with the smell of incense and fish hung out to dry in the sun.

CHEUNG PO TSAI CAVE Map p428
Cheung Chau ferry

This cave, on the southwestern peninsula of the island, is said to have been the favourite hiding place of the notorious pirate Cheung Po Tsai, who once commanded a flotilla of 600 junks and had a private army of 4000 men. He surrendered to the Qing government in 1810 and became an official himself, but his treasure is said to remain hidden here.

It's a 2km walk from Cheung Chau village along Sai Wan Rd, or take a *kaido* (adult/child $3/2) from the cargo ferry pier to the pier at Sai Wan. From here the walk is less than 200m (but uphill).

PAK TAI TEMPLE Map p428
☎ 2981 0663; Pak She Fourth Lane; ◷ 9am-5pm; **Cheung Chau ferry**

This colourful and recently renovated temple from 1783 is the oldest on the island and is the focus of the annual **Cheung Chau Bun Festival** (opposite) in late April or early May. It is dedicated to the Taoist deity Pak Tai, the 'Supreme Emperor of the Dark Heaven', military protector of the state, guardian of peace and order and protector of fisherfolk. Legend tells that early settlers from Guangdong province brought an image of Pak Tai with them to Cheung Chau and, when the statue was carried through the village, Cheung Chau was spared the plague that had decimated the populations of nearby islands. A temple dedicated to the saviour was built six years later.

TIN HAU TEMPLES Map p428
Cheung Chau ferry

Cheung Chau has four temples dedicated to Tin Hau, the empress of heaven and patroness of seafarers. **Pak She Tin Hau Temple** lies 100m northwest of the Pak Tai Temple. **Nam Tan Wan Tin Hau temple** is just north of Morning Beach; **Tai Shek Hau Tin Hau temple** is to the west on Sai Wan Rd. **Sai Wan Tin Hau temple** is west of Sai Wan (Western Bay), on the southwestern tip of the island. You can walk there or catch a *kaido* from the cargo pier.

LANTAU
Eating p193; Sleeping p272

Lantau (Map p427) is a Cantonese word that means 'broken head', but Chinese call Hong Kong's largest island Tai Yue Shan (Big Island Mountain), a name that refers both to its size and elevation. At 144 sq km, Lantau is almost twice the size of Hong Kong Island, and its highest point, Lantau Peak (Fung Wong Shan; 934m), almost double the height of Victoria Peak.

A total of 88,000 people live on Lantau, compared with Hong Kong Island's 1.5 million. They are concentrated in a couple of centres along the south coast, because the interior is so mountainous, though 28,000 have moved into the high-rises of Tung Chung opposite the airport at Chek Lap Kok since 1997, and Discovery Bay on the northeast coast supports 16,000 people. Not everyone on Lantau resides here of their own accord; the island is home to three prisons.

Rock carvings discovered at Shek Pik on the southwestern coast of Lantau suggest that the island was inhabited as early as the Bronze Age 3000 years ago, well before the arrival of the Han Chinese; a stone circle uncovered at Fan Lau may date from Neolithic times. The last Song dynasty emperor passed through here in the 13th century while fleeing the Mongol invaders. He is believed to have held court in the Tung Chung Valley to the north, which takes its name from a local hero who gave up his life for the emperor. Tung Chung is still worshipped by the Hakka people of Lantau, who believe he can predict the future.

Like Cheung Chau, Lantau was once a base for pirates and smugglers, and it was one of the favourite haunts of Cheung Po Tsai. The island was also an important trading post for the British long before they showed any interest in Hong Kong Island.

Lantau is an excellent island on which to escape from the city. More than half of the surface area – 78.5 sq km, in fact – is designated country park and there are several superb mountain trails, including the 70km Lantau Trail, which passes over both Lantau Peak and Sunset Peak (869m); some interesting traditional villages such as Tai O on the west coast; several important religious retreats, including the Po Lin Monastery and the adjacent Tian Tan Buddha, the largest outdoor Buddha statue in the world; and some excellent beaches including Cheung Sha, the longest in Hong Kong.

Orientation

Lantau is the last inhabited island west of Hong Kong Island; next stop is Macau and the Zhuhai SEZ. Lantau has many villages, but the main settlements dot the southern coast. From east to west they are: Mui Wo, the 'capital' and where most of the ferries dock; Pui O and Tong Fuk along South Lantau Rd; and Tai O on the west coast. The New Town of Tung Chung is on the north coast and accessible from Mui Wo by buses that climb steep Tung Chung Rd. Discovery Bay, a self-contained 'bedroom community' to the northeast, can be reached from Mui Wo by ferry.

Until the Lantau Link, the combined road and rail transport connection between Kowloon and Lantau, opened in 1997, the island was accessible only by ferry. That's still the most popular and enjoyable way to go, but today you can reach the island from the rest of the territory by MTR, the Airport Express, a fleet of buses and even by taxi.

Information

The **Country & Marine Parks Authority** (Map p429; ☎ 2984 1066; ☒ 8.30am-noon Mon-Fri, 8.30am-4.30pm Sat & Sun) maintains an information kiosk to the left as you leave the main ferry pier at Mui Wo. **HSBC** (Map p429; ☎ 2984 8271; Mui Wo Ferry Pier Rd) has a branch in Mui Wo and there's an **HSBC ATM** (Tai O Market St) in Tai O, which you'll see as you cross the footbridge from the mainland to the island. The main **post office** (Map p429; Ngan Kwong Wan Rd)

is a short distance west of the footbridge crossing the Silver River in Mui Wo.

Bicycles are available for hire ($10 per hour and $25 per day including overnight) at two central locations a short distance from the ferry pier in Mui Wo: **Friendly Bicycle Shop** (☎ 2984 2278; Ground fl, Shop 12, Mui Wo Centre, 1 Ngan Wan Rd; ☒ 10am-8pm Wed-Mon), just opposite Wellcome supermarket, and **Bike Shop** (☎ 2984 2002; Ground fl, Shop B, Silver Centre, 10 Mui Wo Ferry Pier Rd; ☒ 10am-9pm). They can also be hired from two **bike kiosks** (☎ 2984 7500, 2984 8232) near the Silvermine Beach Hotel in Mui Wo and from several in Pui O village.

The **Lantau Explorer Pass** (☎ 2984 8255; $150) includes return transportation between Central and Mui Wo and a tour of Lantau, with three stops: Cheung Sha Beach (15 minutes), Ngong Ping and Tian Tan Buddha (two hours) and Tai O village (one hour). The Lantau Explorer Bus departs from Mui Wo at 11.45am Monday to Saturday, returning to Mui Wo at 4.30pm. On Sunday and public holidays departure and return times are noon and 4.40pm. Tickets are available from the **New World First Ferry Services Customer Service Centre** (p293) at pier 6 of the Outlying Islands ferry terminal and any HKTB centre.

CHI MA WAN Map p427
Inter-island ferry

Chi Ma Wan, the large peninsula south of Mui Wo that can be reached via the inter-island ferry from Mui Wo and Cheung Chau, is a relatively remote part of Lantau and an

---

TRANSPORT

Ferry Mui Wo pier (Map p429) to pier 6 of Outlying Islands ferry terminal in Central, Cheung Chau (via Chi Ma Wan) and Peng Chau, Tsim Sha Tsui Star Ferry pier (weekend only), and Discovery Bay; Chi Ma Wan pier to Mui Wo and Cheung Chau; Tai O pier to Tuen Mun (via Sha Lo Wan and Tung Chung); Tung Chung New Development pier to Tuen Mun.

Bus Mui Wo bus terminal (Map p429) for buses 1 and N1 (overnight) to Pui O, Cheung Sha, Tong Fuk, Shek Pik, Lung Tsai Ng Garden and Tai O, bus 2 to Shek Pik and Ngong Ping, bus 3M to Tung Chung, bus 4 to Pui O, Cheung Sha and Tong Fuk, bus 7P (Sat afternoon and Sun) to Pui O, and buses A35 and N35 to airport; Tai O (Map p427) for bus 11 to Lung Tsai Ng Garden and Tung Ching, and bus 21 to Lung Tsai Ng Garden and Ngong Ping; Tung Chung MTR station (Map p427) for bus 3M to Mui Wo, bus 11 to Tai O, and bus 23 to Ngong Ping.

Taxi Telephone the call service on ☎ 2984 1328 or 2984 1368. Sample fares to Ngong Ping and the Tian Tan Buddha from Mui Wo and Tung Chung/Tai O/Hong Kong International Airport are $125/45/145.

MTR Tung Chung station (Map p427).

Airport Airport station (Map p427) at Chek Lap Kok.

excellent area for hiking; just be sure to get a map (p316) as the trails are not always clearly defined or well marked.

The Chi Ma Wan ferry pier is on the northeast coast; the large complex just south of the pier is not a hostel but the **Chi Ma Wan Correctional Institution**. There's a decent beach to the south at **Tai Long Wan**. There's budget accommodation at the **Jockey Club Mong Tung Wan Hostel** (p272) on the peninsula's southwestern coast.

DISCOVERY BAY Map p427
Discovery Bay ferry
Lying on the northeastern coast of Lantau, what locals have dubbed 'DB' is very much a world of its own, a bedroom community for professionals who commute to Central. Discovery Bay (Yue Ging Wan in Cantonese) has a fine stretch of sandy beach ringed by high-rises and more luxurious condominiums clinging to the headland to the north – but there is no pressing need to visit except to ogle at residents in their converted golf carts that cost $200,000 a pop. There is a handful of decent restaurants in **Discovery Bay Plaza** just up from the ferry pier and the central plaza and the 27-hole **Discovery Bay Golf Club** (p219) perched in the hills to the southwest.

Until recently Discovery Bay existed in splendid isolation, linked only to the outside by ferries from Central, Lantau and Peng Chau and all but inaccessible from the rest of Lantau even on foot. Now buses make the run to and from Tung Chung and the airport at Chek Lap Kok via the **Discovery Bay Tunnel** and the North Lantau Hwy. A trail leading from the golf course will take you down to Silvermine Bay and the rest of Lantau in a couple of hours.

FAN LAU Map p427
Fan Lau (Divided Flow), a small peninsula on the southwestern tip of Lantau, has a couple of good beaches and the remains of **Fan Lau Fort**, built in 1729 to protect the channel between Lantau and the Pearl River estuary from pirates. It remained in operation until the end of the 19th century and was restored in 1985. The sea views from here are sterling.

To the southeast of the fort is an ancient **stone circle**. The origins and age of the circle are uncertain, but it probably dates from the Neolithic or early Bronze Age and may have been used in rituals.

Signpost for Lantau Trail (below), Lantau

The only way to reach Fan Lau is on foot. To get here from Tai O, walk south from the bus station for 250m and pick up stage No 7 of the coastal **Lantau Trail**, a distance of about 8km. The trail then carries on to the northeast and Shek Pik for another 12km, where you can catch bus 1 back to Mui Wo.

HONG KONG DISNEYLAND Map p427
☎ 1-830 830; www.hongkongdisneyland.com; adult/senior over 65/child 3-11 Mon-Fri $295/170/210, Sat, Sun & holidays $350/250/200; ☻ 10am-9pm Apr-Oct, 10am-7pm Nov-Mar
This 126-hectare theme park overlooking Penny's Bay northeast of Discovery Bay opened in late 2005 after six years of planning and construction. Some 5.6 million visitors a year are expected to visit the four 'lands' (Fantasyland, Adventureland, Tomorrowland and Main Street, USA) and there are two large hotels counting 2100 rooms. The park is linked by rail with the MTR at the new futuristic Sunny Bay station on the Tung Chung line; passengers just cross the platform to board the dedicated train for Disneyland Resort station and the theme park. Journey times from Central/Kowloon/Tsing Yi stations will be 10/21/24 minutes.

LANTAU PEAK Map p427

Known as Fung Wong Shan (Phoenix Mountain) in Cantonese, this 934m-high peak is the second-highest in Hong Kong after Tai Mo Shan (957m) in the New Territories. The views from the summit are absolutely stunning, and on a clear day it is possible to see Macau, and Zhuhai, some 65km to the west.

If you're hiking the length or the first several stages of the **Lantau Trail** (p220) to Ngong Ping, you'll cross the peak. If you want to just climb up from Ngong Ping, the easiest and most comfortable way to make the climb is to spend the night at the SG Davis Hostel, get up at the crack of dawn and pick up the signposted trail at the hostel that runs southeast to the peak. Many climbers get up earlier to reach the summit for sunrise; take a torch and wear an extra layer of clothes, as it can get pretty chilly at the top in the early hours, even in summer.

Another signposted trail leading east from the hostel will take you along the northern slopes of Lantau Peak to **Po Lam Monastery** at Tei Tong Tsai and then south through a valley leading to Tung Chung, from where you can catch the MTR back to Kowloon or Hong Kong or bus 3M to Mui Wo. This charming walk – if you ignore the airport to the north – also takes you past **Lo Hon Monastery** as well as **Tung Chung Fort** (p135) and **Tung Chung Battery** (p135).

LUNG TSAI NG GARDEN Map p427
Bus 1 from Mui Wo, bus 11 from Tung Chung, bus 21 from Ngong Ping

This magical garden southwest of Ngong Ping, with a lotus pond crossed by a rickety **zigzag bridge**, was built by a wealthy merchant in the 1930s in a small valley near where the village of Lung Tsai once stood. The site is rather derelict, but atmospheric nonetheless and the gardens are in excellent condition. You can reach here via a water catchment path and trail from the Tai O Rd, a continuation of South Lantau Rd just west of Keung Shan. Alight from the bus after the Kwun Yam temple on Tai O Rd, which is about 2km past the turnoff for the Tian Tan Buddha. You'll see a country park sign and the start of the water catchment.

MUI WO Map p429
Lantau ferry
Mui Wo (Plum Nest), Lantau's main settlement 'capital', is on Silvermine Bay, so

named for the silver mines that were once worked to the northwest along the Silver River. In fact, many foreign residents refer to Mui Wo as Silvermine Bay.

About a third of Lantau's population lives in the township of Mui Wo and its surrounding hamlets. There are several decent places to stay here and though the options for eating and drinking are few, they are fine.

Silvermine Bay Beach, to the northwest of Mui Wo, has been cleaned up and rebuilt in recent years and is now an attractive place, with scenic views and opportunities for walking in the hills above. There's a complex with toilets, showers and changing rooms open from April to October.

If you have the time, consider hiking out to **Silvermine Waterfall**, the main feature of a picturesque garden near the old **Silvermine Cave** northwest of the town. The waterfall is quite a spectacle during the rainy season, when it swells and gushes; the cave was mined for silver in the latter half of the 19th century but has now been sealed off.

En route to the waterfall you'll pass the local **Man Mo temple**, originally built during the reign of Emperor Shen Zong (1573–1620) of the Ming dynasty and renovated a couple of times in the last century.

You can reach the temple, cave and water-fall by walking west along Mui Wo Rural Committee Rd and then following the marked path north. The 3km walk should take about an hour.

There are several old granite watchtowers in the area, including **Luk Tei Tong Watchtower** on the Silver River and **Butterfly Hill Watchtower** further north. They were built in the late 19th century as safe houses and as coastal defences against pirates.

NGONG PING Map p427
Bus 2 from Mui Wo, bus 21 from Tai O, bus 23 from Tung Chung
Perched 500m up in the western hills of Lantau is the Ngong Ping Plateau, a major drawcard for Hong Kong day-trippers and foreign visitors alike, especially since 1993, when one of the world's largest statues of Buddha was unveiled here.

Po Lin (Precious Lotus; ☺ 6am-6pm) is a huge Buddhist monastery and temple complex that was originally built in 1924. Today it is a fairground as much as a religious retreat, attracting many visitors. Most of the buildings you'll see on arrival are new, with the older, simpler ones tucked away behind them. The 5.7km **Ngong Ping 360** (www.np360.com.hk; adult/child 3-11/senior & student one way $58/28/45, return $88/45/68; ☺ 10am-6pm Mon-Fri, 10am-6.30pm Sat & Sun, 9am-6.30pm certain holidays), a cable car linking Ngong Ping with the centre of Tung Chung (downhill and to the north) was scheduled to open in early 2006. The lower station is just opposite the Tung Chung MTR station; the upper station is at the new 1.5-hectare **Ngong Ping Village** just west of the monastery complex and includes several themed attractions: Walking with Buddha and the Monkey's Tale Theatre, both of which cost $35/18/28 for adults/children aged three to 11/students & seniors, and the Ngong Ping Tea House. The journey takes 20 to 25 minutes, each glassed-in gondola carries 17 passengers and the system can move up to 3500 people per hour.

On a hill above the monastery sits the **Tian Tan Buddha** (☺ 10am-6pm), a seated representation of Lord Gautama some 23m high (or 26.4m with the lotus or just under 34m if you include the podium). There are bigger Buddha statues elsewhere – notably the 71m-high Grand Buddha at Leshan in China's Sichuan province – but apparently these are not seated, outdoors or made of bronze. It weighs 202 tonnes, by the way.

The large bell within the Buddha is controlled by computer and rings 108 times during the day to symbolise escape from what Buddhism terms the '108 troubles of mankind'.

The podium is composed of separate chambers on three different levels. In the first level are six statues of Bodhisattvas, each of which weighs around two tonnes. On the second level is a small **museum** (☎ 2985 5248; admission $23 without meal ticket; ☺ 10am-6pm) containing oil paintings and ceramic plaques of the Buddha's life and teachings. Entry is free if you eat at the monastery's vegetarian restaurant, **Po Lin Vegetarian Restaurant** (p195).

It's well worth climbing the 260 steps for a closer look at the statue and surrounding views. The Buddha's Birthday (p11), a public holiday celebrated in late April or early May, is a lively time to visit, when thousands make the pilgrimage. Visitors are requested to observe some decorum in dress and behaviour. It is forbidden to bring meat or alcohol into the grounds.

A 2.5km concrete footpath to the left of the Buddha statue leads to the **Lantau Tea Garden**, the only one in Hong Kong. The tea bushes are pretty sparse and not worth a detour, but the garden is on the way to the **Hongkong Bank Foundation SG Davis Hostel** (p272) and Lantau Peak and there are tea leaves for sale.

SEEING PINK DOLPHINS

Between 100 and 200 misnamed Chinese white dolphins *(Sousa chinensis)* – they are actually bubble-gum pink – inhabit the coastal waters around Hong Kong, finding the brackish waters of the Pearl River estuary to be the perfect habitat. Unfortunately these glorious mammals, which are also called Indo-Pacific humpback dolphins, are being threatened by environmental pollution, and their numbers are dwindling.

The threat comes in many forms, but the most prevalent – and direct – dangers are sewage, chemicals, over-fishing and boat traffic. Some 200,000 cu metres of untreated sewage are dumped into the western harbour every day, and high concentrations of chemicals such as DDT have been found in tissue samples taken from some of the dolphins. Several dead dolphins have been entangled in fishing nets and, despite the dolphins' skill at sensing and avoiding surface vessels, some have collided with boats.

The dolphins' habitat has also been diminished by the erosion of the natural coastline of Lantau Island during the construction of Hong Kong International Airport, which required land reclamation of 9.5 sq km of seabed and the destruction of many kilometres of natural coastline. The North Lantau Hwy also consumed about 10km of the natural coastline. The Hong Kong Disneyland theme park has also required large amounts of reclamation in Penny's Bay.

Hong Kong Dolphinwatch (☎ 2984 1414; www.hkdolphinwatch.com; 15th fl, Middle Block, 1528A Star House, 3 Salisbury Rd, Tsim Sha Tsui) was founded in 1995 to raise awareness of these wonderful creatures and promote responsible ecotourism. It offers 2½-hour cruises (adult/child under 12/student & senior $320/160/225) to see the pink dolphins in their natural habitat every Wednesday, Friday and Sunday year-round. Guides assemble in the lobbies of the Mandarin Oriental in Central at 8.30am and the Kowloon Hotel in Tsim Sha Tsui at 9am for the bus to Tung Chung via the Tsing Ma Bridge, from where the boat departs; the tours return at 1pm or 1.30pm. About 97% of the cruises result in the sighting of at least one dolphin; if none is spotted, passengers are offered a free trip.

SOUTH LANTAU ROAD Map p427
Bus 1 from Mui Wo & Tai O, bus 2 from Ngong Ping, bus 3 from Tung Chung

Just under 5km southwest of Mui Wo, **Pui O** is the first of several coastal villages along South Lantau Rd. Pui O has a decent beach, but as it's the closest one to Mui Wo it can get very crowded. The village has several restaurants, holiday flats galore and, in season, stalls renting bicycles. There's also a decent restaurant right on Pui O Beach called **Ooh La La!** (p195).

Cheung Sha (Long Sand), at over 3km Hong Kong's longest beach, is divided into 'upper' and 'lower' sections; a trail over a hillock links the two. **Upper Cheung Sha**, with occasional good surf, is the prettier and longer stretch and boasts a modern complex with changing rooms, toilets, showers and a snack bar. **Lower Cheung Sha** village has a beachfront restaurant, **Stoep Restaurant** (p195). **Long Coast Seasports** (☎ 2980 3222; www.longcoast.hk; 29 Lower Cheung Sha Village; ☺ 10am-7pm) is a water-sports centre offering windsurfing, sea kayaking and wakeboarding. Prices vary widely but windsurfing costs from $70/190/280 per hour/half-day/day Monday to Saturday and $90/240/360 on Sunday, while a single kayak rents for $60 for two hours in the week and $60/180 per hour/half-day on Sunday. Some claim because of the Ventura effect on the wind from Tung Chung this is the best windsurfing in Hong Kong, especially from November to March. Long Coast also offers basic accommodation (p272).

The beach at **Tong Fuk**, the next village over from Cheung Sha, is not as nice, but the village has holiday flats, several shops and a popular roadside barbecue restaurant called **Gallery** (p195). To the northwest is the not-so-scenic sprawl of Ma Po Ping Prison.

West of Tong Fuk, South Lantau Rd begins to climb the hills inland before crossing an enormous dam holding back the **Shek Pik Reservoir** (completed in 1963), which provides Lantau, Cheung Chau and parts of Hong Kong Island with drinking water. Just below the dam is the grand-daddy of Lantau's trio of jails, **Shek Pik Prison**. Below the dam to the south but before the prison is another Bronze Age **rock carving** unusual in that it is so far from the coastline.

The trail along the water-catchment area just east of Shek Pik Reservoir, with picnic tables and barbecue pits, offers some of the easiest and most peaceful walking on Lantau. From here you can also pick up the switchback trail to **Dog's Tooth Peak** (539m) from where another trail heads north to Lantau Peak.

TAI O Map p427
Bus 1 from Mui Wo, bus 11 from Tung Chung, bus 21 from Ngong Ping

A century ago this mostly Tanka village on the west coast of Lantau was an important trading and fishing port, exporting salt and fish to China. As recently as the 1980s it traded in IIs (illegal immigrants) brought from China under cover of darkness by 'snakeheads' (smugglers in human cargo) in long narrow boats, sending back contraband such as refrigerators, radios and televisions to the mainland.

Today Tai O is in decline, except perhaps as a tourist destination. A few of the salt-pans still exist, but most have been filled in to build high-rise housing. Older people still make their living from duck farming, fishing, making the village's celebrated shrimp paste and processing salt fish, which you'll see (and smell) everywhere. It remains a popular place for locals to buy seafood – both fresh and dried.

Tai O is built partly on Lantau and partly on a tiny island about 15m from the shore. Until the mid-1990s the only way to cross was via a **rope-tow ferry** pulled by elderly Hakka women. That and the large number of sampans in the small harbour earned Tai O the nickname 'the Venice of Hong Kong'. Though the narrow iron Tai Chung footbridge now spans the canal, the rope-tow ferry is resurrected on some weekends and holidays; drop $1 in the box as you disembark. There are also brief **river boat tours** (☎ 9629 4581, 9645 6652; per 15/25 mins $10/20) departing from the footbridge.

Some of the traditional-style village houses still stand in the centre. A fire in 2000 destroyed many of Tai O's famed **stilt houses** on the waterfront, but when the government tried to raze the rest and relocate residents elsewhere, the move was strongly opposed. The few houses that escaped the fire remain. There are also a number of shanties, their corrugated iron walls held in place by rope, and houseboats that haven't set sail for years – they'd capsize immediately if they tried.

The stilt houses and the local **Kwan Tai temple** dedicated to the god of war are on Kat Hing St. To reach them, cross the bridge from the mainland to the island, walk up Tai O Market St and go right at the Fook Moon Lam restaurant. There are a couple of other temples here, including an 18th-century one erected in honour of Hung Shing, patron of fisherfolk; it's on Shek Tsai Po St, about 600m west of the Fook Lam Moon restaurant.

TRAPPIST MONASTERY Map p427
☎ 2987 6292, 2914 2933; Tai Shui Hang; **kaido from Peng Chau**

Northeast of Mui Wo and south of Discovery Bay at Tai Shui Hang is the Roman Catholic Lady of Joy Abbey – better known as the Trappist Monastery. The monastery is known throughout Hong Kong for its cream-rich milk, sold in half-pint bottles everywhere, but, alas, the cows have been moved to the New Territories and Trappist Dairy Milk now comes from over the border in China.

The Trappists, a branch of the Cistercian order, were founded by a converted courtier at La Trappe in France in 1662 and gained a reputation as being one of the most austere religious communities in the Roman Catholic Church. The Lantau congregation was established at Beijing in the 19th century. All of the monks here now are local Chinese.

Trappist monks take a vow of absolute silence, and there are signs reminding visitors to keep radios and music players turned off and to speak in low tones. Give the guys a break; they're up at 3.15am and in bed by 8pm.

You can reach the monastery on foot by following a well-marked coastal trail from the northern end of Tung Wan Tau Rd in Mui Wo, but it's much easier to get here by *kaido* from Peng Chau, Lantau's little island neighbour to the west. For details see p292.

TUNG CHUNG Map p427
Tung Chung MTR, bus 3 from Mui Wo

In recent years change has come to Tung Chung on Lantau's northern coast at a pace that can only happen in Hong Kong. This previously all-but-inaccessible farming region, with the small village of Tung Chung at its centre, has seen Chek Lap Kok, the mountain across Tung Chung Bay, flattened to build Hong Kong's international airport and a New Town served by the MTR rise up.

As part of the territory's plans to solve the housing crisis, Tung Chung New Town has now become a 760-hectare residential estate. The targeted population of Tung Chung and the neighbouring New Town of Tai Ho is an astonishing 330,000 by 2012.

These developments and transportation improvements have put an end to Tung Chung as a peaceful and secluded spot. But efforts have been made to protect **Tung Chung Old Village**. Buildings may rise no higher than three storeys and each floor can be no larger than 70 sq metres.

Annals record a settlement at Tung Chung as early as the Ming dynasty. There are several Buddhist establishments in the upper reaches of the valley, but the main attraction here is **Tung Chung Fort** (Tung Chung Rd; admission free; ⏱ 10am-5pm Wed-Mon), which dates back to 1832 when Chinese troops were garrisoned on Lantau. The Japanese briefly occupied the fort during WWII. Measuring 70m by 80m and enclosed by granite-block walls, it retains six of its muzzle-loading cannons pointing out to sea.

About 1km to the north are the ruins of **Tung Chung Battery**, which is a much smaller fort built in 1817. All that remains is an L-shaped wall facing the sea, with a gun emplacement in the corner. The ruins were only discovered in 1980, having been hidden for about a century by scrub.

Facing Tung Chung Bay to the southwest in the village of Sha Tsui Tau is double-roofed **Hau Wong Temple**, founded at the end of the Song dynasty. The temple contains a bell dating from 1765 and inscribed by the Qing dynasty emperor, Qian Long.

PENG CHAU
Eating p195

Tiny Peng Chau (Map p429) is fairly flat and not especially beautiful, but it has its own charms. It is perhaps the most traditionally Chinese of the Outlying Islands, with narrow alleyways, crowded housing, a covered wet market near the ferry pier, a couple of small but interesting temples, interesting shops selling everything from Thai goods to New

Age products and everywhere the sound of mahjong tiles being slapped on tables. There are also a few closet-sized restaurants whose sea views have unfortunately been ruined by a massive concrete 'wave reflector' and promenade running along the shore south of the ferry pier.

Until recently the island's economy was supported by fishing and some cottage industries, notably the manufacture of porcelain, furniture and porcelain and metal tubing. These manufacturing industries are now all but dead, having moved to mainland China, though you will find a couple of porcelain and gift shops on Wing Hing St and Wing On St. There's a branch of **HSBC** (☎ 2983 0383; 1 Wing Hing St) nearby. The **post office** is due west near the start of the promenade.

Orientation

Looking not unlike a plumped-out horseshoe jettisoned from Lantau's northeast coast, Peng Chau is just under a square kilometre in area. It is inhabited by around 7000 people, making it far more densely populated than its larger neighbour.

SIGHTS & ACTIVITIES

There are no cars on Peng Chau, and you can walk around it easily in an hour. Climbing the steps up to **Finger Hill** (95m), the island's highest point and topped with the winged Chinese-style **Fung Ping Pavilion**, offers some light exercise and excellent views. To get to it from the ferry pier, walk up Lo Peng St, turn right at the **Tin Hau temple**, containing a century-old 2.5m-long whale bone blackened by incense smoke, and walk south along Wing On St. This gives way to Shing Ka Rd, and Nam Shan Rd leads from here east up to Finger Hill. The water at otherwise-pleasant **Tung Wan Beach**, a five-minute walk from the ferry pier, is too dirty for swimming and is not served by lifeguards.

MA WAN

Ma Wan (Maps pp404–5 & p427) was once famous as the gateway to Kowloon, where foreign ships would drop anchor before entering Chinese waters. If you want to get away from it all, Ma Wan is hardly the place to go. It's got a couple of temples devoted to Tin Hau, a long beach on the east coast at Tung Wan and a massive, high-end residential community called Park Island. Basically you're here to view some startling engineering feats.

Orientation

Ma Wan is a flat, rapidly developing island off the northeastern tip of the Lantau. It is effectively the 'anchor' for the Lantau Link between Hong Kong's largest island and the New Territories.

LANTAU LINK BRIDGES

Maps pp404-5 & p427

Ma Wan ferry

The real reason to come to Ma Wan is to take in the enormity of Tsing Ma Bridge to the east (and, to a lesser extent, Kap Shui Mun Bridge on the western side), which forms the rail and road link connecting Lantau with the New Territories via Tsing Yi Island. While catapulting Ma Wan headlong into the next century, the bridge has guaranteed an end to the island's solitude; it now serves as a huge platform for the civil engineering works overhead. Neighbouring Tsing Yi has a special viewing platform for those particularly interested in really seeing the bridge up close (below).

TSING YI

Tsing Yi (Map pp404–5), disfigured by oil depots and extended by land reclamation, serves as a stepping stone for the gigantic Tsing Ma Bridge, at 1377m, the world's longest suspension bridge. Don't even think about visiting the beaches.

Lantau Link Bridge (opposite), Tsing Yi

Orientation

Tsing Yi is the large island to the east of Ma Wan on the MTR's Tung Chung and the Airport Express lines.

LANTAU LINK VISITORS CENTRE

Map pp404-5

☎ 2495 5825, 2495 7583; admission free;
⏰ 10am-5pm Mon, Tue, Thu & Fri, 10am-6.30pm Sat & Sun; Tsing Yi MTR & green minibus 308

The Lantau Link Visitors Centre and its viewing platform (admission free; ⏰ 7am-midnight Sun-Fri, 7am-1am Sat) is where you can take in the enormity of Tsing Yi Bridge and the Lantau Link, the combined road and rail transport connection between the New Territories and Lantau. The centre contains models, photographs and videos of the construction process – very much a crowd-pleaser for train spotters and the hard-hat brigade.

The visitors centre is in the northwest corner of Tsing Yi Island just to the south of Ting Kau Bridge. To reach it, take the MTR to Tsing Yi station and use exit No A1 and board minibus 308M in Maritime Sq, which will drop you off at the centre's car park.

TUNG LUNG CHAU

Standing guard at the eastern entrance to Victoria Harbour is the island of Tung Lung Chau (Map pp404–5), or 'East Dragon Island', whose position was once considered strategic enough for protection. According to the experts the island is Hong Kong's premier spot for rock climbing (p218).

Orientation

Tung Lung Chau lies to the south of the Clearwater Bay Peninsula across the narrow Fat Tong Mun channel. To the west is Shek O and Big Wave Bay on Hong Kong Island's

---

TRANSPORT

MTR Tsing Yi station (Map pp404–5).

Airport Express Tsing Yi station (Map pp404–5).

Bus Tsing Yi for bus A31 (Long Win) to Kwai Chung and Tsuen Wan MTR; $17; every 15 to 20 minutes from 6am to midnight.

Green minibus Tsing Yi MTR station (Map pp404–5) for bus 308M.

137

east coast. In addition, the northwest tip of the island boasts an important rock carving of what is generally thought to be a dragon. It is quite possibly the oldest such carving in the territory and it is certainly the largest, measuring 2.4m by 1.8m. The ferry pier is close by.

TUNG LUNG FORT Map pp404-5
Tung Lung Chau ferry

Tung Lung Fort, on the northeastern corner of the island, was built in the late 17th or early 18th century and was attacked a number of times by pirate bands before being abandoned in 1810. The fort once consisted of 15 guardhouses and was armed with eight cannons, but little of it remains today except for the outline of the exterior walls. There's an **information centre** (🕑 9am-4pm Wed-Mon) you can visit here.

PO TOI
Eating p196

Po Toi (Map pp404–5) is a solid favourite of weekend holiday-makers with their own seagoing transport. They frequent the seafood restaurants beyond the jetty at **Tai Wan**, the main settlement, in the island's southwest.

Orientation

Po Toi is the largest of a group of four or five islands – one is little more than a huge rock – off the southeastern coast of Hong Kong Island. Hong Kong's territorial border lies just 2km to the south.

SIGHTS & ACTIVITIES

There's some decent walking on Po Toi, a tiny **Tin Hau temple** across the bay from the pier, and, on the southern coast, rock formations that (supposedly) look like a palm tree, a tortoise and a monk, and some mysterious **rock carvings** resembling stylised animals and fish. You can see everything here in an hour.

Walking Tours

Hong Kong Island   140
Central 141
Sheung Wan 142

Kowloon   143
Yau Ma Tei & Mong Kok 143

New Territories   145
Ping Shan Heritage Trail 145
Lung Yeuk Tau Heritage Trail 146

Outlying Islands   147
Cheung Chau 147

Walking Tours

Although much of Hong Kong is best seen on foot, walking around isn't always easy, especially in the business and shopping districts of Central, Causeway and Tsim Sha Tsui. Watch your step – particularly in Wan Chai and Mong Kok, where the pavement is often a workshop – and persevere; you will be rewarded with a world of unique sights, sounds and smells.

Rural Hong Kong is a whole different matter, with the New Territories, the Outlying Islands and even Hong Kong Island itself offering some easy but outstanding nature-trail walks and more arduous hikes (p219).

The 80-page booklet *Hong Kong Walks* is published by the Hong Kong Tourism Board (HKTB). It details nine strolls and hikes in the territory, with three on Hong Kong Island, two in Kowloon, one in the New Territories and three on the Outlying Islands (Cheung Chau, Lamma and Lantau).

Shanghai Street, Tsim Sha Tsui (p89)

HONG KONG ISLAND

Hong Kong Island offers walkers two contrasting worlds: the glittering skyscrapers and colonial relics of Central and the traditional Chinese neighbourhood of Sheung Wan. If you're looking for views, try the 3.5km circuit around Victoria Peak (p76).

CENTRAL ESCALATOR: IT'S NO JOKE

One of Hong Kong's long-standing problems has been that while many people live in the Mid-Levels, the lower portion of the Peak, they work in the skyscraper jungle down below in Central. The roads are narrow and the walk is often more vertical than horizontal, making the journey home on foot a strenuous climb, especially in the humid months. The result has been a rush-hour nightmare of bumper-to-bumper taxis, minibuses and private cars.

Then someone came up with what is officially called the **Central-Mid-Levels Escalator and Walkway System** (☎ 2523 7488) but known simply as the 'Central Escalator' – one of Hong Kong's more unusual forms of transport. Basically, it consists of three moving walkways and 20 elevated escalators that can be reversed; they run down in the morning from 6am to 10am, and up from 10.20am till midnight every day. It's 800m long and runs from the Central Market on Des Voeux Rd, along Cochrane and Shelley Sts in Soho and up to Conduit Rd in the Mid-Levels. It is the longest escalator in the world.

When the government first announced plans to build the system in the late 1980s, many Hong Kong residents thought they were playing an April Fool's joke, particularly because one of the English-language TV stations had done just that several years before, with an announcement that all westbound pedestrian traffic in Central would have to walk on the left-hand side of the street and everyone going east would have to walk on the right-hand side. The Escalator finally opened in 1993, having run some 500% over budget, but no-one is complaining, much less laughing about it now. To judge from the rush-hour crowds – just under 50,000 people make the 20-minute journey every day – the Central Escalator has been a smashing success.

CENTRAL

Begin the walk at the **Star Ferry pier 1** (p291) in Central. With your back to the 2nd-class ferry entrance, Hong Kong's last few **rickshaws 2** (p303) in front of you and **Hong Kong City Hall 3** (p70) to your left, follow the underground walkway to Chater Rd and **Statue Square 4** (p72). Turn left and follow Chater Rd east, with the **Legislative Council Building 5** (p71) on your right and the **Cenotaph 6** (p73) on your left, to **Chater Garden 7** (p71). Walk southwest through the park and cross over Garden Rd to the **Bank of China Tower 8** (p69). Head east along Queen's Rd Central, walk under the flyover and then follow the path to the **Flagstaff House Museum of Tea Ware 9** (p80) in **Hong Kong Park 10** (p79). From here elevated walkways

www.lonelyplanet.com

Walking Tours   HONG KONG ISLAND

WALK FACTS

Start Star Ferry pier, Central
End Central MTR station (entrance/exit K)
Distance 2km
Time One hour
Fuel Stop Mix

west over Cotton Tree Dr, through Citybank Plaza, over Garden Rd and through **Cheung Kong Garden 11** (p70) lead you to **St John's Cathedral 12** (p72). Follow Battery Path past the **Former French Mission Building 13** (p69) to Ice House St. Cross over and walk right (east) along Queen's Rd Central. If you're hungry, **Mix 14** (p157), in the shopping mall of the Standard Chartered Bank building, is a good spot for sandwiches, salads and juices. Next door is the **Hongkong & Shanghai Bank building 15** (p70). Walk through the ground floor plaza to the two **bronze lions 16** (p70) guarding the exit to Des Voeux Rd Central, and follow this road briefly to the west. The closest Central MTR station entrance is then a short distance to the north along the pedestrian walkway between Statue Sq and Prince's Building.

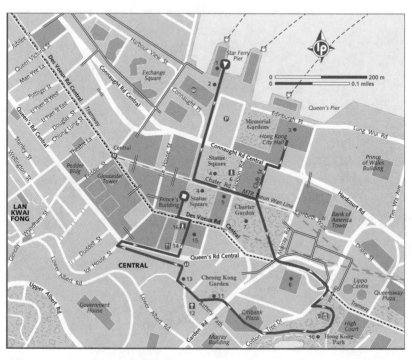

SHEUNG WAN

Begin the tour at the Sutherland St stop of the Kennedy Town tram. Have a look at (and a sniff of) Des Voeux Rd West's **dried seafood shops** 1, then walk south on Sutherland St to Ko Shing St, where there are **herbal medicine traders** 2. At the end of the street, walk northeast along Des Voeux Rd West and turn right into Connaught Rd West, where you'll find **Western Market** 3 (p75) at the corner of Morrison St. Walk south along this street past Wing Lok St and Bonham Strand, which are both lined with shops selling **ginseng root** and **edible birds' nests** 4, and turn right onto Queen's Rd Central. You'll pass **shops** 5 selling paper funeral offerings for the dead. Turn left into **Possession Street** 6

WALK FACTS

Start Kennedy Town tram (Sutherland St stop)
End Sheung Wan MTR station (entrance/exit B)
Distance 1.9km
Time One hour
Fuel Stop Korea Garden

(p74). Take a left into Hollywood Rd then right to ascend Pound Lane to where it meets Tai Ping Shan St. Here, look to the right to spot **Pak Sing Ancestral Hall** 7 (p74) and to the left to find **Kwun Yam Temple** 8 (p74). Turn left into Tai Ping Shan St, then left to descend Upper Station St to the start of Hollywood Rd's **antique shops** 9 (p230). Continuing east on Hollywood Rd brings you to **Man Mo Temple** 10 (p74). Take a short hop to the left down Ladder St to Upper Lascar Row, home of the **Cat Street Market** 11 (p74). Ladder St brings you back to Queen's Rd Central. Cross the road and follow Hillier St to Bonham Strand. On Bonham Strand, head east to **Man Wa Lane** 12 (p74), where you'll find traditional 'chops' (seals) carved. Due north is Des Voeux Rd Central and Connaught Rd Central, where you might have some soup noodles at **Korea House Restaurant** 13 (p162). The Sheung Wan MTR station is a block west of Korea House.

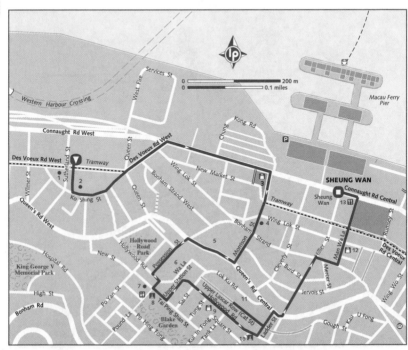

KOWLOON

Like Hong Kong Island, Kowloon offers several different types of walks but the most rewarding is though the workaday but colourful neighbourhoods of Mong Kok and Yau Ma Tei.

YAU MA TEI & MONG KOK

Follow exit A from Prince Edward MTR, walk north up Nathan Rd for 200m, then turn right onto Boundary St. The **Yuen Po Street Bird Garden** 1 (p95) is a 10-minute walk away. Continue out the back and turn right to the **Flower Market** 2 (p95), where some 50 florists sell blooms and plants daily. At the end of the street, turn left onto Sai Yee St, then right onto Prince Edward Rd West. At Tung Choi St turn left again: the first couple of blocks are dominated by bicycle shops and the **Goldfish Market** 3, with up to a dozen shops trading in the extravagantly hued creatures. South of Argyle St, the **Tung Choi Street market** 4 (p246), also known as

WALK FACTS

Start Prince Edward MTR station (entrance/exit A)
End Jordan MTR station (entrance/exit A)
Distance 4.5km
Time Two hours
Fuel Stop Kubrick Bookshop Café

the Ladies' Market, takes over. Turn right at Dundas St; **Trendy Zone** 5 (p232), with cool duds and accessories for guys and gals, is on the corner of Nathan Rd. Cross over and turn left into Shanghai St, where you'll find the **Shanghai Street Artspace** 6 (p28), with some

Jade Market (p94), Yau Ma Tei

Walking Tours

KOWLOON

143

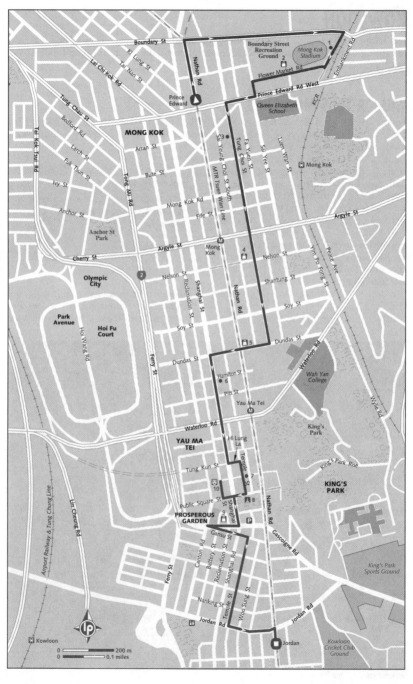

Boundary St

Boundary Street
Recreation
Ground

Mong Kok
Stadium

1

Flower Market Rd

2

KI Lung St

Lai Chi Kok Rd

Tai Nan St

Nathan Rd

Prince Edward Rd West

KCR

Prince
Edward

Queen Elizabeth
School

Tung Chau St

Bedford Rd

MONG KOK

Arran St

Bute St

Sai Yeung Choi St South

Tung Choi St

Fa Yuen St

Sai Yee St

Luen Wan St

Mong Kok

Tai Kok Tsui Rd

Larch St

Fuk Tsun St

Ivy St

Anchor St

Anchor St
Park

Tong Mi Rd

Mong Kok Rd

Fife St

MTR Tsuen Wan Line

Argyle St

Cherry St

Argyle St

Mong
Kok

4

Nelson St

Yim Po Fong St

Peace Ave

**Olympic
City**

2

Nelson St

Reclamation St

Shanghai St

Shantung St

Soy St

Nathan Rd

**Park
Avenue**

**Hoi Fu
Court**

Hoi Wang Rd

Soy St

Dundas St

5

Dundas St

Waterloo Rd

Wah Yan
College

Ferry St

Dundas St

Hamilton St

6

Pitt St

Yau Ma Tei

**King's
Park**

Waterloo Rd

**YAU MA
TEI**

Hi Lung La

King's Park Rise

Wylie Rd

Tung Kun St

Temple St

7

Nathan Rd

**KING'S
PARK**

Airport Railway & Tung Chung Line

Lin Cheung Rd

10

8

Public Square St

Shanghai St

**PROSPEROUS
GARDEN**

9

P

Gascoigne Rd

Gansu St

Canton Rd

Battery St

Reclamation St

Shanghai St

Ferry St

Nanking St

Temple St

Woo Sung St

Jordan Rd

Jordan Rd

Jordan Rd

Jordan

Kowloon Cricket Club
Ground

**King's Park
Sports Ground**

Kowloon

0   200 m
0   0.1 miles

cutting-edge exhibitions. Cut down Hi Lung Lane to Temple St and turn right; the **Temple Street night market 7** (p94) runs right down to Jordan Rd, divided by the **Tin Hau temple 8** (p95) and the **Jade Market 9** (p94). If you want to take a load off your feet, see what's showing at the **Broadway Cinematheque 10** (p214) or have something warm and/or sweet at the attached **Kubrick Bookshop Café** (p184). At Jordan Rd turn east, then south into Nathan Rd to find Jordan MTR station.

NEW TERRITORIES

For the most part the New Territories is about hiking – be it the manageable natural trails like the ones at Pat Sin Leng (p116) and Tai Po Kau (p117), or sections of the more strenuous MacLehose and Wilson trails (p219). There are also a couple of easy signposted walks – one which is just west of Yuen Long, and the other which is on the eastern edge of Fanling – that will take city slickers past

READ IT & WALK

Two walking guides with a different twist are Patricia Lim's *Discovering Hong Kong's Cultural Heritage: The New Territories*, with a dozen walks through traditional areas of the New Territories and lots of cultural information, and *Discovering Hong Kong's Cultural Heritage: Hong Kong and Kowloon*, which has a number of equally interesting but more urban walks.

some of Hong Kong's most important rural architecture – temples, study and ancestral halls, walled villages and the territory's only surviving pagoda. Not all the buildings on these two walks are open to the public.

PING SHAN HERITAGE TRAIL

Alight from the Light Rail at **Ping Shan station 1**, which is five stops to the west of the terminus at Yuen Long. Turn right (north) on Ping Hing St and then left (west) on Ping Ha Rd. The trail begins at the **Hung Shing Temple 2**, built in 1767 in honour of a Tang dynasty official who was later deified and is worshipped by traders and fisherfolk. Just to the west is the 1870 **Kun Ting Study Hall 3**, where the Tangs, the first of the 'Five Clans' to settle in Hong Kong, swotted for their imperial civil service exams during the Qing dynasty. **Ching Shu Hin 4**, the adjacent L-shaped structure, was built in the same year as a guesthouse for prominent visitors and scholars. A couple of hundred metres to the northeast is magnificent **Tang Ancestral Hall** (5; ☽ 9am-1pm & 2-5pm), which dates back 700 years, and the somewhat less impressive **Yu Kiu Ancestral Hall** (6; ☽ 9am-1pm & 2-5pm) next door, dating from the 16th century. They are of a similar design, with three halls and two internal courtyards, and they both retain many original features. The former's ridge tiles from Shiwan near Foshan in Guangdong province are particularly fine. To the northwest, set off on its own, is tiny **Yeung Hau Temple 7**, dedicated to the god Yau Wong, a Song dynasty general renowned for his bravery and loyalty. The trail meanders westward, past an **old well 8** dating back two centuries, and **Sheung Cheung Wai 9**, an inhabited walled village of narrow alleyways and minuscule houses. The trail then turns northwards and leads to **Tsui Sing Lau** (10; ☽ 9am-1pm, 2-5pm), a three-storey hexagonal pagoda of greenish brick built in 1486, and the only such structure in Hong Kong. Tin Shui Wai station on the KCR West Rail is opposite the pagoda. As you won't find much to eat along this short and snappy route, you might consider tucking into some dim sum or sushi at Yuen Long Plaza (p187) in Yuen Long before you set out.

WALK FACTS

Start Ping Shan station on Light Rail
End Tin Shui Wai station on KCR West Rail
Distance 1km
Time One to 1½ hours
Fuel Stop Yuen Long Plaza

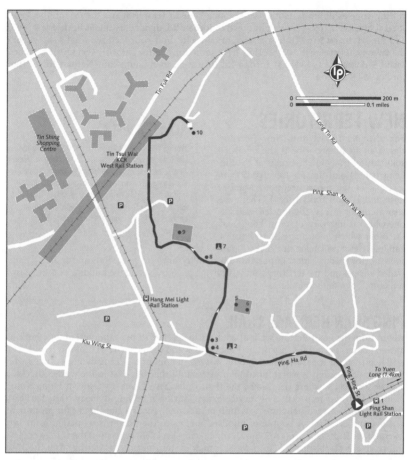

LUNG YEUK TAU HERITAGE TRAIL

Begin this walk along paved roads, which takes in six *wài,* or walled villages, at the end of Lok Tung St in Fanling; it's about a kilometre northeast of the KCR station. Shortly after the start of the trail, you can't help noticing an enormous (and abandoned) two-storey mansion set off in an overgrown lawn to the right. It's called **Shek Lo** 1 and was built in a curious mixture of Western and Chinese architectural styles by a wealthy mainland Chinese in 1924. The first real port of call, though, about 200m to the northeast, is the entrance tower of **Mat Wat Wai** 2, built in the mid-18th century. Another couple of hundred metres to the southeast are the impressive brick enclosing walls of **Lo Wai** (3; ☺ 9am-5pm). Facing this tiny walled village to the east is a lovely **Tin Hau Temple** 4 with two 18th-century bells and the **Tang Chung Ling Ancestral Hall** (5; ☺ 9am-1pm & 2-5pm Wed-Mon),

WALK FACTS

Start Lok Tung St in Fanling (green minibus 54K from Fanling KCR station)
End Siu Hang Tsuen (green minibus 56K to Fanling KCR station)
Distance 4.5km
Time 2½ to three hours
Fuel Stop Fanling market

built in 1525 in honour of the founder of the Tang clan, and one of the largest such structures in the New Territories. The entire hall is richly decorated with fine wood carvings, colourful plaster mouldings and murals. Heading northwest over the next 800m you'll pass three more little villages – **Tung Kok Wai 6**, with an impressive tower; **Wing Ning Tsuen 7**, whose houses are at different heights for feng shui reasons; and **Wing Ning Wai 8** – before reaching **Sin Shut Study Hall 9**, built in 1840 and boasting some fine tiles. Two more walled villages, **San Wai 10** now containing mostly modern buildings, and **Siu Hang Tsuen 11**, where you can pick up the minibus back to the central Fanling. Lively Fanling market (p114), with any number of *daai-pàai-dawng* and noodle shops, is just over a kilometre northwest of the start of the trail.

OUTLYING ISLANDS

The Outlying Islands were made for walking. The best way to 'do' Lamma (p125) is to walk from Yung Shue Wan ferry pier to the one at Sok Kwu Wan. Lantau boasts the 70km Lantau Trail (p220), which is divided into a dozen manageable sections. A walk on Cheung Chau is the best option as it combines scenic beauty with interesting glimpses of traditional southern Chinese culture. To avoid the crowds, stay away at the weekend if possible.

CHEUNG CHAU

From the **Cheung Chau ferry pier 1** (p292) head north along Praya St, where a row of mostly **seafood restaurants 2** (p192) face the harbour. Praya St becomes Pak She Praya Rd after the turn-off for Kwok Man Rd, and from here you can look out at the many junks and sampans moored in the harbour and typhoon shelter. At Pak She Fourth Lane, turn right and immediately in front of you is the colourful **Pak Tai Temple 3** (p129), built in 1783. The **Pak She Tin Hau Temple 4** (p129) is behind, about 100m to the northwest. Leave the Pak Tai Temple behind you and head south down Pak She St. You'll pass a **traditional Chinese house 5** at No 4, with two stone lions on guard outside, several shops selling **traditional Chinese medicine** and **funerary objects 6** and a bakery at No 46, which has small Chinese cakes and buns. Further south, and on the left at the intersection of Pak She St and Kwok Man Rd, is a small **Tou Tei shrine 7**, dedicated to the overworked earth god. San Hing St, which leads off Pak She St after it crosses Kwok Man Rd, has **herbalist shops 8**, and the shops at No 4 and No 50 sell incense and paper hell money to be burned in memory of the dead. As you turn east from San Hing St and enter Tung Wan Rd, you'll see a **sacred banyan tree 9** on the right, which is believed to be inhabited by earth spirits. Tung Wan Rd leads up to the **Hometown Teahouse 10** (p192), where you might stop for a cuppa and a snack, and Tung Wan Beach. Turn right and walk along Cheung Chau

WALK FACTS

Start Cheung Chau ferry pier (ferry from pier 5 in Central)
End Sai Wan (*kaido* to Cheung Chau ferry pier)
Distance 4.5km
Time 2½ hours
Fuel Stop Hometown Teahouse

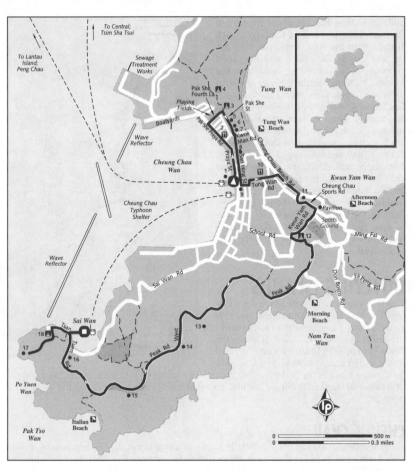

Beach Rd to the 3000-year-old **rock carving** 11 (p127) of two identical geometric designs, just below the Warwick Hotel. Behind the hotel is Cheung Chau Sports Rd; walk up and when you see a pavilion, turn right onto Kwun Yam Wan Rd and past the sports ground below and on your left. Straight on and to the left is the **Kwan Kung Pavilion** 12, a temple built in 1973 and dedicated to the god of war and righteousness, who is also known as Kwan Tai. As you walk down the temple's front steps, turn left onto Peak Rd. After about a kilometre you will pass the **Cheung Chau Meteorological Station** 13, which offers splendid views of the island and sea to the south. Further on is Chung Lok Garden, with its brightly painted stones, and the **Yee Pavilion** 14, which is dedicated to the Chinese poet Zhang Renshi. A bit further south and through the trees to the left is **Cheung Chau Cemetery** 15, affording a quiet and solemn view out to sea. Soon you'll come to a split in the path; the signposted trail to the left leads to Italian Beach, the one to the right carries on to Sai Wan. If you take the latter, you'll soon walk through Lui Kwan Puk, also known as **CARE Village** 16, a small settlement that was set up in 1968 with money from a North American charity. Further on is another signposted fork in the road where you can either turn left for **Cheung Po Tsai Cave** 17 (p129) and the **Sai Wan Tin Hau Temple** 18 (p129), or right for the *kaido* (adult/child HK$3/2) back to Cheung Chau village. Alternatively, follow Sai Wan Rd around the bay and north back to the village (20 to 30 minutes).

Hong Kong Island   151

Central 151
Soho 158
Sheung Wan & the Mid-Levels 161
The Peak 163
Admiralty & Wan Chai 164
Causeway Bay 169
Happy Valley 173
Island East 173
Island South 174

Kowloon   176

Tsim Sha Tsui 176
Tsim Sha Tsui East 183
Yau Ma Tei & Mong Kok 184
New Kowloon 185

New Territories   186

Tsuen Wan 186
Tuen Mun 187
Yuen Long 187
Tai Po & Surrounds 187
Sha Tin 188
Sai Kung 188
Tap Mun Chau 190

Outlying Islands   190

Lamma 190
Cheung Chau 192
Lantau 193
Peng Chau 195
Po Toi 196

Eating

Eating

Hong Kong does not live by dim sum, *chàa-siù-fán* (barbecued pork with rice) and/or *cháau-mìn* (fried noodles) alone, but Chinese food in its various incarnations is clearly what the territory does best (see p34). Still, the surfeit of other cuisines available at the territory's restaurants will have you spoiled for choice and begging for more.

The best source for travellers looking for more restaurant recommendations than we are able to make here is the annual *HK Magazine Restaurant Guide,* which reviews more than 300 eateries throughout the territory. It appears free as an insert in the **HK Magazine** (☎ 2850 5065; asiacity@asia-city.com.hk) sometime in March; extra copies cost $50 ($80 overseas). To order one, contact the magazine's editorial office.

Hong Kong's Best Restaurants, containing 150 rather tame reviews of top-end restaurants in Hong Kong and Macau, is published annually by **Hong Kong Tatler magazine** (www.hktatler.com). *The Guide: Hong Kong's Restaurant Guide* from **bc magazine** (www.bcmagazine.net) has somewhat more critical reviews of 300-plus Hong Kong restaurants in all price categories. Nicole Lade's *HK Cheap Eats,* now in its 2nd edition, lists some 250 restaurants, cafés and *dạai-pàai-dawng* (street stalls) where you should be able to get a meal for under $100.

The Hong Kong Tourism Board (HKTB) distributes an annual booklet called *Best of the Best Culinary Guide,* featuring award-winning local dishes and where to find them. Lonely Planet's *World Food Hong Kong,* while not a restaurant guide per se, will take you on an in-depth culinary tour of the territory.

Busy restaurant, Causeway Bay (p169)

Opening Hours

Restaurants generally open from 11.30am or noon to 2.30pm or 3pm for lunch, and from 6pm or 6.30pm to 11pm for dinner. There are many, many exceptions to this rule, of course. Some pubs' kitchens stay open until 1am, and Chinese noodle shops often run from the early morning until the very wee hours.

How Much?

While a bowl of noodles can cost as little as $10 and fried rice only $20, a proper lunch will set you back at least $60. Anything under $50 for a meal is truly cheap eating. At dinner, a meal for under $100 is budget, $100 to $250 is midrange, $250 to $400 is top end and anything over $400 is luxury.

Booking & Tipping

It's advisable to book ahead in all but the cheapest restaurants, especially on Friday and Saturday nights. Most restaurants add a 10% service charge. If the service was outstanding at an expensive restaurant (but never a cheap or midrange place), you might consider adding another 5% or even 10% on top of the service charge.

Self-Catering

Wellcome and Park 'N' Shop, the two major supermarket chains, have branches all over Hong Kong. City'super is a small chain of gourmet supermarkets with outlets at major malls. Open 24 hours are the ubiquitous 7-Eleven convenience stores; Circle K outlets also abound.

HONG KONG ISLAND

Catering facilities on Hong Kong Island run the gamut from Michelin-level restaurants in five-star hotels and Asian fusion enjoyed at pavement cafés, to an embarrassment of ethnic cuisines – from Indian and Mexican to Chiu Chow and Vietnamese – served in tiny little holes in the wall upstairs, downstairs or in some obscure chamber.

CENTRAL

Though there are many exceptions to the rule, Central is not always the best place to find authentic ethnic cuisine. However, Westernised versions of the same, along with some cutting-edge international and fusion food, are available in spades, especially in Lan Kwai Fong and at the top end of Wyndham St.

AL'S DINER Map p412   American, Deli
☎ 2521 8714; Ground fl, Shop F, 27-39 D'Aguilar St; mains $65-160; ☯ noon-2am Mon-Thu, noon-4am Fri & Sat, noon-2am Sun; Central MTR
A faithful copy of a 1950s chrome and glass American diner, Al's has the usual burgers fit for a giant (from $85 to $158), hot dogs with everything ($65 to $75), chilli con carne ($58), ribs and platters of French fries.

ASSAF Map p412   Lebanese
☎ 2851 6550; Shop B, Ground fl, Lyndhurst Bldg, 37 Lyndhurst Tce; starters $42-55, mains $130; ☯ noon-midnight; Central MTR
This welcoming and cosy place specialises in meze and other tasty titbits; the set dinners are a mixture of six to eight different items. The Assaf brothers also own the **Beyrouth Cafe Central** (Map p412; ☎ 2854 1872; ☯ noon-3am Sun-Thu, noon-6am Sat & Sun), a simple place that does takeaway. Salads, sandwiches, kebabs and meze here cost from $38 to $45. There are good-value set lunches ($68) and dinners (vegetarian/ meat $130/150) as well.

BEIRUT Map p412   Lebanese
☎ 2804 6611; Shop A, Ground fl, 27-39 D'Aguilar St; meze/starters $45-75, mains $95-165; ☯ noon-3pm & 6-11.30pm Mon-Sat, 6-11pm Sun; Central MTR
Beirut is an affable, slightly cramped restaurant that looks out onto Lan Kwai Fong and serves authentic Lebanese dishes like *kibbeh* (Lebanese meatballs) and *lahme bil agine* ('pizza' with minced lamb). Two-/three-course set lunches are $95/115.

BOMBAY DREAMS Map p412   Indian
☎ 2971 0001; 1st fl, Carfield Commercial Bldg, 75-77 Wyndham St; dishes $48-180; ☯ 12.30-2.30pm & 6.30-10.30pm Mon-Sat, noon-3.30pm & 6.30-10.30pm Sun; bus 26
This place is not as all-singin', all-dancin' as its Broadway namesake, but it's close to the pubs of Lan Kwai Fong and serves relatively authentic Indian fare in upmarket surrounds. There's a weekday/Sunday buffet for $98/128 and set dinners for $170 and $190.

CAFÉ Map pp408-9   Café
☎ 2522 0111; Ground fl, Mandarin Oriental, 5 Connaught Rd Central; mains $140-160; ☯ 6.30am-12.30am; Central MTR
Once known as the Mandarin Coffee Shop, this place helped change the face of what are called PPHR (popular-priced hotel restaurants) in the trade. The food is unswervingly excellent, the service always seamless. Sandwiches are $140 to $150, pasta $140 to $185.

FAMILIAR SIGNS

Signs for Café de Coral, Maxim's, Dai Pai Dong, Fairwood and Saint's Alp are familiar everywhere in Hong Kong. These are local fast-food joints where you can get decent Chinese and Western meals in a flash for little cash. Among the best places for sandwiches, soups, salads and baked goods are branches of the Oliver's Super Sandwiches and Délifrance chains. On virtually every corner of the territory and open 24 hours are 7-Eleven outlets – good places for drinks and snacks on the go.

CAFÉ DES ARTISTES Map p412   French

☎ 2526 3880; 1st fl, California Tower, 30-32 D'Aguilar St; starters $85-180, mains $185-295; ☺ noon-2.30pm & 7-10.30pm Mon-Thu, noon-2.30pm & 7-11pm Fri & Sat, 7-10.30pm Sun; Central MTR
This place serves award-winning French provincial food, and the chef introduces a new menu each season. The eatery seems to have grown up since it moved upstairs. Set lunches of two/three courses are $165/185.

CAFÉ SIAM Map p412   Thai

☎ 2851 4803; 40-42 Lyndhurst Tce; starters $52-88, rice & noodle dishes $62-78, mains $65-82; ☺ noon-2.30pm & 6-10.30pm Mon-Thu, noon-11.30pm Fri & Sat, noon-10pm Sun; Central MTR
Perhaps not the best or most authentic Thai restaurant in town, Café Siam serves generous-sized portions of old favourites like *tom ka gai* (coconut-based chicken), green curries and *gung kaprow* (prawns cooked with basil) to a crowd en passant between Soho and Lan Kwai Fong. Can't beat the location.

CHINA TEE CLUB Map pp408-9   International

☎ 2521 0233; Room 101, 1st fl, Pedder Bldg, 12 Pedder St; starters $60-75, mains $110-145; ☺ 11.30am-8pm Mon-Sat; Central MTR
This civilised tea house–cum-restaurant serving both Chinese and Western favourites is perfect for a meal or a cuppa after finishing your shopping at Shanghai Tang (p238) or Blanc de Chine (p233) below. Pasta and vegetarian dishes are $90 to $110.

CITY HALL MAXIM'S PALACE

Map pp408-9   Dim Sum

☎ 2521 1303; 3rd fl, Low Block, Hong Kong City Hall, 1 Edinburgh Pl; dim sum from per person $100; ☺ 11am-3pm & 5.30-11.30pm Mon-Sat, 9am-11.30pm Sun; Central MTR
If you want to experience real, live Hong Kong dim sum, with all its clatter and clutter, head for this place in city hall on a Saturday or Sunday morning.

FINDS Map p412   Scandinavian

☎ 2522 9318; 2nd fl, Lan Kwai Fong Tower, 33 Wyndham St; starters $75-135, mains $165-225; ☺ noon-2.30pm & 7-11pm; bus 26
This wonderful new place, whose name stands for – would you believe? – 'Finland',

---

TOP FIVE CENTRAL RESTAURANTS

- FINDS (left) – Scandinavian exotica in an 'icy' environment
- La Kasbah (opposite) – tasty *tajines* in Levantine caravanserai
- M at the Fringe (p154) – probably the best international restaurant in town
- Vong (p156) – fusion confusion (Southeast Asian and French) with a view
- Yung Kee Restaurant (p156) – have a gander at the best goose dishes in Hong Kong

---

'Iceland', 'Norway', 'Denmark' and 'Sweden', serves light and very tasty Scandinavian food. We love the *scapas* (Scandinavian tapas, for lack of a better term; $38 to $78), especially the tartare of Baltic herring and terrine of pork confit with leek. The surrounds – faux igloo walls, icicle-cum-chandelier, lots of blue tones – will have you thinking that global warming has worked in reverse in old Hong Kong. Good-value set lunch is $168/188 for two/three courses.

FRINGE CLUB Map p412   Vegetarian

☎ 2521 7251; 2nd fl, Dairy Farm Bldg, 2 Lower Albert Rd; set lunch $65; ☺ noon-2pm Mon-Fri; Central MTR
Vegetarians weighing their options in Central at lunch time during the week might try the Western vegetarian buffet available upstairs at the Fringe Club's Volkswagen *fotogalerie*.

GREENLANDS INDIA CLUB

Map p412   Indian

☎ 2522 6098; 1st fl, Yu Wing Bldg, 64-66 Wellington St; starters $38-128, mains $62-98; ☺ 11am-3pm & 6-11.30pm Mon-Sat, 6-11.30pm Sun; Central MTR
Greenlands' low prices and good food ensure that the place is always packed. The lunchtime buffet ($68) and the Friday evening one ($118) are particularly good value.

GUNGA DIN'S CLUB Map p412   Indian

☎ 2523 1439; Lower ground fl, 57-59 Wyndham St; starters $25-35, mains $60-110; ☺ 11.30am-2.30pm & 6-10.30pm Mon-Sat, 6-10.30pm Sun; bus 26
This curry house, which is almost an institution in Hong Kong, serves substantial if not sublime tiffin. It's popular with

long-term expats who remember when Indian food was scarce as hens' teeth in Hong Kong.

HABIBI Map pp408-9 Egyptian
☎ 2544 6198; Shop B & D, Ground fl, 112-114 Wellington St; meze/starters $45-75, mains $120-200; ☺ 11.30am-3pm & 6pm-midnight Mon-Fri, 6pm-midnight Sat; Central MTR

Whether or not Habibi serves strictly authentic Egyptian food is a moot point – the halal food is very good and the setting is the Cairo of the 1930s – all mirrors, tassels, velvet cushions, ceiling fans and hookahs. Set lunches are $80 to $100, set dinners $250 to $290. Habibi's casual and takeaway section, **Habibi Café** (Map pp408-9; ☎ 2544 3886; ☺ 11am-midnight) in Shop A next door is a lot cheaper, with meze from $25 to $40, meze platters $80 to $95, mains $80 to $130 and weekday set lunch $60.

HUNAN GARDEN Map pp408-9 Hunanese
☎ 2868 2880; 3rd fl, The Forum, Exchange Sq, Connaught Rd Central; meals $300 per person; ☺ 11.30am-3.30pm & 5.30-11.30pm; Central MTR

This elegant place specialises in spicy Hunanese cuisine, which is often hotter than the Sichuan variety. The Hunanese fried chicken with chilli is excellent, as are the seafood dishes. Views, overlooking the harbour or into the heart of Central, are a bonus.

INDOCHINE 1929 Map p412 Vietnamese
☎ 2869 7399; 2nd fl, California Tower, 30-32 D'Aguilar St; starters $58-98, mains $125-260; ☺ noon-2.30pm & 6.30-11pm Mon-Thu, noon-2.30pm & 6.30-11.30pm Fri & Sat; Central MTR

It's not cheap and the food quality may have dropped a notch or two over the years, but the colonial Vietnam setting still bewitches. Set lunches are $85 to $148, and set dinners $298 to $415.

IVAN THE KOZAK
Map p412 Ukrainian, Russian
☎ 2851 1193; Lower ground fl, 46-48 Cochrane St; starters $39-119, mains $89-149; ☺ noon-3pm & 6pm-midnight; Central MTR

Blinis and borscht is probably not what springs to mind when you're considering an ethnic dining experience in Hong Kong, but the food here – down-home dishes such as Ukrainian-style borscht ($51), beef Stroganoff ($119), stuffed cabbage rolls ($89) and *vareniki* (Ukrainian dumpling) – is surprisingly authentic and the décor cosy. There's live folk music nightly.

JIMMY'S KITCHEN Map p412 International
☎ 2526 5293; Basement, South China Bldg, 1-3 Wyndham St; meals from per person $300; ☺ noon-3pm & 6-11pm; Central MTR

High on nostalgia and one of the oldest names in the game, Jimmy's, a Hong Kong feature for seven decades, rests on its laurels. The baked onion soup ($50), char-grilled king prawns ($215), seven-pepper steak ($260) and a whole medley of desserts (including its famous baked Alaska, $58) all compete for the diners' attention. There's a branch in Tsim Sha Tsui (p179).

KOH-I-NOOR Map p412 Indian
☎ 2877 9706; 1st fl, California Entertainment Bldg, 34-36 D'Aguilar St; rice & biryani dishes $25-98, mains $44-130; ☺ noon-3pm & 6-11pm Mon-Sat, 6-11pm Sun; Central MTR

This pricier sister-restaurant of the branches in Tsim Sha Tsui (p179) and Sha Tin (p188) serves equally fine northern Indian cuisine. The weekday vegetarian/meat lunch-time buffet is a steal at $48/68.

LA KASBAH Map p412 Maghreb, Middle Eastern
☎ 2525 9493; Basement, 17 Hollywood Rd; starters from $60, mains $105-155; ☺ 6.30-11.30pm Mon-Sat; bus 26

La Kasbah is a Frenchified Maghreb caravanserai serving dishes from Algeria, Tunisia and Morocco, which effectively means meze and *tajine* or couscous. It's good stuff but expensive for what (and where) it is. It has lovely décor in an overly sequined way.

LUK YU TEA HOUSE Map p412 Dim Sum
☎ 2523 5464; 24-26 Stanley St; rice & noodle dishes $65-160, mains $100-350; ☺ 7am-10pm; Central MTR

This old-style teahouse is a museum piece in more ways than one. Most of the staff have been here since the early Ming dynasty and are as grumpy and ill-tempered as an emperor deposed. The booths are uncomfortable, it's not cheap, prices aren't marked on the English menu but the dim sum, served from 7am to 6pm, is really quite delicious.

M AT THE FRINGE Map p412 International

☎ 2877 4000; 1st fl, South Block, Fringe Club, Dairy Farm Bldg, 2 Lower Albert Rd; starters $88-168, mains $138-228; ⏱ noon-2.30pm & 7-10.30pm Mon-Fri, 7-10.30pm Sat & Sun; Central MTR

No one seems to have a bad thing to say about Michelle's. The menu changes constantly and everything is excellent, be it crab soufflé ($128) or slow-baked salted lamb ($218). It's worth saving room for dessert, if you have that kind of self-restraint. Reservations are a must. At lunch starters/mains/desserts are a uniform $68/112/58.

MOZART STUB'N Map pp408-9 Austrian

☎ 2522 1763; 8 Glenealy; starters $46-165, mains $110-198; ⏱ noon-2.30pm & 6-10.45pm Mon-Sat; Central MTR

This classy, almost fastidious Austrian (do not say German) establishment has excellent food and wines and a delightful atmosphere. The dishes may sound Teutonic but they are served in sensible portions.

NING PO RESIDENTS ASSOCIATION
Map p412 Shanghainese

☎ 2523 0648; 4th fl, Yip Fung Bldg, 2-18 D'Aguilar St; starters $60-90, mains $75-250; ⏱ noon-3pm & 6-11pm; Central MTR

The Ning Po offers tasty and well-prepared Shanghainese food and is very popular with expats and locals alike. Communication might be a problem, but persevere; it will be well worth your while.

POST 97 Map p412 International

☎ 2186 1817; 1st fl, Cosmos Bldg, 9-11 Lan Kwai Fong; dishes $50-135; ⏱ 9.30am-1am Mon-Thu, 9.30am-2.30am Fri & Sat, 9.30am-1am Sun; Central MTR

This comfortable, all-day brasserie and café above the Fong serves breakfast ($97), buffet lunches ($125 or $150 to $160 with wine), two-course set lunches ($140) and set dinners ($197); à la carte dishes also are available throughout the day. At night Post 97 turns into a popular bar and gets packed very quickly.

RUGHETTA Map p412 Italian

☎ 2537 7922; Basement, Carfield Commercial Bldg, 75-77 Wyndham St; starters $78-138, mains $178-222; ⏱ noon-3pm & 7pm-midnight Mon-Sat, 7pm-midnight Sun; bus 26

This basement restaurant with a branch in New York City serves faultless 'Roman' (read earthy Italian) cuisine – though it may suffer after being discovered by the cheap lunch crowd. Pasta dishes are $145 to $165.

SAN MARZANO Map p412 Italian

☎ 2850 7898; 21 Lyndhurst Tce; starters $29-55, pasta & pizza $79-103; ⏱ noon-midnight; Central MTR

This is the place for pizza and pasta if you like things, well, familiar. It's part of the UK-based Pizza Express chain and looks it and acts it. Still, it's good value, it's convenient to Lan Kwai Fong and Soho and there's live jazz on Thursday from 8pm.

SCHNURRBART Map p412 German

☎ 2523 4700; Ground fl, 29 D'Aguilar St; mains $78-129; ⏱ noon-2.15pm & 6-10.30pm; Central MTR

'Moustache' serves up hearty Bierstube fare like the best of the wurst and German meatloaf, along with lots and lots of suds. There's also a branch in Tsim Sha Tsui (p180). Both do bar snacks and open-face sandwiches ($30 to $120) as well.

SECRET GARDEN Map pp408-9 Korean

☎ 2801 7990; Shop 5, Ground fl, Bank of America Tower, 12 Harcourt Rd; rice & noodle dishes $100-140, barbecues $100-140; ⏱ noon-3pm & 6-11pm; Central MTR

This authentic and central Korean eatery is highly recommended; you should book in advance during the week – and you'll probably still wait for a table. Try a barbecue with all the little side dishes or the signature ginseng chicken soup ($150).

SHALOM GRILL Map pp408-9 Kosher

☎ 2851 6300; 2nd fl, Fortune House, 61 Connaught Rd Central; starters $15-60, mains $80-180; ⏱ 12.30-3pm & 6.30-10pm Sun-Thu, 12.30-3pm Fri; Central MTR

If it's Ashkenazic and Sephardic glatt kosher food you're after, the Shalom Grill can oblige. Don't expect cordon bleu, but if you're in the mood for felafel or gefilte fish (or you answer to a Higher Authority on matters culinary), this is the place to visit. Shabbat dinner and Saturday lunch can be prearranged and paid for in advance. For something lighter, sandwiches are $30 to $50.

SOHO SOHO Map p412 — Modern British

☎ 2147 2618; Ground fl, The Work Station, 43-45 Lyndhurst Tce; starters $55-90, mains $130-195; ☒ noon-2.30pm & 6.30-10.30pm Mon-Fri, 9am-4pm & 6.30-10.30pm Sat & Sun; Central MTR

More BoHo ('Below Hollywood Rd') than its namesake since its move a couple of hundred metres northward from Soho, SoHo SoHo (so good they had to name it twice) serves creative and comforting British food (crumpet with smoked salmon, herb-crusted roasted cod) to an appreciative audience of expats and Westernised Chinese. There's excellent brunch at the weekend.

SONG Map p412 — Vietnamese

☎ 2559 0997; Lower ground fl, 75 Hollywood Rd; starters $75-90, mains $120-220; ☒ noon-3pm & 7-11pm Mon-Thu, noon-3pm & 7pm-midnight Fri, 7pm-midnight Sat; bus 26

This very stylish though somewhat cramped Vietnamese eatery, down an unnamed alleyway between Peel and Aberdeen Sts, serves refined (some might say overly so) Vietnamese food to the denizens of Soho.

SPAGHETTI HOUSE Map p412 — Italian

☎ 2523 1372; Lower ground fl, 10 Stanley St; starters $24-36, pasta & pizzas $49-104; ☒ 11am-11.30pm Sun-Thu & Sat, 11am-11pm Fri; Central MTR

You probably wouldn't want to take a date to this or any of the seven branches of this cheap-and-cheerful chain, but it's OK for a pizza or bowl of pasta. You'll find another outlet nearby in the IFC Mall (Map pp408–9; ☎ 2147 5543; Shop 2004, 2nd fl, 8 Finance St, Central; ☒ 11am-10:30pm).

STORMY WEATHER

Map p412 — International, Seafood

☎ 2845 5533; Ground & 1st fls, 48 D'Aguilar St; starters $59-88, mains $128-228; ☒ noon-3pm & 6-11pm; Central MTR

This mostly seafood restaurant has an enviable location in Central, on D'Aguilar St just as it doglegs into deepest Lan Kwai Fong. There's a wine bar on the 2nd floor that is a real oasis in an overcrowded desert. Pasta dishes are $118 to $128.

SUPER STAR SEAFOOD RESTAURANT

Map p412 — Chinese, Seafood

☎ 2628 0826; Basement, Wilson House, 19-27 Wyndham St; dishes $70-130; ☒ 10.30am-11pm Mon-Sat, 9.30am-11pm Sun; Central MTR

Though just one of eight branches of yet another chain, the Super Star has some of the best Cantonese fish dishes in Central. Lunch-time dim sum here is legendary among Central office workers.

THAI LEMONGRASS Map p412 — Thai

☎ 2905 1688; 3rd fl, California Tower, 30-32 D'Aguilar St; starters $48-88, rice & noodle dishes $75-98, mains $110-215; ☒ noon-2.30pm & 6.30-11pm Mon-Sat, 6.30-10.30pm Sun; Central MTR

This quiet, discreet and very smart place serves up such treats as pomelo salad, spicy green papaya salad and mussels in red curry. There's a weekday set lunch for $138.

TOKIO JOE Map p412 — Japanese

☎ 2525 1889; Ground fl, 16 Lan Kwai Fong; sushi $20-65, cones & rolls $50-145; ☒ noon-2.30pm & 6.30-11pm Mon-Thu, noon-2.30pm & 6.30-11.30pm Fri & Sat, 6.30-11pm Sun; Central MTR

This place serves sushi and sashimi that's among the freshest in Hong Kong, though there is a full range of hot dishes (including *yakitori*) available as well. There are set lunches for $125 to $165. Joe's flashier kid brother, Kyoto Joe (Map p412; ☎ 2804 6800; Ground fl, 21 D'Aguilar St; Japanese sets $110-160; ☒ noon-3pm & 6pm-midnight Mon-Thu, noon-3pm & 6pm-2am Fri & Sat, 6pm-midnight Sun), just down the hill, is somewhat more expensive and modern, and a venue for drinking as much as dining. There's a *robotayaki* (barbecue) bar in back.

TSUI WAH Map p412 — Cantonese

☎ 2525 6338; Ground fl, 15-19 Wellington St; soup noodles $22-30, rice & noodles $22-58; ☒ 6.30am-4am; Central MTR

Anyone who spends much time in Hong Kong ends up slurping noodles at the territory's favourite late-night eatery at least once. Added bonus: it's something of a pulling place for every persuasion. Western dishes include sandwiches ($16 to $32).

UNCLE WILLIE'S DELI Map p412 — Café, Deli

☎ 2522 7524; Ground fl, 36 Wyndham St; sandwiches $65, pizza & pasta $75-85; ☒ 7.30am-11pm Mon-Sat, 9am-6pm Sun; Central MTR

This is a relaxing café-cum-deli that could be in the Village in New York or London's Soho. It serves some of the best breakfasts in town ($45 to $70). There is a large selection of cakes and tarts for $25 to $30.

VA BENE Map p412 · Italian
☎ 2845 5577; 58-62 D'Aguilar St; starters $108-148, mains $238-288; ☻ noon-3pm & 6.30-11.30pm Mon-Thu, noon-3pm & 6.30pm-midnight Fri, 6.30pm-midnight Sat, 6.30-11.30pm Sun; Central MTR
This smart restaurant bears a striking resemblance to a neighbourhood trattoria in Venice. It's a good choice for a special date or an extravagant celebration. Book ahead; dress smart. There is a set lunch for $178.

VONG Map pp408-9 · Fusion
☎ 2825 4028; 25th fl, Mandarin Oriental, 5 Connaught Rd Central; starters $108-198, mains $248-348; ☻ noon-3pm & 6pm-midnight Mon-Fri, 5pm-midnight Sat & Sun; Central MTR
A jewel of a restaurant in a jewel of a hotel, Vong serves a successful blend of Vietnamese, Thai and French food amid splendid surrounds; the views alone make it all worthwhile. If you really want to see what the chef can do, try the five-course sample menu ($548).

YOROHACHI Map p412 · Japanese
☎ 2524 1251; Ground fl, 6 Lan Kwai Fong; tempura $70-110, set lunches $110-120; ☻ 11am-2.30pm & 6-11pm Mon-Sat; Central MTR
In the heart of Lan Kwai Fong, Yorohachi offers an excellent-value *teppanyaki* grill, hand-rolled sushi and takeaway bento boxes ($85 to $180) at lunch and dinner.

YUNG KEE RESTAURANT
Map p412 · Cantonese
☎ 2522 1624; 32-40 Wellington St; dishes $69-120; ☻ 11am-11.30pm; Central MTR
This long-standing institution is probably the most famous Cantonese restaurant in Central. The roast goose here has been the talk of the town since 1942 (the restaurant farms its own geese for quality control), and its dim sum (2pm to 5.30pm Monday to Saturday, 11am to 5.30pm Sunday) is excellent.

Cheap Eats
BON APPETIT Map p412 · Vietnamese
☎ 2525 3553; 14B Wing Wah Lane; dishes $23-50; ☻ 10am-midnight Mon-Sat; Central MTR
Cheap but tasty dishes for those on a rock-bottom budget are available at this Vietnamese nook in Wing Wah Lane, the northern extension of Lan Kwai Fong and

a scrum of office workers trying to squeeze a decent meal into a short break at lunch time on weekdays. Everything – from snacks and filled baguettes to rice and noodle dishes – costs less than $50.

CAN.TEEN Map pp408-9 · International
☎ 2167 8665; Shop 1081, 1st fl, Two IFC, 8 Finance St; dishes $26-42; ☻ 8am-10pm Mon-Fri, 9.30am-10pm Sat, 9am-9pm Sun; Central MTR
This hybrid Asian 'fast food' place with great views of the harbour has excellent barbecued items, more substantial mains and freshly squeezed juices ($16).

CHIPPY Map p412 · Café, British
☎ 2525 9339; Basement, 51A Wellington St; starters $35, mains $45-85; ☻ 10am-11pm Mon-Wed, 10am-late Thu-Sat, noon-8pm Sun; Central MTR
Craving the taste of home? Well, if home is Blighty this convivial place is where to find real fish and chips ($65 to $85), pies ($55) and bangers and mash ($50). There's also a good range of pasta dishes.

CITY'SUPER Map pp408-9 · Supermarket
☎ 2234 7128; Shop 1040-1049, 1st fl, IFC Mall, 8 Finance St; ☻ 10.30am-9.30pm; Central MTR
Gourmet supermarket with ready-to-eats such as sushi and salads and lots of fresh produce flown in at high prices. Even if you're not in the market, it's worth a browse. There's also a Tsim Sha Tsui branch (Map pp420–1; ☎ 2375 8222; Shop 3001, 3rd fl, Gateway Arcade, Harbour City, 25-27 Canton Rd; ☻ 10am-10.30pm).

CUL-DE-SAC Map p412 · American Fast Food
☎ 2525 8116; Ground fl, 17 Wing Wah Lane; set meals $55; ☻ 11am-1am Mon-Thu, 11am-3.30am Fri & Sat, 6pm-midnight Sun; Central MTR
This well-run little place does fish and chips ($85) and pizza slices ($20 to $25), but it's all about burgers ($55), complex sandwiches ($42 to $48) and submarines ($68). There's a Wan Chai branch (Map pp414–15; ☎ 2529 4116; Shop 5, Ground fl, 89 Lockhart Rd).

GOOD LUCK THAI Map p412 · Thai
☎ 2877 2971, 9128 1781; Ground fl, 13 Wing Wah Lane; dishes $35-120; ☻ 11am-1am Mon-Sat, 4pm-midnight Sun; Central MTR
After sinking a few beers in Lan Kwai Fong, make your way over to this chaotic

but friendly place at the slops end of the Fong's charmingly nicknamed Rat Alley for a cheap fix of late-night Thai food. Fair number of Chinese dishes too.

GRAHAM ST MARKET

Map p412   Produce Market
Graham St; ☺ 6am-8pm; Central MTR
The stalls and shops lining Graham St south of (and up the hill from) Queen's Rd Central to Hollywood Rd are positively groaning with high-quality vegetables and fruit, as well as meat, seafood and other comestibles.

HOT DOG Map p412   American Fast Food
☎ 2543 3555; Shop D, Lower ground fl, Hollywood House, 27-29 Hollywood Rd; hot dogs $20-42; ☺ 24hr; Central MTR
You probably wouldn't cross town for the dogs sold at this minuscule outlet, but it's conveniently located just down from Soho and up from Lan Kwai Fong. Enter from Cochrane St.

LA BAGUETTE

Map p412   Sandwich Shop, Late Night Eats
☎ 2868 3716; Ground fl, 18 Lan Kwai Fong; sandwiches $40-60, small/medium/large pizzas from $48/65/90; ☺ 10am-1am Mon-Thu,10am-5am Fri & Sat, 11am-9pm Sun; Central MTR
This is a great place right on the Fong if you're feeling the need for late-night sandwiches and snacks.

LA FONTAINE Map pp408-9   Café
☎ 2537 2938; Shop 3-5, Ground fl, The Forum, Exchange Sq, Connaught Rd Central; sandwiches $36-58, pasta $60-90; ☺ 7.30am-9pm Mon-Sat, 9.30am-7pm Sun; Central MTR
This little café does proper meals as well as pastries, cakes and sandwiches. You can eat in or take away. Breakfast is $24 to $35, with great omelettes from $65 to $90.

MAK'S NOODLE Map p412   Noodle Bar
☎ 2854 3810; 77 Wellington St; dishes $25-50; ☺ 11am-8pm; Central MTR
This noodle shop sells excellent won ton soup, and the beef brisket noodles, more of a Western taste than a Chinese one, are highly recommended. Go for lunch or eat early; it's shut tight by 8pm.

MIX Map pp408-9   International
☎ 2523 7396; Shop 11, The Cascade, Standard Chartered Bank Bldg, 3 Queens Rd Central; salads $25-28, sandwiches $30-46; ☺ 7am-9.30pm Mon-Thu, 7am-8pm Fri & Sat, 9.30am-7pm Sun; Central MTR
A good and convenient spot to grab a meal on the fly or munch while surfing the in-house Internet. There's a branch in the **IFC Mall** (Map pp408-9; ☎ 2971 0688; Shop 1021, 8 Finance St, Central; ☺ 7am-9.30pm Mon-Sat, 8.30am-8.30pm Sun). Both have great freshly squeezed juices ($24).

OLIVER'S Map pp408-9   Delicatessen
☎ 2810 7710; Shop 201 & 207, 2nd fl, Prince's Bldg, 10 Chater Rd; ☺ 8.30am-8pm; Central MTR
The wood-panelled floors set the tone: this ain't no ordinary supermarket. Matzos or Mexican hot sauce? Got it. There's a great range of international beers, the imported fruit and veggies obviously travel first class, and the delicatessen stocks a wide range of cheeses, sausages, pâtés and wines. Its **Oliver's Super Sandwiches** (Map pp408-9; ☎ 2526 2685; Shop 2, Lower ground fl, Citibank Plaza, 3 Garden Rd; salads $36-39, sandwiches $27-42, pasta $37-39; ☺ 7.30am-8pm Mon-Fri, 7.30am-6pm Sat, 9am-6pm Sun) chain offers cooked breakfasts, sandwiches and cakes. There are also a couple of branches in Tsim Sha Tsui (p183).

PARK 'N' SHOP Map pp408-9   Supermarket
77 Des Voeux Rd Central; ☺ 8am-10.30pm; Central MTR
This is a conveniently located branch of the popular supermarket chain in Central. Enter from Queen Victoria St.

PEARL VIETNAMESE RESTAURANT

Map p412   Vietnamese
☎ 2522 4223; Ground fl, 7 Wo On Lane; dishes $20-30; ☺ 11am-9pm; Central MTR
This tiny place is an inexpensive option for noodles or rice when frequenting the bars of the Fong. It serves cut-price dim sum from 12.30pm to 6pm.

SUNNY & BARBIE Map p412   Korean Fast Food
☎ 2522 8004; Ground fl, California Place, 25 D'Aguilar St; dishes $28-45, set lunch $35-40; ☺ 10am-3am Mon-Thu, 10am-5am Fri & Sat; Central MTR
Did he say Korean fast food? Well with things from the Land of the Morning Calm

Eating

HONG KONG ISLAND

Tsim Chai Kee Noodle (below), Central

the last word in cities from London to Tokyo, why not a late-night shop selling *bibimbab* (rice, egg, meat and vegetables in hot sauce) and Korean noodles to the late-night revellers of Lan Kwai Fong?

TSIM CHAI KEE NOODLE

Map p412   Noodle Bar

☎ 2850 6471; Ground fl, 98 Wellington St; noodles & dumplings from $10; ☼ 9am-9pm; Central MTR

This local shoebox opposite Mak's Noodle is where to head if you want a quick and cheap fix of rice or soup noodles (a major hangover cure). Choose from prawn, fish ball or sliced beef dumpling noodles. You should avoid the main lunch hour (1pm to 2pm) though, unless you want to join the scrum. There is a more upmarket (but less atmospheric) **Central branch** (Map pp408–9; 2581 3369; 61 Connaught Rd Central; ☼ 8am-8pm).

WELLCOME Map pp408-9   Supermarket

3rd fl, The Forum, Exchange Sq, Connaught Rd Central; ☼ 8am-8pm; Central MTR

This branch of the supermarket chain is especially convenient if you're shopping for provisions to take on a picnic to one of the Outlying Islands.

WONG CHI KEI Map p412   Noodle Bar

☎ 2869 1331; 15 Wellington St; soup noodles $18-32, rice & noodles $26-42; ☼ 7.30am-2am; Central MTR

A Hong Kong branch of the Macau stalwart (p365), this is the place to come for excellent (and cheap) noodles from sunup till way past sundown.

XTC ON ICE Map p412   Ice-cream Parlour

☎ 2541 0500; Shop 4B, Ground fl, Cheung Fai Bldg, 45-47 Cochrane St; 2/3 scoops $25/40; ☼ noon-midnight Sun-Thu, noon-4am Fri & Sat; Central MTR

The name may be a mouthful, but when ice cream (sorry, *gelato*) is this good, it just has to be. Choose from up to 20 exotic flavours, including ginger with cinnamon, mango paradise and guava. There's a **Kowloon branch** (Map pp420–1; 2368 3602; Star Ferry Terminal, Tsim Sha Tsui; ☼ 11am-midnight).

SOHO

Soho is awash in restaurants; in fact there is nothing but eateries lining Elgin St. Most of them are in the middle and top-end range in terms of price.

2 SARDINES Map p412   French

☎ 2973 6618; Ground fl, 43 Elgin St; starters $56-110, mains $110-190; ☼ noon-2.30pm & 6-10.30pm; bus 26

This small, independent French bistro deserves the crowds it draws. The namesake fish comes grilled with a yogurt sauce; the roasted rack of lamb is worth trying, too. The wine list leans predictably to the Gallic side and is well chosen. Set lunches ($88) are excellent value.

AL DENTE Map p412   Mediterranean

☎ 2869 5463; Ground fl, 16 Staunton St; starters $45-79, mains $104-218; ☼ 11am-3pm & 6-11pm Mon-Fri, 11am-11pm Sat & Sun; bus 26

This new kid on the block serves surprisingly authentic Mediterranean fare with a Middle Eastern twist at relatively reasonable (for Soho) prices. Try one of the pasta dishes ($82 to $93), a grilled meat dish and the homemade tiramisu.

ARCHIE B'S NEW YORK DELI
Map p412   American, Deli
☎ 2522 1239; Lower ground fl, 7 & 9 Staunton St; sandwiches & burgers $40-100, salads $50; ☺ 11am-11pm; bus 26
This little place just off the Central Escalator serves as authentic East Coast American delicatessen food as you'll find west of the US of A. It's pretty much an eat-and-run kind of place, but the few tables in the small alleyway just off Staunton St may have you lingering over your kosher dill pickle or Dr Brown's Cream Soda.

BLOWFISH Map p412   Japanese
☎ 2815 7868; 20-26 Peel St; sushi & sashimi $30-160, hand-rolls $60-90; ☺ noon-2.30pm & 6-10.30pm Mon-Thu, noon-2.30pm & 6-11.30pm Fri & Sat; bus 26
This classy Japanese eatery, with its long sushi bar, *yakitori* ($28 to $50) and enviable selection of sake, is a colourful and cool place to hang out. Set lunches are $55 to $88.

BOCA Map p412   Fusion
☎ 2548 1717; 65 Peel St; starters $38-78, paella $250-280; ☺ noon-2.30pm & 5pm-midnight Mon-Fri, 11am-4pm & 5pm-midnight Sat & Sun; bus 26
This spot goes down well with expats, who sprawl on the trendy lounges and settees and over-order from the menu offering 'traditional Spanish starters' and 'not so traditional fusion' ones with an Asian twist. Sitting at the very end of Elgin St and boasting a wide frontage, Boca is a prime locale to watch the Soho parade. Weekend brunch is a favourite, with ($245) or without ($109) champers. There's a tapas set lunch for $88.

CARAMBA! Map p412   Mexican
☎ 2530 9963; 26-30 Elgin St; starters $48-63, combination plates $110-128; ☺ noon-midnight; bus 26
Mexican is a cuisine as diametrically opposed to Chinese as you can imagine, but with a blinding selection of tequilas, this *cantina* provides a cosy and intimate venue for a fix of chilli ($95), fajitas, enchiladas and *quesadillas* ($55 to $68). There's brunch from noon to 6pm at the weekend.

CHEDI Map p412   Thai
☎ 2868 4445; Ground fl, 38 Elgin St; starters $58-98, rice & noodle dishes $58-78, mains $92-198; ☺ 11am-11pm; bus 26
This attractive restaurant, with warm yellow backlit walls, serves some of the most authentic Thai food in upbeat, stylish surrounds. There are heaps of choices for vegetarians and – unusual for a Southeast Asian restaurant – the wine list is excellent. The bar stays open till 2am Thursday to Sunday.

CHILLI FAGARA Map p412   Sichuanese
☎ 2893 3330; Shop E, Ground fl, 45-53 Graham St; dishes $48-138; ☺ noon-3pm & 6-11.30pm Mon-Fri, 6-11.30pm Sat & Sun; bus 26
This new hole-in-the-wall in Soho serves reasonably authentic Sichuan fare and is a welcome addition to the short list of quality local eateries open in this part of Central. Make sure you try all three Sichuan tastes: *màa* (spicy), *laat* (hot) and *táam* (mild).

EL TACO LOCO Map p412   Mexican
☎ 2522 0214; Lower ground fl, 7-9 Staunton St; tacos & burritos $15-52; ☺ 11am-11pm; bus 26
Next door and sister to Archie B's New York Deli, 'The Mad Taco' serves up authentic (as the sign informs us) Mexican and Tex-Mex: tacos, burritos and tortilla chips with guacamole.

FAT ANGELO'S Map p412   Italian-American
☎ 2973 6808; Ground fl, 49A-C Elgin St; pasta $88-105, mains $125-188; ☺ noon-midnight; bus 26
Huge portions, free salads, unlimited bread and relatively low prices are the keys to success at this chain of Italian-American restaurants. The set lunch is $118. There are several other branches in Hong Kong, including one in Tsim Sha Tsui (p177).

INDIA TODAY Map p412   Indian
☎ 2801 5959; 1st fl, Million City Bldg, 28 Elgin St; curries & tandoori dishes $72-112; ☺ 11.30am-3pm & 6-11.30pm; bus 26
This upstairs eatery in the thick of Soho, named after a popular Indian news weekly, serves reasonable curries, tandoori dishes and ice-cold beer in a pleasant atmosphere.

KATH+MAN+DU Map p412 Nepalese
☎ 2869 1298; 11 Old Bailey St; starters $38-58, curries & tandoori dishes $88-198; ☪ 11am-3pm & 6-11pm; bus 26
A little over the top in décor (and price), this place is a great choice if you want to try 'nouvelle Nepalese', which we're told is not an oxymoron. It's akin to Indian cuisine but a little milder and sweeter. Set lunches range in price from $58 to $98.

KIYOTAKI JAPANESE RESTAURANT
Map p412 Japanese
☎ 2877 1803; 24 Staunton St; sushi/sashimi platter $150/170, tempura $65-100; ☪ noon-3pm & 6-11pm Mon-Sat, 6-11pm Sun; bus 26
This restaurant is one of the very few budget options for Japanese food in Soho and always packed for that reason. Rice and noodle dishes range from $50 to $110 and a set lunch is $140.

LA COMIDA Map p412 Spanish
☎ 2530 3118; Ground fl, 22 Staunton St; tapas & starters $48-72, mains $148-168; ☪ noon-3pm & 6-11pm; bus 26
This cosy place in the heart of Soho serves authentic Spanish cuisine to the denizens of Soho and Staunton St. Things at La Comida get a bit busy (and service slows down) at the weekend. The paella ($195 to $268 for two) is very good.

LIFE Map p412 Vegetarian
☎ 2810 9777; 10 Shelly St; starters $35-75, mains $75-110; ☪ delicatessen & shop 8am-10.30pm Mon-Fri, 9am-10.30pm Sat & Sun, café & rooftop noon-midnight Mon-Fri, 10am-midnight Sat & Sun; bus 26
This place is a vegetarian's dream, serving vegan food and dishes free of gluten, wheat, onion and garlic. There's a delicatessen and shop on the ground floor, a café on the first and additional seating in the rooftop garden. Snacks are available from $35 to $55.

NEPAL Map p412 Nepalese
☎ 2869 6212; Ground fl, 14 Staunton St; starters $36-88, mains $78-198; ☪ noon-3pm & 6-11pm; bus 26
This was one of the first ethnic restaurants to find its way to Soho, and Nepalese

flavours and treats remain in abundance here. There are some 14 vegetarian choices on the menu.

OLIVE Map p412 Greek, Middle Eastern
☎ 2521 1608; Ground fl, 32 Elgin St; meals from $300 per person; ☪ noon-3pm & 6-11pm; bus 26
We've received very mixed reports about the food at this Greek(ish) Soho restaurant, but with ace Australian chef Greg Malouf (late of M at the Fringe) behind the wheel (if from afar), we know it's going to succeed. Give it a go and stick to the mixed meze ($108).

ORANGE TREE Map p412 Dutch
☎ 2838 9352; 17 Shelley St; starters $58-98, mains $148-178; ☪ 6-10.30pm; bus 26
Modern Dutch food served in a breezy russet setting in the higher reaches of the Central Escalator. Don't get stuck on the sausages – there are lighter dishes like smoked eel. For dessert there are always delicious *poffertjes* (Dutch pancakes) on the menu.

PEAK CAFE BAR Map p412 International
☎ 2140 6877; 9-13 Shelley St; starters & salads $52-98, mains $88-168; ☪ 11am-2am Mon-Fri, 9am-2am Sat, 9am-midnight Sun; bus 26
The fixtures and fittings of the much-missed Peak Cafe, established in 1947, have moved down the hill to this comfy restaurant and bar with excellent nosh and super cocktails. The only thing that's missing now is the view. There are also sandwiches ($68 to $98) and pizza ($88 to $98) available.

RICO'S Map p412 Spanish
☎ 2840 0937; Upper ground fl, 51 Elgin St; tapas & starters $48-90, mains $110-160; ☪ noon-late Mon-Fri, 11am-late Sat & Sun; bus 26
Rico's, a celebrated Mid-Levels tapas bar, has moved down the hill to be closer to the action and comes up a winner. Try the paella ($160 to $220 for two) and a pitcher of sangria ($220) in this candlelit Mediterranean setting.

SHUI HU JU Map p412 Sichuanese
☎ 2869 6927; Ground fl, 68 Peel St; meals from $250 per person; ☪ 6pm-midnight; bus 26
This restaurant, which could almost be in Off Soho, serves earthy dishes from Sichuan

TOP FIVE SOHO RESTAURANTS

- **2 Sardines** (p158) – more consistent and reliable than most other Soho venues
- **Archie B's New York Deli** (p159) – kick-ass delicatessen so authentically American it whistles *Dixie*
- **Life** (opposite) – noncarnivore nirvana on three levels
- **Orange Tree** (opposite) – light modern Dutch food in a breezy setting
- **Shui Hu Ju** (opposite) – traditional Sichuan dishes in traditional surrounds

that have only been gently toned down. The décor is a delight – traditional Chinese with tables separated by latticed screens. It's like dining in one of the neighbouring antiques shops.

STONEGRILL Map p412   International

☎ 2504 3333; Ground fl, 28 Elgin St; steaks & grills $188-308, fish & seafood $168-268; ⏱ noon-3pm & 6.30pm-midnight; bus 26

Don't complain when your food arrives half-cooked – it's supposed to be that way. Steak or fish comes sunny-side up and sizzling on a slab of stone; you turn it over to suit your taste. Whether you consider this a half-baked idea or fall for it, you'll love the excellent New York–style bar. Set lunch is $68 to $148, set dinner $200 to $400.

VEDA Map p412   Indian

☎ 2868 5885; 8 Arbuthnot Rd; starters $58-98, mains $148-238; ⏱ noon-3pm & 6-11pm Mon-Sat, 6-10.30pm Sun; bus 26

We've heard talk that this *über*-stylish and pricey eatery is not measuring up to the same standards as when it first opened its doors and introduced Hong Kong to 'innovative Indian' (eg chicken in coriander and cashew-nut paste, fish steamed with mint). Sunday brunch ($198) still seems to pack in the punters, though. Weekday lunch buffet is $98.

YI JIANG NAN
Map p412   Shanghainese, Northern Chinese

☎ 2136 0886; 33-35 Staunton St; starters $48-98, mains $78-198; ⏱ noon-3pm & 6-11pm; bus 26

This place has excellent (and quite modern in preparation and presentation) Shanghainese and Northern Chinese cuisine served on blackwood tables under bird cages moonlighting as lanterns. Behind the dark wood exterior prevails a subdued, homely atmosphere; service is helpful and friendly.

Cheap Eats

BAGEL FACTORY

Map p412   Sandwich Shop, Bakery

☎ 2951 0755, 2810 7111; Shop B2, Ground fl, 41 Elgin St; filled bagels $16-30, pies & quiches $20; ⏱ 8am-8.45pm; bus 26

This establishment has excellent and quite innovative filled bagels, plus delicious baked goods from the adjoining **Soho Bakery** (⏱ 8am-8.45pm).

CHICKEN ON THE RUN Map p412   Fast Food

☎ 2537 8285; Shop A, Lower ground fl, 1 Prince's Tce; salad bar & dishes $25-60; ⏱ 11.30am-9.30pm; bus 26

This brightly lit and pristine place is where to go if you fancy a half/whole Australian takeaway chicken ($48/90).

LE RENDEZ-VOUS Map p412   Creperie

☎ 2905 1808; 5 Staunton St; galettes & crepes $25-50; ⏱ 10am-midnight; bus 26

This tiny, nautically themed crepe house primarily serves savoury filled *galettes* and sweet crepes, but also does filled baguettes, *croques-monsieur* ($50 to $55) and salads ($30 to $50). The *galettes* come filled with classic combos like mushroom and cheese along with more adventurous spicy inventions.

SHEUNG WAN & THE MID-LEVELS

West of Central, Sheung Wan stands out for two quite disparate cuisines: Chinese (in particular, Chiu Chow) and Korean. For some reason the district has always been a 'Little Korea' and is the best place on Hong Kong Island to look for *bulgogi* (Korean barbecue) and *kimchi* (spicy fermented cabbage). Restaurants in the Mid-Levels cater mostly to local residents who don't feel like making the trek down to Soho or Central.

FUNG SHING RESTAURANT

Map pp408-9   Cantonese

☎ 2815 8689; Ground fl, 7 On Tai St, Sheung Wan; meals from $150 per person; ⏰ 7.30am-11.30pm; Sheung Wan MTR

A cavernous place near the Western Market, the 'Phoenix City' specialises in regional Cantonese cuisine, especially seafood. Dim sum is served from 7.30am to 3pm.

GAIA RISTORANTE

Map pp408-9   Italian

☎ 2167 8200; Ground fl, Grand Millennium Plaza, 181 Queen's Rd Central, Sheung Wan; starters $78-188, mains $158-468; ⏰ noon-3pm & 6.30pm-midnight Sun-Thu, noon-3pm & 6.30pm-1am Fri & Sat; Sheung Wan MTR

At least one *bon vivant* friend considers this the best restaurant in Hong Kong. We love the wood and tile floors, the thin-crust pizzas and the outside tables in the lush plaza.

GRAND STAGE Map pp408-9   Cantonese

☎ 2815 2311; 2nd fl, Western Market, 323 Des Voeux Rd Central, Sheung Wan; dishes $68-128; ⏰ 11.30am-6.15pm & 7pm-midnight; Sheung Wan MTR

This wonderful place, with balcony and booth seating overlooking a huge dance floor in Western Market, features ballroom music and dancing at high tea (2.30pm to 6.15pm) and dinner. The food is fine but come here primarily to kick your heels up.

KOREA HOUSE RESTAURANT

Map pp408-9   Korean

☎ 2544 0007; Ground fl, Honwell Commercial Centre, 119-121 Connaught Rd Central, Sheung Wan; meals $150; ⏰ noon-11pm; Sheung Wan MTR

Korea House, *in situ* since 1965, is acknowledged as having some of the most authentic Korean barbecue, *kimchi* and appetisers (dried fish, pickles etc that come as side dishes to BBQ sizzled at your table) in Hong Kong and is always filled with Korean expats – the ultimate stamp of approval. Enter from Man Wa Lane.

LEUNG HING CHIU CHOW SEAFOOD

RESTAURANT Map pp408-9   Chiu Chow, Seafood

☎ 2850 6666; 32 Bonham Strand West, Sheung Wan; meals from $200 per person; ⏰ 11am-midnight; Sheung Wan MTR

The staple ingredients of Chiu Chow cuisine – goose and duck but especially fish and shellfish – are extensively employed and delectably prepared at this very local place.

LIN HEUNG TEA HOUSE

Map pp408-9   Cantonese

☎ 2544 4556; Ground fl, 160-164 Wellington St; meals from $120 per person; ⏰ 6am-10pm; Sheung Wan MTR

This old-style Cantonese restaurant on the corner of Aberdeen St, packed with older men reading newspapers, extended families and office groups, has decent dim sum served from trolleys. It's a very local place, but staff can rout out an English menu.

PHOENIX Map pp408-9   Modern British

☎ 2546 2110; Ground fl, 29 Shelly St, the Mid-Levels; starters $55-85, mains $115-180; ⏰ 5-11pm Mon-Fri, 9am-11pm Sat & Sun; bus 26

What could lay claim to being the territory's first gastropub when it sat comfortably on the border between traditional Sheung Wan and expat Mid-Levels has moved and is now just another recommendable restaurant along the Central Escalator just above Soho. Still, the food remains well prepared and served in substantial portions. It's a great place for weekend brunch from 9am to 4pm ($55 to $110).

PHUKET'S Map pp408-9   Thai

☎ 2868 9672; Ground fl, Shop D, Peace Tower, 30-32 Robinson Rd, the Mid-Levels; soups & salads $45-85, curries $65-78; ⏰ noon-3pm & 6pm-midnight; bus 3B or 23

This Mid-Levels restaurant is a cosy spot, with a mural of a Thai beach to enhance the mood for an escape to one of Thailand's most popular island destinations. The food (mainly seafood) is not all that authentic, but it's a convenient choice if you're staying in the area and just want some *pad thai* or *guey tiao* noodles. Enter from Mosque Junction.

SHEUNG WAN HO CHOI SEAFOOD

RESTAURANT Map pp408-9   Cantonese, Seafood

☎ 2850 6722; 287-291 Des Voeux Rd Central, Sheung Wan; meals from $200 per person; ⏰ 7am-11pm; Sheung Wan MTR

This place is popular for dim sum ($45 to $80; served from 7.30am to 5pm) and

Lin Heung Tea House (opposite), Sheung Wan

Cantonese seafood. The menu is in Chinese only, so get your pointing finger ready. Enter from Cleverly St.

TAI WOO SEAFOOD RESTAURANT

Map pp408-9   Cantonese, Seafood
☎ 2548 4289; Lower ground fl, 92 Caine Rd, the Mid-Levels; meals from $150 per person; ☽ 10am-11pm; bus 3B or 23
If you're looking for old-style Cantonese cooking at its finest, look no further than 'Great Lake'. The large crab dumplings ($10) are out of this world. You should also try the stewed grouper fin and roast pigeon. There's also a Causeway Bay branch (p172).

THE PEAK

You'd hardly venture all the way up Victoria Peak for a meal; food here takes its place in the queue behind the views and all the attractions of the Peak Tower. But there are a few options from which to choose.

CAFE DECO Map pp408-9   International
☎ 2849 5111; Levels 1 & 2, Peak Galleria, 118 Peak Rd; starters $98-158, curries & tandoori dishes $112-156; ☽ 11.30am-midnight Mon-Thu, 11.30am-1am Fri & Sat, 9.30am-midnight Sun; Peak Tram
With its spectacular harbour views, Art Deco furnishings and live jazz from 7pm to 11pm Monday to Saturday nights, this place need not have made too much effort with the

menu. But the food, while an East-meets-West eclectic thing, is above average, with the bistro dishes, sushi and sashimi plates ($152 to $298) and oyster bar scoring extra points. Breakfast and brunch are served from 9.30am to 2.30pm Saturday and Sunday; there's a set lunch for $88.

GRAPPA'S PEAK PIZZERIA

Map pp408-9   Pizzeria
☎ 2849 4222; Shop 402, 4th fl, Peak Tower, 128 Peak Rd; salads $38-48, pasta & pizza $42-85; ☽ 10am-10pm Mon-Fri, 9am-10pm Sat & Sun; Peak Tram
This is a very useful branch of a popular Italian eatery in Admiralty (p165) to know about, hidden away as it is in the Peak Tower.

PARK 'N' SHOP Map pp408-9   Supermarket
Level 2, Peak Galleria, 118 Peak Rd; ☽ 8am-10pm; Peak Tram
This is a convenient branch of the supermarket chain if you want to stock up on snacks and drinks before embarking on a walk.

PEAK LOOKOUT

Map pp408-9   International, Asian
☎ 2849 1000; 121 Peak Rd; starters $48-$158, mains $110-240; ☽ 10.30am-midnight Mon-Thu, 10.30am-1am Fri, 8.30am-1am Sat, 8.30am-midnight Sun; Peak Tram
East meets West at this swish colonial-style restaurant, with seating indoors in a glassed-in veranda and on the outside

terrace – there's everything from Indian and French to Thai and Japanese on offer. We'll stick to the oysters ($140 to $225 a half-dozen), the barbecue and the views – which are to the south of the island, not the harbour. Breakfast is available at the weekend from 8.30am.

ADMIRALTY & WAN CHAI

Wan Chai (and to a lesser extent Admiralty) is a happy hunting ground for ethnic restaurants. Name your cuisine and MTR, bus or tram it down to the Wanch. You're certain to find it here.

369 SHANGHAI RESTAURANT

Map pp414-15   Shanghainese

☎ 2527 2343; Ground fl, 30-32 O'Brien Rd, Wan Chai; cold dishes $35-50, soups $40-60; ☷ 11am-4am; Wan Chai MTR

Low-key Shanghainese eatery that's nothing like five-star but does the dumpling job well. It's family-run and there are some comfy booths in the front window. It's open late too, so you can come here after a draining dance. Try the signature hot-and-sour soup ($40 to $60) – almost a meal in itself – or the aubergine fried with garlic ($55).

AMERICAN RESTAURANT

Map pp414-15   Northern Chinese

☎ 2527 7277; Ground fl, Golden Star Bldg, 20 Lockhart Rd, Wan Chai; meals from $150 per person; ☷ 11am-11.30pm; Admiralty MTR

The friendly American (which chose its name to attract Yank sailors cruising the Wanch for sustenance while on R&R during the Vietnam War) has been serving decent Northern Chinese cuisine for well over half a century. As you'd expect, the Peking duck ($275) and the beggar's chicken ($310; order in advance) are very good.

BHET GHAT RESTAURANT

Map pp414-15   Nepalese, Indian

☎ 2122 9795; Ground fl, 153 Jaffe Rd, Wan Chai; curries & tandoori dishes $48-119, set lunch $48; ☷ 11.30am-3pm & 6pm-11.30pm Mon-Sat, 6pm-11.30pm Sun; Wan Chai MTR

For heavenly homemade Himalayan treats, head for this eatery just west of Fleming Rd. We love the food here but the carriage-like dining room is a bit cramped for the corpulent.

CAFÉ TOO Map pp408-9   International

☎ 2829 8571; 7th fl, Island Shangri-La Hong Kong, Pacific Place, Supreme Court Rd, Admiralty; starters $90-180, mains $200-260; ☷ 6.30am-10.30pm; Admiralty MTR

This immensely popular food hall has a half-dozen kitchens preparing dishes from around the world, seating for 250 grazers and one of the best lunch/dinner buffets ($250/350 Monday to Saturday, $290/380 Sunday) in town. There's lighter fare as well, including sandwiches ($120 to $180) and rice and pasta dishes ($120 to $170).

CARRIANA CHIU CHOW RESTAURANT

Map pp414-15   Chiu Chow

☎ 2511 1282; 1st fl, AXA Centre, 151 Gloucester Rd, Wan Chai; meals from $150 per person; ☷ 11am-11.30pm; Wan Chai MTR

For Chiu Chow food, the Carriana still rates right up there after all these years. Try the cold dishes (sliced goose with vinegar, crab claws), pork with tofu or Chiu Chow chicken. Enter from Tonnochy Rd.

CHE'S CANTONESE RESTAURANT

Map pp414-15   Cantonese

☎ 2528 1123; 4th fl, The Broadway, 54-62 Lockhart Rd, Wan Chai; meals from $300 per person; ☷ 11am-3pm & 6pm-midnight; Wan Cha MTR

This crème de la crème of Cantonese restaurants serves home-style delicacies and offers a special seasonal menu with a dozen additional dishes. It's highly recommended.

CINE CITTÀ Map pp408-9   Italian

☎ 2529 0199; Ground fl, Starcrest Bldg, 9 Star St, Wan Chai; starters & pasta $98-198, mains $188-268; ☷ noon-3pm & 6pm-12.30am Mon-Fri, 6pm-12.30am Sat & Sun; tram

This very flash restaurant with an Italian film theme is in an area of southwest Wan Chai that is slowly becoming something of a restaurant and nightlife district. The crowd here is more unhip hotel bar than Lan Kwai Fong, though.

CINTA-J

Map pp414-15   Filipino, Indonesian

☎ 2529 6622; Shop G4, Ground fl, Malaysia Bldg, 69 Jaffe Rd, Wan Chai; dishes $50-125; ☷ 11am-3.30am Mon-Fri, 11am-5am Sat & Sun; Wan Chai MTR

This friendly restaurant and lounge has a Southeast Asian menu longer than the Book of Job, which covers all bases from *murtabak* to *gado-gado,* but with a strong emphasis on Pinoy dishes. It turns into a cocktail lounge in the late evening and stays open until 3.30am (5am at the weekend).

COYOTE BAR & GRILL

Map pp414-15   Mexican

☎ 2861 2221; 114-120 Lockhart Rd, Wan Chai; starters $44-63, combination platters $112-128; ☺ noon-3pm & 6-10.45pm Mon-Fri, noon-10.45pm Sat & Sun; Wan Chai MTR

With its warm, mustard-coloured décor and brassy bar, this *cantina* describes itself as 'Mexican with Attitude'. And that's just what it is. There are great margaritas, best enjoyed at happy hour (3pm to 8pm daily), and live Latino sounds at 8.30pm on Saturday. Try the fajitas ($112 to $148).

DAN RYAN'S CHICAGO GRILL

Map pp408-9   American

☎ 2845 4600; Shop 114, Level 1, Pacific Place, 88 Queensway, Admiralty; starters $52-98, mains $95-240; ☺ 11am-midnight Mon-Sat, 9am-midnight Sun; Admiralty MTR

The fare at this re-creation of a Chicago lounge restaurant always satisfies, no matter whether it's the ribs (half/full rack $132/198), steaks ($135 to $240), huge sandwiches ($55 to $120), salads ($98 to $145) or pasta ($98 to $130). There's also a Tsim Sha Tsui branch (p177).

DYNASTY Map pp414-15   Cantonese

☎ 2802 8888; 3rd fl, Renaissance Harbour View Hotel, 1 Harbour Rd, Wan Chai; starters $100-135, rice & noodle dishes $100-160, mains $95-400; ☺ noon-3pm & 6.30-11pm Mon-Sat, 11.30am-3pm & 6.30-11pm Sun; bus 18

Stylish Cantonese restaurant that does a much-lauded daily dim sum. This is a good choice for business lunches; the atmosphere is more hum and hush than the normal dim sum clatter.

EAST OCEAN SEAFOOD RESTAURANT

Map pp414-15   Chinese, Seafood

☎ 2827 8887; 3rd fl, Harbour Centre, 25 Harbour Rd, Wan Chai; meals from $250 per person; ☺ 11am-3pm & 6-11pm; bus 18

TOP FIVE ADMIRALTY & WAN CHAI RESTAURANTS

- **Beijing Shui Jiao Wong** (p168) – northern-style dumplings in a steamy canteen
- **Che's Cantonese Restaurant** (opposite) – Hong Kong celebrities and minor royalty nosh Cantonese delights
- **Liu Yuan Restaurant** (p166) – Shanghainese with a 21st-century spin on it
- **Tan Ta Wan Restaurant** (p167) – where Thai amahs go for a chilli transfusion
- **Vegetarian Court** (p167) – the most upscale grazing ground for veggies – make no bones about it

The East Ocean, which counts some 10 branches or related places in Hong Kong, still serves some of the best and most inventive Cantonese seafood dishes and dim sum ($40 to $85) in town. There's also a Tsim Sha Tsui branch (Map pp420–1; ☎ 2369 1819; 1st fl, Prat Mansion, 26-36 Prat Ave; ☺ 11am-11pm).

GRAPPA'S RISTORANTE

Map pp408-9   Italian

☎ 2868 0086; Shop 132, Ground fl, Pacific Place, 88 Queensway, Admiralty; starters $85-188, mains $128-280; ☺ 9.30am-3pm & 6pm-midnight Mon-Fri, 9.30am-midnight Sat & Sun; Admiralty MTR

This is a top-notch venue for antipasto, fettuccini and other Italian dishes (pizza and pasta are $85 to $130), though not everyone likes dining in a shopping mall. Still, of Grappa's several outlets, this is the best. Breakfast is served from 9.30am to 11.30am Monday to Friday.

HYANG CHON KOREAN RESTAURANT

Map pp414-15   Korean

☎ 2574 5142; 2nd fl, Workingfield Commercial Bldg, 408-412 Jaffe Rd, Wan Chai; meals from $250 per person; ☺ 6pm-4am; Wan Chai MTR

This somewhat expensive Korean restaurant attracts Korean expats and their friends with its authentic ginseng chicken and *bibimbab,* rice served in a sizzling pot topped with thinly sliced beef and cooked and preserved vegetables, which is then bound by a raw egg and flavoured with chilli-laced soy bean paste. Service is friendly and helpful.

JO JO MESS Map pp414-15 — Indian

☎ 2527 3776; 1st fl, Block C, 86-90 Johnston Rd, Wan Chai; dishes $48-95; ☺ noon-3pm & 6-11pm; Wan Cha MTR

A favourite of expats who love Indian food as Indians prepare it, Jo Jo has branched out in recent years, opening three top-class restaurants throughout the territory, including a Central branch (Map pp408–9; 2522 6209; Shop 10G, Ground fl, Bank of America Tower, 12 Harcourt Rd). But this is the original and the most authentic. There's a lunch buffet ($75) on Wednesday and Friday, including a half-pint of beer or other drink. Enter the Wan Chai branch from Lee Tung St.

KOKAGE Map pp408-9 — Japanese

☎ 2529 6138; Ground fl, Starcrest Bldg, 9 Star St, Wan Chai; starters $48-128, rice & noodle dishes $68-168, mains $88-278; ☺ noon-2.30pm & 6-11pm Mon-Thu, noon-2.30pm & 6-11.30pm Fri & Sat, 6-11pm Sun; Admiralty MTR

From the people who brought you Cine Città (and sharing the same building) is this incredibly stylish contemporary Japanese fusion restaurant and *izakaya* (a Japanese-style pub) – almost more Manhattan than Tokyo. Dress up and make sure you've got plastic with you. Sushi and sashimi plates are $180 to $380, hand-roll $98 to $150.

LIU YUAN RESTAURANT

Map pp414-15 — Shanghainese

☎ 2510 0483; 1st fl, CRE Bldg, 303 Hennessy Rd, Wan Chai; meals from $250 per person; ☺ noon-3pm & 6-11pm; Wan Chai MTR

This stylish restaurant serves superb Shanghainese dishes, including things like crab claws cooked with duck egg, and the tiny prawns steamed with tea leaves are superb. Highly recommended.

LOUIS' STEAK HOUSE

Map pp414-15 — Steakhouse

☎ 2529 8933; 1st fl, Malaysia Bldg, 50 Gloucester Rd, Wan Chai; starters $45-70, mains $120-250; ☺ 11.30am-3pm & 6pm-midnight; Wan Chai MTR

This is the sort of place that Hong Kong Chinese used to frequent when they wanted fancy Western cuisine in a Western-style restaurant (eg candles and checked cloths on the tables). It's sort of 1960s, but that's part of Louis' charm. And with

the recent resurgence of interest in steakhouses in Hong Kong, it probably has it made, too.

LUNG MOON RESTAURANT

Map pp414-15 — Cantonese

☎ 2572 9888; 130-136 Johnston Rd, Wan Chai; meals from $150 per person; ☺ 6am-midnight; Wan Chai MTR

The dining experience at this very basic (and friendly) Cantonese restaurant has not changed a great deal since the 1950s, and the prices, while not quite at 1950s levels, are still reasonable. Dim sum is available daily from opening till 5pm.

NICHOLINI'S Map pp408-9 — Italian

☎ 2521 3838; 8th fl, Conrad Hong Kong, 88 Queensway, Admiralty; starters $130-285, mains $275-480; ☺ noon-3pm & 6.30-11pm Mon-Fri, 6.30-11pm Sat, 11am-3pm & 6.30-11pm Sun; Admiralty MTR

This refined restaurant's approach to northern Italian cuisine has won it praise from Italian expats – a certain stamp of approval. Simple yet superb antipasti and shellfish dishes are firm favourites here. It also has an excellent bar. Set lunch/dinner is $288/688.

ONE HARBOUR ROAD

Map pp414-15 — Cantonese

☎ 2588 1234; 7th & 8th fls, Grand Hyatt Hotel, 1 Harbour Rd, Wan Chai; starters $80-165, mains $150-450; ☺ noon-2.30pm & 6.30-10.30pm; bus 18

This is undoubtedly the classiest Chinese restaurant in Hong Kong. In addition to the beautiful design and fabulous harbour view, six pages of gourmet dishes await your perusal, and the dim sum ($30 to $60) is out of this world. Set lunches are $330 and $470, set dinner $650.

PETRUS Map pp408-9 — French

☎ 2820 8590; 56th fl, Island Shangri-La Hotel, Pacific Place, Supreme Court Rd, Admiralty; 2-/3-course set lunch $310/350, 6-/7-course set dinner $800/950; ☺ noon-2.30pm & 6.30-11pm; Admiralty MTR

With its head (and prices) in the clouds, Petrus is one of the finest Western restaurants in Hong Kong. Expect traditional (not nouvelle) French cuisine, some over-the-top décor and stunning harbour views. Coat and tie required for men.

PORT CAFE

Map pp414-15   Buffet, International

☎ 2582 7731; Level 3, Phase 2, Hong Kong Convention & Exhibition Centre, 1 Expo Dr, Wan Chai; buffet $148; ☾ 11.30am-6pm Mon-Sat; bus 18
For stunning views over harbour and Central, fabulous décor and smooth design, try this restaurant in the colossal convention centre. Depending on what's on, the café usually throws on a buffet. If you're into quantity over quality, go straight to Port. Afternoon tea is served from 4pm to 6pm.

R66 Map pp414-15   Buffet, International

☎ 2862 6166; 62nd fl, Hopewell Centre, 183 Queen's Rd E, Wan Chai; buffets $98-308; ☾ noon-2.30pm, 3-5pm (tea) & 6.30-10pm; Wan Chai MTR
R66 – it's on the 62nd, not the 66th floor, as you'd expect – obeys the unwritten code of revolving restaurants by playing cheesy music and serving average buffets (lunch $98 Monday to Saturday, dinner $288 Monday to Thursday, $308 Friday to Sunday). It's best to roll up for an afternoon tea ($66) and go for a twirl in the daylight. To access the lipstick tube–like Hopewell Centre's outfacing bubble lifts, swap at the 17th (lifts are in the alcove opposite lift 6) and 56th floors.

RUTH'S CHRIS STEAKHOUSE

Map pp408-9   Steakhouse

☎ 2522 9090; Ground fl, Lippo Centre, 89 Queensway, Admiralty; starters $60-120, steaks & mains $240-450; ☾ noon-11pm; Admiralty MTR
If you're feeling both flush and carnivorous this is the place to satisfy the craving to spend and eat red meat. It's got the best steaks – Australian Angus beef – in town.

SABAH Map pp414-15   Malaysian

☎ 2143 6626; Shop 4 & 5, Ground fl, 98-108 Jaffe Rd, Wan Chai; starters $38-45, rice & noodle dishes $45-65, mains $40-135; ☾ 7.30am-midnight; Wan Chai MTR
Sabah in the heart of Wan Chai serves Malaysian food tempered for the Hong Kong palate. It's a favourite of office workers; try to avoid 1pm to 2pm. A choice of five set lunches ($48) is available from 11am to 3pm.

SAIGON Map pp414-15   Vietnamese

☎ 2598 7222; Room 2A, 2nd fl, Sun Hung Kai Centre, 30 Harbour Rd, Wan Chai; starters $48-88, mains $78-132; ☾ noon-2.30pm & 6-10.30pm; bus 18

A relatively sterilised version of a Vietnamese restaurant, Saigon has some interesting dishes – pomelo salad with dried shrimps, green papaya and beef salad with chilli ($52 to $65) – and inexpensive set lunches during the week. With the prices on the menu also quoted in renminbi, it's quite clear that it's after the mainland market.

SHABU SHABU Map pp414-15   Japanese

☎ 2893 8806; Ground fl, Kwan Chart Tower, 6 Tonnochy Rd, Wan Chai; sushi & sashimi $25-80, tempura $38-180; ☾ 11.30am-3pm & 6pm-midnight; Wan Chai MTR
This huge place done up in traditional Japanese décor offers a warm welcome and relatively reasonable prices, including rice and noodle dishes from $40 to $70. Enter from Jaffe Rd. There's also a **Tsim Sha Tsui branch** (Map pp420–1; ☎ 2314 4292; Ground fl, 3 Hillwood Rd).

TAN TA WAN RESTAURANT

Map pp408-9   Thai

☎ 2865 1178; Shop 9, Ground fl, Rialto Bldg, 2 Landale St, Wan Chai; starters $40-78, rice & noodle dishes $30-40, mains $40-128; ☾ 11am-11pm Mon-Fri, 11.30am-10.30pm Sat & Sun; Admiralty MTR
This smallish restaurant on the border between Admiralty and Wan Chai serves some of the most authentic Thai food on Hong Kong Island.

THAI BASIL Map pp408-9   Thai

☎ 2537 4682; Shop 005, Lower ground fl, Pacific Place, 88 Queensway, Admiralty; salads $50-80, main dishes $70-100; ☾ 11.30am-11pm; Admiralty MTR
This basement mall restaurant turns out some surprisingly authentic (and quite lovely) Thai dishes. This may not be a destination but it's not a bad stop along the way.

VEGETARIAN COURT

Map pp414-15   Vegetarian

☎ 2845 1199; 2nd fl, CRE Bldg, 303 Hennessy Rd, Wan Chai; dishes $50-140; ☾ noon-3pm & 6-11pm; Wan Chai MTR
Not just another little vegetarian place in Wan Chai, the Vegetarian Court is Shanghainese as well, promising bigger, fuller flavours. If you shun meat but still crave style, come here.

VICEROY RESTAURANT & BAR

Map pp414-15   Indian

☎ 2827 7777; Room 2B, 2nd fl, Sun Hung Kai Centre, 30 Harbour Rd, Wan Chai; starters $32-78, curries & tandoori dishes $68-158; ⓨ noon-3pm & 6-11pm; bus 18

The Viceroy has been an institution in Hong Kong for some two decades: an upmarket Indian restaurant with sitar music and a fun place to watch comedy (p214) at least once a month.

VICTORIA CITY Map pp414-15   Cantonese

☎ 2827 9938; Room 2D, 2nd fl, Sun Hung Kai Centre, 30 Harbour Rd, Wan Chai; meals from $250 per person; ⓨ 11am-3pm & 6-11.30pm; bus 18

Many in Hong Kong consider the dim sum (served 11am to 3pm) here to be the best in the territory. Dinner is a delight too, with many dishes not normally seen in Hong Kong on the menu.

YÈ SHANGHAI Map pp408-9   Shanghainese

☎ 2918 9833; Shop 332, Level 3, Pacific Place, 88 Queensway, Admiralty; starters $44-100, rice & noodle dishes $32-88, mains $76-400; ⓨ 11.30am-3pm & 6-11.30pm; Admiralty MTR

This groovy place takes street-level Shanghainese cuisine and gives it a tweak here and there. The cold drunken pigeon ($100) is a wine-soaked winner and the steamed dumplings are perfectly plump, but sometimes this restaurant goes for clattery style over substance. There's live music from 9.30pm to 11.30pm Thursday to Saturday.

Cheap Eats

BEIJING SHUI JIAO WONG

Map pp414-15   Northern Chinese, Noodle Bar

☎ 2527 0289; 118 Jaffe Rd, Wan Chai; dishes $25-40; ⓨ 7am-11pm Mon-Sat, noon-11pm Sun; Wan Chai MTR

The 'Dumpling King' serves the best (and cheapest) Northern-style dumplings ($31 to $35), *wàw-tip* (pan stickers; $31 to $35) and soup noodles ($22 to $38) in Hong Kong.

DÉLIFRANCE Map pp408-9   Café

☎ 2520 0959; Shop A1-A3, 1st fl, Queensway Plaza, 93 Queensway, Admiralty; soups & salads $12-23, sandwiches & light meals $21-43; ⓨ 7.30am-8pm; Admiralty MTR

A branch of the popular bakery and patisserie can be found just above the Admiralty MTR station.

GENKI SUSHI Map pp408-9   Japanese

☎ 2865 2933; Shop C1, Ground fl, Far East Finance Centre, 16 Harcourt Rd, Admiralty; sushi $9-35, sushi sets $40-235; ⓨ 11am-11pm; Admiralty MTR

This cheap-and-cheerful susherie, popular with young Hong Kong Chinese, doesn't have a written word of English within its four walls, but you'll recognise the logo – not a cringe-making 'smiley face' but a frowning 'meany face'.

GOLDEN MYANMAR

Map pp414-15   Burmese

☎ 2838 9305; Shop 8, Ground fl, 379-389 Jaffe Rd, Wan Chai; dishes $28-48; ⓨ noon-11.30pm Mon-Fri, 3-11.30pm Sat & Sun; Wan Chai MTR

The only Burmese restaurant (we know of) in Hong Kong, this tiny place serves the national cuisine of Myanmar which, with abundant use of peanut oil and a fish sauce more pungent than Thai *nam pla,* might take some getting used to for the uninitiated.

GREAT Map pp408-9   Deli, Food Court

☎ 2918 9986; Lower ground fl, Pacific Place, 88 Queensway, Admiralty; ⓨ 10am-10pm Sun-Fri, 9am-10pm Sat; Admiralty MTR

This food emporium has a large stock of imported comestibles (Western and Asian, with an emphasis on Japanese and Korean), supplying a range of cheeses, preserved meats, breads and chocolates. A quick fix of vegetable curry with rice and a poppadon from one of the stalls is less than $50.

PEPPERONI'S PIZZA Map pp414-15   Italian

☎ 2865 3214; 54 Jaffe Rd, Wan Chai; salads $55-65, pizza $70-125; ⓨ 7am-midnight Mon-Sat, 10am-midnight Sun; Wan Chai MTR

This branch of the celebrated pizzeria is an inexpensive option for pizza and pasta in the Wanch. There is another branch in Sai Kung (p189).

SAIGON BEACH Map pp414-15   Vietnamese

☎ 2529 7823; Ground fl, 66 Lockhart Rd, Wan Chai; noodles & rice $26-40, mains $58-68; ⓨ 11.30am-4pm & 6-10.30pm; Wan Chai MTR

This popular little hole-in-the-wall may not impress at first sight, but the affable service and food makes it well worth sharing a table with strangers, which you undoubtedly will have to do. Set meals for two start at $118.

SHAFFI'S MALIK Map pp414-15   Indian

☎ 2572 7474; Shop 1, Ground fl, Connaught Commercial Bldg, 185 Wan Chai Rd, Wan Chai; starters $18-35, curries & tandoori dishes $48-128; ✆ 11am-3pm & 6-11pm; Wan Chai MTR

This place boasts that it is 'probably the oldest Indian restaurant in town serving the best Indian cuisine'. Both claims are highly debatable, but it's cheap (set lunch is $38), halal and here.

TIM'S KITCHEN

Map pp414-15   Hong Kong Fast Food

☎ 2527 2982; Shop C, Ground fl, 118 Jaffe Rd, Wan Chai; dishes $16-58; ✆ 7am-10pm; Wan Chai MTR

When as many Hong Kong Chinese queue up outside a restaurant at lunch time as they do at Tim's every day, you can be sure that the food is both inexpensive and of good quality. It's a mix of Cantonese staples (fried rice, noodles) with some Hong Kong–style additions (fried pasta).

YOSHINOYA NOODLES

Map pp408-9   Japanese, Noodle Bar

☎ 2520 0953; Shop B, Ground fl, China Hong Kong Tower, 8-12 Hennessy Rd, Wan Chai; soups & noodles $22-40; ✆ 8am-9.30pm Mon-Fri, 8am-10pm Sat & Sun; Admiralty MTR

A decent choice for a quick lunch or some blotter while trawling Wan Chai, this fast-food Japanese place has another 21 outlets around the territory.

ZAMBRA Map pp414-15   Café

☎ 2598 1322; 239 Jaffe Rd, Wan Chai; sandwiches $24, salads $35; ✆ 7.30am-10pm Mon-Thu, 7.30am-11pm Fri & Sat, noon-8pm Sun; Wan Chai MTR

This modern, Western-style café is just the ticket for a quick breakfast (the muffins are excellent) or a sandwich on the hoof. Set lunch is $48 to $68.

CAUSEWAY BAY

Causeway Bay is a strange amalgam of restaurants and cuisines but, apart from a selection of rather slick and overpriced European places on Fashion Walk (otherwise known as Houston St) northeast of the Causeway

MTR station, this is the place for Chinese and other Asian – particularly Southeast Asian – food. Causeway Bay also has a lot of Japanese restaurants because of all the Japanese department stores (and tourists) that used to be based here before the Land of the Rising Sun began to set economically.

ARIRANG Map pp414-15   Korean

☎ 2506 3298; Shop 1105, 11th fl, Food Forum, Times Square, 1 Matheson St; rice & noodle dishes $90-150, hotpot dishes $200-240; ✆ noon-3pm & 6-11pm; Causeway Bay MTR

A branch of the upmarket Korean restaurant chain, with another outlet in Tsim Sha Tsui (p176). There are also the usual barbecues ($88 to $170) and a set lunch for $70.

BANANA LEAF CURRY HOUSE

Map pp414-15   Malaysian, Singaporean

☎ 2573 8187; Ground fl, 440 Jaffe Rd; starters $32-78, mains $54-128; ✆ 11.30am-3pm & 6pm-midnight Mon-Fri, 11.30am-midnight Sat & Sun; Causeway Bay MTR

This large branch of a chain dishes up Malaysian/Singaporean food served on a banana leaf; your hands are the cutlery if you choose to go authentic.

BO KUNG Map pp414-15   Vegetarian

☎ 2506 3377; Room 1203, 12th fl, Food Forum, Times Sq, 1 Matheson St; soups & starters $30-50, mains $48-80; ✆ 11am-11pm; Causeway Bay MTR

If you prefer to eat your vegetables in lofty surrounds, try Bo Kung, which started operations in Vancouver in Canada before moving here.

CHUEN CHEUNG KUI Map pp414-15 Hakka

☎ 2577 3833; 110-112 Percival St; meals from $200 per person; ⏲ 11am-midnight; Causeway Bay MTR

Enlist a Cantonese dining companion or dive in bravely: there's not much English spoken here and the food is challenging. The pulled chicken, a Hakka classic, is the dish to insist upon. ('Gizzard soup' and 'stomach titbit' may be less appealing.)

CHUNG CHUK LAU RESTAURANT

Map pp414-15 Northern Chinese

☎ 2577 4914; 30 Leighton Rd, Causeway Bay; meals from $150 per person; ⏲ 11am-11pm; Causeway Bay MTR

This old standby serves up all the old Northern Chinese favourites – from beggar's chicken to superb onion cakes. If there's a group of you on a budget, head here.

EAST LAKE Map pp414-15 Cantonese

☎ 2504 3311; 4th fl, Pearl City, 22-36 Paterson St; meals from $150 per person; ⏲ 8am-midnight; Causeway Bay MTR

The East Lake, one of the anchor tenants of the mammoth Pearl City building, has a lengthy menu of Cantonese dishes that changes every three months. But its *raison d'être* is to serve appreciative diners afford-able and quite good dim sum (8am to 5pm).

FOREVER GREEN TAIWANESE

RESTAURANT Map pp414-15 Taiwanese

☎ 2890 3448; 93-95 Leighton Rd; dishes $38-188; ⏲ noon-3pm & 6pm-4am; Causeway Bay MTR

Said to be a favourite of actor/director Jackie Chan, Forever Green is Hong Kong's best Taiwanese restaurant, a cuisine that borrows heavily from Fujian cooking. Try such specialities as oyster omelette, fried bean curd and *sàam-bui-gài* (three-cup chicken). Noodle dishes are particularly good value. Enter from Sun Wui Rd.

FORUM Map pp414-15 Cantonese

☎ 2891 2555; 485 Lockhart Rd; meals from $700 per person; ⏲ 11am-2.30pm & 5.30-11pm; Causeway Bay MTR

The Forum's abalone dishes have fans spread across the world and have won countless awards. What restaurant owner Yeung Koon-Yat does with these marvellous molluscs has earned him membership to Le Club des Chefs des Chefs and the

Salted chicken, Chuen Cheung Kui (left), Causeway Bay

moniker 'King of Abalone'. The pan-fried redfish and crunchy-skin chicken are also recommended.

GOLDEN BULL Map pp414-15 Vietnamese

☎ 2506 1028; 11th fl, Food Forum, Times Square, 1 Matheson St; dishes $58-220; ⏲ noon-11.30pm; Causeway Bay MTR

The Bull might not be the best Vietnamese restaurant in Causeway Bay, but it's the most stylish – and highest. There's a branch in Tsim Sha Tsui (p178).

HEICHINROU Map pp414-15 Cantonese

☎ 2506 2333; Shop 1003, 10th fl, Food Forum, Times Square, 1 Matheson St; meals from $150 per person; ⏲ 11.30am-midnight Mon-Fri, 11am-midnight Sat, 10am-midnight Sun; Causeway Bay MTR

This stylish Cantonese restaurant is arguably the most elegant eatery in what makes up the four-level Food Forum (floors 10 to 13) in the Times Square shopping mall. The dim sum ($16 to $45) here is excellent.

HIGASHIYAMA Map pp414-15 Japanese

☎ 2573 7763; 15 Morrison Hill Rd; noodles $38-58, set meals $58-150; ⏲ 11.30am-3.30pm & 5.30pm-midnight; Causeway Bay MTR

For down-to-earth atmosphere, try this unfussy place. It has all the atmosphere of an *izakaya* (Japanese-style pub) and seems to tolerate enthusiastic bouts of sake drinking.

INDONESIAN RESTAURANT 1968

Map pp414-15   Indonesian

☎ 2577 9981; 28 Leighton Rd; rice & noodle dishes $58-78, mains $60-98; ⓨ 11am-11pm; Causeway Bay MTR

This erstwhile dive has recently got a much needed face-lift and has added the year of its founding to its name – just so you won't forget. The food? It still serves pretty authentic *rendang, gado-gado* and the like. There's a Tsim Sha Tsui branch (Map pp420–1; ☎ 2619 1926; 2-4A Observatory Rd), which keeps the same hours.

KOREA RESTAURANT

Map pp414-15   Korean

☎ 2577 9893; Ground fl, 58 Leighton Rd; barbecue & set meals $75-90; ⓨ 11.30am-midnight; Causeway Bay MTR

This is a good choice for an authentic Korean barbecue, but the surrounds are a little frayed and, well, gloomy. Still, it's an inexpensive place for grills and *kimchi*.

KUNG TAK LAM Map pp414-15   Vegetarian

☎ 2881 9966; Ground fl, Lok Sing Centre, 31 Yee Wo St; meals from $120 per person; ⓨ 11am-11pm; Causeway Bay MTR

This long-established place, which serves Shanghai-style meatless dishes, has more of a modern feeling than most vegetarian eateries and is usually packed out. All the vegetables are 100% organic and dishes are free of MSG.

ORPHÉE Map pp414-15   French

☎ 2577 3111; Ground & 1st fls, 1 Hoi Ping Rd; starters $68-78, mains $158-188; ⓨ noon-2.30pm, 3-5.30pm (tea) & 7-10.30pm; Causeway Bay MTR

This minimalist but cosy restaurant *français* is a small pocket of Paris in Causeway Bay. If you feel like a fix of foie gras, this is your choice. There's a more established Tsim Sha Tsui branch (p179). Both offer a three-course set dinner from $168 from Sunday to Thursday and from $188 Friday and Saturday.

PAK LOH CHIU CHOW RESTAURANT

Map pp414-15   Chiu Chow

☎ 2577 1163; 16th fl, Lee Theatre Plaza, 99 Percival St; meals about $250 per person; ⓨ 11am-11pm; Causeway Bay MTR

This is one of the best Chiu Chow restaurants on Hong Kong Island, turning out the most perfect shrimp and crab balls and delectable *sek-làu-gài* (steamed egg-white pouches filled with minced chicken).

QUEEN'S CAFE Map pp414-15   Russian

☎ 2576 2658; Shop D, Ground fl, Eton Tower, 8 Hysan Ave; soups $35-41, mains $72-190; ⓨ noon-11.30pm; Causeway Bay MTR

This eatery has been around since 1952 (though obviously not at the bottom of the same modern high-rise), which accounts for its subdued yet assured atmosphere. The borsch and meat set meals – White Russian dishes that filtered through China after WWII – are pretty good. Try the *za-kuska* ($68 to $180), a mixture of Russian appetisers.

RED PEPPER Map pp414-15   Sichuanese

☎ 2577 3811; 7 Lan Fong Rd; rice & noodle dishes $80-105, mains $95-450; ⓨ 11.30am-midnight; Causeway Bay MTR

If you want to set your palate aflame, try this friendly, long-established eatery's Sichuan-style sliced pork in chilli sauce, accompanied by *daam-daam-mín* (noodles in a spicy peanut broth). Also recommended are the deep-fried beans and sizzling prawns.

SORABOL KOREAN RESTAURANT

Map pp414-15   Korean

☎ 2881 6823; 17th fl, Lee Theatre Plaza, 99 Percival St; meals $150 per person; ⓨ 11.30am-midnight; Causeway Bay MTR

This is the Korean's Korean restaurant, with helpful and informative staff. The barbecues are great and the *kimchi* dishes – notably the summer variety of the piquant and fermented cabbage – are particularly well prepared.

TAI PING KOON

Map pp414-15   International, Chinese

☎ 2576 9161; 6 Pak Sha Rd; starters $38-138, mains $64-190; ⓨ 11am-midnight; Causeway Bay MTR

This place has been around since 1860 and offers an incredible mix of Western and Chinese flavours – what Hong Kong people called 'soy sauce restaurants' in pre-fusion days. Try the borscht ($38) and the smoked pomfret ($140) or roast pigeon ($88).

TAI WOO SEAFOOD RESTAURANT

Map pp414-15   Chinese, Seafood

☎ 2893 9882; 27 Percival St; meals from $150;
🕓 11am-3am Mon-Sat, 10am-3am Sun;
Causeway Bay MTR

Tai Woo is as well known for its vegetarian dishes (try the bean curd with vegetarian crab roe) as it is for its seafood (especially lobster) and fried rice. A dish that has won awards is its crunchy shrimp ball and mini lobster in casserole ($238). Best of all, it's open until very late. There is also a Mid-Levels branch (p163).

TOMOKAZU   Map pp414-15   Japanese

☎ 2833 6339; Shop B, Lockhart House,
441 Lockhart Rd; sushi & sashimi $30-200, rice & noodle dishes $40-82; 🕓 11.30am-3pm & 5.30pm-4.30am; Causeway Bay MTR

For its location and well-prepared Japanese food, Tomokazu is a bargain. It's also the place to go for a fix of noodles or sushi in the wee hours. Set meals cost $50 to $120.

TOWNGAS AVENUE

Map pp414-15   International

☎ 2367 2710; Ground fl, 59-65 Paterson St; starters $42-128, mains $128-188; 🕓 11am-2.30pm & 6.30-10pm; Causeway Bay MTR

This is an odd concept in a Hong Kong restaurant, where the cook is usually to be heard and not seen. This restaurant, operated by a Hong Kong gas utility, allows you to watch chefs at work through a glass screen. You get to keep the recipe of the dish(es) you order and you may even spot the cooker or fridge of your heart's desire: it's also a kitchenware showroom. Set lunch of two/three/four courses is $78/98/118; four-/five-course set dinner is $208/252.

W'S ENTRECÔTE

Map pp414-15   French, Steakhouse

☎ 2506 0133; 6th fl, Express by Holiday Inn, 33 Sharp St East; starters $48-128, steaks $168-210; 🕓 noon-2.30pm & 6-10.30pm; Causeway Bay MTR

This place serves steak almost exclusively in a number of shapes and sizes but with a Gallic twist. Included in the price is a salad and as many frites (chips) as you can squeeze onto your plate. Starters are in the 'foie gras and snails' category. A three-course set lunch is $108 to $138, while a three-course set dinner is $158 to $280.

XIAO NAN GUO

Map pp414-15   Shanghainese, Northern Chinese

☎ 2894 8899; 1st fl, 1-13 Sugar St; meals from $200 per person; 🕓 11.15am-midnight; Causeway Bay MTR

This branch of another famous Shanghai-based chain with the incongruous name of 'Little Southern Country' serves excellent Shanghainese and Northern dishes and is always packed out. The staff is friendly and will help you select dishes, but don't come here for style.

XIN JIN SHI   Map pp414-15   Shanghainese

☎ 2890 1122; Shop 201-203, 2nd fl, Lee Gardens Two, 28 Yun Ping Rd; cold dishes $45-70, mains $60-300; 🕓 noon-3pm & 6-11pm; Causeway Bay MTR

This restaurant exemplifies how the world has turned upside down in Hong Kong in recent years. It's a branch of a successful mainland-based chain, with five restaurants in Shanghai, one in Taipei and another in Osaka. It offers traditional Shanghainese (the cooks are imported) in a modern, very stylish setting. Try one of the clay-pot dishes, such as braised pork meatballs with vegetables ($70).

YIN PING VIETNAMESE RESTAURANT

Map pp414-15   Vietnamese

☎ 2832 9038; Ground fl, 24 Cannon St;
rice & noodle dishes $27-48, hotpot dishes $50-58;
🕓 11am-11.30pm; Causeway Bay MTR

This little place is the 'anchor' Vietnamese restaurant on a street with more than a few of those eateries. Set lunches with soup are a snip at $32 to $45.

Cheap Eats

GENROKU SUSHI   Map pp414-15   Japanese

☎ 2803 5909; 3 Matheson St; sushi $8-36 per pair, sushi sets $75-250; 🕓 11.30am-2am; Causeway Bay MTR

Genroku is Hong Kong's most exotic fast-food chain. The sushi tears around on a conveyor belt and is reasonably fresh. The only drawback is the potentially long wait for seats, especially during the manic 1pm to 2pm lunch hour.

GOGO CAFÉ   Map pp414-15   Café, Fusion

☎ 2881 5598; Ground fl, 11 Caroline Hill Rd;
mains $108-138, set lunches $48-52; 🕓 noon-11pm Mon-Sat; Causeway Bay MTR

This is where East meets West, the place for spaghetti with *mentaiko* (fish roe) or rice with homemade bolognaise sauce. The theme here is part Japanese teahouse, part cool café, and the light meals and homemade desserts make Gogo a good place to re-energise between lunch and dinner. The neighbourhood is predominantly made up of motorcycle shops.

MOON GARDEN TEA HOUSE
Map pp414-15   Cantonese, Teahouse

☎ 2882 6878; 5 Hoi Ping Rd; tea $40-120 per pot, tea & snacks from $120 per person; ✆ noon-midnight; Causeway Bay MTR
The simple cuppa reaches Nirvana at the Moon Garden. Choose from many brews then lose an afternoon perusing tea books, admiring antiques (all for sale) and taking refills from the heated pot beside your table.

HAPPY VALLEY
In general, the restaurants and cafés in Happy Valley cater to local residents, though two places are worth making the trip out – they're both somewhat beyond the racecourse.

ADVENTIST VEGETARIAN CAFETERIA
Map pp406-7   Vegetarian

☎ 2574 6211; 7th fl, Hong Kong Adventist Hospital, 40 Stubbs Rd; soups & starters from $10, mains from $20; ✆ 7-8am, noon-2pm & 5-7pm; bus 6
This is one of the greatest bargains in Hong Kong and anyone can eat all three meals a day here.

AMIGO Map pp414-15   French, International
☎ 2577 2202; Amigo Mansion, 79A Wong Nai Chung Rd; meals from $500 per person; ✆ noon-3pm & 6-midnight; tram
Call us old-fashioned but this old relic with a Spanish name and Gallic twists is a place full of memories. The waiters still wear black tie and white gloves, there's a strolling guitarist, and women are handed roses as they leave. Swoon city…

ISLAND EAST
North Point, traditionally home to a large number of people hailing from Shanghai, can (not surprisingly) boast a number of good Shanghainese eateries. Quarry Bay

has the largest collection of restaurants in the entire district, especially in and around Tong Chong St, a short distance southeast of the Quarry Bay MTR station.

HONG KONG OLD RESTAURANT
Map pp414-15   Shanghainese

☎ 2507 1081; Basement, Newton Hotel Hong Kong, 218 Electric Rd, North Point; starters $70-120, rice & noodle dishes $25-60, mains $70-240; ✆ 11am-3pm & 5-11pm; Fortress Hill MTR
Those in the know say that this hotel restaurant, which is close to the Fortress Hill MTR station, serves some of the best Shanghainese food in Hong Kong. There's also a Tsim Sha Tsui branch (Map pp420–1; ☎ 2722 1812; 4th fl, Miramar Shopping Centre, 1-23 Kimberley Rd; ✆ 11.30am-2.45pm, 6-10.45pm).

JUNE Map pp414-15   Japanese
☎ 2234 6691; Ground fl, 56 Electric Rd, North Point; rice & noodle dishes $50-70, sushi/sashimi plates $250/300; ✆ noon-3pm & 6-11.30pm Tue-Fri, 6-10.30pm Sat-Mon; Tin Hau MTR
By all accounts this place, at the corner of Yacht St and just north of the Tin Hau MTR station, serves the most authentic Japanese food on Hong Kong Island and good-value set lunches ($60 to $100). It's well worth a trip.

NAPA VALLEY OYSTER BAR & GRILL
Map pp406-7   International

☎ 2880 0149; Ground fl, Hoi Wan Bldg, 9 Hoi Wan St, Quarry Bay; starters $66-68, mains $68-82; ✆ 11am-3pm & 6-11pm; Quarry Bay MTR
Despite its name, this modern eatery, a few steps north of (and just off) Tong Chong St, serves classic pasta and meat dishes, though there's an oyster bar offering about a dozen varieties of the bivalves and set lunches for $64 to $78. Best of all there's outside seating, a rare commodity in deepest Quarry Bay.

TUNG LOK HIN Map pp406-7   Fusion
☎ 2250 5022; 2nd fl, Oxford House, Tai Koo Place, Westlands Rd, Quarry Bay; meals from $350 per person; ✆ 11.30am-11.30pm Mon-Fri, 10am-10.30pm Sat & Sun; Quarry Bay MTR
Award-winning Tung Lok Hin, due east of Tong Chong St, is one of the more successful attempts at fusing Chinese and Western

dishes and cooking styles. If cream of tomato soup with shark's fin, and Yunnan ham and mushrooms wrapped in rice pasta don't sound convincing, the proof is in the tasting.

ISLAND SOUTH

The restaurants in this district are as varied and eclectic as the villages and settlements themselves. While the choice is obviously limited in smaller places such as Shek O and Repulse Bay, you'll still manage to eat decent Thai at the former, and enjoy one of the most delightful venues on any coast in the latter. Main St in Stanley offers diners and snackers an embarrassment of choices, and in Aberdeen Harbour you'll find what is – for better or worse – Hong Kong's best-known restaurant.

Shek O
SHEK O CHINESE & THAI SEAFOOD
Map pp406-7   Thai, Cantonese, Seafood
☎ 2809 4426; 303 Shek O Village; dishes $40-140; ⏰ 11.30am-10pm; bus 9 or 309
This hybrid of a place is hardly authentic in either category, but the portions are generous, the staff are convivial and the cold Tsingtao beers just keep on flowing.

Stanley
BAYSIDE BRASSERIE
Map p411   Fusion
☎ 2899 0818; Ground fl, 25 Stanley Market Rd; starters $48-78, mains $78-218; ⏰ 11.30am-11pm; bus 6, 6A, 6X or 260
This waterfront eatery offers a splendid view and an enormous menu, including everything from oysters (from $27 a piece) and pasta and pizzas ($68 to $158) to international and Indian main courses.

BOATHOUSE Map p411   International
☎ 2813 4467; 86-88 Stanley Main St; pasta $109-142, mains $112-228; ⏰ 11am-midnight Sun-Thu, 11am-1am Fri & Sat; bus 6, 6A, 6X or 260
All aboard for nautical overload. Salads, bruschetta and Med-inspired mains make up the bulk of the Boathouse's fleet. Steer for sea views; a table on the roof garden is something to covet. Set lunch/dinner is $98/195.

CHILLI N SPICE Map p411   Asian
☎ 2899 0147; Shop 101, 1st fl, Murray House, Stanley Plaza; starters $40-88, rice & noodle dishes $42-85, mains $48-145; ⏰ noon-11.30pm Mon-Fri, 11am-11.30pm Sat & Sun; bus 6, 6A, 6X or 260
A branch of the ever-growing chain – nine branches at last count – has found its way into Hong Kong's oldest (and reconstructed) colonial building. Expect no surprises, but the venue and views are worth a ringside table.

EL CID CARAMAR Map p411   Spanish
☎ 2899 0858; Shop 102, 1st fl, Murray House, Stanley Plaza; tapas & starters $20-55, mains $150-220; ⏰ noon-11.30pm Mon-Thu, noon-midnight Fri, 11am-midnight Sat, 11am-11pm Sun; bus 6, 6A, 6X or 260
This is one of four restaurants to take up residence in Stanley's historical Murray House. Here they serve a good range of tapas, and with the harbour view and too many *cervezas* (beers) you'll think you're in San Sebastián. Well maybe. Paella for two is $220 to $390. There's also good live music from 7pm to 11pm every day but Monday.

LORD STANLEY AT THE CURRY POT
Map p411   Indian
☎ 2899 0811; Ground fl, 92 Stanley Main St; starters $30-55, mains $55-98; ⏰ 11am-11pm Sun-Thu, 11am-1am Fri & Sat; bus 6, 6A, 6X or 260
The waterfront feels a somewhat odd place to enjoy Indian food, but the surrounds are pleasant and the views to die for. There are some good vegetarian choices here. Set lunches are $88 to $98.

LUCY'S Map p411   International
☎ 2813 9055; 64 Stanley Main St; starters $60-90, mains $160-190; ⏰ noon-3pm & 7-10pm Mon-Thu, noon-3pm & 6.30-10pm Fri, noon-4pm & 6.30-10pm Sat & Sun; bus 6, 6A, 6X or 260
This cool oasis within the hustle and bustle of Stanley Market doesn't overwhelm with choice but with quality food. The menu changes frequently as fresh produce and inspiration arrive, but the offerings tend to honest fusion rather than fancy flimflammery. There's a good selection of wines by the glass. Set dinner of two/three courses for $210/250 is available from Sunday to Thursday only.

STANLEY'S ITALIAN Map p411   Italian
☎ 2813 7313; Shop B, Ground fl, 92 Stanley Main St; starters $46-95, mains $88-126; ☒ 10am-midnight Sun-Thu, 9.30am-midnight Fri & Sat; bus 6, 6A, 6X or 260

Stanley's Italian offers pizza ($78 to $108), pasta ($80 to $94), pints and a ground-level view of the sea. Set lunches are $86 to $138.

CHEAP EATS
DÉLIFRANCE Map p411   Café
☎ 2813 1368; Lower ground fl, Yu Moon House, 17 Stanley New St; soups & salads $12-23, sandwiches & light meals $21-$43; ☒ 7am-7pm Mon-Fri, 7am-7.30pm Sat & Sun; bus 6, 6A, 6X or 260

This is a conveniently located branch of the popular café serving sandwiches, salads, light meals, baked goods and hot drinks.

WELLCOME Map p411   Supermarket
88 Stanley Village; ☒ 8am-10pm; bus 6, 6A, 6X or 260

This supermarket is in the Old Stanley Police Station, a two-storey colonial building dating from 1859, and is convenient for beach supplies, food and drink.

Repulse Bay
VERANDAH RESTAURANT
Map pp406-7   International

☎ 2812 2722; 1st fl, The Repulse Bay, 109 Repulse Bay Rd; starters $145-225, mains $275-310; ☒ noon-2.30pm, 3-5.30pm (tea) & 6.30-10.30pm Tue-Sat, 11am-3pm, 3.30-5.30pm (tea) & 6.30-10.30pm Sun; bus 6, 6A, 6X or 260

In the new-colonial bit of the wavy Repulse Bay condos, the Verandah is hushed and formal, with heavy white tablecloths and demurely clinking cutlery. The Sunday brunch is famous (book ahead); the afternoon tea is the south side's best. Set dinner of three/four/five courses is $598/688/888.

Y-BY-THE-BAY Map pp406-7   Japanese
☎ 2812 2120; Shop G202, The Repulse Bay, 109 Repulse Bay Rd; starters $45-80, sushi & sashimi $70-240, grills $150-280; ☒ 6-10.30pm Mon-Thu, noon-2.30pm & 6-10.30pm Fri-Sun; bus 6, 6A, 6X or 260

This not-so-easy-to-find small restaurant offers excellent, though simply prepared, Japanese food served in a quiet, bamboo-lined garden. One of its special come-ons is an all-you-can-eat *shabu-shabu* (thin slices of beef and vegetables cooked in a broth

TOP FIVE ISLAND EAST & SOUTH RESTAURANTS
- **Boathouse** (opposite) – good salads and Mediterranean-inspired mains on Stanley Bay
- **Hong Kong Old Restaurant** (p173) – the best Shanghainese fare in a Shanghainese neighbourhood
- **Jumbo Kingdom Floating Restaurant** (below) – tacky but fun and oh so Hong Kong
- **Lucy's** (opposite) – cool grazing oasis within the hustle and bustle of Stanley Market
- **Verandah Restaurant** (left)– Repulse Bay's most formal neocolonial restaurant

at the table) chow down for one hour ($99). Rice and noodles hover around $75.

CHEAP EATS
WELLCOME Map pp406-7   Supermarket
Shop G123, 1st fl, The Repulse Bay, 109 Repulse Bay Rd; ☒ 8am-10pm; bus 6, 6A, 6X or 260

This large supermarket can supply you with all your picnic needs.

Aberdeen
JUMBO KINGDOM FLOATING RESTAURANT Map p411   Cantonese

☎ 2553 9111; Shum Wan Pier Dr, Wong Chuk Hang; meals from $250 per person; ☒ 11am-11.30pm Mon-Sat, 7.30am-11.30pm Sun; bus 70 or 70M

The larger of two floating restaurants moored in Aberdeen Harbour and specialising in seafood, the Jumbo is touristy in the extreme and the food is so-so. The interior looks like Beijing's Imperial Palace crossbred with a Las Vegas casino; think of it as a spectacle – a show – and you'll have fun. There's free transport for diners from the pier on Aberdeen Promenade (p87). Dim sum is served from 7.30am to 4.30pm on Sunday. The other floating restaurant, the Tai Pak, is usually reserved for groups and spillovers.

RED DIAMOND CHINESE RESTAURANT Map p411   Cantonese

☎ 2518 8398; Shop 2, 1st fl, Aberdeen Centre, Nam Ning St; meals from $150 per person; ☒ 6am-midnight; bus 70 or 70M

This restaurant is *the* place for dim sum (from $10) in Aberdeen, judging from the hordes of hopefuls waiting for tables, especially weekends. Enter from Chengtu St.

CHEAP EATS
LO YU VIETNAM RESTAURANT

Map p411   Vietnamese

☎ 2814 8460; Shop C, Ground fl, Kong Kai Bldg, 184-188 Aberdeen Main St; starters $15-45, mains $38-108; ⏰ 11am-11pm; bus 70 or 70M

A lot of Vietnamese boat people who made their way to Hong Kong in the late 1970s never made it past the original 'Fragrant Harbour' – Aberdeen's name in Cantonese. Expect authentic and very cheap dishes here.

KOWLOON

Kowloon doesn't have quite the same range of restaurants as Hong Kong Island does, but you will still find an amazing assortment of ethnic eateries in Tsim Sha Tsui. For Chinese soul food, head for Yau Ma Tei or Mong Kok. Kowloon City is renowned for its Thai eateries.

TSIM SHA TSUI

Tsim Sha Tsui can claim the lion's share of ethnic restaurants in Kowloon. If you're looking for something fast, cheap and Chinese, Hau Fook St (Map pp420–1) has food stalls (dishes from about $25). It's a few blocks east of Nathan Rd in Tsim Sha Tsui and isn't included on many tourist maps. Walking north from the intersection of Carnarvon and Cameron Rds, it's the first lane on your right. Most of the places don't have English menus, but you can always point to what your fellow diners are tucking into.

A TOUCH OF SPICE

Map pp420-1   Southeast Asian

☎ 2312 1118; 1st fl, Knutsford 10 Bldg, 10 Knutsford Tce; starters $45-70, curries & seafood dishes $75-165; ⏰ noon-3pm & 6-11.30pm Mon-Sat, 6pm-midnight Sun; Tsim Sha Tsui MTR

This is one of several trendy restaurant/bars stacked up Japanese-style at 10 Knutsford Terrace. This one does Thai curries, Indonesian and Vietnamese noodles and stir-fried dishes. Most meals are good value, unless you go for the seafood.

AQUA Map pp420-1   Fusion

☎ 3427 2288; 29th fl, One Peking Rd, 1 Peking Rd; meals from $400 per person; ⏰ noon-11.30pm; Tsim Sha Tsui MTR

TOP FIVE
DIM SUM RESTAURANTS

- **City Hall Maxim's Palace** (p152) – the most raucous (and genuine) place for dim sum in Central
- **Jade Garden** (p179) – reliable (if predictable) dim sum at a chain restaurant
- **Luk Yu Tea House** (p153) – dim sum with attitude in a traditional teahouse
- **Victoria City** (p168) – excellent dim sum in surprisingly subdued surrounds
- **Zen** (p186) – dim sum with a twist amid stunning Japanese surrounds

This ultra chichi and minimalist place just below a fabulous bar called Aqua Spirit (p204) has a split personality, made up of Aqua Roma and Aqua Tokyo. The food is good but the views are simply astonishing. Afternoon tea is served from 3pm to 6pm.

ARIRANG Map pp420-1   Korean

☎ 2956 3288; Shop 2306-7, 2nd fl, Gateway Arcade, Harbour City, 25-27 Canton Rd; rice & noodle dishes $90-158, barbecues $85-160; ⏰ noon-3pm & 6-11pm; Tsim Sha Tsui MTR

This is a large, brightly lit restaurant that may not be the place for a romantic tête à tête but is great for a group. It's mostly given over to barbecue. If in doubt, order a set lunch ($98). Set dinner for two is $328.

AVENUE Map pp420-1   International

☎ 2315 1118; 1st fl, Holiday Inn Golden Mile, 50 Nathan Rd; starters $65-150, mains $178-208; ⏰ noon-2.30pm & 6-10.30pm Mon-Sat; Tsim Sha Tsui MTR

This wonderful restaurant makes Nathan Rd its focal point and changes the menu according to the season. The vegetarian selection is especially good for such a gourmet restaurant. Set lunch of two/three courses is $160/188, set dinner $308/348.

BALI RESTAURANT Map pp420-1   Indonesian

☎ 2780 2902; 10 Nanking St; dishes $38-48, set lunch from $69; ⏰ noon-11pm; Tsim Sha Tsui MTR

The food is pretty good and the service friendly, but the best thing about the Bali is its superb tackiness: a permanent 'happy birthday' sign, vinyl booths separated by fake brick walls, and a 'resort'-style bar playing tunes from *South Pacific*. Try the nasi goreng, the vegetable curry or the pork satay.

BUSAN KOREAN RESTAURANT

Map pp420-1   Korean

☎ 2376 3385; Ground fl, Kowloon Centre, 29 Ashley Rd; rice & noodle dishes $90-150, barbecues $100-130; ⏰ 10am-11.30pm; Tsim Sha Tsui MTR

This wonderfully authentic place in the bustling hub of touristy Tsim Sha Tsui manages to stay on, despite the nearby competition. Try the barbecued oysters with all the trimmings.

CHANG WON KOREAN RESTAURANT

Map pp420-1   Korean

☎ 2368 4606; 1G Kimberley St; barbecues $100-150; ⏰ 11.30am-5am; Tsim Sha Tsui MTR

If you're looking for truly authentic Korean food, head for this place, just one of several restaurants along a stretch that makes up Tsim Sha Tsui's 'Little Korea'. Try the excellent *bibimbab* ($100).

DAN RYAN'S CHICAGO GRILL

Map pp420-1   American

☎ 2735 6111; Shop 315, 3rd fl, Ocean Terminal, Harbour City, Salisbury Rd; starters & salads $52-145, mains $95-240; ⏰ 11am-midnight Mon-Fri, 10am-midnight Sat & Sun; Star Ferry

The theme at Dan Ryan's is 'Chicago', including a model elevated rail system overhead, and jazz and big-band music on the sound system. It is *the* place for burgers and ribs in Hong Kong and the pasta dishes ($98 to $130) ain't half bad. There's also a branch in Admiralty (p165).

DONG

Map pp420-1   Cantonese

☎ 2315 5166; Arcade 2, Hotel Miramar Hong Kong, 118-130 Nathan Rd; meals from $250 per person; ⏰ 11.30am-2.30pm & 6-10.30pm Mon-Sat, 10.30am-3.30pm & 6-10.30pm Sun; Tsim Sha Tsui MTR

Dong (or 'East') has the classic hotel restaurant interior right down to the cheesy music, but its menu does offer some adventurous Cantonese dishes, including seafood soups and a forest of fungi. Its fusion sister-restaurant, Xi ('West'; ☎ 2315 5155; ⏰ noon-2.30pm & 6-10.30pm), just next door, serves international food with an Asian twist. Both have a set lunch for $138.

DYNASTY

Map pp420-1   Cantonese

☎ 2369 4111, ext 6600; 4th fl, New World Renaissance Hotel, 22 Salisbury Rd; meals from $300 per person, set dinner $490-520; ⏰ 11.30am-2.30pm & 6-11pm Mon-Sat, 11am-3pm Sun; Tsim Sha Tsui MTR

The traditional rosewood furniture, latticed windows and ambience (quiet elegance) of this hotel restaurant make for an unusual (if not particularly authentic) Cantonese dining experience. Specialities include steamed sliced pork with preserved shrimp paste and fresh salmon with rice noodle strips.

EASTERN PALACE CHIU CHOW

RESTAURANT Map pp420-1   Chiu Chow

☎ 2730 6011; Shop 308, 3rd fl, Marco Polo Hongkong Hotel, 3 Canton Rd; meals from $250 per person; ⏰ 11am-11pm; Tsim Sha Tsui MTR

Chiu Chow dim sum is served at this large hotel restaurant from 11am to 4pm daily. Particularly good are the crab and shrimp balls as well as the sliced goose in vinegar.

FAT ANGELO'S

Map pp420-1   Italian, American

☎ 2730 4788; 35 Ashley Rd; pasta $88-175, mains $125-215; ⏰ noon-midnight; Tsim Sha Tsui MTR

This branch of the popular Italian-American restaurant is generous with its portions and seamless in its service. There's also a Soho branch (p159) on Hong Kong Island.

Aqua (opposite), Tsim Sha Tsui

Eating

KOWLOON

FELIX Map pp420-1 — Fusion
☎ 2315 3188; 28th fl, Peninsula Hong Kong, Salisbury Rd; starters $115-250, mains $225-420; ⏱ 6pm-midnight; Tsim Sha Tsui MTR

Felix has a fantastic setting, both inside and out. You're sure to pay as much attention to the views and the Philippe Starck–designed interior as to the fusion food (think lobster nachos, hoisin grilled ribs). Towering ceilings and copper-clad columns surround the Art Deco tables. Even the view from the men's is dizzying. A special lift will whisk you up directly. There's a set dinner for vegetarians for $480.

FOOK LAM MOON Map pp420-1 — Cantonese
☎ 2366 0286; Shop 8, 1st fl, 53-59 Kimberley Rd; meals from $300 per person; ⏱ 11am-11pm; Tsim Sha Tsui MTR

One of Hong Kong's top Cantonese restaurants, the Fook Lam Moon takes care of you from the minute you walk out of the lifts, with cheongsam-clad hostesses waiting to escort you to your table. The enormous menu contains a lot of unusual and expensive dishes (shark's fin, frog, abalone), but there are many old favourites as well. You might sample the pan-fried lobster balls, which are a house speciality.

GADDI'S Map pp420-1 — French
☎ 2315 3171; 1st fl, Peninsula Hong Kong, Salisbury Rd; starters $160-380, mains $390-780; ⏱ noon-2.30pm & 7-11pm; Tsim Sha Tsui MTR

A legend in its own time, Gaddi's still holds onto its reputation as *the* French restaurant in Hong Kong. It has boasted virtually the same menu (and some of the same staff, apparently) for more than three decades.

**TOP FIVE
TSIM SHA TSUI RESTAURANTS**

- **Chang Won Korean Restaurant** (p177) – the spot for *bulgogi* in the heart of Little Korea
- **Felix** (above) – excellent fusion food with Philippe Starck décor as backdrop
- **Fook Lam Moon** (above) – one of Hong Kong's top Cantonese restaurants with a huge menu
- **Orphée** (opposite) – out-of-place minimalist but cosy *restaurant du quartier*
- **Spring Deer** (p180) – the Deer serves some of the crispiest Peking duck in town

---

The atmosphere is a bit stilted, making it hard to relax, but the food will probably keep you excited. A three-course set lunch is $340, while dinner of four/five/six courses is $720/900/1050. Men must wear a jacket.

GAYLORD Map pp420-1 — Indian
☎ 2376 1001; 1st fl, Ashley Centre, 23-25 Ashley Rd; curries & tandoori dishes $66-130, buffet lunch/dinner $88/138; ⏱ noon-3pm & 6-11pm; Tsim Sha Tsui MTR

The first Indian restaurant to open in Hong Kong, the Gaylord has been going strong since 1972. Dim lighting, booth seating and live Indian music set the scene for enjoying the excellent *rogan josh*, dhal and other favourite Indian dishes. There are lots of vegetarian choices ($58 to $66) too.

GOLDEN BULL Map pp420-1 — Vietnamese
☎ 2730 4866; Shop 101, 1st fl, Ocean Centre, Harbour City, 3-9 Canton Rd; rice & noodle dishes $18-60, mains $60-185; ⏱ noon-3pm & 6-11.30pm Mon-Fri, noon-4pm & 6-11.30pm Sat & Sun; Tsim Sha Tsui MTR

The crowds who descend on this place at lunch and dinner are not coming for the atmosphere (noisy) or service (abrupt), but the excellent-quality, low-cost Vietnamese food. There's also a Causeway Bay branch (p170).

HARD ROCK CAFÉ
Map pp420-1 — International
☎ 2375 1323; Ground & 1st fls, Silvercord Shopping Centre, 30 Canton Rd; salads & sandwiches $75-95, burgers $88-90; ⏱ 11am-1am Sun-Thu, 11am-3am Fri & Sat; Tsim Sha Tsui MTR

Why anyone would want to come here is beyond us, but here it is should you need onion rings, chicken strips, a cheap set lunch ($65) and/or a 'Hard Rock Café Kowloon' T-shirt. It's a popular dance space with live music Tuesday to Sunday nights and happy hour is from 4pm to 7pm.

ISLAND SEAFOOD & OYSTER BAR
Map pp420-1 — International, Seafood
☎ 2312 6663; Ground fl, Knutsford 10 Bldg, 10 Knutsford Tce; starters $45-110, mains $160-290; ⏱ noon-3pm & 6pm-midnight; Tsim Sha Tsui MTR

The oyster bar here offers some 20 different varieties of the bivalve, and main courses are available by the half-portion. Pasta and rice dishes cost $95 to $175, and there are set lunches for $68 to $88.

JADE GARDEN Map pp420-1 · Cantonese

☎ 2730 6888; 4th fl, Middle Block, Star House, 3 Salisbury Rd; rice & noodle dishes $55-88, mains $68-200; ✆ 11am-11.30pm Mon-Sat, 10am-11.30pm Sun; Star Ferry

People turn their noses up at the Maxim's chain of 'Garden' restaurants, but they're not half bad, the service is excellent and the food reliable (if somewhat predictable). This branch, just opposite the Tsim Sha Tsui Star Ferry terminal, is particularly well known for its dim sum ($16 to $38), served from 11am to 2.30pm Monday to Friday, till 5pm on Saturday and from 10am to 5pm on Sunday.

JIMMY'S KITCHEN

Map pp420-1 · International

☎ 2376 0327; 1st fl, Kowloon Centre, 29-39 Ashley Rd; starters $50-125, mains $137-260; ✆ 11.30am-3pm & 6-11pm; Tsim Sha Tsui MTR

This place has a lengthy and generous menu that has attracted a loyal following since 1928. There's also a branch in Central (p153).

KING PALACE Map pp420-1 · Cantonese

☎ 2739 3311; 1st fl, Guangdong International Hotel, 18 Prat Ave; meals from $200 per person; ✆ 11am-10pm Sun-Fri, 11am-midnight Sat; Tsim Sha Tsui MTR

This ever-vibrant hotel restaurant serves excellent dim sum from 11am to 2pm daily.

KOH-I-NOOR Map pp420-1 · Indian

☎ 2368 3065; Shop 3-4, 1st fl, Peninsula Mansion, 16C Mody Rd; starters $30-52, curries & tandoori dishes $46-185; ✆ noon-3pm & 6-11.30pm; Tsim Sha Tsui MTR

One of a chain of restaurants, this branch is cheaper and less stylish than its counterpart in Central (p153), but the food is great and the staff friendly. The speciality is North Indian food, though it 'goes south' on Monday. There's a vegetarian/meat lunch buffet ($48/68) on weekdays and a set menu for two/four people for $188/468.

KYOZASA RESTAURANT

Map pp420-1 · Japanese

☎ 2376 1888; 20 Ashley Rd; dishes $48-98; ✆ noon-2.30pm & 6pm-midnight; Tsim Sha Tsui MTR

This colourful and cosy Japanese restaurant has a menu that extends from sushi

to steaks via hotpots. There are reasonably priced set lunches.

KYUSHU-ICHIBAN Map pp420-1 · Japanese

☎ 2314 7889; Ground & 1st fls, 144 Austin Rd; rice & noodle dishes $38-88, mains $48-280; ✆ 11.30am-3pm & 6pm-midnight; Tsim Sha Tsui MTR

This inexpensive Japanese eatery is a favourite with the local young bloods of Tsim Sha Tsui. Sushi is a steal, costing from $28 to $48, and there are some good-value sets.

MERHABA Map pp420-1 · Turkish

☎ 2367 2263; Ground fl, Yiu Pont House, 12 Knutsford Tce; meze & starters $40-70, mains $100-180; ✆ 4pm-2am Mon-Thu, 4pm-3am Fri & Sat, 4pm-midnight Sun; Tsim Sha Tsui MTR

The latest arrival on a street full of restaurants probably not looking for a whole lot more competition is this Turkish establishment with the exciting name of 'Hi', complete with Chinese belly dancer. As always at Turkish restaurants everywhere, it would behove you to stick with the meze and the *raki* (anise-flavoured aperitif not unlike French pastis) and eschew the main courses.

ORPHÉE Map pp420-1 · French

☎ 2730 1128; 18A Austin Ave; starters $53-88, mains $152-182; ✆ noon-2.30pm & 6.45-10.15pm Mon-Thu, noon-2.45pm & 6.45-10.30pm Fri & Sat, noon-2.30pm & 6.45-10.30pm Sun; Tsim Sha Tsui MTR

Entering this minimalist but cosy 'restaurant français' is like stumbling on a small pocket of Paris in deepest Tsim Sha Tsui. If you feel like a fill of *filet de bœuf* or some foie gras, Orphée is the choice. Set lunch is $68 to $78, while a three-course set dinner is $168 on weekdays and $188 at the weekend. There's another branch in Causeway Bay (p171).

PEKING RESTAURANT

Map pp420-1 · Northern Chinese

☎ 2730 1315; 1st fl, 227 Nathan Rd; meals from $150 per person; ✆ 11am-10pm; Tsim Sha Tsui MTR

This no-frills restaurant keeps Peking duck fans merrily chomping away. If the Peking duck ($320) doesn't do it for you, try the tasty Northern-style crab dishes and pastries.

PEP 'N' SPICES Map pp420-1   Asian

☎ 2376 0893; Basement, 10 Peking Rd; starters $48-100, rice & noodle dishes $65-70, mains $55-138; ⏱ noon-3.30pm & 6-11.30pm Mon-Fri, noon-4.30pm & 6-11.30pm Sat & Sun; Tsim Sha Tsui MTR
This friendly place serves anything that happens to be hot and spicy and Asian: from satay to *tom yum gung* (spicy prawn soup). It's a fun restaurant for a group. You can also enter from 8 Ashley Rd. Set lunch is $39 to $50, set dinner for two $148.

RUBY TUESDAY

Map pp420-1   American, International

☎ 2376 3122; Shop 310, 3rd fl, Ocean Terminal, Harbour City, Salisbury Rd; burgers $88-108, mains $144-228; ⏱ 11.30am-11pm; Star Ferry
This place boasts 'starvin' stoppers', a 'serious salad bar' ($88), and 'plentiful platters'; it's just, like, gotta be American. Huge portions.

SALISBURY DINING ROOM

Map pp420-1   International, Buffet

☎ 2268 7000; 4th fl, The Salisbury, 41 Salisbury Rd; lunch/dinner buffet $98/218; ⏱ noon-2.30pm & 6.15-9.30pm; Tsim Sha Tsui MTR
Unlimited sushi and smoked salmon make the buffets at this YMCA-run hotel a pretty good bet. Book ahead if you want a table by the window and unimpeded harbour views. Guzzlers will be glad to note that the dinner buffet includes bottomless glasses of draught beer.

SCHNURRBART Map pp420-1   German

☎ 2366 2986; 9-11 Prat Ave; sandwiches $38-55, mains $85-129; ⏱ noon-3pm & 6-10pm; Tsim Sha Tsui MTR
This is the Kowloon branch of the German eatery. The bar stays open till 2am daily and happy hour lasts from 3pm to 8pm. It's a welcome relief in Tsim Sha Tsui, where you'll find relatively few 'legitimate' (ie nongirlie) bars. The other branch is in Central (p154).

SINGAPORE RESTAURANT

Map pp420-1   Singaporean, Malaysian

☎ 2376 1282; Ground fl, Ashley Centre, 23-25 Ashley Rd; rice & noodle dishes $38-42, satay per dozen $64-90; ⏱ 11am-midnight; Tsim Sha Tsui MTR
Around at least since these two cuisines came from the same country, the Singa-

pore is an institution and was the inspiration behind the restaurant scene in Wong Kar Wai's film *In the Mood for Love*. Try the signature chicken rice.

SPOON BY ALAIN DUCASSE

Map pp420-1   French

☎ 2313 2256; Ground fl, Hotel Inter-Continental Hong Kong, 18 Salisbury Rd; starters & pasta $95-300, mains $240-330; ⏱ 6-11.30pm; Tsim Sha Tsui MTR
This new contemporary French restaurant opened by Michelin-starred chef Ducasse has the hottest tables in Hong Kong, and you should book well in advance, especially for the weekend. The menu is a little disappointing in that nouvelle sort of way, but the décor and the sumptuous harbour view more than make up for it.

SPRING DEER Map pp420-1   Northern Chinese

☎ 2366 4012; 1st fl, Lyton Bldg, 42 Mody Rd; meals from $150 per person; ⏱ noon-3pm & 6-11pm; Tsim Sha Tsui MTR
This is probably Hong Kong's most famous (though not best) Peking restaurant and serves some of the crispiest Peking duck ($280 for the whole bird) in town. This place is extremely popular, so book several days in advance.

SPRING MOON Map pp420-1   Cantonese

☎ 2315 3160; 1st fl, Peninsula Hong Kong, Salisbury Rd; starters $50-90, rice & noodle dishes $50-180, mains $90-220; ⏱ 11.30am-2.30pm & 6-10.30pm Mon-Sat, 11am-3pm & 6-10.30pm Sun; Tsim Sha Tsui MTR
The Peninsula's flagship Chinese restaurant, Spring Moon is Japanese minimalist with bits of Art Deco thrown in. The Cantonese food is excellently prepared, and the surrounds and ambience are stunning.

SWEET DYNASTY

Map pp420-1   Cantonese

☎ 2199 7799; 88 Canton Rd; soups & starters $15-20, mains $38-78; ⏱ 10am-midnight Mon-Thu, 10am-1pm Fri, 7.30am-1am Sat, 7.30am-midnight Sun; Tsim Sha Tsui MTR
Sweet Dynasty has it all, from fine dim sum (weekends only) and tofu soups to bowls of *congee* big enough to swim in. It's a riot at lunch time but somehow, amid all the clatter and kids, Sweet Dynasty retains a sense of style.

TAI FUNG LAU PEKING RESTAURANT

Map pp420-1   Northern Chinese

☎ 2366 2494; 1st fl, Windsor Mansion, 29-31 Chatham Rd South; meals from $150 per person; ⊙ noon-11pm; Tsim Sha Tsui MTR

If you can't get into the Spring Deer (opposite), try this place, which serves some fine Northern specialities, including Peking duck ($240). Enter from Hart Ave.

THREE-FIVE KOREAN RESTAURANT

Map pp420-1   Korean

☎ 2376 1545; Ground fl, 6 Ashley Rd; barbecues $87-130; ⊙ 11am-5pm & 6-11pm; Tsim Sha Tsui MTR

This place is small but sizzlingly popular, especially because of its competitive pricing. There's a set lunch for between $30 and $50 and set dinner for two for $150.

TONY ROMA'S Map pp420-1   American

☎ 2736 6850; Shop 3000, 3rd fl, Miramar Shopping Centre, 132 Nathan Rd; starters $42-77, mains $98-208; ⊙ 11.30am-midnight; Tsim Sha Tsui MTR

The subtitle – 'Famous for Ribs' – says it all. Head to this place or the **Causeway Bay branch** (Map pp414–15; ☎ 2882 3743; Shop 413-418, 4th fl, World Trade Centre, 280 Gloucester Rd) if you crave something that will stick to your, well, you know. A fat slab of what made Eve walk starts at $168, sandwiches and burgers are $68 to $78 and set lunches from $48 to $68.

VALENTINO Map pp420-1   Italian

☎ 2721 6449; Ground fl, Ocean View Court, 27A Chatham Rd South; starters $88-128, mains $178-208; ⊙ noon-11.30pm; Tsim Sha Tsui MTR

This long-established *ristorante italiano* is an upmarket alternative to the pasta and pizza joints of Tsim Sha Tsui. It's a romantic Italian classic with soft lights and nuzzling music. The seasonal menu has super soups and a good range of salads, pasta and pizza ($118 to $158) and meats.

WAN LOONG COURT

Map pp420-1   Cantonese

☎ 2734 3722; Lower level 2, Kowloon Hotel, 19-21 Nathan Rd; meals $300 per person; ⊙ 11am-3pm & 6-11.30pm Mon-Fri, 11am-11.30pm Sat & Sun; Tsim Sha Tsui MTR

There's wonderful Cantonese food with modern touches here; the dim sum (11am to 3pm Monday to Friday, 11am to 6pm Saturday and Sunday) takes some beating. Standouts include steamed beef with tangerine peel and grouper with lemongrass and minced squid. The house-special dessert is t'ai chi cake, a chestnut paste and poppy seed pastry.

WEINSTUBE Map pp420-1   Austrian, German

☎ 2376 1800; 1st fl, Honeytex Bldg, 22 Ashley Rd; mains $99-120; ⊙ noon-1am Mon-Sat; Tsim Sha Tsui MTR

Pfannengebratener fleischkäse (pan-fried meat-loaf), *Schweinshaxe* (Bavarian-style pork knuckle) and other hearty mains await you at this Austro-German wine bar, which has been going strong for over two decades. Happy hour is from 3pm to 8pm Monday to Friday and from noon to 8pm on Saturday.

WU KONG SHANGHAI RESTAURANT

Map pp420-1   Shanghainese

☎ 2366 7244; Basement, Alpha House, 27-33 Nathan Rd; rice & noodle dishes $32-78, mains $60-280; ⊙ 11.30am-midnight; Tsim Sha Tsui MTR

The specialities at this Shanghainese restaurant – cold pigeon in wine sauce and crispy fried eels – are worth a trip across town. Dim sum ($20 to $48) is served all day.

YAN TOH HEEN Map pp420-1   Cantonese

☎ 2721 1211; Shop L059, Lower level, Hotel Inter-Continental Hong Kong, 18 Salisbury Rd; rice & noodle dishes $65-160, mains $130-200; ⊙ noon-3pm & 6-11.30pm Mon-Sat, 1.30am-3.30pm & 6-11.30pm Sun; Tsim Sha Tsui MTR

On the harbour side of the Inter-Con, Yan Toh Heen's menu changes every two to three months, and if the selections get confusing there'll be a waiter hovering nearby to act as tour guide. The assorted seafood in a crispy taro basket is out of this world and the dim sum ($38 to $65) worth a trip.

Cheap Eats

BRANTO Map pp420-1   Indian, Vegetarian

☎ 2366 8171; 1st fl, 9 Lock Rd; dishes $28-57; ⊙ 11am-3pm & 6-11pm; Tsim Sha Tsui MTR

This cheap and excellent 'pure vegetarian Indian club' is where to head if you want to try South Indian dishes. Order a thali, a steel tray of *idlis* (soft rice cakes) and *dosas* with dipping sauces.

CHUNGKING MANSIONS

Map pp420-1   Indian

36-44 Nathan Rd; Tsim Sha Tsui MTR

The greatest concentration of cheap Indian and Pakistani restaurants in Kowloon is in this rabbit warren of hostels and guesthouses. Despite the grotty appearance of the building, many of these 'messes' are quite plush, though somewhat claustrophobic. The food varies in quality, but if you follow the recommendations below you should be in for a cheap and very filling meal. A good lunch will cost from about $50; for $80 to $100 you'll get a blow-out. Only a couple of these places are licensed, but you are usually allowed to BYO.

Delhi Club (☎ 2368 1682; Flat C3, 3rd fl, C Block; ☽ noon-3.30pm & 6-11.30pm) does good-value Indian and Nepalese food, especially the curry and chicken tandoori ($20). Pretty flash by Chungking Mansions standards. **Everest Club** (☎ 2316 2718; Flat D6, 3rd fl, D Block; ☽ 11am-11.30pm) boasts a cornucopia of 'Everest' cuisines but, frankly, standards have fallen in recent years. The Spartan **Islamabad Club** (☎ 2721 5362; Flat C3, 4th fl, C Block; ☽ noon-3.30pm & 6-10.30pm), serves Indian and Pakistani halal food.

Swagat Restaurant (☎ 2722 5350; Flat C3-4, 1st fl, C Block; ☽ noon-3pm & 6-11pm) is one of the most popular messes in Chungking Mansions, probably less to do with the quality of food than its liquor licence, one of the few held by a mess in this building. **Taj Mahal Club** (☎ 2722 5454; Flat B4, 3rd fl, B Block; ☽ 11am-3.30pm & 5.30-11.30pm) is popular with those who like truly hot curries, such as the chicken Madras ($40). This place can do you *raan mussalam* ($275), a leg of lamb cooked in the tandoor and feeding six to eight people, if given advance warning.

DAI PAI DONG

Map pp420-1   Hong Kong Fast Food

☎ 2317 7728; Ground fl, Hanley House, 70 Canton Rd; rice & noodle dishes $28-68, set meals $38-44; ☽ 7.30am-midnight Mon-Sat, 9am-midnight Sun; Tsim Sha Tsui MTR

This modern version of a *chàa-chàan-tèng*, a uniquely Hong Kong café with local dishes, serves meals throughout the day, but it's best to come at breakfast ($15 to $30) or for afternoon tea (2.30pm to 5.30pm) for such oddities as *yìn-yèung* (equal parts coffee and black tea with milk), *líng-lçwk* (boiled cola with lemon and ginger– the ultimate cold cure) and toast smeared with condensed milk.

DELICATESSEN CORNER

Map pp420-1   German, Delicatessen

☎ 2315 1020; Basement 1, Holiday Inn Golden Mile, 50 Nathan Rd; sandwiches $88-95, dishes $96-115; ☽ 9am-9.30pm (shop), 7.30am-11pm (café-restaurant); Tsim Sha Tsui MTR

This is an excellent place to shop for a picnic or just to pause for a pastry and coffee while thumbing through the morning papers. There's a café attached with set lunch/dinner for $108/128.

DELICIOUS CHOW NOODLE

RESTAURANT Map pp420-1   Noodle Bar

☎ 2367 0824; 22 Prat Ave; starters $17-32, mains $28-65; ☽ 7am-3am; Tsim Sha Tsui MTR

This simple and very friendly restaurant is worth trying for a cheap lunch, though the décor is a bit basic.

DÉLIFRANCE Map pp420-1   Café

☎ 2629 1845; Shop G101, Ground fl, The Gateway Arcade, Harbour City, 25-27 Canton Rd; soups & salads $12-23, sandwiches & light meals $21-43; ☽ 7.30am-8pm Sun-Thu, 7.30am-8.30pm Fri & Sat; Tsim Sha Tsui MTR

This is a branch of the popular bakery and patisserie chain noted for its pastries, muffins, submarine sandwiches and quiches (not to mention coffee).

FIRST CUP COFFEE Map pp420-1   Café

☎ 2316 7793; Shop H, Ground fl, 12 Hankow Rd; breakfast $19-22, set lunch $29-35; ☽ 7am-1am; Tsim Sha Tsui MTR

This hole-in-the-wall of a shop serves some excellent gourmet coffees (from $14) and sweet treats as well as light meals. Friendly staff.

HAPPY GARDEN NOODLE &

CONGEE KITCHEN Map pp420-1   Noodle Bar

☎ 2314 9523; 76 Canton Rd; rice & noodle dishes $13-110; ☽ 7am-2am; Tsim Sha Tsui MTR

This is a budget option, with a choice of some 200 rice, noodle and *congee* dishes on the menu, including shrimp won ton noodles ($28). There are also main dishes such as beef in oyster sauce ($55) and roast duck ($45).

OLIVER'S SUPER SANDWICHES

Map pp420-1 — Sandwich Shop

☎ 2367 0881; Shop LG1 & LG1A, Tung Ying Bldg, 100 Nathan Rd; soups & salads $12-38, sandwiches $25-39; ⏰ 7.30am-10.30pm; Tsim Sha Tsui MTR

This is a great place for breakfast, lunch or tea (set menus for $25 to $30). It packs out during lunch hour but is blissfully uncrowded at other times. Enter from Granville Rd. There's another **Tsim Sha Tsui branch** (Map pp420-1; ☎ 2376 2826; Shop 2, Upper ground fl, China Hong Kong City, 33 Canton Rd) to the west.

WELLCOME Map pp420-1 — Supermarket

28 Hankow Rd; ⏰ 8am-10pm; Tsim Sha Tsui MTR

This branch of the supermarket chain is better stocked and maintained than most.

TSIM SHA TSUI EAST

GOMITORI Map pp420-1 — Japanese

☎ 2367 8519; Shop LG5, Lower ground fl, Energy Plaza, 92 Granville Rd; dishes $50-250; ⏰ 7pm-1am Mon-Sat; bus 5C or 8

This *yakitori* restaurant the size of a cupboard will grill you chicken in a variety of ways. It's always packed with Japanese expats – always a good sign.

MARGAUX Map pp420-1 — French

☎ 2733 8750; Mezzanine, Kowloon Shangri-La, 64 Mody Rd; soups & starters $170-235, mains $285-365; ⏰ noon-2.30pm & 6.30-10.30pm Mon-Sat; bus 5C or 8

Margaux is a more relaxed and less pretentious French restaurant than many of its hotel counterparts, though the prices are just as high (if not higher). A three-course set lunch is $250, while dinner of three/four courses is $525/625.

NADAMAN Map pp420-1 — Japanese

☎ 2733 8751; Basement 2, Kowloon Shangri-La, 64 Mody Rd; set lunch $350-400, set dinner $580-700; ⏰ noon-2.30pm & 6-10.30pm; bus 5C or 8

The authentic Japanese food at this restaurant has won it a well-deserved reputation, but the décor falls somewhat short. Though it is expensive, it's worth it, and the set meals at lunch time are very good value.

NEW NORTH SEA FISHING VILLAGE

Map pp420-1 — Cantonese

☎ 2723 6843; 2nd basement, Auto Plaza, 65 Mody Sq; meals from $150 per person; ⏰ 11am-midnight; bus 5C or 8

If you can ignore the cheesy nautical décor, this place is worth a visit for its inexpensive but well-prepared fish dishes. It also has good dim sum.

ROYAL GARDEN CHINESE RESTAURANT Map pp420-1 — Cantonese

☎ 2721 5215; Lower Basement, Royal Garden Hotel, 69 Mody Rd; meals from $250 per person; ⏰ 11.30am-3pm & 6-11pm Mon-Sat, 10am-3pm & 6-11pm Sun; bus 5C or 8

This is a splendid hotel restaurant and is one of the best places in Tsim Sha Tsui for dim sum.

SABATINI Map pp420-1 — Italian

☎ 2733 2000; 3rd fl, Royal Garden Hotel, 69 Mody Rd East; starters $115-195, mains $265-385; ⏰ noon-2.30pm & 6-11pm; bus 5C or 8

Classy Sabatini is a direct copy of its namesake in Rome, with murals on the walls and ceilings and polished terracotta tiles on the floor. Even classic Italian pasta dishes ($160 to $235) such as *fettuccine carbonara* come across as light in the best sense, leaving room to sample the exquisite desserts. Set lunches of two/four courses are $148/250. The wine list is excellent but expensive.

Cheap Eats

GENKI SUSHI Map pp420-1 — Japanese

☎ 2722 6689; Shop G7-G9, Ground fl, East Ocean Centre, 98 Granville Rd; sushi $9-35 per pair, sushi sets $40-235; ⏰ 11.30am-11.30pm; bus 5C or 8

This is a branch of the popular Japanese chain, with cut-rate sushi by the piece and the plate.

GOOD SATAY Map pp420-1 — Malaysian

☎ 2739 9808; Shop 144-148, 1st fl, Houston Centre, 63 Mody Rd; dishes $30-70; ⏰ noon-10pm; bus 5C or 8

This place on the 1st floor of a shopping and office complex doesn't look promising but it serves some of the best (and most authentic) laksa and sate in town. It's packed at lunch.

WOODLANDS Map pp420-1   Indian, Vegetarian

☎ 2369 3718; Shops 5 & 6, Ground fl, Mirror Tower, 61 Mody Rd; meals from $100 per person; ☻ noon-3.30pm & 6.30-10.30pm; bus 5C or 8

If you can't handle the less-than-salubrious surrounds of Chungking Mansions (p182), this place offers inexpensive Indian meals in Tsim Sha Tsui East.

YAU MA TEI & MONG KOK

Temple St, the area around the night market, is a traditional place for cheap eats and snacks. Market cuisine, served from a pushcart, includes fish balls or squid on skewers, and there's a large choice on offer from the nearby stalls. Anything upmarket in this part of Kowloon will usually be inside a hotel of some sort.

MING COURT Map p423   Cantonese

☎ 3552 3388; 6th fl, Langham Place Hotel, 555 Shanghai St, Mong Kok; starters $55, rice & noodle dishes $53-198, mains $60-238; ☻ 11am-2.30pm & 6-10.30pm Mon-Sat, 11am-3pm & 6-10.30pm Sun; Mong Kok MTR

This hotel restaurant serves excellent modern Cantonese fare in a lovely dining room surrounded by replicas of ancient pottery unearthed in the area. Dim sum is served at lunch time daily.

PALM COURT Map pp418-19   Café

☎ 2761 1711; Metropole Hotel, 75 Waterloo Rd, Yau Ma Tei; starters $80-115, mains $85-160; ☻ 6.30am-11.30pm; Mong Kok KCR East Rail

This California-style hotel coffee shop would probably not even merit a mention if it were in the centre of Tsim Sha Tsui, but in deepest, darkest Yau Ma Tei, it's like happening upon an oasis. Sandwiches and set lunches are around $78.

SAKURADA Map p423   Japanese

☎ 2622 6164; 3rd fl, Royal Plaza Hotel, 193 Prince Edward Rd West, Mong Kok; sushi & sashimi $30-120, teppanyaki sets $98-228; ☻ 11.30am-3pm & 6-11pm; Mong Kok KCR East Rail

This place in one of Mong Kok's flashiest hotels is good for a bite after visiting the flower or bird markets. It specialises in *teppanyaki* and *kaiseki* (bite-sized treats to eat with tea or sake). There's a Japanese buffet lunch ($70) as well as set lunches ($68 to $98) available on weekdays.

Cheap Eats

GOOD HOPE NOODLE Map p423   Noodle Bar

☎ 2394 5967; 146 Sai Yeung Choi St South, Mong Kok; dishes $20-36; ☻ 11am-3am; Mong Kok MTR

This busy, late-night noodle shop with no ego problems is known for its won ton soups and shredded pork noodles with spicy bean sauce. This is an eat-and-go sort of place – don't come here if you feel like slurping slowly and lingering.

JOYFUL VEGETARIAN Map p423   Vegetarian

☎ 2780 2230; 530 Nathan Rd, Yau Ma Tei; meals around $60 per person; ☻ 11am-11pm; Yau Ma Tai MTR

This popular restaurant serves up great all-vegetarian meals. The country-style hotpot is made with a ravishing range of fungi and tons of tofu. There's a snack stall out the front of this Buddhist establishment if you're looking for a bite ($2 to $5) on the hoof (ouch!).

KUBRICK BOOKSHOP CAFÉ
Map p423   Café

☎ 2384 5465; Broadway Cinematheque, 3 Public Sq St, Yau Ma Tei; dishes $28-40; ☻ 11.30am-10pm; Yau Ma Tai MTR

This café and bookshop next to the Broadway Cinematheque (p214), with a great range of film-related books, magazines and paraphernalia, serves good coffee and decent pre-flick food such as sandwiches ($30 to $40) and pasta ($36 to $480).

MIU GUTE CHEONG VEGETARIAN RESTAURANT Map pp420-1   Vegetarian

☎ 2771 6218; 31 Ning Po St, Yau Ma Tei; meals from $50 per person; ☻ 11am-11pm; Jordan MTR

Cheap, cheerful and family-oriented vegetarian restaurant. The tofu is fresh and firm, the vegetables are the pick of the market and the tea flows freely. Takeaway dim sum is $3 to $6.

PAK BO VEGETARIAN KITCHEN
Map p423   Chinese, Vegetarian

☎ 2380 2681; Ground fl, Lee Tat Bldg, 785 Nathan Rd, Mong Kok; meals from $60 per person; ☻ 11am-11pm; Mong Kok MTR

This vegetarian restaurant up near Boundary St isn't really worth a detour, but it is here should you be dragging the streets in Mong Kok.

Kubrick Bookshop Café (opposite), Yau Ma Tei

SAINT'S ALP TEAHOUSE

Map p423   Hong Kong Fast Food
☎ 2393 2928, 2785 1023; 134 Sai Yeung Choi St South, Mong Kok; rice & noodle dishes $14-24, main dishes $27-39; ⏰ 11am-12.30am Sun-Thu, 11am-1.30am Fri & Sat; Mong Kok MTR

One in a chain of clean and very cheap snackeries in Hong Kong (look for the footprint logo). It's a great pit stop for Taiwanese-style frothy tea with tapioca drops and Chinese snacks such as shrimp balls, noodles and rice puddings. There's a second **Mong Kok branch** (☎ 2384 0220; Shop 1, Ground fl, 3-5 Fa Yuen St, Mong Kok; ⏰ 11.30am-1am) nearby and a **Tsim Sha Tsui branch** (Map pp420–1; ☎ 2369 8990; 31 Kimberley Rd; ⏰ 11am-midnight).

NEW KOWLOON

About the only reason you'd travel further north than Tsim Sha Tsui specifically for a meal would be for the Thai restaurants in Kowloon City, but there are other options.

AMARONI'S LITTLE ITALY

Map pp418-19   Italian, American
☎ 2265 8818; Shop LG132, Lower ground fl, Festival Walk, 80-88 Tat Chee Ave, Kowloon Tong; starters $49-140, mains $125-220, set lunch $89; ⏰ 11am-midnight; Kowloon Tong MTR

The first rule of American-Italian cuisine is to make it big – Sicilian-style big. And

Amaroni's doesn't stray from that law, dishing up pizza ($120 to $160), pasta ($90 to $120), seafood and steak so large that they make the floor staff strain. Kids get a free feed during the week.

CHONG FAT CHIU CHOW

RESTAURANT Map pp418-19   Chiu Chow
☎ 2383 3114, 2383 1296; 60-62 South Wall Rd, Kowloon City; meals from $150 per person; ⏰ 11am-11pm; bus 5C or 101

While this place isn't easy to get to and communications are limited, it has some of the best and freshest Chiu Chow seafood in the territory. Don't miss the crab dishes, *sek-làu-gài* (chicken wrapped in little egg-white sacs) and the various goose offerings.

FEDERAL RESTAURANT

Off Map pp418-19   Cantonese
☎ 2626 0011; Shop 353, 3rd fl, Hollywood Plaza, 3 Lung Poon St, Diamond Hill; meals from $120 per person; ⏰ 7.30am-midnight; Diamond Hill MTR

This is a bustling restaurant so big that the captains are armed with walkie-talkies to seat diners and have tables cleared. Dim sum is served until mid-afternoon and Cantonese à la carte at dinner. The dim sum menu is in Chinese only – ask your waiter to choose for you or gawp at other tables and point. Federal has another restaurant serving primarily seafood on the same floor at Shop 306.

ISLAM FOOD Map pp418–19   Halal Chinese

☎ 2382 2822; Ground fl, 1 Lung Kong Rd, Kowloon City; meals from $100 per person; ⊙ 11am-11pm; bus 5C or 101

If you fancy trying the cuisine of the Wui (Chinese Muslims), come here. Order the mutton with scallions on a hotplate, or minced beef with pickled cabbage stuffed into sesame rolls.

SNAKE KING Map pp418–19   Snake

☎ 2383 6297; Ground fl, 11 Lung Kong Rd, Kowloon City; soups $50-210; ⊙ 10am-11pm; bus 5C or 101

Should you visit Hong Kong in winter and are anxious to indulge in a taste of one of these slithering beasties, the Snake King can oblige.

ZEN Map pp418–19   Cantonese

☎ 2265 7328; Shop G25, Ground fl, Festival Walk, 80-88 Tat Chee Ave, Kowloon Tong; starters $39-60, mains $80-180; ⊙ 11.30am-3pm & 5.30-11pm Mon-Fri, 11.30am-5pm & 5.30-11pm Sat, 10.30am-5pm & 5.30-11pm Sun; Kowloon Tong MTR

Zen has won praise from the public and restaurateurs alike for its dynamic approach to Chinese cuisine, which is Cantonese served in stunning Japanese surrounds. You'll enjoy mangoes with your prawns and a multitude of dim sum dishes. There's also an **Admiralty branch** (Map pp408–9; ☎ 2845 4555; Shop LG1, Lower ground fl, Pacific Place, 88 Queensway), which keeps the same hours.

Cheap Eats
KOWLOON CITY THAI RESTAURANTS
Map pp418–19   Thai
Bus 5C or 101

Kai Tak airport may have shut down in 1998, but the neighbourhood of Kowloon City to the northeast of Tsim Sha Tsui is still worth a journey. This is Hong Kong's Thai quarter, and the area's restaurants are the place for a *tom yum* (hot and sour Thai soup) and green-curry fix. Among the simplest and most authentic (it attracts Thai domestics by the bucketful) eateries are those below. Kowloon City, packed with herbalists, jewellers, tea merchants and bird shops, is worth a postprandial look round.

One of the most authentic Thai restaurants in the area, **Friendship Thai Food** (☎ 2382

8671; 38 Kai Tak Rd; dishes $32-138; ⊙ 10.30am-3pm & 6-11.30pm) is always full of Thai domestics. **Golden Orchid Thai** (☎ 2716 1269, 2383 3076; 12 Lung Kong Rd; dishes $35-65; ⊙ noon-1am) is slightly more expensive than the Friendship but the food is excellent.

Hot Basil Thai Cuisine (☎ 2718 1088; Ground fl, 31-33 Kai Tak Rd; starters $27-96, rice & noodles $38-55, mains $45-110; ⊙ 11.30am-2.30pm & 5.30-11.30pm Mon-Fri, 11.30am-11.30pm Sat & Sun) serves decent Thai in very upmarket (for this neighbourhood) surrounds, while the **Thai Farm Restaurant** (☎ 2382 0992; Ground fl, 21-23 Nam Kok Rd; ⊙ 11.30am-3pm & 6pm-midnight Mon-Fri, 11.30am-midnight Sat & Sun), with its panelled walls and banquettes, looks like a neighbourhood café in Bangkok. **Wong Chun Chun Thai Restaurant** (☎ 2716 6269; 23 Tak Ku Ling Rd; ⊙ 11am-2am) is an enormous place spread over three floors and keeps later hours than most restaurants in the area.

NEW TERRITORIES
With very few exceptions, the New Territories is not an area offering a surfeit of culinary surprises. The following recommendations are basically to help you find sustenance along the way.

TSUEN WAN
As in most of the New Towns of the New Territories, the happiest hunting grounds for a snack or lunch in Tsuen Wan are in the shopping mall that – inevitably – tops the MTR station. But there are also often surprises further afield.

GRAND BUFFET & BALCONY
Map p424   International

☎ 2409 3226, 2409 3218; 4th fl, Panda Hotel, 3 Tsuen Wah St; starters $98-132, mains $158-178; ⊙ noon-3pm & 6-11pm; Tsuen Wan MTR

You wouldn't travel all the way to Tsuen Wan for these two restaurants sitting side by side in the Panda Hotel, but if you're touring around the area the Grand Buffet is a decent choice for lunch and the more upmarket Balcony does have decent pasta dishes and pizza ($112 to $138). The set meals (lunch buffet $148, set dinner $258 to $288) can also be good value. Take exit B2 from the Tsuen Wan MTR station.

LUK YEUNG GALLERIA Map p424 Food Court
Sau Lau Kok Rd; ⊗ **8am-midnight; Tsuen Wan MTR**
This shopping mall attached to the Tsuen
Wan MTR station has a number of places
to eat, including the usual fast-food outlets
(eg Maxim) as well as a huge **Park 'N' Shop**
(2nd fl; ⊗ 7am-11pm) for the makings of
a picnic. There are some decent food stalls
outside the Tsuen Wan market.

TUEN MUN
You'll find plenty of Chinese restaurants
and noodle shops in Tuen Mun town centre,
but it's best to travel out a way for something unusual and delicious.

MIU FAT MONASTERY
Map pp404-5 Vegetarian
☎ **2461 8567; 18 Castle Peak Rd; lunch $100;**
⊗ **noon-3.30pm; Light Rail line 751**
This restaurant, on the 1st floor of Miu Fat
Monastery in Lam Tei, due north of Tuen
Mun town centre, serves vegetarian meals
at lunch time only.

NANG KEE GOOSE RESTAURANT
Map pp404-5 Cantonese
☎ **2491 0392, 2491 9829; 13 Sham Hong Rd,**
Sun Tsuen, Sham Tseng; cold dishes from $50,
roast goose from $250; ⊗ **10.30am-10.30pm;**
bus 234A or 234B
This restaurant is a bit far-flung from Tuen
Mun for a casual meal, but if you are on
your way to the island of Ma Wan, this is the
place to come. It's the most famous roast-
goose restaurant in a village renowned for
its tasty preparation of the bird – and the
San Miguel brewery is just across the street.

YUEN LONG
Should you feel peckish while in (or passing
through) Yuen Long, there are a number of
restaurants and snack places in Yuen Long
Plaza in the centre of town, just opposite the
Fung Nin Rd LRT stop, including a branch
of **Genki Sushi** (☎ 2476 6233; Shop 281-290,
Level 2; ⊗ 11.30am-11pm) and a **Park 'N' Shop**
(⊗ 8am-11pm) on the ground floor.

KAR SHING RESTAURANT
Map pp404-5 Cantonese
☎ **2476 3228; 3rd fl, Yuen Long Plaza, 249-257**
Castle Peak Rd; meals from $120 per person;
⊗ **noon-4pm & 6-11pm; Yuen Long KCR West Rail**

Excellent dim sum is served from 7am to
4pm at this cavernous Cantonese restaurant in Yuen Long Plaza.

TAI PO & SURROUNDS
Tai Po is not the gourmet centre of the New
Territories, but there are a few decent eater-
ies to choose from in the centre and to the
northwest of Tai Po Market KCR station.
Tai Mei Tuk, the springboard for the Plover
Cove area some 6km to the northeast, boasts
a number of interesting eateries along Ting
Kok Rd, many of them Thai.

CHILI CHILI
Map pp404-5 Asian
☎ **2662 6767; 101 Lung Mei Village, Ting Kok Rd,**
Tai Mei Tuk; rice & noodle dishes $20-50, mains
$58-138, ⊗ **11am-11pm; bus 75K**
The newest and flashiest of the Tai Mei Tuk
eateries, Chili Chili is at the western end of
the strip towards Tai Po. It's a comfortable
place with outside seating and an eclectic
menu (Thai curries, Cantonese noodles etc).

CHUNG SHING THAI RESTAURANT
Map pp404-5 Thai
☎ **2664 5218; 69 Lung Mei Village, Ting Kok Rd, Tai**
Mei Tuk; rice & noodle dishes $26-32, mains $42-108;
⊗ **noon-3pm & 6pm-midnight; bus 75K**
This is the flagship restaurant of the restaurant strip in Tai Mei Tuk, the one that
launched the entire fleet. It remains very
popular for its authentic Thai curries, soups
and fish dishes but caters for less adventurous locals with a few Chinese offerings.

COSMOPOLITAN CURRY HOUSE
Map p424 Indonesian, Malaysian
☎ **2658 6915, 2650 7056; 80 Kwong Fuk Rd, Tai Po;**
curries $49-108, set meals from $28; ⊗ **11.30am-**
5am; Tai Po Market KCR
The Indonesian/Malaysian curries at this Tai
Po institution are excellent, but be sure to
book, especially in the evening.

EMPEROR SUSHI
Map p424 Japanese
☎ **2638 0222; 28-32 Tai Wing Lane, Tai Po;**
sushi $10-50, sashimi $65-100, rice & noodle dishes
$28-33; ⊗ **11.30am-10pm; Tai Po Market KCR**
This little sushi bar, in the popular shopping
area also called Four Lanes Square and
opposite a garden with a fountain, is a cut
above the usual and very centrally located.
Set meals run from $38 to $48.

LITTLE EGRET RESTAURANT

Map pp404-5   International

☎ 2657 6628; Tai Po Kau Interactive Nature Centre, 2 Hung Lam Dr, Tai Po Kau; starters $60-88, mains $72-178; ⚇ 10.30am-6.30pm Mon-Sat, 11am-11pm Sun; bus 70 or 72

In the same complex as the nature centre and the Museum of Ethnology (p117) is this attractive little restaurant serving a mix of dishes – from seafood to pasta ($78 to $98).

MALI-BU Map pp404-5   Thai

☎ 2637 2180; 27A Lung Mei Village, Ting Kok Rd, Tai Mei Tuk; dishes $25-100; ⚇ 11am-11pm; bus 75K

Head for this place for a fix of Thai noodles and/or curry only if the nearby Chung Shing Thai Restaurant is full.

SHALIMAR Map p424   Indian

☎ 2653 7790; 127 Kwong Fuk Rd, Tai Po; starters $20-30, curries & tandoori dishes $35-100; ⚇ 11.30am-3pm & 5.30-11pm; Tai Po Market KCR

If you prefer your curries more subcontinental or you can't get into the Cosmopolitan, the Shalimar is a short distance away to the southeast. Set lunches are $30 to $40, while set dinner for two is $128.

SHA TIN

The multilevel New Town Plaza shopping mall (Map p425) connected to the Sha Tin KCR station has more restaurants and snack bars than you can shake a chopstick at, including a branch of the **Saint's Alp Teahouse** (☎ 2608 9088; Shop A189, 1st fl, New Town Plaza Phase III; ⚇ 11am-11pm).

A-1 RESTAURANT Map p425   International

☎ 2699 0428; Shop 140-151, 1st fl, New Town Plaza Phase I; starters $45-65, mains $70-105; ⚇ 11am-11pm; Sha Tin KCR

The A-1 fills a welcome Western void in an area rife with Chinese and ethnic offerings. It serves the usual dishes – steaks and seafood – and is popular with families at the weekend. The nearby **A-1 Bakery Shop** (☎ 2697 6377) is a bonus for self-caterers.

KAGA JAPANESE RESTAURANT

Map p425   Japanese

☎ 2603 0545; Shop A191-A193A, 1st fl, New Town Plaza Phase III; rice & noodle dishes $52-85, teppanyaki $45-188; ⚇ 11am-3pm & 6-11pm; Sha Tin KCR

Kaga is a bit sterile and the service somewhat abrupt, but the sushi (salmon or yellow tail tuna $14 to $65), grilled eel and tempura ($70 to $90) make up for it.

KOH-I-NOOR map p425   Indian

☎ 2601 4969; Shop A181-182, 1st fl, New Town Plaza Phase III; starters $32-52, curries & tandoori dishes $62-130; ⚇ noon-3pm & 6-11.30pm; Sha Tin KCR

This popular place, with branches in Central (p153) and Tsim Sha Tsui (p179), is a good and stylish choice for North Indian food. A set menu for two is a snip at $188.

ONE ONE PASTA Map p425   Italian

☎ 2699 9449; Shop 451-453, 4th fl, New Town Plaza Phase I; starters $38-68, grills $98-238; ⚇ noon-5pm & 6-11pm; Sha Tin KCR

This large, stylish restaurant in Sha Tin's New Town Plaza has many DIY menus, including pastas ($58 to $92) and stone-grilled things.

SAI KUNG

Sai Kung town is chock-a-block with eateries. Here you'll find curry, pizzas and bangers and mash just as easily as Chinese seafood, but you'd make a special trip here only for that last category.

ALI-OLI Map p425   Bakery, Café

☎ 2792 2655; 11 Sha Tsui Path; meals from $100 per person; ⚇ 7am-7pm; bus 92 or 299

This bakery-cum-café has pizza slices ($9), quiches (whole $65, slice $15), Cornish pasties ($24), Savoy pies ($29 to $38) and assorted loaves, cakes and pies.

CHUEN KEE SEAFOOD RESTAURANT

Map p425   Chinese, Seafood

☎ 2792 9294; Ground fl, 87-89 Man Nin St; meals $150-200 per person; ⚇ 11am-11pm; bus 92 or 299

Chuen Kee, the grandaddy of the Sai Kung seafood restaurants, has three nearby waterfront branches so there'll always be room for you somewhere.

DIA Map p425   Indian

☎ 2791 4466; Shop 2, Block A, Ground fl, 42-56 Fuk Man Rd; starters $35-50, curries & tandoori dishes $65-130; ⚇ 11am-11pm; bus 92 or 299

This stylish place, all blue satin and rattan, serves North Indian cuisine. Set lunch is from $48, while set dinner for two is $228.

TOP FIVE
NEW TERRITORIES RESTAURANTS

- **Chung Shing Thai Restaurant** (p187) – Tai Mei Tuk's flagship restaurant, popular for its authentic Thai dishes
- **Dia** (opposite) – stylish Sai Kung curry house with North Indian cuisine
- **Miu Fat Monastery** (p187) – meatless meals at the monastery's vegetarian restaurant
- **Nang Kee Goose Restaurant** (p187) – far-flung place worth the trip for its famous roast goose
- **Tung Kee Restaurant** (right) – pick of the crop for Cantonese seafood on Sai Kung's waterfront

FIRENZE Map p425   Italian
☎ 2792 0898; 60 Po Tung Rd; starters $25-88, mains $98-118; ☺ noon-11pm; bus 92 or 299
This intimate Italian favourite does full meals as well as excellent pizza ($68 to $120) and pasta dishes ($65 to $78).

HUNG KEE SEAFOOD RESTAURANT
Map p425   Chinese, Seafood
☎ 2792 1348; Shop 4-8, Ground & 1st fls, Siu Yat Bldg, Sai Kung Hoi Pong Sq; meals $150-200 per person; ☺ 6.30am-midnight; bus 92 or 299
See the jumble of glass tanks that ends at the kitchen? That's dinner. Choose your fish or shellfish live from the stall outside and tell the staff how you want it cooked; most want their catch simply steamed with ginger. Looking right out onto the water, Hung Kee has one of the largest selection of seafood in town and dim sum daily from 6.30am to 3.30pm.

INDIAN CURRY HUT Map p425   Indian
☎ 2791 2929, 2791 2333; 64 Po Tung Rd; starters $28-46, curries & tandoori dishes $48-95; ☺ 11.30am-11.30pm; bus 92 or 299
If you can't stand looking at finned creatures from the deep any longer, head for the Indian Curry Hut. This is also the place for vegetarians, with more than a dozen dishes on offer ($46 to $66).

JASPA'S Map p425   International, Fusion
☎ 2792 6388; 13 Sha Tsui Path; starters $65-95, mains $90-160; ☺ 8am-10.30pm Mon-Sat, 9am-midnight Sun; bus 92 or 299
Jaspa's is an upbeat and casual place serving international and fusion food. Weekday

set lunch is $88, while all-day breakfast at the weekend is $88. There's also a **Soho branch** (Map p412; ☎ 2869 0733; 28-30 Staunton St; ☺ 8am-midnight) on Hong Kong Island.

PEPPERONI'S PIZZA
Map p425   Italian
☎ 2791 0394; Lot 1592, Po Tung Rd; starters $45-70, pizzas $70-125; ☺ 11am-11pm; bus 92 or 299
This place serves up some fine pizza and other dishes, and the atmosphere is relaxing and fun.

SAI SQUARE Map p425   International
☎ 2792 8900; Sai Kung Hoi Pong Sq; starters $48-58, rice & pasta dishes $78-88, mains $98-188; ☺ 11am-11pm Mon-Fri, 10am-11pm Sat & Sun; bus 92 or 299
This purpose-built restaurant with a planted rooftop in a waterfront park by Sai Kung Bay is the perfect place to while away a warm Sunday afternoon.

SAUCE Map p425   International
☎ 2791 2348; 9 Sha Tsui Path; starters $54-82, mains $98-135; ☺ 11am-11pm Mon-Fri, 10am-11pm Sat & Sun; bus 92 or 299
This very stylish restaurant on a narrow pedestrian path in the centre of Sai Kung town has outside seating.

STEAMERS BAR & RESTAURANT
Map p425   International
☎ 2792 6991; 23 Chan Man St; breakfast $38-65, mains $45-85; ☺ 8.30am-1am; bus 92 or 299
This bar-restaurant is a very popular place with outside seating. It serves pub grub – bangers and mash ($48), giant burgers ($75) and so on – to a largely expat crowd. Happy hour is 2pm to 9pm Monday to Friday, 5pm to 8pm Sunday.

TUNG KEE RESTAURANT
Map p425   Chinese, Seafood
☎ 2792 7453; 96-102 Man Nin St; meals $150-200; ☺ 6am-11pm; bus 92 or 299
This is the pick of the crop for Cantonese seafood in Sai Kung. It's not cheap, but the food is outstanding. Try to call first – though it has a few other branches, including one on nearby Sai Kung Hoi Pong Sq, to seat you at as an alternative. Dim sum is available daily from 6am to 3pm.

Eating

NEW TERRITORIES

Cheap Eats
SAI KUNG SUPERMARKETS
Map p425   Supermarket
Bus 92 or 299
For self-catering, Sai Kung has both a
Park 'N' Shop (18-20 Fuk Man Rd; ☾ 7.30am-
10.30pm) and a **Wellcome** (Chan Man St;
☾ 7am-10pm).

TAP MUN CHAU
You won't starve to death on remote Tap
Mun, but you also won't have much of a
choice in the way of venues. There's only
one restaurant on this far-flung island, but
the food is good and the staff helpful and
friendly.

NEW HON KEE
Map pp404-5   Chinese, Seafood
☎ 2328 2428; 4 Sai Kung Hoi Pong St; meals under
$100 per person; ☾ 11am-2pm Mon-Fri, 11am-6pm
Sat & Sun; Tap Mun ferry

Squid drying in the sun, Sai Kung (p188)

This seafood restaurant, popular with
islanders and visitors alike, is a short walk
northeast of the ferry pier on the way to
the Tin Hau temple. The grilled prawns and
squid are very good.

OUTLYING ISLANDS
Restaurants and other eateries vary widely
from island to island. Some, like those on
Lantau (and to a large extent Cheung Chau),
are just convenient refuelling stations as you
head for (or return from) your destination.
Others, such as the seafood restaurants in
Sok Kwu Wan on Lamma or on Po Toi, are
destinations in their own right.

LAMMA
Lamma offers the greatest choice of restaurants and cuisines of any of the Outlying Islands. Most people head directly to
Sok Kwu Wan for a fix of Cantonese-style
seafood, but Yung Shue Wan has a vast
and eclectic range, and there are a couple
of other venues elsewhere on the island,
including a famous pigeon restaurant, that
are worth the trip in itself.

Yung Shue Wan
Yung Shue Wan has a large choice of places
to eat. Along its main (and only) street, not
only will you find Chinese restaurants, but
also Western, vegetarian, Thai and even
Indian ones.

BLUE BIRD Map p426   Japanese
☎ 2982 0687; 24 Main St; rice & noodle dishes
$35-50, mains $38-80; ☾ 11.30am-3pm &
5.30pm-12.30am; Lamma (Yung Shue Wan) ferry
This little café-restaurant offers simple but
tasty Japanese dishes – from sushi and
sashimi ($12 to $30) to *teppanyaki* and
tempura.

BOOKWORM CAFÉ
Map p426   Café, Vegetarian
☎ 2982 4838; 79 Main St; breakfast $25-60,
dishes $40-80; ☾ 10am-9pm Mon-Fri, 9am-10pm
Sat, 9am-9pm Sun; Lamma (Yung Shue Wan) ferry
This place is not just a great vegetarian
café-restaurant with fruit juices and organic
wine ($35 per glass, from $198 a bottle),
but a secondhand bookshop and an Internet café ($0.50 per minute) as well.

DELI LAMMA CAFÉ

Map p426   Café, International

☎ 2982 1583; 36 Main St; starters $35-50, mains $70-105; ☽ 9am-1am; Lamma (Yung Shue Wan) ferry

This relaxed café-restaurant serves continental fare leaning towards the Mediterranean, with a fair few pasta dishes and pizzas. It's a great place for breakfast ($35 to $70) and lunch (sandwiches $40 to $60). Excellent bar and views of the harbour.

LAMMA BISTRO Map p426   International

☎ 2982 4343; 44 Main St; mains $60-125; ☽ 5-10pm Mon-Fri, 9am-10pm Sat, 8am-10pm Sun; Lamma (Yung Shue Wan) ferry

This jack of all trades serves breakfast ($35 to $75), snacks and meals. If you're not too hungry, go for a sandwich ($35 to $70); otherwise there is pizza and pasta for $60 to $165. Plenty of outside seating too.

LANCOMBE SEAFOOD RESTAURANT

Map p426   Chinese, Seafood

☎ 2982 0881; Ground & 1st fls; 47 Main St; meals from $150 per person; ☽ 10.30am-midnight; Lamma (Yung Shue Wan) ferry

This popular seafood restaurant has a delightful terrace facing the sea on the 1st floor. The salt and pepper squid and the steamed prawns are excellent.

MAN FUNG SEAFOOD RESTAURANT

Map p426   Chinese, Seafood

☎ 2982 0719; 5 Main St; meals $200 per person; ☽ 11am-10pm; Lamma (Yung Shue Wan) ferry

This friendly place just up from the ferry pier has the main ingredients of its dishes on full, living display. The lobster and prawns are especially recommended here.

PIZZA MILANO Map p426   Italian

☎ 2982 4848; Flat A, Ground fl, 2 Back St; pizzas $50-98, pasta $58-72; ☽ 6-11pm Mon-Fri, noon-11pm Sat & Sun; Lamma (Yung Shue Wan) ferry

If you're looking for pizza, pasta, calzone or crostini, Lamma's only Italian restaurant is the right choice. Small/medium/large pizzas cost from $50/62/98.

SAMPAN SEAFOOD RESTAURANT

Map p426   Chinese, Seafood

☎ 2982 2388; 16 Main St; dishes $42-120; ☽ 6am-10.30pm; Lamma (Yung Shue Wan) ferry

Sampan remains very popular with locals (always a sure sign) for both its seafood and its pigeon dishes. It has dim sum from 6am to 11am daily and boasts a great sea view.

SPICY ISLAND Map p426   Indian

☎ 2982 0830; 23 Main St; starters $20-35, curries & tandoori dishes $35-115; ☽ 11am-midnight; Lamma (Yung Shue Wan) ferry

This place promises (and delivers, say locals) 'genuine Indian cuisine'. You can dine alfresco, and it's become something of a local hang-out, especially when the racing is on. The set lunch/dinner is $45/68.

Hung Shing Yeh

This popular beach southeast of Yung Shue Wan has a convenient waterfront hotel where you can lunch on the terrace. It also boasts one of the most famous nonseafood restaurants on the Outlying Islands.

CONCERTO INN Map p426   Asian, International

☎ 2982 1668, 2836 3388; 28 Hung Shing Yeh Beach; dishes $49-58; ☽ 8am-10pm; Lamma (Yung Shue Wan) ferry

The food is no great shakes at Lamma's only real hotel, but if you're on the beach at Hung Shing Yeh and fancy rice or noodles ($39 to $52), pasta ($49) or a sandwich ($29 to $53), you won't have to travel far.

HAN LOK YUEN Map p426   Cantonese

☎ 2982 0608; 16-17 Hung Shing Yeh Beach; dishes $55-85; ☽ 11am-9.30pm; Lamma (Yung Shue Wan) ferry

This restaurant is famous throughout Hong Kong for its roast pigeon, but make sure to book at the weekend. The quail ($62) and salted prawns ($85) are also exceptional.

Sok Kwu Wan

An evening meal at Sok Kwu Wan is an enjoyable way to end a trip to Lamma. The restaurants line the waterfront on either side of the ferry pier and will be chock-a-block on weekend nights with Chinese and expats who have arrived by ferry, on boats laid on by the restaurants themselves, on company junks or on the ostentatious yachts known locally as 'gin palaces'. Most of the dozen or so restaurants offer the same relatively high-quality seafood at similar prices, but a few places stand out from the pack.

LAMMA HILTON SHUM KEE SEAFOOD
RESTAURANT Map p426 — Chinese, Seafood
☎ 2982 8241; 26 First St; meals $200 per person;
⊙ 10.30am-11.30pm; Lamma (Sok Kwu Wan) ferry
Some people consider this the best seafood
restaurant in Sok Kwu Wan (and, no, it's not
connected with the hotel chain).

RAINBOW SEAFOOD RESTAURANT
Map p426 — Chinese, Seafood
☎ 2982 8100; Shops 1A-1B, Ground fl, 23-24 First St;
meals $200 per person; ⊙ 11am-11pm; Lamma
(Sok Kwu Wan) ferry
The Rainbow, with a waterfront location,
specialises in seafood, especially steamed
grouper, lobster and abalone. A plus is that
when you book a table, you have the option
of being transported by small ferry from
Queen's Pier in Central (up to seven sailings
on weekdays from 2.40pm to 9pm, and up
to a dozen at weekends from 11.30am to
9pm) or from Aberdeen (three optional sailings at 6.15pm, 7.15pm and 8pm).

TAI YUEN RESTAURANT
Map p426 — Chinese, Seafood
☎ 2982 8386, 2982 8391; 15 First St; meals $150-
200; ⊙ 10am-11pm; Lamma (Sok Kwu Wan) ferry
This smaller place offers less frenetic,
friendlier service than most of the other
places in Sok Kwu Wan.

Mo Tat Wan
Surprisingly, in this relatively remote corner of Lamma there's an upmarket Western
restaurant.

COCOCABANA Map p426 — Fusion
☎ 2328 2138; 7 Mo Tat Wan; starters $55-90,
mains $140-165; ⊙ noon-10pm Tue-Sun
This is arguably the most romantic spot on
Lamma. The main menu is a mix of North
African and Mediterranean, but there are
also a half-dozen Asian dishes ($65 to $95).

CHEUNG CHAU
In Cheung Chau village, south of the cargo
pier and at the start of Tai Hing Tai Rd,
there are a number of food stalls with fish
tanks where you can choose your favourite
finned or shelled creatures at more or less
market prices and then pay the stall holders
to cook them the way you like.

Pak She Praya Rd, running northwest off
Praya St, is loaded with seafood restaurants
that face the typhoon shelter and its flotilla
of junks and sampans.

EAST LAKE Map p428 — Cantonese
☎ 2981 3869; 85 Tung Wan Rd; mains $45-85, fish
from $125; ⊙ 10am-9.30pm; Cheung Chau ferry
This Cantonese restaurant, away from the
waterfront and close to Tung Wan Beach, is
popular with locals and expats, especially in
the evening when tables are set up outside.

HING LOK Map p428 — Chinese, Seafood
☎ 2981 9773; 2A Pak She Sixth Lane; mains $50-80,
fish from $120; ⊙ 10am-10.30pm; Cheung Chau ferry
Hing Lok is a tad further north along the
waterfront than neighbour Hong Kee, but
it serves excellent seafood and is within
casting distance of the harbour.

HOMETOWN TEAHOUSE Map p428 — Café
☎ 2981 5038; 12 Tung Wan Rd; snacks $9-18,
afternoon tea $20; ⊙ noon-midnight; Cheung
Chau ferry
This wonderfully relaxed place run by an
amiable Japanese couple serves lunch
and dinner, but the afternoon tea – sushi,
pancake, tea – is what you should come for.
It's convenient to Tung Wan Beach.

HONG KEE Map p428 — Chinese, Seafood
☎ 2981 9916; Ground fl, 11A Pak She Praya
Rd; mains $45-80, fish from $145; ⊙ 10.30am-
10.30pm; Cheung Chau ferry
This is one of the top spots along Pak She
Praya St and should be your first choice. Try
the lobster with black bean sauce.

LONG ISLAND RESTAURANT
Map p428 — Chinese, Seafood
☎ 2981 1678; Ground fl, 51-53 San Hing St; dishes
$42-60; ⊙ 5am-2am; Cheung Chau ferry
This Cantonese restaurant goes several
steps beyond seafood. You can order a
variety of dishes, including hotpot, steamed
pigeon and dim sum, until the wee hours.

NEW BACCARAT Map p428 — Chinese, Seafood
☎ 2981 0606; 9A Pak She Praya Rd; meals from $120
per person; ⊙ 11am-10.30pm; Cheung Chau ferry
Head for this place, the furthest north
along the restaurant strip, if Hong Kee is
too full to fit you in.

SEA DRAGON KING

Map p428 — Chinese, Seafood

☎ 2981 1699; 16 Tai Hing Tai Rd; dishes $45-60, fish from $100; ☯ 10am-11.30pm; Cheung Chau ferry

Sea Dragon King, at the corner of Tai Hing Tai Rd and Praya St, has a wonderful choice of live seafood on display. It's away from the flasher waterfront restaurants and, as a result, is cheaper and more popular with local people.

Cheap Eats

CHEUNG CHAU SUPERMARKETS

Map p428 — Supermarket

Cheung Chau ferry

There is both a **Wellcome** (Praya St; ☯ 8am-midnight) and a **Park 'N' Shop** (cnr Tung Wan Rd & Tai San Back St; ☯ 7.30am-11pm) in Cheung Chau village. These two supermarkets are conveniently located near the ferry pier, so you can stock up on food and drink if you are going hiking or spending the day on the beach. **Park 'N' Shop** (97A Praya St; ☯ 7am-11pm) also has a smaller branch close to the wet market.

LANTAU

The lion's share of Lantau's restaurants is, naturally enough, in Mui Wo (Silvermine Bay), but you certainly won't starve in places further afield such as the settlements along South Lantau Rd, on the Ngong Ping Plateau and in Tai O. Discovery Bay has its own line-up of eateries around Discovery Bay Plaza.

Mui Wo

You'll find a slew of restaurants, noodle shops and bars to the southwest of the ferry pier. There are also some restaurants on the way to Silvermine Bay Beach and on the beach itself. For some pub recommendations, see p206.

BAHÇE Map p429 — Turkish

☎ 2984 0222; Shop 19, Ground fl, Mui Wo Centre, 3 Ngan Wan Rd; meze & starters $28-45, mains $45-80; ☯ 11.30am-11pm Mon-Fri, 10am-11pm Sat & Sun; Lantau ferry

'The Garden' might be a somewhat ambitious name for this small eatery but it has

all our Turkish favourites, including *sigara böreği* (filo parcels filled with cheese) and *yaprak dolmasi* (stuffed vine leaves) as well as kebabs and felafel ($40 to $48).

HIPPO BAR RESTAURANT

Map p429 — Thai, Indian

☎ 2984 0605; Shop D, Ground fl, Grand View Mansion, 11 Mui Wo Ferry Pier Rd; starters $25-30, rice & noodle dishes $38-68, curries & tandoori dishes $38-89; ☯ 10am-midnight; Lantau ferry

We're usually suspicious of places that serve two such disparate cuisines, but if you stick to the Indian dishes at this bar-restaurant hidden in an alley behind the Rome restaurant you'll do fine. Happy hour is from 6pm to 9pm.

LA PIZZERIA Map p429 — Italian

☎ 2984 8933; Ground fl, Grand View Mansion, 11C Mui Wo Ferry Pier Rd; pizza $45-95, mains $77-103; ☯ 10am-3pm, 6-11pm Mon-Fri & 11am-11pm Sat & Sun; Lantau ferry

Most people come here for the pizza, but there are lots of pasta choices ($57 to $65) and main courses such as fajitas ($83) and barbecued spareribs ($115) on the menu.

SILVERMINE BEACH HOTEL

Map p429 — International

☎ 2984 8295; Tung Wan Tau Rd; set meals $138-198; ☯ 11.30am-3pm & 6.30-9.30pm; Lantau ferry

The coffee shop and Chinese restaurant at this relatively flashy hotel is no great shakes, but it can be recommended for its all-you-can-eat buffet (adult/child $138/98) from Sunday to Friday and its barbecue buffet ($198/128) on Saturday.

TOP FIVE
OUTLYING ISLANDS RESTAURANTS

- **Bahçe** (left) – Lantau takes a Turkish twirl with 'the Garden'
- **Han Lok Yuen** (p191) – Lamma restaurant celebrated for its roast pigeon
- **Lamma Bistro** (p191) – jack-of-all-trades eatery with plenty of outside seating
- **Rainbow Seafood Restaurant** (opposite) – multi-outlet place on Sok Kwu Wan Bay
- **Stoep Restaurant** (p195) – Mediterranean-style terrace restaurant on a Lantau beach

Eating OUTLYING ISLANDS

Seafood for sale, Sai Kung (p188)

TAK CHAI KEE SEAFOOD
RESTAURANT Map p429   Chinese, Seafood
☎ 2984 1265; 1 Chung Hau Rd; dishes $50-96;
◷ noon-3pm & 6-10pm; Lantau ferry
This friendly restaurant catches delightful sea breezes from Silvermine Bay and is among the best Chinese restaurants in Mui Wo. Try the chilli prawns ($80), squid with vegetables ($50), chicken with cashew nuts ($50) or crab with ginger ($96).

CHEAP EATS
JAKS Map p429   Café
☎ 2984 7806; Shop N, Ground fl, Seaview Bldg, 1 Ngan Wan Rd; sandwiches & savoury pies $15-30; ◷ 7.30am-10pm Mon, Tue & Thu-Sat, 9am-10pm Sun; Lantau ferry
This place serves everything from soup to hotdogs, but if you're looking for honest-to-goodness English fish and chips ($30 to $95) or fried breakfast ($45), look no further.

MUI WO COOKED FOOD MARKET
Map p429   Cantonese
Ngan Kwong Wan Rd; meals from $35; ◷ 6am-midnight; Lantau ferry
The food isn't great at this series of covered food stalls northwest of the ferry pier, but it's cheap and convenient – especially if you're headed for the beach. Only a few of the stalls and restaurants have English menus, including Yee Henn Seaview Restaurant (☎ 2984 2778), the last restaurant on the western side of the market.

MUI WO MARKET Map p429   Market
Ngan Shek St; ◷ 6am-8pm; Lantau ferry
Silvermine Bay's covered wet market is towards the west after you cross the footbridge over the Silver River. You won't find much fresh fish here after 11am.

MUI WO SUPERMARKETS
Map p429   Supermarket
You'll find a Park 'N' Shop (Mui Wo Ferry Pier Rd; ◷ 8am-10pm) and a Wellcome (Ngan Wan Rd; ◷ 8am-10pm) in the centre of Mui Wo.

ROME RESTAURANT
Map p429   Cantonese, International
☎ 2984 7982; Shop A-B, Ground fl, Grand View Mansion, 11A Mui Wo Ferry Pier Rd; rice dishes $28-37, grills $45-65; ◷ 7am-10.30pm; Lantau ferry
The food – an odd, uniquely Hong Kong mix of Chinese and Western – is not the best, and you may have trouble making yourself understood unless you just point, but Rome is close to the ferry pier.

Discovery Bay
The restaurants in the circular plaza opposite the ferry pier at Discovery Bay (Map p427) offer a wide variety of cuisines.

BREZZA Map p427   Italian
☎ 2914 1906; Shop G01, Ground fl, Block A, Discovery Bay Plaza; starters $35-75, mains $95-145; ◷ noon-10pm; Discovery Bay ferry

Although it does offer more substantial dishes, this Italian place is a good choice for pizza ($75 to $95) and pasta dishes ($80 to $110). It also has pleasant outside seating.

SHOUGON Map p427 Korean

☎ 2987 9299; Shop G07, Ground fl, Discovery Bay Plaza; mains $50-95, barbecues $70-130; ⏰ 11.30am-2.30pm & 5.30-10.30pm Mon-Fri, 11.30am-10.30pm Sat & Sun; Discovery Bay ferry
The Korean food at the Shougon, which has nothing to do with a Japanese shogun by the way, might not be as authentic as what you'd find in Sheung Wan, but it's good nonetheless.

South Lantau Road

Two of the villages along South Lantau Rd, Lantau's main east–west thoroughfare, have decent restaurants from which to choose.

GALLERY Map p427 Middle Eastern, Barbecue

☎ 2980 2582; 26 Tong Fuk Village; starters $35-55, steaks & fish $95-210; ⏰ 6pm-late Mon-Fri, noon-late Sat & Sun; bus 1, 2 or 3
This Middle Eastern(ish) restaurant, on a terrace with an arbour overlooking South Lantau Rd, has some good international dishes and, at the weekend, a decent barbecue, with kebabs and other grills ($95 to $110).

KUNG SHING Map p427 Cantonese

☎ 2980 2711; 35 Lower Cheung Sha Village; mains $45-60, fish dishes from $120; ⏰ 7am-8pm; bus 1, 2 or 3
If you can't get into the Stoep next door, which will happily place your table right on the sand, is a viable alternative. The excellent rice and noodle dishes are $35 to $45.

OOH LA LA! Map p427 French, Mediterranean

☎ 2546 3543; Pui O Beach; shared plates $30-75, cheese/meat fondue for 2 $280-320; ⏰ 10.30am-11.30pm Mon-Sat, 10.30am-10pm Sun; bus 1, 2 or 3
This simple place at the Treasure Island on Lantau (p274) has a meat and seafood barbecue in the summer and fondue in the winter. The terrace directly on the beach is a bonus, as is the Ooh La La! signature Pui-O-Punch.

STOEP RESTAURANT

Map p427 Mediterranean, South African
☎ 2980 2699; 32 Lower Cheung Sha Village; sauces & dips $25 per person, mains $55-150; ⏰ 11am-10pm Tue-Sun; bus 1, 2 or 3
This Mediterranean-style restaurant with a huge terrace right on Lower Cheung Sha Beach has acceptable meat and fish dishes and a South African *braai* (barbecue; $80 to $150). Be sure to book at the weekend.

Ngong Ping

The car park at the Po Lin Monastery is awash with snack bars and kiosks selling vegetarian edibles, but you should try to have a meatless meal inside the monastery complex itself.

PO LIN VEGETARIAN RESTAURANT

Map p427 Cantonese, Vegetarian
☎ 2985 5248; Ngong Ping; snacks $10, set veg meals regular/deluxe $60/100; ⏰ 11.30am-4.30pm; bus 2, 21 or 23
The monastery, in west-central Lantau, has a good reputation for its inexpensive but substantial vegetarian food. The simple restaurant is in the covered arcade to the left of the main monastery building. Buy your ticket there or at the ticket office below the Tian Tan Buddha statue. Sittings are every half-hour.

Tai O

Tai O, a village on the western coast, is famous for its excellent seafood restaurants, many of which display their names in Chinese only.

FOOK MOON LAM Map p427 Cantonese

☎ 2985 7071; 29 Tai O Market St; mains $38-75; ⏰ 5.30am-9.30pm; bus 1, 11 or 21
This relatively upmarket (for Tai O, that is) restaurant serves tasty and not-over-refined dishes. Dim sum is available daily from 5.30am to 10am.

PENG CHAU

Peng Chau has a couple of popular pub-restaurants to the south of the ferry pier that are well worth checking out (see p207). Unfortunately, the construction of a mammoth concrete 'wave reflector' and promenade has robbed them of their lovely sea views, but there is still outside seating out the back in what now look like courtyards.

TYPHOON SHELTER

Map p429   Mediterranean, Pub Grub

☎ 2983 8033; 34 Wing Hing St; mains $45-119; ⏰ 11am-11pm Wed-Mon; Peng Chau ferry

The first of a couple of pub-restaurants lining Wing Hing St, the Typhoon Shelter serves both pizza and pasta dishes ($38 to $95), as well as steaks ($109 to $115) and pub fare like fish and chips ($68).

Cheap Eats
PENG CHAU MARKET

Map p429   Market

Cnr Lo Peng & Po Peng Sts; ⏰ 6am-8pm; Peng Chau ferry

The island's indoor wet market is housed in the same block as the Peng Chau Indoor Recreation Centre near the ferry pier.

WELLCOME Map p429   Supermarket

Lo Peng St; ⏰ 8am-10pm; Peng Chau ferry

You'll find Peng Chau's only supermarket just up from the ferry pier and after the crossing with Po Peng St.

PO TOI
MING KEE SEAFOOD RESTAURANT

Map pp404-5   Chinese, Seafood

☎ 2849 7038; meals about $150 per person; ⏰ 11am-11pm; Po Toi ferry

This is one of a handful of restaurants in the main village of Po Toi Island south of Hong Kong Island, and is by far the most popular with day-trippers. Make sure you book ahead at the weekend.

Entertainment

Drinking 199
  Hong Kong Island 200
  Kowloon 204
  New Territories 205
  Outlying Islands 206

Clubbing 207

Pop, Rock & Jazz 210

Classical Music 212

Cinemas 213
  Hong Kong Island 213
  Kowloon 214

Theatre 214

Comedy 214

Entertainment

When you really want to be wowed after dark, Hong Kong is the seasoned entertainer. Most weeks, half a dozen local arts companies perform anything from Cantonese opera to an English-language version of a Chekhov play. Locally cultivated drama and dance are among the most enjoyable in Asia, and the schedule of foreign performances is often stellar; recent imports have included the incomparable soprano Barbara Hendricks, composer Philip Glass and his ensemble, the Senegalese *mbalax* superstar Youssou N'Dour and Australian pop singer sensation Kylie Minogue. There are some very impressive new venues, especially in New Kowloon and the New Territories.

Nightlife Strips & Districts

Hong Kong Island has the lion's share of the territory's most popular pubs, bars and clubs, plus the cultural venues of Central and Wan Chai, so classical-music concerts, theatre, opera and the like are within easy striking distance.

Much of Central's fun nightlife revolves around Lan Kwai Fong, a narrow alleyway that runs south from D'Aguilar St then dog-legs west. In the not-so-distant past it was an

Lan Kwai Fong (left), Central

area of squalid tenements, rubbish and rats, but it has since been scrubbed, face-lifted and closed to traffic. Lan Kwai Fong's clientele tends to be young, hip and cashed-up; be warned that it can be an expensive area in which to party.

Soho is more geared up for dining than drinking, but there are a couple of bars and clubs worth the trek – on foot or via the Central Escalator – up the hill. Sheung Wan boasts a couple of attractive venues, including a popular gay bar (p208).

Wan Chai has been sleaze territory ever since it was the first port of call for American sailors and GIs on R&R from the battlefields of Vietnam. Much of the western part of the district has cleaned up its act, but hostess bars still line Lockhart Rd. There's lots of zippy club action and late-night cover-band venues throughout the district.

Compared with Wan Chai and the Lan Kwai Fong area of Central, Causeway Bay is relatively tame after dark. Still, there are a few pubs and bars that do a thriving business. The neighbourhoods to the east are not especially attractive for their entertainment venues, though you will find a clutch of pubs and bars in Quarry Bay (especially on and around Tong Chong St).

For the most part, the entertainment scene in Kowloon plays second fiddle to the hot spots of Hong Kong Island. The district is littered with bars and pubs – it's just a bit tackier, less imaginative and more run-down. There are three basic clusters of bars in Tsim Sha Tsui: along Ashley Rd; within the triangle formed by Hanoi Rd, Prat Ave and Chatham Rd; and up along Knutsford Tce, Kowloon's claim to a Lan Kwai Fong.

What's On

To find out what's on in Hong Kong, pick up a copy of HK Magazine (asiacity@asia-city.com.hk), a very comprehensive entertainment-listings magazine that also has lively articles on current trends in the city, reviews of restaurants and bars, and a classified ad pull-out section called *black + white*. It's free, appears on Friday and can be picked up at restaurants, bars, shops and hotels throughout the territory.

Also worth checking out is bc magazine (www.bcmagazine.net), a biweekly guide to Hong Kong's entertainment and partying scene. One of the most useful features in this highly visual and glossy publication is its complete listing of bars and clubs. It is also free and can usually be found alongside copies of *HK Magazine*.

The Hong Kong Arts Centre (www.hkac.org.hk) publishes *Artslink,* a monthly with listings of performances, exhibitions and art-house film screenings. Another invaluable source of information is the monthly Artmap (www.artmap.com.hk), a map with listings, available free at venues throughout the territory.

Tickets & Reservations

Expect to pay around $50 for a seat up the back for the Hong Kong Philharmonic and from about $400 for a performance by the likes of Norah Jones or an international musical such as *Saturday Night Fever*. Bookings for most cultural events can be made by telephone or the Internet with Urbtix (☎ 2111 5999; www.urbtix.gov.hk; ☺ 10am-8pm). Tickets can either be reserved with a passport number and picked up within three days, or paid for in advance by credit card. There are Urbtix windows at the Hong Kong City Hall (Map pp408–9; ☺ 10am-9.30pm) in Central, Queen Elizabeth Stadium in Wan Chai, the Hong Kong Cultural Centre in Tsim Sha Tsui and many Tom Lee Music Company outlets, including the Tsim Sha Tsui Tom Lee Music Company Centre (☎ 2723 9932; 1-9 Cameron Lane; ☺ ticketing 10am-7.30pm daily). The Fringe Theatre and the Academy for Performing Arts use HK Ticketing (☎ 3128 8288; www.hkticketing.com).

You can also book tickets for many films and concerts and a great variety of cultural events over the phone or Internet through Cityline (☎ 2317 6666; www.cityline.com.hk).

DRINKING

Drinking venues in Hong Kong run the gamut from fairly authentic British-style pubs with meat pies, darts and warm beer to stylish lounges where the clothes are straight out of the boutique, the sounds are smooth, the drinks are electric and the buzz is hard-core gossip. Much of Hong Kong's nightlife takes place in top-end hotels where inventive cocktails, skilled bar staff and some of the best views in town attract visitors and locals.

Depending on where you go, beer costs at least $40 a pint (though it's cheaper at happy hour), which is likely to be more expensive than the shirt on your back (if you bought it at a Hong Kong factory outlet). Overall, Lan Kwai Fong in Central is the best – and most expensive – area for bars, though it's the stomping ground of expat and Chinese suits. The pubs in Wan Chai are cheaper and more relaxed, and those in Tsim Sha Tsui generally attract more locals than visitors.

Bars generally open at noon or 6pm and close anywhere between 2am and 6am. Wan Chai bars stay open the latest.

Happy Hour

During certain hours of the day, most pubs, bars and even certain clubs give discounts on drinks (usually one-third to one-half off) or offer two for every one drink purchased. Happy hour is usually in the late afternoon or early evening – 4pm to 8pm, say – but the times vary widely from place to place. Depending on the season, the day of the week and the location, some pubs' happy hours run from midday until as late as 10pm, and some start again after midnight.

HONG KONG ISLAND

Central

APRÈS Map p412

☎ 2524 7722; Upper basement, 79 Wyndham St; ☽ 8am-1pm Mon-Thu, 8am-3am Fri & Sat, 8am-9pm Sun; happy hour 4-9pm; bus 26
This watering hole, decorated in cool purple and silver and with its front open to steep Pottinger St, is also a relaxed bistro with a reasonably priced French-inspired menu (set lunch $95). Enter from Pottinger St.

BAR GEORGE Map p412

☎ 2521 2202; 38-44 D'Aguilar St; ☽ 3pm-4am; happy hour 3-9pm; Central MTR
This large and raucous place is probably Lan Kwai Fong's biggest meat market; if you can't make it here, you won't make it anywhere. There's a lounge section and a dance floor at the back, with a second bar at the dance floor.

BIT POINT Map p412

☎ 2523 7436; Ground fl, 31 D'Aguilar St; ☽ noon-3am Mon-Fri, noon-4am Sat, 4pm-2am Sun; happy hour 4-9pm; Central MTR
Owned by the same lot as Biergarten (p204), Bit Point is essentially a German-style bar where beer drinking is taken very seriously. Most beers here are draught pilsners that you can get in a glass boot if you've got a thirst big enough to kick. Bit Point also serves some pretty solid Teutonic fare (starters $30 to $75, mains $58 to $130), with set lunches still a snip at $59/75 for half/full portions.

CAPTAIN'S BAR Map pp408-9

☎ 2522 0111; Ground fl, Mandarin Oriental, 5 Connaught Rd Central; ☽ 11am-2am Mon-Sat, 11am-1am Sun; Central MTR
This is a clubby, suited place that serves ice-cold draught beer in chilled silver mugs, as well as some of the best martinis in town. This is a good place to talk business, at least until the cover band strikes up at 9pm.

CHAPTER 3 Map p412

☎ 2526 5566; Basement, Amber Lodge, 23 Hollywood Rd; ☽ 5pm-2am Sun-Thu, 5pm-5am Fri, 7pm-5am Sat; happy hour 5-10pm; bus 26
This cheerful, very red bar below the Central Escalator defies its dungeon setting.

It's stylish but less trendy than most bars around here, maintaining a low-key feel and a loyal crowd. Great cocktails. Enter from Cochrane St.

CLUB 64 Map p412

☎ 2523 2801; 12-14A Wing Wah Lane; ☽ 3pm-2am Mon-Thu, 3pm-4am Fri & Sat, 4pm-1am Sun; happy hour 3-9pm Mon-Sat, 4-9pm Sun; Central MTR
The name of this hang-out recalls the date of the Tiananmen Square massacre in Beijing (June 4) in 1989. It's still one of the best bars in town for nonposeurs, journalists, artists, angry young men and women, and those who want simple, unfussy fun. There's jazz on Thursday from 9pm.

DRAGON-I Map p412

☎ 3110 1222; www.dragon-1.com.hk; Upper ground fl, the Centrium, 60 Wyndham St; ☽ noon-midnight Mon-Sat; happy hour 3-9pm Mon-Sat (terrace); bus 26
This fabulous venue on the edge of Soho has both an indoor bar and restaurant and a huge terrace over Wyndham St filled with caged songbirds. You'd almost think you were in the countryside.

DUBLIN JACK Map p412

☎ 2543 0081; Ground fl, Cheung Hing Commercial Bldg, 37-43 Cochrane St; ☽ 11am-1am; happy hour 11am-9pm; bus 26
This Irish pub is *almost* the real thing and a very popular after-hours watering hole for expat soaks. We like the mock-old 'Oirish village' frontage. This is Hong Kong's first (and we guess only) completely smoke-free pub.

GECKO LOUNGE Map p412

☎ 2537 4680; www.gecko.com; Lower ground fl, 15-19 Hollywood Rd; ☽ 4pm-2am Mon-Thu, 4pm-4am Fri & Sat; happy hour 4-10pm; Central MTR
Entered from narrow Ezra's Lane off Cochrane St or Pottinger St, Gecko is an intimate lounge and wine bar run by a friendly French sommelier and wine importer with a penchant for absinthe. The well-hidden DJ mixes good sounds with kooky Parisian tunes and there's usually live music on Tuesday and Wednesday.

GLOBE Map p412

☎ 2543 1941; 39 Hollywood Rd; ☽ 7.30am-1am Mon-Fri, 10am-1am Sat & Sun; happy hour 9am-8pm & midnight-1am Mon-Sat, all day Sun; bus 26

This tiny, unpretentious place gets packed out after work with expats thirsting for one (or more) of the 60 lagers, beers and real ales from around the world available here.

LA DOLCE VITA Map p412

☎ 2186 1888; Cosmos Bldg, 9-11 Lan Kwai Fong; ◷ 11am-2am Mon-Thu, 11.30am-3am Fri, 2pm-3am Sat, 2pm-1am Sun; happy hour 5.30-8pm; Central MTR

This is a popular place for postwork brews, with room to prop on the heart-shaped bar or stand on the terrace and watch the preening mob crawl by.

LE JARDIN Map p412

☎ 2526 2717; 1st fl, Winner Bldg, 10 Wing Wah Lane; ◷ noon-3am Mon-Thu, 4.30pm-3am Fri & Sat; happy hour noon-8pm Mon-Thu, 4.30-8pm Sat; Central MTR

Don't imagine a breezy oasis – 'The Garden' is no more than an enclosed verandah – but this is still an attractive bar with loads of atmosphere. The mostly expat crowd enjoys itself without getting too boisterous.

WHISKEY PRIEST Map p412

☎ 2869 0099; Ground & 1st fls, 12 Lan Kwai Fong; ◷ 4pm-1am Tue-Thu, 4pm-3am Fri & Sat, noon-1am Sun; happy hour 4-10pm Mon-Sat, noon-1pm Sun; Central MTR

The first (and so far only) Irish – thus the 'e' in 'whiskey' – pub to hit Lan Kwai Fong has Guinness, Kilkenny and Harp on tap, and 60 types of whiskey.

Soho & Sheung Wan

BAR 1911 Map p412

☎ 2810 6681; 27 Staunton St, Soho; ◷ 5pm-midnight Mon-Sat; happy hour 5-9pm Mon-Sat; bus 26

This is a refined bar with fine details (stained glass, burlwood bar, ceiling fan) and a 1920s Chinese vibe.

FEATHER BOA Map p412

☎ 2857 2586; 38 Staunton St, Soho; ◷ 5pm-late Tue; bus 26

Feather Boa is a plush lounge hidden behind gold drapes. Part camp lounge, part bordello – part those curtains and order a mango daiquiri ($75). It was once an antiques shop – thus the odd furnishings.

TOP FIVE CLUBS & BARS: CENTRAL, SOHO & SHEUNG WAN

- **Dragon-I** (opposite) – countrylike terrace bar in the heart of Central
- **Drop** (p208) – wallpaper background, chilled crowd
- **Gecko Lounge** (opposite) – great wines and kooky music
- **Om Lounge** (below) – the place where it all makes sense
- **Propaganda** (p209) – if you can make it here, you'll make it anywhere

OM LOUNGE Map p412

☎ 2526 9533; Basement, 41 Staunton St, Soho; ◷ 6pm-2am Sun-Thu, 6pm-4am Fri & Sat; happy hour 6-9pm; bus 26

This incredibly laid-back little lounge just below a tiny temple on Staunton St is filled with atmosphere and candles from the In-Senses shop above it. This place does decent cocktails. Enter from Peel St.

RICE BAR Map pp408-9

☎ 2851 4800; www.rice-bar.com; 33 Jervois St, Sheung Wan; ◷ 7pm-1am Sun-Thu, 7pm-2am Fri, 8pm-3am Sat; happy hour 7-9pm Sun-Fri, 8-9pm Sat; Sheung Wan MTR

Rice is a popular gay bar with a lounge area that sees a bit of dancing as it gets later. It can get very crowded at the weekend.

STAUNTON'S WINE BAR & CAFE Map p412

☎ 2973 6611; 10-12 Staunton St, Soho; ◷ 10am-2am Mon-Fri, 8am-2am Sat & Sun; happy hour 5-9pm; bus 26

Staunton's, at the corner with Shelley St, is swish, cool and on the ball with decent wine, a Central Escalator-cruising scene and a lovely terrace. If you're hungry, there's light fare downstairs and a fabulously re-modelled international restaurant above.

V-13 Map p412

☎ 9803 6650; 13 Old Bailey St, Soho; ◷ 6pm-midnight Mon-Thu, 6pm-late Fri, 6pm-late Sat; happy hour 6-9pm Mon-Sat; bus 26

The 'v' word here could only refer to Russian mouthwash, and there are some 80 vodkas on offer – from chocolate to chilli flavoured. The bar staff know their mixes very well.

Staunton's Wine Bar & Cafe (p201), Soho

Admiralty & Wan Chai

Most of the best bars and pubs line the western ends of Jaffe and Lockhart Rds. As in Lan Kwai Fong, on weekend nights this area is crawling with partygoers.

BRIDGE Map pp414-15

☎ 2865 5586; Shop A-B, 1st fl, Beverly House, 93-107 Lockhart Rd, Wan Chai; ☾ 24hr; happy hour noon-10pm; Wan Chai MTR

This large and airy bar, with great windows overlooking the frenzy of Lockhart Rd, is open 24 hours, serving cocktails to the denizens and the doomed of Wan Chai.

CHAMPAGNE BAR Map pp414-15

☎ 2588 1234 ext 7321; Ground fl, Grand Hyatt Hotel, 1 Harbour Rd, Wan Chai; ☾ 5pm-2am; Wan Chai MTR

Take your fizz in the sumptuous surrounds of the Grand Hyatt's Champagne Room, kitted out in Art Deco furnishings to evoke the Paris of the 1920s. Live blues or jazz happens most evenings and the circular main bar is always busy.

DELANEY'S Map pp414-15

☎ 2804 2880; Ground & 1st fls, One Capital Place, 18 Luard Rd, Wan Chai; ☾ noon-2.30am Sun-Thu, noon-3am Fri & Sat; happy hour noon-9pm; Wan Chai MTR

At this immensely popular Irish watering hole you can choose between the black-and-white–tiled pub on the ground floor and a sports bar and restaurant on the 1st floor. The food is good and plentiful; the kitchen allegedly goes through 400kg of potatoes a week. There's also a branch on Peking Rd in Tsim Sha Tsui (p204).

DEVIL'S ADVOCATE Map pp414-15

☎ 2865 7271; 48-50 Lockhart Rd, Wan Chai; ☾ noon-late Mon-Sat, 1pm-late Sun; happy hour noon-10pm; Wan Chai MTR

This pleasant pub in the thick of things is as relaxed as they come. The bar spills onto the pavement and the staff is charming. 'Devilling Hour' (5pm to 7pm) is even cheaper than happy hour, and there are cheap drinks on Wednesday night.

FENWICK THE DOCK Map pp414-15

☎ 2861 1669; Lower ground fl, 41 Lockhart Rd, Wan Chai; ☾ 5pm-late; happy hour 5-10pm; Wan Chai MTR

This bare-bones basement pub/club on the corner of Fenwick St has a good dance floor.

GROOVY MULE Map pp414-15

☎ 2527 2077; 37-39 Lockhart Rd, Wan Chai; ☾ 4pm-btwn 3am & 5am; happy hour 4-10pm; Wan Chai MTR

Cocktails and shots and the Aussie bar staff – in cork hats, no less – rocking and grooving will keep most punters riveted to their bar stools here. Lots of old-to-young(er) ogling.

HORSE & GROOM Map pp414-15

☎ 2507 2517; Ground fl, 161 Lockhart Rd, Wan Chai; ☾ 4pm-2am Mon-Fri, 6pm-2am Sat & Sun; happy hour 4-9pm Mon-Fri, 6-9pm Sat & Sun; Wan Chai MTR

What used to be called the 'House of Doom´, and a favourite watering hole of hacks and has-beens has gone local.

KANGAROO DOWNUNDER Map pp414-15

☎ 2139 31111; Lower ground fl, The Broadway, 54-62 Lockhart Rd, Wan Chai; ☾ 11am-2am; happy hour 4-9pm; Wan Chai MTR

This well-scrubbed successor to the infamous Kangaroo Pub in Tsim Sha Tsui is more of a lounge bar-cum-restaurant than the erstwhile pub, but it's popular with young Australian and other expats nonetheless.

MES AMIS Map pp414-15

☎ 2527 6680; 81-85 Lockhart Rd, Wan Chai;
🕐 noon-2am Sun-Thu, noon-6am Fri & Sat;
happy hour 4-9pm; Wan Chai MTR
This easy-going bar is in the lap of girly-club land. It has a good range of wines and a Mediterranean-style snacks list. There's a DJ from 11pm on Friday and Saturday. There's also a **Tsim Sha Tsui branch** (Map pp420–1; ☎ 2730 3038; 15 Ashley Rd; 🕐 noon-2am Sun-Thu, noon-3am Fri & Sat; happy hour 4-9pm).

OLD CHINA HAND Map pp414-15

☎ 2865 4378; 104 Lockhart Rd, Wan Chai;
🕐 8am-5am; happy hour noon-10pm;
Wan Chai MTR
This place is hardly recognisable as the gloomy old dive where the desperate-to-drink (no one we know) used to find themselves unhappy but never alone at 3am. Now it's got a generous happy hour, Internet access and set lunches for a mere $49.

RENNIE MAC'S BRASSERIE Map pp414-15

☎ 2520 2300; www.renniemacs.com; Ground fl, Asia Orient Tower, 33 Lockhart Rd; 🕐 10am-2am Mon-Thu, 11am-late Fri & Sat; happy hour noon-9pm Mon-Sat; Wan Chai MTR
This delightful place pays homage to the Scottish Art Nouveau designer Charles Rennie Mackintosh (1868–1928) and is a relaxing place for a late-night drink. In true brasserie style, food (starters $38 to $52, tapas $50 to $68, mains $85 to $95, two-/three-course set meals $88/118) is available throughout the day.

TOP FIVE CLUBS & BARS: ADMIRALTY & WAN CHAI

- **Mes Amis** (above) – late-night spot for that very last one
- **Neptune Disco II** (p209) – unfettered pleasure till the wee (we?) hours
- **Rennie Mac's Brasserie** (above) – great décor in a temple to the Scots designer
- **Tango Martini** (right) – faux skins, real food plus vibes
- **Wanch** (p212) – generous happy hour and live rock and folk nightly

---

SKITZ Map pp414-15

☎ 2866 3277; 1st fl, Jubilee Centre, 18 Fenwick St, Wan Chai; 🕐 24 hr; happy hour 11am-10pm; Wan Chai MTR
This huge sports bar with pool tables and a big screen TV also houses Les Visages (p208), which is fast becoming the most popular dance club in Wan Chai.

TANGO MARTINI Map pp414-15

☎ 2528 0855; 3rd fl, Empire Land Commercial Centre, 81-85 Lockhart Rd, Wan Chai; 🕐 noon-3pm & 6pm-1am Mon-Fri, 6pm-3am Fri & Sat, 6pm-1am Sun; happy hour 6-8pm; Wan Chai MTR
This groovy animal-print restaurant-cum-lounge serves lunch and dinner (starters $88 to $150, mains $160 to $250) but is also perfect for a Wan Chai postprandial. Flux on Sunday ($100) has DJs from 9pm.

WHITE STAG Map pp414-15

☎ 2866 4244; Ground fl, The Broadway, 54-62 Lockhart Rd, Wan Chai; 🕐 noon-late; happy hour noon-10pm; Wan Chai MTR
This is a somewhat subdued (suity, not snooty) pub with open frontage and such filling dishes as sausage and beans ($65), cottage pie ($75), fish and chips ($85) and chilli ($75).

Causeway Bay

BRECHT'S BAR Map pp414-15

☎ 2576 4785; Ground fl, Rita House, 123 Leighton Rd; 🕐 4pm-2am Mon-Thu, 6pm-4am Fri & Sat; happy hour 4-8pm Mon-Sat; Causeway Bay MTR
Brecht's is very small and fairly unusual. It's an arty kind of place given more to intimate, cerebral conversation than serious raging. The décor is pseudo-German, and includes oversized portraits of such charmers as Mao and Hitler.

DICKENS BAR Map pp414-15

☎ 2837 6782; Basement, Excelsior Hong Kong, 281 Gloucester Rd; 🕐 11am-1am Sun-Thu, 11am-2am Fri & Sat; happy hour 5-8pm; Causeway Bay MTR
This evergreen place has been popular with expats and Hong Kong Chinese for decades. There's a weekday curry buffet lunch ($108, including a half-pint of beer), brunch buffet at the weekend ($118, 11.30am to 4pm Saturday and Sunday) and lots of big-screen sports.

Entertainment

DRINKING

TOP FIVE CLUBS & BARS: CAUSEWAY BAY

- **Brecht's Bar** (p203) – small bar where intimate conversation rules
- **Causeway Lounge** (p211) – top of the pops downstairs
- **Dickens Bar** (p203) – reliable place, reliable pints
- **East End Brewery & Inn Side Out** (below) – peanut-strewn sister pubs on a covered terrace
- **Wasabisabi** (p210) – camp lounge in a fab Japanese restaurant

EAST END BREWERY & INN SIDE OUT
Map pp414-15

☎ 2895 2900; Ground fl, Sunning Plaza, 10 Hysan Ave; ☺ 11.30am-1am Sun-Thu, 11.30am-1.30am Fri & Sat; happy hour 2.30-8.30pm; Causeway Bay MTR

These two related pubs flank a central covered terrace where you can while away the hours on a warm evening, sipping beers and throwing peanut shells on the ground. East End has imported microbrews, and also has a Quarry Bay branch (below).

Island East & Island South

CAFÉ EINSTEIN Map pp406-7
☎ 2960 0994; 33 Tong Chong St, Quarry Bay; 11am-1am Mon-Sat; happy hour 4-9pm Mon-Sat; Quarry Bay MTR

This attractive and upbeat bar-bistro, which feels more Lan Kwai Fong than Tong Chong St, has a great bar and lounge with piped jazz and R&B and serves decent food (tapas $50 to $60, set lunch $97) all day from a short but inspired menu.

EAST END BREWERY Map pp406-7
☎ 2811 1907; 23-27 Tong Chong St, Quarry Bay; ☺ 11.30am-2am; happy hour 4-8pm; Quarry Bay MTR

This place out in Quarry Bay is a beer lover's must-visit. You can choose from more than 30 beers and lagers from around the world, including a couple of local microbrews. There's also a Causeway Bay branch (above).

SMUGGLERS INN Map p411
☎ 2813 8852; Ground fl, 90A Stanley Main St, Stanley; ☺ 10am-2am; happy hour 6-9pm; bus 6, 6A, 6X or 260

This scruffy but good-natured place is arguably the most popular pub on the Stanley waterfront. It gets a good mix of people.

KOWLOON
Tsim Sha Tsui
AQUA SPIRIT Map pp420-1
☎ 3427 2288; 30th fl, 1 Peking Rd; ☺ 6pm-1am Sun-Thu, 4.30pm-3am Fri & Sat; Tsim Sha Tsui MTR

This magnificent restaurant-bar on top of one of Kowloon's new skyscrapers is everyone's favourite place for a brew with a view.

BAR Map pp420-1
☎ 2315 3163; 1st fl, Peninsula Hong Kong, Salisbury Rd; ☺ 4pm-midnight; Star Ferry, Tsim Sha Tsui MTR

For mellow 1940s and '50s jazz, don your smoking jacket and sip Cognac at the Peninsula's stylish main watering hole. Your fellow tipplers will be serious business blokes, coutured couples and new money names trying to sound old(er). The music starts around 9.30pm.

BIERGARTEN Map pp420-1
☎ 2721 2302; 5 Hanoi Rd; ☺ 10am-3am Mon-Fri, noon-2am; happy hour 4-9pm; Tsim Sha Tsui MTR

This clean, modern place has a jukebox full of hits (and misses) and Bitburger on tap. It's popular with visiting Germans and others who hanker after such hearty and filling nosh as pork knuckle and sauerkraut ($95). Starters are $38 to $79, mains $52 to $98, and set lunch is $58.

COURTNEY'S Map pp420-1
☎ 2739 7777; 5th fl, The Minden, 7 Minden Ave; ☺ 5pm-2am; Tsim Sha Tsui MTR

This hotel snack room–bar, decorated with original and attractive artwork by local painter Pauline Courtney, has a fabulous outdoor terrace, allowing you to watch the goings-on in lively Minden Ave below.

DELANEY'S Map pp420-1
☎ 2301 3980; Basement, Mary Bldg, 71-77 Peking Rd; ☺ 9am-3am; happy hour 5-9pm; Tsim Sha Tsui MTR

This pub seems more authentically Irish than its Wan Chai counterpart (p202), with lots of dark wood, green felt and a long bar that you can really settle into.

FELIX Map pp420-1

☎ 2315 3188; 28th fl, Peninsula Hong Kong, Salisbury Rd; ⏱ 6pm-2am; Tsim Sha Tsui MTR
Enjoy the fabulous view at the bar connected to Felix restaurant (p178), one of the swankiest eateries in Hong Kong's poshest hotel. Guys, the view from the urinals in the gents' is just one reason to fill your bladders.

LA TASCA Map pp420-1

☎ 2723 1072; 8 Hanoi Rd; ⏱ 11am-4am Mon-Fr, 5pm-4am Sat & Sun; happy hour 5-9pm; Tsim Sha Tsui MTR
La Tasca is more a cantina and bar than a restaurant nowadays and has live music starting from 10pm on Saturdays. But it still does a set lunch ($38 to $42) and food at night, including tasty tapas ($40 to $60) and more substantial main courses ($85 to $95).

NEW WALLY MATT LOUNGE
Map pp420-1

☎ 2721 2568; www.wallymatt.com; 5A Humphreys Ave; ⏱ 5pm-4am; happy hour 5-10pm; Tsim Sha Tsui MTR
The name comes from the old Waltzing Matilda pub, one of the daggiest gay watering holes in creation (see p210). But New Wally Matt is an upbeat and busy place and actually more a pub than a lounge.

ORGAN BAR Map pp420-1

☎ 2376 0389; Basement & Ground fl, Honeytex Bldg, 22 Ashley Rd; ⏱ noon-4am Mon-Fri, 5pm-5am Sat & Sun; happy hour 5-9pm; Tsim Sha Tsui MTR

TOP FIVE CLUBS & BARS: TSIM SHA TSUI

- **Aqua Spirit** (opposite) – brew with a view and cheaper than Felix
- **Bahama Mama's** (p207) – friendly, tropical-themed spot with bopping at the weekend
- **Courtney's** (opposite) – local art on a delightful terrace
- **Ned Kelly's Last Stand** (p212) – yonks-old pub with live big-band jazz nightly
- **Sky Lounge** (right) – departure lounge-like bar with a drop-dead view of Hong Kong Island

---

The erstwhile Amoeba Bar has evolved into the Organ and has big-screen entertainment in the basement from around 9pm. It draws a mainly hip and young Cantonese-speaking crowd.

SKY LOUNGE Map pp420-1

☎ 2369 1111; 18th fl, Sheraton Hong Kong Hotel & Towers, 20 Nathan Rd; ⏱ 4pm-1am Mon-Fri, 2pm-2am Sat & Sun; Tsim Sha Tsui MTR
Before you can pooh-pooh the departure-lounge feel of this big, long lounge, you've already started marvelling at the view. Don't take flight: sit down in a scoop chair, sip something shaken or stirred and scoff international snacks.

TONY'S BAR Map pp420-1

☎ 2723 2726; www.tonys-bar.com; Ground fl, 7-9 Bristol Ave; ⏱ 5.30pm-4am; happy hour 5.30-10pm; Tsim Sha Tsui MTR
This low-key, gay-friendly bar just behind Mirador Mansion (p263) is a relaxed place to come for a drink, with none of that 'last chance for romance' tension found in some other gay venues.

WATERING HOLE Map pp420-1

☎ 2312 2288; Basement, 1A Mody Rd; ⏱ 4pm-1.30am Mon-Sat, 4pm-1am Sun; happy hour 4-10pm; Tsim Sha Tsui MTR
This pub with its imaginative name and central location is a grotty, salt-of-the-earth kind of place popular with both Chinese and expats.

NEW TERRITORIES
Sai Kung Town

DUKE OF YORK PUB Map p425
☎ 2792 8435; Ground fl, 42-56 Fuk Man Rd; ⏱ 11am-2am; happy hour 11am-9pm Wed-Mon, all day Tue; bus 92, 299
This popular pub, just up from the waterfront, has darts and live music at the weekend. It's also OK blotter in the way of fish and chips ($75) or Sunday roast ($70).

POETS Map p425
☎ 2791 7993; 55 Yi Chun St; ⏱ noon-1am Mon-Fri, noon-2am Sat & Sun; happy hour noon-9pm Mon-Fri; bus 92, 299
This workaday pub with literary aspirations is a pleasant place for a pint and does

some substantial pub meals, including beef stew, shepherd's pie and fish and chips ($48 to $58).

XTREME BAR & RESTAURANT Map p425

☎ 2791 7222; 72 Po Tung Rd; ⌚ 4pm-1am Mon-Fri, 11am-3am Sat & Sun; happy hour 4-9pm Mon-Fri, 11am-9pm Sat, 11am-7pm Sun; bus 92, 299
This *über*-styled brasserielike place has raised the bar by a few hundred metres for upmarket drinking venues in Sai Kung town. Food (starters $48 to $118, pasta $78 to $88, mains $78 to $128) is available until just before closing.

OUTLYING ISLANDS

Lamma

Yung Shue Wan has several waterfront boozers worth checking out. You may have to sign a members' book as some operate on club licences.

DIESEL'S BAR Map p426

☎ 2982 4116; 51 Main St, Yung Shue Wan; ⌚ 6pm-late Mon-Fri, noon-late Sat & Sun; happy hour 6-9pm Mon-Fri; Lamma (Yung Shue Wan) ferry
This place next to the Lamma Bistro attracts punters with its Sunday roasts ($75 to $95) and big-screen TV during sports matches.

FOUNTAINHEAD DRINKING BAR
Map p426

☎ 2982 2118; 17 Main St, Yung Shue Wan; ⌚ 5pm-2am Mon-Fri, 3pm-4am Sat & Sun; happy hour all day Mon-Fri; Lamma (Yung Shue Wan) ferry
This place has a good mix of Chinese and expats in regular attendance, decent music and beer at affordable prices.

ISLAND SOCIETY BAR Map p426

☎ 2982 1376; 6 Main St, Yung Shue Wan; ⌚ 6pm-late Mon-Fri, noon-late Sat & Sun; happy hour 6-8pm; Lamma (Yung Shue Wan) ferry
The Island remains the bar of choice for long-term expats living on Lamma, so if you want the lowdown on what's up, head here.

Cheung Chau
MOROCCO'S BAR & RESTAURANT
Map p428

☎ 2986 9767; 117 Praya St; ⌚ 10am-2am or 3am; happy hour 4-9pm Mon-Fri; Cheung Chau ferry

The exodus of expats from Cheung Chau over the past years has left the island all but bereft of quality drinking venues, but there will always be Morocco's on the waterfront. It also does decent Indian food (curries $35 to $50, tandoori dishes $50 to $80).

PATIO CAFÉ Map p428

☎ 2981 8316, 2981 2772; Cheung Chau Windsurfing Water Sports Centre, 1 Hak Pai Rd; ⌚ noon-7pm daily Apr-Nov, noon-7pm Sat & Sun Dec-Mar; Cheung Chau ferry
This open-air, café-cum-pub attached to the windsurfing centre at Tung Wan Beach, known locally as Lai Kam's in honour of its owner, is a Cheung Chau institution. Come here for a sundowner.

Lantau
CHINA BEACH CLUB Map p429

☎ 2983 8931; 18 Tung Wan Tau Rd; ⌚ noon-10pm Thu & Fri, 11am-10pm Sat & Sun; happy hour all day Thu-Sun; Lantau ferry
This pleasant bar has a 185-sq-m rooftop and an open-air balcony overlooking Silvermine Bay Beach. The staff is friendly and helpful and the food is good (starters $55 to $69, mains & grills $75 to $115).

CHINA BEAR Map p429

☎ 2984 9720; Ground fl, Mui Wo Centre, Ngan Wan Rd; ⌚ 10am-3am; happy hour 5-9pm Mon-Fri, 5-8pm Sat & Sun; Lantau ferry
The China Bear is the most popular expat pub-restaurant in Mui Wo, with a wonderful open bar facing the water. Among the pub-grub offerings are fish and chips

---

TOP FIVE CLUBS & BARS: NEW TERRITORIES & OUTLYING ISLANDS

- **China Bear** (above) – Mui Wo bar facing the water and popular with expats
- **Diesel's Bar** (left) – friendly, frenetic place on Lamma with big-screen sports TV
- **Forest Bar & Restaurant** (opposite) – cosy Peng Chau watering hole with five beers on tap
- **Island Society Bar** (left) – Lamma residents' bar of choice near home
- **Xtreme Bar & Restaurant** (left) – a stand-out choice in scruffy Sai Kung

($85), a handy all-day breakfast ($58) and 250g fillet steak ($75). Snacks cost from $20 to $40.

JK'S CLUB Map p427

☎ 2984 0220; Ground fl, 20 Lo Wai Tsuen, Pui O; ⌚ 6pm-late Mon-Fri, noon-late Sat & Sun; bus 1, 2, 3
This place is conveniently located just off the main road in Pui O. The beach is just across the street.

Peng Chau

FOREST BAR & RESTAURANT Map p429

☎ 2983 8837; 38C Wing Hing St; ⌚ 11am-late Tue-Sun; Peng Chau ferry
This cosy bar has five beers on tap and a large outside terrace seating area. The kitchen whips up authentic pan-Asian (mostly Thai) food (snacks $35 to $55, rice and noodle dishes $35 to $50, mains $62 to $130) six days a week.

CLUBBING

Hong Kong has an up-and-running club scene, with venues in Central, Wan Chai and Tsim Sha Tsui where you can dance till you drop or the sun rises, whichever comes first. Many bars stage dance and theme nights.

Most of the club nights take place on Friday and Saturday, but there are some good midweek venues as well. Cover charges range from $100 to as high as $300 when a big-name foreign DJ is mixing, or an internationally recognised band is on stage. On some nights, you may get in free (or for a cheaper cover) if you are among the first 50 or so through the door, dressed in '70s gear (or whatever) on theme nights or a woman.

Hong Kong's most talked about dance parties are one-off raves, held in venues as diverse as the airport hotel and the ferry pier at Kwun Tong. As in any world-class city, the club scene in Hong Kong changes with the speed of summer lightning so it would be in your interest to flip through *HK Magazine* or *bc magazine*. On the web, check out www.hkclubbing.com or www.hkentertainment.com.

1/5 Map pp408-9

☎ 2520 2515; 1st fl, Starcrest Bldg, 9 Star St, Wan Chai; ⌚ 5pm-3am Mon-Thu, 5pm-4am Fri & Sat, 6pm-2am Sun; happy hour 6-9pm Mon-Fri; Admiralty MTR

Pronounced 'one-fifth', this sophisticated lounge bar and club has a broad bar backed by a two-storey drinks selection from which bar staff concoct some of Hong Kong's best cocktails. It gets packed at the weekend but it's still a good place to chill.

BAHAMA MAMA'S Map pp420-1

☎ 9803 6650, 2368 2121; 4-5 Knutsford Tce, Tsim Sha Tsui; ⌚ 5pm-3am Sun-Thu, 5pm-4am Fri & Sat; happy hour 5-9pm & midnight-closing Mon-Thu, 5-9pm Fri & Sat, all day Sun; Tsim Sha Tsui MTR
Bahama Mama's goes for a 'Caribbean island' feel, complete with palm trees and surfboards. It's a friendly spot and stands apart from most of the other late-night watering holes in this part of town. On Friday and Saturday nights there's a DJ spinning and a young crowd out on the bonsai-sized dance floor.

C CLUB Map p412

☎ 2526 1139, 2867 8800; Basement, California Tower, 30-32 D'Aguilar St, Central; ⌚ 6pm-3am Mon-Fri, 9pm-late Sat; happy hour 6-9pm Mon-Fri; Central MTR
This fur-lined club below Lan Kwai Fong reeks of loucheness and is immensely popular. Quality cocktails, sexy house music and hip-hop, and large cushions of velvet, satin and fur. All very red, very black.

CLUB 97 Map p412

☎ 2186 1897; Ground fl, Cosmos Bldg, 9-11 Lan Kwai Fong, Central; ⌚ 6pm-2am Mon-Thu, 6pm-4am Fri, 8pm-4am Sat & Sun; happy hour 6-9pm Mon-Fri, 8-10pm Sun; Central MTR
This schmoozy lounge bar has a popular happy hour (it's a gay event on Friday night) and there's reggae on Sunday. It has a 'members only' policy to turn away the underdressed; make an effort and you're in.

CLUB NU Map p412

☎ 2549 8386; Basement & ground fl, 1-5 Elgin St, Soho; ⌚ 6pm-4am Sun-Fri, 8pm-6am Sat; happy hour 6-9.30pm Mon-Fri; bus 26
What used to be a popular postwork suit hang out called Liquid has metamorphosed into NU, a sophisticated lounge and dance bar with live acid jazz on Monday and Tuesday and DJs serving up funk, soul, R&B, house and hip-hop into the small hours on other nights. The cover charge is $100 on Saturday.

DROP Map p412

☎ 2543 8856; www.drophk.com; Basement, On Lok Mansion, 39-43 Hollywood Rd, Central; ⊕ 7pm-2am Mon & Tue, 7pm-3am Wed, 7pm-4am Thu, 7pm-5am Fri, 9pm-5am Sat; happy hour 7-10pm Mon-Fri; bus 26

Deluxe lounge action, excellent tunes and potent cocktails keep Drop strong on the scene. It's like walking into *Wallpaper* magazine, but the vibe here is unpretentiously inclusive. The members-only policy after 10pm Thursday to Saturday is (flexibly) enforced to keep the dance floor capacity at a manageable 'packed like sardines' level. Enter from Cochrane St.

HOMEBASE Map p412

☎ 2545 0023; 2nd fl, 23 Hollywood Rd, Central; ⊕ 10pm-3am Mon-Fri, 10pm-9am Sat; happy hour 10pm-midnight Mon-Thu & Sat, 8pm-midnight Fri; bus 26

A meet 'n' greet for the styled and beautiful early on, this place turns into a bump 'n' grind after hours (cover $100). It's one of the more popular after-hours venues and one of the few places that is still partying well after dawn in a city that does, in fact, sleep. Great house and breakbeat music, small dance floor. Friday's generous happy hour is for gays and lesbians.

INSOMNIA Map p412

☎ 2525 0957; Lower Ground fl, Ho Lee Commercial Bldg, 38-44 D'Aguilar St, Central; ⊕ 9am-6am Mon-Sat, 2pm-5am Sun; happy hour 5-9pm daily; Central MTR

This is the place to come to when you can't sleep. It's a people-watching place with a wide open frontage, and there's a live band doing covers in the back. Doziest staff this side of Zamboanga City, though. There's

food, too, such as all-day breakfast ($75), fish and chips ($80), sandwiches and burgers ($40 to $55), and snacks ($35 to $60).

JEWEL Map p412

☎ 2541 5988; www.clubjewel.com; 37-43 Pottinger St, Central; ⊕ 3pm-2am Mon & Tue, 3pm-4am Wed, 3pm-2am Thu, 3pm-6am Fri & Sat; happy hour 3-8pm Mon-Sat; Central MTR

This ultracool pearl of a venue is dripping in Asian stone carvings, silk and teak furniture. Getting through the door on Wednesday and at the weekend is a challenge.

JOE BANANAS Map pp414-15

☎ 2529 1811; Ground fl, Shiu Lam Bldg, 23 Luard Rd, Wan Chai; ⊕ noon-5am Mon-Thu, noon-6am Fri & Sat, 4pm-5am Sun; happy hour noon-10pm; Wan Chai MTR

JB's, in Wan Chai forever – or at least since we were bopping and grooving – has dropped its long-standing wet T-shirt/boxers aesthetic and gone for more of a bamboo-bar feel. Unaccompanied females should expect a good sampler of bad pick-up lines; go with friends and have some un-PC fun. Entry is $120 on Friday and Saturday, there are free drinks for women from 6pm to 3am on Wednesday and 'Crazy Hour' (6pm to 8pm daily) is even more generous than happy hour.

LES VISAGES Map pp414-15

☎ 2866 3277; www.skitz-bar.com; 1st fl, Jubilee Centre, 42-46 Gloucester Rd, Wan Chai; ⊕ 10pm-late Tue-Sat, 9pm-1am Sun; Wan Chai MTR

Sharing space with the 24-hour sports bar Skitz (p203), 'The Faces' has both DJs and a resident band called Mystery 5. There's an open bar (men $120, women free) on Wednesday.

GAY & LESBIAN VENUES

What a difference a decade and a half makes… With no more than a couple of grotty speakeasies just over 15 years ago, when homosexual acts between consenting adults over the age of 21 (it's 16 for heterosexuals and lesbians) were finally decriminalised, Hong Kong can now count upwards of two dozen bars and clubs – with more than a third in Central and Tsim Sha Tsui – and just as many gay-oriented saunas scattered throughout the territory. Grab a copy of *G*, a bimonthly gay-centric listings publication brought to you by the same people who publish *HK Magazine* or check out the GayStation (www.gaystation.com.hk) or Gay HK (www.gayhk.com) websites.

On Hong Kong Island, along with Propaganda (opposite) and Works (p210) in Central and the Rice Bar (p201) in Sheung Wan, several other straight clubs have gay nights, including Club 97 (p207) and Homebase (above). In Kowloon, gay or gay-friendly venues include Tony's Bar (p205), Wally Matt Lounge (p210) and New Wally Matt Lounge (p205).

MANHATTAN CLUB ING Map pp414-15

☎ 2836 3690; 4th fl, Renaissance Harbour View Hotel, 1 Harbour Rd, Wan Chai; ☿ 5pm-4am Mon-Fri, 9.30pm-4am Sat; happy hour 5pm-4am Mon & Tue, 5-8pm Wed, 5-9pm Thu & Fri; bus 18
Supremely decked-out club with lounges, a long bar, popular theme nights and a serious attitude. It's popular with a suave Cantonese crowd so dress to impress (no sandals, sneakers or tank tops). There's free entry and drinks for fashionable ladies on Thursday night. Men pay $160 (including one drink) or $120 before 11pm.

NEPTUNE DISCO II Map pp414-15

☎ 2865 2238; Basement, 98-108 Jaffe Rd, Wan Chai; ☿ 4pm-6am Mon-Fri, 2pm-6am Sat & Sun; happy hour 4-9pm Mon-Fri, 2-9pm Sat; Wan Chai MTR
Neptune II is a fun club with a mostly Filipino crowd and a rockin' Pinoy covers band. If everything's closing and you can't bear to stop dancing, this is the place to come. It really rocks at the Sunday afternoon tea dance (men/women $100/50, including one drink), starting at 2pm.

NEW MAKATI PUB & DISCO Map pp414-15

☎ 2866 3928; 1st fl, 94-100 Lockhart Rd; ☿ 4pm-5am; happy hour 4-9pm; Wan Chai MTR
It has to be said: you can't go lower than this sleazy pick-up joint, complete with dimly lit booths and Filipino amahs – it's named after a district of Manila – who just wanna have fun. But the natives are friendly and it's a good place to dance the morning away.

PROPAGANDA Map p412

☎ 2868 1316; Lower ground fl, 1 Hollywood Rd, Central; ☿ 9pm-4am Tue-Thu, 9pm-6am Fri & Sat; happy hour 9pm-1.30am Tue-Thu; Central MTR
Propaganda is still the premier gay dance club and meat market; everyone gay ends up here at some point on a weekend night. It's free from Tuesday to Thursday but cover charges ($120 to $160) apply on Friday and Saturday (which gets you into Works, p210, on Friday). Enter from Ezra's Lane, which runs between Pottinger and Cochrane Sts.

RED ROCK Map p412

☎ 2868 3884; Lower ground fl, 57-59 Wyndham St, Central; ☿ noon-3pm & 5pm-2am Mon-Thu, 11am-2pm & 5pm-5am Fri & Sat; happy hour 5-8pm Mon-Fri; Central MTR

Neptune Disco II (left), Wan Chai

This attractive place, backing onto the walkway above Lan Kwai Fong, is a very successful chameleon: a decent Italian restaurant at lunch and dinner (set lunch $87, starters $20 to $60, pasta and pizza $35 to $80, mains $70-90) and a popular dance venue by night (cover $100). A dozen cocktails and as many shooters go for half-price at happy hour.

RICK'S CAFÉ Map pp420-1

☎ 2311 2255, 2367 2939; Ground fl, Luna Ct, 53-59 Kimberley Rd, Tsim Sha Tsui; ☿ 5pm-late Mon-Sat; happy hour 5-10pm Mon-Sat; Tsim Sha Tsui MTR
Rick's, one of Tsim Sha Tsui's better-known venues, has a cheesy 'Casablanca' décor, complete with palm trees and stacks of neon. The large dance floor is usually a writhing knot of Western men and Filipino girls. Be sure to check out the fabulous 'piano bar'.

VENUE Map pp414-15

☎ 3105 8990; www.venue.com.hk; Ground fl, 15-19 Luard Rd, Wan Chai; ☿ 4pm-late Mon-Sat; happy hour 4-9pm; Wan Chai MTR
Clubby crowds groove to hip-hop and R&B. Thursday night is Industry Night (film, fashion, club), when women get free drinks.

WALLY MATT LOUNGE Map pp420-1

☎ 2367 6874; 3A Granville Circuit, Tsim Sha Tsui; ☻ 5pm-4am; happy hour 5-10pm; Tsim Sha Tsui MTR
Cantopop karaoke and 'It's Raining Men' add to the ambience in this boy zone. It's industrial but there are just enough seats to retreat to with a drink and watch the action.

WASABISABI Map pp414-15

☎ 2506 0009; 13th fl, Times Square, 1 Matheson St; ☻ 6pm-midnight Sun-Thu, 6pm-3am Fri & Sat; happy hour 6-8pm; Causeway Bay MTR
This Japanese restaurant in the Times Square shopping mall, with out-of-this-world décor (cable vines, rondo lounges, faux birch forest) transforms each night into the camp Lipstick Lounge.

WORKS Map p412

☎ 2868 6102; 1st fl, 30-32 Wyndham St, Central; ☻ 7pm-2am; happy hour 7-10.30pm Mon-Fri; Central MTR
Propaganda's sister club, Works is where most gay boyz out on the town start the evening and sees some heavy FFFR (file-for-future-reference) cruising till it's time to move on to the P. There's a cover ($60 to $100) at the weekend.

POP, ROCK & JAZZ

Cantopop is the name for the local pop music (p29). If you give it a chance, you'll discover some worthwhile tunes (or ones that you won't be able to get out of your head for your entire stay here).

There are usually a few decent rock bands (both local and imported) playing around town, and numerous bars have house bands that play dance music. Hotel bars and clubs have Filipino bands that can play 'Hotel California' and 'Love Is a Many-Splendored Thing' in their sleep (and yours).

Judging from the closure of a couple of key venues in recent years, jazz seems to be losing a lot of its traditional following in Hong Kong; there's only a couple of venues in Central and Tsim Sha Tsui. World music

---

HOSTESS WITH THE LEASTEST (ON)

Hostess clubs come in two varieties in Hong Kong: the sleaze pits mostly found on Lockhart Rd in Wan Chai, and the more 'respectable' establishments in Tsim Sha Tsui East. The difference is that the former blatantly try to cheat customers, while the latter don't need to – they're upfront about their astronomical prices. The respectable hostess clubs offer live music, featuring Filipino bands and topless dance shows. An evening out in any of these places could easily cost $1000 or more.

Be wary of places where an aggressive tout, often female, stands at the entrance, and tries to persuade you to go inside. It's likely that there will be signs on the front door announcing 'Drinks Only $40' and naughty pictures to, er, arouse your interest. Inside, a cocktail waitress, wearing nothing but her knickers, will serve you a drink. She will probably be friendly and chat for a few minutes. It will be one of the most expensive conversations of your life: the bill you're presented with will be at least $500.

When (or if) you protest, staff will undoubtedly point to the tiny sign posted on the wall behind a vase that informs you of the $460 service charge for talking to the waitresses. If you balk at paying the fee or don't have the cash, don't be surprised when two gorillas suddenly appear at your elbows, ready to frogmarch you to the nearest ATM.

Club Bboss (Map pp420–1; ☎ 2369 2883; Lower ground fl, New Mandarin Plaza, 14 Science Museum Rd, Tsim Sha Tsui East; ☻ 1pm-4am; happy hour 1-4.30pm; Tsim Sha Tsui MTR) Hong Kong's biggest and most garish hostess bar is so overwhelming it will have you stammering too. It's a ridiculous scene: chauffeured to your table in a mock Roller, extravagant floor shows (at 9.20pm, 10.15pm and 11.10pm), babes and men drinking Cognac by the tumbler. Bring along a well-fattened wallet; entry costs from $450 to $1200 depending on the time of your arrival.

Club de Millennium (Map pp420–1; ☎ 2368 8013; 10th & 11th fls, BCC Bldg, 25-31 Carnarvon Rd, Tsim Sha Tsui; ☻ 8.30pm-4am; Tsim Sha Tsui MTR) If you've got the dosh, this club will most likely let you partake of its high-class giggly sleaze, where hostesses are rented by the minute and drinks are expensive. There are lavish harem-style lounges done up as Gucci, Versace and Starck showrooms. Enter from Hanoi Rd and pay from $150 for the privilege.

Today's Tonnochy Nightclub (Map pp414–15; ☎ 2573 8223; 1-5 Tonnochy Rd, Wan Chai; ☻ 1pm-4am; Wan Chai MTR) This, the classiest of the Wan Chai hostess clubs, is more on the 'respectable' side, positively dripping with Sino-baroque (Hapsburg meets Qing dynasty?) furnishings and features. There are shows (don't ask) every night from 9.30pm till midnight.

is generally a staged event, with big international acts booked at the Hong Kong Arts Centre or Hong Kong City Hall.

48TH STREET CHICAGO BLUES

Map pp420-1

☎ 2723 7633; Shop G4, Ground fl, 2A Hart Ave, Tsim Sha Tsui; ☽ 5.30pm-2am; happy hour 5.30-9pm Mon-Sat, 5-8pm Sun; Tsim Sha Tsui MTR
This intimate bar in Tsim Sha Tsui has live music (mostly jazz and blues) from 10.30pm nightly.

BLUE DOOR JAZZ CLUB Map p412

☎ 2858 6555; 5th fl, Cheung Hing Commercial Bldg, 37-43 Cochrane St, Central; ☽ 10pm-late Sat; bus 26
This is a relaxed but very serious jazz venue with excellent music from 10.30pm on Saturday and good food from its Sichuanese restaurant one floor up.

BOHEMIAN LOUNGE Map p412

☎ 2526 6099; 3-5 Old Bailey St, Soho ☽ 4.30pm-12.30am Mon-Wed, 4pm-2am or 3am Thu-Sun; happy hour 5-9pm; bus 26
This long, narrow watering hole is a great place for a libation anytime, but try to make it on Thursday after 9pm or Friday or Saturday after 10pm when live jazz kicks in.

CARNEGIE'S Map pp414-15

☎ 2866 6289; Ground fl, 53-55 Lockhart Rd, Wan Chai; ☽ 11am-late Mon-Sat, 5pm-late Sun; happy hour 11am-9pm Mon-Sat; Wan Chai MTR
This place displays a lot of rock memorabilia, which makes it all seem a bit Hard Rock Café-ish. From 9pm on Friday and Saturday, however, the place fills up with revellers. There's unlimited free vodka from 10pm to 11pm on Tuesday, free champers at 9pm on Wednesday, and 'Magnificent Seven' cocktails priced at $25 at 9pm on Thursday. 'Crazy Hour' – 6pm to 7pm daily – is cheaper than happy hour.

CAUSEWAY LOUNGE Map pp414-15

☎ 2890 6665; Basement, Causeway Cnr, 18 Percival St, Causeway Bay; ☽ 5pm-2am Mon-Thu, 5.30pm-2.30am Fri-Sun, happy hour 5-9pm; Causeway Bay MTR
This slick lounge has live folk music from 6pm to 9pm on weekdays and a resident quartet plays pop favourites from 9pm to 1am Monday to Saturday.

CAVERN Map p412

☎ 2121 8969; Shop 1, Lower ground fl, Lan Kwai Fong Tower, 33 Wyndham St, Central; ☽ 6pm-late Mon-Sat; Central MTR
Hong Kong's first (and only) supper club, the Cavern is effectively a showcase for two tribute bands: Sixties Mania Showband, done up in mop-head haircuts and bell-bottoms, and the Rolling Bones, a great Filipino band. Music starts at 9pm Monday to Saturday, a four-course meal is $285 and there's a cover of $100. Enter from D'Aguilar St.

CHASERS Map pp420-1

☎ 2367 9487; Ground fl, Carlton Bldg, 2-3 Knutsford Tce, Tsim Sha Tsui; ☽ 4pm-6am Mon-Fri, noon-6am Sat & Sun; happy hour 4-10pm Mon-Fri, noon-10pm Sat & Sun; Tsim Sha Tsui MTR
This friendly, classy pub has a live Filipino covers band nightly from around 9.30pm. Before the band cranks up, there's a jukebox to party along to and DJs after the band takes its bows. There's dancing most nights; the weekend sees a major sweat-fest.

DUSK TILL DAWN Map pp414-15

☎ 2528 4689; Ground fl, 76-84 Jaffe Rd, Wan Chai; ☽ noon-5am Mon-Fri, 3pm-6am Sat & Sun; happy hour 5-11pm; Wan Chai MTR
This fun place has live music from 10.30pm with an emphasis on beats and vibes so irresistible your booty'll get shaking. The dance floor can be packed, but the atmosphere is usually fun and friendly. Food (set lunch $60 Monday to Friday, set dinner $85 nightly) sticks to easy fillers like pies and burgers.

EDGE Map p412

☎ 2523 6690; www.edgehk.com; Shop 2, Ground fl, The Centrium, 60 Wyndham St, Central; ☽ 6pm-3am Tue-Thu, 6pm-6am Fri & Sat; happy hour 6-10pm Tue-Sat; Central MTR
This spacious venue just up the hill from Lan Kwai Fong has three bars, a restaurant and a live-music room, with gigs (R&B, hip hop and rock) from 10pm during the week and from 10.30pm at the weekend.

FRINGE GALLERY Map p412

☎ 2521 7251; www.hkfringe.com.hk; Ground fl, Fringe Club, 2 Lower Albert Rd, Central; ☽ noon-midnight Mon-Thu, noon-3am Fri & Sat; happy hour 3-9pm Mon-Thu, 3-8pm Fri & Sat; Central MTR
The Fringe, a friendly and eclectic venue on the border of the Lan Kwai Fong quadrant,

MAJOR VENUES

Hong Kong has at last arrived on the big-name concert circuit, and a growing number of internationally celebrated bands and solo acts, including the likes of REM, U2, Norah Jones, Diana Krall, Sting and k.d. lang, perform in Hong Kong regularly.

Big concerts are usually held at either the 12,500-seat **Hong Kong Coliseum** (Map pp420–1; ☎ 2355 7233; 9 Cheong Wan Rd, Hung Hom; Hung Hom MTR), located behind the KCR station, and **Queen Elizabeth Stadium** (Map pp414–15; ☎ 2591 1347; www.lcsd.gov.hk/qes; 18 Oi Kwan Rd, Wan Chai; Wan Chai MTR). The sound is abysmal in the former, and you'd get better acoustics in an empty aircraft hanger than at the latter.

Two other venues are the **HITEC Rotunda** (Map pp418–19; ☎ 2620 2222; www.hitec.com.hk; 1 Trademart Dr, Kowloon Bay; Kowloon Bay MTR) and the New Wing of the **Hong Kong Convention & Exhibition Centre** (HKCEC; Map pp414–15; ☎ 2582 8888; www.hkcec.com; 1 Expo Dr, Wan Chai; bus 18, Wan Chai MTR). These are not huge venues, so the ticket prices are usually quite high.

Smaller acts are sometimes booked into the **Ko Shan Theatre** (Map pp418–19; ☎ 2740 9222; www.lcsd.gov.hk/kst; 77 Ko Shan Rd, Hung Hom). The sound at this venue isn't great either, but the back portion of the seating area is open air, and most of the seats offer a good view of the stage.

has original music in its gallery/bar from 10.30pm on Friday and Saturday, with jazz, rock and world music getting the most airplay. There's a pleasant rooftop bar open in the warmer months.

HARI'S Map pp420-1

☎ 2369 3111 ext 1345; Mezzanine, Holiday Inn Golden Mile, 50 Nathan Rd, Tsim Sha Tsui; ☽ 5pm-2am; happy hour 5-9pm Mon-Sat, 5pm-2am Sun; Tsim Sha Tsui MTR

Is it tacky or classy (or neither)? You decide after you've had a couple of speciality martinis (there are over a dozen to challenge you). There's live music, from 6.15pm weekdays, 8.45pm Saturday and 7.30pm Sunday.

NED KELLY'S LAST STAND Map pp420-1

☎ 2376 0562; 11A Ashley Rd, Tsim Sha Tsui; ☽ 11.30am-2am; happy hour 11.30am-9pm; Tsim Sha Tsui MTR

Ashley Rd in Tsimsy has its own little time warp in this tribute to the 19th-century Australian bushranger and folk hero. A great tradition continues with Ned Kelly's Big Band playing jazz nightly from 9.30pm till 1am. Food is available and there's never a cover charge.

WANCH Map pp414-15

☎ 2861 1621; 54 Jaffe Rd, Wan Chai; ☽ noon-2am Sun-Thu, noon-4am Fri & Sat; happy hour noon-10pm Mon-Thu, noon-8pm Fri-Sun; Wan Chai MTR

This place, which derives its name from what everyone calls the district, has live music (mostly rock and folk with the occasional solo guitarist thrown in) seven nights a week from 9pm. Jam night is Monday from 8pm. If you're not here for the music it can be a dubious scene – the Wanch is basically a pick-up joint.

CLASSICAL MUSIC

In Hong Kong there are classical music concerts performed every week by one of the local orchestras or a foreign ensemble. Many performances are held at the **Hong Kong Cultural Centre** (Map pp420–1; ☎ 2734 2009; www.hkculturalcentre.gov.hk; 10 Salisbury Rd, Tsim Sha Tsui; Tsim Sha Tsui MTR), just east of the Star Ferry terminal, and home to the Hong Kong Philharmonic and the Hong Kong Chinese Orchestra. It is well worth stopping by there to pick up a monthly schedule.

On Hong Kong Island some of the most important venues are the **Hong Kong Academy for the Performing Arts** (Map pp414–15; ☎ 2584 8500, bookings 3128 8288; www.hkapa.edu; 1 Gloucester Rd, Wan Chai; Wan Chai MTR), **Hong Kong City Hall** (Map pp408–9; ☎ 2921 2840, bookings 2734 9009; www.cityhall.gov.hk; 5 Edinburgh Place, Central; Star Ferry, Central MTR), next to the Star Ferry terminal and the **Hong Kong Arts Centre** (Map pp414–15; ☎ 2582 0200, bookings 2734 9009; www.hkac.org.hk; 2 Harbour Rd, Wan Chai; Wan Chai MTR).

The New Territories also has several important cultural centres: **Kwai Tsing Theatre** (Map pp404–5; ☎ 2408 0128; www.lcsd.gov.hk/ktt; 12 Hing Ning Rd, Kwai Chung; Kwai Fong MTR), **Sha Tin Town Hall** (Map p425; ☎ 2694 2542; www.lcsd.gov.hk/stth; 1 Yuen

Wo Rd, Sha Tin; Sha Tin KCR East Rail), **Tuen Mun Town Hall** (Map pp404–5; ☎ 2450 4202; www.lcsd.gov.hk/tmth; 3 Tuen Hi Rd, Tuen Mun; Tuen Mun KCR West Rail), **Tsuen Wan Town Hall** (Map p424; ☎ 2414 0144; www.lcsd.gov.hk/twth; 72 Tai Ho Rd, Tsuen Wan; Tsuen Wan MTR) and **Yuen Long Theatre** (Map pp404–5; ☎ 2476 1029; www.lcsd .gov.hk/ylt; 9 Tai Yuk Rd, Yuen Long; Yuen Long KCR West Rail).

CINEMAS

Hong Kong has some 55 cinemas with 185 screens. Most show local films (with English subtitles) or Hollywood blockbusters dubbed into Cantonese, but a few – Cine-Art House in Wan Chai, the Broadway Cinematheque in Yau Ma Tei and the UA Pacific Place in Admiralty – screen more interesting current releases and art-house films.

Cinemas usually screen five sessions (very roughly at 12.30pm, 2.30pm, 5.30pm, 7.30pm and 9.30pm) weekdays, with extra screenings at 4pm and 11.30pm on Saturday, Sunday and public holidays. You must select a seat when you buy a ticket, which costs between $45 and $75, depending on the location and whether you can claim a concession. Tickets are usually cheaper (eg $40 to $50) at matinées, the last screening of the day at weekends and on holidays (usually 11.30pm) or on certain days of the week (eg Tuesday at the UA Pacific Place).

Almost all Hong Kong films showing in Hong Kong have both Chinese and English subtitles. You can confirm that the film has English subtitles by checking its Censorship Licence in the cinema.

Both the *HK Magazine* and the *South China Morning Post* have listings for film screenings.

HONG KONG ISLAND
Central

You won't find many cinemas in Central but there is one comfortable choice.

PALACE IFC CINEMA Map pp408–9
☎ 2388 6268; Podium L1, IFC Mall, 8 Finance St; Central MTR
This new eight-screen cinema complex in the IFC Mall is arguably the most advanced and comfortable in the territory.

Admiralty & Wan Chai

Certain cultural organisations based in this area show foreign films from time to time, including the **Alliance Française** (Map pp414–15; ☎ 2527 7825; 1st & 2nd fl, 123 Hennessy Rd, Wan Chai) and the **Goethe-Institut** (Map pp414–15; ☎ 2802 0088; 13th & 14th fl, Hong Kong Arts Centre, 2 Harbour Rd, Wan Chai).

For both art-house and mainstream films, Wan Chai has two of the best and most comfortable cinemas in the territory.

AGNÈS B CINEMA Map pp414-15
☎ 2582 0200; Upper basement, Hong Kong Arts Centre, 2 Harbour Rd, Wan Chai; bus 18
This recently renamed cinema – it was the Lim Por Yen Theatre for years – is the place for classics, revivals, alternative screenings and travelling film festivals.

CINE-ART HOUSE Map pp414-15
☎ 2827 4820; Ground fl, Sun Hung Kai Centre, 30 Harbour Rd, Wan Chai; bus 18
This alternative cinema specialises in English-language films.

UA PACIFIC PLACE Map pp408-9
☎ 2869 0322; Level 1, Pacific Place, 88 Queensway, Admiralty; Admiralty MTR
It's blessedly easy to sink yourself into the comfort offered by one of Hong Kong's plushest cinemas. Its great sound system ensures you won't miss a whisper.

Causeway Bay & Island East

Causeway Bay is packed with cinemas but, with few exceptions, most of them show Hollywood blockbusters and Hong Kong and mainland films. Further east is Hong Kong's most important film-watching venue, the Hong Kong Film Archive.

HONG KONG FILM ARCHIVE Map pp406-7
☎ 2739 2139, bookings 2734 9009; 50 Lei King Rd, Sai Wan Ho MTR
This is the place to find out what lies (or perhaps lurks) behind Hong Kong's film industry. The archive houses more than 4300 films, runs a rich calendar of screenings (local and foreign movies) and exhibits natty posters and other fine film paraphernalia.

WINDSOR CINEMA Map pp414–15

☎ 2388 3188; 1st fl, Windsor House, 311 Gloucester Rd, Causeway Bay; Causeway Bay MTR

This comfortable cineplex with four screens
is just west of Victoria Park.

KOWLOON
Tsim Sha Tsui

GRAND OCEAN CINEMA Map pp420–1

☎ 2377 2100; Marco Polo Hong Kong Hotel
Shopping Arcade, Zone D, Harbour City, 3 Canton Rd,
Tsim Sha Tsui; Star Ferry

The Grand Ocean screens the usual
blockbusters.

Yau Ma Tei & New Kowloon

AMC FESTIVAL WALK Map pp418–19

☎ 2265 8545; Upper ground fl & Levels 1 & 2,
Festival Walk, 80-88 Tat Chee Ave, Kowloon Tong;
Kowloon Tong MTR

This complex with 11 screens at Hong
Kong's poshest mall is the largest cinema in
the territory.

BROADWAY CINEMATHEQUE
Map p423

☎ 2388 3188; Ground fl, Prosperous Garden,
3 Public Square St, Yau Ma Tei; Yau Ma Tei MTR

This is an unlikely place for an alternative
cinema, but it's worth coming up for new
art-house releases and rerun screenings.
The Kubrick Bookshop Café (p184) next
door serves good coffee and decent pre-
flick food.

THEATRE

Local theatre groups (p30) mostly perform
at the Shouson Theatre of the Hong Kong
Arts Centre, the Academy for Performing
Arts, the Hong Kong Cultural Centre and
Hong Kong City Hall (p212). Performances
are usually in Cantonese, though there
are usually summaries in English available.
Smaller troupes occasionally present plays
in English at one of the two theatres at the
Fringe Club.

CHINESE OPERA UNMASKED

The best time to see and hear Chinese opera – not the
easiest form of entertainment to catch in Hong Kong
these days – is during the Hong Kong Arts Festival
(p10) in February/March, and outdoor performances
are staged in Victoria Park during the Mid-Autumn
Festival. At other times, you might take your chances
at catching a performance at the Temple Street night
market (p94), but the most reliable venue for opera
performances year round is the Sunbeam Theatre
(below) in North Point.

FRINGE STUDIO & O² THEATRE
Map p412

☎ 2521 7251, bookings 3128 8288; www.hkfringe
.com.hk; Ground & 1st fls, Fringe Club, 2 Lower
Albert Rd; ☽ 8pm during performances (days vary);
Central MTR

These intimate theatres, each seating up to
100 people, host eclectic local and international performances (average ticket price
is $80) in English and in Cantonese.

SUNBEAM THEATRE Map pp406–7

☎ 2856 0161, 2563 2959; Kiu Fai Mansion, 423 King's
Rd, North Point; tickets $40-320; North Point MTR

Cantonese and other Chinese opera (p31)
can be seen at this theatre throughout the
year. Performances generally run for about
a week, and are usually held five days a
week in the evening at 7.30pm, with occasional matinées at 1pm or 1.30pm. The
theatre is directly above the North Point
MTR station (exit A4), on the north side of
King's Rd, near the intersection with Shu
Kuk St.

COMEDY

The only venue with regularly scheduled
comedy acts in Hong Kong at present is the
Viceroy Restaurant & Bar's **Punchline Comedy
Club** (Map pp414–15; ☎ 2827 7777; 2nd fl,
Sun Hung Kai Centre, 30 Harbour Rd, Wan
Chai; bus 18), with local and imported acts,
every third Thursday, Friday and Saturday
from 9pm to 11pm. Entry costs $260; Indian
buffet dinner (from 7pm to 11pm) is $120.

Watching Sport 216
Cricket 216
Football 216
Horse Racing 216
Rugby 217

Outdoor Activities 217
Beach Swimming 217
Bird Watching 217
Bowling 217
Climbing 218
Cycling 218
Fishing 218
Golf 218
Hiking 219
Horse Riding 222
Kayaking & Canoeing 222
Martial Arts 222
Running 223
Scuba Diving 223
Skating 223
Squash 224
Tennis 224
Windsurfing & Wakeboarding 224
Yachting & Sailing 225

Health & Fitness 225
Gyms & Fitness Clubs 225
Swimming Pools 225
Therapy Clinics 226
Yoga 226

Activities ■

Activities

Hong Kong people revel in watching live sporting events – especially if there's the possibility of a flutter. But if you're feeling more active than passive about sports while in the territory, getting involved can be as simple as slipping into some swimming togs, grabbing the handlebars of a rental bike or unrolling a yoga mat.

WATCHING SPORT

Sporting events are well covered in the sports section of Hong Kong's English-language newspapers. Many of the annual events don't fall on the same day or even in the same month every year, so contact the Hong Kong Tourism Board (HKTB; ☎ 2508 1234; www .discoverhongkong.com) for further information.

CRICKET

Hong Kong has two cricket clubs: the very exclusive **Hong Kong Cricket Club** (Map pp406–7; ☎ 2574 6266; 137 Wong Nai Chung Gap Rd), above Deep Water Bay on Hong Kong Island, and the **Kowloon Cricket Club** (Map pp420–1; ☎ 2367 4141; 10 Cox's Rd, Tsim Sha Tsui), where the Hong Kong International Cricket Sixes is held in early November. This two-day match sees teams from Australia, New Zealand, Hong Kong, England, Kenya, India, Pakistan, Sri Lanka and South Africa battle it out in a speedier version of the game. For information contact the **Hong Kong Cricket Association** (Map pp414–15; ☎ 2504 8102; www.hkca.cricket .org; Room 1019, Sports House, 1 Stadium Path, Causeway Bay).

FOOTBALL

Hong Kong has a fairly lively amateur soccer league. Games are played at the **Happy Valley Sports Ground** (Map pp414–15; ☎ 2895 1523; Sports Rd, Happy Valley), a group of pitches inside the Happy Valley Racecourse, and at **Mong Kok Stadium** (Map p423; ☎ 2380 0188; 37 Flower Market Rd, Mong Kok). For match schedules and venues, check the sports sections of the English-language newspapers or contact the **Hong Kong Football Association** (☎ 2712 9122; www.hkfa.com; 55 Fat Kwong St, Ho Man Tin). The big football event of the year is the Carlsberg Cup, which is held on the first and fourth days of the Chinese New Year (late January/early February).

HORSE RACING

Horse racing is Hong Kong's biggest spectator sport, probably because until recently it was the only form of legalised gambling in the territory apart from the Mark Six Lottery, and no-one likes to wager like the Hong Kong Chinese. There are about 80 meetings a year at two racecourses: one in Happy Valley (p83) on Hong Kong Island with a capacity for 35,000 punters and the newer and larger one at Sha Tin (p119) in the New Territories accommodating 85,000.

The racing season is from September to June, with most race meetings at Happy Valley taking place on Wednesday at 7pm or 7.30pm and at Sha Tin on Saturday or Sunday afternoon. Check the website of the **Hong Kong Jockey Club** (HKJC; ☎ 2966 8111, information hotline ☎ 1817; www.hong kongjockeyclub.com) for details, or pick up a list of race meetings from any HKTB information centre.

You have three choices if you want to attend a meeting. You can join the crowds and pay $10 to sit in the public area or, if you've been in Hong Kong for less than 21 days and are over 18 years of age, you can buy a tourist ticket ($100 to $150, depending on the race), which allows you to jump the queue, sit in the members' enclosure and walk around next to the finish area. These can be purchased at the gate on the day of the race, or up to two days in advance at any branch of the HKJC. Make sure to bring along your passport as proof. The last choice is to join one of the racing tours (p83) sponsored by the HKTB.

The HKJC maintains off-track betting centres around the territory, including a **Central branch** (Map pp408–9; Unit A1, Ground fl, CMA Bldg, 64 Connaught Rd Central), a **Wan Chai branch** (Map pp414–15; Shop A, Ground fl, Allied Kajima Bldg, 134-145 Gloucester Rd, enter from Stewart St) and a **Tsim Sha Tsui branch** (Map pp420–1; Ground fl, Eader Centre, 39-41 Hankow Rd).

Red-letter days at the races include the Chinese New Year races in late January or early February, the Hong Kong Derby in March, the Queen Elizabeth II Cup in April, and the Hong Kong International Races in December. For information on horse racing in Macau, see p331.

RUGBY

The **Rugby World Cup Sevens** (www.hksevens .com.hk) sees teams from all over the world come together in Hong Kong in late March for three days of lightning-fast 15-minute matches at the 40,000-seat **Hong Kong Stadium** (Map pp414–15; ☎ 2895 7895; www.lcsd .gov.hk/stadium) in So Kon Po, a division of Causeway Bay. Even non–rugby fans scramble to get tickets (adult/child under 13 for $1000/350), because the Sevens is a giant, international, three-day party. For inquiries and tickets, contact the **Hong Kong Rugby Football Union** (Map pp414–15; ☎ 2504 8311; www.hk rugby.com; Room 2001, Sports House, 1 Stadium Path, So Kon Po).

OUTDOOR ACTIVITIES

Hong Kong offers countless ways to have fun and keep fit. From tennis and squash courts to cycling and hiking trails, you'll hardly be stumped for something active to do during your visit here.

Information & Venues

One excellent, all-round option is the **South China Athletic Association** (SCAA; Map pp414–15; ☎ 2577 6932; www.scaa.org.hk; 5th fl, Sports Complex, 88 Caroline Hill Rd, So Kon Po), east of the Happy Valley Racecourse and south of Causeway Bay. The SCAA has facilities for badminton, billiards, bowling, tennis, squash, table tennis, gymnastics, fencing, yoga, judo, karate and golf (among other activities) and short-term membership for visitors is $50 per month. Another good place to know about

is the nearby **Hong Kong Amateur Athletic Association** (Map pp414–15; ☎ 2504 8215; www .hkaaa.com; Room 2015, Sports House, 1 Stadium Path, So Kon Po).

Hong Kong Outdoors (www.hkoutdoors.com) is an excellent website for all sorts of active pursuits.

BEACH SWIMMING

The most accessible beaches are on the southern side of Hong Kong Island, but the best ones are on the Outlying Islands and in the New Territories. For a list of beaches deemed safe enough for swimming and their water-quality gradings, check the website of the **Environmental Protection Department** (www.info.gov.hk/epd).

Hong Kong's 41 gazetted beaches are staffed by lifeguards from 9am to 6pm daily from April to October (from 8am to 7pm on Saturday and Sunday from June to August) and the shark nets at the 30 beaches that have them are inspected. From the first day of the official swimming season until the last, expect the beaches to be chock-a-block on weekends and holidays. When the swimming season is officially declared over, the beaches become deserted – no matter how hot the weather.

At most of the beaches you will find toilets, showers, changing rooms, refreshment stalls and sometimes cafés and restaurants.

For information on Hong Kong's swimming pools, see p225.

BIRD WATCHING

Birders in Hong Kong will have their work cut out for them: some 450 species have been spotted in the territory. The best area is **Mai Po Marsh** (p112), but others include **Tai Po Kau Nature Reserve** (p117), **Shing Mun Country Park** (p221) and **Po Toi** (p138). The **Hong Kong Bird-Watching Society** (☎ 2667 4537; www.hkbws.org .hk; GPO Box 12460, Central) is a font of information and can arrange organised visits to local birding venues. Ask for its free brochure *Bird Watching in Hong Kong*.

BOWLING

Some of the best facilities are on the 1st floor of the Sports Complex at the **SCAA** (left). About 60 lanes are open from 10am to 12.30am Monday to Friday and from 9am to 12.30am Saturday, Sunday and holidays.

Games cost $18 to $30, depending on the time of day and day of the week.

In Kowloon and the New Territories, bowling alleys tend to be located in the backwaters. One of the most accessible is **Sha Tin Super Bowl** (Map p425; ☎ 2648 2815; Level 4, City One Plaza Sha Tin, Ngan Shing St, Sha Tin). Games are $25 to $45.

CLIMBING

Climbers might contact the **Hong Kong Mountaineering Union** (Map pp414–15; ☎ 2504 8124; www.hkmu.org.hk; Room 1013, Sports House, 1 Stadium Path, So Kon Po), which supposedly offers courses in leisure, rock and sport climbing, but you'll find out a lot more – and make better contacts – by browsing the **Hong Kong Climbing** (www.hong kongclimbing.com) website. According to these guys, **Tung Lung Chau** (p137) has the highest concentration of quality sport climbs in Hong Kong and is the territory's premier climbing spot.

CYCLING

There are bicycle paths in the New Territories, mostly around Tolo Harbour. The paths run from Sha Tin to Tai Po and continue up to Tai Mei Tuk. You can rent bicycles in these three places, but the paths get very crowded on the weekends. Bicycle rentals are also available at Shek O on Hong Kong Island and on Lamma, Cheung Chau and Lantau.

Although the **Hong Kong Cycling Association** (Map pp414–15; ☎ 2504 8176; www.cycling .org.hk; Room 1015, Sports House, 1 Stadium Path, So Kon Po) mainly organises races, you can try it for information.

Mountain biking is no longer banned in Hong Kong's country parks and there is a fine, ever-growing network of trails available in 10 of them, including Sai Kung and Lantau South Country Parks. You must apply for a permit in writing, in person or by fax through the **Country & Marine Parks Authority** (Map pp418–19; ☎/fax 2317 0482; 5th fl, 303 Cheung Sha Wan Rd, Sham Shui Po). For information check out the website of the **Hong Kong Mountain Bike Association** (www .hkmba.org); for equipment (and first-hand advice) talk to the helpful staff at the **Flying Ball Bicycle Co** (☎ 2381 3661; 201 Tung Choi St, Mong Kok; ☉ 10am-8pm Mon-Sat, 10.30am-7pm Sun).

FISHING

While there are almost no restrictions on deep-sea fishing, it's a different story at Hong Kong's 17 freshwater reservoirs, where the season runs from September to March and there are limits on the quantity and size of fish (generally various types of carp and tilapia) allowed. A licence from the **Water Supplies Department** (Map pp414–15; ☎ 2824 5000; 1st fl, Immigration Tower, 7 Gloucester Rd, Wan Chai) costs $24 and is valid for three years.

For something a little less, well, wild, head for the **Tai Mei Tuk Fish Farm** (Map pp404–5; ☎ 2662 6351; Tai Mei Tuk; weekday/weekend per hr $15/30, all-day package $110; ☉ 9am-10pm Mon-Fri, 8am-10pm Sat & Sun), a large artificial pond by the harbour stocked with freshwater fish. Rods cost $10 to rent.

GOLF

Most golf courses in Hong Kong are private but do open to the public at certain times – usually weekdays only. Greens fees for visitors vary, but range from $450 for two rounds at the nine-hole **Deep Water Bay Golf Club** (Map pp406–7; ☎ 2812 7070; 19 Island Rd, Deep Water Bay) on Hong Kong Island, where nonmembers can play weekdays only, to $1400 at the **Hong Kong Golf Club** (Map pp404–5; ☎ 2670 1211; Fan Kam Rd, Fanling, New Territories), which has three 18-hole courses.

One of the most dramatic links to play in Hong Kong – for the scenery if not the par – is the 36-hole **Jockey Club Kau Sai Chau Public Golf Course** (Map pp404–5; ☎ 2791 3388; www.kscgolf.com) on the island of Kau Sai Chau, which is linked by regular ferry with Sai Kung town, northeast of Kowloon (p122). Greens fees for 18 holes of play by nonresidents range from $275 to $640 on weekdays and $395 to $940 at the weekend. Be sure to bring your passport and handicap card.

It costs from $100 to $300 to rent clubs and $30 to $65 to rent golf shoes; caddies are $165 to $275 for 18 holes. Other courses in Hong Kong include those below.

Clearwater Bay Golf & Country Club (Map pp404–5; ☎ 2719 1595; www.cwbgolf.org; 139 Tau Au Mun Rd, Clearwater Bay; greens fees $1200-1400) This 27-hole course lies at the tip of the Clearwater Bay Peninsula in the New Territories.

Discovery Bay Golf Club (Map p427; ☎ 2987 7273; Discovery Bay, Lantau; greens fees $1200-1400) Perched high on a hill, this 27-hole course has impressive views of the Outlying Islands.

Shek O Golf & Country Club (Map pp406–7; ☎ 2809 2117; Shek O Rd, Shek O; greens fees $500) You'll find this 18-hole course located on the southeastern edge of Hong Kong Island.

If you're content with just teeing off (again and again), the Jockey Club Kau Sai Chau Public Golf Course has a **driving range** (☎ 2791 3341; weekday/weekend $110/150, club rental $15; ⏰ 7.30am-6pm Mon, Wed & Thu, 11am-8pm Tue, 7am-10pm Fri-Sun). There's also the **Sai Kung Ho Chung Driving Range** (Map pp404–5; ☎ 2243 6222; 88 Ho Chung Rd, Sai Kung; $100-120, club rental $20; ⏰ 5.30-11pm Mon-Fri, 8am-9pm Sat & Sun), and the more centrally located **OGC Golf City** (☎ 2522 2111; www.ogcgolfcity.com; Kai Fuk Rd, Kowloon Bay; $100-120; ⏰ 7am-midnight), with 150 bays on the old Kai Tak airport runway in Kowloon. The closest MTR stop is Kowloon Bay.

For more information contact the **Hong Kong Golf Association** (Map pp414–15; ☎ 2504 8659; www.hkga.com; Room 2003, Sports House, 1 Stadium Path, So Kon Po).

HIKING

Hong Kong is an excellent place for hiking, and there are numerous trails on Hong Kong Island, in the New Territories and on the Outlying Islands. The four main ones are the **MacLehose Trail** (p220), at 100km the longest in the territory; the 78km-long **Wilson Trail** (p222), which runs on both sides of Victoria Harbour; the 70km-long **Lantau Trail** (p220); and the **Hong Kong Trail** (p220), which is 50km long.

When hiking or trekking in Hong Kong some basic equipment is required. Most important is a full water bottle. Other useful items include trail snacks, a weatherproof jacket, a sun hat, toilet paper, maps and a compass. Boots are not necessary; the best footwear is a good pair of running shoes.

Hikers should remember that the high humidity during spring and summer can be enervating. October to March is the best season for arduous treks. At high elevations, such as parts of the Lantau and Mac-Lehose Trails, it can get very cold so it's essential to bring warm clothing.

Mosquitoes are a nuisance in spring and summer, so a good mosquito repellent is necessary. Snakes are rarely encountered.

Maps

Good hiking maps will save you a lot of time, energy and trouble. The **Map Publication Centres** (p317) stock the excellent Countryside Series of topographical maps as well as the unfolded hiking maps ($30) produced by the Country & Marine Parks Authority for each of Hong Kong's four main trails: the 1:15,000 *Hong Kong Trail,* the 1:35,000 *Wilson Trail,* the 1:25,000 *MacLehose Trail* and the 1:20,000 *Lantau Trail.* The four trail maps are also available from the **Government Publications Office** (p235) in Central.

Accommodation

The **Country & Marine Parks Authority** (☎ 2420 0529; http://parks.afcd.gov.hk) of the Agriculture, Fisheries & Conservation Department maintains 29 no-frills camp sites in the New Territories and 10 in the Outlying Islands for use by hikers. They are all free and are clearly labelled on the Countryside Series and four trail maps. Camping is prohibited on the 41 gazetted public beaches patrolled by lifeguards, but is generally OK on more remote beaches.

You can camp at the hostels managed by the **Hong Kong Youth Hostels Association** (HKYHA; ☎ 2788 1638; www.yha.org.hk) with the exception of the Jockey Club Mount Davis hostel on Hong Kong Island and Bradbury Lodge at Tai Mei Tuk in the New Territories. The fee, which allows you to use the hostel's toilet and washroom facilities, is $16 for HKYHA or Hostelling International (HI) members, or $25 for nonmembers. See p251 for details.

Organised Hikes

The **YWCA** (☎ 3476 1340; www.ywca.org.hk) arranges group hikes around such areas as Silvermine to Pui O, Shek O to Chai Wan and other popular routes. An excellent group is the **Saturday Hikers Club of Hong Kong** (http://groups.yahoo.com/group/saturday hikers), which organises informal hikes in the countryside most Saturdays from October to May. Serious hikers might consider joining in the annual **Trailwalker event** (www .oxfamtrailwalker.org.hk), a gruelling 48-hour race across the MacLehose Trail in the New Territories in November, organised since 1986 by Oxfam Hong Kong (☎ 2520 2525).

If you would like to do some hiking in the countryside – either individually or in a group – but you would prefer to be shown the way Walk Hong Kong (☎ 9359 9071, 9187 8641; www.walkhongkong.com) takes guided nature walks in southwestern Hong Kong Island (eg Dragon's Back), the New Territories (eg Kam Shan and Shing Mun Country Parks) and Lantau Island. They last between four and eight hours and cost from $300 to $600, including lunch.

Natural Excursion Ideals (☎ 2486 2112, 9300 5197; www.kayak-and-hike.com) offers both hiking and kayaking trips to Hoi Ha, Tap Mun Chau and Tai Long Wan in the New Territories. It has a fab five-hour tour of the harbour around Sai Kung at 9am on Tuesday and Thursday that will take you by unique 'fast-pursuit craft' to the otherwise inaccessible Bluff Island and the fishing village of Sha Kiu Tau. The price ($595) includes a seafood lunch and all gear, including a mask and snorkel.

HONG KONG TRAIL

Starting from the Peak Tram upper terminus on the Peak, the 50km-long Hong Kong Trail (Map pp408–9) follows Lugard Rd to the west and drops down the hill to Pok Fu Lam Reservoir near Aberdeen, before turning east and zigzagging across the ridges. The trail traverses four country parks: 2.7-sq-km Pok Fu Lam Country Park south of Victoria Peak, 4.2-sq-km Aberdeen Country Park east of the Peak, 13-sq-km Tai Tam Country Park on the eastern side of the island and 7-sq-km Shek O Country Park in the southeast. Tai Tam is the most beautiful of the four, with its dense emerald woods and trickling streams. The Hong Kong Trail skirts the northern side of Tai Tam Reservoir, the largest body of water on the island.

It's possible to hike the entire trail – a total of eight stages from the Peak to Big Wave Bay – in one day, but it's quite a slog and requires about 15 full hours. Most hikers pick a manageable section to suit, such as stage No 1 from the Peak to Pok Fu Lam Reservoir Rd (7km, two hours). Note that there are no designated camp sites along the Hong Kong Trail.

Apart from gaining stage No 1 of the trail on the Peak, you can reach stage No 6 (Tai Tam) on bus 6 from the Central bus terminal below Exchange Square, bus 14 from Sai Wan Ho, and stage No 7 (Tai Tam Bay and Shek O) on buses 9 and 309 (Sunday only) from Shau Kei Wan MTR station.

LANTAU TRAIL

The 70km-long Lantau Trail (Map p427) follows the mountain tops from Mui Wo and then doubles back at Tai O along the coast to where it started. It takes just over 24 hours to walk in full, but the trail is divided into a dozen manageable stages ranging from 2.5km (45 minutes) to 10.5km (three hours).

A realistic approach is to tackle the trail's first four stages (17.5km, seven hours), which take in the highest and most scenic parts of the trail and can be accessed from Mui Wo or, conversely, from the Po Lin Monastery and SG Davis Hostel at Ngong Ping. Note that the walk can be treacherous in certain steep sections. Stage No 1 (2.5km, 45 minutes) of the Lantau Trail from Mui Wo follows boring South Lantau Rd but there's an alternative, more scenic path from Mui Wo to Nam Shan, where stage No 2 begins, via Luk Tei Tong.

The western part of the trail, which follows the southwestern coast of Lantau from Tai O to Fan Lau and then up to Shek Pik (stage Nos 7 to 9), is also very scenic.

MACLEHOSE TRAIL

The 100km MacLehose Trail (Map pp404–5), the territory's longest hiking path, spans the New Territories from Tuen Mun in the west to Pak Tam Chung on the Sai Kung Peninsula in the east. The trail follows the ridge, goes over Tai Mo Shan, at 957m Hong Kong's highest peak, and passes close to Ma On Shan (702m), the territory's fourth-tallest mountain. The trail is divided into 10 stages, ranging in length from about 4.6km (1½ hours) to 15.6km (five hours).

You can access the MacLehose trail by public transport at many points (see the list at the end of this section), but arguably the most convenient is reached by catching bus 51 on Tai Ho Rd North, just north of the Tsuen Wan MTR station, and getting off where Route Twisk meets Tai Mo Shan Rd. This is the beginning (or the end) of stage No 9 of the trail. From there you have the choice of heading east towards Tai Mo Shan and Lead Mine Pass (9.7km, four hours) or west to the Tai Lam Chung Reservoir, through Tai Lam Country Park (54 sq km), and eventually all the way to Tuen Mun (22km, 7½ hours), which is the western end of the trail. From Tuen Mun town centre, you can catch bus 260X or 63X to Yau Ma Tei and Tsim Sha Tsui.

Another, perhaps more enjoyable, way to reach the trail is to take green minibus 82 from Shiu Wo St, due south of the Tsuen Wan MTR station. This will drop you off at Pineapple Dam, adjacent to the Shing Mun Reservoir in 14-sq-km Shing Mun Country Park; the new **Shing Mun Country Park Visitor Centre** (Map pp404–5; ☎ 2498 1362; ☯ 9.30am-4.30pm Wed-Mon) is on the western edge of the reservoir. You can follow the Pineapple Dam Nature Trail past several picnic and barbecue areas and around the reservoir itself. The signposted Shing Mun Arboretum has 70 varieties of fruit and other trees, plus medicinal plants.

Running south from the Shing Mun Reservoir is stage No 6 of the MacLehose Trail, which will take you by Smugglers' Ridge and past some pretty dramatic scenery. The trail leads west and then south alongside Kowloon Reservoir to Tai Po Rd (4.6km, 1½ hours). From here stage No 5 of the trail heads east past a hill called Eagle's Nest, through woodland and up Beacon Hill, named after a lookout station positioned here under Qing-dynasty Emperor Kang Xi, who fired up a beacon when enemy ships sailed into view.

From there stage No 5 of the trail runs along a ridge to Lion Rock, from where there is a path leading north to **Amah Rock** (p118). The MacLehose Trail circumvents Lion Rock but you can clamber up the path leading to it. Be warned, though – it's a tough climb.

Coming down from Lion Rock, the MacLehose Trail leads you to Sha Tin Pass. From here you can either head south a short distance along the road and pick up green minibus No 37M at Tsz Wan Shan estate heading for Wong Tai Sin MTR in Kowloon, or walk north along a path to Sha Tin (about 2km) and jump on the KCR. If you carry on along stage No 4 of the MacLehose Trail, it will take you into the heart of Ma On Shan Country Park via Tate's Cairn (577m) and Buffalo Hill.

Other places to access the MacLehose Trail (from east to west):

Pak Tam Chung (stage No 1) Bus 94 from Sai Kung town.

Pak Tam Au (stage Nos 2 & 3) As above.

Kei Ling Rd (stage Nos 3 & 4) Bus 299 from Sha Tin or Sai Kung town.

Ma On Shan (stage No 4) Bus 99 from Sai Kung town to Nai Chung (descend at Sai Sha Rd).

Tai Po Rd (stage No 6) Green minibus 81 from Tsuen Wan or bus 81C from the Hung Hom KCR station.

Tuen Mun (stage No 10) Buses 53 and 60M from Tsuen Wan or bus 63X from Nathan Rd in Tsim Sha Tsui or Yau Ma Tei.

WALKING & NATURE GUIDES TO LEAD THE WAY

Exploring Hong Kong's Countryside: A Visitor's Companion by Edward Stokes is a well-written and illustrated 185-page guidebook distributed free by the HKTB. It provides excellent background information and the maps are good.

Peter Spurrier's new *Hiker's Guide to Hong Kong* will guide you along the four main trails and introduce you to 10 shorter ones.

Hong Kong Hikes: The Twenty Best Walks in the Territory by Christian Wright and Tinja Tsang is unique in that it consists of 20 laminated loose-leaf cards for hikes on Hong Kong Island, the Outlying Islands and the New Territories that can be unclipped and slotted into the transparent plastic folder provided.

Magic Walks, which comes in four volumes and is good for 50 relatively easy hikes throughout the territory, is written by Kaarlo Schepel, almost a legend among Hong Kong walkers.

Hong Kong Pathfinder: 23 Day-Walks in Hong Kong by Martin Williams is based on the author's 'Day Away' column in the *South China Morning Post*.

A lovely pictorial dealing with the countryside is *The MacLehose Trail* by Tim Nutt, Chris Bale and Tao Ho.

The Birds of Hong Kong and South China by Clive Viney, Karen Phillips and Lam Chiu Ying is the definitive guide for spotting and identifying the territory's feathered creatures and an excellent guide to take along while hiking in the New Territories.

A specialist title but a welcome addition to Hong Kong's walking guides bookshelf is *Ruins of War: A Guide to Hong Kong's Battlefields and Wartime Sites* by Ko Tim Keung and Jason Wordie, which includes a lot of walking in the countryside.

WILSON TRAIL

Wilson Trail (Maps pp404–5 and pp406–7), which is 78km in length – 82.5km long if you include the MTR harbour crossing – is unusual in that its southern section (two stages, 11.4km, 4½ hours) is on Hong Kong Island, while its northern part (eight stages, 66.6km, 26½ hours) crosses the eastern harbour to Lei Yue Mun in New Kowloon and then carries on into the New Territories.

The trail begins at Stanley Gap Rd, about 1km to the north of Stanley; bus 6, 6A, 6X and 260 from Central pass the beginning of the trail about 2km short of Repulse Bay. The first steeply rising section of the trail is all concrete steps. You soon reach the summit of Stanley Mound (386m), topped by a pavilion. The summit is also known as the Twins (or Ma Kong Shan in Cantonese). On a clear day you'll have an excellent view of Stanley, Repulse Bay and as far as Lamma. The trail continues north over Violet Hill (Tsz Lo Lan Shan), where it meets the Hong Kong Trail, and passes by Mt Butler, drops down into the urban chaos and terminates at the Quarry Bay MTR station. Those who wish to carry on should then take the MTR across to Yau Tong on the Tseung Kwan O line and pick up the trail outside the station.

From there the trail zigzags south to Lei Yue Mun before turning sharply north again into the hills. The trail then takes a westward turn, heading over the summit of Tate's Cairn, and passes Lion Rock and Beacon Hill. The path makes another sharp turn northward, continues through Shing Mun Country Park, returns to civilisation near Tai Po, then disappears into the hills again at Pat Sin Leng Country Park before ending at Nam Chung Reservoir on the Starling Inlet, not far from Shau Tau Kok and Hong Kong's border with Shenzhen and the mainland.

Parts of the Wilson Trail overlap with the Hong Kong Trail on Hong Kong Island and with the MacLehose Trail in the New Territories, particularly in the area east of Tai Mo Shan.

HORSE RIDING

The Hong Kong Jockey Club's **Tuen Mun Public Riding School** (Map pp404–5; ☎ 2461 3338; Lot No 45, Lung Mun Rd, Tuen Mun;

ⓧ 9am-6pm Tue-Sun) in the New Territories offers private lessons for about $360 per hour, as does the club's **Pok Fu Lam Public Riding School** (Map pp406–7; ☎ 2550 1359; 75 Pok Fu Lam Reservoir Rd) in southeastern Hong Kong Island.

KAYAKING & CANOEING

The **Cheung Chau Windsurfing Water Sports Centre** (Map p428; ☎ 2981 8316) located at Tung Wan Beach rents out single/double kayaks for $50/80 per hour. These are also available at the **St Stephen's Beach Water Sports Centre** (Off Map p411; ☎ 2813 5407; Wong Ma Kok Path; ⓧ 9am-noon & 1-4pm Wed-Mon) located in Stanley.

Canoeing facilities are available through the **Tai Mei Tuk Water Sports Centre** (Map pp404–5; ☎ 2665 3591) at Tai Mei Tuk in the New Territories. You can also inquire at the **Wong Shek Water Sports Centre** (Map pp404–5; ☎ 2328 2311; Wong Shek pier, Sai Kung) in the New Territories.

Natural Excursion Ideals (☎ 2486 2112, 9300 5197; www.kayak-and-hike.com) has organised kayaking trips ($595) to Hoi Ha, Tap Mun Chau and Tai Long Wan in the New Territories. **Dragonfly** (☎ 2577 6319; www.dragonfly.com.hk) has similar excursions on offer.

MARTIAL ARTS

The **HKTB** (☎ 2508 1234), through its Cultural Kaleidoscope program, offers free one-hour t'ai chi lessons at 8am on Monday, Wednesday, Thursday and Friday on the waterfront promenade outside the Hong Kong Cultural Centre (Map pp420–1) in Tsim Sha Tsui. On Sunday from 2.30pm to 4.30pm a display of traditional Chinese martial arts takes place at Kung Fu Corner near Sculpture Walk in Kowloon Park (Map pp420–1).

Fightin' Fit (Map p412; ☎ 2526 6648; www.fightinfit.com.hk; 2nd fl, World Trust Tower, 50 Stanley St, Central)

Hong Kong Chinese Martial Arts Association (Map pp414–15; ☎ 2504 8164; Room 1008, Sports House, 1 Stadium Path, So Kon Po)

Hong Kong Tai Chi Association (Map p423; ☎ 2395 4884; 11th fl, Lee On Bldg, 56-62 Argyle St, Mong Kok)

Hong Kong Wushu Union (Map pp414–15; ☎ 2504 8226; www.hkwushu.com.hk/; Room 1017, Sports House, 1 Stadium Path, So Kon Po) Has classes for children.

Wan Kei Ho International Martial Arts Association
(Map pp408–9; ☎ 2544 1368, 9885 8336; www.kung fuwan.com; 3rd fl, Yue's House, 304 Des Voeux Rd Central, Sheung Wan)

Wing Chun Yip Man Martial Arts Athletic Association
(Map pp420–1; ☎ 2723 2306; Flat A, 4th fl, Alpha House, 27-33 Nathan Rd, Tsim Sha Tsui) Charges $500 a month for three lessons a week (two or three hours each) and has a six-month intensive course (six hours a day, six days a week) for $5000.

RUNNING

Good places to run on Hong Kong Island include Harlech and Lugard Rds on the Peak, Bowen Rd above Wan Chai, the track in Victoria Park and the racecourse at Happy Valley (as long as there aren't any horse races on it!). In Kowloon a popular place to run is the Tsim Sha Tsui East Promenade.

For easy runs followed by brewskis and good company, contact the **Hong Kong Hash House Harriers** (www.hkhash.com), the main local branch of a lively organisation with members worldwide, or the **Ladies' Hash House Harriers** (☎ 2881 0748; www.hkladieshash .com). The inappropriately named **Ladies Road Runners Club** (www.hklrrc.org) allows men to join in the fun. Another group that organises runs is **Athletic Veterans of Hong Kong** (www .avohk.org).

Every Sunday from 8am to 10am between April and July, and from 7am to 9am between August and November, the **Adventist Hospital** (Map pp406–7; ☎ 2835 0555; Wong Nai Chung Gap Rd, Happy Valley) organ-ises a running clinic. It will set you back $450 as a new member, $350 if you're a returning member.

SCUBA DIVING

Hong Kong has some surprisingly worth-while diving spots, particularly in the far northeast, and there is certainly no short-age of courses. One of the best sources of information for courses and excursions is Sai Kung–based **Splash Hong Kong** (☎ 2792 4495, 9047 9603). Other outfits giving lessons and organising dives include the following:

Bunn's Divers (Map pp414–15; ☎ 3422 3322; Mezza-nine, Chuen Fung House, 188-192 Johnston Rd, Wan Chai; ☺ 11am-8pm Mon-Sat, noon-7pm Sun) Organises dives in Sai Kung on Sunday for about $400.

Ocean Sky Divers (Map pp420–1; ☎ 2366 3738; 1st fl, 17-19 Lock Rd, Tsim Sha Tsui; ☺ 10.30am-9pm Apr-Nov, 11.30am-9pm Dec-Mar) This dive shop runs PADI courses and organises local dives for $290 to $990.

SKATING

The **Hong Kong Federation of Roller Sports** (Map pp414–15; ☎ 2504 8203; www.rollersports .org.hk; Room 1016, Sports House, 1 Sta-dium Path, So Kon Po) can provide infor-mation on venues around the territory.

There are several major ice-skating rinks in Hong Kong, with Cityplaza Ice Palace in Quarry Bay and Festival Walk Glacier in Kowloon Tong by far the best. They both have two separate sessions on weekdays and up to three at the weekend.

Activities

OUTDOOR ACTIVITIES

KUNG FU & YOU

Chinese *gùng-fū* (kung fu) is the basis for many Asian martial arts. There are hundreds of styles of martial arts that have evolved since about AD 500, including *mó-seut*, which is full of expansive strides and strokes and great to watch in competition; *wíng-chèun*, the late actor and martial arts master Bruce Lee's original style, indigenous to Hong Kong, which combines blocks, punches and low kicks; and the ever-popular *taai-gík* (t'ai chi), the slow-motion 'shadow boxing' that has been popular for centuries.

As you can see every morning in the parks throughout Hong Kong, t'ai chi is the most visible and commonly practised form of kung fu today. Not only is it a terrific form of exercise, improving your muscle tone, developing breathing muscles and promoting good health in general, it also forms a solid foundation for any other martial arts practice. Its various forms are characterised by deep, powerful stances, soft and flowing hand techniques and relaxed breathing.

In China martial arts were traditionally passed down through patriarchal family lines and seldom taught to outsid-ers, as these skills were considered far too valuable to spread indiscriminately. During the Cultural Revolution, when all teachings outside Maoist philosophy were suppressed, the practice of innocuous-looking t'ai chi was allowed, helping kung fu to live on when so much of traditional culture had disappeared.

Ice skating at Festival Walk Glacier (below), Kowloon Tong

Cityplaza Ice Palace (Map pp406–7; ☎ 2844 8688; 1st fl, Cityplaza 2, 18 Tai Koo Shing Rd, Quarry Bay; admission Mon-Fri $45-50, Sat & Sun $60; ☺ 9.30am-10pm Mon-Fri, 7.30am-10pm Sat & Sun)

Festival Walk Glacier (Map pp418–19; ☎ 2265 8888; Upper Ground fl, Festival Walk Shopping Centre, 80-88 Tat Chee Ave, Kowloon Tong; admission Mon-Fri $40-50, Sat & Sun $60; ☺ 8.30am-10pm Mon-Fri, 8.30am-10pm Sat, 1-10pm Sun)

Skyrink (Map pp418–19; ☎ 2307 9365; Dragon Centre, 8th fl, 37K Yen Chow St, Sham Shui Po; admission Mon-Fri $35-40, Sat & Sun $50; ☺ 9am-10pm Mon-Fri, 9am-10pm Sat & Sun)

SQUASH

There are almost 80 squash centres scattered around the territory. The **Hong Kong Squash Centre** (Map pp408–9; ☎ 2521 5072; 23 Cotton Tree Dr; per half-hour $27; ☺ 7am-11pm) has some of the most modern facilities, with 17 courts bordering Hong Kong Park in Central. There are three squash courts at **Queen Elizabeth Stadium** (Map pp414–15; ☎ 2591 1331; 18 Oi Kwan Rd, Wan Chai) and **Kowloon Park Sports Centre** (Map pp420–1; ☎ 2724 3120; 22 Austin Rd, Tsim Sha Tsui).

TENNIS

The **Hong Kong Tennis Centre** (Map pp406–7; ☎ 2574 9122; Wong Nai Chung Gap Rd; per hr day/evening $42/57; ☺ 7am-11pm), with 17 courts, is on the spectacular pass in the hills between Happy Valley and Deep Water Bay on Hong Kong Island. It's usually only easy to get a court during working hours. Other courts available include the following:

Bowen Road Sports Ground (Map pp408–9; ☎ 2528 2983; Bowen Dr, the Mid-Levels; ☺ 6am-7pm) Four courts.

King's Park Tennis Courts (Map pp418–19; ☎ 2385 8985; 6 Wylie Path, Yau Ma Tei; ☺ 7am-11pm) Six courts.

Victoria Park (Map pp414–15; ☎ 2890 5127; Hing Fat St, Causeway Bay; ☺ 6am or 7am-11pm) Fourteen courts.

WINDSURFING & WAKEBOARDING

Windsurfing is extremely popular in Hong Kong; the territory's only Olympic gold medal (Atlanta, 1996) to date was won in this sport. The best months for windsurfing are October, November and December, when a steady northeast monsoon wind blows. Boards and other equipment are available for rent at **St Stephen's Beach Water Sports Centre** (Off Map p411; ☎ 2813 5407) in Stanley on Hong Kong Island, at the **Windsurfing Centre** (Off Map p425; ☎ 2792 5605) in Sha Ha just north of Sai Kung in the New Territories, at the **Cheung Chau Windsurfing Water Sports Centre** (Map p428; ☎ 2981 8316) on Cheung Chau and at **Long Coast Seasports** (Map p427; ☎ 2980 3222) located on Lantau.

The **Windsurfing Association of Hong Kong** (Map pp414–15; ☎ 2504 8255; www.windsurfing .org.hk; Room 1001, Sports House, 1 Stadium Path, So Kon Po) has courses for juniors.

Wakeboarding has grown tremendously in popularity in recent years. Deep Water Bay is a popular area for the sport, but for other venues contact the Hong Kong Wakeboarding Association, which shares an address and a website with the **Hong Kong Water Ski Association** (Map pp414–15; ☎ 2504 8168; www.waterski.org.hk; Room 1025, Sports House, 1 Stadium Path, So Kon Po).

YACHTING & SAILING

Even if you're not a member, you can check with any of the following yachting clubs to see if races are being held and whether an afternoon's sail is possible.

Aberdeen Boat Club (Map p411; ☎ 2552 8182; 20 Shum Wan Rd, Aberdeen)

Aberdeen Marina Club (Map p411; ☎ 2555 8321; 8 Shum Wan Rd, Aberdeen)

Hebe Haven Yacht Club (Map pp404–5; ☎ 2719 9682; 10½ Milestone, Hiram's Hwy, Pak Sha Wan)

Royal Hong Kong Yacht Club (Map pp414–15; ☎ 2832 2817; Hung Hing Rd, Kellett Island, Causeway Bay)

A major sailing event in Hong Kong is the Hong Kong–Manila yacht race, which takes place every two years. Phone the Royal Hong Kong Yacht Club or the **Hong Kong Sailing Federation** (Map pp414–15; ☎ 2504 8159; www .sailing.org.hk; Room 1009, Sports House, 1 Stadium Path, So Kon Po) for details.

If there is a group of you, you should consider hiring a junk for the day or evening. Eight hours of vessel hire, plus a captain and deck hand, are usually included in the price. **Jubilee International Tour Centre** (Map pp408–9; ☎ 2530 0530; www.jubilee.com.hk; Room 604, 6th fl, Far East Consortium Bldg, 121 Des Voeux Rd Central; ◷ 8.30am-5.30pm Mon-Fri, 8.30am-1pm Sat) hires out vessels for up to 25 people for from $1800 on weekdays and $2500 at the weekend.

In addition, the restaurant chain **Jaspa's** (p189) has two junks – one carrying 26 people and the other 40 – for rent. An evening or daytime junk party, including all drinks and a full menu prepared and served on board, costs $550/200/100 for adults/children aged five to 13/children aged one to five. Note that there must be a minimum

of 14 passengers. The boat can pick up or drop off guests at either Sai Kung or Causeway Bay. Ring **Jaspa's Party Junk** (☎ 2869 0733; www.jaspasjunk.com) or consult the website for details.

HEALTH & FITNESS

Hong Kong is bursting at the seams with gyms, yoga studios, spas and New Age clinics offering everything from aromatherapy and foot care to homeopathy. And if your hotel doesn't have a swimming pool, there are three dozen public ones to choose from.

GYMS & FITNESS CLUBS

Getting fit is big business in Hong Kong, with the largest slices of the pie shared out among a few big names. The **South China Athletic Association** (p217) has a massive (1000-sq-metre) gym, with modern exercise machinery and an aerobics room, as well as a sauna, a steam room and massage (monthly membership $250). The following two are notable in that they offer short-term memberships.

California Fitness (Map p412; ☎ 2522 5229; www .californiafitness.com; 1 Wellington St, Central; daily $150; ◷ 6am-midnight Mon-Sat, 8am-10pm Sun) Asia's largest health club has six outlets in Hong Kong, including a **Wan Chai branch** (Map pp414–15; ☎ 2877 7070; 88 Gloucester Rd), which keeps the same hours.

Pure Fitness (Map p412; ☎ 2970 3366; www.pure-fit .com; 1st-3rd fls, Kinwick Centre, 32 Hollywood Rd, Soho; daily $200; ◷ 6am-midnight Mon-Sat, 8am-10pm Sun) This favourite of the Soho set (entered from Shelley St) has a **Central branch** (Map pp408–9; ☎ 8129 8000; 3rd fl, IFC Mall, 8 Finance St, Central), which is open the same hours.

SWIMMING POOLS

Hong Kong has 36 swimming pools that are open to the public. There are excellent pools in Tsim Sha Tsui's **Kowloon Park** (p91) and in Victoria Park (p82) in Causeway Bay. Most pools are closed between November and March, but heated indoor pools, such as the **Morrison Hill Public Swimming Pool** (Map pp414–15; ☎ 2575 3028; 7 Oi Kwan Rd, Wan Chai; adult/child $19/9) and the one in the basement of the **South China Athletic Association** (Map pp414–15; ☎ 2890 7736; 88 Caroline Hill Rd, So Kon Po; adult/child $22/10) are open all year.

THERAPY CLINICS

Feel like giving your tootsies a pamper? Or how about your nostrils an olfactory feast? You can at one of Hong Kong's therapy clinics.

DK Aromatherapy (Map p412; ☎ 2771 2847; Ground fl, 16A Staunton St, Central; ☿ noon-10pm) This is the place to come if you're looking for value for scents (full body aromatherapy treatment $500 to $550).

Happy Foot Reflexology Centre (Map p412; ☎ 2544 1010; 11th & 13th fls, Jade Centre, 98-102 Wellington St, Central; ☿ 10am-midnight) Foot/body massage starts at $198/250 for 50 minutes.

Healing Plants (Map p412; ☎ 2815 5005; info@ehealingplants.com; 17 Lyndhurst Tce, Central; ☿ 10am-8pm Mon-Sat, noon-7pm Sun) Acupuncture, reflexology, Swedish massage and homeopathic doctors at hand.

YOGA

Yoga in all its forms is as popular in Hong Kong as it is everywhere else in the world.

Q Yoga (Map p412; ☎ 2521 4555; www.q-yoga.com; 3rd fl, Winning Centre, 46-48 Wyndham St, Central; ☿ 8am-10pm Mon-Fri, 8am-7pm Sat) Hong Kong's poshest yoga studio offers ashtanga, hatha and vinyasa hot yoga classes starting at just under $1300 per month with unlimited attendance.

Yoga Central (Map p412; ☎ 2982 4308; www.yogacentral.com.hk; 4th fl, 13 Wyndham St, Central; ☿ variable hours) Offering hatha yoga with an iyengar spin and Pilates, this well-established studio has beginner and intermediate classes Monday to Saturday costing from $120/200 per one-/two-hour class.

Yoga Fitness (Map p412; ☎ 2851 8353; www.yoga-fitness.com; 5th fl, Sea Bird House, 22-28 Wyndham St, Central; ☿ variable hours) This place offers hatha instruction for $140 per class or $499 for five classes in a month.

Shopping

Hong Kong Island 233
Central 233
Sheung Wan 240
Admiralty & Wan Chai 240
Causeway Bay 242

Kowloon 243
Tsim Sha Tsui 243
Yau Ma Tei & Mong Kok 247
New Kowloon 248

Shopping

Shopping in Hong Kong is not just about buying stuff: it's a social activity, a form of recreation, and a way of life for many people, both locals and expatriates. Though it isn't the bargain basement it once was, Honkers still wins for variety and for its passionate embrace of competitive consumerism. Any international brand worthy of its logo has at least one outlet here, and there is a slew of local brands worth spending your money on. Clothing (off the peg or tailored), shoes, jewellery, luggage and, to a lesser degree nowadays, cameras and electronic goods (p230) are the city's strong suits.

There is no sales tax in Hong Kong, so the marked price is the price you'll pay. Credit cards are widely accepted, except in markets, but it's rare for traders to accept travellers cheques or foreign currency as payment. Sales assistants in department or chain stores rarely have any leeway to give discounts, but you can try bargaining in owner-operated stores and certainly in markets.

Digital cameras for sale (p232)

The Hong Kong Tourism Board (HKTB) produces a handy 300-page book called *A Guide to Quality Shops and Restaurants,* which lists shops that are HKTB members. It is available for free at its information outlets (p323).

Shopping Areas

The main shopping areas are Central and Causeway Bay on Hong Kong Island and Tsim Sha Tsui in Kowloon. Nathan Rd in Tsim Sha Tsui is the main tourist strip, and one of very few places where you'll find merchants poised to rip you off (see the boxed text, opposite), especially when buying electronic goods or photographic equipment. Central is good for clothing (usually midrange to top end), as well as books, cameras and antiques. Causeway Bay has a lot of department stores and low-end clothing outlets. For market shopping see the boxed text, p246.

Warehouse sales and factory extras can be found along Granville Rd in Tsim Sha Tsui, in Causeway Bay and on Ap Lei Chau, the island opposite Aberdeen. Most of these deal in ready-to-wear garments, but there are a few that also sell carpets, shoes, leather goods, jewellery and imitation antiques. Often prices aren't that much less than in retail shops, and it's important to check purchases carefully, as refunds are rarely given and many articles are factory seconds and imperfect.

Opening Hours

In the Central and Western districts, daily shop hours are generally from 10am to between 6pm and 7.30pm, and in Causeway Bay and Wan Chai many will stay open until 9.30pm or 10pm. In Tsim Sha Tsui, Mong Kok and Yau Ma Tei, they close around 9pm and in Tsim Sha Tsui East at 7.30pm. Some smaller shops close for major holidays – sometimes for up to a week – especially during Chinese New Year.

Winter sales are during the first three weeks in January and the summer ones in late June and early July.

DEFENSIVE SHOPPING, BLOW BY BLOW

How you shop is important in Hong Kong. The territory is *not* a nest of thieves just waiting to rip you off, but there are a lot of pitfalls just waiting for the uninitiated to fall into, and the longer you shop in Hong Kong, the more likely it is that you'll run into a shopkeeper who is crooked.

Whatever you are in the market for, always check prices in a few shops, take your time and return to a shop several times if necessary. Don't buy anything expensive in a hurry and always get a manufacturer's guarantee or warranty that is valid worldwide. When comparing camera prices, for example, make sure you're comparing not only the same camera body but also the comparable lenses and any other accessories included.

The most common way for shopkeepers in Hong Kong to cheat tourists is to simply overcharge. In the tourist shopping district of Tsim Sha Tsui, you'll rarely find price tags on anything. Checking prices in several shops therefore becomes essential. But Hong Kong merchants weren't born yesterday; they know tourists comparison-shop. So staff will often quote a reasonable or even low price on a big-ticket item, only to get the money back by overcharging on accessories.

Spotting overcharging is the easy part though. Sneakier tricks involve merchants removing vital components that should have been included for free (like the connecting cords for the speakers on a stereo system) and demanding more money when you return to the shop to get them. You should be especially wary if staff want to take the goods into the back room to 'box it up'. Another tactic is to replace some of the good components with cheap or imitation ones.

Watch out for counterfeit-brand goods. Fake labels on clothes are the most obvious example, but there are fake Rolex watches, fake Gucci leather bags, even fake electronic goods. Pirated CDs and DVDs are a positive steal (in more ways than one) but are of poor quality and rapidly deteriorate.

Hong Kong's customs agents have cracked down on the fake cameras and electronic goods, and the problem has been pretty much solved. However, counterfeit brand-name watches remain very common and are constantly being flogged by the irritating touts patrolling Nathan Rd. If you discover that you've been sold a fake brand-name watch by a shopkeeper when you thought you were buying the genuine article, call the **police** (☎ 2527 7177).

If you have any trouble with a dodgy merchant, call the HKTB's **Quality Tourism Services** (QTS; ☎ 2806 2823; www.qtshk.com) if the shop is a tourist-board member (the HKTB logo will be displayed on the front door or in some other prominent place). Otherwise, contact the **Hong Kong Consumer Council** (☎ 2929 2222; www.consumer.org .hk) weekdays between 9am and 5.45pm.

If you are determined to take legal action against a shopkeeper, the **Small Claims Tribunal** (Map pp414–15; ☎ 2582 4084, 2582 4085; 4th fl, Wan Chai Tower, 12 Harbour Rd, Wan Chai; 🕑 9am-1pm & 2-5pm Mon-Fri, 9am-noon Sat; Wan Chai MTR) handles civil cases involving up to a maximum of $50,000. The **Community Advice Bureau** (Map pp408–9; ☎ 2815 5444; www.cab.org.hk; Room 16C, Right Emperor Commercial Bldg, 122 Wellington St, Central; 🕑 9.30am-4.30pm Mon-Fri) will help you find a lawyer.

Bargaining

Bargaining is a way of life at retail outlets throughout Hong Kong, with the exception of department stores and clothing chain shops, where the prices marked are the prices paid. Some visitors operate on the theory that you can get the goods for half the price originally quoted. Many Hong Kong residents believe that if you can bargain something down that low, then you shouldn't be buying from that shop anyway. If the business is that crooked – and many are, particularly in the Tsim Sha Tsui tourist ghetto – it will probably find other ways to cheat you (such as selling you electronic goods with missing components or no international warranty).

Price tags are supposed be displayed on all goods. If you can't find a price tag you've undoubtedly entered one of those business establishments with 'flexible' – ie rip-off – prices.

Duty Free

The only imported goods on which there is duty in Hong Kong are alcohol, tobacco, perfumes, cosmetics, cars and certain petroleum products. In general, almost anything – from cameras and electronics to clothing and jewellery – will be cheaper when you buy it outside duty-free shops.

Warranties & Guarantees

Every guarantee should carry a complete description of the item (including the model and serial numbers), as well as the date of purchase, the name and address of the shop it was purchased from, and the shop's official name chop (stamp).

Many imported items come with a warranty registration with the words 'Guarantee only valid in Hong Kong'. If it's a well-known brand, you can often return this card to the importer in Hong Kong to get a warranty card for your home country.

A common practice is to sell grey-market equipment (ie imported by somebody other than the official local agent). Such equipment may have no guarantee at all or the guarantee may only be valid in the country of manufacture (which will probably be either China or Japan).

Refunds & Exchanges

Most shops are loath to give refunds, but they can usually be persuaded to exchange purchases that haven't been soiled or tampered with. Make sure you get a detailed receipt that enumerates the goods as well as the amount and payment method.

There is really no reason to put a deposit on anything unless it is an article of clothing being made for you or you've ordered a new pair of glasses. Some shops might ask for a deposit, if you're ordering an unusual item that's not normally stocked, but this isn't a common practice.

Shipping Goods

Goods can be sent home by post, and some shops will package and post the goods for you, especially if it's a large item. It's a good idea to find out whether you will have to clear the goods at the country of destination. If the goods are fragile, it is sensible to buy 'all risks' insurance. Make sure you keep all the receipts.

Smaller items can be shipped from the post office. **United Parcel Service** (UPS; ☎ 2735 3535) also offers services from Hong Kong to some 40 countries worldwide. It ships by air and accepts parcels weighing up to 70kg. **DHL** (☎ 2400 3388) is another option.

What to Buy

ANTIQUES

Hong Kong has a rich and colourful array of Asian, especially Chinese, antiques on offer, but serious buyers will restrict themselves to the reputable antique shops and auction houses only; Hong Kong imports many forgeries and expert reproductions from China and Southeast Asia. Just remember that most of the really good pieces are in private collections and are often sold either through Christie (p234) or Sotheby (p238), especially at their auctions in spring (April/May) and autumn (October/November).

Most of Hong Kong Island's antique shops are bunched along Wyndham St and Hollywood Rd in Central and Sheung Wan. The shops at the western end of Hollywood Rd tend to be cheaper in price and carry more dubious 'antiques'. Some of them stock a range of old books and magazines, Chinese propaganda posters, badges from the Cultural Revolution and so on. It's easy to get lost in some of these dusty holes in the wall, but be cautious – tread carefully through this minefield of reproductions. When it comes to buying antiques and curios, there are relatively few places of interest in Kowloon.

For Chinese handicrafts and other goods (hand-carved wooden pieces, ceramics, paintings, cloisonné, silk garments), the main places to go are the large China-run emporiums scattered throughout the territory, such as Chinese Arts & Crafts (p240) and Yue Hwa Chinese Products Emporium (p247).

CARPETS

While carpets are not a huge bargain in Hong Kong, there is a good selection of both new and antique silk and wool ones in several areas. Imported carpets from Afghanistan, China,

India, Iran, Pakistan, Tibet and Turkey are widely available; some of the new Iranian ones with contemporary designs are stunning. The best carpets have a larger number of knots per square inch (over 550) and are richer in detail and colour than cheaper carpets. Older carpets are dyed with natural vegetable dye. Silk carpets are often hung on the wall rather than used on the floor. The bulk of Hong Kong's carpet and rug shops are clustered around Wyndham St in Central, although there are some large retailers located in Wan Chai as well.

CLOTHING

The best places to find designer fashions and top-end boutiques are in the big shopping centres and malls, especially Landmark (p236) in Central, Pacific Place (p241) in Admiralty and Festival Walk (p248) in Kowloon Tong. The best hunting grounds for warehouse sales and factory extras are generally in Tsim Sha Tsui at the eastern end of Granville Rd; check out Austin Ave and Chatham Rd South as well. On Hong Kong Island, Jardine's Bazaar in Causeway Bay has low-cost garments and there are several sample shops and places to pick up cheap jeans in Lee Garden Rd. The street markets (p246) in Temple St in Yau Ma Tei and Tung Choi St in Mong Kok have the

CLOTHING SIZES

Measurements approximate only, try before you buy

Women's Clothing

Aus/UK	8	10	12	14	16	18
Europe	36	38	40	42	44	46
Japan	5	7	9	11	13	15
USA	6	8	10	12	14	16

Women's Shoes

Aus/USA	5	6	7	8	9	10
Europe	35	36	37	38	39	40
France only	35	36	38	39	40	42
Japan	22	23	24	25	26	27
UK	3½	4½	5½	6½	7½	8½

Men's Clothing

Aus	92	96	100	104	108	112
Europe	46	48	50	52	54	56
Japan	S		M	M		L
UK/USA	35	36	37	38	39	40

Men's Shirts (Collar Sizes)

Aus/Japan	38	39	40	41	42	43
Europe	38	39	40	41	42	43
UK/USA	15	15½	16	16½	17	17½

Men's Shoes

Aus/UK	7	8	9	10	11	12
Europe	41	42	43	44½	46	47
Japan	26	27	27½	28	29	30
USA	7½	8½	9½	10½	11½	12½

cheapest clothes. You may also try Li Yuen St East and Li Yuen St West, two narrow alleyways linking Des Voeux Rd Central with Queen's Rd Central. They are a jumble of inexpensive clothing, handbags, backpacks and costume jewellery.

For midpriced items, Causeway Bay and Tsim Sha Tsui, particularly east of Nathan Rd, are good hunting grounds.

Although many people still frequent Hong Kong's tailors, getting a suit or dress made is no longer a great bargain. Remember that you usually get what you pay for; the material is often good but the work may be shoddy. Remember that most tailors will require a 50% nonrefundable deposit and the more fittings you have, the better the result.

COMPUTERS

Hong Kong is a popular place to buy personal computers and laptops. While prices are competitive, it is also important to pay careful attention to what you buy and where you buy it.

You may have your own ideas about what kind of computer you want to buy, but if you're just visiting Hong Kong you would be wise to choose a brand-name portable computer with an international warranty, such as Hewlett-Packard, Compac or Acer.

Be careful: you may be hit with a steep import tax when you return to your home country. Save your receipt; the older the machine, the less you're likely to pay in import duty. The rules in many countries say that the machine is tax exempt if over a year old.

Most people buy their computers in Kowloon, where there are loads of centres selling computers and related equipment, there's a much greater choice and prices are lower, but 'caveat emptor' is the phrase to bear in mind as you browse. Hong Kong Island does have a couple of reasonable computer arcades – **Windsor House** (Map pp414–15; 311 Gloucester Rd, Causeway Bay) and the Wan Chai Computer Centre (p242).

ELECTRONIC GOODS

Sham Shui Po in northwestern Kowloon is a good neighbourhood to search for electronic items. You can even buy and sell second-hand goods. If you take exit A2 from the MTR at Sham Shui Po station, you'll find yourself on Apliu St, one of the best places in Hong Kong to search for the numerous plug adaptors you'll need if you plan to use your purchase in Hong Kong, Macau and/or the mainland.

Mong Kok is another great neighbourhood in which to look for electronic gadgetry. Starting at Argyle St and heading south, explore all the side streets running parallel to Nathan Rd, such as Canton Rd, Tung Choi St, Sai Yeung Choi St, Portland St, Shanghai St and Reclamation St.

There are also quite a few electronics shops in Causeway Bay, their windows stuffed full of digital cameras, DVD and CD players and iPods. Locals generally avoid these places – apparently many of these shops are under the same ownership, ensuring that the prices remain high throughout the area.

It's best to avoid the electronics shops in Tsim Sha Tsui, especially those along Nathan Rd or just off it, as many are skilled at fleecing foreign shoppers.

GEMS & JEWELLERY

The Chinese attribute various magical qualities to jade, including the power to prevent ageing and accidents. The circular disc with a central hole worn around many Hong Kong necks (including ours) represents heaven in Chinese mythology. If you're interested in looking at and possibly purchasing jade, head for the Jade Market (p94) in Yau Ma Tei. Unless you're fairly knowledgeable about jade, though, it's probably wise to limit yourself to modest purchases.

Opals are said to be the best value in Hong Kong because this is where opals are cut. Hong Kong also carries a great range of pearls. Diamonds aren't generally a good deal, because the world trade is mostly controlled by a cartel. Hong Kong does not have a diamond-cutting industry and must import from Belgium, India, Israel and the USA. Nonetheless, jewellery exporting is big business in Hong Kong, because other gemstones are imported, cut, polished, set and re-exported using cheap labour. In theory, this should make Hong Kong a cheap place to purchase jewellery. In reality, retail prices are only marginally lower than elsewhere.

A couple of reputable jewellery-shop chains, including King Fook (p236) and Tse Sui Luen (p239), will issue a certificate that states exactly what you are buying and guarantees that the shop will buy it back at a fair market price. If you've bought something and want to know its value, you can have it appraised. There is a charge for this service, and some stones (such as diamonds) may have to be removed from their setting for testing. You can contact **Hong Kong Jewellers' & Goldsmiths' Association** (☎ 2543 9633) for a list of the approved appraisers. One company that does appraisals is **Valuation Services** (☎ 2869 4350; GPO Box 11996, Hong Kong).

The only carved-ivory products being sold here *legally* are those that were manufactured before a 1989 ban came into effect or those made of marine ivory. Ivory retailers must have all sorts of documentation to prove where and when the goods were made.

TOP FIVE MICRO MALLS

Crammed into old buildings, above MTR stations, up escalators and in back lanes are Hong Kong's malls of micro-shops (p16) selling designer threads, a kaleidoscope of kooky accessories and a colourful closet of funky footwear. This is where Hong Kong's youngest mall-trawlers go for clothes, trinkets and to capture the moment on sticker machines. The best shopping is done from 3pm to 10pm, when *all* the shops are open.

- **Beverley Commercial Centre** (Map pp420–1; 87-105 Chatham Rd South, Tsim Sha Tsui; Tsim Sha Tsui MTR) Enter via the passage north of Observatory Rd.
- **Island Beverley** (Map pp414–15; 1 Great George St, Causeway Bay; Causeway Bay MTR)
- **Rise Commercial Centre** (Map pp420–1; 5-11 Granville Circuit, Tsim Sha Tsui; Tsim Sha Tsui MTR)
- **Trendy Zone** (Map p423; Chow Tai Fook Centre, 580A Nathan Rd, Mong Kok; Mong Kok MTR)
- **Up Date Mall** (Map pp420–1; 36-44 Nathan Rd, Tsim Sha Tsui; Tsim Sha Tsui MTR)

LEATHER GOODS & LUGGAGE

Most of what gets sent to the Hong Kong market from China is export quality, but check carefully because there is still a lot of rubbish on sale. All the big brand names such as Louis Vuitton and Gucci are on display in Hong Kong department stores, and you'll find some local vendors in the luggage business. If you're just looking for a casual bag or daypack, try Li Yuen St East and Li Yuen St West in Central or Stanley Market (p86).

PHOTOGRAPHIC EQUIPMENT

When shopping for a camera, keep in mind that you should never buy one that doesn't have a price tag. This will basically preclude most of the shops in Tsim Sha Tsui. One of the best spots in Hong Kong for buying photographic equipment is Stanley St in Central and competition is keen. Everything carries price tags, though some low-level bargaining may be possible. Tsim Sha Tsui has a couple of shops on Kimberley Rd dealing in used cameras and there are plenty of photo shops on Sai Yeung Choi St in Mong Kok.

WATCHES

Shops selling watches are ubiquitous in Hong Kong and you can find everything from a Rolex to Russian army timepieces and diving watches. As always, you should avoid the shops that do not have price tags on the merchandise. The big department stores and City Chain (p234) are fine, but compare prices.

HONG KONG ISLAND

Central and Causeway Bay are the main shopping districts on Hong Kong Island, with Wan Chai lagging pretty far behind.

CENTRAL

Central has a mix of midrange to top-end shopping centres and street-front retail; it's popular with locals and tourists alike. This is a good place to look for cameras, books, antiques and designer threads. The Landmark shopping mall in Central has designer boutiques, shops selling crystal and so on. The IFC Mall is for high fashion.

AMOURS ANTIQUES

Map p412   Antiques; Clothing & Accessories
☎ 2803 7877; 45 Staunton St; ⊙ 12.30-9.30pm Sun-Thu, 12.30-10.30pm Fri & Sat; bus 26
This wonderful shop stocks antique (well, old) rhinestone jewellery, frocks and a darling clutch of beaded and tapestry bags dating from the early 20th century.

ANGLO-CHINESE FLORIST

Map p412   Flowers
☎ 2921 2986; Ground fl, Winway Bldg, 50 Wellington St; ⊙ 8am-10pm Mon-Sat, 9am-9pm Sun; Central MTR
If you've been invited to someone's home and you wish to bring flowers – as is *de rigueur* here – stop by Anglo-Chinese. Nobody does them better.

ARCH ANGEL ANTIQUES

Map p412   Antiques
☎ 2851 6848; 53-55 Hollywood Rd;
⊙ 9.30am-6.30pm; bus 26
Though the specialities are antique and ancient porcelain and tombware, Arch Angel packs a lot more into its three floors: there's everything from mahjong sets and terracotta horses to palatial furniture. It also operates an art gallery, **Arch Angel Fine Art** (Map p412; ☎ 2854 4255; 38 Peel St; ⊙ 9.30am-6.30pm), across the road that deals in paintings by Vietnamese artists.

BEVERLEY BOUTIQUE

Map pp408-9   Leather Goods
☎ 2840 1069; Shop 2 & 4, Ground fl, Cascade, Standard Chartered Bank Bldg, 4-4A Des Voeux Rd Central; ⊙ 9am-7pm Mon-Sat; Central MTR
This hole-in-the-wall shop has excellent-quality bags. You'll also find a range of wallets and briefcases in fine and exotic leathers.

BLANC DE CHINE

Map pp408-9   Clothing & Accessories
☎ 2524 7875; Room 201 & 203A, 2nd fl, Pedder Bldg, 12 Pedder St; ⊙ 10am-7pm Mon-Sat, noon-5pm Sun; Central MTR
This sumptuous store specialises in traditional men's Chinese jackets, off the rack or made to measure. There's also a lovely selection of silk dresses for women. The satin bed linens are exquisite (as are the old ship's cabinets in which they are displayed).

BLOOMSBURY BOOKS Map pp408-9　Books

☎ 2526 5387; 2nd fl, Club Lusitano Bldg, 16 Ice House St; ☺ 9am-7pm Mon-Fri, 9am-6pm Sat; Central MTR

The delightful bookshop carries an tremendous selection of business, legal and other professional titles but, in deference to its name, leans on the literary side as well. There's an brilliant children's section. You can also enter the Club Lusitano Building from Duddell St.

BOOKAZINE Map pp408-9　Books

☎ 2522 1785; Shop 309-313A, 3rd fl, Prince's Bldg, 10 Chater Rd; ☺ 9.30am-7.30pm Mon-Sat, 10.30am-6.30pm Sun

Bookazine operates a half-dozen atmosphere-free chain stores that are dotted all around the territory and this is the largest. Each shop stocks a dependable range of books, titles of local interest, magazines and stationery. There's also a branch in **Admiralty** (Map pp408–9; ☎ 2866 7522; Shop C, Upper ground fl, Far East Finance Centre, 16 Harcourt Rd).

CARAVAN Map p412　Carpets

☎ 2547 3821; 65 Hollywood Rd; ☺ 10am-7pm; bus 26

A shop called Caravan with an owner named Driver? Trustworthy rug-sellers travel all over Asia to stock this nicely cluttered shop. The range of Afghan and Tibetan carpets is especially notable among a varied rug range.

CARPET CENTRE

Map p412　Clothing & Accessories

☎ 2850 4993; Shop A, Lower ground fl, 29 Hollywood Rd; ☺ 10am-9pm; bus 26

No, you're not being asked to don a dhurry… This place has pashmina shawls, ranging in price from $350 to $900, and exotic slippers fit for a sultana. Enter the store from Cochrane St.

CHINE GALLERY Map p412　Antiques

☎ 2543 0023; www.chinegallery.com; 42A Hollywood Rd; ☺ 10am-6pm Mon-Sat, 1-6pm Sun; bus 26

The carefully restored furniture – the lacquered cabinets are fab – at this shop come from all over China, and hand-knotted rugs are sourced from remote regions such as Xinjiang, Ningxia, Gansu, Inner Mongolia and Tibet. It sells statues and collectibles too.

CHRISTIE Map pp408-9　Auction House

☎ 2521 5396; Room 2203-2208, 22nd fl, Alexandra House, 16-20 Chater Rd; Central MTR

Christie has regular sales in ceramics, jade, modern and jadeite jewellery, stamps, snuff bottles, works of art, traditional and contemporary Chinese paintings and calligraphic works. It holds its spring (May) and autumn (November) pre-auction previews in the Hong Kong Convention & Exhibition Centre in Wan Chai.

CIGAR EXPRESS CENTRAL Map p412　Cigars

☎ 2110 9201; Shop 4A, Ground fl, Cheung Fai Bldg, 45-47 Cochrane St; ☺ 11am-11pm Mon-Sat, noon-6pm Sun; Central MTR

This branch of a Hong Kong chain sells everything from a $23 Honduran Quintero stogy to a hand-rolled Cuban Cohiba Double Corona for $315 a pop.

CIGARRO Map pp408-9　Cigars

☎ 2810 1883; Shop 5, Ground fl, St George's Bldg, 2 Ice House St; ☺ 10am-9pm Mon-Fri, 10am-8pm Sat, noon-6pm Sun; Central MTR

Sometimes you do need a fat cigar to feel like you're making it big in the big city. Or do you? This smoke shop in Central comes to the rescue with Cuban, Dominican, Nicaraguan and other fine stogies.

CITY CHAIN Map p412　Watches

☎ 2259 9020; Ground fl, Man Yee Bldg, 67 Queen's Rd Central; ☺ 10am-8pm; Central MTR

City Chain stocks every type of wristwatch imaginable – from the stylish and dress-up to the funky and glitzy. It has some two dozen outlets in Hong Kong, including one in Admiralty (Map pp408–9; ☎ 2845 9403; Shop 112, 1st fl, Pacific Place, 88 Queensway; ☺ 11am-9pm) and one in Tsim Sha Tsui (Map pp420–1; ☎ 2739 4110; Shop D, Ground fl, 16D Carnarvon Rd; ☺ 10am-10.30pm).

DYMOCKS Map pp408-9　Books

☎ 2522 1012; Star Ferry Concourse; ☺ 8am-10.30pm Mon-Sat, 9am-10.30pm Sun; Star Ferry, Central MTR

Australia's biggest bookshop chain offers a solid mainstream selection of page-turners, travel books and magazines. There's a larger branch in **Central** (Map pp408–9; ☎ 2117 0360; Shop 2007-2011, 2nd fl, IFC Mall, 8 Finance St; ☺ 9am-9pm).

EU YAN SANG Map pp408-9   Medicine

☎ 2544 3870; 152-156 Queen's Rd Central;
⏰ 9am-7.30pm; Central MTR

Traditional Chinese medicine is extremely popular in Hong Kong, both as a preventative and a cure. Eu Yan is probably the most famous practice in town and the doctors speak good English. It's also an interesting place to browse as many of the healing ingredients are displayed and explained. There's also a branch in **Tsim Sha Tsui** (Map pp420–1; ☎ 2366 8321; 11-15 Chatham Rd South; ⏰ 10am-8.30pm).

EVERBEST PHOTO SUPPLIES

Map p412   Photographic Equipment

☎ 2522 1985; 28B Stanley St; ⏰ 9am-7pm; Central MTR

This extremely reliable shop is where many of Hong Kong's professional photographers buy their equipment.

FLOW ORGANIC BOOKSHOP

Map p412   Books

☎ 2964 9483, 8104 0822; www.flowagain.com; 1st & 2nd fls, 40 Lyndhurst Tce; ⏰ noon-7pm; bus 26
Quite what makes this secondhand and exchange bookstore 'organic' is anyone's guess, but it does have a focus on spiritual and New Age literature. On the 2nd floor are Chinese-language books and relaxation tapes and CDs. Enter from Cochrane St.

FOOK MING TONG TEA SHOP

Map pp408-9   Food & Drink

☎ 2295 0368; Shop 1016, 1st fl, IFC Mall, 8 Finance St; ⏰ 10am-9pm; Central MTR
Carefully chosen teas of various ages and propensities – from gunpowder ($8 for 37.55g) to Nanyan Ti Guan Yin Crown Grade ($780 for 150g) – and tea-making accoutrements. There's also a branch in **Tsim Sha Tsui** (Map pp420–1; ☎ 2735 1077; Shop 3225, Level 3, Gateway Arcade, Harbour City, 25-27 Canton Rd; ⏰ 10.30am-8pm Mon-Sat, 11am-8pm Sun).

GOVERNMENT PUBLICATIONS OFFICE

Map pp408-9   Books, Maps

☎ 2537 1910; Room 402, 4th fl, Murray Bldg, 22 Garden Rd; ⏰ 9am-6pm Mon-Fri, 9am-noon Sat; bus 3B, 12 or 40M
All publications, including hiking maps, that have been produced by the Hong Kong government are available from here.

HING LEE CAMERA COMPANY

Map p412   Photographic Equipment

☎ 2544 7593; 25 Lyndhurst Tce; ⏰ 9.30am-7pm Mon-Sat, 11am-5pm Sun; bus 26
Hing Lee is a reputable photographic supply outlet. Come here for new and second-hand 35mm camera bodies and lenses, as well as midrange compact and digital cameras.

HMV Map pp408-9   Music

☎ 2739 0268; 1st fl, Central Bldg, 1-3 Pedder St; ⏰ 9am-10pm; Central MTR
This Aladdin's cave of music not only has Hong Kong's largest choice of CDs, DVDs and cassettes, but also a great range of music-related literature. There are branches in **Causeway Bay** (Map pp414–15; ☎ 2504 3669; 1st fl, Windsor House, 311 Gloucester Rd; ⏰ 10am-11pm Mon-Fri, 10am-11.45pm Sat & Sun) and **Tsim Sha Tsui branch** (Map pp420–1; ☎ 2302 0122; Sands Bldg, Ground-4th fls, 12 Peking Rd; ⏰ 9am-11.45pm).

HOBBS & BISHOPS FINE ART

Map p412   Antiques

☎ 2537 9838; 28 Hollywood Rd; ⏰ 10am-5.30pm Mon-Sat; bus 26
This shop smelling of beeswax specialises in lacquered Chinese wooden furniture from the 19th and early 20th centuries. Its taste leans towards the sleek and handsome rather than gilded and showy pieces.

HONEYCHURCH ANTIQUES

Map p412   Antiques

☎ 2543 2433; 29 Hollywood Rd; ⏰ 10am-6pm Mon-Sat; bus 26
This fine shop, run by an American couple for more than four decades, specialises in antique Chinese furniture, jewellery and Chinese export and antique English silver.

HONG KONG BOOK CENTRE

Map pp408-9   Books

☎ 2522 7064; www.swindonbooks.com; Basement, On Lok Yuen Bldg, 25 Des Voeux Rd Central; ⏰ 9am-6.30pm Mon-Fri, 9am-5.30pm Sat, summer only 1-5pm Sun; Central MTR
This basement shop has a vast selection of books and magazines, including a mammoth number of business titles.

IFC MALL Map pp408-9 — Shopping Mall

☎ 2295 3308; www.ifc.com.hk; 8 Finance St; ⏰ 10.30am-10pm; Central MTR

A bright shopping centre with 200 high-fashion boutiques linking the One and Two IFC towers and the Four Seasons Hotel (under construction). The Hong Kong Airport Express Station is downstairs.

INDOSIAM Map p412 — Books, Antiques

☎ 2854 2853; 1st fl, 32 Lyndhurst Tce; ⏰ 2-7pm

Hong Kong's first (and only) truly antiquarian bookshop deals in rare titles relating to Asian countries. It's particularly strong in Thailand, China and the former French colonies (eg Vietnam, Cambodia, Laos).

JOINT PUBLISHING Map pp408-9 — Books

☎ 2868 6844; 9 Queen Victoria St; ⏰ 10.30am-7.30pm Mon-Sat, 1-6pm Sun; Central MTR

This primarily Chinese-language bookshop has a good range of English-language books about China, and CDs and DVDs for studying the language. It's also strong in local and China maps. Most English-language titles are on the mezzanine floor. There are 15 other JP outlets, many in MTR stations, including a branch in Wan Chai (Map pp414–15; ☎ 2838 2081; 158 Hennessy Rd; ⏰ 11am-9pm).

JOYCE Map pp408-9 — Clothing & Accessories

☎ 2810 1120; Ground fl, New World Tower, 16 Queen's Rd Central; ⏰ 10.30am-7.30pm Mon-Sat, 11am-7pm Sun; Central MTR

This multidesigner store is a good choice if you're pressed for time: Issey Miyake, Alexander McQueen, Comme des Garçons, Chloë, Pucci, Yohji Yamamoto and several Hong Kong fashion designers are just some of the designers whose wearable wares are on display. There's another branch of Joyce in Admiralty (Map pp408–9; ☎ 2523 5944; Shop 334, 3rd fl, Pacific Place, 88 Queensway), which keeps the same hours. For the same duds at half the price, visit Joyce Warehouse (Off Map p411; ☎ 2814 8313; 21st fl, Horizon Plaza Arcade, 2 Lee Wing St, Ap Lei Chau; ⏰ 10am-7pm Tue-Sat, 11am-7pm Sun), opposite the Aberdeen waterfront.

KARIN WEBER GALLERY

Map pp408-9 — Antiques, Fine Art

☎ 2544 5004; www.karinwebergallery.com; 20 Aberdeen St; ⏰ 11am-7pm Mon-Sat, 1-7pm Sun; bus 26

Karin Weber has an enjoyable mix of Chinese country antiques and contemporary Asian artworks. She also gives short lectures on antiques and the scene in Hong Kong and is able to arrange antique-buying trips into Guangdong for serious buyers.

KING FOOK Map p412 — Jewellery

☎ 2822 8573; Ground fl, King Fook Bldg, 30-32 Des Voeux Rd Central; ⏰ 9.30am-7pm; Central MTR

King Fook, with a grandiose gilded entrance, stocks a large range of watches, top-end fountain pens and baubles. There's another branch in Tsim Sha Tsui (Map pp420–1; ☎ 2313 2788; Shop G1, Miramar Shopping Centre, 118-130 Nathan Rd; ⏰ 10am-10pm).

LANDMARK Map pp408-9 — Shopping Mall

☎ 2525 4142; www.centralhk.com; 12-16 Des Voeux Rd Central; ⏰ 10.30am-7.30pm; Central MTR

The most central of all shopping centres, the Landmark has high fashion and good eating in a pleasant, open space, but a recent relaunch has driven out everything but five-star brands.

LANE CRAWFORD

Map pp408-9 — Department Store

☎ 2118 3388; Level 3, IFC Mall, 8 Finance St; ⏰ 10am-9pm; Central MTR

This branch of Hong Kong's original Western-style department store, the territory's answer to Harrods in London, is the flagship now that the store on Queen's Rd Central has closed. There are branches in Admiralty (Map pp408–9; ☎ 2118 3668; 1st & 2nd fls, Pacific Place, 88 Queensway; ⏰ 10am-9pm), Causeway Bay (Map pp414–15; ☎ 2118 3638; Ground & 1st fls, Times Square, 1 Matheson St; ⏰ 10am-9pm Sun-Thu, 10am-10pm Fri & Sat) and Tsim Sha Tsui (Map pp420–1; ☎ 2118 3428; Ground & 1st fls, Ocean Terminal, Harbour City, Salisbury Rd; ⏰ 10am-9pm).

LINVA TAILOR

Map p412 — Clothing & Accessories

☎ 2544 2456; Ground fl, 38 Cochrane St; ⏰ 9.30am-6.30pm Mon-Sat; bus 26

This is the place to come to have your own cheongsam (see p16) stitched up. Bring your own silk or choose from Miss Tong's selection.

King Fook (opposite), Central

tea boxes and well-presented gift packs of various cuppas. A great bonus is that you can try before you buy. Enter the store from Ladder St.

MANDARIN ORIENTAL FLOWER & GIFT SHOP Map pp408-9 Gifts & Souvenirs
☎ 2840 1974; Shop 13-14, Mezzanine fl, Mandarin Oriental, 5 Connaught Rd Central; ☀ 8.30am-7.30pm Mon-Fri, 9am-6pm Sat, 10am-5pm Sun; Central MTR
Crockery, cushion covers, chopsticks, tasteful souvenirs and a small selection of jewellery, all of the highest quality, are available.

MIR ORIENTAL CARPETS
Map p412 Carpets
☎ 2521 5641; Ground fl, New India House, 52 Wyndham St; ☀ 10am-6.30pm Mon-Sat, 11am-5pm Sun; bus 26
This two-floor shop is the largest stockist of fine rugs in Hong Kong, with thousands of carpets from around the world flying in and out of the store. It is the top specialist in town for Persian carpets.

MIU MIU Map pp408-9 Clothing & Accessories
☎ 2523 7833; Shop B24, Basement 1, Landmark, 1 Pedder St; ☀ 10am-6pm Mon-Sat, 11am-7pm Sun; Central MTR
Super-cute and creative threads for neo-adults on sale here. The shoes are exceptionally stylish.

MOUNTAIN FOLKCRAFT
Map p412 Gifts & Souvenirs
☎ 2523 2817; 12 Wo On Lane; ☀ 9.30am-6.30pm Mon-Sat; Central MTR
This is one of the nicest shops in Central for folk craft and is piled with bolts of batik and sarongs, clothing, wood carvings, lacquerware and papercuts made by ethnic minorities in China and other Asian countries. The shop attendants are friendly, and prices, while not cheap, are not outrageous either.

NEW WING HING DISPENSARY
Map pp408-9 Medicine
☎ 2523 0980; 85 Queen's Rd Central; ☀ 10am-7pm Mon-Sat; Central MTR
New Hing Wing offers personal and informed service and will never let you down. Enter from Queen Victoria St.

LITTLE MISSES & MINI MASTERS
Map pp408-9 Clothing & Accessories
☎ 2156 1118; Shop 307, 3rd fl, Prince's Bldg, 10 Chater Rd; ☀ 10am-7pm; Central MTR
Horrible name but this children's shop, owned and managed by expats, has some of the most stylish clothing imaginable for kids.

LIULIGONGFANG
Map pp408-9 Gifts & Souvenirs
☎ 2973 0820; Shop 20-22, Ground fl, Central Bldg, 1-3 Pedder St; ☀ 10am-7.30pm Mon-Sat, 10am-7pm Sun; Central MTR
Exquisite coloured-glass objects, both practical (vases, candle holders, jewellery) and ornamental (figurines, crystal Buddhas, breathtaking sculptures) from renowned Taiwanese glass sculptor Loretta Yang Hui-Shan are on display (and sale) here. There's a branch in **Admiralty** (Map pp408-9; ☎ 2918 9001; Shop 320, 3rd fl, Pacific Place, 88 Queensway; ☀ 10.30am-8pm).

LOCK CHA TEA SHOP
Map pp408-9 Food & Drink
☎ 2805 1360; Ground fl, 290B Queen's Rd Central; ☀ 11am-7pm; bus 26
This favourite shop sells Chinese teas of infinite variety as well as tea sets, wooden

OCEAN OPTICAL

Map pp408-9 — Optical Goods

☎ 2868 5670; Shop 5, Ground fl, The Cascade, Standard Chartered Bank Bldg, 4-4A Des Voeux Rd Central; ◷ 9.30am-7.30pm Mon-Sat, 10.30am-6pm Sun; Central MTR

Both frames and lenses can be cheaper (in some case, much cheaper) in Hong Kong than what you would pay at home, and we do not know of a better optician in Hong Kong than Ocean Optical. There's a branch in Tsim Sha Tsui (Map pp420–1; ☎ 2735 0611; Shop 326, 3rd fl, Ocean Centre, Harbour City, 3-9 Canton Rd).

OLYMPIA GRAECO-EGYPTIAN

COFFEE Map p412 — Food & Drink

☎ 2522 4653; Ground fl, 24 Old Bailey St; ◷ 10am-7pm Mon-Sat; bus 26

This place has been around since, well, anyone can remember, and it definitely still grinds the best beans in town. The house bean – Java Mocha – costs $96.80 a kilogram.

PHOTO SCIENTIFIC

Map p412 — Photographic Equipment

☎ 2525 0550; 6 Stanley St; ◷ 9am-7pm Mon-Sat; Central MTR

This is the favourite of Hong Kong's resident pros. You'll almost certainly find equipment elsewhere for less, but Photo Scientific has a rock-solid reputation with labelled prices, no bargaining, no arguing and no cheating.

PO KEE FISHING TACKLE

Map pp408-9 — Sporting Goods

☎ 2544 1035; 6 Hillier St; ◷ 10am-6.30pm Mon-Sat; Sheung Wan MTR

The guys at Po Kee have got the market cornered – hook, line and sinker – on fishing supplies.

PRINCE'S BUILDING

Map pp408-9 — Shopping Mall

☎ 2504 0704; www.centralhk.com; 10 Chater Rd; ◷ 10am-8pm; Central MTR

You may find the layout of Prince's Building to be poky and disorientating, but it's worth a look for its speciality fashion, toy and kitchenware shops. Good place to bring the kids as almost the entire 3rd floor is given over to children's shops.

SHANGHAI TANG

Map pp408-9 — Clothing & Accessories

☎ 2525 7333; Basement & ground fl, Pedder Bldg, 12 Pedder St; ◷ 10am-8pm Mon-Sat, 11am-7pm Sun; Central MTR

This stylish shop has sparked something of a fashion wave in Hong Kong with its updated versions of traditional yet neon-coloured Chinese garments. It also stocks accessories and delightful gift items. Custom tailoring is available.

SOHO WINES & SPIRITS

Map p412 — Food & Drink

☎ 2530 1182; 37 Staunton St; ◷ 11am-11pm; bus 26

Its name notwithstanding, this place's forte is in its large selection of beer and spirits. If it's not here, it probably isn't made or drunk any longer.

SOTHEBY Map pp408-9 — Auction House

☎ 2524 8121; 5th fl, Standard Chartered Bank Bldg, 4-4A Des Voeux Rd Central; Central MTR

Sotheby usually holds its auction previews in April/May and October/November at the Island Shangri-La Hotel in Admiralty. Like Christie, it also has regular sales in ceramics, jade, modern and jadeite jewellery, stamps, snuff bottles, works of art, traditional and contemporary Chinese paintings and calligraphic works.

TAI SING FINE ANTIQUES

Map p412 — Antiques

☎ 2525 9365; 12 Wyndham St; ◷ 10.30am-6pm Mon-Sat; Central MTR

Tai Sing has been selling quality Chinese antiques for more than half a century, with a special focus on porcelain. Two of the shop's six floors are now devoted to European furniture, including a dandy assembly of Art Deco pieces.

TAI YIP ART BOOK CENTRE

Map p412 — Books

☎ 2524 5963; Room 101-102, 1st fl, Capitol Plaza, 2-10 Lyndhurst Tce; ◷ 10am-7pm Mon-Fri, 10am-6.30pm Sat & Sun; Central MTR

Tai Yip has a terrific selection of books about anything that is Chinese and artsy: calligraphy, jade, bronze, costumes, architecture, symbolism. This is a good place to look deeper if you're planning on buying art in Hong Kong. There are outlets in several of Hong Kong's museums including the **Hong Kong Museum of Art** (p90).

TERESA COLEMAN FINE ARTS

Map p412   Antiques

☎ 2526 2450; Ground fl, 79 Wyndham St; ⏰ 9.30am-6pm Mon-Sat; bus 26

This is the finest shop in Hong Kong for purchasing antique Chinese textiles, including rare *chi fu*, the formal court robes of valuable silk worn by the Chinese emperor, princes and imperial ministers. The shop also deals in Chinese export paintings from the 18th and 19th centuries and antique fans.

TIBETAN GALLERY Map p412   Antiques

☎ 2530 4863; Shop A, Yu Yuet Lai Bldg, 43-55 Wyndham St; ⏰ 10am-6pm Mon-Sat; bus 26

This shop has an impressive selection of Tibetan religious art and artefacts, including mini-altars. There's a large showroom on the 1st floor.

TOTO Map pp408-9   Clothing & Accessories

☎ 2869 4668; Shop 212, 2nd fl, Prince's Bldg, 10 Chater Rd; ⏰ 10am-7pm Mon-Sat; Central MTR

Jump suits and other togs for under-twos; everything made by this Hong Kong brand is 100% cotton.

TOY MUSEUM Map pp408-9   Toys

☎ 2869 9138; Shop 320, 3rd fl, Prince's Bldg, 10 Chater Rd; ⏰ 10am-7pm Mon-Sat, noon-5pm Sun; Central MTR

Top-of-the-line teddy bears, action men, Beanie Babies and Pokemon paraphernalia are crammed into a tight space here. There's a great collection of old GI Joes for dads to amuse themselves with and a toy hospital too.

TSE SUI LUEN Map p412   Jewellery

☎ 2921 8800; Ground fl, Commercial House, 35 Queen's Rd Central; ⏰ 10am-8pm Mon-Sat, 10am-7pm Sun; Central MTR

This is the most sparkling of Tse Sui Luen's dozen or so outlets and is worth visiting for its sheer opulence or garishness – however you see it. There's another branch in **Tsim Sha Tsui** (Map pp420–1; ☎ 2926 3210; Shop A & B, Ground fl, 190 Nathan Rd; ⏰ 10am-10.30pm).

WANKO Map pp408-9   Clothing & Accessories

☎ 2523 0520; Shop 209, Ground fl, Chinese Bank Bldg, 31-37 Des Voeux Rd Central; ⏰ 11am-10pm; Central MTR

Soft spring-colour skirts and blouses, as well as sharper business attire, are all on offer here. Of course, some people shop here just to be able to say: 'I got it at Wanko'.

WATSON'S WINE CELLAR

Map p412   Food & Drink

☎ 2869 2210; 2 Staunton St; ⏰ noon-10pm; bus 26

The choice at this wine emporium is enormous and the staff are always willing to assist. There's a branch in **Causeway Bay** (Map pp414–15; ☎ 2895 6975; Basement, Windsor House, 311 Gloucester Rd).

WATTIS FINE ART Map p412   Antiques

☎ 2524 5302; www.wattis.com.hk; 2nd fl, 20 Hollywood Rd; ⏰ 10am-6pm Tue-Sat, 1-5pm Sun; bus 26

No place in Hong Kong has a better collection of antique maps for sale than Wattis Fine Art. The selection of old photographs of Hong Kong and Macau is also very impressive. You enter the shop from Old Bailey St.

X GAME SPORTING GOODS

Map p412   Sporting Goods

☎ 2366 9293; Shop A1, Ground fl, Wilson House, 19-27 Wyndham St; ⏰ 11am-8pm Mon-Fri, 10am-7pm Sat; Central MTR

This is a choice spot for windsurfing equipment and supplies, as well as surfwear. There's a branch in **Causeway Bay** (Map pp414–15; ☎ 2881 8960; 1st fl, 11 Pak Sha Rd; ⏰ noon-9pm).

Shopping

HONG KONG ISLAND

TOP FIVE ANTIQUE SHOPS

- **Amours Antiques** (p233) – fun, almost kitsch, accessories
- **Chine Gallery** (p234) – top-of-the-crop antique furniture and rugs
- **Hobbs & Bishops Fine Art** (p235) – sleek, refined furniture and extras
- **Teresa Coleman Fine Arts** (left) – the finest spot for antique Chinese textiles
- **Wattis Fine Art** (above) – the best place in Hong Kong for antique maps, prints and photographs

SHEUNG WAN

For antiques and curios, head for Hollywood Rd, which starts in Central and ends up in Sheung Wan, where there is a long string of shops selling Asian items. Some of the really good spots have genuine finds, but beware of what you buy. There are also a couple of big department stores here.

SINCERE Map pp408-9 Department Store

☎ 2830 1016, 2544 2688; Ground fl, Wing Shan Tower, 173 Des Voeux Rd Central; 🕑 10am-7.30pm; Sheung Wan MTR

Sincere carries everything, but is most memorable for its line of clothing, particularly menswear.

WING ON Map pp408-9 Department Store

☎ 2852 1888; 211 Des Voeux Rd Central; 🕑 10am-7.30pm; Sheung Wan MTR

'Forever Peaceful' is notable for being locally owned. It carries a range of goods but is especially well known for electronics and household appliances. There is another branch located in **Tsim Sha Tsui** (Map pp420–1; ☎ 2710 6288; 345 Nathan Rd; 🕑 10.30am-10pm).

ADMIRALTY & WAN CHAI

Admiralty, bordering Wan Chai, has Hong Kong Island's glitziest shopping mall, Pacific Place, just opposite (and connected by elevated walkway to) the Admiralty MTR station. Wan Chai is a good spot for medium- and low-priced clothing, sporting goods and footwear, but the area caters mainly for locals. The district has little glamour, but it is well worth hunting for bargains.

AL-SHAHZADI PERSIAN CARPET GALLERY Map pp414-15 Carpets

☎ 2834 8396; 265 Queen's Rd East, Wan Chai; 🕑 10am-6pm Tue-Sun; bus 6, 6A or 6X

This shop has quality new carpets from Afghanistan, Iran and Russia and antique Chinese ones. It's off the beaten track so pricing is competitive.

BUNN'S DIVERS

Map pp414-15 Sporting Goods

☎ 3422 3322; Mezzanine, Chuen Fung House, 188-192 Johnston Rd, Wan Chai; 🕑 11am-8pm Mon-Sat, noon-7pm Sun; Wan Chai MTR

Masks, snorkels, fins, regulators, tanks – this is Hong Kong's longest-established dive shop.

CHINESE ARTS & CRAFTS

Map pp408-9 Department Store

☎ 2523 3933; Shop 230, Pacific Place, 88 Queensway, Admiralty; 🕑 10.30am-7.30pm; Admiralty MTR

Mainland-owned CAC is probably the best place to buy quality bric-a-brac and other Chinese trinkets in Hong Kong; it's positively an Aladdin's department store of souvenirs. On Hong Kong Island there's also a branch in **Central** (Map p412; ☎ 2901 0338; Ground fl, Asia Standard Tower, 59 Queen's Rd Central; 🕑 10.30am-7.30pm) and a huge branch in **Wan Chai** (Map pp414–15; ☎ 2827 6667; Lower Block, China Resources Bldg, 26 Harbour Rd; 🕑 10.30am-7.30pm). There are two branches in Kowloon: in **Tsim Sha Tsui** (Map pp420–1; ☎ 2735 4061; 1st fl, Star House, 3 Salisbury Rd; 🕑 10am-9.30pm) and in the Nathan Hotel building in **Yau Ma Tei** (Map pp420–1; ☎ 2730 0061; Ground fl, 378 Nathan Rd; 🕑 10.30am-9.30pm).

COSMOS BOOKS Map pp414-15 Books

☎ 2866 1677; Basement & 1st fl, 30 Johnston Rd, Wan Chai; 🕑 10am-8pm; bus 6, 6A or 6X

This independently owned chain, with an outlet in **Tsim Sha Tsui** (Map pp420–1; ☎ 2367 8699; 96 Nathan Rd; 🕑 10.30am-9pm), has a good selection of China-related books in the basement. Upstairs are English-language books (nonfiction is strong) plus one of Hong Kong's best stationery departments. Enter the Wan Chai store from Lun Fat St and the Tsimsy store from Granville Rd.

DESIGN GALLERY

Map pp414-15 Gifts & Souvenirs

☎ 2584 4146; Hong Kong Convention & Exhibition Centre, 1 Harbour Rd, Wan Chai; 🕑 10am-7.30pm Mon-Fri, 10am-7pm Sat, noon-7.30pm Sun; bus 18

Supported by the Hong Kong Trade Development Council, this shop showcases local design in the form of jewellery, toys, ornaments and gadgets. It's a chaotic – but often rewarding – gaggle of goodies.

HONG KONG RECORDS

Map pp408-9 Music

☎ 2845 7088; Shop 252, 2nd fl, Pacific Place, 88 Queensway, Admiralty; 🕑 10am-8.30pm Mon-Thu, 10am-9pm Fri-Sun; Admiralty MTR

This local outfit has a good selection of Cantonese and international sounds, including traditional Chinese, jazz, classical and contemporary music. There's also a good range of VCDs of both Chinese films and Western movies with Chinese subtitles. There's also a **Kowloon Tong branch** (Map pp418–19; ☎ 2265 8299; Shop L1-02, Level 1, Festival Walk, 80-88 Tat Chee Ave; 🕙 11.30am-9.30pm Sun-Thu, 11.30am-10pm Fri & Sat).

KELLY & WALSH Map pp408-9   Books
☎ 2522 5743; Shop 236, 2nd fl, Pacific Place, 88 Queensway, Admiralty; 🕙 10.30am-8pm Sun-Thu, 10.30am-8.30pm Fri & Sat; Admiralty MTR
This smart shop has a good selection of art, design and culinary books, and the staff know the stock well. Books for children are shelved in a handy kids' reading lounge. There's also a **Central branch** (Map pp408–9; ☎ 2810 5128; Shop 305, 3rd fl, Exchange Square Tower I; 🕙 8.30am-7pm Mon-Fri, 8.30am-5pm Sat).

KENT & CURWEN
Map pp408-9   Clothing & Accessories
☎ 2840 0023; Shop 372, 3rd fl, Pacific Place, 88 Queensway, Admiralty; 🕙 10am-7.30pm Sun-Thu, 10am-8pm Fri & Sat; Admiralty MTR
Distinguished suits, dress shirts, ties, cufflinks and casual tops for the gentleman who'd rather look to the manor born than arriviste broker.

KING & COUNTRY
Map pp408-9   Gifts & Souvenirs
☎ 2525 8603; Shop 362, 3rd fl, Pacific Place, 88 Queensway, Admiralty; 🕙 10.30am-8pm Mon-Sat, 11am-7pm Sun; Admiralty MTR
This shop has models and miniatures, mostly a military bent (the American War of Independence and so forth). But there are also charming street models of old Hong Kong: building frontages, a Chinese wedding procession, even an 'amah with baby and chicken'.

KUNG FU SUPPLIES
Map pp414-15   Sporting Goods
☎ 2891 1912; Room 6A, 6th fl, Chuen Fung House, 188-192 Johnston Rd, Wan Chai; 🕙 10am-7pm Mon-Sat, 1-7pm Sun; bus 6, 6A or 6X

If you need to stock up on martial arts accessories or just want to thumb through a decent collection of books, Kung Fu Supplies is the place to go. The staff here is very helpful.

PACIFIC CUSTOM TAILORS
Map pp408-9   Clothing & Accessories
☎ 2845 5377; Shop 110, 1st fl, Pacific Place, 88 Queensway, Admiralty; 🕙 9.30am-7.30pm Mon-Sat; Admiralty MTR
This is one of our favourite bespoke tailors in Hong Kong. It'll make or copy anything; turnaround on most items is two or three days, including two fittings. Count on about $3500 for a suit.

PACIFIC PLACE Map pp408-9   Shopping Mall
☎ 2844 8988; www.pacificplace.com.hk; 88 Queensway, Admiralty; 🕙 10.30am-11pm; Admiralty MTR
Piped jazz, free telephones and the classiest (and widest) range in town can all be found at Pacific Place, our favourite mall in Hong Kong.

SEIBU Map pp408-9   Department Store
☎ 2971 3333; 1st & 2nd fls, Pacific Place, 88 Queensway, Admiralty; 🕙 10.30am-8pm Sun-Wed, 10.30am-9pm Thu-Sat; Admiralty MTR
This Japanese department store is a shadow of its former self, but still has a decent food emporium called **Great** (p168) in the basement.

SUNMARK CAMPING EQUIPMENT
Map pp414-15   Outdoor Gear
☎ 2893 8553; 1st fl, 121 Wan Chai Rd, Wan Chai; 🕙 noon-8pm Mon-Sat, 1.30-7.30pm Sun; bus 6, 6A or 6X
Head here for hiking and camping gear and waterproof clothing of all sorts. Enter from Bullock Lane.

VIVIENNE TAM
Map pp408-9   Clothing & Accessories
☎ 2918 0238; Shop 209, 2nd fl, Pacific Place, 88 Queensway, Admiralty; 🕙 11am-8pm Sun-Thu, 11am-9pm Fri & Sat; Admiralty MTR
Adventurous women's foundation pieces and accessories from New York–based designer Tam, who was trained in Hong Kong.

Seibu (p241), Admiralty

WAH TUNG CHINA ARTS

Map pp408-9   Gifts & Souvenirs

☎ 2520 5933; 8 Queen's Rd East, Wan Chai; ⏰ 10am-8pm Mon-Sat, 11am-7pm Sun; Admiralty MTR

Wah Tung, the world's largest supplier of hand-decorated ceramics, has some 18,000 items on display at this showroom, just east of Pacific Place. You'll find everything from brightly painted vases and ginger jars to repro Tang dynasty figurines. There's also a branch in Central (Map p412; ☎ 2543 2823; 59 Hollywood Rd; ⏰ 11am-6pm).

WAN CHAI COMPUTER CENTRE

Map pp414-15   Computers

1st fl, Southorn Centre, 130-138 Hennessy Rd, Wan Chai; ⏰ 10.30am-7pm Mon-Sat; Wan Chai MTR

This place, on the northern edge of South-orn Playground, is a cut above Hong Kong's computer emporiums.

WISE KIDS Map pp408-9   Toys

☎ 2868 0133; Shop 134, 1st fl, Pacific Place, 88 Queensway, Admiralty; ⏰ 10am-8pm Sun-Wed, 10am-9pm Thu-Sat; Admiralty MTR

Nothing to plug in, nothing with batteries: Wise Kids concentrates on kids generating energy with what's upstairs. Along with stuffed toys, card games and things to build, there are practical items for parents such as toilet-lid locks and carry-alls. There's also a branch in Central (Map pp408–9; ☎ 2377 9888; Shop 301, 3rd fl, Prince's Bldg, 10 Chater Rd; ⏰ 10am-7pm).

CAUSEWAY BAY

Causeway Bay has perhaps the largest weekend crowds and the broadest spectrum in terms of price. It is a crush of department stores and smaller outlets selling designer and street fashion, electronics, sporting goods and household items. In this area you'll also stumble upon lively street markets. Jardine's Bazaar (actually a street) and the area behind it are home to stalls and shops peddling cheap clothing, luggage and footwear. The area is also home to the huge Times Square shopping mall.

CAMPER Map pp414-15   Clothing & Accessories

☎ 2882 9310; Ground fl, 1A Kingston St; ⏰ noon-10pm; Causeway Bay MTR

Emblazoned with thought-provoking slogans and aphorisms, Camper is one of the most popular outlets in Hong Kong for locally designed fashion.

CHUNG YUEN ELECTRICAL CO

Map pp414-15   Electronic Goods

☎ 2506 3515; Shop 727-728, Times Square, 1 Matheson St; ⏰ 11am-9.30pm; Causeway Bay MTR

Fair-minded, fixed-price electronics store with a good selection of iPods and other personal sound systems, DVD players and organisers. There's also a larger branch in Tsim Sha Tsui (Map pp420–1; ☎ 2736 8323; Shop 306-307, Ocean Centre, Harbour City, 3-9 Canton Rd; ⏰ 11am-8.30pm).

CITYPLAZA Map pp406-7   Shopping Mall

☎ 2568 8665; www.cityplaza.com.hk; 18 Tai Koo Shing Rd, Tai Koo Shing, Quarry Bay; ⏰ 10.30am-10pm; Tai Koo MTR

The largest shopping centre in eastern Hong Kong Island, with 180 shops, Cityplaza is directly linked up to the MTR. Being further from the main business district, it charges retailers lower rents, which can translate into lower prices for shoppers. There's a Wing On department store branch here, as well as an ice-skating rink. From Tai Koo Shing MTR use exit D2.

D-MOP Map pp414-15   Clothing & Accessories

☎ 2203 4130; Shop B, Ground fl, 8 Kingston St; ⏰ noon-10pm Mon-Sat, noon-9pm Sun; Causeway Bay MTR

This is the main outlet for one of Hong Kong's edgier designer lines.

DADA CABARET VOLTAIRE

Map pp414-15   Clothing & Accessories

☎ 2890 1708; Shop F-13A, 1st fl, Fashion Island, 47 Paterson St; ⏰ 12.30-10pm; Causeway Bay MTR
Sells ragged rainbow-coloured clothing also sported by the staff. Just one of many fine shops in the Fashion Island micro mall.

IN SQUARE Map pp414-15   Computers

10th-12th fl, Windsor House, 311 Gloucester Rd; ⏰ 11am-9pm; Causeway Bay MTR
This landmark building in Causeway Bay houses dozens of reliable computer shops, selling both hardware and software.

MITSUKOSHI Map pp414-15   Department Store

☎ 2576 5222; 500 Hennessy Rd; ⏰ 10.30am-10pm; Causeway Bay MTR
Mitsukoshi has cheap clothing, lots of crockery and household goods, food outlets and a **Park 'N' Shop** (⏰ 7.30am-11pm), which is in the lowest level and can also be entered from Kai Chiu and Lee Garden Rds, from behind the store.

MOUNTAINEERING SERVICES

Map pp414-15   Outdoor Gear

☎ 2541 8876; Ground fl, 271 Gloucester Rd; ⏰ 11am-7.45pm; Causeway Bay MTR
This excellent and centrally located shop sells climbing and hiking gear.

SISTER Map pp414-15   Clothing & Accessories

☎ 2504 1016; Shop 331, 3rd fl, Island Beverley, 1 Great George St; ⏰ 2-11pm; Causeway Bay MTR
This 'trendy fashion store' sells young Hong Kong designer wear verging on the wacky.

SOGO Map pp414-15   Department Store

☎ 2833 8338; www.sogo.com.hk; 555 Hennessy Rd; ⏰ 10am-10pm; Causeway Bay MTR
This Japanese-owned store, in the hub of Causeway Bay, has 12 well-organised floors and more than 37,000 sq metres of retail space. The range is mind-boggling: over 20 brands of ties just for starters. Eclectic departments include the Barbie Counter and the Character's Shop.

SPY Map pp414-15   Clothing & Accessories

☎ 2893 7799; Shop C, Ground fl, 11 Sharp St East; ⏰ noon-11pm; Causeway Bay MTR
Tame yet trendy everyday wear, such as slacks and short-sleeved shirts. It has two

other outlets, including one in **Tsim Sha Tsui** (Map pp420-1; ☎ 2366 5866; Shop 406-407, 4th fl, Rise Commercial Centre, 5-11 Granville Circuit; ⏰ 2-11pm).

TIMES SQUARE Map pp414-15   Shopping Mall

☎ 2118 8900; www.timessquare.com.hk; 1 Matheson St; ⏰ 10am-10pm; Causeway Bay MTR
Some 10 floors of retail organised by type. There are restaurants on the 10th to 13th floors and snack bars, cafés and a supermarket in the basement.

WALTER MA

Map pp414-15   Clothing & Accessories

☎ 2838 7655; Ground fl, 33 Sharp St East; ⏰ noon-10pm Mon-Fri, noon-10.30pm Sat & Sun; Causeway Bay MTR
Sophisticated women's wear from 'the voice of Hong Kong fashion'.

KOWLOON

Shopping in Kowloon is a bizarre mix of the down at heel and the glamorous, and an afternoon's stroll through its shopping quarters should yield quite a few surprises.

TSIM SHA TSUI

Nathan Rd is the main tourist strip, a huge avenue with side streets full of camera, watch and electronic shops, and leather and silk emporiums. Although this is the part of town where you're most likely to get ripped off, Tsim Sha Tsui is also home to a large number of above-board designer and signature shops. Some of these are found in Nathan Rd, but the bulk are in Harbour City, a labyrinthine shopping complex with a mall that stretches nearly 1km from the Star Ferry terminal north along Canton Rd. Many hotels in Tsim Sha Tsui have very upmarket boutique shopping arcades, most notably the Peninsula and the Hotel Inter-Continental.

ALAN CHAN CREATIONS

Map pp420-21   Gifts & Souvenirs

☎ 2723 2722; www.alanchancreations.com; Shop 5A, Basement, Peninsula Hong Kong, Salisbury Rd; ⏰ 9.30am-7pm; Tsim Sha Tsui MTR
Alan Chan has designed everything – from airport logos to soy-sauce bottles – and

now lends his name to stylish souvenirs, such as clothing and ceramic pieces. Some items he has a direct hand in, others he simply approves of.

CHINESE CARPET CENTRE

Map pp420-1   Carpets

☎ 2736 1773; Shop L021, Ground fl, New World Centre, 18-24 Salisbury Rd; 🕙 10am-8pm; bus 5C or 8

This place has a excellent selection of new Chinese carpets and rugs. There's another branch in **Tsim Sha Tsui East** (Map pp420–1; ☎ 2730 7230; Shop 5, Ground fl, Houston Centre, 63 Mody Rd; 🕙 10am-8pm).

CURIO ALLEY Map pp420-1   Gifts & Souvenirs

🕙 10am-8pm; Tsim Sha Tsui MTR

This is a fun place to shop for name chops, soapstone carvings, fans and other Chinese bric-a-brac. It's found in an alleyway, between Lock and Hankow Rds, just south of Haiphong Rd.

DAVID CHAN PHOTO SHOP

Map pp420-1   Photographic Equipment

☎ 2723 3886; Shop 15, Ground fl, Champagne Court, 16 Kimberley Rd; 🕙 10am-8pm Mon-Sat; Tsim Sha Tsui MTR

This dealer, one of the most reliable in Hong Kong, sells both new and antique cameras.

GIGA SPORTS

Map pp420-1   Outdoor Gear

☎ 2115 9930; Shop 244-247, 2nd fl, Ocean Terminal, Harbour City, Salisbury Rd; 🕙 10am-8pm; Star Ferry

This large store has a wide range of sports equipment, backpacks, clothing and footwear.

GOLF CREATION

Map pp420-1   Sporting Goods

☎ 2721 8860; Shops 12 & 15, Ground fl, Hong Kong Pacific Centre, 28 Hankow Rd; 🕙 10.30am-8.30pm Mon-Sat, 11am-6.30pm Sun; Tsim Sha Tsui MTR

This shop keeps upwardly mobile Hong Kong Chinese equipped with the kit of their favourite new game.

HARBOUR CITY Map pp420-1   Shopping Mall

☎ 2118 8666; www.harbourcity.com.hk; 3-9 Canton Rd; 🕙 10am-9pm; Tsim Sha Tsui MTR

This is an enormous place, with 700 shops, 50 food and beverage outlets and five cinemas in four separate zones. Every major brand is represented.

I.T Map pp420-1   Clothing & Accessories

☎ 2736 9152; Shop 1030, 1st fl, Miramar Shopping Centre, 1-23 Kimberley Rd; 🕙 noon-10pm; Tsim Sha Tsui MTR

This shop and the women's-only **b+ab** shop next door both sell the cute, trendy gear that abounds in Hong Kong. There are i.t shops in all the major shopping areas including in **Causeway Bay** (Map pp414–15; ☎ 2506 0186; Shop 517, 5th fl, Times Square, 1 Matheson St).

KING SING JEWELLERY

Map pp420-1   Jewellery

☎ 2735 7021; Shop 14, Ground fl, Star House, 3 Salisbury Rd; 🕙 9.30am-7.30pm Mon-Sat, 9.30am-6.30pm Sun; Star Ferry

A long-standing jeweller with a wide selection of diamonds, pearls and gold items. The sales staff is pleasant and not pushy.

KS AHLUWALIA & SONS

Map pp420-1   Sporting Goods

☎ 2368 8334; 8C Hankow Rd; 🕙 10am-7.45pm Mon-Sat, 10am-5pm Sun; Tsim Sha Tsui MTR

Long established, this store is well stocked with golf gear, tennis racquets, cricket bats, shirts and balls. It's cash only and no prices are marked, so haggle away.

LIDS Map pp420-1   Clothing & Accessories

☎ 3523 0626; Shop 2, Park Hotel, 61-65 Chatham Rd South; 🕙 11am-11pm; Tsim Sha Tsui MTR

This is the place to come for headgear – from baseball caps begging to be turned back to front, to helmets for cyclists, rollerbladers and skateboarders.

MINAMOTO KITCHOAN

Map pp420-1   Food & Drink

☎ 2368 6582; Shop G1, Ground fl, Tung Ying Bldg, 100 Nathan Rd; 🕙 10.30am-10.30pm; Tsim Sha Tsui MTR

The folk here go to unbelievable lengths to make sweets so artistic that merely popping them into your mouth seems crude. Do it anyway and make it the *tosenka* (a big peach whose stone is replaced by a baby green peach) or *reika* (Japanese jelly flavoured with plum wine).

MING'S SPORTS COMPANY

Map pp420-1   Sporting Goods

☎ 2376 1387; Ground fl, 53 Hankow Rd; ⏰ 10am-7pm Mon-Sat, 11am-5pm Sun; Tsim Sha Tsui MTR
This is an excellent place to buy gear for tennis or golf.

MONITOR RECORDS Map pp420-1   Music

☎ 2809 4603; Shop 5, Ground fl, Fortune Tce, 4-16 Tak Shing St; ⏰ noon-10pm; Jordan MTR
One of Hong Kong's few independent music stores, this is a well-presented operation that specialises in indie and imported sounds you wouldn't even bother asking for anywhere else.

OCEAN SKY DIVERS

Map pp420-1   Sporting Goods

☎ 2366 3738; 1st fl, 17-19 Lock Rd; ⏰ 10.30am-9pm Apr-Nov, 11.30am-9pm Dec-Mar; Tsim Sha Tsui MTR
This new kid on the block is giving Bunn's a run for its money with the whole range of diving and snorkelling gear in stock.

OM INTERNATIONAL

Map pp420-1   Jewellery

☎ 2366 3421; 1st fl, Friend's House, 6 Carnarvon Rd; ⏰ 9.30am-6pm Mon-Sat; Tsim Sha Tsui MTR
This place has an excellent selection of saltwater and freshwater pearls, and there's a whole lot more on offer than what you see. The staff is scrupulously honest, helpful and friendly.

ONESTO PHOTO COMPANY

Map pp420-1   Photographic Equipment

☎ 2723 4668; Shop 2, Ground fl, Champagne Court, 16 Kimberley Rd; ⏰ 10am-9pm; Tsim Sha Tsui MTR
This retail establishment, also known as the Kimberley Camera Company, has price tags on all of its equipment (a rare find in Tsim Sha Tsui), but there's always some latitude for bargaining.

OPAL MINE Map pp420-1   Jewellery

☎ 2721 9933; Shop G & H, Ground fl, Burlington Arcade, 92-94 Nathan Rd; ⏰ 9.30am-7pm; Tsim Sha Tsui MTR
This place, more of a museum than a shop, has a truly vast selection of Australian opals that makes for fascinating viewing and buying, should you be so tempted.

TOP FIVE
SHOPS FOR GIFTS & SOUVENIRS

- **Alan Chan Creations** (p243) – stylish souvenirs from the man who has designed almost everything in Hong Kong
- **Chinese Arts & Crafts** (p240) – the best place in town for quality Chinese bric-a-brac
- **Curio Alley** (opposite) – the strip for low-cost trinkets and mementos
- **Liuligongfang** (p237) – renowned glass sculptor hawks her creations here
- **Shanghai Tang** (p238) – retro Chinese duds in neon colours

PONTI FOOD & WINE CELLAR

Map pp420-1   Food & Drink

☎ 2721 8770; Shop 3, Ground fl, Hong Kong Pacific Centre, 28 Hankow Rd; ⏰ 11am-8.30pm Mon-Sat, 11am-8pm Sun; Tsim Sha Tsui MTR
Ponti stocks a huge range of both table and vintage wines and periodically holds attractive bin-end sales. There's also a **Central branch** (Map pp408–9; ☎ 2810 1000; Shop B2, 1st basement, Alexandra House, 16-20 Chater Rd; ⏰ 10.30am-8pm Mon-Sat, 10.30am-7.30pm Sun).

PREMIER JEWELLERY

Map pp420-1   Jewellery

☎ 2368 0003; Shop G14-15, Ground fl, Holiday Inn Golden Mile Shopping Mall, 50 Nathan Rd; ⏰ 10am-7.30pm Mon-Sat, 10.30am-4pm Sun; Tsim Sha Tsui MTR
This third-generation family firm is directed by a qualified gemologist and one of our favourite places to shop. The selection isn't huge, but if you're looking for something particular, give it a day's notice to have a selection ready in time for your arrival. Staff can also help you design your own piece.

SAM'S TAILOR

Map pp420-1   Clothing & Accessories

☎ 2367 9423; Shop K, Burlington Arcade, 92-94 Nathan Rd; ⏰ 10am-7.30pm Mon-Sat, 10am-noon Sun; Tsim Sha Tsui MTR
It's not certain that Sam's is the best tailor in Hong Kong, but it's the most aggressively marketed and best known. Sam's has stitched up everyone – from royalty and rock stars to us.

Shopping

KOWLOON

STAR COMPUTER CITY

Map pp420-1   Computers

**2nd fl, Star House, 3 Salisbury Rd; ☺ 10am-8pm;
Star Ferry**

This is the largest complex of retail
computer outlets in Tsim Sha Tsui, with
some two dozen shops. Have a look at
Reptron (☎ 2730 2891; Shop A1, 2nd fl;
☺ 10.30am-7.30pm) for desktops, laptops
and PDAs, and **2C Company** (☎ 2730 4382;
Shop D1-2, 2nd fl; ☺ 10am-8pm) for accessories – modem protectors, various adaptors and the cables that could be just
what you need to get roadworthy.

SWINDON BOOKS Map pp420-1   Books

☎ 2366 8001; 13-15 Lock Rd; ☺ 9am-6.30pm
Mon-Thu, 9am-7.30pm Fri & Sat, 12.30-6.30pm Sun;
Tsim Sha Tsui MTR
This is one of the best 'real' (as opposed to
'supermarket') bookshops in Hong Kong.
There's another outlet in **Tsim Sha Tsui** (Map
pp420–1; ☎ 2730 0183; Shop 370, 3rd fl,
Ocean Centre, Harbour City, 3-9 Canton Rd;
☺ 10.30am-8pm Mon-Fri, 10.30am-8.30pm
Sat, 12.30-8pm Sun).

TOM LEE MUSIC COMPANY

Map pp420-1   Music

☎ 2723 9932; 1-9 Cameron Lane; ☺ 10am-8pm
Sun-Thu, 10am-9pm Fri & Sat; Tsim Sha Tsui MTR
Tom Lee, who has almost 20 branches
across the territory, is Mr Music in Hong
Kong and the man to see if you're looking
for Western musical instruments, including guitars, flutes, recorders and the odd
mouth organ.

TRAVELLERS' HOME Map pp420-1   Books

☎ 2380 8380; travelbookshop@yahoo.com.hk;
2nd fl, 55 Hankow Rd; ☺ noon-9pm Mon-Sat,
1-7.30pm Sun; Tsim Sha Tsui MTR
This one-stop shop sells both new and
used travel books (roughly at a ration of
30% to 70%), schedules travel talks and
hosts photo exhibitions. There's a small
café corner and a message board, and it
has become something of a meeting place
for travellers in Tsim Sha Tsui.

TRAVELMAX Map pp420-1   Outdoor Gear

☎ 3188 4271; Shop 270-273, 2nd fl, Ocean Terminal,
Harbour City, Salisbury Rd; ☺ 10.30am-9pm;
Star Ferry
Travelmax sells both lightweight and cold-
weather outdoor gear; kids' sizes are available. There's a good range of Eagle Creek
travel products here, too.

WWW.IZZUE.COM

Map pp420-1   Clothing & Accessories

☎ 2992 0612; Shop 2225, 2nd fl, Gateway Arcade,
Harbour City, 25-27 Canton Rd; ☺ 11am-9pm; Tsim
Sha Tsui MTR
Simple, energetic and comfortable styles in
this chain of super-groovy boutiques. There
are 15 outlets throughout the territory,
including a branch in **Central** (Map pp408–9;
☎ 2868 4066; Upper ground fl, 10 Queen's
Rd Central; ☺ 10.30am-7.30pm).

TO MARKET, TO MARKET...

For budget shopping, there's no better place to start than at one of Hong Kong's busy covered or street markets.

The biggest one in the territory is the **Temple Street night market** (p94) in Yau Ma Tei, which basically runs parallel
to (and west of) Nathan Rd from Jordan Rd in the south to Man Ming Lane in the north and is divided by Tin Hau Temple.
It is the place to go for cheap clothes, watches, pirated CDs and DVDs, fake labels, footwear, cookware and everyday
items, as well as *dqai-pàai-dawng* (open-air street stall) food. The best time to visit is between 7pm and 10pm.

The **Tung Choi St market** (Map p423; ☺ noon-11.30pm), two blocks east of Nathan Rd and the Mong Kok MTR
station, mainly sells cheap clothing. It is sometimes called Ladies' Market to distinguish it from Men's St (the Temple
Street night market) because the stalls in the latter once sold only menswear. Though there are still a lot of items on sale
for women on Tung Choi St, vendors don't discriminate and anyone's money will do nowadays. Vendors start setting up
their stalls as early as noon, but it's best to get here between 1pm and 6pm when there's much more on offer.

There are other bustling markets on **Apliu St** (Map pp418–19; ☺ noon-9pm) in Sham Shui Po, one block west of
Sham Shui Po MTR station, and in the streets running off Tai Po's **Four Lane Sq** (Map p424) in the New Territories.

If you're looking strictly for clothing, try **Jardine's Bazaar** (Map pp414–15) in Causeway Bay. A bit more upmarket
and a tourist attraction in its own right is **Stanley Market** (p86), in the village of that name on southern Hong Kong
Island. Another market worth visiting is **Western Market** (p75) near the Macau ferry terminal in Sheung Wan.

Shopping

KOWLOON

YAU MA TEI & MONG KOK

To the north of Tsim Sha Tsui, Yau Ma Tei and Mong Kok cater mostly to local shoppers and offer good prices on clothing, sporting goods, camping gear, footwear, computers and other daily necessities. There's nothing very exotic available here, but for your everyday items they're popular spots, and it is fun to see how the local people shop and to check out what they are buying.

CHAMONIX ALPINE EQUIPMENT

Map p423   Outdoor Gear

☎ 2770 6746; 1st fl, On Yip Bldg, 395 Shanghai St, Yau Ma Tei; ☽ 11am-8pm Mon-Sat, noon-7pm Sun; Yau Ma Tei MTR

Far-flung but worth the trip, this Mong Kok shop, run by an avid mountaineer, has a wide range of camping, hiking and climbing equipment.

FLYING BALL BICYCLE CO

Map p423   Sporting Goods

☎ 2381 3661; 201 Tung Choi St, Mong Kok; ☽ 10am-8pm Mon-Sat, 10.30am-7pm Sun; Mong Kok MTR

This place is the No 1 choice for locals and expats alike, and serious cyclists will be able to find a great selection of bikes and accessories.

LANGHAM PLACE MALL

Map p423   Shopping Mall

☎ 3520 2800; 8 Argyle St, Mong Kok; ☽ 10.30am-11pm; Mong Kok MTR

This 15-storey super mall has some 300 shops that stay open till as late as 11pm. The focal point of the mall is the high-tech Digital Sky where special events take place.

MONG KOK COMPUTER CENTRE

Map p423   Computers

8-8A Nelson St, Mong Kok; ☽ 1-10pm; Mong Kok MTR

This centre has three floors of computer shops. In general, it's geared more towards the resident Cantonese-speaking market than foreigners, but you can normally get better deals here than in Tsim Sha Tsui. Check out **Winframe System** (☎ 2300 1238; Shop 106-107) on the 1st floor.

MOUNTAINEER SUPERMARKET

Map p423   Outdoor Gear

☎ 2398 2898; 424-428 Portland St, Mong Kok; ☽ 1.30-8pm Mon-Fri, noon-8pm Sat, 12.45-8pm Sun; Mong Kok MTR

This is a great spot for climbing equipment and outfits.

RAG BROCHURE

Map p423   Clothing & Accessories

☎ 2391 4660; Shop 4, Basement, Trendy Zone, Chow Tai Fook Centre, 580A Nathan Rd, Mong Kok; ☽ 1-10pm; Mong Kok MTR

One of a crush of fashion outlets in this micro mall selling new and vintage gear for guys and gals.

WING SHING PHOTO SUPPLIES

Map p423   Photographic Equipment

☎ 2396 6886; 57 Sai Yeung Choi St South, Mong Kok; ☽ 10am-10pm Mong Kok MTR

We've received letters from readers praising the quality of the service and the competitive prices at Wing Shing. We like the hours; the boys in the north always try harder.

WISE MOUNT SPORTS

Map p423   Outdoor Gear

☎ 2787 3011; Ground fl, 75 Sai Yee St, Mong Kok; ☽ 11.30am-10.30pm Mong Kok MTR

This is a long-standing family-run shop with camping gear, swimming goggles, pocket knives, compasses, hard-wearing bags and even sports trophies for sale.

YUE HWA
CHINESE PRODUCTS EMPORIUM

Map pp420-1   Department Store

☎ 2384 0084; 301-309 Nathan Rd, Yau Ma Tei; ☽ 10am-10pm

This enormous place, with seven floors of ceramics, furniture, souvenirs and clothing, has absolutely everything the souvenir-hunting tourist could possibly want, as well as bolts of silk, herbs, clothes, porcelain, luggage, umbrellas and kitchenware. There are two branches in Tsim Sha Tsui: one northeast of the Star Ferry pier on **Kowloon Park Dr** (Map pp420–1; ☎ 2317 5333; 1 Kowloon Park Dr) that's entered from Peking Rd, and the other on the eastern edge of Kowloon Park on **Nathan Rd** (Map pp420–1; ☎ 2368 9165; 54-64 Nathan Rd).

TOP FIVE BOOKSHOPS

- **Bloomsbury Books** (p234) – excellent independent bookshop for professional as well as literary titles
- **Indosiam** (p236) – Hong Kong's only real antiquarian bookshop
- **Page One** (right) – what Hong Kong's largest bookshop lacks in atmosphere it makes up for in its volume of volumes
- **Swindon Books** (p246) – helpful, knowledgeable staff make this bookshop a delight
- **Tai Yip Art Book Centre** (p238) – the best selection of Chinese art and culture titles in the territory

YUET WAH MUSIC COMPANY

Map p423   Music

☎ 2385 6880; 464 Nathan Rd, Yau Ma Tei; ☽ 9.30am-7pm; Jordan MTR

Hong Kong is generally not a great place for Chinese musical instruments; there are a few shops along Wan Chai Rd between Johnston and Morrison Hill Rds in Wan Chai, but what is on offer is generally not good value for money. Yuet Wah is arguably the best retail outlet for quality Chinese instruments at competitive prices – from two-stringed *yi-wú* to *gú* (drums) and *bat* (brass cymbals).

NEW KOWLOON

Shopping venues in New Kowloon run the gamut from glittering shopping malls, such as Festival Walk in Kowloon Tong, to the cut-price computer centres of Sham Shui Po.

FESTIVAL WALK Map pp418-19 Shopping Mall

☎ 2844 2222; www.festivalwalk.com.hk; 80-88 Tat Chee Ave, Kowloon Tong; ☽ 10am-midnight; Kowloon Tong MTR, KCR

Festival Walk is a huge and glittering shopping mall with Hong Kong's largest cinema and ice-skating rink. There's a good middle-range selection of some 200 shops and around two dozen restaurants here as well.

GOLDEN COMPUTER ARCADE

Map pp418-19   Computers

Basement & 1st fl, 146-152 Fuk Wa St, Sham Shui Po; ☽ 10am-10pm; Sham Shui Po MTR

This centre sells computers and components as well as software, VCDs and DVDs.

NEW CAPITAL COMPUTER PLAZA

Map pp418-19   Computers

1st & 2nd fls, 85-89 Un Chau St, Sham Shui Po; ☽ 10am-10pm; Sham Shui Po MTR

This emporium of computer shops has a good range of stock and helpful staff who can produce enough English to close a sale.

PAGE ONE Map pp418-19   Books

☎ 2778 2808; Shop LG1 30, Lower ground fl, Festival Walk, 80-88 Tat Chee Ave, Kowloon Tong; ☽ 10.30am-10pm Sun-Thu, 10.30am-10.30pm Fri & Sat; Kowloon Tong MTR

A chain, yes, but one with attitude. Page One has Hong Kong's best selection of art and design magazines and books; it's also strong on photography, literature, film and children's books. There's also a smaller branch in **Tsim Sha Tsui** (Map pp420–1; ☎ 2730 6080; Shop 3202, 3rd fl, Gateway Arcade, Harbour City, 25-27 Canton Rd).

Hong Kong Island 253

Central, Soho & the Mid-Levels 253
Admiralty & Wan Chai 254
Causeway Bay 256
Island East 259

Kowloon 259

Tsim Sha Tsui 260
Tsim Sha Tsui East & Hung Hom 266
Yau Ma Tei & Mong Kok 267

New Territories 269

Tsuen Wan 270
Tai Mo Shan 270
Tai Mei Tuk 270
Sha Tin 270
Sai Kung Peninsula 271

Outlying Islands 271

Lamma 271
Cheung Chau 272
Lantau 272

Sleeping

Sleeping

There are three basic types of accommodation in Hong Kong: deluxe and top-end hotels, some of which count among the finest in the world; adequate but generally uninspiring midrange hotels; and cramped hostels and guesthouses at the budget level. Within each category there is a good deal of choice, and you should be able to find a comfortable place to stay at your price.

Accommodation costs are generally higher in Hong Kong than most other Asian cities, but cheaper than those in Europe and the USA. It is worth bearing in mind that in recent years many guesthouses and hotels have dropped their prices, and that midrange and even some top-end hotels are offering big discounts (especially to walk-ins during the shoulder and low seasons) on their posted rates, which are the ones listed in this chapter.

Hong Kong's two high seasons are from March to April and October to November, though things can be tight around Chinese New Year (late January or February) as well.

Mandarin Oriental (p254), Central

Outside these periods, rates drop (sometimes substantially) and little extras can come your way: room upgrades, late checkouts, free breakfast and complimentary cocktails. If the hotel seems a bit quiet when you arrive, it can be worth asking for an upgrade.

Reservations

Making an advance reservation for accommodation is not essential outside peak periods, but it can save you a lot of time, hassle and, depending on the season, money. If you fly into Hong Kong without having booked anything, the **Hong Kong Hotels Association** (Map pp420–1; HKHA; ☎ 2375 8380, 2375 3838; www.hkha.org; 508-511 Silvercord Tower Two, 30 Canton Rd, Tsim Sha Tsui; Star Ferry, Tsim Sha Tsui MTR), which deals with almost 90 of the territory's hotels, has reservation centres located inside Halls A and B (level 5) of Hong Kong International Airport. It can book you into a midrange or top-end hotel room for as much as 50% cheaper than if you were to walk in yourself.

Booking through a travel agent can also garner substantial discounts, sometimes as much as 40% off the walk-in price. If you're in Hong Kong and want to book either a midrange or luxury hotel, call or email **Phoenix Services Agency** (Map pp420–1; ☎ 2722 7378; info@phoenixtrvl.com; Room 1404, 14th fl, Austin Tower, 22-26 Austin Ave, Tsim Sha Tsui; ⏰ 9am-6pm Mon-Fri, 9am-1pm Sat) or **Traveller Services** (Map pp420–1; ☎ 2375 2222; www.taketraveller.com; Room 1012, 10th fl, Silvercord Tower One, Silvercord, 30 Canton Rd, Tsim Sha Tsui; ⏰ 9am-1pm & 2-6pm Mon-Fri, 9am-1pm Sat).

Hotels

Hong Kong's deluxe hotels are unique places, with individual qualities that propel them above the rest. Expect discreet, smooth-as-silk service, large baths, superlative climate control, extensive cable TV with Internet access, dataports, top-of-the-range food and beverage outlets and prices from about $3000 per room. A few such hotels – the Peninsula, Mandarin Orien-

tal and Island Shangri-La, for example –
offer comfort, amenities and service that
compete with or surpass that of the world's
finest five-star hotels.

Top-end hotels, starting at a minimum
of $1600, are in spiffy locations: they also
have smart, comfortable rooms with excellent air-con, in-house movies and a good
variety of room-service options. Amenities
include business facilities, bars and restaurants, and fluent English-speaking staff.

Midrange hotels tend to be generic business and/or tourist establishments with little
to distinguish one from another. Rooms are
spacious enough (if you don't plan on play-
ing Twister in the evening), and usually have a bath, limited cable TV and room service. Most
have some sort of business centre with Internet access as well. Sometimes there is not a
great deal to distinguish midrange from top-end hotels, except perhaps a certain ambience
and sense of style.

Prices in the midrange category start anywhere from about $700 (minimum) for a double
room, though the average price is closer to around $1000. At the very least, rooms will have
a separate bathroom with shower, bath and toilet, plus air-con, telephone and TV.

The majority of Hong Kong's budget hotels – a dying breed (as opposed to guesthouses
and hostels) – are in Kowloon, with many on or near Nathan Rd. Though most budget
hotel rooms are very small, the places listed here are clean and cheerily shabby rather than
grim and grimy. Most have telephones, TVs, air-con and private bathrooms; if not, we've
said so. Anything under $700 should be considered budget.

Hotels in Hong Kong add 10% service and 3% government tax to your bill, something
guesthouses and hostels usually do not do. The rates quoted in this book do not include
these charges.

TOP FIVE HOTELS

- **Grand Hyatt Hotel** (p255) – stunning outlets, seamless service and a lobby that screams 'Wow!'
- **Jia** (p257) – designer Philippe Starck comes to town and opens a boutique hotel
- **Mandarin Oriental** (p254) – the last word in style and 'face' on Hong Kong Island
- **Minden** (p261) – an eclecticist's dream, where East and West really do meet
- **Peninsula Hong Kong** (p92) – the one and only 'grand dame of Kowloon'

Cheap Sleeps

Budget accommodation in Hong Kong amounts to guesthouses, many of which offer
dormitory accommodation for those on very tight budgets, and official hostels, most of
which are located in very remote areas of the New Territories. The **Country & Marine Parks Authority** (☎ 2420 0529; http://parks.afcd.gov.hk) maintains about 38 basic camp sites in the
New Territories and Outlying Islands that are intended for walkers and hikers (see p219
for details).

GUESTHOUSES

Dominating the lower end of the accommodation market are guesthouses, usually a block
of tiny rooms squeezed into a converted apartment or two. Often there are several guesthouses operating out of the same building. Your options are greater if there are two of
you; find a double room in a clean guesthouse for $150 to $200 and your accommodation
costs will fall sharply.

Some guesthouses are relatively swish, with doubles for up to $400. Depending on the
season and location, try to negotiate a better deal as a lot of places will be eager to fill empty
rooms. Most guesthouses now offer some sort of Internet access.

HOSTELS

The **Hong Kong Youth Hostels Association** (HKYHA; Map pp418–19; ☎ 2788 1638; www.yha.org
.hk; Room 225-227, Block 19, Upper Shek Kip Mei Estate, Shek Kip Mei St; Shek Kip Mei
MTR) maintains seven hostels affiliated with Hostelling International (HI). It sells HKYHA
and HI cards (p311). If you intend on buying a membership card at one of the hostels, be
sure to take along a visa-sized photo and some identification.

Sleeping

TOP FIVE GUESTHOUSES

- **Booth Lodge** (p269) – no-nonsense affordable accommodation and service with a smile
- **Garden Hostel** (p264) – featuring *the* terrace where travellers meet
- **Hong Kong Hostel** (p258) – best value for money on Hong Kong Island
- **Rent-a-Room Hong Kong** (p265) – all the comforts of home, within spitting distance of Tsimsy
- **Salisbury** (p265) – YMCA reliability with views as rich as the Peninsula's, next door

All HKYHA hostels have separate toilets and showers for men and women, and cooking facilities, including free gas, refrigerators and utensils. They provide blankets, pillows and sheet bags, though you may prefer to take your own. Most hostels have lockers available.

Prices for a bed in a dormitory range from $30 to $65 a night, depending on the hostel and whether you are a junior (under 18 years of age) or senior member.

Only three of the hostels are open daily. Jockey Club Mount Davis Hostel (p254) allows check-in from 2pm till 11pm daily, while Bradbury Lodge (p270) and Hong-kong Bank Foundation SG Davis Hostel (p272) are open to guests from 4pm to 11pm Sunday to Friday and 2pm to 11pm on Saturday. The four other hostels usually open on Saturday night and the eve of public holidays only. All hostels are shut between 11pm and 7am and checkout is between 10am and noon on weekdays and between 11am and 1pm on Sunday. Travellers are not normally permitted to stay more than three days, but this can be extended if the hostel has room.

If making a booking more than three days in advance, ring or email the HKYHA head office. International computerised bookings are also possible. To reserve a bed less than three days before your anticipated stay, call the hostel directly. The phone numbers of the individual hostels are listed in the relevant sections of this chapter.

Rental Accommodation

A one-bedroom apartment in the Mid-Levels will cost anywhere from $10,000 a month. That same apartment will go for somewhat less in Tsim Sha Tsui or Wan Chai. The districts on eastern Hong Kong Island, western Hong Kong Island (eg Kennedy Town) and northeastern or northwestern Kowloon are more affordable – you may even find a one-bedroom apartment (roughly 60 sq metres) for as little as $4000 a month. The most expensive place is the Peak, where rents can easily top $100,000 a month. A guide to prices and availability can be found on the website www.gohome.com.hk.

Apartments are generally rented out with little or no furniture, but used furnishings can easily be bought from departing foreigners. Check the noticeboards at pubs and supermarkets, particularly around expatriate housing areas. Also check the classified advertisements of the weekend English-language papers and *HK Magazine* or the website www.asiaxpat.com. Estate agents usually take a fee equivalent to two weeks' rent. Other upfront expenses include a deposit, usually equal to two months' rent, and, of course, the first month's rent in advance.

Long-term accommodation on the Outlying Islands and in the Sai Kung area of the New Territories offers far better value than the equivalent on Hong Kong Island or in Kowloon. You can still rent a three-bedroom apartment with a roof terrace on Lamma for less than $7000 a month or a shared flat or room for as little as $2000 a month. Things to weigh in the balance, however, include transportation costs and the time spent commuting. A one-way ferry trip to Lamma, for example, costs a minimum of $11 from Monday to Saturday ($14 on Sunday) and takes 25 to 35 minutes. Allow 40 minutes to an hour (and $20) for the journey via the MTR and green minibus to Sai Kung from Central. Though nowhere near as cheap, Discovery Bay on Lantau's southeast coast is another affordable option.

Those staying in Hong Kong for between one and three months may be interested in serviced apartments: relatively high-priced flats that are rented out for the short term have become more and more common, particularly in and around Central. Some of these are listed in this chapter. Many hotels (eg Garden View International Hotel in Central, the Empire Hotel Hong Kong, Harbour View International House and Wharney Guangdong Hotel in Wan Chai, and the Caritas Lodge and YMCA International House in Yau Ma Tei) offer extraordinarily good-value, long-term packages at certain times throughout the year, depending on the season.

Sleeping

HONG KONG ISLAND

The lion's share of Hong Kong Island's luxury hotels are in Central and Admiralty and cater predominantly to the business market. Wan Chai and Causeway Bay count some top-end hotels as well, but the former is better for midrange accommodation and the latter for guesthouses, especially on or around Paterson St. During the low season, guesthouses often struggle to fill beds and rooms; most will offer discounts to anyone staying longer than a few nights.

CENTRAL, SOHO & THE MID-LEVELS

BAUHINIA FURNISHED SUITES

Map pp408-9   Serviced Apartments

☎ 2156 3000; www.apartments.com.hk; 119-120 Connaught Rd Central; per month 1-bedroom $13,000-18,000, 2-bedroom $17,000-36,000; Central MTR

This very central outfit has more than 110 furnished and serviced flats on offer. Prices usually depend on whether you want an open or enclosed kitchen, and include daily cleaning, broadband access, all cooking utensils and crockery, and laundry facilities. Enter from Man Wah Lane.

BISHOP LEI INTERNATIONAL HOUSE

Map pp408-9   Hotel

☎ 2868 0828; www.bishopleihtl.com.hk; 4 Robinson Rd, the Mid-Levels; s/d from $1080/1280, ste from $1880; bus 23 or 40

This 203-room hotel is not sitting in the lap of luxury and is a bit away from the action, but it is a short walk to the Zoological & Botanical Gardens and has its own swimming pool and gym. The rack rates are reduced by more than half during the low season, with standard singles and doubles quoted at under $500.

EDEN Map pp408-9   Hotel

☎ 2851 0303; 148 Wellington St, Central; s & d $750-1050; Central MTR

It may call itself a 'boutique hotel in Central', but with rates posted as '3 hours extended (sic) session' and the like, we know what this place is up to… Still, it is probably the most luxurious knock-up shop you've ever stayed in. Rooms are comfortable but small, with down-filled bedding, spa baths in some, and mirrors to inspect yourself from any and every angle. Now that will be something to write on the postcards.

GARDEN VIEW INTERNATIONAL HOUSE Map pp408-9   Hotel

☎ 2877 3737; www.ywca.org.hk; 1 MacDonnell Rd, Central; s & d from $1250, ste from $2300, biweekly/monthly packages from $7000/10,000; green minibus 1A

Straddling the border of Central and the Mid-Levels, the YWCA-run Garden View (133 rooms) overlooks the Zoological & Botanical Gardens. Accommodation here is plain but comfortable enough (there's good air-con) and there's an outdoor swimming pool on the roof. Daily rates drop substantially in the low season, typically from $600 to $750 for a single or double and from $1200 for a suite.

HANLUN HABITATS

Map pp408-9   Serviced Apartments

☎ 2868 0168; www.hanlunhabitats.com; 21st fl, Winway Bldg, 50 Wellington St, Central; Central MTR

This agency has three properties with serviced and furnished flats that are within striking distance of each other in the Mid-Levels and easily accessible via the Central Escalator to Central and Soho. Daisy Court (☎ 2533 7203; fax 2810 1870; 31 Shelley St, the Mid-Levels) has one-bedroom flats measuring about 45 sq metres for $16,500 to $19,500 a month, depending on the floor and the view. Peach Blossom (☎ 2234 8202; fax 2537 7080; 15 Mosque St, the Mid-Levels) has one- and two-bedroom flats of about 50 or 60 sq metres for between $24,000 and $32,000. Lily Court (☎ 2822 9508; fax 2521 9529; 28 Robinson Rd, the Mid-Levels) has two-bedroom flats of about 65 sq metres for between $20,500 and $28,000 a month.

ICE HOUSE Map p412   Serviced Apartments

☎ 2836 7333; www.icehouse.com.hk; 38 Ice House St, Central; 350/450-sq-m studios per night $700/900; Central MTR

In terms of location, this property is one of the coolest deals in Central. Situated next to the Fringe Club and up the hill from Lan Kwai Fong, Ice House has 64 standard and superior open-plan 'suites' spread over 13 floors that are bright, colourfully decorated, and have a small kitchenette and a work area with Internet access. It's become a favourite of visiting journalists, who water at the Foreign Correspondents' Club next door. The down side is that some of the rooms on the top floors are very noisy, and service at every level is cavalier at best. Weekly/monthly rates start at $4500/$12,000 in the low season.

MANDARIN ORIENTAL

Map pp408-9   Hotel

☎ 2522 0111; www.mandarinoriental.com; 5 Connaught Rd Central; s & d $2950-4200, ste from $5500; Central MTR

The Mandarin is not architecturally as impressive as its counterpart in Kowloon, the Peninsula, but it has a healthy dose of old-world charm. Styling is subdued – the décor in its 541 rooms and suites is just about to get a major makeover – and service, food and atmosphere are stellar throughout. If you're on business and want to give or get good face, splash out and stay here. Its restaurant **Vong** (p156), on the 25th floor, is renowned as much for its views as for its fusion food, and **Café** (p151) is the best hotel 'coffee shop' in town.

RITZ-CARLTON HONG KONG

Map pp408-9   Hotel

☎ 2877 6666; www.ritzcarlton.com; 3 Connaught Rd Central; s & d $3400-4600, ste from $7800; Central MTR

This is a truly beautiful hotel, with 245 plush guestrooms and suites that manage to be cosy and incredibly distinguished at the same time. Views from harbour-side rooms are – surprise, surprise – breathtaking, but the best view in the hotel may have to be the one from the outdoor pool. Lie back and soak up the skyline.

Cheap Sleeps

JOCKEY CLUB MOUNT DAVIS HOSTEL

Map pp406-7   Hostel

☎ 2817 5715; www.yha.org.hk; Mt Davis Path, Kennedy Town; dm under/over 18 $40/65, 2-/3-/4-/6-bed r $150/225/300/450; bus 5A, minibus 54

Hong Kong Island's only official hostel is a very clean and quiet 163-bed property on the top of Mt Davis, in the northwest part of the island. It has great views of Victoria Harbour and there are cooking and laundry

facilities, a TV and recreation room, and secure lockers. The only problem is that it's so far away from everything; call ahead to make sure there's a bed before you make the trek out. The hostel is open daily throughout the year; check-in time is from 2pm to 11pm. You can check out at noon any day of the week. Camping is prohibited here.

There are several ways to reach Jockey Club Mount Davis Hostel, depending on where you're coming from. The easiest way is to catch the hostel shuttle bus ($10) from the **Shun Tak Centre** (Map pp408-9; 200 Connaught Rd, Sheung Wan), from where the ferries to Macau depart, but there are only five departures a day: at 9.30am, 4.30pm, 7pm, 9pm and 10.30pm. (Buses leave the hostel for the Shun Tak Centre at 7.30am, 9am, 10.30am, 1pm and 6.30pm daily.) Alternatively, you can catch bus No 5A from Admiralty or minibus No 54 from the Outlying Islands ferry terminal and alight at Felix Villas, at the junction of Victoria Rd and Mt Davis Rd. From there, walk back 100m. Look for the hostel association sign and follow Mt Davis Path (not Mt David Rd). The walk is about 2km. A taxi from Central costs about $30.

YWCA BUILDING

Map pp408-9   Serviced Apartments

☎ 2915 2345; www.ywca.org.hk; 38C Bonham Rd, the Mid-Levels; s/d $440/880, ste from $1760, monthly packages from $6600; bus 23, 40 or 40M

This 99-room block of serviced apartments, arguably the only budget 'hotel' on the island, is not in the most convenient of locations, but it's accessible via bus Nos 23, 40 and 40M from Admiralty and Central, open to men and women, and reasonably cheap. There are TVs and phones with IDD in the rooms, a laundry and a decent coffee shop on the 1st floor. All rooms require minimum stay of seven nights.

ADMIRALTY & WAN CHAI

CHARTERHOUSE HOTEL

Map pp414-15   Hotel

☎ 2833 5566; www.charterhouse.com; 209-219 Wan Chai Rd, Wan Chai; s $950-1600, d $1500-1700, ste from $2000; Wan Chai MTR

This 277-room property on the leafy side of Wan Chai is a pretty good deal. You're almost getting top-end accommodation for midrange rates. And if you feel up to it, you can always sing for your supper at the fun Nightingale karaoke bar on the 2nd floor.

CONRAD HONG KONG

Map pp408-9   Hotel

☎ 2521 3838; www.conrad.com.hk; Pacific Place, 88 Queensway, Admiralty; s & d $2950-3650, ste from $5200; Admiralty MTR

This elegantly unstuffy 513-room hotel above Pacific Place gets enthusiastic reviews for its attention to business travellers' needs, and its restaurants Nicholini's (p166) and the Chinese Golden Leaf. The lobby lounge-bar is a gossipy, corporate hang-out.

COSMOPOLITAN HOTEL

Map pp414-15   Hotel

☎ 3552 1111; www.cosmopolitanhotel.com.hk; 387-397 Queen's Rd East, Wan Chai; s $1500-2300, d $1600-2500, ste from $3800; Wan Chai MTR

The Cosmopolitan, directly opposite the Happy Valley racetrack, is the place for punters. Once the headquarters of Xian Hua, the New China News Agency (thus the office block look, the oddly shaped rooms and the high ceilings), this new hotel caters to those with less-demanding tastes, though there are a couple of decent outlets, all 454 rooms have broadband and the eight themed suites have enormous plasma TV screens. One unique feature is a computer-generated machine that produces custom-made pillows for guests after

their specifications have been taken. Check the Internet for promotional rates that are often half the quoted ones.

EMPIRE HOTEL HONG KONG

Map pp414-15   Hotel

☎ 2866 9111; www.asiastandard.com; 33 Hennessy Rd, Wan Chai; s $1200-1800, d $1300-2000, ste from $2200, weekly/biweekly/monthly packages from $3850/7000/13,500; Wan Chai MTR

With its sunny staff, pleasant rooms, outdoor swimming pool and fitness centre on the 21st-floor terrace, and the basement Wu Kong Shanghai Restaurant (11am-11pm) – a branch of the more established one of that name in Tsim Sha Tsui (p181) – the 360-room Empire is a good option and an easy hop from the Hong Kong Convention & Exhibition Centre. Enter from Fenwick St.

GRAND HYATT HOTEL

Map pp414-15   Hotel

☎ 2588 1234; www.hongkong.hyatt.com; 1 Harbour Rd, Wan Chai; s $2600-4000, d $2650-4250, ste from $4400; bus 18

This hotel is one of the most sumptuous in town and as technologically up to date as any. Each of its 556 rooms is charged with a self-contained work station and enormous marble bath. Its gourmet Chinese restaurant One Harbour Road (p166) is celebrated with good reason, and the Champagne Bar (p202) is one of the classiest places to tipple in town. The stunning Plateau, a 7500-sq-metre spa complex with every treatment imaginable (available to both hotel guests and visitors), is an oasis on the 11th floor. The hotel also has 28 exclusive rooms and suites.

HARBOUR VIEW INTERNATIONAL HOUSE Map pp414-15   Hotel

☎ 2802 0111; www.harbour.ymca.org.hk; 4 Harbour Rd, Wan Chai; s $1200-1600, d $1200-1850, biweekly/monthly packages from $6300/12,000; bus 18

Right next door to the Hong Kong Arts Centre and a mere stroll to the Hong Kong Convention & Exhibition Centre and Wan Chai ferry terminal, this 320-room, YMCA-run hotel is excellent value. It offers simply furnished but adequate rooms, most of which look out over Victoria Harbour, and exceptionally friendly and helpful staff. Room rack rates drop by as much as 40% in the slower months.

Sleeping

HONG KONG ISLAND

ISLAND SHANGRI-LA HONG KONG

Map pp408-9   Hotel

☎ 2877 3838; www.shangri-la.com; Pacific Place, Supreme Court Rd, Admiralty; s $2400-3700, d $2600-3900, ste from $5800; Admiralty MTR
The 56-storey Shangri-La's sterile exterior conceals its swish sophistication; its 565 guestrooms are among the loveliest in Hong Kong. The hotel has a wonderful atrium and bubble lifts link the 39th and 56th floors. Take a quick ride up; you'll catch a glance of the hotel's signature 60m-high painting, a mountainous Chinese landscape said to be the largest in the world. Facilities include an outdoor spa and a 24-hour business centre. Among its fabulous outlets is the French restaurant **Petrus** (p166) and the innovative **Café TOO** (p164).

LUK KWOK HOTEL

Map pp414-15   Hotel

☎ 2866 2166; www.lukkwokhotel.com; 72 Gloucester Rd, Wan Chai; s $1500-1800, d $1650-1950, ste from $3600; bus 18
The original Luk Kwok, which featured as the Nam Kok brothel in *The World of Suzie Wong*, has long since been demolished and it's now a 196-room hotel housed in a not-unattractive modern tower block. There aren't that many frills or outlets here (business and fitness centres, a half-baked French restaurant), but the staff is eager to please and you're close to the convention centre and the bustle (and hustle) of Wan Chai.

RENAISSANCE HARBOUR VIEW HOTEL

Map pp414-15   Hotel

☎ 2802 8888; www.renaissancehotels.com; 1 Harbour Rd, Wan Chai; s & d $2500-3100, ste from $4000; bus 18
This spectacular, 860-room hotel adjoins the almost-in-the-water Hong Kong Convention & Exhibition Centre, ensuring steady suit-and-tie custom and marvellous harbour views from 65% of the guestrooms. Leisure travellers will appreciate turbaned doormen, informed concierges and some excellent outlets, including the Chinese restaurant **Dynasty** (p165) and the flashy nightclub **Manhattan Club Ing** (p209) on the 4th floor. The Harbour View has the largest outdoor pool of any hotel in town – naturally it looks over the harbour – and also has kiddies' pools.

SOUTH PACIFIC HOTEL HONG KONG

Map pp414-15   Hotel

☎ 2572 3838; www.southpacifichotel.com.hk; 23 Morrison Hill Rd, Wan Chai; s & d $1000-2000, ste from $2300; Wan Chai MTR
This flash, 272-room mirrored tower has a rather odd location in southern Wan Chai, but you'll be closer to the traditional back streets of the district and to the open green spaces around Queen Elizabeth Stadium. Just minutes away is Wan Chai and its nightlife.

WESLEY HONG KONG

Map pp408-9   Hotel

☎ 2866 6688; www.grandhotel.com.hk; 22 Hennessy Rd, Wan Chai; s & d $800-2000, monthly packages $8800-26,000; Wan Chai MTR
This central, 22-storey property with 251 rooms offers some of the best deals on the island, but there are very few facilities and the service is all but nonexistent. Rates depend on the size of the room: a 26-sq-metre Economy costs $800 and a 56 -sq-metre Deluxe Plus is $2000. Rates vary according to the season.

WHARNEY GUANGDONG HOTEL

HONG KONG Map pp414-15   Hotel

☎ 2861 1000; www.gdhhotels.com; 57-73 Lockhart Rd, Wan Chai; s & d $1000-1800, ste from $2400, weekly/monthly packages from $3300/10,800; Wan Chai MTR
Noteworthy for its rooftop swimming pool and outdoor whirlpool, the 358-room Wharney is a midrange option in the heart of Wan Chai with decent weekly and monthly packages. The so-called Departure Lounge bar offers a nice respite for weary departing guests awaiting late-night flights.

CAUSEWAY BAY
EXCELSIOR HONG KONG

Map pp414-15   Hotel

☎ 2894 8888; www.excelsiorhongkong.com; 281 Gloucester Rd; s & d $2100-2900, ste from $4000; Causeway Bay MTR
Part of the Mandarin Oriental Group of hotels – always a sure sign of quality – and a Causeway Bay landmark, this 884-room hotel offers some decent outlets, including the long-serving **Dickens Bar** (p203), fabulous harbour views and very convenient

shopping. With all the shops in the area, however, the lobby is always a bit of a madhouse.

EXPRESS BY HOLIDAY INN

Map pp414-15   Hotel

☎ 2295 6509; www.ichotelsgroup.com; 33 Sharp St East; s & d $600-1400; Causeway Bay MTR

Very much geared to business and other travellers on a budget, the 269-room Holiday Inn Express, located in a block next to the Times Square shopping mall, houses half a dozen fine eateries, including W's Entrecôte (p172), and delivers what it promises: consistent and affordable accommodation.

JIA Map pp414-15   Boutique Hotel

☎ 3196 9000; www.jiahongkong.com; 1-5 Irving St; s & d $1600, ste from $2400; Causeway Bay MTR

After a couple of false starts (cf Eden, Rosedale on the Park), Hong Kong has finally got a bona fide boutique hotel. And with French design guru Philippe Starck the inspiration behind it, 'Home' (its name in Mandarin) has created not just a splash but a tidal wave. The 57-room hotel has all sorts of Starck touches and whimsies – postmodern/baroque furnishings, the word 'Dream' emblazoned above the bed, a normal key to open the door, as well as the latest in music and Internet technology – but the rooms are a tad what Monsieur

Starck would call *serré* (cramped). Its two restaurants – Y's, a bistro serving Asian 'street food', and Opia, an Australian-style restaurant encompassing Asian fusion – no doubt will take Hong Kong by storm (as will the Shanghai Tang–designed staff uniforms).

METROPARK HOTEL

Map pp414-15   Hotel

☎ 2600 1000; www.metroparkhotel.com; 148 Tung Lo Wan Rd; s & d $900-1800, ste from $2600; Causeway Bay MTR

This flashy tower, overlooking Victoria Park and managed by a department of China Travel Service, makes the most of its easterly location, with 70% of its 243 rooms boasting sweeping city-harbour views through floor-to-ceiling windows. Openplan rooms offer generous workspace and broadband Internet for those who like to mix business with a bit of pleasure. Expect some substantial discounts – often 50% – during the low season.

PARK LANE HONG KONG

Map pp414-15   Hotel

☎ 2293 8888; www.parklane.com.hk; 310 Gloucester Rd; s & d $2000-3600, ste from $5000; Causeway Bay MTR

With restful views of Victoria Park to the east and the shoppers' paradise of Causeway

JIA (above), Causeway Bay

Bay to the west, the Park Lane is the perfect hotel for those who want to be both in and out of the action. Depending on the season, you should be able to get at least a third off the rack rate.

REGAL HONGKONG HOTEL

Map pp414-15   Hotel

☎ 2890 6633; www.regalhongkong.com; 88 Yee Wo St; s & d $2300-4000, ste from $6000; Causeway Bay MTR

Though double glazing keeps the traffic of busy Yee Wo St at bay, this 425-room Sino-baroque palace dripping with gilt may be a bit too central and, well, shiny for some. The rooftop Roman-style *piscina* (pool), all mosaics and columns supporting nothing, is over the top in the nicest possible way.

ROSEDALE ON THE PARK

Map pp414-15   Hotel

☎ 2127 8606; www.rosedale.com.hk; 8 Shelter St; s $1180-1480, d $1280-1580, ste from $1880/1980, weekly/monthly packages from $4300/15,800; Causeway Bay MTR

This property touts itself as Hong Kong's first 'cyber boutique hotel'. If the truth be known, it's a bit big for a boutique hotel, but its rooms are attractively appointed and its location opposite Victoria Park excellent. Each guestroom has broadband and the rooftop Sky Zone Lounge boasts a 'cyber corner'. Amazingly the hotel offers some generous weekly and monthly packages.

SHAMA Map pp414-15   Serviced Apartments

☏ 2202 5555; www.shama.com; 7th fl, 8 Russell St, Causeway Bay; studios per month from $17,000, 1-/2-bedroom apt per month from $23,500/60,500; Causeway Bay MTR

Among the most attractive serviced apartments in Hong Kong are these ones, in a block opposite Times Square shopping mall. Ranging from fairly spacious studio flats to two-bedroom apartments, they're all tastefully furnished and exceedingly comfortable. Features and extras include broadband Internet connection, VCD and DVD equipment, laundry facilities on each floor and membership to a half-dozen California Fitness Centres scattered around the territory. There are also branches in Central, Soho and Wan Chai; contact the **Shama main office** (Map p412; ☎ 2522 3082; www.shama.com; 8th fl, Wyndham Pl, 40-44 Wyndham St, Central) for details.

Cheap Sleeps

ALISAN GUEST HOUSE

Map pp414-15   Guesthouse

☎ 2838 0762; http://home.hkstar.com/~alisangh; Flat A, 5th fl, Hoito Ct, 275 Gloucester Rd; s $280-320, d $320-350, tr $390-450; Causeway Bay MTR

This excellent and spotlessly clean, family-run place has 21 rooms with air-conditioning, private showers and toilets, and Internet access. The multilingual owners are always willing to please and can organise China visas. Enter from 23 Cannon St.

CAUSEWAY BAY GUEST HOUSE

Map pp414-15   Guesthouse

☎ 2895 2013; www.cbgh.net; Flat B, 1st fl, Lai Yee Bldg, 44A-D Leighton Rd; s/d/tr $250/350/450; Causeway Bay MTR

On the south side of Causeway Bay and wedged between a pub and a church (enter from Leighton Lane), this comfortable, seven-room guesthouse can get booked up quickly so phone ahead. All rooms are quite clean and have private bathrooms.

CHUNG KIU INN Map pp414-15   Guesthouse

☎ 2895 3304; www.chungkiuinn.com.hk; Flat P, 15th fl, Hong Kong Mansion, 1 Yee Wo St; s $220-280, d $280-350, tr $400-450; Causeway Bay MTR

This hostel, with three dozen rooms spread over the 9th and 15th floors of the same building, is tidy but the rooms are small. Cheaper rooms with shared bathrooms are available. You may have trouble communicating as the owner speaks no English.

HONG KONG HOSTEL

Map pp414-15   Hostel, Guesthouse

☎ 2895 1015, 9353 0514; www.wangfathostel.com.hk; Flat A2, 3rd fl, Paterson Bldg, 47 Paterson St; dm $120, s/d/tr from $240/280/420; Causeway Bay MTR

This excellent 120-room series of ever-expanding hostels and guesthouses, incorporating the long-established **Wang Fat Hostel** on the same floor and the **Asia Hostel** on the 6th floor, is just about the best deal on Hong Kong Island. It's quiet and clean and most of the rooms have private phones, TVs and fridges. There are also cooking and laundry facilities, a computer room with three terminals offering free Internet access, safe-deposit boxes and phonecards for sale. Dorm rooms have between four and five beds. Cheaper rooms with shared bathrooms are available.

JETVAN TRAVELLERS' HOUSE

Map pp414-15   Guesthouse

☎ 2890 8133; jetvanhus@yahoo.com; Flat A, 4th fl, Fairview Mansion, 51 Paterson St; s & d $350, tr $450; Causeway Bay MTR

This rather cramped but upbeat place has 18 spotless rooms (those that have shared bathrooms incur cheaper rates) and a friendly owner.

NOBLE HOSTEL Map pp414-15   Guesthouse

☎ 2576 6148; www.noblehostel.com.hk; Flat A3, 17th fl, Great George Bldg, 27 Paterson St; s/d $280/340; Causeway Bay MTR

This is certainly one of the best-value guesthouses on Hong Kong Island. Each one of the 45 rooms is squeaky clean and is equipped with a private phone, fridge and air-conditioning. Some cheaper rooms have shared bathrooms.

ISLAND EAST
North Point
CITY GARDEN HOTEL HONG KONG

Map pp406-7   Hotel

☎ 2887 2888; www.citygarden.com.hk; 9 City Garden Rd; s & d $1100-2500, ste from $3600; Fortress Hill MTR

Readers have nice things to say about this 613-room, exceptionally well-turned-out hotel, not only for its service and generous discounting policy (biweekly/monthly packages from $8200/13,800), but also for

---

TOP FIVE HOTEL RESTAURANTS

- Hong Kong Old Restaurant (p173; Newton Hotel Hong Kong) – Shanghai surprises again and again
- Nadaman (p183; Kowloon Shangri-La) – probably the best Japanese food in town
- Spoon by Alain Ducasse (p180; Hotel Inter-Continental Hong Kong) – seeing (Michelin) stars over Hong Kong
- Vong (p156; Mandarin Oriental) – fusion food and views to die for (or over)
- Wan Loong Court (p181; Kowloon Hotel Hong Kong) – dim sum at its finest

---

the all-day barbecue ($78; ☺ noon-10.30pm) featuring Malaysian and Singapore flavours that's held in Garden Plus, the covered and leafy terrace fronting the hotel. The closest MTR stop is Fortress Hill (exit A) on the Island line. Enter the hotel from the corner of Electric Rd and Power St.

NEWTON HOTEL HONG KONG

Map pp414-15   Hotel

☎ 2807 2333; www.newtonhk.com; 218 Electric Rd; s & d $900-1600, ste from $2600; Fortress Hill MTR

This 362-room hotel, on the corner of Oil St, is a real find. Sure it's in less-than-sexy North Point, but the Fortress Hill MTR station (exit A) is just opposite, and you can easily walk to Causeway Bay through Victoria Park if you prefer. Its Hong Kong Old Restaurant (p173) has some of the best Shanghainese food in town.

KOWLOON

Kowloon is home to an incredible cross section of society, from the well-heeled residents of Kowloon Tong and Ho Man Tin to the tenement dwellers of Mong Kok and Kowloon City. Those with a sense of style and a lot of cash will also be impressed. Hong Kong's poshest hotel, the Peninsula, is here in Tsim Sha Tsui, within spitting distance of the infamous Chungking Mansions, a crumbling block stacked with dirt-cheap hostels and guesthouses. Of course, a huge range of other hotels and guesthouses can be found in Kowloon catering to all budgets between these two extremes.

When you mention the words 'hotel' and 'Hong Kong', many people think of the Peninsula, which opened in 1928 and is the matriarch of the territory's luxury hotels. Across from the Peninsula is the Inter-Continental, which has a much more modern feel to it and fabulous views. These are Kowloon's two 'face' hotels.

Tsim Sha Tsui East, an area of reclaimed land to the northeast of Tsim Sha Tsui, is weighted down with top-end hotels. It's not very convenient for the MTR, but the terminus of the KCR East Rail (East Tsim Sha Tsui station) is nearby and most of the hotels run shuttle buses to Tsim Sha Tsui proper and/or to Central. You'll find many more top-end hotels lining Nathan Rd as it travels north from the harbour.

TSIM SHA TSUI
BP INTERNATIONAL HOTEL
Map pp420-1   Hotel

☎ 2376 1111; www.bpih.com.hk; 8 Austin Rd; s & d $1000-2100, ste from $3100; Jordan MTR
This enormous, 535-room hotel, owned by the Scout Association of Hong Kong and named after Robert Baden-Powell, founder of the World Scout Movement, overlooks Kowloon Park from its northwest corner and is relatively convenient to most places of interest in Tsim Sha Tsui. The public areas are quite flash, the rooms dowdy but comfortable and some of the more expensive ones have good harbour views. There are family rooms with bunk beds available, making this a good option if you're travelling with kids. A self-service laundry room and free broadband access are on site. Haggle before you book; depending on the season and day of the week, prices are often reduced by 50%.

EMPIRE KOWLOON Map pp420-1   Hotel
☎ 2685 3000; www.asiastandard.com; 62 Kimberley Rd; s & d $1400-2200, ste from $2800; Tsim Sha Tsui MTR
This 302-room sister hotel of the Empire (p255) on Hong Kong Island houses state-of-the-art technical features, 'exciting' bathrooms, 'trendy excellent restaurants' and a truly magnificent indoor atrium swimming pool and spa. It's an easy stroll from here to just about anywhere in Tsimsy. Check the website for promotions.

GUANGDONG INTERNATIONAL HOTEL
Map pp420-1   Hotel

☎ 2739 3311; www.gdhhotels.com; 18 Prat Ave; s & d $1080-1680, ste from $2280; Tsim Sha Tsui MTR
This mainland-owned pile of grey polished granite has 245 rooms towering over the heart of Tsim Sha Tsui. Among its recently renovated outlets, the Cantonese restaurant King Palace (p179) is recommended.

HOLIDAY INN GOLDEN MILE
Map pp420-1   Hotel

☎ 2369 3111; www.goldenmile-hk.holiday-inn.com; 50 Nathan Rd; s $2100-3050, d/tw $2500-3150, ste from $5800; Tsim Sha Tsui MTR
The 600 guestrooms are pricey for what they are, but they're Holiday Inn reliable. Among the excellent outlets are the bril-

liant restaurant Avenue (p176) on the 1st floor, the schmoozy Hari's (p212) on the mezzanine level and Delicatessen Corner (p182) for all your picnic needs in the basement.

HOTEL INTER-CONTINENTAL
HONG KONG Map pp420-1   Hotel
☎ 2721 1211; www.hongkong-ic.intercontinental .com; 18 Salisbury Rd; s & d $3300-3900, ste from $5500; Tsim Sha Tsui MTR
The Hotel Inter-Continental is to rock stars what the Pen is to royalty. This hotel, which boasts arguably the finest waterfront position in the territory, tilts at modernity while bowing to colonial traditions, such as a fleet of navy-blue Rolls Royces, doormen liveried in white and incessant brass polishing. The emphasis on service ensures a lot of return custom. The restaurants – including the superb Yan Toh Heen (p181) and the renowned Spoon by Alain Ducasse (p180) – are top-class, and the Lobby Lounge bar has comfy armchairs and the best view in Hong Kong. Even if you don't stay here, drop by for a taste of its signature Nine Dragons Cocktail.

HOTEL MIRAMAR HONG KONG
Map pp420-1   Hotel

☎ 2368 1111; www.miramarhk.com; 118-130 Nathan Rd; s & d $1200-2000, ste from $3800; Tsim Sha Tsui MTR
This landmark (and very central hotel) is excellent value for its category and location. It has some fine outlets, including the restaurants Dong and Xi (p177), and the Miramar Shopping Centre is just across Kimberley Rd.

IMPERIAL HOTEL Map pp420-1   Hotel
☎ 2366 2201; www.imperialhotel.com.hk; 30-34 Nathan Rd; s $950-1700, d $1100-2000; Tsim Sha Tsui MTR
The 225 rooms with faded-pink bedspreads and bathrooms are prim, proper and squeaky clean. The hotel is so well located that the noise of Nathan Rd leaks right into the street-facing rooms – light sleepers should request a back room. It's no great shakes, but you won't do much better on Nathan Rd for this price.

KIMBERLEY HOTEL Map pp420-1   Hotel
☎ 2723 3888; www.kimberleyhotel.com.hk; 28 Kimberley Rd; s $1100-1750, d $1200-1850, ste from $2150; Tsim Sha Tsui MTR

The 546-room Kimberley Hotel isn't a glamorous property, but it's one of the better midrange hotels in Tsim Sha Tsui. You'll find assured staff and good rooms and facilities, including golf nets and a fabulous hot and cold spa bath. The lobby, a leafy and cool oasis up from the bustle, is on the 2nd floor. Summer rates are half the quoted ones.

KNUTSFORD Map pp420-1   Hotel
☎ 3119 0088; www.knutsfordhotel.com; 39 Kimberley Rd; s & d $950-1800, ste from $2600; Tsim Sha Tsui MTR
This 166-room hotel, formerly the Royal Windsor, is ideally situated for anyone intending to do a lot of shopping in Tsimsy. The hotel wins an award for the inspired name of its lounge bar: Bonkers (☒ 4.30pm-2am, happy hour 4.30-8pm).

KOWLOON HOTEL HONG KONG
Map pp420-1   Hotel
☎ 2929 2888; www.thekowloonhotel.com; 19-21 Nathan Rd; s $1300-2550, d $1400-2650, ste from $3600; Tsim Sha Tsui MTR
Part of the Peninsula stable, the 736-room Kowloon Hotel has an 'also ran' feel about it, with its over-the-top lobby and views of the back of the Peninsula. Nevertheless, the hotel is popular for its unflappable service, decent rooms and the wonderful restaurant Wan Loong Court (p181), located in the basement. Rates drop dramatically off season.

LANGHAM HOTEL HONG KONG
Map pp420-1   Hotel
☎ 2375 1133; www.langhamhotels.com/langham /hongkong; 8 Peking Rd; s & d $2200-3600, ste from $6000; Tsim Sha Tsui MTR
The elder sister of the Langham Place Hotel (p267), the 488-room Langham is a five-star hotel in the heart of Tsim Sha Tsui. It has some stunning outlets of its own and is just round the corner from the restaurants and bars of Ashley and Peking Rds.

MARCO POLO HONGKONG HOTEL
Map pp420-1   Hotel
☎ 2113 0088; www.marcopolohotels.com; Harbour City, 3-9 Canton Rd; s & d $2450-3750, ste from $4900; Star Ferry, Tsim Sha Tsui MTR
The 664-room Marco Polo Hongkong is the linchpin in the Marco Polo Hotel group's Canton Rd trio, all of which are in

the Harbour City complex. The first, the Marco Polo Hongkong, is closest to the Star Ferry and the most highly priced; it has an outdoor pool and plenty of shopping in the attached mall. The 433-room Marco Polo Gateway (Map pp420–1; 13 Canton Rd; s $2050-2350, d $2150-2450, ste from $3650) is a flash hotel with good business facilities, while the smaller Marco Polo Prince (Map pp420–1; 23 Canton Rd; s $2050-2350, d $2150-2450, ste from $3650), at the northern end of Harbour City, is the slick little sister, with 394 smart rooms.

MINDEN Map pp420-1   Hotel
☎ 2739 7777; www.theminden.com; 7 Minden Ave; s & d $900-1500, ste from $2500; Tsim Sha Tsui MTR
This almost boutique 64-room hotel, on recently pedestrianised Minden Ave, is chock-a-block with Asian and Western antiques, curios and furnishings accumulated by owner and pack rat Robert WH Wand. It's an odd mixture but comfortable (the sofas are stuffed with goose down) in a personalised, eclectic kind of way. The Drawing Room, used for meetings and functions, looks as though it was moved lock, stock and barrel from an English stately home. Courtney's (p204) is a welcome addition to Tsim Sha Tsui's surprisingly meagre selection of quality watering holes.

PARK HOTEL Map pp420-1   Hotel
☎ 2366 1371; www.parkhotel.com.hk; 61-65 Chatham Rd South; s $1100-1900, d $1200-2000, ste from $2600; Tsim Sha Tsui MTR
An ongoing renovation at this 430-room hotel has seen standards (and prices) go up. Family suites are available from $4000, the history and science museums are just over the road and the hustle of Granville Rd is a block away. Enter from Cameron Rd.

PENINSULA HONG KONG
Map pp420-1   Hotel
☎ 2920 2888; www.peninsula.com; Salisbury Rd; s & d $3000-4900, ste from $5600; Tsim Sha Tsui MTR
Lording it over the southern tip of Kowloon, Hong Kong's finest hotel evokes colonial elegance and actually does resemble an oversized throne. Some 300 classic European-style rooms boast Internet access, CD and DVD players, as well as the requisite (and sumptuous) marble bathrooms. Many

rooms in the Pen's 20-storey annexe offer spectacular harbour views; in the original building, you'll have to make do with the glorious interior décor. Some of the outlets, such as the French restaurant **Gaddi's** (p178), the fusion **Felix** (p205) and the Cantonese **Spring Moon** (p180) are the best eating spots of their class in the territory.

PINNACLE APARTMENT

Map pp420-1   Serviced Apartments

☎ 2734 8288; www.pinnacleapartment.com; 8 Minden Ave; per month 1-bedroom apt $15,800-24,500, 2-bedroom apt $22,200-35,000; Tsim Sha Tsui MTR

This elegant block of serviced apartments, on lively Minden Ave in the heart of the Tsim Sha Tsui nightlife area, has four different size apartments available ranging in size from 47 to 90 sq metres. Some have harbour views. The staff here is delightful.

ROYAL PACIFIC HOTEL & TOWERS

Map pp420-1   Hotel

☎ 2736 1188; www.royalpacific.com.hk; China Hong Kong City, 33 Canton Rd; s $1180-2500, d $1280-2600, ste from $2500; Tsim Sha Tsui MTR

Choose between cheaper rooms in the hotel wing or flashier rooms in the harbour-facing tower – some 675 in total. The location is convenient: there's a walkway to Kowloon Park, leading onto Nathan Rd and the MTR station. At the back, the hotel is connected to the ferry terminal from where boats sail to Macau and China. It's also a mere skip to the shopping overkill of Harbour City. You'll find reception on the 3rd floor.

SHERATON HONG KONG HOTEL &

TOWERS Map pp420-1   Hotel

☎ 2369 1111; www.sheraton.com/hongkong; 20 Nathan Rd; s $2200-4200, d $2400-4400, ste hotel/towers from $4200/5600; Tsim Sha Tsui MTR

This very American 782-room hostelry (the ground floor is the 1st floor, escalators travel on the right), at the start of Nathan Rd, is as central as you'll find in Tsim Sha Tsui. Choose between rooms in the hotel or the towers, which offer superior harbour views (and higher prices). The **Sky Lounge** (p205), on the 18th floor, is worth a visit for the stunning harbour views. Reception is on the 2nd floor.

STANFORD HILLVIEW HOTEL

Map pp420-1   Hotel

☎ 2722 7822; www.stanfordhillview.com; 13-17 Observatory Rd; s & d $880-1580, ste from $2380; Tsim Sha Tsui MTR

This 163-room hotel is a very good choice, set back from Nathan Rd in a quiet, leafy little corner of Tsim Sha Tsui, but just down the road from the food, fun and frolicking of Knutsford Tce. The rooms are forgettable but clean and well-maintained. Enter from Knutsford Tce.

Cheap Sleeps

Say 'budget accommodation' and 'Hong Kong' in the one breath and everyone thinks of **Chungking Mansions** (Map pp420–1; 36-44 Nathan Rd, Tsim Sha Tsui; Tsim Sha Tsui MTR), a place like no other in the world. This huge, ramshackle high-rise dump of a place in the heart of Tsim Sha Tsui caters for virtually all needs – from finding a bed and a curry lunch to buying a backpack and getting your hair cut – and more.

You may be put off by the undercurrent of sleaze and the peculiar odours – a potent mixture of cooking fat, incense and shit – but don't seek sanctuary in the lifts; they're like steel coffins on cables. Perhaps the best introduction to Chungking is Wong Kar Wai's cult film *Chungking Express* (1994), which captures all the sleaze in a haunting series of stories.

For years there had been talk about tearing down this eyesore and fire trap. A crackdown on fire-safety violations finally came at the end of 1993, and many guesthouses were forced to shut down. Others survived by upgrading and installing smoke

---

TOP FIVE HOTEL BARS

- **Champagne Bar** (p202; Grand Hyatt Hotel) – bubbly and blues
- **Courtney's** (p204; Minden) – original artwork five floors above the madness
- **Dickens Bar** (p203; Excelsior Hong Kong) – still the place for a pint in CB
- **Felix** (p205) – Hong Kong's swishest gin palace, bar none
- **Sky Lounge** (p205; Sheraton Hong Kong Hotel & Towers) – where things take off, before and after a cocktail

alarms, sprinklers and walls made of fire-proof material. The block is now partially under renovation.

Much of the character of Chungking Mansions has changed. Many of the guesthouses now serve as long-term boarding houses for workers from developing countries in the Indian subcontinent and Africa, and matchbox rooms are often occupied by two, three or even four people. Backpackers have started migrating to guesthouses in other buildings, but Chungking Mansions is still the cheapest place to stay in Hong Kong and the place to meet fellow travellers and zany characters. One thing travellers should really guard against is drugs; a few grams of hashish in your backpack could leave you in a lot of trouble.

The entrance to Chungking Mansions is via Chungking Arcade, a parade of shops that faces Nathan Rd. You will find lifts labelled A to E with hostels in each block listed. There are just two cramped and over-worked lifts for each 17-storey block, and long queues form at 'rush hour'. Otherwise there're always the less-than-salubrious stairs. Be grateful for the stray cats as they keep the rats in check.

Despite the dilapidated appearance, most of the little guesthouses are OK – generally clean and often quite comfortable, though rooms are usually the size of cupboards. Standards do, however, vary; your best bet is to opt for the hotels that have a high percentage of foreign travellers.

Bargaining for a bed or room is always possible, though you won't get very far in the high season. You can often negotiate a cheaper price if you stay more than, say, a week, but never try that on the first night – stay one night and find out how you like it before handing over more rent. Once you pay, there are usually no refunds. Always be sure to get a receipt; paying for a room in advance so that you can have it on a certain day is not advised.

The rooms will typically come with air-conditioning and TV, although the phones are often communal and located in the lobby. Local telephone calls are free from residential phones in Hong Kong, so be suspicious if staff charge you. Many guesthouses can get you a Chinese visa quickly, most have Internet access and some have a laundry service. Also, be prepared for varying levels of English fluency among guesthouse owners and concierges. Mobile phone numbers have been included here as many of the guesthouse owners and managers engage in all sorts of other businesses and often lock their establishments during the day.

Chungking Mansions is also a cheap place to eat Indian and other subcontinental food (see p182).

Chungking Mansions is not the only budget block in Tsim Sha Tsui. **Mirador Mansion** (Map pp420–1; 58-62 Nathan Rd, Tsim Sha Tsui; Tsim Sha Tsui MTR), above an arcade of that name between Mody and Carnarvon Rds, is a scaled-down version of Chungking Mansions, but considerably cleaner and roomier. Much of the back-packer clientele has moved here in recent years, with the result that there can be heavy queues for the lifts during peak hours. **Golden Crown Court** (Map pp420–1; 66-70 Nathan Rd, Tsim Sha Tsui; Tsim Sha Tsui MTR), opposite the southeast corner of Kowloon Park, has undergone a transformation in recent years and now offers a host of clean, smart guesthouses.

CHUNGKING HOUSE

Map pp420-1   Guesthouse

☎ 2366 5362; chungkinghouse@yahoo.com.hk; 4th & 5th fls, A Block, Chungking Mansions, 36-44 Nathan Rd; s $150-250, d $250-350; Tsim Sha Tsui MTR

This place covering two floors – with two receptions and a total of 80 rooms – is pretty swish by the standards of Chungking Mansions.

COSMIC GUEST HOUSE

Map pp420-1   Hostel, Guesthouse

☎ 2369 6669; info@cosmicguesthouse.com; Flats A1-A2, F1-F4, 12th fl, Mirador Mansion, 58-62 Nathan Rd; dm $60, s & d $160-200, big d $220-240; Tsim Sha Tsui MTR

This is a very clean and quiet guesthouse with big and bright rooms and a very helpful owner. The security is top grade.

DRAGON INN Map pp420-1   Guesthouse

☎ 2368 2007; dragoninn@netvigator.com; Flats B3 & B5, 3rd fl, B Block, Chungking Mansions, 36-44 Nathan Rd; s/d/tr $150/200/300; Tsim Sha Tsui MTR

This super spotless and relatively large (21 rooms) place doubles as the Dragon International Travel Agency, with cheap air tickets and other services available in-house.

Sleeping

KOWLOON

FIRST-CLASS GUEST HOUSE

Map pp420-1   Guesthouse

☎ 2724 0595; fax 2724 0843; Flat D1, 16th fl, Mirador Mansion, 58-62 Nathan Rd; s/d $160/200; Tsim Sha Tsui MTR

While its name may be a little ambitious, the First-Class Guest House is hygienic and fresh and the staff friendly. All 20 rooms have private bathrooms.

GARDEN GUEST HOUSE

Map pp420-1   Guesthouse

☎ 2368 0981, 9057 5265; Flat C5, 16th fl, C Block, Chungking Mansions, 36-44 Nathan Rd; s $120, d $150-180; Tsim Sha Tsui MTR

This is a clean place much favoured by backpackers. There's another **branch** (☎ 2366 0169; Flat C5, 7th fl) in the same block.

GARDEN HOSTEL

Map pp420-1   Hostel, Guesthouse

☎ 2311 1183; fax 2721 2085; Flat F4, 3rd fl, Mirador Mansion, 58-62 Nathan Rd; dm $60, s & d with shower $200, d with shared shower $180; Tsim Sha Tsui MTR

This place is owned by the irrepressible Sam 'Mr Kung Fu' Lau, who also runs **Wing Chun Yip Man Martial Arts Athletic Association** (p222). It's a great place for meeting other travellers and the open terrace is a delight on a warm evening. There are laundry facilities, the lockers are like Fort Knox and the staff speaks good English.

GOLDEN CROWN GUEST HOUSE

Map pp420-1   Guesthouse

☎ 2369 1782; fax 2368 1740; Flats B2 & H, 5th fl, Golden Crown Court, 66-70 Nathan Rd; s/d $250/280; Tsim Sha Tsui MTR

This sanitary place, one of the better guesthouses in Golden Crown Court, was recently renovated and has a pleasant owner. There are a total of eight rooms.

HUNG KIU GUEST HOUSE

Map pp420-1   Guesthouse

☎ 2312 1505, 9370 2325; fax 2311 4258; Flat C3, 8th fl, Mirador Mansion, 58-62 Nathan Rd; s $120, d $180-200; Tsim Sha Tsui MTR

This is a relatively new and very clean place with a affable and helpful young Chinese manager.

KYOTO GUEST HOUSE

Map pp420-1   Guesthouse

☎ 2721 3574, 9077 8297; Flat A8, 15th fl, A Block, Chungking Mansions, 36-44 Nathan Rd; s with shared shower $80, d & tw with private shower from $130; Tsim Sha Tsui MTR

This guesthouse, run by Mrs Kam, is basic but comfortable.

LILY GARDEN HOSTEL

Map pp420-1   Hostel, Guesthouse

☎ 2724 2612, 9053 2900; fax 2312 7681; Flat A9, 3rd fl, Mirador Mansion, 58-62 Nathan Rd; dm $70, s $150-250, d $200-300, tr $250-350; Tsim Sha Tsui MTR

Lily Garden has small but tidy rooms. It is part of a group of guesthouses under the same management as the **New Osaka Guest House** (☎ 2724 2612; Flat F2, 5th fl), also in Mirador Mansion. Go directly to either or visit **reception** (☎ 2606 7778) in shop 18 on the ground floor of Mirador Mansion.

LUCKY GUESTHOUSE

Map pp420-1   Guesthouse

☎ 2367 3522, 9373 8779; fax 2367 3325; Flat A11, 7th fl, Mirador Mansion, 58-62 Nathan Rd; s/d/tr $150/200/300; Tsim Sha Tsui MTR

This eight-room place is shipshape and the owner speaks excellent English.

MAN HING LUNG HOTEL

Map pp420-1   Guesthouse

☎ 2722 0678, 2311 8807; http://home.hkstar .com/~mhlhotel; Flat F2, 14th fl, Mirador Mansion, 58-62 Nathan Rd; s $120-150, d $150-200, tr $210-240; Tsim Sha Tsui MTR

This decent place, which likes to call itself a hotel, has clean rooms, broadband and laundry facilities. If you need a roommate to share costs, the very friendly manager, Mr Chan, will put you in with another traveller for $80. He can also arrange China visas.

NEW SHANGHAI GUEST HOUSE

Map pp420-1   Guesthouse

☎ 2311 2515; Flat D2, 16th fl, D Block, Chungking Mansions, 36-44 Nathan Rd; s/d $150/260; Tsim Sha Tsui MTR

This is an old-style guesthouse run by pleasant Mrs Cheung. It's clean and there's a laundry service.

PARK GUEST HOUSE

Map pp420-1   Guesthouse

☎ 2368 1689; fax 2367 7889; Flat A1, 15th fl,
A Block, Chungking Mansions, 36-44 Nathan Rd;
s with shared bathroom $108, s/d with private
bathroom $120/150; Tsim Sha Tsui MTR

All 45 rooms in this welcoming guesthouse
have air-con. It comes recommended by
readers. Room 1509 has a sliver of a sea
view.

PEKING GUEST HOUSE

Map pp420-1   Guesthouse

☎ 2723 8320, 9464 3684; fax 2366 6706;
Flat A1-A2, 12th fl, A Block, Chungking Mansions,
36-44 Nathan Rd; s $120-150, d $150-200, tr $280;
Tsim Sha Tsui MTR

Peking has friendly management, the place
is spotless and all rooms have a bathroom.

RENT-A-ROOM HONG KONG

Map pp420-1   Guesthouse

☎ 2366 3011, 9023 8022; www.rentaroomhk.com;
Flat A, 2nd fl, Knight Garden, 7-8 Tak Hing St, Tsim
Sha Tsui; dm $150, s/d/tr/q with shared bathroom
from $300/360/480/600, with private bathroom
from $350/450/700/900; Jordan MTR

This fabulous place, run by Thomas Tang,
has 50 positively immaculate rooms in a
block around the corner from the Jordan
MTR station. Each room has TV, telephone
(no charge for local calls), high-speed Internet access and a fridge.

SALISBURY Map pp420-1   Hostel, Hotel

☎ 2268 7000; www.ymcahk.org.hk; 41 Salisbury Rd;
dm/s $210/675, d $750-950, ste from $1300;
Star Ferry

If you can manage to book a room at the
YMCA-run Salisbury, you'll be rewarded
with professional service and excellent
exercise facilities, including a six-lane swimming pool and fitness centre on the 1st
floor and a climbing wall on the 2nd floor.
The 365 rooms and suites are comfortable
but simple so keep your eyes on the harbour; that view would cost you at least five
times as much at the Peninsula next door.
The four-bed dormitory rooms on the 9th
floor are a bonus, but there are restrictions:
check-in is at 2pm; no-one can stay more
than seven consecutive nights; and walk-in
guests aren't accepted if they've been in
Hong Kong for more than 10 days.

Salisbury (below), Tsim Sha Tsui

SEALAND HOUSE Map pp420-1   Guesthouse

☎ 2368 9522; www.sealandhouse.com.hk; Flat D,
8th fl, Majestic House, 80 Nathan Rd; s $250-300,
d $280-380; Tsim Sha Tsui MTR

This eight-room place, towering above
Nathan Rd, is small but clean and very
bright. It's a good independent choice over
the guesthouses in Mirador or Chungking
Mansions. Enter from Cameron Rd.

STAR GUEST HOUSE

Map pp420-1   Guesthouse

☎ 2723 8951; www.starguesthouse.com; Flat B,
6th fl, 21 Cameron Rd; s/d with shared bathroom $220/
250, s/d with private bathroom $250/300, tr with
private bathroom $400-450; Tsim Sha Tsui MTR

This excellent guesthouse and its sister
property just up the road, the **Lee Garden
Guest House** (Map pp420–1; ☎ 2367 2284;
charliechan@iname.com; 8th fl, D Block, 36
Cameron Rd), with a total of 45 rooms, are
owned and run by the charismatic Charlie
Chan, who can arrange most things for you,
including China visas ($300) delivered in a
day. Long-term stayers get good discounts.

Sleeping   KOWLOON

TOM'S GUEST HOUSE

Map pp420-1   Guesthouse

☎ 2722 6035, 9194 5923; fax 2366 6706; Flat B7, 16th fl, B Block, Chungking Mansions, 36-44 Nathan Rd; s $130-160, d $150-250; Tsim Sha Tsui MTR

Tom's, a clean, friendly and popular place, can also be entered from C Block (Flat C1, 16th fl). There's another large branch located in A Block (☎ 2722 4956; Flat A5, 8th fl) so you should always be able to find a room here.

TRAVELLERS HOSTEL

Map pp420-1   Hostel, Guesthouse

☎ 2368 7710; mrspau@yahoo.com.hk; Flat A1-A4, 16th fl, A Block, Chungking Mansions, 36-44 Nathan Rd; dm $60-65, s/d with shared shower $80/100, d with private shower $120; Tsim Sha Tsui MTR

This popular hostel is a landmark in this building, and cooking facilities, cable TV, student discounts and Internet access are available. The Travellers Hostel is probably the best place to meet fellow travellers in Chungking Mansions.

WELCOME GUEST HOUSE

Map pp420-1   Guesthouse

☎ 2721 7793, 9838 8375; guesthousehk@hotmail .com; Flat A5, 7th fl, A Block, Chungking Mansions, 36-44 Nathan Rd; s with shared shower $100, s with private shower $120-150, d with private shower $180-200; Tsim Sha Tsui MTR

This place is a cut above the rest in Chungking Mansions and its name says it all. The owner, John Wah, is exceptionally friendly, speaks excellent English and operates a small souvenir shop and gem showroom on site. What's more, it has a laundry service.

YAN YAN GUEST HOUSE

Map pp420-1   Guesthouse

☎ 2366 8930, 9489 3891; fax 2721 0840; Flat E1, 8th fl, E Block, Chungking Mansions, 36-44 Nathan Rd; s $100-130, d $150-200; Tsim Sha Tsui MTR

This is one of the last of the Chinese-owned guesthouses in the overwhelmingly subcontinental E Block of Chungking Mansions. The swish New Yan Yan Guesthouse (☎ 2723 5671; Flat E5, 12th fl), in the same block, is managed by the same people.

TSIM SHA TSUI EAST & HUNG HOM

GRAND STANFORD INTER-CONTINENTAL

Map pp420-1   Hotel

☎ 2721 5161; www.hongkong.intercontinental.com; 70 Mody Rd, Tsim Sha Tsui East; s & d $2500-3300, ste from $4000; bus 5C or 8

This 579-room, five-star palace is one of the nicest top-range hotels in Tsim Sha Tsui East and offers excellent discounts, depending on the season and the day of the week. Unfortunately part of its harbour view is marred by the unsightly Hung Hom Bypass.

HARBOUR PLAZA METROPOLIS

Map pp420-1   Hotel

☎ 3160 6888; www.harbour-plaza.com/hpme; 7 Metropolis Dr, Hung Hom; s $1600-2700, d $1700-2800, ste from $3200; bus 5C or 8

Directly behind the Hong Kong Coliseum and just southeast of the Hung Hom train station, this 690-room hotel is the place to stay if you expect to be travelling into China at the crack of dawn or attending a lot of late-night concerts. It has everything you would expect of a hotel in this category; the Metropolis Mall, to which it is connected by walkway, is an extra. Reception is on Level 7.

HOTEL NIKKO HONGKONG

Map pp420-1   Hotel

☎ 2739 1111; www.hotelnikko.com.hk; 72 Mody Rd, Tsim Sha Tsui East; s & d $2000-3000, ste from $5000; bus 5C or 8

Another almost faceless Tsim Sha Tsui East hotel, this time with 462 guestrooms and loads of tourists from the mainland. It's not a very efficiently run place, but the harbour views are striking.

KOWLOON SHANGRI-LA

Map pp420-1   Hotel

☎ 2721 2111; www.shangri-la.com; 64 Mody Rd, Tsim Sha Tsui East; s $2500-4050, d $2700-4250, ste from $4300; bus 5C or 8

This 700-room extravaganza is almost (but not entirely) as swish as its sister hotel in 'new' Wan Chai, the Island Shangri-La Hong Kong (p256), but the views and its eight bars and restaurants, including the superb French **Margaux** (p183) and the Japanese **Nadaman** (p183) are stunning. We love the enormous murals of imperial Chinese scenes in the lobby.

REGAL KOWLOON HOTEL
Map pp420-1   Hotel

☎ 2722 1818; www.regalhotel.com; 71 Mody Rd, Tsim Sha Tsui East; s & d $1400-2500, ste from $4000; bus 5C or 8

This 600-room, somewhat cheesy hotel, in a block rising up for 15 storeys, is a bargain by Tsim Sha Tsui East standards, but the oatmeal and blush-pink décor that seems to sneak into every room and outlet may grate.

ROYAL GARDEN HOTEL
Map pp420-1   Hotel

☎ 2721 5215; www.rghk.com.hk; 69 Mody Rd, Tsim Sha Tsui East; s $2100-2600, d $2250-2750, ste from $3700; bus 5C or 8

The 422-room Royal Garden, often overlooked, gets our vote for being the best-equipped hotel in Tsim Sha Tsui East and one of the territory's most attractive options. From the chic blonde-wood-and-chrome lobby and atrium to the rooftop sports complex (25m pool, putting green and tennis court with million-dollar views), the Royal Garden kicks ass. **Sabatini** (p183), on the 3rd floor, is one of the best Italian restaurants in Hong Kong.

YAU MA TEI & MONG KOK
DORSETT SEAVIEW HOTEL
Map p423   Hotel

☎ 2782 0882; www.dorsettseaview.com.hk; 268 Shanghai St, Yau Ma Tei; s $880-1280, d $1280-1580, ste from $2400; Yau Ma Tei MTR

This hotel does a big trade in group tours from China. The 257 guestrooms in this tall, thin building are fine, and the Temple St and Jade Markets and Nathan Rd retail area are all within easy reach. The Tin Hau temple is practically outside the front door.

EATON HOTEL
Map pp420-1   Hotel

☎ 2782 1818; www.eaton-hotel.com; 380 Nathan Rd, Yau Ma Tei; s & d $1750-4100, ste from $3100; Yau Ma Tei MTR

This 468-room, recently upgraded hotel in the huge New Astor Plaza complex has a grand lobby and a number of fine outlets, including the glass-fronted **Planter's Bar** (☎ 2710 1866; ☽ 4pm-1am Mon-Thu, 5pm-2am Fri-Sat, happy hour 5-9pm) on the 4th floor, where you'll also find reception and a delightfully leafy courtyard just off it. Booking on the Internet can halve the quoted rates. Enter the hotel from Pak Hoi St.

LANGHAM PLACE HOTEL
Map p423   Hotel

☎ 3552 3388; www.langhamhotels.com/langhamplace/hongkong; 555 Shanghai St, Mong Kok; s & d $2200-3000, ste from $3500; Mong Kok MTR

Peering out from one of the 665 guestrooms of this colossal tower hotel, you'd never suspect for a moment that you were in Mong Kok. It's a triumph for the district and special guestroom features include multifunction IP phones, DVD players, marble bathrooms with 'rain shower' plus bath, and room safes that can fit (and recharge) a laptop. **Ming Court** (p184) serves excellent dim sum. Reception is on the 4th floor and the hotel is linked to the **Langham Place Mall** (p247).

MAJESTIC HOTEL Map pp420-1   Hotel
☎ 2781 1333; www.majestichotel.com.hk; 348 Nathan Rd, Yau Ma Tei; s & d $950-1850, ste from $3000; Yau Ma Tei MTR

This 387-room hotel, housed in a 15-storey glass tower, is just north of the Jordan MTR station (enter the Majestic from Saigon St). Reception is on the 1st floor. Excellent-value weekly/monthly packages are available for $3430/10,800.

METROPOLE HOTEL
Map pp418-19   Hotel

☎ 2761 1711; www.metropole.com.hk; 75 Waterloo Rd, Yau Ma Tei; s & d $900-1700, ste from $3500; Mong Kok KCR East Rail, Yau Ma Tei MTR

This 487-room baroque palace, managed by a China Travel Service department, is a bit out of the way, but has some excellent facilities, including a huge outdoor swimming pool on the roof and the coffee shop, **Palm Court** (p184). Check out the 50m-wide mural *Magnificent China* rising above the podium. Seasonal promotions will lower the quoted rates by at least 35%.

NATHAN HOTEL Map pp420-1 Hotel
☎ 2388 5141; www.nathanhotel.com; 378 Nathan Rd, Yau Ma Tei; s & d $880-1280, ste from $1480; Yau Ma Tei MTR

The partially renovated Nathan Hotel is surprisingly quiet and pleasant; even the cheapest of its 166 rooms are spacious, clean and serene. It's in a good location, right near the Jordan MTR station and Temple St; we like the moustachioed and turbaned doorman. Enter from Pak Hoi St.

NEWTON HOTEL KOWLOON
Map p423 Hotel
☎ 2787 2338; www.newtonkln.com; 66 Boundary St, Mong Kok; s & d $750-1200, ste from $2200; Prince Edward MTR

If you don't mind being in a noisy neighbourhood, the Prince Edward MTR is an easy five-minute walk from this 168-room hotel and you're close to the Mong Kok market, clothes stalls and noodle shops. The hotel itself is reasonable for the price – no surprises here – but is not of the same standard as its sister property, the Newton Hotel Hong Kong (p259) in North Point.

ROYAL PLAZA HOTEL
Map p423 Hotel
☎ 2928 8822; www.royalplaza.com.hk; 193 Prince Edward Rd West, Mong Kok; s & d $1580-1800, ste from $3200; Mong Kok KCR East Rail

The plushness is a bit overdone, but the 671-room Royal Plaza is comfortable and central; the bird and flower markets are on the other side of Prince Edward Rd. The heated no-steam bathroom mirrors are a stroke of genius, the large outdoor pool with underwater music is a lounge lizard's nirvana and some rooms have kitchenettes. The Mong Kok KCR station is accessible through the adjoining Grand Century Place shopping centre, making this a handy spot if you've business in the New Territories or China. Its Japanese restaurant Sakurada (p184) is excellent.

SHAMROCK HOTEL
Map pp420-1 Hotel
☎ 2735 2271; www.shamrockhotel.com.hk; 223 Nathan Rd, Yau Ma Tei; s $900-1500, d $1100-1700, ste from $2500; Yau Ma Tei MTR

The Shamrock offers decent value for its category and location; the quoted rates are rarely what you'll pay. The beds can be a bit spongy and the décor pedestrian, but the 158 guestrooms are well sized, clean and airy, and there are excellent kitsch lounges outside the lifts. Jordan MTR is right outside the door and there's a decent seafood restaurant on site.

STANFORD HOTEL
Map p423 Hotel
☎ 2781 1881; www.stanfordhongkong.com; 118 Soy St, Mong Kok; s $780-1480, d $830-1480; Mong Kok MTR

This 194-room hotel is equidistant from the Mong Kok MTR and KCR stations and a hop, skip and a jump to the bird and flower markets.

YMCA INTERNATIONAL HOUSE
Map p423 Hostel, Guesthouse
☎ 2771 9111; www.ymcaintlhousehk.org; 23 Waterloo Rd, Yau Ma Tei; dm $220, s & d $680-1180, ste from $1600; weekly/monthly packages from $3000/8500; Yau Ma Tei MTR

Though a bit out of the way, the 427-room YMCA, with all the mod cons, is a steal for what it offers, so book well in advance. It is open to men and women.

Cheap Sleeps
New Lucky House (Map pp420–1; 300-306 Nathan Rd, Yau Ma Tei), with its main entrance on Jordan Rd, is a block with a heap of hostels and guesthouses in a slightly better neighbourhood than the places further south in Tsim Sha Tsui. Accommodation located here includes the Hakka's, Ocean and Overseas guesthouses.

ANNE BLACK GUEST HOUSE
Map pp418-19 Guesthouse
☎ 2713 9211; www.ywca.org.hk; 5 Man Fuk Rd, Yau Ma Tei; s & d with shared bath $350-600, with private bathroom $400-1000, monthly packages from $6600; Yau Ma Tei MTR

This 169-room, YWCA-run guesthouse, which accommodates both women and men, is located near Pui Ching and Waterloo Rds in Mong Kok, behind and uphill from a petrol station. There are laundry facilities and a decent restaurant here and conveniently almost half of the rooms are singles.

BOOTH LODGE Map p423   Guesthouse
☎ 2771 9266; http://boothlodge.salvation.org.hk; 11 Wing Sing Lane, Yau Ma Tei; s & d $640-1500; Yau Ma Tei MTR

Run by the Salvation Army, this 53-room place is Spartan and clean but comfortable too. Promotional rates for standard singles and doubles are a rock-bottom $420 to $540. Rates include breakfast. Reception is on the 7th floor.

CARITAS BIANCHI LODGE
Map p423   Guesthouse
☎ 2388 1111; cblresv@bianchi-lodge.com; 4 Cliff Rd, Yau Ma Tei; s/d/tr $720/820/1020; s weekly/monthly packages from $2240/7500, d from $2450/8400; Yau Ma Tei MTR

This 90-room hotel-cum-guesthouse is run by a Catholic social-welfare organisation. Though it's just off Nathan Rd (and a goalie's throw from Yau Ma Tei MTR station), the rear rooms are very quiet and some have views onto King's Park. All rooms have private bathroom and breakfast is included. Promotional rates throughout the year bring rates down as low as $360/410/510 for a single/double/triple.

CARITAS LODGE
Map pp418-19   Guesthouse
☎ 2339 3777; reservation@caritas-lodge.com; 134 Boundary St, Mong Kok; s/d/tw $350/400/560, s weekly/monthly packages from $1960/5940, d from $2310/7140; Mong Kok KCR East Rail

With just 40 rooms, this place is a lot smaller and just as nice as its sister-guesthouse, Caritas Bianchi Lodge, but it's a bit further afield. Still, you couldn't get much closer to the bird market, and the New Territories is (officially) just across the road. Breakfast is included in the price of the room.

HAKKA'S GUEST HOUSE
Map pp420-1   Guesthouse
☎ 2771 3656; fax 2770 1470; Flat L, 3rd fl, New Lucky House, 300 Nathan Rd, Yau Ma Tei; s $200-250, d $250-300, tr $300-350; Jordan MTR

This is the nicest guesthouse of those found in New Lucky House and each of the nine ultraclean guestrooms has a telephone, TV, air-con and shower. The affable and helpful owner, Kevin Koo, is a keen hiker and he will often invite guests out along with him for country walks on Sunday.

NEW KINGS HOTEL
Map p423   Hotel
☎ 2780 1281; newkings@netvigator.com; 473 Nathan Rd, Yau Ma Tei; s $550-600, d $650-750; Yau Ma Tei MTR

The newly upgraded New Kings Hotel may look somewhat off the track, but it's hard by the Yau Ma Tei MTR station (you enter the hotel from Wing Sing Lane). It's a smallish (72 rooms) but long-established place and the Temple Street night market is nearby.

OCEAN GUEST HOUSE
Map pp420-1   Guesthouse
☎ 2385 0125; fax 2771 4083; Flat G, 11th fl, New Lucky House, 300 Nathan Rd, Yau Ma Tei; s/d $200/250; Jordan MTR

All eight rooms in this rather comfy place have TVs, telephone, air-con and private shower.

OVERSEAS HOUSE
Map pp420-1   Guesthouse
☎ 2384 5079; fax 2780 9831; Flat G, 9th fl, New Lucky House, 300 Nathan Rd, Yau Ma Tei; s/d $180/250; Jordan MTR

This place is clean and friendly. Though it no longer contains an in-house travel agency, it can still arrange China visas for travellers.

NEW TERRITORIES

The New Territories does not offer travellers a tremendous choice in terms of accommodation, but there are five official and independent hostels, usually to be found in the more remote parts of the region. Remember, too, that walkers and hikers can pitch a tent at any one of 28 New Territories camp sites managed by the **Country & Marine Parks Authority** (☎ 2420 0529; http://parks.afcd .gov.hk).

TSUEN WAN

PANDA HOTEL Map p424 | Hotel

☎ 2409 1111; www.pandahotel.com.hk;
3 Tsuen Wah St; s $850-1550, d $1000-1700,
ste from $1600/1750, weekly/monthly packages
from $3388/8388; Tsuen Wan MTR

This 1025-room hotel, the largest in the
New Territories by far, has some decent
outlets, including the restaurant **Grand
Buffet** (p186). The Panda is less than 1km
southeast of the Tsuen Wan MTR station. To
reach it, take exit B2 from the MTR station,
head south down Tai Ho Rd then turn left
on Tsuen Wan Market St, which leads into
Kwan Mun Hau St. Enter from Kwan Mun
Hau St; reception is on the 3rd floor.

TAI MO SHAN

SZE LOK YUEN HOSTEL

Map pp404-5 | Hostel

☎ 2488 8188; www.yha.org.hk; camping members/
nonmembers $16/25, dm under/over 18 years $30/45;
bus 51

This 92-bed hostel, a few kilometres north
of Tsuen Wan, is usually only open on
Saturday and on the eve of public holidays (telephone the HKYHA in advance on
☎ 2788 1638). It's in the shadow of Hong
Kong's highest peak and at this elevation
it can get pretty chilly at night so come
prepared. There are cooking facilities, but
you should buy food supplies while in
Tsuen Wan as none are available at the
hostel. Check-in is usually from 2pm to
11pm. To get here take bus No 51 from the
Tsuen Wan MTR station (exit A) and alight
at Tai Mo Shan Rd. Follow Tai Mo Shan Rd
for about 4kms, pass the car park and turn
onto a small concrete path on the right-
hand side. This leads directly to the hostel.

TAI MEI TUK

BRADBURY LODGE

Map pp404-5 | Hostel

☎ 2662 5123; www.yha.org.hk; 66 Tai Mei Tuk Rd;
dm under/over 18 years $35/55, d/q $150/240;
bus 75K

Bradbury Lodge (not to be confused with
Bradbury Hall in Sai Kung) is the HKYHA's
flagship hostel in the New Territories. It has
94 beds and is open seven days a week
year-round. Check-in is from 4pm to 11pm

(from 2pm on Saturday). Bradbury Lodge is
next to the northern tip of the Plover Cove
Reservoir dam wall, a few hundred metres
south of Tai Mei Tuk. Camping is not permitted here.

SHA TIN

ASCENSION HOUSE

Map p425 | Hostel

☎ 2691 4196; www.achouse.com; 33 Tao Fong
Shan Rd; dm $125; Sha Tin KCR East Rail

This 11-bed place, affiliated with the Lu-
theran Church, is one of the best deals in
Hong Kong as the price of a bed includes
free laundry service and three meals. To
get here, take the KCR East Rail to Sha Tin
station, leave via exit B and walk down
the ramp, passing a series of old village
houses on the left. Between them is a
set of steps. Go up these, follow the path
and when you come to a roundabout, go
along the uphill road – Pak Lok Path – to
your right. After about 150m you'll come
to a small staircase and a sign pointing
the way to Ascension House on the right.
When you reach the fork in the path and
the Tao Fong Shan Christian Centre, bear
to the right and you'll soon come to more
steps leading up to Ascension House.
The walk should take between 15 and 20
minutes. A taxi from the station in Sha Tin
will cost around $20.

REGAL RIVERSIDE HOTEL

Map p425 | Hotel

☎ 2649 7878; www.regalhotel.com; 34-36 Tai Chung
Kiu Rd; s & d $1200-2300, ste from $3500; Sha Tin
KCR East Rail

This 830-room hotel overlooks the Shing
Mun River, northeast of Sha Tin town centre. It has quite a spacious health club and
a large outdoor swimming pool on a leafy
terrace. Special promotions can cut quoted
rates in half.

ROYAL PARK HOTEL

Map p425 | Hotel

☎ 2601 2111; www.royalpark.com.hk;
8 Pak Hok Ting St; s & d $1200-1800, ste from $2800;
Sha Tin KCR East Rail

The 448-room Royal Park is next to the
New Town Plaza shopping mall. Its **Royal Park
Chinese Restaurant** (☎ 2601 2111, ext 3939;
🕑 lunch 11am-3pm Mon-Sat, 9am-3pm Sun,

dinner 6-11pm), on the 2nd floor, is one of the best in Sha Tin. It has dim sum continuously on Sunday. Special deals and packages are available on the Internet.

SAI KUNG PENINSULA
BRADBURY HALL
Map pp404-5   Hostel
☎ 2328 2458; www.yha.org.hk; Chek Keng, Sai Kung; camping members/nonmembers $16/25, dm under/over 18 years $30/45; bus 94
This 92-bed HKYHA hostel is right on the harbour facing Chek Keng pier. In the past it's been open at the weekend and on the eve of public holidays only; telephone the HKYHA on ☎ 2788 1638 in advance to check. To reach Chek Keng by bus from Sai Kung town, catch No 94 headed for Wong Shek and alight at Pak Tam Au (it's the fourth bus stop after the entrance to Sai Kung Country Park near the top of a hill). Take the footpath at the side of the road heading east and walk for about half an hour to Chek Keng. Bradbury Hall is another 10 minutes to the northeast.

PAK SHA O HOSTEL
Map pp404-5   Hostel
☎ 2328 2327; www.yha.org.hk; Hoi Ha Rd, Sai Kung; camping members/nonmembers $16/25, dm under/over 18 years $30/45; bus 94
This large HKYHA hostel with 112 beds is southwest of Hoi Ha Bay and the marine park. Like Bradbury Hall, it too is not open every day. Call the HKYHA on ☎ 2788 1638 for details. To reach the hostel, take bus No 94 from Sai Kung town and get off at Ko Tong village. Walk about 100m along Pak Tam Rd and turn left onto Hoi Ha Rd. A sign about 30m ahead shows the way to Pak Sha O. Count on walking for 30 to 40 minutes. A taxi from Sai Kung will cost $95.

OUTLYING ISLANDS
There are not many hotels per se on the Outlying Islands, though you'll find one each on Lamma and Cheung Chau and several on Lantau. There are guesthouses on these three islands as well.

During the warmer months and at the weekends throughout most of the year, estate agencies set up booking kiosks for rental apartments and holiday villas near the ferry piers on Cheung Chau and at Mui Wo (Silvermine Bay) on Lantau.

The HKYHA has two hostels on Lantau, and the **Country & Marine Parks Authority** (☎ 2420 0529; http://parks.afcd.gov.hk) maintains 10 basic camp sites for hikers along the Lantau Trail and a single one on Tung Lung Chau.

LAMMA
BALI HOLIDAY RESORT
Map p426   Holiday Homes
☎ 2982 4580; fax 2982 1044; 8 Main St, Yung Shue Wan; s/d Sun-Fri $280/380, Sat $560/760; Lamma (Yung Shue Wan) ferry
An agency rather than a resort as such, Bali Holiday Resort has a total of some 30 studios and apartments sprinkled around the island. All have TVs, fridges and air-con and some have sea views.

CONCERTO INN
Map p426   Hotel
☎ 2982 1668, 2836 3388; www.concertoinn .hk; 28 Hung Shing Yeh Beach, Hung Shing Yeh; Sun-Fri s & d $480-630, tr & q $730, Sat & public holidays s & d $780-930, tr & q $1060; Lamma (Yung Shue Wan) ferry
This beachfront hotel, southeast of Yung Shue Wan, is quite some distance from the action, so you should stay here only if you really want to get away from it all. There's also a decent café-restaurant (p191).

JACKSON PROPERTY AGENCY
Map p426   Holiday Homes
☎ 2982 0606, 9055 3288; fax 2982 0636; 15 Main St, Yung Shue Wan; Lamma (Yung Shue Wan) ferry
This property agency has studios and apartments for rent on Lamma. All of them have TVs, private bathrooms, microwaves and fridges; some also offer sea views. The cost starts at $250 per night for two people from Sunday to Friday and goes up to between $450 and $500 on Saturday.

MAN LAI WAH HOTEL
Map p426   Guesthouse
☎ 2982 0220; ericiris123@netvigator.com; 2 Po Wah Garden, Yung Shue Wan; r Mon-Fri $300-350, Sat & Sun $500; Lamma (Yung Shue Wan) ferry
This eight-room hotel (or, rather, guesthouse) greets you as you get off the ferry

and begin to walk up Main St. All rooms have air-con and private shower and some have little balconies.

CHEUNG CHAU

Cheung Chau is not particularly well set up for overnighters. Depending on the day of the week and the season, up to half a dozen booths just opposite the ferry pier and another couple north along Praya St rent out studios and apartments. There is also the Warwick Hotel on Tung Wan Beach.

CHEUNG CHAU
ACCOMMODATION KIOSKS

Map p428   Holiday Homes

Cheung Chau Ferry Pier; Cheung Chau ferry
Agents with booking kiosks on the Cheung Chau *praya* include **Bela Vista** (☎ 2981 7299), **Island Resorts** (☎ 2981 3201) and **Cheung Chau Holidays** (☎ 2981 6623), but unless you have a smattering of Cantonese or a Chinese friend in tow, you may have difficulty getting what you want at a fair price (though there are photo albums illustrating what's on offer both outside and in). Expect to pay from $180 to $200 a night for a studio accommodating two people from Sunday to Friday, and from $300 to $400 on Saturday.

WARWICK HOTEL Map p428   Hotel

☎ 2981 0081; www.warwickhotel.com.hk;
**Cheung Chau Sports Rd, Tung Wan Beach;
s & d with mountain/sea view Mon-Fri $620/690,
Sat & Sun $890/990, ste from $1320/1890,
weekly/monthly packages from $3500/12,000;
Cheung Chau ferry**
This six-storey, 71-room carbuncle on the butt of Tung Wan Beach is the only game in town, but it does offer wonderful views across the sea to Lamma and Hong Kong Islands. Ignore the rack rates; heavy discounts are available here.

LANTAU

As on Lamma and Cheung Chau during the summer, and at weekends the rest of the year, you can rent holiday rooms and apartments from kiosks set up at the Mui Wo ferry pier.

The HKYHA has two hostels on Lantau, one a stone's throw from the Tian Tan Bud-

dha in Ngong Ping and the other in a remote area of the Chi Ma Wan Peninsula. The hostels are open to HKYHA/HI cardholders only, but membership is available if you pay the nonmember's rate for six nights here or at other HKYHA hostels.

You can also find another three decent accommodation options along Silvermine Bay Beach.

HONGKONG BANK FOUNDATION
SG DAVIS HOSTEL

Map p427   Hostel

☎ 2985 5610; www.yha.org.hk; Ngong Ping;
**camping members/nonmembers $16/25, dm under/
over 18 years $30/45, d $150; bus 2, 21 or 23**
This 46-bed hostel (open daily) is a 10-minute walk from the bus stop near the Tian Tan Buddha statue in Ngong Ping and is the ideal place to stay if you want to watch the sun rise at nearby Lantau Peak. Check-in is from 4pm to 11pm (from 2pm on Saturday). From the bus stop, take the paved path to your left as you face the Tian Tan Buddha, pass the public toilets on your right and the Lantau Tea Garden on your left and follow the signs to the mazelike steps going up to the hostel. If you visit in winter be sure to bring warm clothing for the evenings and early mornings.

JOCKEY CLUB
MONG TUNG WAN HOSTEL

Map p427   Hostel

☎ 2984 1389; www.yha.org.hk; Mong Tung Wan;
**camping members/nonmembers $16/25, dm under/
over 18 years $30/45; bus 1, 4, 7P or A35**
This tranquil, 88-bed property, along the waterfront on the southeastern side of the Chi Ma Wan Peninsula, is jointly operated by the HKYHA and the Hong Kong Jockey Club. In the past it's been open at the weekend and on the eve of public holidays only, so telephone the HKYHA on ☎ 2788 1638 in advance for advice. From Mui Wo, take bus 1, 4 or 7P (or bus A35 from Hong Kong International Airport) and jump out at Pui O. Follow the footpath across the fields from the bus stop and continue along Chi Ma Wan Rd until it leaves the sea edge. At a sharp bend in the road at Ham Tin, turn right onto the footpath by the sea and follow it to the hostel – about a 45-minute walk. Alternatively, you can take

a ferry to Cheung Chau and hire a sampan (this should cost about $150, it will be more in the evening) to the jetty at Mong Tung Wan.

LONG COAST SEASPORTS

Map p427   Guesthouse

☎ 2980 3222; www.longcoast.hk; 29 Lower Cheung Sha Village; r Sun-Thu $280, Fri & Sat $400; weekly package from $1600; bus 1, 2 or 3

This new windsurfing centre (see p134) offers basic accommodation in four double rooms with private bathrooms, two of which (rooms 1 and 4) have sea views. The catch is you must become a member of LCS ($500) to stay here, but the first night's accommodation is free. It can organise beachside barbecues for $90 per person and use of broadband is $20 per day.

MUI WO ACCOMMODATION KIOSKS

Map p429   Holiday Homes

Mui Wo Ferry Pier; Lantau ferry

Kiosks run by Brilliant Holiday (☎ 2984 2662) and others let out rooms and apartments on Lantau and have photos of them on display. Expect to pay $150 on weekdays and $250 at the weekend for a double room or studio. Not all the places are in Mui Wo (ie within walking distance of the ferry pier); many are along Cheung Sha Beach and in Pui O village.

MUI WO INN Map p429   Hotel

☎ 2984 7225; fax 2984 1916; Tung Wan Tau Rd, Silvermine Bay Beach; s & d Sun-Fri $280-350, Sat $400-520; Lantau ferry

This 20-room place is the last hotel on the beach and can be identified by the ring of faux-classical statues in front. It's a bit ragged around the edges but is a friendly place to stay. Rates include breakfast.

REGAL AIRPORT HOTEL

Map p427   Hotel

☎ 2286 8888; www.regalhotel.com; 9 Cheong Tat Rd, Hong Kong International Airport; s & d $2400-4500, ste from $6000; Airport Express

A simple undercover shuffle from the airport terminal is this stylish hotel with more than 1100 sleek and easily accessible rooms, many with futuristic runway views. There's a splashy indoor/outdoor pool complex, half a dozen restaurants and fun

Pui O Beach, in front of Treasure Island on Lantau (p274), Lantau

games rooms (one for adults, one for kids). Soundproofing ensures the only noise is that of your own making. Rooms available for day use (six hours between 8am and 10pm) cost $700 or $800, depending on the season.

SEAVIEW HOLIDAY RESORT

Map p429   Hotel

☎ 2984 8877; fax 2984 8787; 11 Tung Wan Tau Rd, Silvermine Bay Beach; d/tr/q Sun-Fri $250/300/400, Sat $350/400/600; Lantau ferry

The Seaview is by far the cheapest place to stay along the beach, but it is not as nice as the other two hotels here.

SILVERMINE BEACH HOTEL

Map p429   Hotel

☎ 2984 8295; www.resort.com.hk; Tung Wan Tau Rd, Silvermine Bay Beach; s & d $880-1380, monthly packages from $6000; Lantau ferry

This 128-room hotel (the 'Savoy' of Mui Wo) has rooms that look out to the hills, sideways to the bay and directly onto the bay. A good-value barbecue buffet is held in the coffee shop and Chinese restaurant in the evening, and there's an attractive pool. Eschew the rooms in the South Wing for those in the superior New Wing. Rates are negotiable, depending on the day of the week and the season.

TREASURE ISLAND ON LANTAU

Map p427   Guesthouse

☎ 2546 3543, 9645 8871; www.treasureislandhk .com; Pui O Beach; r Sun-Thu $500, Fri & Sat $700; bus 1, 2, 3 or 7P

This little guesthouse and Ooh La La! restaurant (p195), directly on the beach in Lower Cheung Sha village, offers basic accommodation (including breakfast) in six rooms.

Excursions ◼

Shenzhen   277
Zhuhai   282

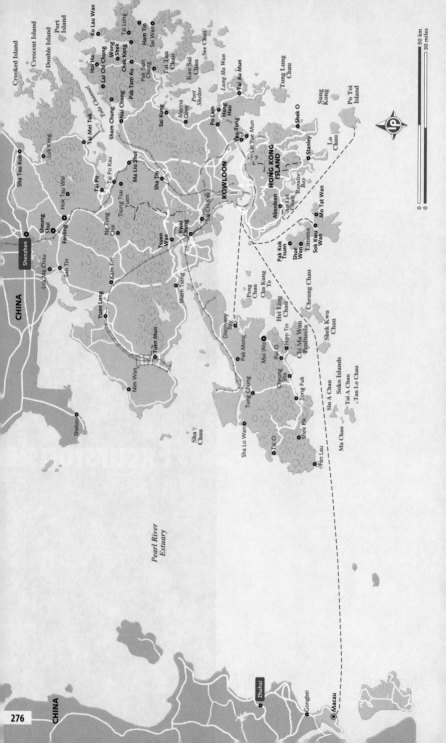

Excursions

Within very easy reach of Hong Kong and Macau are two of China's five original 'Special Economic Zones': Shenzhen and Zhuhai. The two could hardly be more different. While the former is a temple to Mammon, with an edgy, almost lawless feel to it, Zhuhai is a laid-back and very green university city. Both offer bargain shopping, cut-rate services (massage, manicures, tailoring etc) and a glimpse at the direction in which 21st-century China is heading.

SHENZHEN

Shenzhen (population 752,200), the 'Special Economic Zone' (SEZ) straddling the Hong Kong border to the north, is China's richest city. It is a restricted zone and, in theory, Chinese nationals require a special pass even to enter it, much less live and work there. The majority of foreigners who come here are on business or looking for bargains at the innumerable factory outlets and shops. If you buy your visa ($150) at the border with Hong Kong (not recommended due to the queues), your stay will be limited to the confines of the Shenzhen SEZ only and valid for just five days. Without a proper Chinese visa (p306), you cannot travel north into the rest of China, not even to Guangzhou. The border is open from 6.30am to midnight.

Shenzhen was no more than a tiny fishing village when it won the equivalent of the National Lottery and became a SEZ in 1980. Developers added a stock market, international hotels and towering office blocks and the world as Shenzhen knew it came to an abrupt end. Indeed, the only fishnets you're likely to see in these parts nowadays will be on the legs of the city's formidable hordes of hookers.

City centre, Shenzhen (above)

Nowadays Shenzhen – the name refers to Shenzhen City (Shēzhèn Shì in Mandarin), opposite the border crossing at Lo Wu (Luóhú), the Shenzhen SEZ and Shenzhen County (Shēzhèn Xiàn), which extends several kilometres north of the SEZ – is essentially an extended shopping mall for Hong Kong residents, much to the chagrin of the SAR's retailers. It's also a good place for cheap (legitimate and otherwise) massage and dim sum. It's true that Shenzhen has been a fabulous commercial success, but it remains a place without much culture or spirit. Still, it's an easy way to have a glimpse at the mainland and there are a few things to see and do.

In Litchi Park (Lìzhī Gōngyuán), **Shenzhen Museum**, contains some 20,000 jade, porcelain and bronze artefacts and has halls devoted to ancient Shenzhen, zoology and underwater life.

Shenzhen Art Gallery, in Donghu Park (Dōnghú Gōngyuán) to the northeast, for the most part hosts special exhibits, usually modern Chinese art.

Some 12km to the east of Shenzhen City is one of the world's most unusual attractions: a 40,000-ton decommissioned Soviet aircraft carrier called **Minsk World**, complete with choppers and MiG fighter planes parked on the deck. You can scramble up and down the ship's five levels, viewing sailors' bunks, old propaganda posters, exhibits on space travel and missiles, missiles and more missiles. Real *Boy's Own* stuff, this.

Shenzhen Sea World, further east and about 30km from the centre, is chock-a-block with aquariums and tanks filled with creatures from the briny deep. Most people come to see the shows and performances here, though: trapeze acts, dancing with sharks, dolphin synchronised swimming and so on.

SIGHTS & ACTIVITIES	(p280)
Diwang Commercial Building 地王商业大厦	(see 4)
Gen Gen 根根	(see 12)
Jian Fu Mei Health & Beauty Centre 靓富美	(see 12)
Mang Bing Massage Centre 盲병	(see 12)
Shenzhen Museum 深圳博物馆	1 A2

EATING	🍴 (p281)
BBC Restaurant	(see 12)
Chow Phaya Thai Restaurant 昭帕耶泰国餐馆	2 D2
Food Stalls	3 C2
Friday Café 星期五咖啡	4 B2
King Elephant Restaurant 金象皇粤菜楼	(see 12)
Laurel (branch)	(see 12)
Laurel 丹桂轩	(see 13)
Noodle King 面点王	5 C2
Noodle King 面点王	6 C1
Ocean King Restaurant 海上皇酒家	7 C2
Taj Indian Restaurant	8 C2

DRINKING	(p280)
BJ'zz.com Bar	9 D2
Henry J Bean's Bar & Grill	(see 17)

ENTERTAINMENT	(p280)
Bar Leo	(see 10)
Citic City Plaza 中信城市广场	10 A2
Class Club	(see 13)

SHOPPING	(p280)
Dongmen Market 东门市场	11 D1
Luohu Commercial City 罗湖商业城	12 C3

SLEEPING	🛏 (p281)
Century Plaza Hotel 新都酒店	13 C2
Gold Hotel 富丽华大酒店	14 D1
Guangdong Hotel 粤海酒店	15 D2
Petrel Hotel 海燕大酒店	16 C2
Shangri-La Hotel 香格里拉大酒店	17 C3
Shenzhen Hotel 深圳酒店	18 C2
Wah Chung International Hotel 华中国际酒店	19 C2

TRANSPORT	(p282)
Buses to Shekou	20 C2
Local Bus Station	21 C3
Local Minibuses	22 C3
Luohu Bus Station 罗湖汽车站	(see 12)
Shenzhen Train Station 深圳火车站	23 C3
Taxi Stands	24 C3

INFORMATION	(p279)
Bank of China (branch) 中国银行分行	25 C2
Bank of China 中国银行	26 C3
China Travel Service Shenzhen 深圳中国旅行社	27 C2
HSBC 汇丰银行	28 C2
Post Office 邮局	29 C1
Public Security Bureau 公安局	30 B1
Shenzhen Grandland International Travel Agency 深圳市巨邦国记旅行社	(see 18)
Shenzhen Tourist Information Centre 深圳市游客咨询处	31 C3

Some 15km west of Shenzhen City and about halfway to the port of Shekou (Shékǒu) are several theme parks, with everything from a miniature Great Wall and an Eiffel Tower 'that stands erect' to a 'bird's view of thousands of years of Chinese culture'. They're pretty naff, but it's always a treat to watch other people having fun. You can walk between the theme parks easily enough, but a mini-monorail run by the **Shenzhen Happy Line Tour Co** links the three as well as several other sights.

Splendid China is a hum-drum assembly of China's sights in miniature. Contiguous to Splendid China and included in the admission price, **China Folk Culture Village** recreates two dozen ethnic minority villages and a number of dwellings. Famous monuments of the world are scrutinised at **Window of the World**, the next park over.

Of course, for Hong Kong people Shenzhen is mostly about shopping (see the boxed text, p280) and shoppers' first port of call should be **Luohu Commercial City**, which greets you as you emerge from customs and immigration. Here there are corridors after corridors of stalls selling ceramics, curios, knockoff handbags, clothing and DVDs. Retail shops are open 10.30am to 8.30pm but hairdressers, massage parlours etc usually open earlier and close later.

As well as shopping, Luohu Commercial City offers all sorts of services – from massage and facials to hair styling and nail painting. Two of the best places for massage are **Mang Bing Massage Centre** on the 2nd floor and **Jian Fu Mei Health & Beauty Centre** on the 4th floor. The latter also does excellent facials. **Gen Gen** on the 3rd floor specialises in reflexology. Try the foot massage.

Popular for tailored suits and skirts, electronic goods, custom-made drapes and cheap ready-to-wear is the area around **Dongmen Market**, which is just off Dongmen Lu. Be warned that this is pickpocket territory so keep your valuables safe. An invaluable book to guide you is the recently updated *Shop in Shenzhen: An Insider's Guide* ($95/US$12) by Ellen McNally, available in bookshops throughout Hong Kong and online from Amazon.

Finding a venue for a quiet drink or a raucous knees-up after a hard day of shopping and bargaining is easy. Most of the top-end hotels have international-style bars, including **Henry J Bean's Bar & Grill** at the Shangri-La Hotel, with occasional live music, and **BJ'zz.com Bar** at the Shenzhen Landmark Hotel, with a resident jazz band playing nightly. **Class Club** at the Century Plaza, with an LED wall and two separate halls, is one of the most popular dance clubs in Shenzhen. In town there's also a bunch of places on 'Bar St' below Citic City Plaza (Zhōngxìn Chéngshì Guǎngchǎng), including **Bar Leo**. To the north, under the stands at Shenzhen City Stadium, a club called **Chicago Club** has become a Shenzhen institution.

Further afield in the port of Shekou are a number of bars frequented by locals and resident expats alike, including **McCawley's Irish Bar & Restaurant**, with a great rooftop beer garden, **Soho Restaurant & Night Club**, a popular dance club with super, up-to-date décor, and **X-Ta-Sea**, a raucous American-style sports bar with a couple of pool tables, darts and large dance floor.

Information

Bank of China (Zhōngguó Yínháng; 23 Jianshe Lu; ☺ 8.30am-5pm Mon-Fri, 9am-4pm Sat & Sun); **Heping Lu branch** (Zhōngguó Yínháng Fēnháng; 1197 Heping Lu; ☺ 8.30am-5pm Mon-Sat) You can use either Chinese renminbi (or yuan, abbreviated 'Y') or Hong Kong dollars in Shenzhen, but if you choose the latter make sure you get your change back in Hong Kong currency, which is worth about 6%.

China Travel Service Shenzhen (CTS; Zhōngguó Lǚxíngshè Shēnzhèn; ☎ 0755-8225 8447; 3023 Renmin Nanlu; ☺ 9am-6pm)

HSBC (Renmin Nanlu; ☺ 9am-5pm Mon-Fri) This branch of the Hong Kong bank is on the east side of the Century Plaza Hotel.

Internet Access You can get onto the Internet at most of the hotels listed in this chapter for an average Y10 per hour.

Post office (Yóujú; 3002 Jianshe Lu; ☺ 9am-8pm)

Public Security Bureau (PSB; gōng'ānjú; ☎ 0755-2446 3999; 4018 Jiefang Lu)

Shenzhen Grandland International Travel Agency (Shēnzhènshì Jùbāng Guójì Lǚxíngshè; ☎ 0755-2515 5555; Shenzhen Hotel, 3085 Shennan Donglu; ☺ 8am-8pm) This agency is in the lobby of the Shenzhen Hotel and good for plane tickets.

Shenzhen Happy Line Tour Co (☎ 0755-2690 6000; adult/child under 12 Y35/18; ☺ 9.30am-7pm; Huáqiáo Chéng metro)

Shenzhen Tourist Information Centre (Shēnzhènshì Yóukè Wènxùnchù; ☎ 0755-8200 3220, 0755-8236 5043; Ground fl, West Exit Hall, Luohu Train Station; ☺ 8am-1pm & 2-6pm) This undersupplied and understaffed place is opposite the Felicity Hotel; to reach it use the footbridge west of the Luohu Commercial City.

Websites Visit Shenzhen (www.visitshenzhen.com) is a great website on the city. For entertainment options, check out the expat-run Shenzhen Party (www.shenzhenparty.com).

Sights

Bar Leo (☎ 0755-2598 9898; Ground fl, Shop A4, Citic City Plaza, 1093 Shennan Zhonglu, Futian District; ⏰ 11am-2am; Kēxué Guǎn metro)

BJ'zz.com Bar (☎ 0755-8217 2288 ext 504; 3rd fl, Landmark Hotel, 3018 Nanhu Lu; ⏰ 6pm-2am, happy hour 6-9pm & midnight-2am)

Chicago Club (☎ 0755-8325 9715; Shenzhen City Stadium, Sungang Xilu & Shangbu Beilu; ⏰ 9pm-2am; bus 4, 9, 209 & 420)

China Folk Culture Village (Zhōngguó Mínzú Wénhuà Cūn; 中国民族文化村; ☎ 0755-2660 0626; www.china fcv.com; adult/child under 12 incl entry to Splendid China Y120/60; ⏰ 9am-10pm; Huáqiáo Chéng metro)

Class Club (☎ 0755-8236 3999; www.classclubsz.com; 5th fl, Century Plaza Hotel, 1 Chunfeng Lu; ⏰ 9pm-late)

Dongmen Market (Dōngmén Shìháng; Hubei Lu; ⏰ 10am-8pm)

Gen Gen (Gēngēn; ☎ 0755-8232 3435; Shop 3028, 3rd fl, Luohu Commercial City; ⏰ 9am-11pm)

Henry J Bean's Bar & Grill (☎ 0755-8233 0888 ext 8270; 2nd fl, Shangri-La Hotel; ⏰ 5pm-1am Sun-Thu, 5pm-2am Fri & Sat, happy hour 5-8.30pm)

Jian Fu Mei Health & Beauty Centre (Jiàn Fù Měi; ☎ 0755-8233 8178; Shop 4028, Luohu Commercial City; ⏰ 8.30am-11pm) Massage Y88 to Y128, facials from Y90.

Luohu Commercial City (Luóhú Shāngyè Chéng; ☎ 0755-8233 8178; Renmin Nanlu; ⏰ 6.30am-midnight)

Mang Bing Massage Centre (Máng Bǐng; ☎ 0755-8232 1703; Shop 2028, 2nd fl, Luohu Commercial City; ⏰ 8am-11pm) Expect to pay between Y60 and Y110 for an hour's massage.

McCawley's Irish Bar & Restaurant (☎ 0755-2668 4496; Ground fl, Shop 118, Sea World, Taizi Lu, Shekou; ⏰ 11.30am-2am; bus 204 or 226)

Minsk World (Míngsīkè Hángmǔ Shìjiè; 明思克航母世界; ☎ 0755-2535 5333, 0755-2525 1415; Shatoujiao, Dapeng Bay, Yantian District; adult/child under 12 Y100/50; ⏰ 9.30am-6pm; bus 103 or 205)

Shenzhen Art Gallery (Shēnzhèn Měishùguǎn; 深圳美术馆; ☎ 0755-2540 9307; Aiguo Lu; admission Y5, free on Fri; ⏰ 9am-5pm Tue-Sun; bus 3, 106, 208 or 351)

Shenzhen Museum (Shēnzhèn Bówùguǎn; ☎ 0755-8210 2993; 6 Tongxin Lu; adult/student Y10/5; ⏰ 9am-5pm Tue-Sun; Kēxué Guǎn metro, bus 3, 12, 101, 102 or 104)

Shenzhen Sea World (Shēnzhèn Hǎiyáng Shìjiè; 深圳海洋世界; ☎ 0755-2506 2986; www.szxms.com.cn; Xiaomeisha Recreation Centre, Yantian District; adult/child under 12 Y100/50; ⏰ 9.30am-8.30pm; bus 103, 360 or 380)

Soho Restaurant & Night Club (☎ 0755-2669 2148, 2669 0148; Taizi Lu, Shekou; ⏰ 11am-2am; bus 204 or 226)

Splendid China (Jǐnxiù Zhōnghuá; 锦绣中华; ☎ 0755-2660 0626; www.chinafcv.com; adult/child under 12 incl entry to China Folk Culture Village Y120/60; ⏰ 9am-6pm; Huáqiáo Chéng metro)

X-Ta-Sea (☎ 0755-2686 7649; Taizi Lu, Shekou; ⏰ noon-2am, happy hour noon-9.30pm)

Window of the World (Shìjiè Zhīchuāng; 世界之窗; ☎ 0755-2690 2840, 0755-2660 8000; www.szwwco.com; adult/child under 12 Y120/60; ⏰ 9am-9pm; Shìjiè Zhīchuāng metro)

TALLY, HO *TAI TAI*!

Mrs Ho is a *tai tai*. *Tai tai* simply means 'Mrs' and, strictly speaking, every married Chinese woman is a *tai tai*. But *tai tai* in southern China – and especially Hong Kong – has a somewhat different connotation. *Tai tais* are the well-to-do, leisured wives of successful businessmen. They lunch, take tea in the lobby of the Peninsula Hotel, gossip with their friends (mostly via mobile phone) and play mahjong. And they shop, especially in Shenzhen, for *tai tais* – however wealthy – are always in search of a bargain.

Mrs Ho took us to Shenzhen the first time we visited. No, that's not strictly true. In fact, the incomparable *HK Magazine* (p199) had recently run a cover story about a *tai tai* named Ho who would board the KCR East Rail for Lo Wu in the morning at least once a week, spend the day shopping, nibbling and being pampered and return at the end of the day thoroughly relaxed, satiated and clothed – at half the price it would have cost her in Hong Kong.

Mrs Ho 'took' us for a tour of the Luohu Commercial City, then for lunch at the Laurel and to her favourite massage parlour (legitimate of course – after all, Mrs Ho is a married women with children!) for an hour's worth of foot rubbing after pounding the pavements of the SEZ all day. We did stop short of following Mrs Ho into the manicurist's where, 'feeling particularly whimsical', she had tiny flowers, butterflies and birds painted on each fingernail. That was, we thought, beyond the call of duty – for a guidebook writer.

Some people are snide about *tai tais*, dismissing them as lazy, self-indulgent creatures whose main concern is the quality of the oolong tea and the price of the knockoff Louis Vuitton bag. But we – and now you – know differently. *Tai tais* have got something to teach us all.

Eating

BBC Restaurant (☎ 0755- 8232 1773; Shop 3008, 3rd fl, Luohu Commercial City; starters Y32-48, salads Y25-56, pasta Y28-45, mains Y48-88; ⏰ 8am-10.30pm) This is one of the few options in Luohu Commercial City for Western food and most of the staff speak reasonable English.

Casa Blanca (☎ 0755-2667 6968; Ground fl, Yin Bing Building, Taizi Lu, Shekou; dishes Y50-85; ⏰ 11am-3pm & 6-9pm) This upmarket Western eatery does some fine Tex-Mex (Y60) and pasta dishes (Y60 to Y65).

Chow Phaya Thai Restaurant (Zhāopàyē Tàiguó Cānguǎn; ☎ 0755-8225 9988; Shenzhen Lido Hotel, 2007 Dongmen Nanlu; starters Y20-40, salads Y42-75, mains Y53-140; ⏰ 10am-midnight) Don't expect Bangkok-standard cuisine at this hotel restaurant, but if you need a fix of *tom yom gung* (spicy prawn soup) or *pad thai* noodles, the Chow Phaya can oblige.

Friday Cafe (Xīngqīwǔ; ☎ 0755-8246 0757; Ground fl, Diwang Commercial Building, Jiefang Lu; dishes from Y25; ⏰ 7am-1am) This attractive, renovated café-restaurant is in one of the most striking modern buildings in Shenzhen.

King Elephant Restaurant (Jīnxiànghuáng Yuècài Lóu; ☎ 0755-8232 5650; Shop 4008, 4th fl, Luohu Commercial City; meals from Y120 per person; ⏰ 7am-11pm) If the queue at the Laurel is too long, try this alternative in the Luohu Commercial City for its dim sum (Y6 to Y18).

Laurel (Dānguìxuān; ☎ 0755-8232 3888; 2nd fl, Century Plaza Hotel, 1 Chungfeng Lu; meals from Y150 per person; ⏰ 7am-11pm; **Luohu Commercial City branch** (☎ 0755-8232 3668; Shop 5010, 5th fl, Luohu Commercial City; ⏰ 7am-11pm) This is one of the finest Chinese restaurants in town; expect to have to wait in a queue. Dim sum is served from opening till 3pm daily.

Muslim Hotel Restaurant (Músīlín Bīngguǎn Dà Cānguǎn; 穆斯林宾馆大餐馆; ☎ 0755-8225 9664; Ground fl, Muslim Hotel, 2013 Wenjing Nan Lu; dishes Y28-45; ⏰ 10am-11pm) If you fancy trying *huí* (Chinese Muslim) food (eg various beef and mutton dishes, onion cakes) head for this hotel done up like a mock mosque. What's more, it's all halal.

Noodle King (Miàndiàn Wáng; ☎ 0755-8205 8099; 4 Jiefang Lu; ⏰ 8am-midnight; **Renmin Nanlu branch** (☎ 0755-8222 2348; 3021 Renmin Nanlu; dishes Y10-15; ⏰ 8.30am-10.30pm) This popular budget noodle chain has a line-up of chefs from whom you request dumplings, noodles and vegetable dishes.

Ocean King Restaurant (Hǎishàng Huáng Jiǔjiā; ☎ 0755-8223 9000; 1116 Jianshe Lu; meals per person from Y100; ⏰ 7am-10pm) This is one of Shenzhen's best seafood restaurants and is always packed.

Taj Indian Restaurant (☎ 0755-8236 2782; Ground fl, Lianhua Building, Renmin Nanlu; starters Y20-30, tandoori & curry Y20-45; ⏰ 10am-11.45pm) If you need a fix of something spicy, head for this authentic South Indian curry house in the complex opposite the Century Plaza Hotel. The *idlis* (soft rice cakes) and chicken Chettinad are excellent.

Sleeping

Hotels in Shenzhen discount deeply during the week, slicing as much as 50% off the regular rack rate, though you should ask for a discount at any time. This is also partially offset by the 10% or 15% tax/service charge levied by many hotels.

Century Plaza Hotel (Xīndū Jiǔdiàn; ☎ 0755-8232 0888; www.szcenturyplaza.com; 1 Chunfeng Lu; s & d Y1320-1430, ste from Y1980) The 401-room Century Plaza is a better deal than the Shangri-La as it sometimes cuts its published rates in half and has more comprehensive facilities, including the Laurel restaurant (left) and Class dance club (opposite).

Gold Hotel (Fùlìhuá Dàjiǔdiàn; ☎ 0755-8218 0288; www.goldhotel.com.cn; 2098 Shennan Donglu; s Y480, d Y680-850, ste from Y1180) A discount of between 35% and 45% off the published price makes what is actually a 210-room, top-end hotel an excellent deal. The Jade Sauna on the 11th floor is a delight.

Guangdong Hotel (Yuèhǎi Jiǔdiàn; ☎ 0755-8222 8339; www.gdhotels.com; 3033 Shennan Donglu; s & d Y888-1188, ste from Y1988) The 278 rooms – relatively large by Shenzhen standards – at this three-star hotel are attractive and comfortable and a steal when 45% is knocked off the rack rate.

Petrel Hotel (Hǎiyàn Dàjiǔdiàn; ☎ 0755-8223 2828; www.petrel-hotel.com; Haiyan Building, Jiabin Lu; s & d Y336-456, ste from Y576) This hotel has 242 rooms spread over 14 floors of an office tower. Expect a discount of at least 25% during the week.

Shangri-La Hotel (Xiānggélǐlā Dàjiǔdiàn; ☎ 0755-8223 0888; www.shangri-la.com; 1002 Jianshe Lu; s Y1450-1650, d Y1600-1800, ste from Y2300) Despite all the competition this luxurious hotel still keeps its prices up there in the stars. But it'll throw in a lot of extras on nondiscounted rates. The hotel's big swimming pool is set in leafy surrounds.

Shenzhen Hotel (Shēnzhèn Dàjiǔdiàn; ☎ 0755-8235 1666; fax 0755-8222 4922; 3085 Shennan Donglu; s & d Y328-368, tr Y368, ste from Y668) At the intersection of Jianshe Lu and Shennan Donglu, this central 100-room place isn't much to look at from the outside but has a nice interior with comfortable rooms. Discounts of 20% to 25% apply.

Wah Chung International Hotel (Huázhōng Guójì Jiǔdiàn; ☎ 0755-8223 8060; fax 0755-8222 1439; 3041 Shennan Donglu; s Y298-318, d & tw Y368-408, tr Y478-518, ste from Y880) The Wah Chung has a central location and 170 recently renovated rooms. Count on a weekday discount of at least 20%.

TRANSPORT

For more detailed information about getting from Hong Kong to Shenzhen, see p304.

Distance from Hung Hom station 35km

Direction from Hung Hom station North

Travel time from Hung Hom station 40 minutes by KCR East Rail train

Distance from Macau's Inner Harbour to Shekou About 115km

Direction from Macau's Inner Harbour to Shekou Northeast

Travel time from Macau's Inner Harbour to Shekou 90 minutes by ferry

Boat There are 13 jet-cat departures ($110 to $130) daily between **Shekou port** (☎ 0755-2669 5600) and Hong Kong (Y108/125 day/night sailing, 50 minutes) between 7.45am and 9.30pm. Seven go to the Macau ferry pier in Central, with the rest heading for the China ferry terminal in Kowloon. The same number of boats leave Hong Kong for Shekou between 7.45am and 9pm. Three ferries a day also link Shekou with Macau; for details see p375. You can also reach Zhuhai (Y70, one hour) from Shekou every half-hour from 7.30am to between 5.30pm and 6.30pm, depending on the season.

Bus While the majority of people travel to Shenzhen from Hong Kong by train, most big hotels in Hong Kong run minivans to and from that destination for between $60 and $100 (Y80 and Y120 from Shenzhen) one way. In Shenzhen intercity buses depart from Luohu bus station (Luóhú qìchēzhàn) beneath Luohu Commercial City, and there are frequent departures to Chaozhou (Cháozhōu; Y160, five hours), Guangzhou (Guǎngzhōu; Y60, 1½ hours), Humen (Hǔmén; Y35, one hour), Shantou (Shàntóu; Y150, four hours), Xiamen (Xiàmén; Y210, eight hours) and Zhongshan (Zhōngshān; Y70, 1½ hours). Shenzhen has a cheap and efficient network of buses and minibuses costing Y1 to Y3.

Metro Shenzhen's first two metro lines (Y2 to Y5) opened in late 2004 after much delay. Line No 1, the more useful for visitors, stretches from the Luohu border crossing to the Windows of the World theme park.

Taxi In Shenzhen **taxis** (☎ 0755-8322 8000) cost Y12.5 (Y16.10 from 11pm to 6am) for the first 3km, with each additional 250m another Y0.60.

Train The Kowloon-Canton Railway East Rail (1st/2nd class $66/33, 40 minutes) is the fastest and most convenient transport to Shenzhen from Hong Kong (p304). From Shenzhen there are frequent local trains (Y70, two hours) and high-speed trains (Y80, 55 minutes) to Guangzhou.

ZHUHAI

Like Shenzhen to the northeast, Zhuhai is a 'Special Economic Zone' (SEZ). But 'the pearl of the sea' has never reached the level of success (or excess) of its well-heeled stepsister across the Pearl River estuary. So much the better for residents and travellers, for this city of 460,600 people is one of the cleanest and greenest metropolises in China and an important university centre. Zhuhai is close enough to Macau that a day trip is possible.

Travellers who visited here in the 1980s will remember Zhuhai as a small agricultural town with a few rural industries and a peaceful beach, a place to stop for lunch on the way to Cuiheng, where Dr Sun Yat Sen, the founder of the Republic of China, was born in 1866. But that's all history and the Zhuhai of today not only has the usual SEZ skyline of glimmering five-star hotels and big factories, bargain shopping and pulsating bars and clubs, it also has its own spotless and ultramodern airport.

The city of Zhuhai is divided into three main districts. Gongbei (Gǒngběi; 拱北), which straddles the Macau border, is the main tourist district, with hotels, restaurants and shops; Gongbei Port (Gǒngběi Kǒu'àn) is the large modern complex that visitors pass through en route from the SAR. To the northeast is Jida (Jídà; 吉大), the eastern part of which contains some large waterfront hotels and resorts as well as Jiuzhou Harbour (Jiǔzhōu Gǎng; 九州港), where Hong Kong, Shenzhen and Guǎngdōng passenger ferries arrive and depart. Xiangzhou (Xiāngzhōu; 香洲) is the northernmost part of Zhuhai City and has many government buildings, housing blocks and a busy fishing port.

Zhuhai is not overly endowed with sights and activities, but there are one or two attractions of note, a couple of theme parks, some pretty city parks and a few destinations further afield that are worthy of a visit.

The **Zhuhai City Museum** is housed in a dozen galleries on two floors of a building in Jida made to look like a Ming dynasty compound. It contains a small but interesting collection of copperware (drinking vessels, temple bells, figurines etc), some of which date back 5000 years; Tibetan art and artefacts, including gilded cups formed from human skulls; and scroll paintings and calligraphy.

North of the museum at the eastern edge of **Xiangshan Park**, the austere **Revolutionary Martyrs' Memorial** is dedicated to local victims of the Japanese executed during WWII. Walk towards the pagoda at the top of the steps to reach the park.

Parks in Jida include the waterfront **Haibin Park** (Hǎibìn Gōngyuán; 海滨公园), with hills on both sides, palm trees, statues and an amusement park, and **Paradise Park**, noted

for its 'boulder forest' covering **Paradise Hill** (Shíjǐng Shān; 石景山) behind and the **Paradise Hill Cable Car**, which takes you to the top.

In the bay between the two parks is the **Zhuhai Fisher Girl**, an 8.7m-high statue of a young woman holding a pearl – the symbol of the city – over her head. In fact, pearls are still farmed off the coast to the northeast.

A couple of kilometres northwest of Gongbei is **New Yuan Ming Palace**, a massive theme

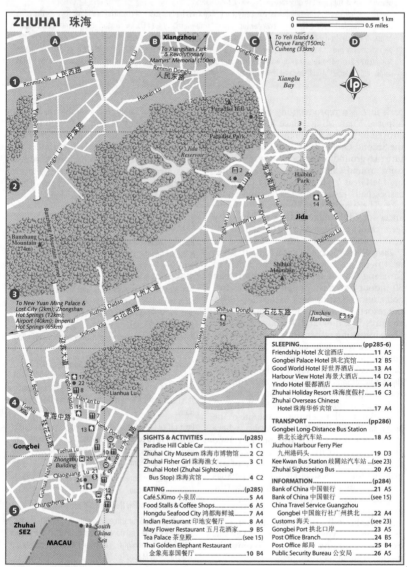

SLEEPING	(pp285–6)
Friendship Hotel 友谊酒店	11 A5
Gongbei Palace Hotel 拱北宾馆	12 B5
Good World Hotel 好世界酒店	13 A4
Harbour View Hotel 海景大酒店	14 D2
Yindo Hotel 银都酒店	15 A4
Zhuhai Holiday Resort 珠海度假村	16 C3
Zhuhai Overseas Chinese	
Hotel 珠海华侨宾馆	17 A4

TRANSPORT	(pp286)
Gongbei Long-Distance Bus Station	
拱北长途汽车站	18 A5
Jiuzhou Harbour Ferry Pier	
九州港码头	19 D3
Kee Kwan Bus Station 歧關站汽车站	...(see 23)
Zhuhai Sightseeing Bus	20 A5

INFORMATION	(p284)
Bank of China 中国银行	21 A5
Bank of China 中国银行	(see 15)
China Travel Service Guangzhou	
Gongbei 中国旅行社广州拱北	(see 23)
Customs 海关	(see 23)
Gongbei Port 拱北口岸	23 A5
Post Office Branch	24 B5
Post Office 邮局	25 B4
Public Security Bureau 公安局	26 A5

SIGHTS & ACTIVITIES	(p285)
Paradise Hill Cable Car	1 C1
Zhuhai City Museum 珠海市博物馆	2 C2
Zhuhai Fisher Girl 珠海渔女	3 C1
Zhuhai Hotel (Zhuhai Sightseeing	
Bus Stop) 珠海宾馆	4 C2

EATING	(p285)
Café.S.Kimo 小泉居	5 A4
Food Stalls & Coffee Shops	6 A5
Hongdu Seafood City 鸿都海鲜城	7 A4
Indian Restaurant 印地安餐厅	8 A4
May Flower Restaurant 五月花酒家	9 B5
Tea Palace 茶皇殿	(see 15)
Thai Golden Elephant Restaurant	
金象苑泰国餐厅	10 B4

ZHUHAI 珠海

0 ————— 1 km
0 ————— 0.5 miles

283

BRANDED IN THE SEZ

It's easy – and unfair – to mock the prose of non-native speakers of English, but when it comes to Chinese brand names it becomes irresistible.

Fancy a pair of Pansy Y-fronts, boys? Wake up in the morning with a Golden Cock (that's an alarm clock) and take your pleasure with a Imperial Concubine cup of tea (not forgetting to light up a Long Life cigarette) after refreshing yourself with Horse Head facial tissues. For your faithful Golden Cock you should avoid White Elephant batteries, but the Moon Rabbit variety should have it going like a, well, bunny. Rambo toilet paper must be the toughest stuff around and definitely preferable to the Thumbs Up brand. No one is sure what the ginseng product with the name of Gensenocide is supposed to do exactly – revive or annihilate.

China is not alone in its commercial creativity: Hong Kong has had its share of colourful brand names over the years too. Until the late 1980s, the most popular toothpaste in the territory was Darkie, featuring a portrait of a broadly grinning minstrel on each tube. Realising that the world had indeed entered the 20th century some eight decades previously, the product's marketing team launched a TV campaign to transform its image. 'We're changing our name!' said an overexcited voiceover as an animated minstrel gave the 'k' a good solid kick and an 'l' miraculously appeared in its place. 'To Darlie!' And then, as if by magic, all was right with the world.

park that is a reproduction of the original imperial Yuan Ming Palace in Beijing destroyed by British and French forces during the Second Opium War. It is a huge adventure playground of reproduced scenic sights from around China and the world, including the Great Wall of China and European castles, halls, restaurants, temples and a huge lake. There are lavish 30-minute performances staged throughout the day. The entry fee includes admission to **Lost City**, a huge adventure and water park just next door.

Zhongshan Hot Springs, a resort about 12km northwest of Zhuhai near the town of Sanxiang (Sānxiāng; 三乡), has more than 30 indoor hot-spring pools as well as two golf courses. Dating back to the mid-1980s, the resort was one of the first foreign joint ventures in China and, frankly, the whole place is looking rather run-down. However, if you're a real enthusiast of either activity, you might want to take a dip, have a massage or even spend a night at the 313-room **Zhongshan Hot Springs Hotel**, whose higher-priced rooms (80 in total) have hot-spring tubs.

The small village of **Cuiheng** (Cuìhēng; 翠亨), 33km north of Zhuhai, is the site of the **Dr Sun Yat Sen Residence Memorial Museum**, where the revolutionary hero was born in 1866 and returned to live with his parents for four years in 1892. A solemn place of pilgrimage for Chinese of all political persuasions, the museum recreates the house (the original was torn down in 1913) where Sun grew up and the village compound includes a remarkable collection of furniture and objects from everyday life. The main hall has exhibits examining his life and accomplishments, with signs in English.

Imperial Hot Springs is a massive resort some 65km to the west of Zhuhai City in Doumen (Dǒumén; 斗门) and has a number of thermal open-air pools as well as rooms with their own hot-spring tubs, where you can soak away the fatigue and grime of touring Zhuhai or have one of three types of massage (Shanghai/Hong Kong/Thai).

Information

Bank of China (Zhōngguó Yínháng; cnr Yingbin Dadao & Yuehai Donglu; ✉ 8.30am-5pm Mon-Fri, 10am-4pm Sat & Sun) Next to the Yindo hotel; **Lianhua Lu branch** (Zhōngguó Yínháng Fēnháng; 41 Lianhua Lu; ✉ 8.30am-5pm Mon-Fri, 10am-4pm Sat & Sun) Most shops, restaurants and hotels accept Hong Kong dollars and Macau patacas (MOP) as well as Chinese renminbi (or yuan, abbreviated 'Y'). ATMs at both banks and elsewhere are linked to several international money systems, including Cirrus, Maestro and Plus.

China Travel Service Guangzhou Gongbei (CTS; Zhōngguó Lǚxíngshè Guǎngzhōu Gǒngběi; ☎ 0756-888 5777, 0756-813 6525; 33 Yingbin Dadao; ✉ 8am-midnight) This helpful office is next to the Zhuhai Overseas Chinese Hotel.

Post office (Yóujú; 1043 Yuehai Donglu; ✉ 8am-8pm); **Qiaoguang Lu branch** (18 Qiaoguang Lu; ✉ 8am-8pm) Both post offices sell telephone cards, though you can make IDD calls from your room in most hotels.

Public Security Bureau (Gōng'ānjú; ☎ 0756-887 2872; 1038 Yingbin Dadao)

Tourist Information Hotline (☎ 336 6908)

Visas Visas valid for three days only (MOP$150) are available on the 2nd floor of Gongbei Port at the **border** (✉ 7.30am-midnight). You would do better to buy one in advance in Macau (p374).

Sights

Dr Sun Yat Sen Residence Memorial Museum (Sūn Zhōngshān Gùjū Jìniànguǎn; 孙中山故居纪念馆; ☎ 0760-550 1691; Cuiheng Dadao, Cuiheng; adult/child Y20/10; ☯ 9am-5pm) Board bus 10 along Yingbin Dadao in Zhuhai. Alight at the terminus, walk 10 minutes past the gate to the next bus stop and board bus 12.

Haibin Park (Hǎibīn Gōngyuán; 海滨公园; Haibin Nanlu; ☯ 8am-10pm) The **amusement park** (☯ 8am-7pm) has rides costing Y2 to Y5.

Imperial Hot Springs (Yù Wēnquán; 御温泉; ☎ 0756-579 7128; www.imperial-hot-spring.com; Doumen) Amenities and services include open-air thermal pools (Y128 to Y200 for two hours) and massage (from Y198 to Y298). Buses 602 and 609 from Zhuhai will take you to the resort in just under 1½ hours.

Lost City (Mènghuàn Shuǐchéng; 梦幻水城; ☎ 0756-861 0388; ☯ 10.30am-6pm Mon-Fri, 9.30am-6.30pm Sat & Sun May, Jun, Sep & Oct, 9am-9pm Jul & Aug)

New Yuan Ming Palace (Yuánmíng Xīnyuán; 圆明新园; ☎ 0756-861 0388; www.ymy.com.cn; cnr Jiuzhou Dadao & Lanpu Lu; adult/child Y120/80; ☯ 9am-9pm; bus 1, 13, 60 or 99) Entry fee includes admission to Lost City.

Paradise Hill Cable Car (Shíjǐng Shān Suǒdào; 石景山索道; ☎ 0756-213 6477, 0756-211 3078; adult one way/return Y25/50, child Y20/30; ☯ 8am-9pm)

Paradise Park (Shí Jǐngshān Gōngyuán; 石景山公园; Haibin Beilu; admission Y2; ☯ 8am-9pm) Next to the Paradise Hill Cable Car there are go-karts for rent (for five/10 minutes Y25/40).

Revolutionary Martyrs' Memorial (Lièshì Língyuán; 烈士陵园; ☎ 8am-6pm; bus 3, 13 or 99)

Xiangshan Park (Xiāngshān Gōngyuán; 香山公园; Fenghuang Bei Lu) To the edge of the park is the Revolutionary Martyrs' Memorial.

Zhongshan Hot Springs (Zhōngshān Wēnquán; 中山温泉; ☎ 0760-668 3888; www.zshs.com; admission Y108; ☯ 8.30am-1.30am) Services here include massage (eg two-hour foot massage Y188). Buses headed for Zhongshan (Zhōngshān; 中山) from Zhuhai drop you by the entrance to the resort, from where it's a 500m walk along a tree-lined avenue to the hotel.

Zhuhai City Museum (Zhūhǎishì Bówùguǎn; ☎ 0756-332 4116; 191 Jianshan Lu; admission Y10; ☯ 9am-5pm; bus 2, 30 or 26)

Zhuhai Fisher Girl (Zhūhǎi Yúnǚ; Xianglu Bay) Reach this city landmark on bus 99.

Zhuhai Sightseeing Bus (☎ 0756-337 8821, 0756-337 8381) Two lines – the east line (Y3, every 30 minutes, 7am-8pm) and the west line (Y2, every 20 minutes, 7am-8pm) – take in all the sights in Zhuhai. Both depart from along Yingbin Dadao in Gongbei and the Zhuhai Hotel next to the Zhuhai City Museum in Jida.

Eating

Gongbei near the Macau border has restaurants, night markets and street hawkers. Try Lianhua Lu for bakeries and a few basic restaurants serving Cantonese food.

Café E.S. Kimo (Xiǎoquán Jū; ☎ 0756-828 0635; 92 Yuehua Lu; dishes Y23-36; ☯ 10am-3am) This popular Chinese fast-food chain, with several branches in Macau, is the place for salads, sandwiches and snacks.

Deyue Fang (Déyuè Fǎng; 得月舫; ☎ 0756-217 3283; Minting Garden, Yeli Island; meals per person from Y100; ☯ 11am-3pm & 5-10.30pm) This opulent place is where to go if you want to impress or be impressed. It's a floating restaurant specialising in seafood moored just off Yeli Island in Xiangzhou Harbour. A golf cart will pick you up and deliver you to your table.

Hongdu Seafood City (Hóngdū Hǎixiān Chéng; ☎ 0756-888 8333; 1138 Yuehai Donglu; meals per person from Y85; ☯ 7am-9.30pm) This enormous and very popular place spread over several floors serves excellent seafood dishes as well as simple vegetable and meat ones.

Indian Restaurant (Yìndì'ān Cāntīng; ☎ 0756-815 0615; 2100 Lian'an Lu; dishes Y26-78; ☯ 9am-4am) No, not curries and tandoori dishes, but wigwams, tomahawks and waitresses dressed up as squaws. Lots of steaks and burgers cooked on stone grills, no scalps.

May Flower Restaurant (Wǔyuèhuā Jiǔjiā; ☎ 0756-818 1111; 31 Shuiwan Lu; meals per person Y100; ☯ 7am-2.30pm & 5pm-midnight) This place opposite the Gongbei Palace specialises in Cantonese seafood and clay pot dishes.

Tea Palace (Chá Huángdiàn; ☎ 0756-888 3388; Ground fl, Yindo Hotel, cnr Yingbin Dadao & Yuehai Lu; per person from Y60; ☯ 8am-5pm) This delightful space serves traditional Chinese brews and snacks. It's an excellent spot to head for in order to chill out.

Thai Golden Elephant Restaurant (Jīnxiàngyuàn Tàiguó Cāntīng; ☎ 0756-815 9890; 87-97 Shuiwan Lu; dishes Y25-75; ☯ 11am-midnight) Don't expect Bangkok-style authenticity from this cosy Thai place, but the *tom yum gung* is a reasonable facsimile.

Sleeping

Relatively few travellers stay in Zhuhai apart from those on business. There's not much demand for budget accommodation, so prices are generally midrange to top end (though heavy discounting during the week can blur those distinctions). Most hotels add a 10% to 15% service charge to the bill.

Friendship Hotel (Yǒuyì Jiǔdiàn; ☎ 0756-813 1818; fax 0756-813 5505; 2 Youyi Lu, Gongbei; s Y368-418, d Y388-418, ste from Y568) This modern hotel, opposite the border crossing, will cut its quoted prices by half if you

TRANSPORT

For more detailed information about getting from Macau to Zhuhai, see p374.

Distance from Macau ferry pier 2km

Direction from Macau ferry pier North

Travel time from Macau ferry pier 20 minutes by bus

Distance from Hong Kong's Macau ferry pier in Central about 65km

Direction from Hong Kong's Macau ferry pier in Central West

Travel time from Hong Kong's Macau ferry pier in Central 70 minutes by high-speed ferry

Boat Jetcats between Zhuhai and Hong Kong (Y150, 70 minutes) depart six times a day between 8am and 5pm from **Jiuzhou Harbour** (☎ 0756-333 3359, Hong Kong ☎ 852-2858 3876) for the China ferry terminal in Kowloon, and eight times a day from 9am to 9.30pm for the Macau ferry pier in Central. A high-speed ferry operates between Jiuzhou Harbour and Shenzhen's port of Shekou (Shékǒu; Y70, one hour). There are departures every half-hour from 8am and between 5.30pm and 6.30pm, depending on the season. They leave from Shekou at the same frequency between 7.30am and 5.30pm or 6.30pm. Local buses 3, 12, 25 and 26 all go to the harbour.

Bus In Macau buses 3, 5, 9 and 10 all go to the Border Gate (Portas de Cerco). You can also enter the Zhuhai SEZ via the less-busy **Cotai Frontier Post** (☿ 9am-8pm). Macau bus 15, 21 or 26 will drop you off at the crossing; a shuttle bus will then take you over the Lotus Bridge. In Zhuhai, air-conditioned buses for Guangzhou (Guǎngzhōu; Y55 to Y75, 2½ hours) leave from **Gongbei long-distance bus station** (☎ 0756-888 5218, 0756-888 8554) on Youyi Lu every 20 minutes between 6am and 10pm. Buses to other points in China depart from either this station or the **Kee Kwan Bus Station** (☎ 0756-818 6705) below the shopping centre at Gongbei Port. Destinations include Dongguan (Dōngguǎn; Y60 to Y70, 2½ hours), Foshan (Fóshān; Y60 to Y70, three hours), Humen (Hǔmén; Y50 to Y65, two hours), Kaiping (Kāipíng; Y40 to Y55, 3½ hours), Shantou (Shàntóu; Y160 to Y180, seven hours), Shenzhen (Shēnzhèn; Y80 to Y90, 2½ hours), Zhaoqing (Zhàoqìng; Y55 to Y70, 4½ hours) and Zhongshan (Zhōngshān; Y15 to Y20, one hour). Most of the top-end hotels have bus service to and from Hong Kong (Y150, 2½ hours). Zhuhai's local buses are clean, efficient and, at Y2, very cheap.

Taxi A taxi from the Macau ferry pier to the border will cost about MOP$20. In Zhuhai **taxis** (☎ 863 2033) have meters; flag-fall is Y10 for the first 3km and Y0.60 for each additional 250m. A taxi ride from the border with Macau to Jiuzhou Harbour costs around Y20.

ask. Should you arrive late or have to depart early, this is an excellent choice. There's a bank in the lobby; just think of the convenience.

Gongbei Palace Hotel (Gōngběi Bīnguǎn; ☎ 0756-888 6833; fax 0756-888 1900; 21 Shuiwan Lu, Gongbei; s Y280, d Y280-380, tr Y450-580, ste from Y680) Its advertised rates notwithstanding, this over-the-top 220-room hotel by the waterfront – Disneyland meets Imperial China – has singles/doubles for as low as Y180/230.

Good World Hotel (Hǎo Shìjiè Jiǔdiàn; ☎ 0756-888 0222; fax 0756-889 2061; 82 Lianhua Lu, Gongbei; s & d Y300, tr Y440, ste from Y550) This cheerily named place offers reasonable rooms (180 in total) for a remarkable 'unquoted' rate of Y180 (Y200 at the weekend) for a single or double.

Harbour View Hotel (Hǎijǐng Jiǔdiàn; ☎ 0756-332 2888; hvhbc@pub.zhuhai.gd.cn; Haibin Beilu, Jida; s & d Y880-1180, suites from Y1480) The latest caravanserai to park itself on the waterfront, this 383-room pile is more a resort than a hotel, and has all the mod-cons as well as four bowling lanes, tennis courts, indoor games and a huge, fan-shaped outdoor swimming pool.

Yindo Hotel (Yíndū Jiǔdiàn; ☎ 0756-888 3388; yindobc@pub.zhuhai.gd.cn; cnr Yingbin Dadao &

Yuehai Lu; s & d Y860-1240, ste from Y1360) This 310-room landmark hotel next to the main Bank of China is one of the best places to stay within striking distance of the border. Outlets include a decent Western restaurant called **Huntress Grill** (☿ 11am-2.30pm & 5.30-10.30pm) on the 2nd floor and the Tea Palace (p285).

Zhongshan Hot Springs Hotel (Zhōngshān Wēnquán Bīnguǎn; 中山温泉兵馆; ☎ 0760-668 3888; s & d Y380-660, ste from Y720) The higher priced rooms – some 80 in all – at this sprawling, 313-room hotel have their own hot-spring tubs.

Zhuhai Holiday Resort (Zhūhǎi Dùjià cūn; ☎ 0756-333 3838; www.zhuhai-holitel.com; 9 Shihua Donglu; s & d Y880-980, ste from Y1380) This five-star complex with spacious grounds and some eight restaurants hugs the coast northeast of Gongbei near Jiuzhou Harbour. Its amenities include a bowling alley, tennis courts, club house, go-kart racing, a sauna and a great outdoor pool.

Zhuhai Overseas Chinese Hotel (Zhūhǎi Huáqiáo Bīnguǎn; ☎ 0756-888 6288; fax 0756-888 5119; 35 Yingbin Dadao, Gongbei; s & d Y368-398, ste from Y498) This friendly, 197-room hotel is a block north of Yuehai Lu. It has quite a good fitness centre and sauna.

Air	288
Airlines 288	
Airport 289	
To/From the Airport 289	

Bicycle	291

Boat	291
Star Ferry 291	
Other Cross-Harbour Ferries 292	
New Territories Ferries 292	
Outlying Islands Ferries 292	
Other Boats 296	

Bus	296
Routes & Schedules 297	
Night Buses 297	

Car & Motorcycle	297
Driving Licence & Permits 297	
Hire 298	
Road Rules 298	

Minibus	298
Red Minibus 298	
Green Minibus 299	

Mass Transit Railway	299

Taxi	300

Train	301
Kowloon-Canton Railway 301	
Light Rail 301	

Tram	302
Peak Tram 302	

Travel & Tourist Passes	303

Transport To/From China	304
Air 304	
Land 304	
Sea 305	
Visas 306	

Transport

Transport

AIR

Hong Kong is a major gateway to China and much of East and Southeast Asia. Consequently, the international air service is excellent, and competition keeps the fares relatively low (to most places except China) compared with other countries in the region. Rip-offs here are not unknown though; be sure to use reputable travel agents only. Specific information on air travel to and from Macau and China can be found on p374 and p304, respectively.

Tickets are normally issued the day after booking, but you usually pick up the really cheap tickets (actually group fares) at the airport from the 'tour leader' just before the flight. Check these tickets carefully as there may be errors (eg the return portion of the ticket being valid for only 60 days from when you paid – or thought you paid – for a ticket that should be good for six months).

You can generally get a good idea of what fares are available at the moment by looking in the classified section of the *South China Morning Post*. Otherwise try any of the following websites:

Bargain Holidays (www.bargainholidays.com)

Cheap Flights (www.cheapflights.co.uk)

ebookers (www.ebookers.com)

Last Minute (www.lastminute.com)

Travelocity (www.travelocity.com)

You'll find travel agencies everywhere in Hong Kong but the following are among the most reliable and offer the best deals on air tickets:

Aero International (Map pp408–9; ☎ 2543 3800; www.ticketscentre.com; Room 603, 6th fl, Cheung's Bldg, 1-3 Wing Lok St, Sheung Wan; ⊙ 9.15am-5.30pm Mon-Fri, 9.15am-1pm Sat) Convenient to Central; enter from Wing Wo St.

Concorde Travel (Map p412; ☎ 2526 3391; www.concorde-travel.com; 1st fl, Galuxe Bldg, 8-10 On Lan St, Central; ⊙ 9.30am-5.30pm Mon-Fri, 9am-1pm Sat) This is a long-established and highly dependable agency owned and operated by expats.

Natori Travel (Map p412; ☎ 2810 1681; fax 2810 8190; Room 2207, Melbourne Plaza, 33 Queen's Rd Central; ⊙ 9am-7pm Mon-Fri, 9am-4pm Sat) Readers have long used and recommended this place.

Phoenix Services Agency (Map pp420–1; ☎ 2722 7378; info@phoenixtrvl.com; Room 1404, 14th fl, Austin Tower, 22-26 Austin Ave, Tsim Sha Tsui; ⊙ 9am-6pm Mon-Fri, 9am-1pm Sat) Phoenix is one of the best places in Hong Kong to buy air tickets, get China visas and seek travel advice.

Traveller Services (Map pp420–1; ☎ 2375 2222; www.taketraveller.com; Room 1012, 10th fl, Silvercord Tower One, Silvercord, 30 Canton Rd, Tsim Sha Tsui; ⊙ 9am-1pm & 2-6pm Mon-Fri, 9am-1pm Sat) Very reliable for good-value air tickets.

AIRLINES

More than 70 international airlines operate between Hong Kong International Airport and some 130 destinations around the world. You can check flight schedules in the monthly booklet *Hong Kong & Macau Airline Timetable* ($35), available at newsstands everywhere, or on its website (www.hktimetable.com).

Among the major airlines serving Hong Kong are the following:

Air New Zealand (Map pp408–9; NZ; ☎ 2862 8988; Suite 1701, 17th fl, Jardine House, 1 Connaught Pl, Central)

British Airways (Map pp408–9; BA; ☎ 2822 9000; 24th fl, Jardine House, 1 Connaught Pl, Central)

China Airlines (Map pp408–9; CI; ☎ 2868 2299; Suite 901-907, 9th fl, One Pacific Pl, 88 Queensway, Admiralty)

China Eastern/China Southern Airlines (Map pp408–9; MU/CZ; ☎ 2861 0322; 4th fl, CNAC Group Bldg, 10 Queen's Rd Central)

Dragonair (Map pp408–9; KA; ☎ 3193 3888; Room 4611, Cosco Tower, 183 Queen's Rd Central)

Northwest Airlines (Map pp408–9; NW; ☎ 2810 4288; Room 1908, 19th fl, Cosco Tower, 183 Queen's Rd Central)

Qantas Airways (Map pp408–9; QF; ☎ 2822 9000; 24th fl, Jardine House, 1 Connaught Pl, Central)

Singapore Airlines (Map pp408–9; SQ; ☎ 2520 2233; 17th fl, United Centre, 95 Queensway, Admiralty)

United Airlines (Map pp408–9; UA; ☎ 2810 4888; 29th fl, Gloucester Tower, The Landmark, 11 Pedder St, Central)

Virgin Atlantic Airways (Map pp408–9; VS; ☎ 2532 6060; 8th fl, Alexandra House, 16-20 Chater Rd, Central)

AIRPORT

Hong Kong International Airport (Map p427; ☎ 2181 0000; www.hkairport.com), which was the world's largest civil engineering project when it opened in mid-1998, is on Chek Lap Kok, a small island off the northern coast of Lantau. It is connected to the mainland by several spans. Among them is the 2.2km-long Tsing Ma Bridge, which is one of the world's largest suspension bridges and is capable of supporting both road and rail transport, including the 34km-long Airport Express high-speed train from Hong Kong Island to Chek Lap Kok via Kowloon.

The futuristic passenger terminal, designed by British architect Sir Norman Foster, consists of eight levels, with check-in on level seven, departures on level six and arrivals on level five. Outlets – including bank branches, moneychangers and five ATMs – total 150, and there are more than 30 cafés, restaurants and bars, and more than 280 check-in counters.

The **Hong Kong Tourism Board** (HKTB; ☎ 2508 1234; www.discoverhongkong.com) maintains information centres on level five (see p323). On the same level you'll also find branches of **China Travel Service** (CTS; ☎ 2261 2472, 2261 2062; www.chinatravel1.com; ☽ 8.45am-10pm), which can issue China visas, and counters run by the **Hong Kong Hotels Association** (HKHA; ☎ 2383 8380, 2769 8822; www.hkha.org; ☽ 6am-midnight); for details see p250. Be advised that the HKHA deals with midrange and top-end hotels only and does not handle hostels, guesthouses or other such budget accommodation.

If you are booked on a scheduled (but *not* a charter) flight and are taking the Airport Express to the airport, most airlines allow you to check in your bags and receive your boarding pass on the day of your flight at the in-town check-in counters at the Hong Kong Island or Kowloon Airport Express stations between 5.30am and 12.30am. You are required, however, to check yourself in at least 90 minutes before your flight. Some airlines, including Cathay Pacific Airways, China Airlines and Thai Airways, allow check-in a full day before your flight. See the airport's website for details.

Departure Tax

Hong Kong's airport departure tax – $120 for everyone over the age of 12 – is always included in the price of the ticket. Those travelling to Macau by helicopter (see p374) must pay the same amount.

TO/FROM THE AIRPORT

The Airport Express line of the Mass Transit Railway (MTR) is the fastest – and most expensive – way to get to and from Hong Kong International Airport. A gaggle of much cheaper buses connect the airport with Lantau, the New Territories, Kowloon and Hong Kong Island.

Airport Express

Airport Express (AEL; ☎ 2881 8888; www.mtr .com.hk) has trains departing from Hong Kong station in Central every 10 to 12 minutes from 5.50am to 12.48am, calling at Kowloon and Tsing Yi stations before arriving at Airport station. The last train leaves the airport for all three stations at 12.48am. Running at speeds of up to 135km/h, trains make the journey from Central/Kowloon/ Tsing Yi in only 23/20/12 minutes.

From Central/Kowloon/Tsing Yi one-way adult fares are $100/90/60, with children three to 11 years paying half-fare. Adult return fares, valid for a month, are $180/160/ 110. A same-day return is equivalent to a one-way fare.

Airport Express has two shuttle buses on Hong Kong Island (H1 and H2) and five in Kowloon (K1 to K5), with free transfers for passengers between Hong Kong and Kowloon stations and major hotels. The buses run every 12 to 24 minutes between 6.18am and 11.10pm. Schedules and routes are available at Airport Express and MTR stations and on the Airport Express website.

Boat

High-speed ferries run by **New World First Ferry Services** (☎ 2131 8181; www.nwff.com.hk) link Tung Chung New Development ferry pier opposite the airport (and accessible from the terminal on bus S56) with Tuen Mun in the New Territories. Ferries depart from Tuen Mun every 20 to 30 minutes between 5.40am and 11pm; the first ferry from Tung Chung pier leaves at 6am and the last at 11.20pm and the journey takes 18 minutes (one way adult/child and senior $15/10).

Bus

Most major areas of Hong Kong Island, Kowloon, the New Territories and Lantau are connected to the airport by bus, of which there is a huge choice. The buses are run by different companies; for details see p296.

The most useful for travellers are the Citybus 'airbuses' A11 ($40) and A12 ($45), which go to or near the major hotel and guesthouse areas on Hong Kong Island, and the A21 ($33), which serves similar areas in Kowloon. These buses have plenty of room for luggage, and announcements are usually made in English, Cantonese and Mandarin notifying passengers of hotels at each stop. But they are also the most expensive; there are cheaper options, such as taking 'external' bus E11 ($21) to Hong Kong Island or 'shuttle' bus S1 ($3.50) to Tung Chung and then the MTR to Kowloon or Central. There are also quite a few night (designated 'N') buses costing from $20 to $31.

Bus drivers in Hong Kong do not give change, but it is available at the ground transportation centre at the airport, as are Octopus cards (p303). Normal returns are double the one-way fare. Unless otherwise stated, children aged between three and 11 and seniors over 65 pay half-fare.

Some of the New Territories buses terminate at MTR stations, from where you can reach destinations in Kowloon and on Hong Kong Island at a lower cost than the more direct buses. You can also reach Shenzhen and other points in southern China directly from the airport (p304).

The following lists give the bus numbers, service providers, routes, one-way fares and frequencies for the airport buses most useful for visitors.

BUSES TO HONG KONG ISLAND

A11 (Citybus) Sheung Wan, Central, Admiralty, Wan Chai, Causeway Bay, North Point Ferry Pier; $40; every 15 to 30 minutes from 6.10am to midnight.

E11 (Citybus) Tung Chung, Tsing Ma, Kowloon Station, Sheung Wan, Central, Admiralty, Wan Chai, Causeway Bay, Tin Hau MTR; $21; every 15 to 20 minutes from 5.20am to midnight.

N11 (Citybus) Same routing as E11; $31; every 30 minutes from 12.15am to 4.45am.

A12 (Citybus) Tsing Ma, Kowloon Station, Wan Chai, North Point, Quarry Bay, Sai Wan Ho, Shau Kei Wan, Chai Wan, Siu Sai Wan; $45; every 20 to 30 minutes from 6am to midnight.

BUSES TO KOWLOON

A21 (Citybus) Sham Shui Po, Mong Kok, Yau Ma Tei, Jordan, Tsim Sha Tsui MTR, Tsim Sha Tsui East, Hung Hom KCR; $33; every 10 to 15 minutes from 6am to midnight.

N21 (Citybus) Tung Chung, Mei Foo Sun Chuen, Lai Chi Kok MTR, Mong Kok, Tsim Sha Tsui Star Ferry pier; $23; every 20 minutes from 12.20am to 5am.

BUSES TO THE NEW TERRITORIES

A31 (Long Win) Tsing Yi, Kwai Chung, Tsuen Wan MTR; $17; every 15 to 20 minutes from 6am to midnight.

N31 (Long Win) Same routing as A31; $20; every 20 to 30 minutes from 12.20am to 5.05am.

BUSES TO LANTAU

A35 (New Lantao) Tong Fuk village, Mui Wo; $14 ($23 on Sunday and public holidays); every 40 to 60 minutes from 6.30am to 12.25am.

N35 (New Lantao) Same routing as A35; $20 ($30 on Sunday and public holidays); departures at 1.30am, 3am and 5am.

S1 (Citybus) Tung Chung MTR; $3.50; every six to 10 minutes from 5.30am to midnight.

S56 (Citybus) Tung Chung New Development pier (ferries to/from Tuen Mun); $3.50; every 30 minutes from 6am to 11.20pm.

DB02R (Discovery Bay Transportation Services) Discovery Bay; $28; every 30 minutes, 24 hours.

Taxi

In addition to the fares listed, passengers taking a taxi to or from the airport at Chek Lap Kok are required to pay the $30 toll for using the Lantau Link road and bridge network in both directions.

Destination	Fare ($)
Aberdeen (Hong Kong Island)	375
Causeway Bay (Hong Kong Island)	335
Central (Hong Kong Island)	335
Kwun Tong MTR (Kowloon)	320
Mui Wo (Lantau)	130
Sai Kung (New Territories)	355-370
Sha Tin (New Territories)	300
Tsim Sha Tsui Star Ferry (Kowloon)	270
Tsuen Wan (New Territories)	200-235
Tung Chung (Lantau)	30-35

There are limousine service counters in the arrivals hall and at the ground transportation centre, including **Parklane Limousine Service** (☎ 2261 0303; www.hongkonglimo.com) and **Intercontinental Hire Cars** (☎ 2261 2155; www.trans-island.com.hk). In a car seating up to four people, expect to pay from $450 to destinations in urban Kowloon and from $500 to Hong Kong Island.

BICYCLE

Cycling in urbanised Kowloon or Hong Kong Island would be suicide, but in the quiet areas of the islands (including southern Hong Kong Island) or the New Territories, a bike can be a lovely way to get around. It's not really a form of transport, though – the hilly terrain will slow you down (unless you're mountain biking) – but more recreational. Be advised that bicycle-rental shops and kiosks tend to run out of bikes early on weekends if the weather is good (see p218).

BOAT

Despite Hong Kong's comprehensive road and rail public-transport system, the territory still relies very much on ferries to get across the harbour and to reach the Outlying Islands.

Hong Kong's cross-harbour ferries are faster and cheaper than buses and the MTR. They're also great fun and afford stunning views. Since the opening of the Lantau Link, ferries are not the only way to reach Lantau, but for the other Outlying Islands, they remain the only game in town.

Smoking is prohibited on all ferries; the fine is a hefty $5000. With the exception of Star Ferry services from Central to Hung Hom and Wan Chai to Hung Hom, the cross-harbour ferries ban the transport of bicycles. You can, however, take bicycles on the ordinary ferries to the Outlying Islands.

STAR FERRY

You can't say you've 'done' Hong Kong until you've taken a ride on a **Star Ferry** (☎ 2367 7065; www.starferry.com.hk), that wonderful fleet of a dozen electric-diesel vessels with names like *Morning Star*, *Celestial Star* and *Twinkling Star*. Try to take your first trip on a clear night from Kowloon to Central. It's not half as dramatic in the opposite direction.

The Star Ferry operates on four routes, but the most popular one is the run between Tsim Sha Tsui and Central. The coin-operated turnstiles do not give change, but you can get this from the ticket window (unnecessary, of course, if you're carrying an Octopus card).

For details on the special four-day tourist pass valid on trams and the Star Ferry, see p303.

The four Star Ferry routes:

Central (Star Ferry pier)–Tsim Sha Tsui Adult lower/upper deck $1.70/2.20, child $1.20/1.30, seniors free; seven minutes; every six to 12 minutes from 6.30am to 11.30pm.

Central (Star Ferry pier)–Hung Hom Adult/child $5.30/2.70, seniors free; 15 minutes; every 15 to 20 minutes from 7am to 7.20pm Monday to Friday, every 20 minutes from 7am to 7pm Saturday and Sunday.

Wan Chai–Tsim Sha Tsui Adult/child $2.20/1.30, seniors free; eight minutes; every eight to 20 minutes from 7.30am to 11pm Monday to Saturday, every 12 to 20 minutes from 7.40am to 11pm Sunday.

Wan Chai–Hung Hom Adult/child $5.30/2.70, seniors free; 10 minutes; every 15 to 20 minutes from 7.08am to 7.17pm Monday to Friday, every 20 to 22 minutes from 7.08am to 7.10pm Saturday and Sunday.

Transport

BICYCLE

BORNE ON A STAR

There are few modes of transport anywhere that can claim they sparked a riot, but Hong Kong's Star Ferry can. In 1966, when Communist China was in the grip of the Cultural Revolution, agitators used the ferry company's fare increase of 5c as a pretext for fomenting violent demonstrations. The disturbances continued for almost a year.

Mention of the Star Ferry service between Pedder's Wharf (now reclaimed land) and Tsim Sha Tsui first appeared in an 1888 newspaper article. At that time, boats sailed 'every 40 minutes to one hour during all hours of the day' except on Monday and Friday, when they were billeted for coal delivery. Service has continued ever since, with the only major suspension occurring during WWII. The Star Ferry was something of a war hero; during the Japanese invasion, boats were used to evacuate refugees and Allied troops from the Kowloon Peninsula before the service was suspended for more than four years.

Until the Cross-Harbour Tunnel opened in 1978 and the first line of the MTR two years later, the Star Ferry was the only way to cross the harbour. At rush hour long queues of commuters would back up as far as the General Post Office on the Hong Kong Island side and Star House in Kowloon.

OTHER CROSS-HARBOUR FERRIES

Three other ferry companies operate cross-harbour ferries: **Discovery Bay Transportation Services** (☎ 2987 7351; www.hkri.com) makes trips from Central to Tsim Sha Tsui East; **New World First Ferry** (☎ 2131 8181; www.nwff .com.hk) has ferries from North Point to Hung Hom and Kowloon City; and the **Fortune Ferry Co** (☎ 2994 8155) has a service linking North Point and Kwun Tong.

Central (Queen's pier)–Tsim Sha Tsui East Adult $4.50, child and senior $2.30; five minutes; every 20 minutes from 7.40am to 8.20pm (from 8am on Sunday).

North Point–Hung Hom Adult $4.50, child and senior $2.30; seven minutes; every 20 minutes from 7.20am to 7.20pm.

North Point–Kowloon City Adult $4.50, child and senior $2.30; 11 minutes; every 20 minutes from 7.10am to 7.30pm.

North Point–Kwun Tong Adult $5, child and senior $2.50; 12 minutes; every 30 minutes from 7am to 7.30pm.

NEW TERRITORIES FERRIES
Sai Kung Peninsula & Tap Mun Chau

Boats operated by the **Tsui Wah Ferry Service** (☎ 2527 2513, 2272 2022; www.traway.com .hk) link the east-central New Territories near Chinese University with the Sai Kung Peninsula and Tap Mun Chau. From the pier at Ma Liu Shui, ferries cruise through Tolo Harbour to Tap Mun Chau and back, calling at various villages on the Sai Kung Peninsula both outbound and inbound.

Ferries leave Ma Liu Shui at 8.30am and 3pm daily, arriving at Tap Mun Chau at 10am and 4.20pm respectively, from where they continue on to Ko Lau Wan, Chek Keng and Wong Shek (weekdays/weekend $16/25). They leave for Ma Liu Shui at 11.10am and 5.30pm. On Saturday, Sunday and public holidays an extra ferry leaves Ma Liu Shui at 12.30pm, arriving and departing from Tap Mun Chau at 1.45pm.

An easier – and faster – way to reach Tap Mun Chau, with many more departures, is by *kaido* (p296) from Wong Shek pier, which is the last stop on bus 94 from Sai Kung town. The *kaidos*, operated by Tsui Wah Ferry Service, run about once every two hours (there's a total of six sailings, with

two callings at Chek Keng) from 8.30am to 6.30pm Monday to Friday ($8), and hourly (there are 12 sailings, with two stops at Chek Keng) between 8.30am and 6.35pm at the weekend and on public holidays ($12). Be aware that the last sailing back from Tap Mun Chau is at 6pm from Monday to Friday and 6.05pm at the weekend.

If you've missed the boat or can't be bothered waiting for the next, the private sampans at Wong Shek pier, which seat up to three people in addition to the driver, charge from $60 per trip to or from the island.

Tung Ping Chau

You can reach Tung Ping Chau from Ma Liu Shui, near the Chinese University, on ferries operated by **Tsui Wah Ferry Service** (☎ 2527 2513; www.traway.com.hk), but only at the weekend and on public holidays. Ferries depart from Ma Liu Shui at 9am and 3.30pm on Saturday, returning at 5.15pm. The single ferry on Sunday and public holidays leaves Ma Liu Shui at 9am, returning from Tung Ping Chau at 5.15pm. Only return tickets ($80) are available, and the trip takes 1¾ hours. The Sunday morning ferry could well be booked out, so call ahead to check availability.

OUTLYING ISLANDS FERRIES

The main Outlying Islands are all linked to Hong Kong by regular ferry services. Fares are cheap and the ferries are comfortable and usually air-conditioned. They have toilets, and some have a basic bar that serves snacks and cold drinks. The ferries can get very crowded on Saturday afternoon and all day Sunday, especially in the warmer months. They depart early and return in the evening.

There are two types of ferries: the large 'ordinary ferries', which, with the exception of those to Lamma, offer ordinary and deluxe classes; and the smaller 'fast ferries' – hovercraft that have one class only and cut travel time by between 10 and 20 minutes but cost between 50% and 100% more. 'Weekday' fares apply from Monday to Saturday; prices are higher on Sunday and public holidays. Unless stated otherwise, children aged three to 11 years, seniors over 65 years and people with disabilities pay half-fare on both types of ferries and in both classes. Return is double the single fare.

The main operator serving the Outlying Islands is **New World First Ferry** (NWFF; ☎ 2131 8181; www.nwff.com.hk), which has a **customer service centre** (Map pp408–9; Pier 6, Outlying Islands ferry pier; ☯ 10am-2pm & 3-7pm Mon & Wed-Fri, 10am-1.30pm Tue, 10.30am-3.30pm Sat & Sun). NWFF boats sail to/from Cheung Chau, Peng Chau and Lantau, and connect all three via an inter-island service. The **Hong Kong & Kowloon Ferry Co** (HKKF; ☎ 2815 6063; www.hkkf.com .hk) serves destinations on Lamma only and also has a **customer service centre** (Map pp408–9; Pier 4, Outlying Islands ferry pier; ☯ 9am-6pm).

Ferry timetables are subject to slight seasonal changes. They are prominently displayed at all ferry piers, or you can read them on the ferry companies' websites.

Tickets are available from booths at the ferry piers, but avoid queuing at busy times by using an Octopus card or putting the exact change into the turnstile as you enter.

If your time is limited, you can go on an organised tour (p66) or even hire your own junk (p225).

The NWFF's Island Hopping Pass allows unlimited rides for a day on ordinary ferries to Lantau, Cheung Chau and Peng Chau. The pass costs $30 Monday to Saturday and $40 on Sunday. For $10 per trip you can upgrade to deluxe class or the fast ferry.

Lamma
TO/FROM CENTRAL
Both Yung Shue Wan and Sok Kwu Wan are served by HKKF ferries from pier 4 (Map pp408–9) at the Outlying Islands ferry pier in Central. Ordinary and fast ferries depart Central for Yung Shue Wan approximately every half-hour to an hour (with additional sailings around 8am and 6pm) from 6.30am to 12.30am. The last boat to Central from Yung Shue Wan leaves at 11.30pm. The trip on the ordinary ferry takes 35 minutes, and the adult one-way fare is $11 ($14 on Sunday and public holidays). The fast ferries, which take just 20 minutes, cost $16 ($20 on Sunday and public holidays).

From Central, fast ferries (only) reach Sok Kwu Wan in 25 minutes and cost $14 ($18 on Sunday and public holidays). Ferries leave every 1½ hours or so, with the first departing Central at 7.20am and the last at 11.30pm. The last ferry to Central from Sok Kwu Wan is at 10.40pm.

TO/FROM ABERDEEN
Fast ferries (only) link the pier at Aberdeen Promenade with Yung Shue Wan ($12) via Pak Kok Tsuen ($6) some 10 times a day, with the first ferry leaving Aberdeen at 6.30am and the last at 8.15pm Monday to Saturday. There are up to 15 ferries on Sunday and public holidays, with the first leaving Aberdeen at 7.30am and the last at 7.30pm. The last ferry for Aberdeen leaves Yung Shue Wan at 8.45pm and Pak Kok Tsuen at 9pm Monday to Saturday. On Sunday and public holidays, the last sailing times are 8pm from Yung Shue Wan and 8.10pm from Pak Kok Tsuen.

There is also a smaller ferry – more like a *kaido*, really – run by **Chuen Kee Ferry** (☎ 2982 8225, 2375 7883; www.ferry.com.hk) between Aberdeen and Sok Kwu Wan; all but two stop at Mo Tat Wan along the way. The journey between Aberdeen and Mo Tat Wan takes 23 minutes, and it's another seven minutes from there to Sok Kwu Wan. The adult fare is $8 ($12 in the evening and on Sunday and public holidays); between Mo Tat Wan and Sok Kwu Wan it costs $3 ($4).

There are up to 13 departures from Aberdeen to Sok Kwu Wan from Monday to Saturday between 6.40am and 10.50pm, leaving roughly every 1½ hours. In the other direction there are the same number of daily departures from Monday to Saturday between 6am and 10.10pm. On Sunday and public holiday, the service increases to 19 trips in each direction. Boats depart approximately every 45 minutes; the earliest and latest boats from Aberdeen are 6.40am and 10.50pm. From Sok Kwu Wan, the earliest and latest trips are 6am and 10.10pm.

A sampan from Aberdeen to Sok Kwu Wan/Yung Shue Wan will cost about $80/100 during the day and double that or more in the wee hours, when drunken revellers who have missed the last ferry back from Central are trying to get home. If you should be in the same boat – as it were – don't panic; there's usually at least one other person willing to split the cost.

Cheung Chau
TO/FROM CENTRAL
Ordinary and fast ferries for Cheung Chau depart from pier 5 (Map pp408–9) at the Outlying Islands ferry pier in Central approximately every half-hour between 6.15am (6.30am on Sunday and holidays)

Transport

BOAT

and 12.30am. There are then fast ferries at 1.30am and 4.15am until normal daytime services begin again. The last ferry back to Central from Cheung Chau leaves at 11.45pm (11.30pm on Sunday), but don't worry if you miss it; there are fast ferries at 2.20am and 5.10am seven days a week and an ordinary one at 5.50am Monday to Saturday (6am on Sunday and holidays).

The trip on the ordinary ferry takes 48 minutes, and the adult one-way fare in ordinary class is $10.50 ($15.70 on Sunday and public holidays). The fares for deluxe class, which allows you to sit on the open-air deck at the stern, are $16.80 and $25, respectively. The fast ferries, which run as frequently as the ordinary ones and take just 32 minutes, cost $21 ($31 on Sunday and public holidays).

TO/FROM TSIM SHA TSUI

On Saturday, Sunday and public holidays only, fast ferries depart for Cheung Chau via Mui Wo on Lantau from the northern side of the Tsim Sha Tsui Star Ferry pier. The one-way fare is $31, and the voyage takes 55 minutes. Boats leave Tsim Sha Tsui at 2pm, 4pm and 6pm on Saturday, and every two hours between 10am and 6pm on Sunday and public holidays. The return ferries from Cheung Chau run at 3.05pm, 5.05pm and 7.05pm on Saturday and every two hours between 11.05am and 7.05pm on Sunday and public holidays.

INTER-ISLAND SERVICE

An ordinary inter-island ferry ($8.40 all sectors) links Cheung Chau with Mui Wo (usually via Chi Ma Wan on Lantau) and Peng Chau seven days a week. The first ferry leaves Cheung Chau at 6am, and the last ferry is at 10.50pm; boats depart approximately every 1½ hours. From Cheung Chau, it takes 20 minutes to reach Chi Ma Wan, 30 to 45 minutes to Mui Wo and 50 to 75 minutes to Peng Chau.

Lantau

The main entry port for vessels serving Lantau proper is Mui Wo, which is known as Silvermine Bay in English. You can, however, also reach Lantau destinations from other ports: Discovery Bay from Central, the Chi Ma Wan Peninsula from Cheung Chau, the Trappist Monastery from Peng Chau, and Tai O and Tung Chung from Tuen Mun in the New Territories.

MUI WO TO/FROM CENTRAL

Both ordinary and fast ferries depart for Mui Wo from pier 6 (Map pp408–9) at the Outlying Islands ferry pier in Central approximately every half-hour between 6.10am (7am on Sunday and public holidays) and 12.30am. Between those times there is a 3am fast ferry to Mui Wo via Peng Chau. The last ferry from Mui Wo to Central is at 11.30pm, though there is a fast ferry at 3.40am, which calls at Peng Chau along the way.

The journey on the ordinary ferry takes 48 minutes, and the adult one-way fare is $10.50/16.80 in ordinary/deluxe class ($15.70/25 on Sunday and public holidays). The fast ferries, which take 31 minutes, cost $21 ($31 on Sunday and public holidays).

MUI WO TO/FROM TSIM SHA TSUI

At the weekend and on public holidays only, ferries depart for Mui Wo from the Tsim Sha Tsui Star Ferry pier in Kowloon. Fast ferries leave Tsim Sha Tsui every two hours between 2pm and 6pm on Saturday and between 10am and 6pm on Sunday and public holidays. The return ferries from Mui Wo are at the same frequency between 2.40pm and 6.40pm on Saturday and between 10.40am and 6.40pm on Sunday and public holidays, calling at Cheung Chau en route. The one-way fare is $31 and the trip to Mui Wo takes about 35 minutes.

MUI WO & THE INTER-ISLAND SERVICE

The ordinary inter-island ferry ($8.40) links Mui Wo with Cheung Chau (via Chi Ma Wan mostly) and Peng Chau 20 times a day. The first ferry leaves Mui Wo for Cheung Chau at 6am and for Peng Chau at 6.35am; the last ferry to Cheung Chau is at 10.20pm and to Peng Chau at 11.20pm. From Mui Wo it takes 20 to 25 minutes to reach Peng Chau, 15 to 20 minutes to Chi Ma Wan and 40 to 50 minutes to Cheung Chau.

TO/FROM THE TRAPPIST MONASTERY

For details on how to reach the Trappist Monastery on Lantau's northeast coast, see opposite.

TO/FROM DISCOVERY BAY

High-speed ferries run by the Discovery Bay Transportation Service (☎ 2987 7351; www.hkri .com) leave from pier 3 (Map pp408–9) at the Outlying Islands ferry pier in Central every 10 to 30 minutes between 6.30am and 1am; after that time there are additional sailings at 1.30am (on weekends only), 2am, 2.30am (on weekends only), 3.30am and 5am until the daytime schedule resumes. Similar services run from Discovery Bay to Central. Tickets are $27 and the trip takes 25 to 30 minutes.

Ferries run by **Peng Chau Rental Kaito** (☎ 9033 8102) depart from Mui Wo for Discovery Bay between 7.45am and 6.45pm Monday to Friday and up to nine times at the weekend. From Discovery Bay to Mui Wo, sailings are between 7.15am and 6.15pm Monday to Friday, and there are up to nine sailings on Saturday and Sunday. Tickets cost $10 and the trip takes between 15 and 20 minutes.

You can also reach Discovery Bay from Peng Chau (right).

TO/FROM CHI MA WAN

The ordinary inter-island ferry ($8.40) linking Cheung Chau and Mui Wo calls at the Chi Ma Wan ferry pier on the northeastern corner of the peninsula six times a day (with the first at 6.15am and the last at 8.30pm) heading for Cheung Chau, and five times a day going to Mui Wo (the first at 6.55am and the last at 7.05pm), from where it carries on to Peng Chau.

TO/FROM TAI O

There are NWFF ferries linking the Tai O berthing pier on Wing On St and Tuen Mun in the New Territories (via Sha Lo Wan and the Tung Chung New Development pier on Lantau's north coast) daily at 9.45am, 12.15pm, 4.15pm and 7.15pm, with an additional sailing at 2.15pm on Sunday. The trip takes between 50 minutes and an hour and costs $15 ($25 on Sunday). On Sunday and public holidays there are three direct sailings ($25; 30 minutes) to Tuen Mun (at 10.45am, 1.45pm and 5.45pm) departing from Tai O's Shek Tsai Po pier, which is about 1.2km west of the centre.

TO/FROM TUNG CHUNG

Another service run by NWFF links Tung Chung New Development pier with Tuen Mun in the New Territories. Ferries depart from Tuen Mun every 20 minutes from 5.40am to 11pm, with the return boats leaving Tung Chung between 20 and 30 minutes later (6am to 11.20pm). The trip takes 17 minutes and costs $15 ($10 for concession).

Peng Chau

TO/FROM CENTRAL

Ordinary and fast ferries leave for Peng Chau approximately once every 45 minutes between 7am and 12.30am from pier 6 (Map pp408–9) at the Outlying Islands ferry pier in Central. There's also a 3am fast ferry to Peng Chau that carries on to Mui Wo on Lantau. The last ferry from Peng Chau to Central is at 11.30pm (11.35pm on Sunday), though there is a fast ferry at 3.25am.

The journey on the ordinary ferry takes 38 minutes, and the adult one-way fare is $10.50/16.80 in ordinary/deluxe class ($15.70/25 on Sunday and public holidays). The fast ferries, which take 25 minutes, cost $21 ($31 on Sunday and public holidays).

INTER-ISLAND SERVICE

An ordinary inter-island ferry ($8.40) links Peng Chau with Mui Wo and (frequently) Chi Ma Wan on Lantau, as well as Cheung Chau, up to 11 times a day. The first ferry leaves Peng Chau at 5.40am for all three destinations; the last ferry to Mui Wo is at 11.40pm. Boats take 20 minutes to reach Mui Wo, 40 minutes to Chi Ma Wan and 70 minutes to Cheung Chau.

TO/FROM
THE TRAPPIST MONASTERY

Peng Chau is the main springboard for the Trappist Monastery, with up to 10 sailings a day. **Peng Chau Rental Kaito** (☎ 9033 8102) sails sampans to Tai Shui Hang pier from the auxiliary pier southeast of the main Peng Chau ferry pier daily between 7.45am and 5pm. They return from the monastery between 8.10am and 5.10pm.

TO/FROM DISCOVERY BAY

Peng Chau Rental Kaito (☎ 9033 8102) links Peng Chau with Discovery Bay every 30 minutes to an hour, with up to 20 sailings a day between 6.30am and 10pm, from the pier southeast of the main Peng Chau ferry. The last boat from Discovery Bay sails at 10.15pm.

Ma Wan

TO/FROM CENTRAL

Ferries run by **Park Island Transport** (☎ 2946 8888; www.pitck.com.hk) and essentially servicing the high-end residential community on

Ma Wan depart from pier 2 (Map pp408–9) at the Outlying Islands ferry pier in Central every 15 to 30 minutes from 6.30am to 1.30 and then run hourly until the normal schedule resumes. The one-way fare is $16 and the trip takes 22 minutes.

TO/FROM TSUEN WAN

Boats run by Park Island Transport leave the ferry pier in Tsuen Wan, which is due south of the KCR West Rail's Tsuen Wan West station in the New Territories, for Ma Wan every 15 to 30 minutes between 6.55am and 11.55pm (6.40am to 11.40pm from Ma Wan to Tsuen Wan). The one-way fare is $5 and the trip takes just 10 minutes.

Tung Lung Chau

At the weekend only, ferries run by **Lam Kee Kaido** (☎ 2560 9929) heading for Joss House Bay on the Clearwater Bay Peninsula from Sai Wan Ho, east of Quarry Bay on Hong Kong Island, stop at Tung Lung Chau en route. On Saturday, boats sail from Sai Wan Ho at 9am, 10.30am, 3.30pm and 4.45pm, departing from Tung Lung Chau a half-hour later. On Sunday and public holidays there are boats from Sai Wan Ho at 8.30am, 9.45am, 11am, 2.15pm, 3.30pm and 4.45pm; they return from Tung Lung Chau at 9am, 10.20am, 1.45pm, 3pm, 4pm and 5.30pm. The trip takes a half-hour, and the one-way fare is $28/14 for adults/children under 12.

To catch the ferry, take the MTR's Island line to Sai Wan Ho and then use exit A. Follow Tai On St north until you reach the quayside. The ride to Joss House Bay from Tung Lung Chau is significantly shorter than the one from Sai Wan Ho. If you're in a hurry coming back, get off there and catch bus No 91 to the Choi Hung MTR station.

Po Toi Island

A ferry run by **Po Toi Kaido Services** (☎ 2554 4059) leaves Aberdeen for Po Toi on Tuesday, Thursday and Saturday at 9am, returning from the island at 10.30am. On Sunday a single boat leaves Aberdeen at 8am, but there are also departures at 10am and 11.30am from **St Stephen's Beach Water Sports Centre** (Map p411; ☎ 2813 5407; Wong Ma Kok Path) in Stanley. Boats return from Po Toi at 3pm, 4.30pm and 6pm. A same-day return fare is $40 and the journey takes about 35 minutes.

OTHER BOATS

Sea and harbour transport is not limited to scheduled ferries in Hong Kong. You may encounter several other types of boats as you travel further afield.

Kaidos (small- to medium-sized 'ferries') are able to make short runs on the open sea. Only a few *kaido* routes operate on regular schedules (eg the ones from Peng Chau to the Trappist Monastery and Discovery Bay, and from Aberdeen to Sok Kwu Wan on Lamma); most simply adjust supply to demand. *Kaidos* run most frequently at weekends and public holidays.

Sampans are motorised launches that can only accommodate a few (usually four) people. Sampans are generally too small to be considered seaworthy, but they can safely zip you around typhoon shelters like the ones at Aberdeen and Cheung Chau.

Bigger than a sampan but smaller than a *kaido*, *walla wallas* (water taxis that operate in Victoria Harbour) are a dying breed. Most of the customers are sailors stationed on ships anchored in the harbour. On Hong Kong Island look for them at Queen's pier on the east side of the Star Ferry pier. On the Kowloon side, they can sometimes be found southeast of the Star Ferry pier in Tsim Sha Tsui.

BUS

Hong Kong's extensive bus system offers a bewildering number of routes that will take you just about anywhere in the territory. Since the northern side of Hong Kong Island and Kowloon are so well served by the MTR, most visitors use the buses primarily to explore the southern side of Hong Kong Island and the New Territories.

Although buses pick up and discharge passengers at stops along the way, on Hong Kong Island the most important bus stations are the bus terminus below Exchange Square in Central (Map pp408–9) and the one at Admiralty (Map pp408–9). From these stations you can catch buses to Aberdeen, Repulse Bay, Stanley and other destinations on the southern side of Hong Kong Island. In Kowloon the bus terminal at the Star Ferry pier in Tsim Sha Tsui is the most important, with buses to Hung Hom station and points in eastern and western Kowloon. Almost all New Towns in the New Territories are important transport hubs, though Sha Tin is particularly so, with buses travelling as far afield as Sai Kung, Tung Chung and Tuen Mun.

Bus fares range from $1.20 to $45, depending on the destination and how many sections you travel. Fares for night buses cost from $12.80 to $23. Payment is made into a fare box upon entry so, unless you're carrying an ever-so-convenient Octopus card (p303), have plenty of coins handy, as the driver does not give change.

Hong Kong's buses are usually double-deckers. Many buses have easy-to-read LCD displays of road names and stops in Chinese and sometimes in English, and TV screens to entertain you as you roll along. Buses serving the airport and Hung Hom train station have luggage racks.

Hong Kong's buses are run by a half-dozen private operators, carrying just over four million passengers a day (ie 37% of the total daily public-transport volume). Though it's much of a muchness as to who's driving you from A to B or even C, you may want to check the routings on their websites.

Citybus (☎ 2873 0818; www.citybus.com.hk)

Discovery Bay Transportation Services (☎ 2987 7351; www.hkri.com)

Kowloon Motor Bus Co (☎ 2745 4466; www.kmb.com.hk)

Long Win Bus Co (☎ 2261 2791; www.kmb.com.hk)

New Lantao Bus Company (☎ 2984 9848; www.new lantaobus.com)

New World First Bus Services (☎ 2136 8888; www.nwfb.com.hk)

ROUTES & SCHEDULES

There are no good bus maps and, because buses are run by so many different private operators, there is no longer a comprehensive directory for the whole territory. Your best option is Universal Publications' *Hong Kong Guidebook* or *Hong Kong Directory* (p316), which include the *Public Transport Boarding Guide* in (mostly) Chinese and (some) English.

The HKTB has useful leaflets on the major bus routes, and the major bus companies detail all their routes on their websites. You might also try the Yellow Pages Map website (www.ypmap.com).

NIGHT BUSES

Most buses run from about 5.30am or 6am until midnight or 12.30am, but there are a handful of useful night bus services in addition to the ones linking the airport with various parts of the territory. Citybus' N121, which operates every 15 minutes between 12.45am and 5am, runs from the Macau ferry bus terminus through Central and Wan Chai on Hong Kong Island and through the Cross-Harbour Tunnel to Chatham Rd North in Tsim Sha Tsui East before continuing on to eastern Kowloon and Ngau Tau Kok ($12.80).

Bus No N122, also run by Citybus with the same fare and schedule, runs from North Point ferry bus terminus on Hong Kong Island, through the Cross-Harbour Tunnel to Nathan Rd and on to Mei Foo Sun Chuen in the northwestern part of Kowloon. You can catch these two buses near the tunnel entrances on either side of the harbour.

Other useful night buses that cross the harbour include the N118, which runs from Siu Sai Wan in the northeastern part of Hong Kong Island to Sham Shui Po in northwest Kowloon via North Point and Causeway Bay ($12.80); and the N170, which runs from Wah Fu, a large estate near Aberdeen in the southwest of Hong Kong Island, through Wan Chai and Causeway Bay before crossing over to Kowloon and travelling as far as Sha Tin in the New Territories ($23).

Useful night buses on Lantau include the N1 ($16; $25 Sundays and public holidays) linking Mui Wo and Tai O at 2.50am (3.45am from Tai O) and the N35 ($20; $35 on Sunday and public holidays) between Mui Wo (1.30am, 3.30am and 4.30am) and the airport (1.30am, 3am and 5am).

CAR & MOTORCYCLE

It would be sheer madness for a newcomer to consider driving in Hong Kong. Traffic is heavy, the roads can get hopelessly clogged and the ever-changing network of highways and bridges with its new numbering system is complicated in the extreme. And if driving the car doesn't destroy your holiday sense of spontaneity, parking the damn thing will. If you are determined to see Hong Kong under your own steam, do yourself a favour and rent a car with a driver.

DRIVING LICENCE & PERMITS

Hong Kong allows most foreigners over the age of 18 to drive for up to 12 months with their valid local licenses. It's still a good idea to carry an International Driving Permit (IDP) as well. This can be obtained from your local automobile association for a reasonable fee (eg $80 in Hong Kong).

Anyone driving in the territory for more than a year will need a Hong Kong licence valid for 10 years ($900). Apply to the **Licensing Division of the Transport Department** (Map pp408–9; ☎ 2804 2600; www.info.gov.hk /td; 3rd fl, United Centre, 95 Queensway, Admiralty; ◷ 9am-4pm Mon-Fri & 9-11.30am Sat).

HIRE

Car-hire firms accept International Driving Permits or driving licences from your home country. Drivers must usually be at least 25 years of age. Daily rates for small cars start at just under $700, but there are weekend and weekly deals available. For example, **Avis** (Map pp420–1; ☎ 2890 6988; Ground fl, Shop 46, Peninsula Centre, 67 Mody Rd, Tsim Sha Tsui East; ◷ 9am-6pm Mon-Fri, 9am-4pm Sat & Sun) will rent you a Toyota Corolla or Honda Civic for the weekend (from 2pm on Friday to 10.30am Monday) for $1360; the same car for a day/week costs $680/3000. Rates include unlimited kilometres.

If you're looking for a car with a driver, contact **Ace Hire Car Service** (Map pp406–7; ☎ 2572 7663; www.acehirecar.com.hk; 16 Min Fat St, Happy Valley), which charges between $160 and $250 per hour (minimum three to five hours, depending on the location). Avis' chauffeur-driven cars are much more expensive: $300 to $400 with a minimum of four hours on weekdays and six hours on Saturday and Sunday.

ROAD RULES

Vehicles drive on the left-hand side of the road in Hong Kong, as in the UK, Australia and Macau, but *not* in mainland China. Seat belts must be worn by the driver and all passengers, in both the front and back seats. Police are strict and give out traffic tickets at the drop of a hat.

MINIBUS

Minibuses are vans with no more than 16 seats. They come in two varieties – red and green. Red minibuses are cream-coloured with a red roof or stripe, and pick up and discharge passengers wherever they are hailed or asked to stop (but not in restricted zones or at busy bus stops). Maxicabs, commonly known as 'green minibuses', are cream-coloured with a green roof or stripe, and operate on fixed routes.

There are 4350 minibuses running in the territory. About 40% are red minibuses and 60% green.

RED MINIBUS

Red minibuses can be handy for short distances, such as the trip from Central to Wan Chai or Causeway Bay, and you can be assured of a seat – by law, passengers are not allowed to stand. The destination is displayed on the front in large Chinese characters, usually with a smaller English translation below.

The problem for non-Chinese-speakers is not getting on but getting off. There are no buttons or bells, so you must call out your stop – and minibus drivers rarely speak English. If you call out, 'stop here, please', there is a pretty good chance the driver will do so, but otherwise try the Cantonese version, *yiu lawk* (have to get down), or simply *lày-do `m-gòi* (here, please).

Minibus fares range from $2 to $20. The price to the final destination is displayed on a card propped up in the windscreen, but this is often only written in Chinese numbers. Fares are equal to or higher than those on the bus, but drivers often increase their fares on rainy days, at night and during holiday periods. You usually hand the driver the fare when you get off, and change is given. You can use your Octopus card on certain routes.

If you're in Central, the best place to catch minibuses to Wan Chai and other points east is the Central bus terminus below Exchange Square. If heading west towards Kennedy Town, walk to Stanley St, near Lan Kwai Fong.

There are a few minibuses that cross the harbour late at night, running between Wan Chai and Mong Kok. In Wan Chai minibuses can be found on Hennessy and Fleming Rds. In Kowloon you may have to trudge up Nathan Rd as far as Mong Kok or over to the Hung Hom station before you'll find one. Minibuses to the New Territories can be found at the Jordan and Choi Hung MTR stations in Kowloon.

Transport MINIBUS

GREEN MINIBUS

Green minibuses operate on some 352 routes, more than half of which are in the New Territories, and serve designated stops. Fares range from $2.50 to $22.50, according to distance. You must put the exact fare in the cash box as you descend (no change is given) or, on some routes, use your Octopus card.

In Tsim Sha Tsui the No 6 green minibus ($4.30) runs from Hankow Rd to Tsim Sha Tsui East and Hung Hom station every five minutes or so between 6.30am and 12.05pm. On Hong Kong Island the No 1 green minibus ($7.40) leaves Lung Wui Rd just east of Hong Kong City Hall and the Star Ferry pier in Central for the Peak every five to 12 minutes from 6.30am to midnight.

MASS TRANSIT RAILWAY

The **Mass Transit Railway** (MTR; Map p417; ☎ 2881 8888; www.mtr.com.hk), Hong Kong's underground rail system and universally known as the 'MTR', is a phenomenon of modern urban public transport. Sleek, pristine and *always* on time, it is also rather soulless.

Though it costs more than other forms of public transport in Hong Kong, the MTR is the quickest way to get to most destinations in the urban areas. Trains run every two to 10 minutes from around 6am to sometime between 12.30am and 1am.

The MTR travels on just under 88km of track and is made up of seven lines, including the Airport Express (p289) and the new Disneyland Resort line. It serves 53 stations and carries 2.3 million passengers a day.

The Island line (blue) extends along the northern coast of Hong Kong Island from Sheung Wan in the west to Chai Wan in the east. The Tsuen Wan line (red) runs from Central station and travels alongside the Island line as far as Admiralty, where it crosses the harbour and runs through central Kowloon, terminating at Tsuen Wan in the New Territories.

The Kwun Tong line (green), which begins at Yau Ma Tei, shares that and two subsequent stations with the Tsuen Wan line; at Prince Edward it branches off and heads for eastern Kowloon, crossing the KCR East Rail line at Kowloon Tong before joining the Tseung Kwan O line at Yau Tong and terminating at Tiu Keng Leng in the southeastern New Territories.

The Tseung Kwan O line (purple) starts at North Point and hits Quarry Bay before crossing the eastern harbour and terminating at Po Lam in the southeastern New Territories. The Tung Chung line (orange) shares the same rail lines as the Airport Express, but stops at two additional stations in Kowloon (Kowloon and Olympic) along the way. It terminates at Tung Chung, a New Town on Lantau that offers cheaper transport options to and from the airport.

The MTR connects with the KCR East Rai at Tsim Sha Tsui and Kowloon Tong stations. It meets the KCR West Rail at Nam Cheong and Mei Foo.

For short hauls, the MTR is not great value. If you want to cross the harbour from Tsim Sha Tsui to Central, for example, at $9/4.5 per adult/child (or $7.90/4 with an Octopus card) the MTR is more than four times the price of the Star Ferry, with none of the views, and the journey is only marginally faster. If your destination is further away – North Point, say, or Kwun Tong – the MTR is considerably faster than a bus or minibus and about the same price. If possible, it's best to avoid the rush hours: 7.30am to 9.30am and 5pm to 7pm weekdays and Saturday morning, when 85% of the 1050 MTR carriages are in use.

Travelling by the MTR is so easy: everything, from the ticket-vending machines to the turnstiles, is automated. The system uses the stored-value Octopus card (p303), really the only way to go, and single-journey tickets with a magnetic coding strip on the back. When you pass through the turnstile, the card is encoded with the station identification and time. At the other end, the exit turnstile sucks in the ticket, reads where you came from, the time you bought the ticket and how much you paid. If everything is in order, it will let you through. If you have underpaid (by mistake or otherwise), you can make up the difference at an MTR service counter; there are no fines since no one gets out without paying. Once you've passed through the turnstile to begin a journey you have 90 minutes to complete it before the ticket becomes invalid.

Ticket prices range from $4 to $26 ($3.80 and $23.10 with an Octopus card); children and seniors pay between $3 and $13 ($2.40 and $11.60 with a card), depending on the destination. Ticket machines accept $10 and $20 notes and $10, $5, $2, $1 and 50c coins and dispense change. The machines have a touch screen with high-lighted destinations. You can also buy tickets from MTR service counters and get change from the Hang Seng bank branches located in most stations.

Smoking, eating and drinking are not permitted in MTR stations or on the trains, and violators are subject to a fine of $5000. You are not allowed to carry large objects or bicycles aboard trains either, though back-packs and suitcases are fine.

There are no toilets in any of the MTR stations. Like the 90-minute limit on a tick-et's validity, the reasoning behind this is to get bodies into stations, bums on seats (or hands on straps), and bodies out onto the street again as quickly as possible. The sys-tem works, and very few people complain.

MTR exit signs use an alphanumerical system and there can be as many as a dozen to choose from. We give the correct exit for sights and destinations wherever pos-sible in the Sights chapter, but you may find yourself studying the exit table from time to time and scratching your head. There are always maps of the local area at each exit.

Should you leave something behind on the MTR, you can contact the **lost property office** (☎ 2861 0020; ☿ 8am-8pm) at Ad-miralty MTR station.

TAXI

Hong Kong taxis are a bargain compared with those in other world-class cities. With more than 18,000 cruising the streets of the territory, they're easy to flag down.

When a taxi is available, there should be a red 'For Hire' sign illuminated on the meter that's visible through the windscreen. At night the 'Taxi' sign on the roof will be lit up as well. Taxis will not stop at bus stops or in restricted zones where a yellow line is painted next to the kerb.

The law requires that everyone in a ve-hicle wears a seat belt. Both driver and passenger(s) will be fined if stopped by the police, and most drivers will gently remind you to buckle up before proceeding.

'Urban taxis' – those in Kowloon and on Hong Kong Island – are red with silver roofs. New Territories taxis are green with white tops, and Lantau taxis are blue.

Hong Kong Island and Kowloon taxis tend to avoid each others' turf as the drivers'

street geography on the other side of the har-bour can be pretty shaky. Hong Kong Island and Kowloon taxis maintain separate ranks at places such as Hung Hom train station and the Star Ferry pier and will sometimes refuse to take you to the 'other side'. In any case, if you're travelling from Hong Kong Island to Kowloon (or vice versa), choose the correct cab as you'll save on the tunnel toll. New Territories taxis are not permitted to pick up passengers in Kowloon or on Hong Kong Island at all.

The rate for taxis on Hong Kong Island and Kowloon is $15 for the first 2km and $1.40 for every additional 200m; waiting costs $1.40 per minute. In the New Territo-ries it's $12.50 for the first 2km and $1.20 for each additional 200m; waiting costs $1.20 per minute. On Lantau the equiva-lent charges are $12 and $1.20, and $1.20 for per-minute waiting. There is a luggage fee of $5 per bag but, depending on the size, not all drivers insist on this payment. It costs an extra $5 to book a taxi by tele-phone. Try to carry smaller bills and coins; most drivers are hesitant to make change for anything over $100. You can tip up to 10%, but most Hong Kong people just leave the little brown coins and a dollar or two.

Passengers must pay the toll if a taxi goes through many of Hong Kong's harbour or mountain tunnels or uses the Lantau Link to Tung Chung or the airport. Though the Cross-Harbour Tunnel costs only $10, you'll be required to pay $20 if, say, you take a Hong Kong taxi from Hong Kong Island to Kowloon. If you manage to find a Kow-loon taxi returning 'home', you'll pay only $10. (It works the other way round as well, of course.) If you cross the harbour via the Western Harbour Tunnel you must pay the $15 toll plus $15 for the return unless you can find a cab heading for its base. Similarly, if you use the Eastern Harbour Crossing you may have to pay the $15 toll twice.

There's no way of avoiding the whopping great toll of $30 in both directions when a taxi uses the Lantau Link, however.

There is no double charge for the other roads and tunnels: Aberdeen ($5); Lion Rock ($8); Shing Mun ($5); Tate's Cairn ($10); Tai Lam ($22); and Tseung Kwan O ($3).

It's not as hard as it used to be, but you may have some trouble hailing a cab during rush hour, when it rains or during the driver shift-change period (around 4pm daily). Taxis are also in higher demand after midnight. There are no extra late-night charges and no extra passenger charges, though some taxis are insured to carry four passengers and some five. You can tell by glancing at the licence plate.

Some taxi drivers speak English well; others don't have a word of the language. It's never a bad idea to have your destination written down in Chinese.

Though most Hong Kong taxi drivers are scrupulously honest, if you feel you've been ripped off, take down the taxi or driver's licence number (usually displayed on the sun visor in front) and call the **taxi complaints hotline** (☎ 2889 9999), the **police report hotline** (☎ 2527 7177) or the **Transport Department hotline** (☎ 2804 2600) to lodge a complaint. Be sure to have all the relevant details: when, where and how much. If you leave something behind in a taxi, ring the **Road Co-op Lost & Found hotline** (☎ 187 2920); most drivers turn in lost property.

TRAIN

The MTR underground system notwithstanding, Hong Kong has two 'real' train systems that are crucial for travellers getting around in the New Territories and/or heading for China.

KOWLOON-CANTON RAILWAY

Also known as the 'KCR', the **Kowloon-Canton Railway** (Map pp404–5; ☎ 2929 3399; www .kcrc.com) is made up of two lines. KCR East Rail, which commenced in 1910, is a single-line, 35.5km-long commuter railway running from the new East Tsim Sha Tsui station in southern Kowloon to Lo Wo on the border with mainland China. It serves some 14 stations and carries 800,000 passengers a day. The tracks are the same as those used by the express trains to cities in Guangdong province as well as to Shanghai and Beijing, but the trains are different and look more like MTR carriages. Ma On Shan Rail, which branches off from KCR East Rail at Tai Wai and serves nine stations, opened in December 2004 but is of limited use to travellers. A KCR East Rail spur running from Sheung Shui to Lok Ma Chau on the mainland border is under construction.

The KCR West Rail, a separate 30.5km-long line that opened in late 2003, links Nam Cheong station in Sham Shui Po with Tuen Mun via Yuen Long, stopping at nine

stations. Eventually it will be linked to the KCR East Rail at East Tsim Sha Shui, with stops at Kowloon West and Canton Road.

The KCR is a quick way to get to the New Territories, and the ride offers some nice vistas, particularly between the Chinese University and Tai Po Market stations on the KCR East Rail. You can transfer from the MTR to the KCR East Rail at Tsim Sha Tsui and Kowloon Tong stations. On the KCR West Rail, there is interchange with the Tung Chung MTR line at Nam Cheong, with the Tsuen Wan line at Mei Foo and with the Light Rail (see below) at Yuen Long, Tin Shui Wai, Siu Hong and Tuen Mun.

KCR trains run every five to eight minutes, except during rush hour, when they depart every three to eight minutes. The first KCR East Rail train leaves East Tsim Sha Tsui at 5.28am and the last departs from Lo Wu at 12.30am, a half-hour after the border between Hong Kong and Shenzhen closes. The KCR West Rail runs from 6am to sometime between 12.15am and 12.40am. The trip from Nam Cheong to Tuen Mun on the KCR West Rail takes 30 minutes.

KCR fares are cheap, starting at $3.50, with a half-hour ride to Sheung Shui from East Tsim Sha Tsui costing just $12.50 (1st class is double) and the 40-minute trip to Lo Wu $36.50 ($73). Children and seniors pay reduced fares of between $1.80 and $17.40. Paying with an Octopus card brings down fares considerably.

The KCR runs some 129 feeder buses on 18 routes via its **KCRC Bus Service** (☎ 2602 7799; www.kcrc.com) but these are generally of interest only to residents of housing estates within striking distance of the KCR East and West Rails and the Light Rail.

LIGHT RAIL

The KCR's **Light Rail** (Map pp404–5; ☎ 2929 3399; www.kcrc.com) system began operations in 1988 and has been extended several times since. It is rather like a modern, air-conditioned version of the trams in Hong Kong, but it's much faster, reaching speeds of up to 70km/h. It runs along 36km of track parallel to the road and stops at 68 designated stations, carrying some 320,000 passengers a day.

Until recently, only those travellers visiting the temples of the western New Territories made much use of the Light Rail as it essentially was just a link between the New

Towns of Tuen Mun and Yuen Long. But with the opening of the KCR West Rail, it is an important feeder service for the KCR and, by extension, the MTR.

There are 11 Light Rail lines connecting various small suburbs with Tuen Mun to the south and Yuen Long to the northeast, both of which are on the KCR West Rail. The system operates from about 5.30am to between 12.15am and 12.45am. Trams run every four to 20 minutes, depending on the line and time of day. Fares are $4 to $5.80, depending on the number of zones (from No 1 to No 5) travelled; children aged three to 11 and seniors over 65 pay from $2 to $2.90. If you don't have an Octopus card, you can buy single-journey tickets from vending machines on the platforms.

The system of fare collection is unique in Hong Kong: there are no gates or turnstiles and customers are trusted to validate their ticket or Octopus card when they board and exit. That trust is enforced by frequent spot checks, however, and the fine is 50 times the maximum adult fare – $290 at present.

TRAM

Hong Kong's venerable old trams, operated by **Hongkong Tramways Ltd** (☎ 2548 7102; www .info.gov.hk/td/eng/transport/tram.html) are tall and narrow double-decker street-cars, the only all double-deck wooden-sided tram fleet in the world. They roll (and rock) along the northern coast of Hong Kong Island on 16km of track, carrying some 240,000 passengers daily.

The electric tram line first began operating in 1904 on what was then the shoreline of Hong Kong Island. This helps to understand why roads curve and dogleg in ways that don't seem quite right. Try to get a seat at the front window on the upper deck for a first-class view while rattling through the crowded streets: tall passengers will find it uncomfortable standing up as the ceiling is low, but there is more space at the rear of the tram on both decks.

Trams operate from 6am to between 12.30am and 1am daily and run every two to 10 minutes, but they often arrive bunched together. Be prepared to elbow your way through the crowd to alight, particularly on the lower deck.

Hong Kong's trams are not fast but they're cheap and fun; in fact, apart from the Star Ferry (p291), no form of transport

is nearer and dearer to the hearts of most Hong Kong people. For a flat fare of $2 (children three to 11 and seniors over 65 $1), dropped into a box beside the driver as you descend, you can go as far as you like, whether it's one block or to the end of the line. You can also use your Octopus card.

Tram routes often overlap. Some start at Kennedy Town and run to Shau Kei Wan, while others run only part of the way; one turns south and heads for Happy Valley. The longest run, covering the entire length of the system from Shau Kei Wan to Kennedy Town (with a change at Western Market), takes about 1½ hours. The six routes from west to east are Kennedy Town–Western Market; Kennedy Town–Happy Valley; Kennedy Town–Causeway Bay; Sai Ying Pun (Whitty St)–North Point; Sheung Wan (Western Market)–Shau Kei Wan; and Happy Valley–Shau Kei Wan.

PEAK TRAM

The Peak Tram is not really a tram but a cable-hauled funicular railway that has been climbing, since 1888, some 396m along a steep gradient to the highest point on Hong Kong Island. It is thus the oldest form of public transport in the territory.

While a few residents on the Peak and in the Mid-Levels actually use it as a form of transport – there are four intermediate stops before you reach the top – the Peak Tram is intended to transport visitors and locals to the attractions, shops and restaurants in the Peak Tower and Peak Galleria (p77).

The **Peak Tram** (Map pp408–9; ☎ 2522 0922, 2849 7654; www.thepeak.com.hk; one way/return adult $20/30, child 3-11 $6/9, senior over 65 years $7/14; one way intermediary stops adult/child/senior $18/5/6) runs every 10 to 15 minutes from 7am to midnight, making between one and four stops (Kennedy Rd, MacDonnell Rd, May Rd and Barker Rd) along the way in about seven minutes. It's such a steep ride that the floor is angled to help standing passengers stay upright. Running for more than a century, the tram has never had an accident – a comforting thought if you start to have doubts about the strength of that cable. It carries 8500 passengers a day.

The lower tram terminus is behind the **St John's Building** (Map pp408–9; 33 Garden Rd, Central). The upper tram terminus is in the **Peak Tower** (Map pp408–9; 128 Peak Rd).

Avoid going on Sunday and public holidays when there are usually long queues. Octopus cards can be used.

Between 10am and 11.45pm, open-deck (or air-conditioned) bus 15C takes passengers between the Star Ferry pier and Pedder St in Central and the lower tram terminus.

TRAVEL & TOURIST PASSES

The Octopus card (☎ 2266 2266; www.octopus cards.com), originally designed for the MTR and seven other forms of transport (thus the eight-armed 'octopus' connection), is valid on most forms of public transport in Hong Kong and will even allow you to make purchases at retail outlets across the territory (such as 7-Eleven convenience stores and Wellcome supermarkets). All you do is touch fare-deducting processors installed at stations and ferry piers, on minibuses, in shops etc with the Octopus card and the fare is deducted, indicating how much credit you have left.

The Octopus card comes in three basic denominations: $150 for adults, $100 for students aged 12 to 25, and $70 for children aged three to 11 and seniors ('elders' here) over 65. All cards include a refundable deposit of $50. If you want to add more money to your card, just go to one of the add-value machines or the ticket offices located at every MTR station. The maximum amount you can add is $1000, and the card has a maximum negative value of $30, which is recovered the next time you reload (thus the $50 deposit). Octopus fares are between 5% and 10% cheaper than ordinary fares on the MTR, KCR, Light Rail systems and certain green minibuses.

You can purchase Octopus cards at ticket offices or customer service centres in MTR, KCR and LRT stations, New World First Bus customer service centres as well as Outlying Islands ferry piers on both sides.

The much-advertised Airport Express Tourist Octopus card is not really worth the microchip embedded into it. The card costs $220 (including $50 deposit) and allows one trip on the Airport Express, three days' unlimited travel on the MTR and $20 usable value on other forms of transport. For $300 you get two trips on the Airport Express and the same benefits. At the end of your trip you can claim your deposit back (plus any part of the $20 'usable value' still on the card) or keep the card, emblazoned with that lovely word 'tourist', as a souvenir. For shorter stays there's the Tourist MTR 1-Day Pass ($50), valid on the MTR for 24 hours.

A special tourist ticket allowing unlimited rides on the Star Ferry (Central and Wan Chai to Tsim Sha Tsui only) as well as the trams for four days is available for $30. It's not much of a deal; you'd have to take almost 15 trips over that period just to break even. If you want to include the Star Ferry routes serving Hung Hom, the pass costs $54.

WHERE HAVE ALL THE RICKSHAWS GONE?

Rickshaws appeared in Hong Kong soon after *jinriksha* (literally, 'person strength vehicle') were invented in mid-19th-century Japan as a more 'humane' alternative to the back-breaking sedan chairs. By 1895 there were already some 700 registered and licensed in the colony; the figure jumped to an estimated 5000 by WWI. Towards the end of the war there were even 60 rickshaws registered in the name of brothels, which were used to deliver courtesans to their customers.

In the mid-1920s, despite competition from buses, trams and other forms of mechanised transport, rickshaws held tight, numbering more than 3000 and still playing a vital role in Hong Kong's transport network. Over the next 15 years, rickshaws dwindled away until there were only a few hundred left at the start of WWII. But the lack of fuel and access to other forms of transport during and after the war gave rickshaws a new lease of life; by the late 1940s there were around 8000 back trawling the streets of the colony.

It was the peak before a rapid decline; taxis and private cars swept rickshaws off the roads in the 1950s and 1960s. There was a busy trade to the bars and brothels of Wan Chai for a time during the Vietnam R&R years of the 1960s and early 1970s, but for the most part rickshaws had ceased to be a means of transport and had become a tourist attraction.

The last new rickshaw licence was issued in 1975, when there were still nearly 100 left on the streets. By the early 1980s the numbers had been halved, and the rickshaw fleet eventually contracted to the tiny group that still hangs out at the Star Ferry pier on the Hong Kong Island side, waiting to take visitors on a short jaunt around the car park or to pose for photographs. By the early 1990s rickshaw numbers had fallen to less than 20 and by 2005 they were truly an endangered species. Just a couple were manned and two lay idle, with prominent 'For Sale' signs hanging from the back.

TRANSPORT TO/FROM CHINA

AIR

There are relatively few bargain airfares between Hong Kong and China as the government regulates the prices. Depending on the season, seats can be difficult to book due to the enormous volume of business travellers and Chinese tourists, so book well in advance. Some normal return fares valid for a year from Hong Kong are Beijing $2300, Chengdu $2500, Guangzhou $600, Kunming $2300 and Shanghai $2000. One-way fares are a bit more than half the return price.

You should be able to do better than that, however, on both scheduled and charter flights, especially in summer. To Beijing, China Southern Airlines has a fixed return ticket for as low as $1600. An open ticket valid for 30 days on the same carrier is $2200 and a 90-day one on Dragonair costs $3000.

If you plan to fly to a destination in China from Hong Kong, you can save at least 30% on the above fares by heading for Shenzhen by bus (below) and boarding the aircraft at Huangtian Airport there.

LAND

The only way in and out of Hong Kong by land is to cross the 30km border with mainland China. The options for surface travel to and from China have increased dramatically since the handover, with buses and trains departing throughout the day to destinations as close as Shenzhen and as far as Beijing. Travellers should be aware that, although the Hong Kong Special Administrative Region (SAR) is an integral part of China, visas are still required to cross the border to the mainland (see p306).

The border crossing at Lo Wu opens at 6.30am and closes at midnight. The crossing at Lok Ma Chau is open round the clock.

Bus

You can reach virtually any major destination in neighbouring Guangdong province by bus from Hong Kong. With KCR East Rail services so fast and cheap, however, few buses call on Shenzhen proper, though most of the big hotels run minivans to

and from that destination for around $100 one way. One-way fares from Hong Kong to other mainland destinations include Changsha $280, Dongguan $70 to $100, Foshan $100, Guangzhou $75 to $100, Huizhou $100, Kaiping $150, Shantou $180 to $200, Shēnzhèn's Huangtian Airport $110, Xiamen $350 and Zhongshan $80 to $130.

Buses are run by a multitude of transport companies and depart from locations around the territory; the list that follows is only a sampling. Schedules vary enormously according to carrier and place, but buses leave throughout the day and departures are frequent.

CTS Express Coach (☎ 2365 0118; http://ctsbus.hkcts.com) Buses depart from locations throughout Hong Kong, including the CTS **main branch** (Map pp408–9; ☎ 2853 3888; 78-83 Connaught Rd Central) and the CTS **Wan Chai branch** (Map pp414–15; ☎ 2832 3888; Southorn Centre, 130-138 Hennessy Rd) on Hong Kong Island and from just south of the CTS **Mong Kok branch** (Map p423; ☎ 2789 5888; 62-72 Sai Yee St) in Kowloon.

Eternal East Cross Border Coach (Map pp420–1; ☎ 3412 6677; www.eebus.com; 13th fl, Kai Seng Commercial Centre, 4-6 Hankow Rd, Tsim Sha Tsui; ☉ 7am-8pm) Buses leave from just outside the Hang Seng Bank next door.

Motor Transport Company of Guangdong and Hong Kong (GDHK; ☎ 2317 7900; www.gdhkmtc.com) Buses bound for destinations throughout Guangdong leave from the **Cross-Border Coach Terminus** (Map pp420–1; ☎ 2317 7900; Ground fl, Hong Kong Scout Centre, 8 Austin Rd, Tsim Sha Tsui; ☉ 6.30am-7pm), which is entered from Scout Path.

Trans-Island Limousine Service (☎ 3193 9333; www .trans-island.com.hk) Cars and vans leave from Portland St opposite the Hotel Concourse Hong Kong (Map p423).

In addition, at Chek Lap Kok buses run by **CTS Express Coach** (☎ 2261 2472), **Eternal East Cross Border Coach** (☎ 2261 0176) and **Gogobus** (☎ 2261 0886; www.gogobus.com) link Hong Kong International Airport with many points in southern China, including Dongguan ($100), Foshan ($130 to $150), Guangzhou ($100) and Shenzhen ($100).

Train

Reaching Shenzhen is a breeze. Just board the KCR East Rail at East Tsim Sha Tsui station (1st/2nd class $73/36.50) or at any other KCR East Rail station along the way (such as Hung Hom, Kowloon Tong or Sha Tin) and ride it to Lo Wu; China is a couple of hundred metres away. The first train to Lo Wu leaves East Tsim Sha Tsui station at 5.28am, the last at 11.05pm, and the trip takes about 40 minutes. For more details on KCR services, see p301.

The most comfortable way to reach Guangzhou by land is via the Kowloon–Guangzhou express train (usually via Dongguan), which covers the 182km route in approximately 1¾ hours. High-speed intercity trains leave Hung Hom station for Guangzhou East train station 12 times a day between 7.30am and 7.15pm, returning from that station the same number of times from 8.35am to 9.23pm. One-way tickets cost $230/190 in 1st/2nd class for adults and $115/95 for children aged five to nine. Adults/children are allowed one piece of luggage, weighing up to 20kg/10kg. Additional bags cost $3.90 per 5kg.

There are also direct rail links between Hung Hom and both Shanghai and Beijing. Trains to Beijing West train station (hard/soft sleeper from $574/934, 24 hours) depart on alternate days at 3pm and travel via Guangzhou East, Changsha and Wuhan, arriving at 3.18pm the following day. Trains to Shanghai (hard/soft sleeper from $508/825, 23 hours) also depart on alternate days at 3pm and pass through Guangzhou East and Hangzhou East stations, arriving at 1.38pm the following day.

There is one daily departure to Zhaoqing (adult/child $235/117.50) via Dongguan, Guangzhou East and Foshan at 2.20pm, arriving in Zhaoqing at 6.30pm. The train departs Zhaoqing at 9.37am, reaching Hung Hom at 1.38pm.

Immigration formalities at Hung Hom are completed before boarding; you won't get on the train without a visa for China. Passengers are required to arrive at the station 45 minutes before departure. To reach Hung Hom station from Tsim Sha Tsui by public transport, take the KCR East Rail for one stop, bus 5C from the Star Ferry pier or the No 6 or 8 green minibus from Hankow Rd.

One-way and return tickets can be booked 60 days in advance though CTS (p306), including at CTS Hung Hom station branch (☎ 2334 9333; ✆ 6.30am-8pm) and at KCR East Rail stations in Hung Hom, Mong Kok, Kowloon Tong and Sha Tin. Tickets booked with a credit card via the Tele-Ticketing Hotline (☎ 2947 7888) must be collected at least one hour before departure.

A cheaper but much less convenient option is to take the KCR East Rail train to Lo Wu, cross through immigration into Shenzhen and catch a local train from there to Guangzhou. There are frequent local trains (Y70, two hours) and high-speed trains (Y80, 55 minutes) throughout the day.

SEA

Regularly scheduled ferries link the China ferry terminal (Map pp420–1; Canton Rd, Tsim Sha Tsui) in Kowloon and/or the Macau ferry pier (Map pp408–9; 200 Connaught Rd, Sheung Wan) on Hong Kong Island with a string of towns and cities on the Pearl River delta – but not central Guangzhou or Shenzhen. For sea transport to/from Macau, see p374.

TurboJet (☎ 2921 6688; www.turbojet.com .hk) runs high-speed ferries ($189, one hour) leaving the China ferry terminal for Fuyong ferry terminal (Shenzhen airport) six to eight times a day between 7.30am and 5.30pm. There are five or six return sailings from Fuyong ($171) starting at 9am, with the last at 5pm. One boat a day leaves the Macau ferry pier in Central at 8am. Return sailings are at 5.50pm, 7pm and 8.30pm.

CMSE Passenger Transport (☎ 2858 0909) runs some 13 Jetcats (day/night sailing $110/130, one hour) that link Hong Kong with Shekou, a port about 20km west of Shenzhen town and easily accessible by bus or taxi to the centre, from 7.45am to 9pm daily. Seven of these (between 7.45am and 7pm) leave from the China ferry terminal in Kowloon, while the rest (9am to 9pm) go from the Macau ferry pier on Hong Kong Island. Return sailings from Shekou are from 7.45am to 9.30pm.

Zhuhai can also be reached from Hong Kong on seven ferries a day ($170, 70 minutes) from the China ferry terminal in Tsim Sha Tsui (from 7.30am to 5.30pm) and on the same number from the Macau ferry pier in Sheung Wan (8.40am to 9.30pm) on ferries operated by the Chu Kong Passenger Transportation Company (☎ 2858 3876; www.cksp.com .hk). The 14 return sailings from Zhuhai ($148) run between 8am and 9.30pm.

Chu Kong also has ferries from the China ferry terminal in Tsim Sha Tsui to a number of other ports in southern Guangdong province, including Humen (Taiping; $160, 90 minutes, three a day at 9am, 1.45pm and 5.30pm), Kaiping ($185, four hours, daily at 8.30am), Nanhai in Pingzhou ($168, 2¾ hours, twice daily at 8.40am and 4pm), Shunde ($168, 110 minutes, six sailings between 7.30am and 6pm), Zhongshan ($194, 90 minutes, eight or nine sailings from 8am to 8pm) and Zhaoqing ($200, 3¾ hours, daily at 8.15).

Ferries run by **Expert Fortune** (☎ 2375 0688, 2517 3494) link the China ferry terminal with Nansha ($130, five sailings daily) between 8am and 3.30pm, with return sailings ($100) between 9.30am and 5pm or 5.30pm. One daily ferry departs from the Macau ferry pier at 8.20am.

Departure Tax

The $19 departure tax levied when leaving Hong Kong by sea is usually included in the ticket price.

VISAS

Everyone except Hong Kong Chinese residents must have a visa to enter mainland China. Holders of Canadian, Australian, New Zealand and most European Union passports – but *not* British or American ones (at the time of writing) – can get a visa on the spot for $150 at the Lo Wu border crossing, the last stop on the Kowloon-Canton Railway's East Rail. This particular visa limits you to a maximum stay of seven days within the confines of the Shenzhen Special Economic Zone (SEZ) *only*. Since the queues for these visas are usually serpentine and the wait interminable, it is highly recommended that you shell out the extra money and get a proper China visa even if you're headed just for Shenzhen.

If you would like to arrange your visa yourself, you can go to the **Visa Office of the People's Republic of China** (Map pp414–15; ☎ 3413 2424; 7th fl, Lower Block, China Resources Centre, 26 Harbour Rd, Wan Chai; ☯ 9am-noon & 2-5pm Mon-Fri). Visas processed in one/two/three days for

'reciprocal countries' cost $400/300/150. Visas for double entry/multiple entry valid six months/multiple entry valid for a year cost $220/400/600 (plus $150/250 if you require express/urgent service). You must supply two photos, which can be taken at photo booths in the MTR or at the visa office for $35. Any photo-processing shop can also oblige.

Visas can be arranged by **China Travel Service** (CTS; ☎ 2789 5401; www.chinatravel1 .com), the mainland-affiliated agency; a good many hostels and guesthouses; and most Hong Kong travel agents, including those listed on p288.

China Travel Services Offices

There are almost three dozen China Travel Services (CTS) offices in Hong Kong, including the six listed below.

HONG KONG ISLAND

Causeway Bay (Map pp414–15; ☎ 2808 1131; Room 606, 6th fl, Hang Kung Centre, 2-20 Paterson St; ☯ 9am-7pm Mon-Fri, 9am-5pm Sat)

Central (Map p412; ☎ 2522 0450; Ground fl, China Travel Bldg, 77 Queen's Rd Central; ☯ 9am-6pm Mon-Fri, 9am-5pm Sat, 9.30am-12.30pm & 2-5pm Sun)

Wan Chai (Map pp414–15; ☎ 2832 3888; Ground fl, Southorn Centre, 130-138 Hennessy Rd; ☯ 9am-7pm Mon-Fri, 9am-5pm Sat, 9.30am-12.30pm & 2-5pm Sun)

KOWLOON

Mong Kok (Map p423; ☎ 2789 5888, 2789 5970; 1st & 2nd fl, Tak Po Bldg, 62-72 Sai Yee St; ☯ 9am-7pm Mon-Fri, 9am-5pm Sat, 9.30am-12.30pm & 2-5pm Sun)

Tsim Sha Tsui (Map pp420–1; ☎ 2315 7188; 1st fl, Alpha House, 27-33 Nathan Rd; ☯ 9am-7pm Mon-Fri, 9am-5pm Sat, 9.30am-5pm Sun)

NEW TERRITORIES

Sha Tin (Map p425; ☎ 2692 7773; Shop 438C, 4th fl, New Town Plaza I; ☯ 9am-9pm)

Accommodation 308
Addresses 308
Business 308
Business Hours 308
Children 308
Climate 309
Consulates 310
Courses 310
Cultural Centres 311
Customs 311
Disabled Travellers 311
Discount Cards 311
Electricity 312
Emergency 312
Gay & Lesbian Travellers 312
Health 313
Holidays 314
Identity Card 314
Internet Access 315
Laundry 315
Left Luggage 315
Legal Matters 316
Libraries 316
Maps 316
Medical Services 317
Money 318
Newspapers & Magazines 319
Passport 320
Photography 320
Places of Worship 320
Post 320
Radio 321
Taxes & Refunds 321
Telephone 321
Television 322
Time 322
Tipping 322
Toilets 323
Tourist Information 323
Universities 323
Useful Organisations 324
Visas 324
Websites 324
Weights & Measures 325
Women Travellers 325
Work 325

Directory ■

Directory

ACCOMMODATION

The accommodation options in this guide are listed alphabetically by area for mid- and top-range hotels, followed by a separate 'cheap sleeps' section.

For details on accommodation costs in Hong Kong, on seasonal variations and useful agencies and websites for finding and booking hotels see p250.

ADDRESSES

Addresses in Hong Kong are fairly straight-forward. In general the apartment (or office) number and floor precede the name of the building, street address and district. There are no postal codes. In Hong Kong (and in this book), the 1st floor is the floor above the ground floor. Virtually every business and residential building here has a guard or concierge and a table displaying the names of the occupants.

About the only problem you may have in finding your way in Hong Kong is deter-mining the appropriate exit for your desti-nation from the MTR (p299).

BUSINESS

Hong Kong is not all about business, but it remains an important aspect of its ethos and character. Some useful business contacts:

American Chamber of Commerce (Map pp408–9; ☎ 2526 0165; www.amcham.org.hk; Room 1904, 19th fl, Bank of America Tower, 12 Harcourt Rd, Central) The most active overseas chamber of commerce in Hong Kong.

Chinese General Chamber of Commerce (Map pp408–9; ☎ 2525 6385; www.cgcc.org.hk; 4th fl, Chinese General Chamber of Commerce Bldg, 24-25 Connaught Rd, Central) Authorised to issue Certificates of Hong Kong origin for trade.

Chinese Manufacturers' Association of Hong Kong (Map pp408–9; ☎ 2545 6166; www.cma.org.hk; 3rd fl, CMA Bldg, 64-66 Connaught Rd, Central) Operates testing laboratories for product certification and can also issue Certificates of Hong Kong origin.

Hong Kong General Chamber of Commerce (Map pp408–9; ☎ 2529 9229; www.chamber.org.hk; 22nd fl, United Centre, 95 Queensway, Admiralty) Services for foreign executives and firms, such as translation, serviced offices, secretarial help and printing.

Hong Kong Labour Department (Map pp408–9; ☎ 2717 1771; www.labour.gov.hk;16th fl, Harbour Bldg, 38 Pier Rd, Central) Contact this department for labour-relations problems and queries.

Hong Kong Trade Development Council (HKTDC; Map pp414–15; ☎ 2584 4333; www.tdctrade.com; 38th fl, Office Tower, Convention Plaza, 1 Harbour Rd, Wan Chai) Cosponsors and participates in trade fairs, publishes a wealth of material on Hong Kong markets.

Hong Kong Trade & Industry Department (Map p423; ☎ 2392 2922; www.tid.gov.hk; Room 908, 700 Nathan Rd, Trade & Industry Department Tower, Mong Kok) Key source for trade information, statistics, government regula-tions and product certification (enter from Fife St).

TDC Business Info Centre (Map pp414–15; ☎ 2248 4000; http://infocentre.tdctrade.com; New Wing, Hong Kong Convention & Exhibition Centre, 1 Expo Dr, Wan Chai; ☎ 9am-8pm Mon-Fri, 9am-5pm Sat, noon-5pm Sun) Run by the HKTDC, the centre is well stocked with relevant books, periodicals and reference materials.

BUSINESS HOURS

Office hours in Hong Kong are from 9am to either 5.30pm or 6pm on weekdays and often (but increasingly less so) from 9am to noon or 1pm on Saturday. The weekday lunch hour is usually from 1pm to 2pm. Banks are open from 9am to 4.30pm or 5pm weekdays and 9am to 12.30pm on Saturday.

Shops that cater to tourists keep longer hours, but almost nothing opens before 9am. As a rule of thumb, assume a place will be open from 10am to 7pm daily. For specifics, see p228.

Museums are generally open from 10am to between 5pm and 9pm and are closed one day a week (usually Monday, Tuesday or Thursday).

Restaurants are open 11.30am or noon to 2.30pm or 3pm; dinner is usually from 6pm or 6.30pm to 11pm.

CHILDREN

Hong Kong is a great travel destination for kids (see the boxed text, p124), though the crowds, traffic and pollution might be off-putting to some parents. Food and sanita-tion is of a high standard, and the territory is jam-packed with things to entertain the young 'uns. As a starting point, get a copy of the HKTB's *Hong Kong Family Fun Guide* or download it from the HKTB website http://www.discoverhongkong.com/eng /travelneeds/family/index.jhtml.

Lonely Planet's *Travel with Children* includes all sorts of useful advice for those travelling with their little ones.

Most public transport and museums offer half-price fares and admission fees to children under the age of 12, but combination family tickets are rare. Hotels can recommend baby-sitters if you've got day-time appointments or want a night out sans child. Otherwise call **Rent-A-Mum** (Map p412; ☎ 2523 4868; rentamum@netvigator.com; 12A Amber Lodge, 21-25 Hollywood Rd, Central; per hr $110-160).

CLIMATE

Both Hong Kong and Macau have a sub-tropical climate characterised by hot, humid summers and cool, relatively dry winters.

October, November and most of December are the best months to visit. Temperatures are moderate, the skies are clear and

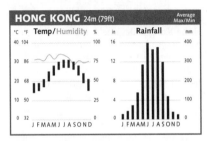

the sun shines. January and February are cloudy and cold but dry. It's warmer from March to May, but the humidity is high, and the fog and drizzle can make getting around difficult. The sweltering heat and humidity from June to August can make sightseeing a sweaty proposition, and it is also the rainy season. September is a grand month if you like drama; the threat of a typhoon seems to loom every other day.

The very informative **Hong Kong Observatory** (Map pp420–1; ☎ 2926 8200; www.hko.gov .hk; 134A Nathan Rd, Tsim Sha Tsui) issues weather reports on ☎ 187 8066 and on their website. The hotline for cyclone warnings is ☎ 2835 1473.

TYPHOON!

A typhoon is a violent tropical cyclone, a massive whirlpool of air currents often tens of kilometres high and hundreds of kilometres wide. Feeding off moisture, tropical cyclones can only survive over warm oceans – once typhoons hit land, they quickly die out. The 'eye' of the cyclone is generally tens of kilometres wide and basically is a column of descending air, which is much calmer than the surrounding vortex.

Cyclones can last for as long as a few weeks, but not all will mature into typhoons. Only about half the cyclones in the South China Sea ever reach typhoon ferocity. The gradation of tropical cyclones ascends as follows: tropical depression (with winds up to 62km/h); tropical storm (up to 87km/h); severe tropical storm (up to 117km/h); and typhoon (118km/h or more).

Although some two dozen typhoons develop in the South China Sea each year, and a quarter of those reach within 800km of Hong Kong, the territory is a small target, so the chances of a direct hit – within 100km – are slim.

There is a numbering system to warn of typhoons broadcast on all media. No 1 (its visual symbol being the letter 't') means that a tropical cyclone is within 800km of Hong Kong. No 3 (an upside-down 't') – there is no No 2 – warns that winds of up to 62km are blowing in Victoria Harbour, there is a risk of Hong Kong being hit and that people should take precautions such as securing flower pots on balconies and terraces. The system then jumps to No 8 (a triangle), which means that there are sustained winds of between 63km/h and 117km/h. People are instructed to stay indoors and to fix adhesive tape to exposed windows to reduce the damage caused by broken glass, while businesses shut down and ferries stop running. No 9 (a double triangle) warns that gale- or storm-force winds are increasing, and No 10 (a cross) is the most severe, with winds reaching upward from 118km/h and gusts exceeding 220km/h.

Only 13 typhoons have reached No 10 since the end of WWII, despite an average of 16 appearing in the vicinity each year. The most famous ones in recent years were Typhoon Wanda (1962), the most ferocious of all, delivering hourly mean wind speeds of 133km/h and peak gusts of 259km/h; Typhoon Ellen (1983), which killed 22 people and injured over 300; and Typhoon York (1999), which had the No 10 signal up the longest of any other typhoon – 11 hours.

Rain, which can fall so heavily in Hong Kong that it sounds like a drum roll as it hits the pavement, can cause deadly landslips. Hong Kong also has a 'heavy rain warning system' that is colour-coded – in ascending degrees of severity – amber, red and black.

CONSULATES

Hong Kong is definitely one of the world's most consulate-clogged cities. You'll find a complete list of consulates in the Yellow Pages.

Australia (Map pp414–15; ☎ 2827 8881; 23rd fl, Harbour Centre, 25 Harbour Rd, Wan Chai)

Canada (Map pp408–9; ☎ 2810 4321; 11th-14th fl, Tower One, Exchange Sq, 8 Connaught Pl, Central)

France (Map pp408–9; ☎ 3196 6100; 26th fl, Tower II, Admiralty Centre, 18 Harcourt Rd, Admiralty)

Germany (Map pp408–9; ☎ 2105 8744; 21st fl, United Centre, 95 Queensway, Admiralty)

Ireland (Map pp414–15; ☎ 2527 4897; 6th fl, Chung Nam Bldg, 1 Lockhart Road, Wan Chai) Honorary consulate.

Japan (Map pp408–9; ☎ 2522 1184; 46th-47th fl, Tower I, Exchange Sq, 8 Connaught Pl, Central)

Netherlands (Map pp408–9; ☎ 2522 5127; Room 5702, 57th fl, Cheung Kong Centre, 2 Queen's Road Central)

New Zealand (Map pp414–15; ☎ 2877 4488; Room 6508, 65th fl, Central Plaza, 18 Harbour Rd, Wan Chai)

South Africa (Map pp414–15; ☎ 2577 3279; Room 2706-2710, 27th fl, Great Eagle Centre, 23 Harbour Road, Wan Chai)

UK (Map pp408–9; ☎ 2901 3000; 1 Supreme Court Rd, Admiralty)

USA (Map pp408–9; ☎ 2523 9011; 26 Garden Rd, Central)

COURSES

The **Community Advice Bureau** (Map pp408–9; ☎ 2815 5444; www.cab.org.hk; Room 16C, Right Emperor Commercial Bldg, 122-126 Wellington St, Central; ☺ 9.30am-4.30pm Mon-Fri) is a fabulous source of information on courses of all kinds in Hong Kong. The **YMCA** (☎ 2369 2211; www.ymca.org.hk) and the **YWCA** (☎ 3476 1340; www.ywca.org .hk) both offer a range of cultural classes and three-month courses, from basic Cantonese and mahjong to yoga and t'ai chi.

For visual arts, check with the **Hong Kong Museum of Art** (☎ 2721 0116), the **Hong Kong Visual Arts Centre** (☎ 2521 3008) or the **Hong Kong Arts Centre** (☎ 2582 0200). The **Fringe Club** (☎ 2521 7251; 2 Lower Albert Rd, Central) offers any number of courses and workshops.

The Cultural Kaleidoscope Meet the People program organised by the **HKTB** (☎ 2508 1234) will whet your appetite to learn more about everything from Chinese tea and opera to t'ai chi and jade. It is unique in that it allows you to visit galleries, antique shops, jewellers to grade peals and jade, teahouses, even a feng shui master's studio and a t'ai chi class. It's an excellent way to learn first-hand about Hong Kong Chinese culture. For details on times and locations see the HKTB website www.discoverhong kong.com.

Cooking

Hong Kong is a good place to learn about or hone you skills in the art of Chinese cookery.

Chinese Cuisine Training Institute (Map pp406–7; ☎ 2538 2373; www.ccti.vtc.edu.hk; 7th fl, Pokfulam Training Centre Complex, 145 Pok Fu Lam Rd, Pok Fu Lam) Three-hour afternoon courses ($288 to $408) covering the full spectrum of Chinese cooking.

Chopsticks Cooking Centre (Map p423; ☎ 2336 8433; cauyeung@netvigator.com; Ground fl, 8A Soares Ave, Mong Kok) Introductory ($100,1½ hours), regional cookery ($150, four hours) and full-day ($250, six hours) courses available at this long-established school.

Home Management Centre (Map pp406–7; ☎ 2510 2828; www.hec.com.hk; 10th fl, Electric Centre, 28 City Garden Road, North Point) You can learn simple Chinese dishes in two hours at the HMC for $200 or the basics of Thai, Vietnamese or Indian cuisine at more intensive courses.

Towngas Cooking Centre (Map pp414–15; ☎ 2576 1535; www.towngascooking.com; Basement, Leighton Centre, 77 Leighton Rd, Causeway Bay) The centre has classes in a vast range of Chinese cooking styles ($100 to $300) as well as such specialised subjects as Italian bread and pizza-making and candy-making. There's also a **Tsim Sha Tsui branch** (Map pp420–1; ☎ 2367 2707; Shop L030, New World Centre, 18-24 Salisbury Rd).

Language

The New Asia-Yale-in-China Chinese Language Centre at the **Chinese University of Hong Kong** (Map pp404–5; ☎ 2609 6727; www .cuhk.edu.hk/clc; Fong Shu Chuen Bldg, Ma Liu Shui, New Territories) offers regular courses in Cantonese and Mandarin. There are four terms a year – four- and 11-week summer sessions and two regular 15-week terms in spring and autumn. The cost of the four-week summer term is $8000, the 11-week session $18,960 while the 15-week semesters are $23,700. Another good place for learning Cantonese, Mandarin and other Asian languages is Hong Kong University's **School of Professional and Continuing Education** (☎ 2559 9771; http://hkuspace.hku.hk; Room 304, 3rd fl, TT Tsui Bldg, Pok Fu Lam Road, Pok Fu Lam).

A number of private language schools cater to individuals or companies. These schools offer more flexibility and even dispatch teachers to companies to teach the whole staff. For one-on-one instruction, expect to pay $200 plus per hour. Language schools to consider:

Essential Chinese Language Centre (Map pp408–9; ☎ 2544 6979; www.eclc.com.hk; 6th fl, Jim's Commercial Bldg, 102-104 Des Voeux Rd Centre)

Hong Kong Institute of Languages (Map p412; ☎ 2877 6160; www.hklanguages.com; 6th fl, Wellington Plaza, 56-58 Wellington St, Central)

CULTURAL CENTRES

Opening hours for cultural centres vary according to the department (library, media centre, gallery etc) and what's on exhibit.

Alliance Française (Map pp414–15; ☎ 2527 7825; www.alliancefrancaise.com.hk; 1st & 2nd fl, 123 Hennessy Rd, Wan Chai) This place has a library and offers a wide range of cultural activities.

British Council (Map pp408–9; ☎ 2913 5100; www.britishcouncil.org.hk; 3 Supreme Court Rd, Admiralty) Provides English-language classes, sponsors cultural programs, has Internet access (1st floor) and a useful **Customer Services Centre** (☑ 9am-8.30pm Mon-Fri, 9am-6pm Sat).

Goethe-Institut (Map pp414–15; ☎ 2802 0088; www.goethe.de/hongkong; 13th & 14th fl, Hong Kong Arts Centre, 2 Harbour Rd, Wan Chai) German classes, films, exhibitions and lectures.

CUSTOMS

Even though Hong Kong is a duty-free port, there are items on which duty is still charged. Import taxes on cigarettes and, in particular, alcohol are high (100% on spirits, 80% on wine, 40% on beer).

The duty-free allowance for visitors arriving into Hong Kong (including those coming from Macau and mainland China) is 200 cigarettes (or 50 cigars or 250g tobacco) and 1L of alcohol (wine or spirits). Apart from these limits there are few other import taxes, so you can bring in reasonable quantities of almost anything.

Firecrackers and fireworks are banned in Hong Kong but not in Macau and mainland China, and people crossing the border are sometimes thoroughly searched for these. Customs officers are on high alert for drug smugglers. If you're arriving from Thailand or Vietnam, be prepared for a rigorous examination of your luggage.

DISABLED TRAVELLERS

People with disabilities have to cope with substantial obstacles in Hong Kong, including the stairs at many MTR and KCR stations, as well as pedestrian overpasses, narrow and crowded footpaths and steep hills. On the other hand, some buses are accessible by wheelchair, taxis are never hard to find, most buildings have lifts (many with Braille panels) and MTR stations have Braille maps with recorded information. Wheelchairs can negotiate the lower decks of most ferries.

For further information about facilities and services for disabled travellers in Hong Kong contact either of the following:

Joint Council for the Physically and Mentally Disabled (Map pp414–15; ☎ 2864 2929; www.hkcss.org.hk; Room 1204, 12th fl, Duke of Windsor Bldg, 15 Hennessy Rd, Wan Chai)

Hong Kong Sports Association for the Physically Disabled (☎ 2602 8232; www.hksap.org)

DISCOUNT CARDS
Hong Kong Museums Pass

This pass allows multiple entries to six of Hong Kong's museums: Hong Kong Museum of Coastal Defence on Hong Kong Island; the Hong Kong Science Museum, Hong Kong Museum of History, Hong Kong Museum of Art and Hong Kong Space Museum (excluding Space Theatre) in Kowloon; and the Hong Kong Heritage Museum in the New Territories. Passes valid for seven consecutive days cost $30; passes valid for a half-year cost $50/25 for adults/seniors over 60 and students; and a full-year pass is $100/50. Passes are available from HKTB outlets and participating museums. Please note that these half-dozen museums are all free on Wednesdays.

Hostel Card

A Hostelling International (HI) card or the equivalent is of relatively limited use in Hong Kong as there are only seven HI-affiliated hostels here and most are in remote locations in the New Territories. If you arrive without a card and want to stay in one of these hostels, you can buy one from the **Hong Kong Youth Hostels Association** (HKYHA; Map pp418–19; ☎ 2788 1638; www.yha.org.hk; Room 225-227, Block 19, Shek Kip Mei

Estate, Nam Cheong St, Kowloon) for $180. Hong Kong residents over/under age 18 pay $110/50.

You are allowed to stay at any of Hong Kong's HKYHA hostels without a membership card, but you will have to buy a 'Welcome Stamp' ($30) for each night of your stay. Once you've stayed six nights, you are issued your own card.

Seniors Card

Many attractions in Hong Kong offer discounts for people over 60 or 65. Most of Hong Kong's museums are either free or half-price for those over 60 and most forms of public transport offer a 50% discount to anyone over 65. A passport or ID with a photo should be sufficient proof of age.

Student, Youth & Teacher Cards

The International Student Identity Card (ISIC), a plastic ID-style card with your photograph, provides discounts on some forms of transport and cheaper admission to museums and other sights. If you're aged under 26 but not a student, you can apply for an International Youth Travel Card (IYTC) issued by the Federation of International Youth Travel Organisations (FIYTO), which gives much the same discounts and benefits. Teachers can apply for the International Teacher Identity Card (ITIC).

Hong Kong Student Travel, based at **Sincerity Travel** (Map pp420–1; ☎ 2730 3269; Room 833-834, 8th fl, East Block, Star House, 3 Salisbury Rd, Tsim Sha Tsui; ☯ 10am-7pm Mon-Fri & 10am-6.30pm Sat) can issue you any of these cards for $100 in a week or $150 in just a day. Make sure you bring your student ID or other credentials along with you.

ELECTRICITY

The standard is 220V, 50Hz AC. Hong Kong's plug and socket system can be a bit confusing at first. The vast majority of electric outlets are designed to accommodate the British three square pins, but some take three large round prongs and others three small pins. Not surprisingly, inexpensive plug adaptors are widely available in Hong Kong, even in supermarkets.

EMERGENCY

Hong Kong is generally a very safe place but, as everywhere, things can go awry. Although it is safe to walk around just about anywhere in the territory after dark, it's best to stick to well-lit areas. Tourist districts such as Tsim Sha Tsui are heavily patrolled by the police. In the event of a real emergency, ring ☎ 999.

Hong Kong does have its share of local pickpockets and thieves. Carry as little cash and as few valuables as possible, and if you put a bag down, keep an eye on it. This also applies to restaurants and pubs, particularly in touristed areas such as the Star Ferry piers and the Peak Tram. If your bag doesn't accompany you to the toilet, don't expect to find it when you return.

If you are robbed, you can obtain a loss report for insurance purposes at the police station in the area in which the crime occurred. For locations and contact details of police stations in Hong Kong, visit www.info.gov.hk/police and click on 'Telephone'.

If you run into legal trouble, call the **Legal Aid Department** (☎ 2537 7717; ☯ 8.45am-1pm & 2-5.15pm Mon-Fri, 9am-noon Sat, 24hr hotline), which provides residents and visitors with representation, subject to a means and merits test. Other important numbers include the following:

Auxiliary Medical Service (AMS) hotline (☎ 2762 2033)

Bushfire Control Centre hotline (☎ 2720 0777)

Police (general inquiries ☎ 2860 2000, report hotline ☎ 2527 7177)

St John Ambulance Brigade (Hong Kong Island ☎ 2576 6555, Kowloon ☎ 2713 5555, New Territories ☎ 2639 2555, territory-wide ☎ 2530 8032)

Tropical Cyclone Warning (☎ 2835 1473)

GAY & LESBIAN TRAVELLERS

The gay scene in Hong Kong has undergone quite a revolution over a few short years. It was only in 1991 that the Crimes (Amendment) Ordinance removed criminal penalties for homosexual acts between consenting adults over the age of 18. Since that time gay groups have been lobbying for legislation to address the issue of discrimination on the grounds of sexual orientation. Despite these changes, however, Hong Kong Chinese society remains fairly conservative, and it can still be risky for gays and lesbians to come out to family members or their employers.

Useful organisations:

Chi Heng Foundation (☎ 2517 0564; www.chiheng foundation.com; GPO Box 3923, Central, Hong Kong) Umbrella unit for gay and lesbian associations and groups in Hong Kong.

Horizons (☎ 2815 9268, 9776 6479; www.horizons.org.hk; GPO Box 6837, Central, Hong Kong; hotline 🕑 7.30-10.30pm Tue & Thu) Phone service that can provide information and advice to local and visiting gays, lesbians and bisexuals.

Queer Sisters (☎ 2314 4348; www.qs.org.hk; GPO Box 9313, Central, Hong Kong; 🕑 7.30-10pm Thu & 8-10pm Fri) Information and assistance organisation for lesbians.

HEALTH

The Severe Acute Respiratory Syndrome (SARS) outbreak of 2003 notwithstanding (see the boxed text, p51), health conditions in the region are good. Travellers have a low risk of contracting infectious diseases, apart from travellers' diarrhoea, which is common throughout Asia. The health system (p317) is generally excellent.

Diseases
DENGUE FEVER

This is caught from mosquito bites. Until recently it was unheard of in Hong Kong yet some 30 cases were reported in 2004 but the outbreak claimed no lives.

This viral disease is transmitted by mosquitoes but unlike the malaria mosquito, the *Aedes aegypti* mosquito, which transmits the dengue virus, is most active during the day, and is found mainly in urban areas, in and around human dwellings. Signs and symptoms of dengue fever include a sudden onset of high fever, headache, joint and muscle pains (hence its old name, 'breakbone fever') and nausea and vomiting. A rash of small red spots sometimes appears three to four days after the onset of fever.

You should seek medical attention as soon as possible if you think you may be infected. A blood test can exclude malaria and indicate the possibility of dengue fever. There is no specific treatment for dengue. Aspirin should be avoided, as it increases the risk of haemorrhaging. The best prevention is to avoid mosquito bites at all times by covering up, using insect repellents containing the compound DEET and mosquito nets.

GIARDIA

This is a parasite that often jumps on board when you have diarrhoea. It then causes a more prolonged illness with intermittent diarrhoea or loose stools, bloating, fatigue and some nausea. There may be a metallic taste in the mouth. Avoiding potentially contaminated foods and always washing your hands can help to prevent giardia.

HEPATITIS A

This virus is common in Hong Kong and Macau and is transmitted through contaminated water and shellfish. It is most commonly caught at local island seafood restaurants. Immunisation and avoiding local seafood restaurants should prevent it.

HEPATITIS B

Whilst this is common in the area, it can only be transmitted by unprotected sex, sharing needles, treading on a discarded needle, or receiving contaminated blood in very remote areas of China.

INFLUENZA

Hong Kong has a bad flu season over the winter months from December to March. Symptoms include a cold (runny nose etc) with a high fever and aches and pains. You should wash your hands frequently, avoid anybody you know who has the flu, and think about getting a flu shot before you travel.

TRAVELLERS' DIARRHOEA

To prevent diarrhoea, avoid tap water unless it has been boiled, filtered or chemically disinfected (eg with iodine tablets); only eat fresh fruits and vegetables if cooked or peeled; be wary of dairy products that might contain unpasteurised milk; and be highly selective when eating food from street vendors.

If you develop diarrhoea, be sure to drink plenty of fluids, preferably an oral rehydration solution containing lots of salt and sugar. A few loose stools don't require treatment but, if you start experiencing more than four or five stools a day, you should start taking an antibiotic (usually a quinolone drug) and an antidiarrheal agent (such as loperamide). If diarrhoea is bloody, or persists for more than 72 hours, or is accompanied by fever, shaking chills or severe abdominal pain you should seek medical attention.

Directory

HEALTH

Environmental Hazards
MOSQUITOES

Mosquitoes are prevalent in Hong Kong. You should always use insect repellent and if bitten use hydrocortisone cream to reduce swelling.

SNAKES

There are many snakes in Hong Kong and some are deadly, but you are unlikely to encounter any. Still, always take care when bushwalking. Go straight to a public hospital if bitten; private doctors do not stock antivenin.

WATER

Avoid drinking the local water as its quality varies enormously and depends on the pipes in the building you're in. Bottled water is a safer option or you can boil tap water for three minutes.

Online Resources

The World Health Organization publishes a superb book called *International Travel and Health*, which is revised annually and is available free online at www.who.int/ith.

Recommended Immunisations

Since most vaccines don't produce immunity until at least two weeks after they're given, visit a physician four to eight weeks before departure. Ask your doctor for an International Certificate of Vaccination (or 'yellow booklet'), which will list all of the vaccinations you've received.

If your health insurance doesn't cover you for medical expenses abroad, consider supplemental insurance (see www.lonelyplanet .com/travel_links for more information).

There are no required vaccinations for entry into Hong Kong or Macau unless you have travelled from a country infected with yellow fever. In this case, you will have to show your yellow-fever vaccination certificate. Recommended immunisations for Hong Kong and Macau:

Hepatitis A and B Given (Twinrix) 1ml at day 1, day 30 and six months. Minimal soreness at injection site. You are not immune until after the final shot.

Influenza shot 0.5ml is recommended if you are travelling in the winter months and especially if you are over 60 years or have a history of chronic illness. It lasts for one year. You should not have the shot if you are allergic to eggs.

Polio syrup 0.5ml orally every 10 years. There are no side effects.

Tetanus and diphtheria (DT) 0.5ml every 10 years. It will cause a sore arm and redness at the injection site.

Do not have any of these immunisations if you are pregnant or breastfeeding. Talk to your doctor about possible alternatives.

HOLIDAYS

Western and Chinese culture combine to create an interesting mix – and number – of public holidays in Hong Kong and Macau. Determining the exact date of some of them is tricky as there are traditionally two calendars in use: the Gregorian solar (or Western) calendar and the Chinese lunar calendar.

The following are public holidays in both Hong Kong and Macau (unless noted otherwise). For Macau-specific holidays, see p377.

New Year's Day 1 January

Chinese New Year 29 January 2006, 18 February 2007, 7 February 2008

Easter 14–17 April 2006, 6-9 April 2007, 21–24 March 2008

Ching Ming 5 April

Buddha's Birthday 5 May 2006, 24 May 2007, 12 May 2008

Labour Day 1 May

Dragon Boat (Tuen Ng) Festival 31 May 2006, 19 June 2007, 8 June 2008

Hong Kong SAR Establishment Day 1 July (not Macau)

Mid-Autumn Festival 6 October 2006, 25 September 2007, 14 September 2008

China National Day 1 & 2 October

Cheung Yeung 30 October 2006, 19 October 2007, 7 October 2008

Christmas Day 25 December

Boxing Day 26 December

IDENTITY CARD

Hong Kong residents are required to carry a government-issued Hong Kong Identity Card with them at all times and this rule is strictly enforced. As a visitor, you are required to carry your passport; it is the only acceptable form of identification as far as the police are concerned.

Anyone over the age of 11 who stays in Hong Kong for longer than 180 days must apply for a Hong Kong ID. Inquire at the Immigration Department's **ID-issuing**

office (Map pp414–15; ☎ 2824 6111; www
.immd.gov.hk; 8th fl, Immigration Tower,
7 Gloucester Rd, Wan Chai; ☿ 8.45am-
4.30pm Mon-Fri & 9-11.30am Sat). Be sure
to take your passport and other documents
with you.

INTERNET ACCESS

The Internet is very popular in computer-
literate Hong Kong, and the territory was
the first place in the world to be totally
accessible by broadband. Virtually every
business has a website and just about anyone you're likely to do business with can be
contacted by email.

Internet service providers (ISPs) most
often used in Hong Kong include **PCCW's Netvi-
gator** (☎ 183 3833; www.netvigator.com),
HKNet (☎ 2110 2288; www.hknet.com), **CPC-
Net** (☎ 2331 8123; www.cpcnet-hk.com) and
Yahoo (☎ 2895 5769; www.yahoo.hk).

Most hotels and hostels have Internet access. You'll also be able to log on for free at
major MTR stations (eg Central and Tsim
Sha Tsui) and many public libraries, including the Causeway Bay branch of the Central
Library (p316). All it takes to log on to one
of up to a half-dozen terminals at the **Pacific
Coffee Company** (www.pacificcoffee.com) is the
purchase of a coffee ($15 to $36) or a piece
of cake ($12 to $25).

Among some of the best (ie fast machines,
good locations, number of terminals) private Internet cafés:

Cyber Clan (Map pp420–1; ☎ 2723 2821; South Base-
ment, Golden Crown Court, 66-70 Nathan Rd, Tsim Sha
Tsui; membership $5, per hr $10 midnight-noon Mon-Fri,
$13 noon-midnight Mon-Fri, all day Sat & Sun; ☿ 24 hr)
Enter this round-the-clock place from Carnarvon Rd.

Cyber Pro Internet (Map pp414–15; ☎ 2836 3502;
Basement, 491-499 Lockhart Rd, Causeway Bay; per hr
$16/10 11am-midnight/midnight-7am Sun-Thu, $18/13 Fri
& Sat; ☿ 11am-midnight) This huge place is packed with
young-uns playing games.

IT. Fans (Map pp408–9; ☎ 2542 1868; Ground &
mezzanine fl, Man On Commercial Bldg, 12-13 Jubilee St,
Central; membership $10, per hr members/nonmembers
$16/20 Mon-Thu, $18/22 Fri-Sun; ☿ 10am-5am) This
massive and very central place has 100 monitors and
serves real food.

Just Online Cyber Cafe (Map p423; ☎ 2374 1723;
Basement, SB Commercial Bldg, 478 Nathan Rd, Yau Ma
Tei; adult/student per hr $12/10; ☿ 24hr) This basement
café is fairly rough and ready but its opening hours are
about right.

Pacific Coffee Company (Map pp408–9; ☎ 2868 5100;
shop 1022, 1st fl, IFC Mall, 1 Harbour View St, Central;
☿ 7am-11pm Sun-Thu, 7am-midnight Fri & Sat) There's
another **Central branch** (Map p412; ☎ 2537 1688; 23
Hollywood Rd, Central; ☿ 7am-midnight Mon-Thu,
7am-1am Fri & Sat, 8am-midnight Sun) and a **Tsim
Sha Tsui branch** (Map pp420–1; ☎ 2735 0112, Shop
G31-G32A, Miramar Shopping Center, 132 Nathan Road;
☿ 7am-midnight Mon-Thu, 7am-1am Fri & Sat, 8am-
midnight Sun). Internet is free for customers.

Shadowman Cyber Cafe (Map pp420–1; ☎ 2366 5262;
Ground fl, Karlock Bldg, 7 Lock Rd, Tsim Sha Tsui; ☿ 8am-
midnight Mon-Fri, 9am-11.30pm Sat & Sun) This is a small
but convivial place to check emails, surf the web and have
lunch (sandwiches $38 to $45, set meal $45). The first 20
minutes are free with your purchase, then it's $10 every
15 minutes.

LAUNDRY

Laundries are easy to find everywhere in
Hong Kong – hey, this *is* China – though
they're *never* self-service. Most hotels, guesthouses and even some hostels have a laundry
service. Prices at local laundries are normally
$28 to $32 for the first 3kg, and then $8 to
$12 for each additional kilogram.

Drycleaners are easy to spot and some
laundries offer that service as well. Both
prices and quality vary enormously but expect to pay from $25 for a dress shirt, from
$35 for a skirt, and from $60 for a suit.

The following are recommended laundries and dry-cleaners:

Martinizing (Map pp408–9; ☎ 2525 3089; Ground fl,
7 Glenealy, Central; ☿ 8.30am-7pm Mon-Sat)

New Furama Dry-Cleaning (Map pp408–9; ☎ 2537
2217; Shop 1C, Ground fl, Bank of America Tower,
12 Harcourt Rd, Central; ☿ 8am-7pm Mon-Sat)

Sunshine Laundry (Map pp420–1; ☎ 2377 9804;
Shop 12, Ground fl, National Court, 19-24 Tak Hing St,
Tsim Sha Tsui; ☿ 7.30am-8.30pm)

Wei Wei Dry Cleaner & Laundry (Map p412;
☎ 2522 9818; 26 Old Bailey St, Soho; ☿ 7.30am-
8.30pm Mon-Sat)

LEFT LUGGAGE

There are left-luggage lockers in major KCR
train stations, including the Hung Hom station, the West Tower of the Shun Tak Centre in Sheung Wan, from where the Macau
ferry departs, and the China ferry terminal
in Tsim Sha Tsui. Luggage costs between $20
and $30 for up to two hours (depending on

the locker size) and between $25 and $35 for every 12 hours after that. The Hong Kong Airport Express station has a left-luggage office open from 6am to 1am. There's also a counter on level 5 (arrivals hall) of **Hong Kong International Airport** (☎ 2261 0110; ☿ 5.30am-1.30am). Storage here costs $35 for up to three hours, $50 for up to 24 hours and $120 for up to 48 hours. It's $80 for each 24-hour period after that.

Generally the machines don't use keys but spit out a numbered ticket when you have deposited your money and closed the door. You have to punch in this number when you retrieve your bag so keep it somewhere safe or write the number elsewhere. Some lockers have a maximum storage time of three days, so read the instructions carefully.

If you're going to visit Macau or the mainland and you'll be returning to Hong Kong, most hotels and even some guesthouses and hostels have left-luggage rooms and will let you leave your gear behind, even if you've already checked out and won't be staying on your return. There is usually a charge for this service but be sure to inquire first.

LEGAL MATTERS

Hong Kong has a serious drug problem, much of it supplied by the Triads. There are estimated to be more than 40,000 drug addicts in Hong Kong, 75% of whom are hooked on heroin, which they generally smoke – the process is called 'chasing the dragon' – rather than inject. Some female addicts finance their habit by working in the sex industry; others resort to pickpocketing, burglary and robbery.

Professional smugglers often target Westerners to carry goods into countries like Vietnam and India, where those goods are prohibited or the import taxes are high. The theory is that customs agents are less likely to stop and search foreigners. These small-time smuggling expeditions, or 'milk runs', either earn the Westerner a fee or a free air ticket to another destination. But smuggling is very, very risky.

Most foreigners who get into legal trouble in Hong Kong are involved in drugs. *All* forms of narcotics are illegal in Hong Kong. It makes no difference whether it's heroin, opium, 'ice', ecstasy or marijuana – the law makes no distinction. If police or customs officials find dope or even smoking equip-

ment in your possession, you can expect to be arrested immediately. If you do run into legal trouble, contact the **Legal Aid Department** (☎ 2537 7717; ☿ 24hr hotline).

LIBRARIES

Hong Kong has an extensive public library system – some 69 in total – and you will find a list on the Internet at www.hkpl.gov .hk. The most useful for travellers is the **City Hall Public Library** (Map pp408–9; ☎ 2921 2555; ☿ 10am-7pm Mon-Thu, 10am-9pm Fri, 10am-5pm Sat & Sun & some public holidays) spread over eight floors of the High Block of City Hall, opposite Queen's Pier in Central. With a passport and a deposit of $130 per item, foreign visitors can get a temporary library card (3rd floor), which allows them to borrow up to six books and other materials from the library for 14 days at any one time.

In Causeway Bay the even larger **Central Library** (Map pp414–15; ☎ 2921 0500; 66 Causeway Rd; ☿ 10am-9pm Thu-Tue, 1-9pm Wed, 10am-7pm some public holidays) has lending sections, children's and young adult libraries, some two dozen terminals with Internet available to the public, and a wonderful reading room on the 5th floor with around 4000 international periodicals.

MAPS

Decent tourist maps are easy to come by in Hong Kong, and they're usually free. The HKTB hands out copies of the bimonthly *The Hong Kong Map* at its information centres. It covers the northern coast of Hong Kong Island from Sheung Wan to Causeway Bay and part of the Kowloon Peninsula, and has inset maps of Aberdeen, Hung Hom, Kowloon City, Kowloon Tong, Sha Tin, Stanley and Tsuen Wan.

Another free map you'll find everywhere is the *AOA Street Map*, but it's full of advertising and difficult to use.

Lonely Planet's *Hong Kong City Map* ($60) has five separate maps with varying scales, a street index and an inset map of Hong Kong's rail network.

Universal Publications (UP; www.up.com.hk) produces many maps of Hong Kong, including the 1:80,000 *Hong Kong Touring Map* ($22) and the 1:9000 *City Map of Hong Kong & Kowloon* ($25). It publishes

Directory

LEGAL MATTERS

detailed street maps of Hong Kong Island and Kowloon ($22 each), with scales below 1:8000.

The *Hong Kong Official Guide Map* ($45), produced by the **Survey and Mapping Office of the Lands Department** (www.info.gov.hk/landsd /mapping), has both street and district maps and is available from most bookshops.

If you're looking for greater detail, topographical accuracy and good colour reproduction, it's worth investing in the *Hong Kong Guidebook* ($60), a street atlas to the entire territory published by UP and updated annually. Compiled in English and Chinese, it also includes useful information such as ferry timetables, hotel listings and a separate booklet called the *Public Transport Boarding Guide*, which is the only complete listing of bus and minibus routes available in Hong Kong. A larger format version of this, the *Hong Kong Directory* ($70) also includes the transport guide; the pocket-size *Palm Atlas of Hong Kong* ($42) does not.

Along with everything from flying charts to plans of the New Towns in the New Territories, the Survey and Mapping Office produces a series of eight *Countryside Series* maps that are useful for hiking in the hills and country parks. They are available from two **Map Publication Centres**: the **North Point branch** (Map pp406–7; ☎ 2231 3187; 23rd fl, North Point Government Offices, 333 Java Rd; ⏰ 9am-5pm Mon-Fri & 9am-noon Sat) and the **Yau Ma Tei branch** (Map pp420–1; ☎ 2780 0981; 382 Nathan Rd; ⏰ 9am-5pm Mon-Fri & 9am-noon Sat).

Each of the six *Countryside Series* maps is 1:25,000, with larger-scale inset maps. One of them covers Hong Kong Island and surrounds: *Hong Kong Island & Neighbouring Islands* ($50). Three maps are devoted to the New Territories: *North-West New Territories* ($45); *North-East & Central New Territories* ($50) and *Sai Kung & Clearwater Bay* ($50). For the islands, there's *Outlying Islands* ($50), with large-scale maps of Cheung Chau, Lamma, Peng Chau, Ma Wan, Tung Lung Chau and Po Toi, and *Lantau Island & Neighbouring Islands* ($50), essentially a 1:25,000-scale map of Hong Kong's largest island, with several larger-scale inset maps.

Most bookshops stock Universal Publications' 1:32,000-scale *Lantau Island, Cheung Chau & Lamma Island* ($25), which is laminated and contains useful transport information, and its 1:54,000 *Tseung Kwan O, Sai Kung, Clearwater Bay* ($25).

If you're heading for any of Hong Kong's four major trails, you should get a copy of the trail map produced by the Country & Marine Parks Authority, which is available at the Map Publication Centres.

MEDICAL SERVICES

The standard of medical care in Hong Kong is generally excellent but expensive. Always take out travel insurance before you travel. Healthcare is divided into public and private, and there is no interaction between the two. In the case of an emergency, all ambulances (☎ 999) will take you to a government-run public hospital where, as a visitor, you will be required to pay $570 for using emergency services. Treatment is guaranteed in any case; people who cannot pay immediately will be billed later. While the emergency care is excellent, you may wish to transfer to a private hospital once you are stable.

There are many English-speaking general practitioners, specialists and dentists in Hong Kong, who can be found through your consulate (p310), private hospital or the Yellow Pages. If money is tight, take yourself to the nearest public hospital emergency room and be prepared to wait. The general inquiry number for hospitals is ☎ 2300 6555.

Public and private hospitals with 24-hour accident and emergency departments:

HONG KONG ISLAND

Hong Kong Central Hospital (Map p412; ☎ 2522 3141; 1B Lower Albert Rd, Central) Private.

Matilda International Hospital (Map pp406–7; ☎ 2849 0700, 24hr help line 2849 0111; 41 Mt Kellett Rd, The Peak) Private.

Queen Mary Hospital (Map pp406–7; ☎ 2855 3838; 102 Pok Fu Lam Rd, Pok Fu Lam) Public.

KOWLOON

Hong Kong Baptist Hospital (Off Map pp418–19; ☎ 2339 8888; 222 Waterloo Rd, Kowloon Tong) Private.

Princess Margaret Hospital (Map pp404–5; ☎ 2990 1111, 24hr help line 2990 2000; 2-10 Princess Margaret Hospital Rd, Lai Chi Kok) Public.

Queen Elizabeth Hospital (Map pp420–1; ☎ 2958 8428; 30 Gascoigne Rd, Yau Ma Tei) Public.

NEW TERRITORIES

Prince of Wales Hospital (Map p425; ☎ 2632 2415; 30-32 Ngan Shing St, Sha Tin) Public.

TRADITIONAL MEDICINE

Traditional Chinese medicine is extremely popular in Hong Kong, both for prevention and cure and the main body overseeing it is the **Chinese Medicine Council of Hong Kong** (Map pp414–15; ☎ 2121 1888; www.cmchk.org.hk; 37 fl, Wu Chung House, 213 Queen's Rd East, Wan Chai). **Eu Yan Sang** (p235) in Central and elsewhere is probably the most famous traditional-medicine dispensary in town, and many of the doctors speak English. The store is also an interesting place to browse, as many of the healing ingredients are displayed and explained.

There are many pharmacies in Hong Kong and Macau. They bear a red and white cross outside and there should be a registered pharmacist available. Though many medications can be bought over the counter without a prescription in Hong Kong, you should check it is a known brand and that the expiry date is valid. Birth-control pills, pads, tampons and condoms are available over the counter in these dispensaries as well as stores such as Watsons and Mannings.

MONEY

Consult the inside front cover for a table of exchange rates and refer to the boxed text, p18, for information on costs.

ATMs

Hong Kong automated teller machines (ATMs) can be found almost everywhere and are usually linked up to international money systems such as Cirrus, Maestro, Plus and Visa Electron. Some HSBC so-called Electronic Money machines offer cash withdrawal facilities for Visa and Master-Card holders; American Express cardholders have access to Jetco ATMs and can withdraw local currency and travellers' cheques at the Express Cash ATMs in town.

Changing Money

One of the main reasons why Hong Kong has become a major financial centre is because it has no currency controls; locals and foreigners can bring/send in or take out as much money as they like.

Banks in Hong Kong generally offer the best rates, though three of the biggest ones –

HSBC, Standard Chartered and the Hang Seng Bank – levy a $50 commission for each transaction on non-account holders. If you're changing the equivalent of several hundred US dollars or more, the exchange rate improves, which usually makes up for the fee.

There are licensed moneychangers, such as Chequepoint, abundant in touristed areas, including Tsim Sha Tsui and the Shun Tak Centre, from where ferries depart for Macau. While they are convenient (usually open on Sunday and holidays and late into the evenings) and take no commission per se, the less-than-attractive exchange rates offered are equivalent to a 5% commission. These rates are clearly posted, though if you're changing several hundred US dollars or more you might be able to bargain for a better rate. Before the actual exchange is made, the moneychanger is required by law to give you a form to sign that clearly shows the amount due to you, the exchange rate and any service charges. And try to avoid the exchange counters at the airport: they offer some of the worst rates in Hong Kong. The rates offered at hotels are only marginally better.

One moneychanger that we've been using since the ink was still wet on the Treaty of Nanking is **Wing Hoi Money Exchange** (Map pp420–1; ☎ 2723 5948; Ground fl, shop No 9B, Mirador Mansion Arcade, 58 Nathan Rd, Tsim Sha Tsui; ⊗ 8.30am-8.30pm Mon-Sat, 8.30am-7pm Sun). They'll change just about any currency as well as travellers cheques.

No foreign currency black market exists in Hong Kong. If anyone on the street does approach you to change money, assume it's a scam.

Credit Cards

The most widely accepted credit cards in Hong Kong are Visa, MasterCard, American Express (Amex), Diners Club and JCB – and pretty much in that order. When signing credit card receipts, make sure you always write 'HK' in front of the dollar sign if there isn't one already printed there.

If you plan to use a credit card make sure you have a high enough credit limit to cover major expenses such as car hire or airline tickets. Alternatively, leave your card in credit when you start your travels. And don't just carry one card, go for two: an American Express or Diners Club card with a MasterCard or Visa card. Better still, combine cards and travellers cheques so you have something to fall back on if an ATM swallows your card or the bank won't accept it.

Some shops in Hong Kong may try to add a surcharge to offset the commission charged by credit companies, which can range from 2.5% to 7%. In theory, this is prohibited by the credit companies, but to get around this many shops will offer a 5% discount if you pay cash. It's your call.

If a card is lost or stolen you must inform both the police (☎ 2527 7177) and the issuing company as soon as possible; otherwise, you may have to pay for the purchases that the unspeakable scoundrel has racked up on your card. Some 24-hour numbers for cancelling cards:

American Express (☎ 2811 6888)

Diners Club (☎ 2860 1888)

JCB (☎ 2366 7211, 2877 5280)

MasterCard (☎ 800 966 677)

Visa (☎ 800 900 782)

The Visa number may be able to help you (or at least point you in the right direction) should you lose your Visa card but, in general, you must deal with the issuing bank in the case of an emergency. Round-the-clock emergency bank numbers:

Chase Manhattan Bank (☎ 2890 8188)

Citibank (☎ 2860 0333)

HSBC (☎ 2748 8080)

Standard Chartered Bank (☎ 2886 4111)

Currency

The local currency is the Hong Kong dollar (HK$), which is divided into 100 cents. Bills are issued in denominations of $10 (purple and rose), $20 (grey), $50 (blue), $100 (red), $500 (brown) and $1000 (yellow). There are little copper coins worth 10¢, 20¢ and 50¢, silver-coloured $1, $2 and $5 coins and a nickel and bronze $10 coin.

Hong Kong notes are issued by three banks: HSBC (formerly the Hongkong & Shanghai Bank), the Standard Chartered Bank and the Bank of China (all but the $10 bill).

For exchange rates see the inside front cover, or check out the FX Converter website (www.oanda.com/convert/classic).

Personal Cheques

Personal cheques are still widely used (and accepted) in Hong Kong; a group of diners will often write separate cheques to pay for their share of a meal. If you plan to stay for a while in Hong Kong – or even travel around Asia and return here – you might open a bank account here. There is no need to be a Hong Kong resident, and current and savings accounts can be opened in Hong Kong dollars or most other major currencies.

Travellers Cheques

Travellers cheques offer protection from theft but are becoming less common due to the preponderance of ATMs. Most banks will cash travellers cheques, and they all charge a fee, often irrespective of whether you are an account holder or not. HSBC charges 0.375% of the total exchanged, Standard Chartered adds a flat $50 commission and Hang Seng charges $60.

If any cheques go missing, contact the issuing office or the nearest branch of the issuing agency immediately. American Express (☎ 3002 1276) can usually arrange replacement cheques within 24 hours.

NEWSPAPERS & MAGAZINES

There are two principal English-language newspapers available in Hong Kong. The daily broadsheet South China Morning Post (www.scmp.com; $7), which has always toed the government line – before and after the handover – has the larger circulation and is read by more Hong Kong Chinese than expatriates. Its classified advertisement sales have placed it among the world's most profitable newspapers in the past. The tabloid Hong Kong Standard (www .thestandard.com.hk; $6), published from Monday to Saturday (weekend edition), is generally more rigorous in its local reporting. It dubs itself 'Greater China's Business Newspaper', though it's hard to see how it can claim that sobriquet. The Beijing mouthpiece China Daily (www.china daily.com.cn) also prints a Hong Kong English-language edition of its paper.

The *Asian Wall Street Journal* as well as regional editions of *USA Today*, the *International Herald Tribune* and the *Financial Times* are printed and are available in Hong Kong.

Directory

NEWSPAPERS & MAGAZINES

Hong Kong also has its share of English-language periodicals, including a slew of home-grown (and Asian-focused) business magazines. *Time*, *Newsweek* and *The Economist* are all available in the current editions.

PASSPORT

A passport is essential for visiting Hong Kong, and if yours is within six months of expiration get a new one. If you'll be staying for some time in Hong Kong, it's wise to register with your consulate. This makes the replacement process much simpler if you lose your passport or it is stolen.

Hong Kong residents are required to carry an officially issued identification card at all times (p314). Visitors should carry their passports with them at all times, as the immigration authorities do frequent spot checks to catch illegal workers and those who overstay their visas, and this is the only form of identification acceptable to the Hong Kong police.

PHOTOGRAPHY

Airport Security

You will have to put your camera and film through the X-ray machine at Hong Kong International Airport. The machines are film-safe for most kinds of film. Professional photographers using ultra-sensitive film (eg ASA 1000) do need to worry about this, especially if the film is repeatedly exposed. One way to combat the problem is to put the film in a protective lead-lined bag, though it's probably safer and easier to have the film hand-inspected (if possible).

Film & Equipment

Almost everything you could possibly need in the way of photographic accessories is available in Hong Kong. Stanley St on Hong Kong Island is the place to look for reputable camera stores.

Photo developing is relatively inexpensive; to develop a roll of 36 exposures and have them printed costs from $50 for size 3R and from $60 for size 4R. Processing and mounting slide film is $50. Most photo shops will take four passport-size photos of you for $35 or $40. Some of the best photo-processing in town is available at

Color Six (Map p412; ☎ 2526 0123; Ground fl, 28A Stanley St, Central; ◷ 8.30am-7pm Mon-Fri, 8.30am-4pm Sat). Not only can colour slides be professionally processed in just three hours, but many special types of film, unavailable elsewhere in Hong Kong, are on sale here.

PLACES OF WORSHIP

The following places either offer services themselves, or will tell you when and where services are held. You should also check the Yellow Pages for a more comprehensive list of Hong Kong churches, temples and synagogues.

Anglican (Church of England; ☎ 2523 4157; St John's Cathedral, 4-8 Garden Rd, Central)

Baha'i (☎ 2367 6407; Flat C-6, 11th fl, Hankow Centre, 1C Middle Rd, Tsim Sha Tsui)

Christian Scientist (☎ 2524 2701; Church of Christ, Scientist, 31 MacDonnell Rd, Central)

Hindu (☎ 2572 5284; Hindu Temple, 1B Wong Nai Chung Rd, Happy Valley)

Jewish (☎ 2529 2621; Ohel Leah Synagogue, 70 Robinson Rd, the Mid-Levels)

Mormon (Church of Jesus Christ of the Latter-Day Saints; ☎ 2910 2910 for venue)

Muslim (☎ 2724 0095; Kowloon Mosque & Islamic Centre, 105 Nathan Rd, Tsim Sha Tsui)

Quaker (Society of Friends; ☎ 2656 5656; David Kwok Hall, St John's Cathedral Annexe Bldg, 3 Garden Rd, Central)

Roman Catholic (☎ 2523 0384; The Cathedral, 16 Caine Road, Mid-Levels)

Sikh (☎ 2572 4459; Khalsa Diwan Sikh Temple, 371 Queen's Rd East, Wan Chai)

POST

Hong Kong Post (☎ 2921 2222; www.hongkong post.com) is generally excellent; local letters are often delivered the same day they are sent and there is Saturday delivery. The staff at most post offices speak English, and the lavender-coloured mail boxes with lime-green posts are clearly marked in English.

Receiving Mail

If a letter is addressed c/o Poste Restante, GPO Hong Kong, it will go to the GPO on Hong Kong Island. Pick it up at counter No 29 from 8am to 6pm Monday to Saturday only. If you want your letters to go to Kowloon, have them addressed as follows: c/o Poste Restante, Tsim Sha Tsui Post Office, 10 Middle Rd, Tsim Sha Tsui, Kowloon. Mail is normally held for two months.

Sending Mail
On Hong Kong Island, the **General Post Office** (Map pp408–9; 2 Connaught Place, Central; ☻ 8am-6pm Mon-Sat, 9am-2pm Sun) is just west of the Star Ferry. In Kowloon, the **Tsim Sha Tsui Post Office** (Map pp420–1; Ground fl, Hermes House, 10 Middle Rd, Tsim Sha Tsui; ☻ 8am-6pm Mon-Sat, 9am-2pm Sun) is just east of the southern end of Nathan Rd. Post office branches elsewhere keep shorter hours and usually don't open on Sunday.

You should allow five days for delivery of letters, postcards and aerogrammes to the UK, Continental Europe and Australia and five to six days to the USA.

COURIER SERVICES
Private companies offering courier delivery service include the following. All four companies have pick-up points around the territory. Many MTR stations have DHL outlets, including the **DHL Central branch** (☎ 2877 2848) next to exit F, and the **Admiralty MTR branch** (☎ 2529 5778), next to exit E.

DHL International (☎ 2400 3388)

Federal Express (☎ 2730 3333)

TNT Express Worldwide (☎ 2331 2663)

UPS (☎ 2735 3535)

POSTAL RATES
Local mail is $1.40 for up to 30g. Airmail letters and postcards are $2.40/4.50 to Asia (excluding Japan) and $3/5.30 elsewhere for the first 20/30g and $1.20 and $1.30 respectively for each additional 10g. Aerogrammes are a uniform $2.30.

SPEEDPOST
Letters and small parcels sent via Hong Kong Post's **Speedpost** (☎ 2921 2277; www .hongkongpost.com/speedpost) should reach any of some 216 destinations worldwide within four days and are automatically registered. Speedpost rates vary enormously according to destination; every post office has a schedule of fees and a timetable.

RADIO
Hong Kong's most popular English-language radio stations are RTHK Radio 3 (current affairs and talkback; 567AM, 1584AM, 97.9FM & 106.8FM); RTHK Radio 4 (classical music; 97.6-98.9FM); RTHK Radio 6 (BBC World Service relays; 675AM); AM 864 (hit parade; 864AM); and Metro Plus (news; 1044AM). The *South China Morning Post* publishes a daily schedule of radio programs.

TAXES & REFUNDS
There is no sales tax in Hong Kong. The only 'visible' tax visitors are likely to encounter is the 3% government tax on hotel rates.

TELEPHONE
International Calls & Rates
Hong Kong's country code is ☎ 852. To call someone outside Hong Kong, dial ☎ 001, then the country code, the local area code (you usually drop the initial zero if there is one) and the number. Country codes:

Australia (☎ 61)

Canada (☎ 1)

China (mainland) (☎ 86)

France (☎ 33)

Germany (☎ 49)

Japan (☎ 81)

Macau (☎ 853)

Netherlands (☎ 31)

New Zealand (☎ 64)

South Africa (☎ 27)

United Kingdom (☎ 44)

United States (☎ 1)

Remember that phone rates in Hong Kong are cheaper from 9pm to 8am on weekdays and throughout the weekend. If the phone you're using has the facility, dial ☎ 0060 first and then the number; rates will be cheaper at any time.

International direct dial calls to almost anywhere in the world can be made from most public telephones in Hong Kong, but you'll need a phonecard. These are available as stored-value Hello cards ($50 and $100) and as Smartcards (five denominations from \$50 to \$500). The former allow you to call from any phone – public or private – on your penny, by punching in a PIN code. You can buy phonecards at any PCCW branch, 7-Eleven and Circle K convenience stores, Mannings pharmacies and Wellcome supermarkets.

PCCW (☎ 2888 2888, 1000 hotline; www .pccw.com), the erstwhile Hong Kong Telecom and now known as Pacific Century Cyber Works, has retail outlets called i.Shops (☎ 2888 0008; www.pccwshop.com) throughout the territory, where you can buy phonecards, mobile phones and accessories. The most convenient shops for travellers are the Central branch (Map pp408–9; Ground fl, 161-163 Des Voeux Rd Central; ☻ 10am-8pm Mon-Sat, noon-7pm Sun) and the Tsim Sha Tsui branch (Map pp420–1; Shop G3, Ground fl, Hotel Miramar, 118-130 Nathan Rd; ☻ 10am-10pm). There's also a Causeway Bay branch (Map pp414–15; Ground fl, 42-44 Yee Woo St; ☻ 10am-10pm Mon-Sat, 11am-9pm Sun).

Local Calls & Rates

All calls made from private phones in Hong Kong are local calls and therefore free. From public pay phones calls cost \$1 for five minutes. The pay phones accept \$1, \$2, \$5 and \$10 coins. Hotels charge between \$3 and \$5 for local calls.

All landline numbers in the territory have eight digits (except ☎ 800 toll-free numbers), and there are no area codes.

Mobile Phones

Hong Kong has the world's highest per-capita usage of mobile telephones, and they work everywhere, including in tunnels and on the MTR. Any GSM-compatible phone can be used here.

PCCW i.Shops have mobile phones and accessories along with rechargeable SIM chips for sale at \$180 and \$280. Local calls work out to cost between 30¢ and 50¢ a minute (calls to the mainland are about \$1 a minute) and top-up cards are \$88 and \$180. Handsets can be hired from Hong Kong CSL (☎ 2888 1010; www.hkcsl.com), which maintain 1010 outlets in Hong Kong, including a Central branch (Map p412; ☎ 2918 1010; Ground fl, Century Square, 1-13 D'Aguilar St; ☻ 8.30am-11pm) and a Tsim Sha Tsui branch (Map pp420–1; ☎ 2910 1010; Ground fl, Canton House, 82-84 Canton

Rd; ☻ 8.30am-11pm), for as little as \$35 a day. CSL's prepaid SIM cards come in a variety of price options, depending if and where you need roaming services; top-up cards, which are also available at 7-Eleven and Circle K convenience stores, are \$99 and \$200.

Useful Numbers

The following are some important telephone numbers and codes; for emergency numbers see p312. Both the telephone directory and the Yellow Pages can be consulted online (p324).

Coastal Waters & Tidal Information (☎ 187 8970)

International Credit Card Calls (☎ 10011)

International Dialling Code (☎ 001)

International Directory Inquiries (☎ 10015)

International Fax Dialling Code (☎ 002)

Local Directory Inquiries (☎ 1081)

Reverse-Charge/Collect Calls (☎ 10010)

Time & Temperature (☎ 18501)

Weather (☎ 187 8066)

TELEVISION

Hong Kong's four free terrestrial TV stations are run by two companies: Television Broadcasts (TVB) and Asia Television (ATV). Each runs a Cantonese-language channel (TVB Jade and ATV Home) and an English one (TVB Pearl and ATV World). The program schedule is listed daily in the *South China Morning Post* and in a weekly Sunday supplement.

There are some 30 pay cable channels and a variety of satellite channels.

TIME

Hong Kong does not have daylight-saving time. Hong Kong time is eight hours ahead of GMT; 13 hours ahead of New York; 16 hours ahead of San Francisco; eight hours ahead of London; the same in Singapore, Manila and Perth; and two hours behind Sydney.

TIPPING

As a place Hong Kong isn't particularly conscious of tipping and there is no obligation to tip, say, taxi drivers; just round the fare up or you can throw in a dollar or two more. It's almost mandatory to tip hotel staff $10 to $20, and if you make use of the porters at the airport, $2 to $5 a suitcase is normally expected. The porters putting your bags on a push cart at Hong Kong or Kowloon Airport Express station do not expect a gratuity, though; it's all part of the service.

Most hotels and many restaurants add a 10% service charge to the bill. Check for hidden extras before you tip; some midrange hotels charge $3 to $5 for each local call when they are actually free throughout the territory, and some restaurants consistently get the bill wrong. If using the services of a hotel porter, it's customary to tip them at least $10.

TOILETS

Hong Kong has never had as many public toilets as other world-class cities but that is changing rapidly, with new ones being built and old ones refurbished and reopened. They are always free to use. Almost all public toilets have access for people with disabilities and baby-changing shelves in both men's and women's rooms. Equip yourself with tissues, though; public toilets in Hong Kong are often out of toilet paper.

TOURIST INFORMATION

The enterprising and energetic **Hong Kong Tourism Board** (HKTB; ☎ 2508 1234; www .discoverhongkong.com) is one of the most helpful and useful in the world. Staff are welcoming and have reams of information. Most of its literature is free, though they also sell a few useful publications and books, as well as postcards, T-shirts and souvenirs.

Before you depart, check the HKTB website (www.discoverhongkong.com), which should be able to answer any question you could possibly have. While on the ground and in Hong Kong phone the **HKTB Visitor Hotline** (☎ 2508 1234; ☉ 8am-6pm) if you have a query, a problem or you're lost. They're always able (and, what's more, keen) to help.

HKTB Visitor Information & Service Centres can be found on Hong Kong Island, in Kowloon, at Hong Kong International

Airport on Lantau and in Lo Wu on the border with the mainland. Outside these centres and at several other places in the territory you'll be able to find iCyberlink screens from which you can conveniently access the HKTB website and database 24 hours a day.

Hong Kong International Airport HKTB Centres
(Map p427; Chek Lap Kok; ☉ 7am-11pm) There are centres in Halls A and B on the arrival level and the E2 transfer area.

Hong Kong Island HKTB Centre (Map pp414–15; Causeway Bay MTR station, near exit F; ☉ 8am-8pm)

Kowloon HKTB Centre (Map pp420–1; Star Ferry Concourse, Tsim Sha Tsui; ☉ 8am-8pm)

Lo Wu HKTB Centre (Map pp404–5; 2nd fl, Arrival Hall, Ko Wu Terminal Bldg; ☉ 8am-6pm)

Other excellent sources for information are listed following:

Community Advice Bureau (Map pp408–94; ☎ 2815 5444; www.cab.org.hk; Room 16C, Right Emperor Commercial Bldg, 122-126 Wellington St, Central; ☉ 9.30am-4.30pm Mon-Fri) Will answer questions for anyone about anything but primarily directed at new Hong Kong residents trying to get their feet on the ground.

Hong Kong Information Services Department
(☎ 2842 8777; www.info.gov.hk) Can answer specific questions or direct you to the appropriate government department.

UNIVERSITIES

Hong Kong has a total of eight universities. **Hong Kong University** (Map pp406–7; ☎ 2859 2111; www.hku.hk), established in 1911, is the oldest and most difficult to get into. Its campus is in Pok Fu Lam on the western side of Hong Kong Island. The **Chinese University of Hong Kong** (Map pp404–5; ☎ 2609 6000; www.cuhk.edu.hk), that was established in 1963, is most applicants' second choice. It is situated on a beautiful campus at Ma Liu Shui, which is north of Sha Tin in the New Territories.

The **Hong Kong University of Science & Technology** (Map pp404–5; ☎ 2358 6000; www.ust.hk) admitted its first students in 1991, and is situated at Tai Po Tsai in Clearwater Bay in the New Territories.

The other five universities are based in Kowloon and include the **Hong Kong Polytechnic University** (Map pp420–1; ☎ 2766 5111; www.polyu.edu.hk) in Hung Hom, which was set up in 1972.

USEFUL ORGANISATIONS

Hong Kong Consumer Council (Map pp408–9; ☎ 2929 2222; www.consumer.org.hk; Ground fl, Harbour Bldg, 38 Pier Rd, Central) Can help with complaints about dishonest shopkeepers and other rip-offs.

Royal Asiatic Society (☎ 2813 7500; www.royalasiatic society.org.hk; GPO Box 3864, Central) Organises lectures, field trips of cultural and historical interest and puts out publications.

Royal Geographical Society (☎ 2583 9700; www.rgshk .org.hk; GPO Box 6681, Central) Organises lectures by high-profile local and foreign travellers, as well as hikes and field trips.

World Wide Fund for Nature Hong Kong (WWFHK; ☎ 2526 4473, 2526 1011; www.wwf.org.hk; 1 Tramway Path, Central)

VISAS

The vast majority of travellers, including citizens of Australia, Canada, the European Union (EU), Israel, Japan, New Zealand and the USA, are allowed to enter the Hong Kong SAR without a visa and stay 90 days. Holders of British or EU United Kingdom passports can stay up to 180 days without a visa, but British Dependent Territories and British Overseas citizens not holding a visa are only allowed to remain 90 days. Holders of most African (including South African), South American and Middle Eastern passports do not require visas for a visit of 30 days or less.

If you do require a visa, you must apply beforehand at the nearest Chinese consulate or embassy; for addresses and contact information consult the website www.immd .gov.hk/ehtml/embassy.htm.

If you plan on visiting mainland China, you must have a visa; for details, see p306.

Visitors have to show that they have adequate funds for their stay (a credit card should do the trick) and that they hold an onward or return ticket. Ordinary visas cost $135 (or the equivalent in local currency), while transit visas are $70.

Visitors are not permitted to take up employment, establish any sort of business or enrol as students while visiting on a tourist visa. If you want to work or study, you must apply for an employment or student visa beforehand. It is very hard to change your visa status after you have arrived in Hong Kong. Anyone wishing to

stay longer than the visa-free period must apply for a visa before travelling to Hong Kong. For details on applying for a work permit, see opposite.

Visa Extensions

In general, visa extensions ($135) are not readily granted unless there are special or extenuating circumstances, such as cancelled flights, illness, registration in a legitimate course of study, legal employment, or marriage to a local.

For more information contact the **Hong Kong Immigration Department** (Map pp414–15; ☎ 2852 3047; www.info.gov.hk/immd; 5th fl, Immigration Tower, 7 Gloucester Rd, Wan Chai; ☺8.45am-4.30pm Mon-Fri & 9-11.30am Sat).

WEBSITES

The Lonely Planet website, www.lonely planet.com, is a good start for many of Hong Kong's more useful links. Other helpful sites:

Asiaxpat (www.asiaxpat.com) Lifestyle – restaurants, nightlife, trends – but advertorial.

bc magazine (www.bcmagazine.net) Nightlife and entertainment from one of Hong Kong's top nightlife freebies.

Business in Asia (www.business-in-asia.com)

Census and Statistics Department (www.info.gov.hk /censtatd) All the facts and figures you need (or don't).

Doing Business in Hong Kong (www.business.gov.hk)

Gay Hong Kong (www.gayhk.com) The nightlife scene in Hong Kong for visitors and locals alike.

HK Clubbing (www.hkclubbing.com)

Hong Kong Antiquities and Monuments Office (www.amo.gov.hk) Hong Kong's listed monuments and sites.

Hong Kong Information Services Department (www.info.gov.hk)

Hong Kong Leisure and Cultural Services Department (www.lcsd.gov.hk)

Hong Kong News.Net (www.hongkongnews.net)

Hong Kong Observatory (www.weather.gov.hk)

Hong Kong Outdoors (www.hkoutdoors.com)

Hong Kong Tourism Board (www.discoverhongkong.com)

Hong Kong Transport Department (www.info.gov.hk/td)

Hong Kong Yearbook (www.info.gov.hk/yearbook/2003 /eindex.html)

Hong Kong Yellow Pages (www.yp.com.hk)

Jobs DB (www.jobsdb.com/hk)

South China Morning Post (www.scmp.com.hk)

Yellow Pages Maps (www.ypmap.com) Includes maps as well as phone numbers and addresses.

YPExpat (www.ypexpat.com) Lifestyle website for expatriates.

WEIGHTS & MEASURES

Although the international metric system (see the inside front cover) is in official use in Hong Kong, traditional Chinese weights and measures are still common. At local markets, meat, fish and produce are sold by the *léung*, equivalent to 37.8g, and the *gàn* (catty), which is equivalent to about 600g. There are 16 *léung* to the *gàn*. Gold and silver are sold by the tael, which is exactly the same as a *léung*.

WOMEN TRAVELLERS

Respect for women is deeply ingrained in the Chinese culture. Despite the Confucian principle of the superiority of men, women in Chinese society often call all the shots and can wield a tremendous amount of influence at home, in business and in politics.

Hong Kong is a safe city for women, although common-sense caution should be observed, especially at night. Few women – visitors or residents – complain of bad treatment, intimidation or aggression. Having said that, some Chinese men regard Western women as 'easy' and have made passes at foreigners – even quite publicly. If you are sexually assaulted call the **Hong Kong Rape Hotline** (☎ 2375 5322).

Other useful organisations:

Hong Kong Federation of Women (Map pp414–15; ☎ 2833 6518; hkfw.org; Ground fl, 435 Lockhart Rd, Wan Chai)

International Women's League (Map pp420–1; ☎ 2782 2207; 2nd fl, Boss Commercial Bldg, 28 Ferry St, Jordan)

WORK

Travellers on tourist visas are barred from accepting employment in Hong Kong. It is possible to obtain work 'under the table', but there are stiff penalties for employers

who are caught hiring foreigners illegally. Still, to earn extra money many foreigners end up teaching English or doing some other kind of work – translating, modelling, acting in Chinese films, waiting on tables or bartending. Few – if any – restaurants or bars will take the risk and hire you if you don't have a Hong Kong ID card these days.

For professional jobs, registering with Hong Kong personnel agencies or headhunters is important; check out the **Jobs DB** website (www.jobsdb.com/hk). **Drake International** (Map pp408–9; ☎ 2848 9288; www.drakeintl.com; 19 fl, Chekiang First Bank Centre, 1 Duddell St, Central) is an international employment agency that often advertises work in Hong Kong. You can always check the classified advertisements in the local English-language newspapers. The Thursday and Saturday editions of the *South China Morning Post* or the Friday edition of the *Hong Kong Standard* are particularly helpful. *HK Magazine* also has a jobs section.

Recruit (www.recruit.com.hk) and **Jiu Jik** (Job Finder; www.jiujik.com) are free jobseeker tabloids available on Wednesdays and Fridays at the majority of MTR stations. There are also the **Job Market Weekly** (www.jobmarket.com.hk; $3) and **Career Times** (www.careertimes.com.hk; $3), available at most newsagents.

Work Permits

To work legally here you need to have a work permit. The Hong Kong authorities require proof that you have been offered employment, usually in the form of a contract. The prospective employer is obligated to show that the work you plan to do cannot be performed by a local person. If you're planning on working or studying in Hong Kong, it could be helpful to have copies of transcripts, diplomas, letters of reference and other professional qualifications in hand.

In general, visitors must leave Hong Kong in order to obtain a work permit, returning only when it is ready; unfortunately Macau and the mainland do not qualify as interim destinations. Exceptions are made, however, especially if the company urgently needs to fill a position. Work visas are generally granted for between one and three years. Extensions should be applied for at least a month before the visa expires.

From overseas, applications for work visas can be made at any Chinese embassy or consulate (p324). In Hong Kong, contact the **Immigration Department** (Map pp414–15; ☎ 2824 6111; www.info.gov.hk/immd; 2nd fl, Immigration Tower, 7 Gloucester Rd, Wan Chai; ◷ 8.45am-4.30pm Mon-Fri & 9-11.30am Sat) for information on how to apply.

Introducing Macau   328

City Life   329
  Macau Calendar 329
  Culture 330
  Economy 333
  Government & Politics 334

Arts   334

Food   335

History   337

Sights   341

Macau Peninsula
    Walking Tour   361

Eating   362

Entertainment   367

Activities   369

Shopping   370

Sleeping   371

Transport   374

Directory   376
  Books 376
  Business Hours 376
  Climate 376
  Customs 376
  Discount Cards 376
  Emergency 376
  Holidays 377
  Internet Access 377
  Left Luggage 377
  Maps 377
  Medical Services 377
  Money 377
  Post 377
  Telephone 378
  Tourist Information 378
  Visas 378
  Websites 378

Macau ▮

Macau

INTRODUCING MACAU

Lying 65km to the west of Hong Kong, but predating it by almost 300 years, Macau was the first European enclave in Asia. When China resumed sovereignty over what is now called the Special Administrative Region (SAR) of Macau in 1999, it was by far the oldest.

Macau is a fascinating mix of cultures – a fusion of Mediterranean and Asian architecture, food, lifestyles and temperaments. It is a city of cobbled backstreets, baroque churches, ancient stone fortresses and exotic street names etched on *azulejos*, the distinctive Portuguese blue enamel tiles. There is a surfeit of interesting (and important) Chinese temples and restored colonial villas, and the cemeteries of Macau are the final resting places of many European and American missionaries, painters, soldiers and sailors who died at 'Macao Roads.' You will also find many good hotels, excellent restaurants and lively casinos here.

Most Western travellers who visit Macau spend just a few hours here on a whistle-stop tour, and many who travel to Hong Kong don't bother coming to Macau at all. That's a pity, for it's one of those 'treasure chest' sorts of places where something new can be found at every step and on every visit.

Macau has always been a popular destination for Hong Kong residents. In general, Hong Kong Chinese go to gamble at the casinos while foreigners make the trip to enjoy a little bit of the Mediterranean on the South China Sea. And beyond that there's a whole lot more.

In some regards, Macau is almost unrecognisable from how it was even a decade ago. Hong Kong Chinese had always looked down upon Macau as a sleepy, dirty, impoverished backwater, with nothing to recommend it except legalised gambling and cheap dim sum. Before the Portuguese colonial government departed in 1999, it spent some MOP$70 million on renovating and refurbishing civil buildings, churches, gardens and public squares; the place is now a colourful palette of pastels and ordered greenery.

At the same time, the post-handover government has spent a fortune on ambitious infrastructural projects and tourist facilities (see p341) in an effort to claim the prestigious title 'recreational centre of southern China'. The majority of this will cater to the enormous quantity of tourists from the mainland, whose numbers have almost doubled the total annual visitors to Macau since China began allowing residents of Guangdong, Beijing and Shanghai to visit Macau as individuals in mid-2003.

Getting to Macau from Hong Kong has never been easier, with high-speed ferries now running between the two territories virtually every 15 minutes. Go to Macau and stay a night or even two, and you'll discover something pretty, old, curious or tasty around every corner.

Traditional blue tile work, Largo do Senado (p361), Central Macau Peninsula

CITY LIFE
MACAU CALENDAR

No matter when you visit, you're likely to find a festival or some special event taking place in Macau. Chinese New Year (see the boxed text, p11) is chaotic in Macau, and hotel rooms are a prized commodity during this period. Still, it's a colourful time to visit, as the city literally explodes with bangers and fireworks – they're legal here – and the streets are filled with a carnival atmosphere. The Macau Formula 3 Grand Prix (p333) is also a peak time for visitors. For more information on events in Macau, check out the website of the **Macau Government Tourist Office** (MGTO; www.macautourism .gov.mo). For dates of Macau's public holidays, see p377 and p314. For information on festivals and events celebrated both here and in Hong Kong, see p10.

February/March
PROCESSION OF
THE PASSION OF OUR LORD
A 400-year-old tradition on the first Saturday of Lent in which a colourful procession bears a statue of Jesus Christ from Macau's Church of St Augustine to Macau Cathedral, where it spends the night and is carried back the following day. This will fall on 4 March in 2006, 24 February in 2007 and 9 February in 2008.

MACAU ARTS FESTIVAL
www.icm.gov.mo
Macau's red-letter arts event kicks off the cultural year with music, drama and dance from both Asia and the West.

April/May
A-MA FESTIVAL
This festival honours Tin Hau (known here as A-Ma), the patroness of fisherfolk and one of the territory's most popular goddesses. The best place to see the festival is at the A-Ma Temple in the Inner Harbour. This festival will fall on 9 May in 2006, 29 April in 2007 and 28 April in 2008.

BIRTHDAY OF THE LORD BUDDHA/
FEAST OF THE DRUNKEN DRAGON
On this public holiday, Buddha's statue is taken from monasteries and temples and ceremoniously bathed in scented water. This day also marks the Feast of the Drunken Dragon, which features dancing dragons in the streets of the Inner Harbour and a lot of legless merrymakers. This will fall on 5 May in 2006, 24 May in 2007 and 12 May in 2008.

PROCESSION OF
OUR LADY OF FATIMA
The procession goes from Macau Cathedral to the Chapel of Our Lady of Penha to commemorate a series of apparitions by the Virgin Mary to three peasant children at Fatima in Portugal in 1917. This falls on 13 May each year.

MACAU OPEN GOLF TOURNAMENT
www.sport.gov.mo
Part of the Asian PGA Tour, this event is held at the Macau Golf & Country Club on Coloane and attracts the region's best golfers.

June
DRAGON BOAT FESTIVAL
The Dragon Boat festival is also known as Tuen Ng (Double Fifth) as it falls on the fifth day of the fifth moon. This festival commemorates the death of Qu Yuan, a poet-statesman of the 3rd century BC, who

---

MACAU'S TOP FIVE

- a visit to the **ruins of the Church of St Paul** (p345) and an escalator ride up to **Monte Fort** (p345) and the **Macau Museum** (p344)
- a climb (not necessarily to the tippity-top) up the **Macau Tower** (p355)
- a stroll along Praia Grande and a visit to the **A-Ma Temple** (p355)
- a visit to the **Taipa House Museum** (p359) and a lunch of *caldo verde* (kale soup thickened with potatoes) and *bacalhau* (dried salted cod) at a Portuguese restaurant in **Taipa Village** (p365)
- a night out gambling at one of Macau's flashy new **casinos** (p331)

hurled himself into the Mi Lo River in Hunan province to protest against a corrupt government; dragon-boat races take place and traditional rice dumplings are eaten in memory of the event. The festival will fall on 31 May in 2006, 19 June in 2007 and 8 June in 2008.

MACAU LOTUS FLOWER FESTIVAL
The symbol of Macau is the focus of this festival, which sees lotuses blossoming in parks, gardens and ponds throughout Macau.

July
FIVB WOMEN'S VOLLEYBALL GRAND PRIX
www.sport.gov.mo
This is one of the most important women's volleyball tournaments in the region.

September/October
MACAU INTERNATIONAL FIREWORKS DISPLAY CONTEST
This event, the largest of its kind in the world, adds a splash of colour to the Macau night sky in autumn.

October/November
MACAU INTERNATIONAL MUSIC FESTIVAL
www.icm.gov.mo
This two-week festival is a heady mix of opera, musicals, visiting orchestras and other musical events.

ONE-DAY ITINERARY

If you only have a day in Macau, start by following the **walking tour** (p361) to get a feel for the lay of the land and Macau's living history. Spend an hour or so in the **Macau Museum** (p344) to answer all the questions you'll now have, and walk to **Yes Brazil** (p365) – via the **ruins of the Church of St Paul** (p345) – for lunch. In the afternoon, hop on a bus for **Taipa** (p358) and stroll through the village to Avenida da Praia and the three-part **Taipa House Museum** (p359). In the evening you should also walk along peninsular Macau's more dramatic Avenida da Praia Grande, stopping for a while at the **Lisboa Casino** (opposite) to see what all the fuss is about. Have a sundowner drink or two along the **'Lan Kwai Fong'** (p367) strip in NAPE and dinner at the atmospheric **Clube Militar de Macau** (p363) before catching the ferry back to Hong Kong.

MACAU FORMULA 3 GRAND PRIX
www.macau.grandprix.gov.mo
Approximately 30 national championship drivers compete to take the chequered flag in Macau's premier sporting event. The Grand Prix is held in the third week of November.

December
MACAU INTERNATIONAL MARATHON
www.sport.gov.mo
Like its Hong Kong counterpart, this running event, which takes place on the first Sunday in December, also includes a half-marathon.

CULTURE
Traditional culture among the Chinese of Macau is by and large indistinguishable from that of Hong Kong (p12). However, the Portuguese minority has a vastly different culture – one that has evolved under a number of different influences, including the Roman, Moorish, French, Spanish, Flemish and Italian cultures. Colonial Portuguese architecture survives throughout Macau, and Portuguese food is to be found in abundance.

Macanese culture is different again, with a unique cuisine, set of festivals and traditions, and even its own dialect called *patuá*. The *do* (traditional woman's outfit) has long disappeared, though you may catch a glimpse of it at certain festivals.

Portuguese and Chinese – Cantonese being the more widely spoken dialect – are both official languages of Macau. For key phrases and words in Cantonese and Portuguese, see p380.

For the vast majority – more than 90% – of Macau Chinese people, Taoism and Buddhism are the dominant religions (see p14). Four and a half centuries of Portuguese Christian rule left its mark, however, and the Roman Catholic Church is very strong in Macau, with an estimated 30,000 (about 6% of the population) adherents. Macau consists of a single diocese, directly responsible to Rome.

Gambling

CASINOS

At the time of writing, Macau had 18 casinos, an increase of 50% in just two years, and many, many more are on the way.

Although the games in Macau are somewhat different from those played in Las Vegas and elsewhere (see the boxed text, p332), the same basic principles apply. No matter what the game, the casino enjoys a built-in mathematical advantage. In the short term, anyone can hit a winning streak and get ahead, but the longer you play, the more certain it is that the odds will catch up with you and you will lose.

The legal gambling age in Macau is 18 years (21 for Macau residents). Photography is absolutely prohibited inside the casinos. Men cannot wear shorts, even relatively long ones, or a singlet (undershirt) unless they have a shirt over it. Women wearing shorts or sleeveless tops are refused entry, the same for anyone wearing thongs (flip-flops) as footwear.

None of the local casinos in Macau offers the atmosphere or level of service considered minimal elsewhere, but with the end of the casino monopoly held by Sociedade de Turismo e Diversões de Macau (STDM) in 2002 and the arrival of two consortia from Las Vegas, that's beginning to change.

Most of Macau's casinos are located at big hotels, and include the **Casa Real Casino** (Map pp430–1; ☎ 726 288; International Centre, Casa Real Hotel, 1118 Avenida do Dr Rodrigo Rodrigues), the **Fortuna Casino** (Map pp430–1; ☎ 982 1328; Fortuna Hotel, 63 Rua da Cantão), the **Golden Dragon Casino** (Map pp430–1; ☎ 361 999; Hotel Golden Dragon, Quarteirão 3, Lotes C & F, ZAPE), the **Diamond Casino** (Map pp430–1; ☎ 786 424; Holiday Inn Macau, 82-86 Rua de Pequim), the **Casino Kingsway** (Map pp430–1; ☎ 701 111; 230 Rua de Luís Gonzaga Gomes), the **Lisboa Casino** (Map pp430–1; ☎ 375 111; Hotel Lisboa, 2-4 Avenida de Lisboa), the **Mandarin Oriental Casino** (Map pp430–1; ☎ 564 297; Mandarin Oriental, 956-1110 Avenida da Amizade) and the **Galaxy Casino** (Map pp430–1; ☎ 886 688; Waldo Hotel, Quarteirão 6, Lote J, ZAPE) on the peninsula, and the **Macau Jockey Club Casino** (Map p433; ☎ 837 788; Grandview Hotel, 142 Estrada Governador Albano de Oliveira), **Greek Mythology Casino** (Map p433; ☎ 835 223; Hotel New Century, 889 Avenida Padre Tomas Pereira) and the **Marina Casino** (Map p433; ☎ 838 333; Pousada Marina Infante, Marina da Taipa Sul, Cotai), all on Taipa.

Independent casinos include the **Macau Palace Casino** (Map pp430–1; ☎ 346 701; Avenida da Amizade), a 'floating casino' moored in the Outer Harbour southwest of the ferry terminal, the **Jai Alai Casino** (Map pp430–1; ☎ 726 086; Jai Alai Complex, Travessa do Reservatório), the **Kam Pek Casino** (Map pp430–1; ☎ 780 168; Rua de Foshan), close to the Lisboa Hotel, and **Pharaoh's Palace Casino** (Map pp430–1; ☎ 788 111; 3rd fl, Landmark Macau, Avenida da Amizade). The **Legend Club** (Map pp430–1; ☎ 788 822), two floors above Pharaoh's Palace, is for high-spending members and their guests only. The mammoth **Sands Macau** (Map pp430–1; ☎ 883 388; Avenida da Amizade), which has more than 300 gaming tables and hundreds of state-of-the-art slot and poker machines, is the first of what will be an avalanche of American-style casinos.

HORSE RACING

Regular flat racing takes place at the Taipa racetrack (hipodromo da Taipa) of the **Macau Jockey Club** (Jockey Clube de Macau; Map p433; ☎ 821 188, racing information hotline ☎ 820 868, Hong Kong hotline ☎ 800 967 822; www.macauhorse.com; Estrada Governador Albano de Oliveira; admission MOP$20) through most of the year, usually on Saturday or Sunday from 2pm, and midweek (generally Tuesday or Wednesday) from 5pm. Summer recess lasts from late August to mid-September.

DOG RACING

Macau's **Canidrome** (Map pp430–1; ☎ 221 199, racing information hotline ☎ 333 399, Hong Kong hotline ☎ 800 932 199; www.macaudog.com; Avenida do General Castelo Branco;

admission MOP$10), in the northern part of the Macau Peninsula, is the only facility for greyhound racing in Asia. Greyhound races are held on Monday, Thursday, Friday, Saturday and Sunday at 7.30pm. There are 16 to 18 races per night, with six to eight dogs chasing a mechanical rabbit around the 455m oval track at speeds of up to 60km/h. If you want to sit in the members' stands it costs MOP$80 weekdays and MOP$120 at the weekend.

SOME FUN & GAMES IN MACAU

Baccarat

Also known as *chemin de fer* (railroad), this has become the card game of choice for the upper crust of Macau's gambling elite. Baccarat rooms are always the classiest part of any casino, and the minimum wager is high – MOP$1000 at some casinos. Two hands are dealt simultaneously: a player hand and a bank hand. Players can bet on either (neither is actually the house hand), and the one that scores closest to nine is the winner. The casino deducts a percentage if the bank hand wins, which is how the house makes its profit. If the player understands the game properly, the house enjoys only a slightly better than 1% advantage over the player.

Blackjack

Also known as 21, this card game is easy to play, although it requires some skill to play it well. The dealer takes a card and gives another to the players. Face cards count as 10, aces as one or 11. Cards are dealt one at a time – the goal is to get as close as possible to 21 (blackjack) without going over. If you go over 21 you 'bust', or lose. Players are always dealt their cards before the dealer, so if they bust they will always bust before the dealer does. This is what gives the casino the edge over the player. If the dealer and player both get 21, it's a tie and the bet is cancelled. If players get 21, they win even money plus a 50% bonus. Dealers must draw until they reach 16, and stand on 17 or higher. The player is free to decide when to stand or when to draw.

Boule

This is very similar to roulette, except that boule is played with a ball about the size of a billiard ball, and there are fewer numbers – 24 numbers plus a star. The payoff is 23 to one on numbers. On all bets (numbers, red or black, odd or even), the casino has a 4% advantage over players.

Daai-sai

Cantonese for 'big little', this game is also known as *sìk-bó* (dice treasure) or *chàai sìk* (guessing dice) and remains popular in Macau. The game is played with three dice. The dice are placed in a covered glass container, the container is then shaken and you bet on whether the toss will be from three to nine (small) or 10 to 18 (big). However, you lose on combinations where all three dice come up the same (2-2-2, 3-3-3 etc) unless you bet directly on three of a kind. For betting *daai-sai* the house advantage is 2.78%. Betting on a specific three of a kind gives the house a 30% advantage.

Fàan-tàan

This ancient Chinese game is practically unknown in the West. The dealer takes an inverted silver cup and plunges it into a pile of porcelain buttons, then moves the cup to one side. After all bets have been placed, the buttons are counted out in groups of four. You have to bet on how many will remain after the last set of four has been taken out.

Pàai-gáu

This is a form of Chinese dominoes similar to mahjong. One player is made banker and the others compare their hands against the banker's. The casino doesn't play, but deducts a 3% commission from the winnings for providing the gambling facilities.

Roulette

The dealer spins the roulette wheel in one direction and tosses a ball the other way. Roulette wheels have 36 numbers plus a zero, so your chance of hitting any given number is one in 37. The payoff is 35 to one, which is what gives the casino its advantage. Rather than betting on a single number, it's much easier to win if you bet odd versus even, or red versus black numbers, which only gives the house a 2.7% advantage. If the ball lands on zero, everyone loses to the house (unless you also bet on the zero).

Sport

The recently expanded **Macau Stadium** (Estádio de Macau; Map p433; ☎ 838 208; www.sport
.gov.mo; Avenida Olímpica), next to the Macau Jockey Club on Taipa Island, seats 16,250
people and hosts international soccer matches, and track-and-field and athletics competi-
tions. On the first Sunday in December the Macau International Marathon starts and
finishes here. The impressive **Macau Dome** (Map p433) on Coloane was built to host the 2005
East Asian Games and the 2007 Indoor Asian Games. Its main arena seats more than 7000
spectators.

Another organisation that may be worth contacting for details of forthcoming events is
the **Macau Sports Institute** (Instituto do Desporto de Macau; Map pp430–1; ☎ 580 762, 881 836;
Macau Forum, Avenida do Doutor Rodrigo Rodrigues).

GRAND PRIX

The biggest sporting event of the year is the Macau Formula 3 Grand Prix, held in the third
week of November. The 6.2km Guia circuit (see Map pp430–1) starts near the Lisboa Hotel
and follows the shoreline along Avenida da Amizade, going around the reservoir and back
through the city. It is a testing series of twists and turns – including the infamous Melco
hairpin – that calls on drivers' reserves of skill and daring. The Grand Prix, which celebrated
its golden jubilee in 2003, attracts many international contestants as well as spectators; some
70,000 people flock to see it and accommodation is tight.

Certain areas in Macau are designated as viewing areas for the races. Streets and alleys
along the track are blocked off, so it's unlikely that you'll be able to find a decent vantage
point without paying for it. Prices for seats in the Reservoir Stand are MOP$150/250 for
a single day/package (which includes practise days and qualifying events before the start
of the actual races) and from MOP$400 to MOP$600 at the Lisboa and Grand Stands
(MOP$700 for the package). To watch just the practise days and qualifying events costs
MOP$20/30 from the Grand/Lisboa Stand and is free from the Reservoir Stand. For ticket
inquiries and bookings call ☎ 796 2268 or consult www.macau.grandprix.gov.mo.

ECONOMY

Tourism and the spin of the roulette wheel still drive Macau's economy, and gambling
remains Macau's major cash cow.

In 2002 the Macau government awarded gambling concessions to two American companies, thereby ending the 40-year gambling monopoly held by STDM, Stanley Ho's
'Macau Tourism and Amusement Com-
pany.' Gambling concessions contribute
some 63% of government revenue through
betting tax, which accounts for a third of
the total GDP.

Tourism usually generates almost half
of Macau's GDP, and about a third of the
labour force works in some aspect of it.
In 2004 Macau welcomed some 16.7 million tourists and visitors, an astonishing
increase of 45% over the previous year and
almost 35 times its population. Visitors
from the mainland accounted for 57% of
total arrivals, with most of the balance coming from Hong Kong, Taiwan, Japan and
the USA. As a result of this phenomenal
boost, Macau's economy expanded a record
28% in 2004.

Macau has various light industries, such
as textile, garment, toy and fireworks pro-
duction, but factories have slowed down and

Galaxy Casino (p331), Macau Peninsula

many companies have moved across the border. Unemployment in Macau is currently around 4.2%.

GOVERNMENT & POLITICS

The executive branch of the Macau SAR government is led by the chief executive, who is chosen by an electoral college made up of 200 local representatives. Edmund Ho, a popular Macau-born banker, was selected for his second (and, by law, final) five-year term in 2004.

The Legislative Assembly, which sits in its own purpose-built assembly hall on reclaimed land in the Nam Van Lakes area, now permanently consists of 29 members, 12 of whom are directly elected in geographical constituencies, 10 chosen by interest groups and seven appointed by the chief executive.

Like Hong Kong, Macau has primary courts, intermediate courts and a Court of Final Appeal.

POPULATION & PEOPLE

Macau's population is approximately 480,000, with an impressive annual growth rate of 4%. Population density is more than 17,500 people per square kilometre, and the northern part of the peninsula is one of the most densely populated areas in the world. Coloane Island has remained essentially rural, but Taipa Island is rapidly becoming an urban extension of peninsular Macau.

The population is about 95% Chinese. Fewer than 2% of Macau residents are Portuguese and the rest are Macanese (people of mixed Portuguese, Chinese and/or African blood) or Filipino.

ARTS

PAINTING

Macau can lay claim to having spawned or influenced a number of artists. Their work is on display in the Gallery of Historical Pictures of the Macau Museum of Art (p355).

The most important Western artist to have lived in Macau was George Chinnery (see the boxed text, below). Other influential European painters who spent time in Macau include the Scottish physician Thomas Watson (1815–60), who was a student of Chinnery and lived in Macau from 1845 to 1856; Frenchman Auguste Borget (1808–77), who spent some 10 months in 1838 and 1939 painting Macau's waterfront and churches; and watercolourist Marciano António Baptists (1856–1930), who was born in Macau.

Guan Qiaochang (1825–60), another of Chinnery's pupils, was a Chinese artist who painted in the Western style and worked under the name Lamqua. His oil portraits of mandarins and other Chinese worthies are particularly fine.

GEORGE CHINNERY: CHRONICLER OF MACAU

Though George Chinnery may enjoy little more than footnote status in the history of world art, as a chronicler of his own (colonial Macau) and his times (the early 19th century) he is without peer. In the absence of photography, taipans ('big bosses' of large companies) and mandarins turned to trade art (commissioned portraiture), and Chinnery was the master of the genre. Today he is known less for his formal portraits and paintings of factory buildings and clipper ships than for his landscapes and sometimes fragmentary sketches of everyday life.

Chinnery was born in London in 1774 and studied at the Royal Academy of Arts before turning his hand to portrait painting in Dublin. He sailed for India in 1802 and spent the next 23 years in Madras and Calcutta, where he earned substantial sums (up to UK£500 a month) as a popular portrait painter to British colonial society and spent most of it on his opium addiction. He fled to Macau in 1825 to escape spiralling debts, Calcutta's 'cranky formality' and his wife (whom he described as 'the ugliest woman I ever saw in my life'), and took up residence at 8 Rua de Inácio Baptista (Map p432), just south of the Church of St Lawrence. He lived at this address until his death from stroke in 1852.

Although Chinnery is sometimes 'claimed' by Hong Kong (the Mandarin Oriental hotel even has a bar named after him), he visited the colony only once, during the hot summer of 1846. Although he was unwell and did not like it very much, he managed to execute some vivid sketches of the place.

Two of the best galleries for viewing contemporary Macau and other art are **Tap Seac Gallery** (Galeria Tap Seac; Map pp430–1; ☎ 335 140; 95 Avenida de Conselheiro Ferreira de Almeida; admission free; ☒ 10am-7pm), which is situated just west of the Sun Yat Sen Memorial Home (p358), and **Ox Warehouse** (Armazem de Boi; Map pp430–1; ☎ 530 026; www .olhartspace.org.mo; cnr Avenida do Almirante Lacerda & Avenida do Coronel Mesquita; admission free; ☒ noon-7pm Wed-Mon), near the Canidrome and home to a group of avant-garde artists who work in a variety of media.

ARCHITECTURE

Portuguese architectural styles reflect a variety of forms, from Romanesque and Gothic through to baroque and neoclassical, and these are best seen in Macau's churches. Two excellent examples are the **Chapel of St Joseph Seminary** (p343), completed in 1758, and the **Church of St Dominic** (p343), a 17th-century replacement of a chapel built in the 1590s.

Civic buildings worth close inspection are the **Leal Senado** (p344), erected in 1784 but rebuilt after it was damaged by a typhoon a century later; the **Dom Pedro V Theatre** (p344), built in 1860; **Government House** (p344), dating from 1849; and the exquisite villas that now form the **Taipa House Museum** (p359).

Macau counts upwards of 50 skyscrapers, but only a few are memorable. **Macau Tower** (p355), a 338m-tall copy of the Sky Tower in Auckland, New Zealand, is the world's 10th-tallest building. The landmark **Bank of China** (Map pp430–1; Avenida do Doutor Mario Soares) is an attractive, 38-floor (163m) structure clad in pinkish granite.

LITERATURE

Macau's home-grown writers are not insignificant; you'll sample their work at the Macau Museum (p344).

First and foremost in literature was Portugal's national poet, Luís de Camões (1524–80), who was banished from Portugal to Goa and then apparently to Macau in the 16th century. He is said to have written part of his epic poem *Os Lusiadas* (The Lusiads), which recounts the 15th-century voyage of Vasco da Gama to India, during the two years he lived in the enclave, but there is no firm evidence that he was ever even in Macau.

The teacher, judge, opium addict and Symbolist poet (author of such works as *Clepsidra*) Camilio de Almeida Pessanha (1867–1926) lived in Macau for the last 30 years of his life; he is buried in the Cemetery of St Michael the Archangel (p343). Local-born writers include Henrique de Senna Fernandes (1923–), author of the *Nam Wan* collection of short stories and the novel *The Bewitching Braid*, and the much beloved Macanese writer José dos Santos Ferreira (1919–93), known as Adé, who wrote in *patuá*, a dialect forging Portuguese and Cantonese. A statue in honour of Adé, who wrote plays, operettas and poems, stands in the Jardim des Artes along Avenida da Amizade, opposite the Landmark Macau building, and you can hear a recording of him reading his poetry in the Macau Museum.

FOOD

Eating (see p362) – be it Portuguese or Macanese 'soul food', Chinese dim sum or the special treats available from street stalls and night markets – is one of the most rewarding aspects of a visit to Macau. One thing to remember, though: people eat dinner relatively early here, and in some restaurants the dining room is all but empty by 9pm.

The most popular alcoholic tipple in Macau is *vinho verde*, a crisp, dry, slightly effervescent 'green' wine from Portugal that goes down a treat with salty Portuguese food and spicy Macanese dishes. You may also try one of the fine wines from Dão, Douro or Alenquer.

PORTUGUESE & MACANESE

Portuguese cuisine is meat-based and not always particularly refined. It makes great use of olive oil, garlic and *bacalhau* (dried salted cod), which can be prepared in many different ways. The cuisine sometimes combines meat and seafood in one dish, such as *porco*

SAMPLING THE MENU

Listed here are a few of the dishes you are likely to encounter on your travels through Macau.

Entradas (Appetisers)

chouriço assado – grilled Portuguese sausage
croquetes de carne – minced beef croquettes

pastéis de bacalhau – dried Portuguese cod cakes

Sopas (Soups)

caldo verde – Portuguese kale soup with chouriço, thickened with potato

sopa de marisco – seafood soup

Marisco (Shellfish)

açorda de marisco – seafood and mashed bread casserole
ameijoas 'Bulhão Pato' – clams with garlic, coriander and olive oil
arroz de marisco – mixed seafood rice

camarão frito com alho e piri-piri – deep-fried prawns with garlic and chilli
caril de carangueijo – crab curry
casquinha – stuffed crab

Peixe (Fish)

bacalhau á 'Brás' – sautéed bacalhau with potatoes and egg
bacalhau á 'Zé do Pipo' – baked, dried cod with mashed potato

lulas recheadas – stuffed squid
sardinhas na brasa – grilled sardines

Carne (Meat)

bife de vitela grelhado na brasa com batata frita – grilled veal steak and chips
caldeirada de borrego – lamb, potato and white wine stew
carne de porco á Alentejana – sautéed pork and clams
coelho á caçadora – rabbit stew

feijoada – pork knuckle, *chouriço*, red bean and cabbage stew
galinha á Africana – grilled chicken cooked with coconut, garlic and chillies
minchi – minced beef or pork cooked with potato
porco balichão tamarino – pork cooked with tamarind and shrimp paste

Sobremesas (Desserts)

fatias de tomar – cakelike dessert made with egg yolks and syrup
pudim de ovos – caramel egg pudding

serradura – cream and condensed milk pudding topped with crumbled biscuits

à Alentejana, a tasty casserole of pork and clams. Some favourite dishes are *caldo verde* (a soup of green kale – a type of cabbage – thickened with potatoes), *pasteis de bacalhau* (codfish croquettes), *sardinhas grelhadas* (grilled sardines), and *feijoada* (a casserole of beans, pork, spicy sausages, potatoes and cabbage).

Macanese food borrows a lot of its ingredients and tastes from Chinese and other Asian cuisines, as well as from those of former Portuguese colonies in Africa and India. It is redolent of coconut, tamarind, chilli, jaggery (palm sugar) and shrimp paste.

The most famous Macanese speciality is *galinha áfricana* (African chicken), in which the bird is prepared in coconut, garlic and chillies. As well as cod, there are plenty of other fish and seafood: shrimps, prawns, crabs, squid and white fish. Sole, a tongue-shaped flat fish, is a Macanese delicacy. The contribution from the former Portuguese enclave of Goa, on the west coast of India, is spicy prawns.

Other Macanese favourites include *casquinha* (stuffed crab), *porco balichão tamarino* (pork cooked with tamarind and shrimp paste), *minchi* (minced beef or pork cooked with potatoes, onions and spices), and baked rice dishes made with cod, prawns or crab. Maca-

Macau

FOOD

nese desserts include *pudim*, which is basically crème caramel, and *serradura*, a calorie-rich 'sawdust' pudding made with crushed biscuits, cream and condensed milk. If you want to try the latter while touring around, visit **Serradura** (Map pp430–1; ☎ 332 880; Ground fl, Tin Fok Bldg, 15 Avenida do Coronel Mesquita; ☯ noon-11pm), a shop selling bite-sized (MOP$6.50) and large (MOP$56) versions of the rich dessert. *Pastéis de nata* is a scrumptious egg-custard tartlet eaten warm.

Dining in Macau (www.dininginmacau.com) is a quarterly advertorial freebie, but a good source of information about some 40 restaurants nonetheless. You may also have a flip through the **Macau Food Guide** (www.cityguide.gov.mo/food/food_e.htm), available for free at the tourist office.

OTHER CUISINES

Macau is not just about Macanese and Portuguese food. Some people swear that the dim sum here is far better than anything you'll find in Hong Kong. Thai food, one of the great contributions of the Thai bar girls working here, can be excellent, especially in the area just east of the Cemetery of St Michael's the Archangel.

HISTORY

EARLY SETTLEMENT

Archaeological finds from digs around Hác Sá and Ká Hó Bays on Coloane Island suggest that Macau has been inhabited since Neolithic times (from 4000 BC). Before the arrival of the Portuguese, Macau had a relatively small number of inhabitants, mainly Cantonese-speaking farmers and fisherfolk from Fujian.

THE ARRIVAL OF THE PORTUGUESE

In 1510 and 1511 the Portuguese routed Arab fleets at Goa on the west coast of India and Malacca on the Malay Peninsula. At Malacca they encountered several junks with Chinese captains and crews. Realising that the so-called Chins, about whom Portuguese mariners and explorers had heard reports a century earlier, were not a mythical people at all but natives of 'Cathay', the land that Marco Polo had visited and written about 2½ centuries earlier, a small party sailed northwards to try to open up trade with China.

The first Portuguese contingent, led by Jorge Álvares, set foot on Chinese soil in 1513 at a place they called Tamaō, today known as Shangchuan Island, about 80km southwest of the mouth of the Pearl River.

Portugal's initial contacts with China were not successful and, despite the establishment of several small trading posts along the southern Chinese coast, a permanent base seemed beyond its grasp. However, in 1553 an official basis for trading was set up between the two countries, and the Portuguese were allowed to settle on Shangchuan. The exposed anchorage there forced the Portuguese traders to abandon the island that same year, and they moved to Lampacau, an island closer to the Pearl River estuary.

To the northeast of Lampacau was a small peninsula where the Portuguese had frequently dropped anchor. Known variously as Amagau, Aomen and Macau (see the boxed text, p338), the peninsula had two natural harbours – an inner one on the Qianshan waterway facing the mainland, and an outer one in a bay on the Pearl River – and two sheltered islands to the south. In 1557 officials at Guangzhou allowed the Portuguese to build temporary shelters on the peninsula in exchange for customs dues and rent. The Portuguese also agreed to rid the area of the pirates that were endemic at the time.

A TRADING POWERHOUSE

Macau grew rapidly as a trading centre, largely due to the fact that Chinese merchants were forbidden to leave the country by imperial decree. Acting as agents for the Chinese merchants, Portuguese traders took Chinese goods (including porcelain and silks) to Goa

WHAT'S IN A NAME?

The name 'Macau' is derived from the name of the goddess A-Ma, better known in Hong Kong as Tin Hau. At the southwestern tip of Macau Peninsula, and facing the Inner Harbour, stands the A-Ma Temple, which dates back to the early 16th century. Many people believe that when the Portuguese first arrived and asked the name of the place, 'A-Ma Gau' (Bay of A-Ma) was what they were told.

According to legend, A-Ma, a poor girl looking for passage to Guangzhou, was turned away by wealthy junk owners. Instead a poor fisherman took her on board; shortly afterwards a storm blew up, wrecking all the junks but leaving the fishing boat unscathed. When it returned to the Inner Harbour, A-Ma walked to the top of nearby Barra Hill and, in a glowing aura of light, ascended to heaven. The fisherman built a temple on the spot where they had landed (which was, in fact, on the water's edge until land reclamation early in the last century set it further inland).

In modern Cantonese, 'Macau' is Ou Mun (Aomen in Mandarin), meaning 'Gateway of the Bay'.

and exchanged them for cotton and textiles. The cloth was then taken to Malacca, where it was traded for spices and sandalwood. The Portuguese would then carry on to Nagasaki in Japan, where the cargo from Malacca was exchanged for Japanese silver, swords, lacquerware and fans that would be traded in Macau for more Chinese goods.

During the late 16th century the Portuguese in Macau were at the forefront of all international commerce between China and Japan. But the territory was not just gaining in economic strength. Such was Macau's growing status and importance that when the Holy See established the bishopric of Macau in 1576, it included both China and Japan under its jurisdiction. By 1586 Macau was large enough and important enough for the Portuguese Crown to confer upon it the status of a city: *Cidade de Nome de Deus* (City of the Name of God).

THE GOLDEN YEARS

By the beginning of the 17th century, Macau supported several thousand permanent residents, including about 900 Portuguese. The rest were Christian converts from Malacca and Japan and a large number of slaves from colonial outposts in Africa, India and the Malay Peninsula. Large numbers of Chinese had moved into Macau from across the border, and they worked there as traders, craftspeople, hawkers, labourers and coolies; by the close of the century, their numbers had reached 40,000.

Trade was the most important activity, but Macau had also become a centre of Christianity in Asia. Priests and missionaries accompanied Portuguese ships, although the interests of traders and missionaries were frequently in conflict.

Among the earliest missionaries was Francis Xavier (later canonised) of the Jesuit order, who spent two years (1549 to 1551) in Japan attempting to convert the local population before turning his attention to China. He was stalled by the Portuguese, who feared the consequences of his meddling in Chinese affairs, but made it as far as Tamaõ, where he developed a fever and died in December 1552 at age 46. Subsequently it was Jesuit missionaries, not traders, who were able to penetrate China beyond Macau and Guangzhou.

The Portuguese who stayed in Macau, along with their Macanese descendants, created a home away from home. Their luxurious villas overlooking the Praia Grande, now the enclosed Baia da Praia, and splendid baroque churches were paid for with the wealth generated by their monopoly on trade with China and Japan. These buildings included the Jesuit Church of Madre de Deus (later the Church of St Paul, p345), hailed as the greatest monument to Christianity in the Far East when dedicated in 1602.

PORTUGUESE DECLINE

Portugal's decline as an imperial power came as quickly as its rise. In 1580 Spanish armies occupied Portugal and for more than 60 years three Spanish kings were to rule over the country and its empire. In the early years of the 17th century, the Dutch, embroiled in the Thirty Years' War with Spain, moved to seize the rich Portuguese enclaves of Macau,

Nagasaki and Malacca. In June 1622 some 13 Dutch warships carrying 1300 men attacked Macau but retreated when a shell fired by a Jesuit priest from one of the cannons on Monte Fort hit a stock of gunpowder and blew the Hollanders out of the water.

The Japanese soon became suspicious of Portuguese and Spanish intentions and closed its doors to foreign trade in 1639. Two years later, Dutch harassment of Portuguese commerce and trading interests ended with the capture of Malacca. The Portuguese would no longer be able to provide the Chinese with the Japanese silver needed for their silk and porcelain or with spices from the Malay Peninsula.

www.lonelyplanet.com

A CHANGE OF STATUS

The overthrow of the moribund Ming dynasty in 1644 saw a flood of refugees unleashed on Macau. In 1684 the most corrupt of the new Manchu rulers, the so-called *hoppo* (*hói poi* in Cantonese) – the customs superintendent who held the monopoly on trade with foreigners – set up an office in the Inner Harbour.

At the same time religious infighting weakened the status of Macau as a Christian centre. In what became known as the Rites Controversy, the Jesuits maintained that central parts of Chinese belief – eg ancestor worship and Confucianism – were not incompatible with the Christian faith. The Dominicans and Franciscans, equally well represented in Macau and elsewhere in the Far East, disagreed. It took an edict by Pope Clement XI in 1715 condemning the rites as idolatrous to settle the matter and this stopped further missionary expansion into China.

In the mid-18th century Chinese authorities created the *cohong*, a mercantile monopoly based in Guangzhou that dealt with foreign trade. Numerous restrictions were placed on Western traders, including limitations on the amount of time they could reside in Guangzhou. Macau in effect became an outpost for all European traders in China, a position it held until the British took possession of Hong Kong in 1841.

Until the mid-19th century the history of Macau was a long series of incidents involving the Portuguese, Chinese and British as the Portuguese attempted to maintain a hold on the territory. But as time progressed and the troublesome British wrestled concession after concession out of China, the Portuguese grew bolder.

The Treaty of Nanking (1842) had ceded the island of Hong Kong in perpetuity to the British; the Treaty of Tientsin (1860) gave them Kowloon on the same terms. The Portuguese

Macau 1835, engraving by Thomas Allom (supplied by Macau Tourist Bureau)

felt that they too should take advantage of China's weakness and push for sovereignty over the territory they had occupied for three centuries. Negotiation began in 1862, although it was not until 1887 that a treaty was signed in which China effectively recognised Portuguese sovereignty over Macau forever.

With the advent of the steamship and then other motorised vessels, there were fewer transshipments from Chinese ports through Macau and more direct transactions between the mainland and Hong Kong. Macau's future economy would be greatly assisted by the legalisation of gambling in the 1850s, but by the close of the 19th century the ascent of the British colony and the decline of the Portuguese territory had become irreversible.

MACAU IN THE 20TH CENTURY

By the turn of the 20th century Macau was little more than an impoverished backwater, its glory days all but forgotten. It did, however, continue to serve as a haven for Chinese refugees fleeing war, famine and political oppression. Among them was Sun Yat Sen, founder of the republic of China, who lived in Macau before the 1911 Revolution. Even the birth of the Portuguese republic in 1910 had little effect on the sleepy outpost.

In the mid-1920s large numbers of Chinese immigrants doubled the number of Macau residents to 160,000. A steady stream of refugees from the Sino-Japanese War meant that by 1939 the population had reached 245,000. During WWII many people from Hong Kong and China, as well as Asian-based Europeans, took refuge in Macau, as the Japanese respected Portugal's neutrality; by 1943 the population stood at 500,000. There was another influx of Chinese refugees in 1949 when the Communists took power in China, and from 1978 until about 1981 Macau was a haven for Vietnamese boat people. Macau was made an overseas province of Portugal in 1951.

Macau's last great upset occurred in 1966 and 1967, when China's Cultural Revolution spilled over into the territory. Macau was stormed by Red Guards, and violent riots resulted in some of them being shot and killed by Portuguese troops. The government proposed that Portugal abandon Macau forever, but China refused to hear of it, fearing the loss of foreign trade through the colony.

In 1974 a revolution restored democracy in Portugal and the new left-wing government began to divest Portugal of the last remnants of its empire, including Mozambique and Angola in Africa and East Timor in the Indonesian archipelago. Power brokers in Lisbon tried to return Macau to China as well, but the word from Beijing was that China wished Macau to remain as it was – at least for the time being.

THE END OF PORTUGUESE RULE

Once the Joint Declaration over Hong Kong had been signed by Britain and China in 1984, the latter turned its attentions to the future of Macau. Talks began in 1986 and an agreement was signed the following April.

Under the so-called Sino-Portuguese Pact, Macau would become a 'Special Administrative Region' (SAR) of China. The date set was 20 December 1999, ending 442 years of Portuguese rule. Like Hong Kong, the Macau SAR would enjoy a 'high degree of autonomy' for 50 years in all matters except defence and foreign affairs, under the slogan 'one country, two systems'.

The basic law for Macau differed from its Hong Kong equivalent in that holders of foreign passports were not excluded from holding high-level posts in the post-handover administration (apart from the position of chief executive). There was also no stipulation that China would station troops of the People's Liberation Army (PLA) in Macau after the return of the territory to China, though it did just that.

Macau had directly elected some of the members of its Legislative Assembly since the assembly's founding in 1976 but, unlike Hong Kong, it did not rush through proposals to widen the franchise or speed up democratisation at the last minute. The existing legislature continued to serve throughout the handover, unlike that in the British territory.

But not everything went so smoothly. Macau residents were pleased when Portugal gave everyone born in Macau the right to a Portuguese passport, allowing them to live anywhere in the European Union – something the UK had refused Hong Kong Chinese people. However, not everyone in Macau benefited from Portugal's move. Until 1975 any Chinese refugee reaching Macau could obtain residency (after that anyone caught sneaking into the territory was considered an illegal immigrant and sent back). As a result, as much as 70% of the population had not actually been born in Macau and therefore didn't qualify for Portuguese citizenship.

The years 1996 to 1998 were a grim showdown for Macau and its all-important tourism industry – an escalating number of gangland killings took place. Some 40 people were killed as senior Triad leaders jostled for control of the lucrative gambling rackets, and one international hotel was raked with AK-47 gunfire. On 8 May 1998 alone, 14 cars and motorcycles and a couple of shops were engulfed in flames when Triad members, protesting the arrest of their boss, Wan Kwok 'Broken Tooth' Koi, let off a string of firebombs. Needless to say, the violence scared tourists off in a big way; arrivals fell by some 36% in August 1997.

As the handover approached, China put pressure on Portugal to clean up its act. The government issued a new anti-Triad law calling for a lengthy prison term for anyone found to be a senior leader. Koi was arrested and sentenced to 15 years, and many other Triad members, including post-1997 imports from Hong Kong, fled overseas.

THE HANDOVER & MACAU AFTER 1999

The handover ceremony on 20 December 1999 was as stage-managed as the one held 2½ years earlier in Hong Kong. The following day 500 PLA soldiers drove down from Zhuhai. There are now an estimated 10,000 troops stationed here, though they have no responsibility for internal security.

In the past decade Macau has launched a series of enormous public works projects. The completion of Macau's US$11.8-billion airport in 1995 was one of the most ambitious, as was the construction of a deep-water port on the northeastern side of Coloane Island.

Land-reclamation projects have been equally ambitious. The one along the Praia Grande, Macau's historic waterfront, buffeted by the NAPE reclaimed area, has created two large freshwater lakes. The causeway linking Taipa and Coloane, once a narrow two-lane raised road, is now a reclaimed area called Cotai that's almost the size of Taipa and has a six-lane highway.

Heading west from Cotai is the US$25-million Lotus Flower Bridge, which opened in 2000, linking Macau with Hengqing Island in the Zhuhai Special Economic Zone (SEZ). A border checkpoint opened four years later. To handle the anticipated increase in motor-vehicle traffic brought on by the airport and the Taipa City high-rise housing development on Taipa, a second bridge was built between the island and peninsular Macau in 1994 and a third bridge, a typhoon-proof covered span linking the peninsula's southwest corner with western Taipa, opened in 2004.

Other grand ongoing projects include the Ponte 16 and Macau Fisherman's Wharf theme parks on the Inner and Outer Harbours respectively and the East Asia Satellite TV City in Cotai. But the most ambitious project by far is the proposed 36km-long, US$3.7-billion, six-lane cross-delta bridge linking Macau and Zhuhai with Hong Kong via Tai O on Lantau Island. The Y-shaped bridge would reduce the present four-hour journey by car between Zhuhai and Hong Kong to 20 minutes.

SIGHTS

Macau is a tiny but ever-growing place. Nowadays it has a total land area of 27.3 sq km, which takes in the peninsula (8.7 sq km), Taipa Island (6.3 sq km), Coloane Island (7.6 sq km) and Cotai (from 'Coloane' and 'Taipa'; 4.7 sq km), the artificial isthmus linking the last two.

Macau is divided here into three main sections: the Macau Peninsula, which is attached to mainland China to the north; the middle island of Taipa, directly south of the peninsula

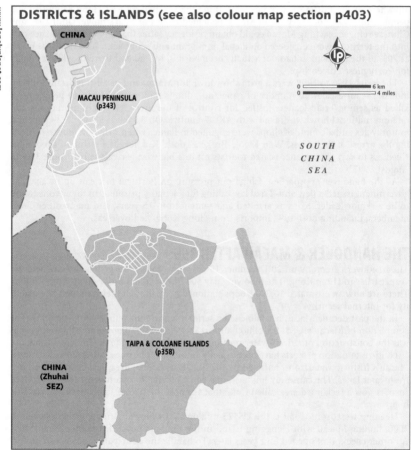

DISTRICTS & ISLANDS (see also colour map section p403)

CHINA

MACAU PENINSULA
(p343)

SOUTH
CHINA
SEA

0 — 6 km
0 — 4 miles

TAIPA & COLOANE ISLANDS
(p358)

CHINA
(Zhuhai
SEZ)

and linked to it by the 2.5km-long Ponte Governador Nobre de Carvalho (Macau-Taipa Bridge), the 4.5km-long Ponte da Amizade (Friendship Bridge) and the new 2.2km-long covered, typhoon-proof Sai Van Bridge; and Coloane Island, which is south of Taipa and connected to it by the 2.2km-long Cotai causeway.

ORGANISED TOURS

Tours booked on the ground in Macau are generally much better value than those booked in Hong Kong, though the latter include transportation to and from Macau and sometimes a side trip across the border to Zhuhai. Tours from Hong Kong are usually one-day whirlwind tours, departing for Macau in the morning and returning to Hong Kong on the same evening. **Gray Line** (in Hong Kong ☎ 2368 7111; www.grayline.com.hk) offers such a tour for HK$690/

HK$720 weekdays/weekends (child under 10 HK$620/HK$650).

Quality Tours organised by the MGTO and tendered to agents such as **Gray Line** (Map pp430–1; ☎ 336 611; Rua do Campo; ⏰ 8am-7pm) take around 6½ hours (adult/child under 10 including museum tickets MOP$98/MOP$78).

The Tour Machine, run by **Avis Rent A Car** (Map pp430–1; ☎ 336 789; www.avis.com.mo; Room 1022, Ground fl, Macau ferry terminal; ⏰ 8am-7pm), is a replica 1920s-style English bus that seats nine people and

Macau

SIGHTS

runs on fixed routes in about two hours past some of Macau's most important sights (adult/child under 12 MOP$150/MOP$80). You're allowed to disembark, stretch your legs and take photos along the way. There are two departures a day – at 11am and 3pm – from the Macau ferry terminal.

MACAU PENINSULA

You'll find the lion's share of Macau's museums, churches, gardens, old cemeteries and important colonial buildings on the peninsula and, in July 2005, UNESCO recognised this wealth by adding the Historic Centre of Macau, comprising 25 distinct sites, to its World Heritage list. If you're after more-active pursuits, such as cycling, hiking and swimming, head for the islands (p369).

Central Macau Peninsula

Avenida de Almeida Ribeiro – called San Ma Lo (New St) in Cantonese – is the peninsula's main thoroughfare. It starts at the delightful Leal Senado and ends at the Inner Harbour, effectively dividing the narrow southern peninsula from central and northern Macau. The avenue's southern extension, Avenida do Infante Dom Henrique, runs from Avenida da Praia Grande to the Outer Harbour, just below the landmark Lisboa Hotel. In the centre of this long thoroughfare is the charming square, Largo do Senado.

CEMETERY OF ST MICHAEL THE ARCHANGEL
Map pp430-1
Cemitério de São Miguel Arcanjo; 2A Estrada do Cemitério; ☺ 8am-6pm
This cemetery, northeast of Monte Fort, contains tombs and sepulchres that can only be described as baroque ecclesiastical works of art. Near the main entrance is the Chapel of St Michael (Capela de São Miguel; ☺ 10am-6pm), a doll-sized, pea-green church with a tiny choir loft and pretty porticoes.

CHAPEL OF ST JOSEPH SEMINARY
Map p432
Capela do Seminário São José; Rua do Seminário; ☺ 10am-5pm
To the southwest of the Dom Pedro V Theatre is the Chapel of St Joseph, consecrated

in 1758 as part of a Jesuit seminary. Its 19m-high domed ceiling has exceptionally fine acoustics, and the church is used as a concert venue.

CHINESE READING ROOM Map p432
Rua de Santa Clara; ☺ 9am-noon & 7-10pm Tue-Sat, 9am-10pm Sun
This attractive octagonal structure, with its double stone staircase and little round tower, is a wonderful mix of Chinese and Portuguese styles that could only be found in Macau. Opposite are the lovely St Francis Garden (Jardim de São Francisco; Map pp430-1) and the 17th-century St Francis Barracks (Quartéis de São Francisco; Map pp430-1), which houses the Macau Security Forces Museum (Museu das Forças de Segurança de Macau; Map pp430-1; ☎ 559 999; Calçada dos Quartéis; admission free; ☺ 9am-5.45pm Mon-Fri, 9am-5pm Sat & Sun) and its two rooms of exhibits relating to the police and their work.

CHURCH OF ST AUGUSTINE Map p432
Igreja de Santo Agostinho; Largo de São Agostinho; ☺ 10am-6pm
Southwest of Largo do Senado via Rua Central is the Church of St Augustine. Though its foundations date from 1586, the present church was built in 1814. The high altar has a statue of Christ bearing the cross, which is carried through the streets during the Procession of the Passion of Our Lord on the first Saturday of Lent (p329).

CHURCH OF ST DOMINIC Map p432
Igreja de São Domingos; Largo de São Domingos; ☺ 8am-6pm
A fine example of ecclesiastical baroque architecture, this imposing church, northeast of Largo do Senado, is an early-17th-century replacement of a chapel built by the Dominicans in the 1590s. Today it contains the Treasury of Sacred Art (Tresouro de Arte Sacra; ☎ 367 706; admission free; ☺ 10am-6pm), an Aladdin's cave of ecclesiastical art and liturgical objects exhibited on three floors.

CHURCH OF ST LAWRENCE Map p432
Igreja de São Lourenço; Rua de São Lourenço; ☺ 10am-6pm Tue-Sun, 1-2pm Mon
Southwest along Rua de São Lourenço (enter from Rua da Imprensa Nacional) is Macau's most fashionable church. The

original was built of wood in the 1560s but was reconstructed in stone in the early 19th century and has a magnificent painted ceiling. One of the church towers once served as an ecclesiastical prison.

CULTURAL CLUB Map p432
Clube Cultural; ☎ 921 811; www.culturalclub.net; 390 Avenida de Almeida Ribeiro; admission free; 🕑 10.30am-8pm
Housed in the same building as the Pawn-shop Museum, the Cultural Club claims to look at various aspects of everyday life in Macau, though it really is little more than a themed shop. There's a library devoted to the work of martial-arts novelist Louis Cha (Ching Yung in Cantonese, Jin Yong in Mandarin) on the 1st floor and a lovely teahouse on the 2nd.

DOM PEDRO V THEATRE Map p432
Teatro Dom Pedro V; ☎ 939 646; Calçada do Teatro
Opposite the Church of St Augustine, this colonnaded, neoclassical theatre built in 1858 is the oldest European theatre in China and is sometimes used for cultural performances.

GOVERNMENT HOUSE Map pp430-1
Sede do Governo; cnr Avenida da Praia Grande & Travessa do Padré Narciso
South of the Church of St Lawrence is monu-mental Government House, a pillared, rose-coloured building erected for a Portuguese noble in 1849. It's now the headquarters of various branches of the Macau SAR govern-ment, including the Secretariat for Security.

Opposite Government House, the 80m-high Cybernetic Fountains (🕑 1-10pm Mon-Fri, 10am-10pm Sat & Sun), in artificial Lagos de Nam Van (Nam Van Lake), play colourful water games on and off throughout the day.

HONG KUNG TEMPLE Map p432
Hong Kung Miu; cnr Rua das Estalagens & Rua de Cinco de Outubro; 🕑 8am-6pm
This temple, in a market district west of Monte Fort, was built in 1750 and dedi-cated to Kwan Yu, the god of war and other things (see the boxed text, p12). His image is the one in the middle of the main altar, flanked by his son and standard-bearer. The temple gets particularly busy in May and June, when two festivals in the god's honour are celebrated.

LEAL SENADO Map p432
163 Avenida de Almeida Ribeiro
Facing Largo do Senado to the west is Macau's most important historical building, the 18th-century 'Loyal Senate', which now houses the Instituto para os Assuntos Cívi-cos e Municipais (IACM; Civic and Municipal Affairs Bureau) and the mayor's office. It is so-named because the body sitting here refused to recognise Spain's sovereignty dur-ing the 60 years that it occupied Portugal.

In 1654, a dozen years after Portuguese sovereignty was re-established, King João IV ordered a heraldic inscription to be placed inside the senate's entrance hall, and this can still be seen today. To the right of the entrance hall is the IACM Gallery (☎ 988 4180; admission free; 🕑 9am-9pm Tue-Sun), which features changing exhibits. On the 1st floor is the Senate Library (☎ 572 233; admission free; 🕑 1-7pm Mon-Sat), which has a collection of some 18,500 books, and wonderful carved wooden furnishings and panelled walls.

MACAU CATHEDRAL Map p432
A Sé Catedral; Largo da Sé; 🕑 8am-6pm
East of Largo do Senado is the cathedral, a not particularly attractive structure con-secrated in 1850 to replace an earlier one badly damaged in a typhoon. The cathe-dral, which was completely rebuilt in 1937, has some notable stained-glass windows and is the focus for most major Christian festivals and holy days in Macau.

MACAU MUSEUM Map pp430-1
Museu de Macau; ☎ 357 911; Praceta do Museu de Macau, Fortaleza do Monte; adult/child under 11, student & senior over 60 MOP$15/8, admission free on 15th of month; 🕑 10am-6pm Tue-Sun
This wonderful museum within Monte Fort tells the story of the hybrid territory of Macau through a host of multimedia and other special effects. It's definitely worth visiting for a couple of hours.

On the 1st level, the Genesis of Macau exhibit takes you through the early history of the territory, with parallel developments in the East and the West compared and contrasted. The section devoted to the territory's religions is excellent, as is the recreated Macau street, with many different examples of architecture.

On the 2nd level (Popular Arts & Tradi-tions of Macau), you'll see and hear every-

Macau

SIGHTS

Exhibit, Macau Museum (opposite), Central Macau Peninsula

thing from a re-created firecracker factory, and a *chá gordo* (fat tea) of 20 dishes enjoyed on a Sunday, to the recorded cries of street vendors selling items such as brooms, tea and scrap metal. You can also hear a recording of the poet José dos Santos Ferreira (1919–93), known as Adé, reading from his work in local dialect.

The top floor illustrates 'Contemporary Macau' and focuses on its architecture, literature and urban-development plans.

MONTE FORT Map pp430-1
Fortaleza do Monte; 6am-7pm May-Sep, 7am-6pm Oct-Apr

On a hill and accessible by an escalator just east of the ruins of the Church of St Paul, Monte Fort was built by the Jesuits between 1617 and 1626 as part of the College of the Mother of God. Barracks and storehouses were designed to allow the fort to survive a two-year siege, but the cannons were fired only once: during the aborted attempt by the Dutch to invade Macau in 1622 (p338).

MUSEUM OF THE HOLY HOUSE OF MERCY Map p432
Núcleo Museológico da Santa Casa da Misericórdia; 573 938; 2 Travessa da Misericórdia; adult/student & senior over 65 MOP$5/free; 10am-1pm, 2.30-5.30pm Mon-Sat

The lovely Santa Casa da Misericórdia (Holy House of Mercy), on the southeastern side

of Largo do Senado, was established in 1569 and is the oldest social institution in Macau. It served as a home for orphans and prostitutes in the 18th century, and its patron was the Macanese trader Martha Merop (1766–1828), heroine of Austin Coates' *City of Broken Promises*. Today it is a two-room museum containing items related to the house, including religious artefacts; Chinese, Japanese and European porcelain; the skull of its founder and Macau's first bishop, Dom Belchior Carneiro; and a portrait of Merop painted shortly before her death.

MUSEUM OF SACRED ART & CRYPT
Map pp430-1

Museu de Arte Sacra e Cripta; Rua de São Paolo; admission free; 9am-6pm

This small museum, in the chancel of the Church of St Paul to the northwest of the façade contains polychrome carved wooden statues, silver chalices, monstrances and oil paintings, including a copy of a 17th-century painting depicting the martyrdom of 26 Japanese Christians by crucifixion at Nagasaki in 1597. The adjoining crypt contains the remains of the martyrs, as well as those of Vietnamese and other Japanese Christians killed in the 17th century. Also here is the recently unearthed tomb of Alessandro Valignano, the Jesuit who founded the College of the Mother of God and is credited with establishing Christianity in Japan.

PAWNSHOP MUSEUM Map p432
Casa de Penhores Tradicional; 921 811; 396 Avenida de Almeida Ribeiro; admission MOP$5; 10.30am-7pm, closed 1st Mon of month

Pawnshops can be traced back to the 17th century in Macau. They flourished during difficult times, especially the Sino-Japanese War (1938–45). This museum is housed in the former Tak Seng On (Virtue and Success) pawnshop built in 1917 and incorporates the fortress-like eight-storey granite tower with slotted windows where goods were stored on racks or in safes.

RUINS OF THE CHURCH OF ST PAUL
Map pp430-1

Ruinas de Igreja de São Paulo; Rua de São Paulo; admission free

The façade is all that remains of this Jesuit church, built in the early 17th century, but with its wonderful statues, portals and engravings, some consider the ruins of the Church of St Paul to be the greatest monument to Christianity in Asia.

Constructed on one of Macau's seven hills, the church was designed by an Italian Jesuit and completed by early Japanese Christian exiles and Chinese craftsmen in 1602. The church was abandoned after the expulsion of the Jesuits in 1762 and a military battalion was stationed here. In 1835 a fire erupted in the kitchen of the barracks, destroying everything but the front of the structure and the stone steps leading to it.

The façade has been described as a 'sermon in stone' and a *Biblia pauperum*, a 'Bible of the poor', to help the illiterate understand the Passion of Christ and the lives of the saints.

At the top is a dove, representing the Holy Spirit, surrounded by stone carvings of the sun, moon and stars. Beneath the Holy Spirit is a statue of the Infant Jesus surrounded by stone carvings of the implements of the Crucifixion (the whip, crown of thorns, nails, ladder and spear). In the centre of the 3rd tier stands the Virgin Mary being assumed bodily into heaven along with angels and two flowers: the peony, representing China, and the chrysanthemum, a symbol of Japan. To the right of the Virgin is a carving of the tree of life and the apocalyptic woman (Mary) slaying a seven-headed hydra; the Chinese characters next to her read 'the holy mother tramples the heads of the dragon'. To the left of the central statue of Mary, a 'star' guides a ship (the Church) through a storm (sin); a carving of the devil is to the left.

The 4th tier has statues of four Jesuit doctors of the Church (from left to right): Blessed Francisco de Borja; St Ignatius Loyola, the founder of the order; St Francis Xavier, the apostle of the Far East; and Blessed Luís Gonzaga.

Southern Macau Peninsula

Southern Macau Peninsula encompasses three areas: that around the extensively renovated Macau Forum and Tourist Activities Centre; the rectangle of reclaimed land called NAPE to the south; and the southwest corner of the peninsula.

The Macau Forum (Forum de Macau) and the Tourist Activities Centre (Centro de Actividades Turísticas; CAT) stand side by side on Rua de Luís Gonzaga Gomes to

the east of central Macau. The former is a conference and exhibition space; the latter houses two worthwhile museums.

GRAND PRIX MUSEUM Map pp430-1
Museu do Grande Prémio; ☎ 798 4108; Basement, CAT, 431 Rua de Luís Gonzaga Gomes; adult/child under 11 & senior over 60/child under 19 MOP$10/free/5, adult with Macau Wine Museum MOP$20; ⊗ 10am-6pm Wed-Mon

Cars from the Macau Formula 3 Grand Prix, including the bright-red Triumph TR2 driven by Eduardo de Carvalho that won the first Grand Prix in 1954, are on display, while simulators let you test your racing skills.

MACAU WINE MUSEUM Map pp430-1
Museu do Vinho de Macau; ☎ 798 4188; Basement, CAT, 431 Rua de Luís Gonzaga Gomes; adult/child under 11 & senior over 60/child under 19 MOP$15/free/5, adult with Grand Prix Museum MOP$20; ⊗ 10am-6pm Wed-Mon

For the most part, this museum is a rather inert display of wine racks, barrels, presses and tools used by wine makers, as well as a rundown of Portugal's various wine regions, but some of the more recent wines of the more than 1000 on display are available for tasting, which is included in the entry fee.

NAPE

The rectangular area of reclaimed land called NAPE – pronounced 'NA-pay' and short for Novos Aterros do Porto Exterior (New Reclaimed Land of the Outer Harbour) – separates the Outer Harbour from what was once Baia da Praia (now a large artificial lake). NAPE is primarily an area of casinos, bars and restaurants, but there are several interesting sights here as well.

Bordering NAPE to the east is **Macau Fisherman's Wharf** (Map pp430–1; www.fishermanswharf.com.mo), an ambitious 'theme park' built partially on reclaimed land that was nearing completion at the time of writing. The park will combine attractions, hotels, shops and restaurants, and be divided into sections. **Dynasty Wharf** will focus on Chinese history and culture; **East Meets West** will have a 30m-high working volcano, an Africa Fort funfair for kids and the Greek Square leisure and performance park; and **Legend Wharf** will feature landmarks from around the world.

(Continued on page 355)

Macau SIGHTS

1 *Lin Heung Tea House (p162), Sheung Wan* **2** *Hong Kong–style food – spicy fried squid* **3** *Ginseng at a roadside shop, Yau Ma Tei (p184)* **4** *Making won ton noodle soup, Central (p151)*

1 *Front window of Yung Kee Restaurant (p156), Central*
2 *Dragon fruit, Graham St Market (p157), Central* 3 *Dried foods, Shanghai St shop, Mong Kok (p184)* 4 *Fish drying in the sun at Tai O (p134), Lantau*

1 *Morning joggers, Avenue of the Stars (p93), Tsim Sha Tsui* **2** *Pui O Beach (p134), Lantau* **3** *Cable cars, Ocean Park (p88), Aberdeen* **4** *Jumbo Kingdom Floating Restaurant (p175), Aberdeen Marina, Aberdeen*

1 *Morning t'ai chi (p222), Tsim Sha Tsui* 2 *Moongate, Kowloon Walled City Park (p97), Kowloon* 3 *Duk Ling junk (p66), Hong Kong Harbour* 4 *Dusk at Peak Tower (p77), the Peak*

1 *Worshipper, A-Ma Temple (p355), Macau Peninsula* 2 *Back streets of Macau (p328), Macau Peninsula* 3 *Crowds on Largo do Senado (p343), Macau Peninsula* 4 *Portuguese cannon, Monte Fort (p345), Macau Peninsula*

1 *Ruins of the Church of St Paul (p345), Macau Peninsula* **2** *Lotus pond, Lou Lim Ioc Garden (p357), Macau Peninsula* **3** *Tending a grave – Cemetery of St Michael the Archangel (p343), Macau Peninsula* **4** *Massive fruit decorations for the Mid-Autumn Festival, in front of the Chapel of St Francis Xavier (p359), Coloane Island*

1 *Sumptuous seafood, Mandarin Oriental (p372), Macau Peninsula*
2 *Stir-fried dishes from a Macau street stall (p362)* 3 *Pastéis de nata, a warm egg-custard tart* 4 *Dim sum (p36)*

1 *Neon signs of Lisboa Casino (p331), Macau Peninsula* 2 *Neon street lights, Macau (p328)* 3 *Lisboa Hotel (p372), Macau Peninsula* 4 *Crazy Paris Show (p369), Macau Peninsula*

(Continued from page 346)

HANDOVER OF
MACAU GIFTS MUSEUM Map pp430-1
Museu das Ofertas sobre a Transferência de Sobera-
nia de Macau; ☎ 791 9800; Avenida Xian Xing Hai;
admission free; ⏰ 10am-7pm Tue-Sun

This new museum, housed in a three-storey
hall next to the Macau Cultural Centre, displays art pieces and handicrafts presented
by China's various provinces and regions
(including Hong Kong) to Macau to mark
the return of Chinese sovereignty in 1999.
Some are kitsch in the extreme (eg Chong-
qing's *Centuries of the Yangtze River,* Guangdong's *Nation of One Mind*), while others
exhibit the work of Chinese craftspeople
at their best. Needless to say, it's a crowd-
pleaser among visitors from the mainland.

KUN IAM STATUE Map pp430-1
Estátua de Kun Iam; Avenida Doutor Sun Yat Sen

The bizarre 20m-high bronze monument to
the goddess of mercy, emerging Venus-like
from a 7m-high lotus in the Outer Harbour,
is actually quite restful once you've entered
Kun Iam's 'blossom'. This is the two-level **Kun
Iam Ecumenical Centre** (Centro Ecuménico Kun
Iam; ☎ 751 516; admission free; 10.30am-
6pm Sat-Thu), where information is available
on Buddhism, Taoism and Confucianism.
The statue is connected to the mainland
by a 60m-long footbridge.

MACAU CULTURAL CENTRE Map pp430-1
Centro Cultural de Macau; ☎ 700 699, 555 555;
www.ccm.gov.mo; Avenida Xian Xing Hai;
⏰ 9am-7pm Tue-Sun

This US$100-million centre is the territory's
prime venue for theatre, opera and other
cultural performances. The Macau Museum
of Art is part of the centre, and a walkway
connects it with a large tower standing in
the harbour. Free guided tours in English
depart from the main lobby at 10.30am on
Friday, but be sure to book in advance.

MACAU MUSEUM OF ART Map pp430-1
Museu de Arte de Macau; ☎ 791 9814; www.art
museum.gov.mo; Avenida Xian Xing Hai; adult/
senior over 65/child under 12 & student MOP$5/
free/3, admission free Sun; ⏰ 10am-7pm Tue-Sun

Located within the Macau Cultural Centre,
the museum is an enormous five-storey
complex with over 10,000 sq metres of floor

space. There's a library with art-related titles
and Internet access (p377) on the ground
floor. On the 1st floor are ticket offices, a
café and lecture halls. The 2nd floor is given
over to temporary exhibits, the 3rd floor
has the Gallery of Historical Pictures (mostly
Western art) and the 4th floor contains Chinese painting, calligraphy and porcelain.

SOUTHWEST CORNER
The southwestern tip of the Macau Peninsula has a number of important historical
sights, as it should – it was the first area of
territory to be settled.

A-MA TEMPLE Map pp430-1
Templo de A-Ma; Rua de São Tiago da Barra;
⏰ 10am-6pm

North of Barra Hill, this temple – called Ma
Kok Miu in Cantonese – is dedicated to
the goddess A-Ma, who is better known
as Tin Hau (see the boxed text, p338). The
original temple on this site was probably
already standing when the Portuguese
arrived, although the present one may only
date back to the 17th century. At the main
entrance is a large boulder with a coloured
relief of a *lorcha,* a traditional sailing vessel
of the South China Sea. The faithful make
a pilgrimage here during the A-Ma Festival
sometime between late April and early May.

AVENIDA DA REPÚBLICA Map pp430-1
Avenida da Praia Grande and Rua da Praia
do Bom Parto form an arc that leads into
Avenida da República, one of the prettiest
avenues in Macau. Towering above it is the
former **Bela Vista Hotel**, whose rooms hold
enough stories to fill several volumes. It is
now the residence of the Portuguese
consul general. A short distance southwest
is the **Santa Sancha Palace** (Palacete de Santa
Sancha; Estrada de Santa Sancha), erstwhile
residence of Macau's Portuguese governors
and now used to accommodate state guests.

MACAU TOWER Map pp430-1
Torre de Macau; www.macautower.com.mo;
Largo da Torre de Macau; ⏰ 10am-9pm Mon-Fri,
9am-9pm Sat & Sun

Macau Tower, at 338m the 10th-tallest
freestanding structure in the world, stands
on the narrow isthmus of land southeast of
Avenida da República. The squat building
at its base is the **Macau Convention & Entertainment Centre** (☎ 933 339).

Macau **SIGHTS**

Apart from housing **observation decks** (adult/child 3-12 & senior over 65 MOP$70/35) on the 58th and 61st floors, and a bunch of restaurants and bars, including the revolving **360° Café** on the 60th floor and the **180° Lounge** a floor below it, the Macau Tower doesn't 'do' anything – not even relay broadcast signals. As a result, a New Zealand–based extreme-sports company called **AJ Hackett** (☎ 988 8656) has been allowed to organise all kinds of adventure climbs.

The truly intrepid will go for the Mast Climb (MOP$700 to MOP$1000, depending on when you do it and how many are in your group), in which you go up and down the mast's 100m of vertical ladders to the top in two hours. The Skywalk (weekdays/weekends MOP$100/MOP$120) is a twirl around the covered walkway – you're attached to a lanyard – under the pod of the tower (on the 57th floor) and 216m above ground. The Skywalk X (MOP$160/MOP$190) is a rail-less walk around the *outer* rim, some 233m high, on the 61st floor. The faint-hearted may try something closer to terra firma: the Flying Fox (MOP$30) is a 70m 'flight' on a zip line from one of the tower legs into a large net; the Ironwalk (MOP$60) is an 8m-high walk via rope ladder around the legs of the tower, with a Flying Fox finish; and Long Ironwalk (MOP$80) is a vertical version of the Ironwalk, some 23m up.

MARITIME MUSEUM Map pp430-1

Museu Marítimo; ☎ 595 481; 1 Largo do Pagode da Barra; adult/senior over 65/child 10-17 Mon & Wed-Sat MOP$10/free/5, Sun MOP$5/free/3; ⊙ 10am-5.30pm Wed-Mon

Opposite the A-Ma Temple, the Maritime Museum is neither Macau's biggest nor its best, but its collection of boats and other artefacts related to Macau's seafaring past is interesting nonetheless. Particularly good are the mock-ups of a Hakka fishing village and the displays of the long, narrow boats that are raced during the Dragon Boat Festival (p329) in June. There's also a small aquarium.

PENHA HILL Map pp430-1

Colina da Penha

Towering above the colonial villas along Avenida da República is Penha Hill, from where you'll get an excellent view of the central area of Macau and across the Pearl River into China. The **Bishop's Palace** (built in 1837) is here, as is the **Chapel of Our Lady of Penha** (Capela de Nostra Señora da Penha; ⊙ 9am-5.30pm), once a place of pilgrimage for sailors.

Northern Macau Peninsula

The northern part of the peninsula, encompassing everything northwards from the Luís de Camões Garden in the west and Guia Fort in the east to the border with the mainland, was more recently developed than the southern and central areas. Nevertheless, there are quite a few important historic sites in this district and some divine gardens.

CASA GARDEN Map pp430-1

13 Praça de Luís de Camões

This restored (but once again decaying) colonial villa, east of the Luís de Camões Garden, was the headquarters of the British East India Company when it was based in Macau in the early 19th century. Today the villa houses the **Oriental Foundation** (Fundação Oriente; ☎ 554 699; www.foriente.pt), an organisation founded in 1996 to promote Portuguese culture worldwide, and an **exhibition gallery** (☎ 398 1126; admission free; ⊙ 10am-5.30pm Mon-Fri, 10am-7pm daily during special exhibitions), which houses both permanent and temporary exhibits of Chinese antiques, porcelain and contemporary art.

FIRE SERVICES MUSEUM Map pp430-1

Museu de Bombeiros; ☎ 572 222; 2-6 Estrada de Coelho do Amaral; admission free; ⊙ 10am-6pm daily

Housed in the former headquarters of the Macau fire brigade, the museum holds a small but interesting collection of old fire trucks from the 1940s and '50s, a manual pump from 1877, lots of helmets and boots, and the requisite sliding pole.

GUIA FORT Map pp430-1

Colina da Guia

The fortress (built in 1638) atop Guia Hill, the highest point on the peninsula, was originally designed to defend the border with China, but it soon came into its own as a lookout post, and storm warnings were sounded from the bell in the **Chapel** of Our Lady of Guia (Capela de Nostra Señora da Guia; 🕐 9am-5.30pm Tue-Sun), built in 1622. The walls of the little church have interesting frescoes only discovered recently, and there's a colourful choir loft above the main entrance. On the floor below is a tombstone with the inscription (in Latin): 'Here lies at this gate the remains of a Christian, by accident, for his body does not deserve such an honourable sepulchre'. The identity of the deceased and his 'crime' have remained a mystery since he was buried here in 1687. The 15m-tall **Guia Lighthouse** (Farol da Guia; 1865), next to the chapel, is the oldest lighthouse on the China coast. Guia Hill is littered with old bunkers, relics of both WWII and the Cold War.

The easiest way to reach the top of Guia Hill is to hop on the little **Guia Cable Car** (Teleférico da Guia; one way/return MOP$2/3) that runs from 8am to 6pm Tuesday to Sunday from just outside the entrance of the attractive **Flora Garden** (Rua do Túnel; 🕐 6am-7pm), off Avenida de Sidónio Pais.

KUN IAM TEMPLE Map pp430-1
Kun Iam Tong; Avenida do Coronel Mesquita; 🕐 **10am-6pm**

Dating from 1627, this is the most active (and interesting) Buddhist temple in Macau. Rooms adjacent to the main hall honour the goddess of mercy with a collection of pictures and scrolls. Note some of the reliefs at the front, which were damaged during the Cultural Revolution.

The first treaty of trade and friendship between the USA and China (1844) was signed at a stone table in the terraced gardens at the back; a tablet marks the spot.

LIN FUNG TEMPLE Map pp430-1
Lin Fung Miu; Avenida do Almirante Lacerda; 🕐 **10am-6.30pm**

This complex, built in 1592 as a Taoist temple but now dedicated to Kun Iam, is where mandarins from Guangdong province would stay when they visited Macau. The most celebrated of these visitors was Lin Zexu (p54), the commissioner charged with stamping out the opium trade, who stayed here in September 1839. The **Lin Zexu Memorial Hall** (Museu de Lin Zexu; ☎ 550 166; tourist adult/local adult/child under 8 & senior over 65 MOP$10/5/3; 🕐 9am-5pm Tue-Sun), with its old photographs, a model of a Chinese war junk and opium-smoking paraphernalia, recalls his visit.

LOU LIM IOC GARDEN Map pp430-1
Jardim de Lou Lim Ioc; 10 Estrada de Adolfo de Loureiro; 🕐 **6am-9pm**

This cool and leafy garden contains huge shade trees, lotus ponds, golden bamboo groves, grottoes and a bridge with nine turns (since evil spirits can only move in straight lines). Local people use the park to practise t'ai chi or play traditional Chinese musical instruments.

The renovated Victorian-style **Lou Lim Ioc Garden Pavilion** (Pavilhão do Jardim de Lou Lim Ioc; ☎ 988 4128; admission free; 🕐 9am-9pm Tue-Sun), which is in the centre of the pond and connected to the mainland by little bridges, is used for temporary exhibits and for recitals during the Macau International Music Festival (p330) in late October/November.

LUÍS DE CAMÕES GARDEN Map pp430-1
Jardim de Luís de Camões; Praça de Luís de Camões; 🕐 **6am-10pm**

This lovely garden is a pleasant and shady place popular with local Chinese, who use it to 'walk' their caged songbirds, play Chinese chequers or just sit and chat. In the centre of the park is the **Camões Grotto** (Gruta de Camões), which contains a 19th-century bust of the one-eyed national poet of Portugal, Luís de Camões (see p335).

OLD PROTESTANT CEMETERY
Map pp430-1
15 Praça de Luís de Camões; 🕐 **8.30am-5.30pm**

To the east of the Casa Garden is the final resting place of many early non-Portuguese residents of Macau, including English, Scots, Americans and Dutch. As Church law forbade the burial of non-Catholics on hallowed ground, there was nowhere to inter Protestants who died here, and they were often buried clandestinely in the nearby hills. The governor finally allowed a local merchant to sell some of his land to the British East India Company, and the cemetery was established in 1821. A number of old graves were then transferred to the cemetery, which explains the earlier dates on some of the tombstones.

Among the better-known people interred in this well-kept cemetery are the artist George Chinnery (see the boxed text, p334) and Robert Morrison (1782–1834), the first Protestant missionary to China and author of the first Chinese-English dictionary.

SUN YAT SEN MEMORIAL HOME
Map pp430-1

Casa Memorativa de Doutor Sun Yat Sen;
☎ 574 064; 1 Rua de Silva Mendes; admission free;
🕑 10am-5pm Wed-Mon

Around the corner from the Lou Lim Ioc
Garden, this museum is dedicated to the
founder of the Chinese Republic, Dr Sun
Yat Sen (1866–1925). Dr Sun practised
medicine at the Kiang Wu Hospital on Rua
Coelho do Amaral for a few years before
turning to revolution and seeking to overthrow the Qing dynasty. The house, built in
the mock Moorish style popular at the time,
contains a collection of flags, photos and
documents relating to the life and times
of the 'Father of the Nation'. It replaces the
original house, which blew up while being
used as an explosives store. Sun's first wife,
Lu Muzhen, died in the upstairs back bedroom in 1952.

TAIPA & COLOANE ISLANDS

A visit to Macau's two islands perfectly
rounds off a trip to the territory. While
peninsular Macau is where the vast majority of the territory's population lives,
works and makes merry, Coloane and, to
a much lesser extent nowadays, Taipa are
oases of calm and greenery. Striking pastel-
coloured colonial villas and civic buildings
preside over quiet lanes and a couple of
decent beaches, there's ample opportunity
for walking and cycling, and the Portuguese
and Macanese restaurants of Taipa Village
alone are worth the trip.

Taipa Island

When the Portuguese first sighted Taipa
(Tam Chai in Cantonese, Tanzai in Mandarin), it was actually two islands. Over the
centuries the pair was joined together by silt
pouring down from the Pearl River. Reclamation has almost succeeded in doing the
same thing to Taipa and Coloane.

Traditionally an island of duck farms and
boat yards, with enough small fireworks
factories to satisfy the insatiable demand
for bangers and crackers, Taipa is rapidly
becoming urbanised. The construction of
Taipa City, a large high-rise housing development in the centre of the island, is a major
ongoing project, a new stadium has been
built and new hotels are planned.

TAIPA WALK

After visiting the Taipa House Museum, walk up the
steps to the 1885 **Church of Our Lady of Carmel**
(Map p433) from the western end of Avenida da
Praia. The colonial **library** (Map p433), opposite, is
a recent reproduction, replacing the original that had
been pulled down illegally. Surrounding it are the
pretty **Carmel Gardens** (Map p433) and just north
is **Calçada do Carmo**, a positively delightful stepped
lane lined with ancient banyans.

Following Avenida de Carlos da Maia will take you
past an **old police school** (Map p433) and into Rua
da Correia Silva, which leads to a small early-19th-
century **Tin Hau temple** (Map p433) on Largo Governador Tamagnini Barbosa. Northeast, just off Rua do
Regedor, is **Pak Tai Temple** (Map p433), dedicated to
the guardian of peace and order. The Taipa **market**
(Map p433) is housed in a building at the end of the
street. There's a weekly **crafts market** (🕑 noon-
9pm Sun) in Largo de Camões.

Resisting the onslaught, however, is a
parade of baroque churches and buildings,
Taoist and Buddhist temples and overgrown
esplanades.

FOUR-FACED BUDDHA SHRINE
Map p433

O Buda de Quatro Faces; cnr Estrada Governador
Albano de Oliveira & Rua de Fat San
Northeast of the Macau Jockey Club
racetrack's main entrance, this Buddhist
shrine, guarded by four stone elephants
and festooned with gold leaf and Thai-style
floral bouquets, recalls the Erawan shrine in
Bangkok. Apparently it was erected shortly
after the racetrack opened, when punters encountered a string of bad luck. It's a
popular place to pray and make offerings
before race meetings.

POU TAI TEMPLE Map p433
Pou Tai Un; 5 Estrada Lou Lim Ieok; 🕑 9am-6pm
This Buddhist temple is the largest temple
complex on the islands. The main hall,
dedicated to the Three Precious Buddhas,
contains an enormous bronze statue of
Lord Gautama, and there are brightly
coloured prayer pavilions and orchid greenhouses scattered around the complex. The
temple also contains a popular **vegetarian
restaurant** (p366).

TAIPA HOUSE MUSEUM Map p433

Casa Museum da Taipa; ☎ 827 103; Avenida da Praia; adult/child under 12 & senior over 65/student MOP$5/free/3, admission free Sun; ☺ 10am-6pm Tue-Sun

The five lime-green villas facing the water were built in 1921 by wealthy Macanese as summer residences and three of them collectively form this unusual museum. The two houses east of where Avenida da Praia meets Rua do Supico are used for receptions and special exhibitions; the three to the west house permanent collections.

The first of the houses that form the museum, the House of the Regions of Portugal (Casa das Regiões de Portugal) contains costumes and examines traditional ways of life in Portugal. The House of the Islands (Casa das Ilhas) looks at the history of Taipa and Coloane, with interesting displays devoted to the islands' traditional industries: fishing and the manufacture of oyster sauce, shrimp paste and fireworks. The last is the Macanese House (Casa Macaense), a residence done up in traditional local style that looks like the *dom e doña* (husband and wife) residing here just left. The mix of furnishings – heavy blackwood furniture and Chinese cloisonné with statues and pictures of saints and the Sacred Heart – offers a snapshot of life in Macau in the early 20th century.

TAIPA VILLAGE Map p433

This village to the south of the island, once on the water and now landlocked, has somehow managed to retain its charm. It is a tidy sprawl of traditional Chinese shops and some excellent restaurants, punctuated here and there by grand colonial villas, churches and ancient temples. Down along what was once the seafront and is now an artificial lake, Avenida da Praia is a tree-lined esplanade with wrought-iron benches and old-world charm. It's the perfect place for a leisurely stroll.

Coloane Island

A haven for pirates until the beginning of the last century, Coloane (Lo Wan in Cantonese, Luhuan in Mandarin) fought off the last assault by buccaneers on the South China Sea in 1910, and the island still celebrates the anniversary of the victory on 13 July. Nowadays Coloane attracts large numbers of visitors to its sleepy main village and sandy coastline.

A-MA STATUE Map p433

Estátua da Deusa A-Ma; Estrada do Alto de Coloane

This colossal 20m statue of the goddess who gave Macau its name (see the boxed text, p338), atop Alto de Coloane (176m), was hewn from a form of white jade quarried in Fangshang near Beijing and was erected in 1998. Below it is enormous Tian Hou Temple (☺ 8am-7.30pm), which, together with the statue, will form the core of A-Ma Cultural Village, a cultural and religious complex containing a museum, retreat and medical centres, a vegetarian restaurant and handicraft shops. Within the temple, A-Ma takes pride of place in the centre, flanked by Man Cheung and Kwan Yu (see the boxed text, p12). Painted panels on the walls recall key events in the life of the goddess.

A free bus departs for the statue and temple from the ornamental gate at the corner of Estrada de Seac Pai Van and Estrada do Alto de Coloane every half-hour from 8am to 6pm. Otherwise you can reach both by following the Coloane Trail (Trilho de Coloane; p370) from Seac Pai Van Park.

CHAPEL OF ST FRANCIS XAVIER Map p433

Capela de São Francisco Xavier; Avenida de Cinco de Outubro; ☺ 10am-8pm

This delightful little church on the waterfront was built in 1928 to honour St Francis Xavier. He had been a missionary in Japan, and Japanese Catholics still come to Coloane to pay their respects. For many years a fragment of the saint's arm bone was kept in the chapel, but it has now been moved to St Joseph Seminary on the Macau Peninsula.

In front of the chapel are a monument and fountain surrounded by four cannonballs that commemorate the successful – and final – routing of pirates in 1910.

CHEOC VAN BEACH Map p433

Estrada de Cheoc Van

About 1.5km down Estrada de Cheoc Van, which runs east and then southeast from Coloane Village, is the beach at Cheoc Van (Bamboo Bay). There are public changing rooms and toilets and, in season, lifeguards (☺ 10am-6pm Mon-Sat, 9am-6pm Sun May-Oct) on duty.

COLOANE VILLAGE Map p433

The only true settlement on the island, Coloane Village is still largely a fishing

Hác Sá Beach (below), Coloane Island

village in character (particularly at the northern end), although in recent years tourism has given the local economy a big boost. The village is a fascinating relic of the Macau that once was, and strolling along the narrow lanes, flanked by temples and colourful shops is a joy.

The bus drops you off in the village's attractive **main square**; Coloane **market** is on the eastern side. To the west is the waterfront; China is just across the channel. From here a sign points the way north to the **Sam Seng Temple** (2 Rua dos Navegantes), which is so small it's more like a family altar. Just past the temple is the village pier and beyond that, to the northeast, about a dozen **junk-building sheds**. Junks are still built here – it takes about two months to make one – but a fire in 1999 destroyed many of the sheds.

HÁC SÁ BEACH Map p433

Hác Sá (Black Sand) is a much larger and more popular bathing spot than Cheoc Van. The sand is indeed a grey to blackish colour and makes the water look somewhat dirty (especially at the tide line), but it's perfectly clean. On a clear day you can just make out the mountaintops on Hong Kong's Lantau Island. Lifeguards keep the same schedule here as on Cheoc Van Beach.

SEAC PAI VAN PARK Map p433

☎ 870 277; Estrada de Seac Pai Van; admission free; ☒ 9am-6pm Tue-Sun

About 1km south of the causeway (ie the end of Cotai), this 20-hectare park, built

in the wooded hills on the western side of the island, has somewhat unkempt gardens sprouting species of plants and trees from around the world, a children's **zoo**, a **lake** with swans and other waterfowl, and a decaying walk-through **aviary** (☒ 9am-5pm Tue-Sun), which contains a number of rare birds. The **Museum of Nature & Agriculture** (Museu Natural e Agrário; ☎ 827 277; admission free; ☒ 10am-6pm Tue-Sun), housed in two small buildings, has traditional farming equipment, dioramas of Coloane's ecosystem and displays cataloguing a wide range of the island's fauna, flora and geology.

TEMPLES Map p433

Southeast of the Chapel of St Francis Xavier, between Travessa de Caetano and Travessa de Pagode, is a small **Kun Iam Temple** – just an altar inside a little walled compound really. If you walk just a little further to the southeast, you'll find the considerably larger and more interesting **Tin Hau Temple** up in Largo Tin Hau Miu.

At the southern end of Avenida de Cinco de Outubro in Largo Tam Kong Miu, the **Tam Kong Temple** is dedicated to the Taoist god of seafarers, who may be a deification of the Song-dynasty boy emperor Duan Zong (see p53). To the right of the main altar is a long whale bone, which has been carved into a model of a boat, complete with a dragon's head and a crew of men in pointed hats. Stroke the dragon's head and tail for good luck.

MACAU PENINSULA WALKING TOUR

www.lonelyplanet.com

Begin your tour of the peninsula in **Largo do Senado** 1, the beautiful 'Square of the Senate' in the heart of Macau, which is accessible from the ferry terminal on bus 3. On the south side of the square facing Avenida de Almeida Ribeiro is the **main post office** 2, built in 1931,

and nearby is the restored **Museum of the Holy House of Mercy** 3 (p345). From here, walk to the northeastern end of the square. Overlooking Largo de São Domingos is the **Church of St Dominic** 4 (p343), with its distinctive green shutters and doors. On the southern side of this square, you'll spot a narrow road called Travessa de São Domingos. Follow this up to Largo da Sé and **Macau Cathedral** 5 (p344). Travessa da Sé leads down into Rua de São Domingos.

WALK FACTS

Distance 2.5km
Duration 2½ hours
Start Largo do Senado
End Maritime Museum

tom of the hill and follow Rua de São Domingos and its extension, Rua de Pedro Nolasco da Silva, to the corner with Calçada do Monte. Just visible across the garden to the east is the **Consulate General of Portugal** 6, housed in an exquisite colonial mansion. Begin climbing up

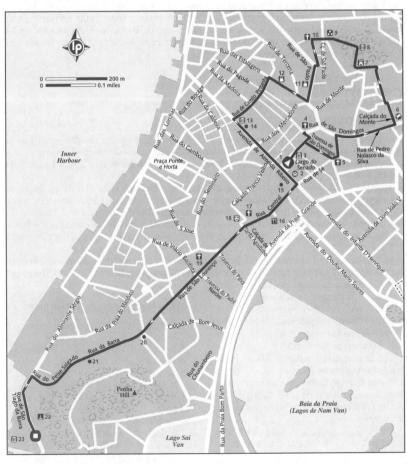

Macau

MACAU PENINSULA WALKING TOUR

Calçada do Monte, and once you reach Travessa do Artilheiros, turn left. A cobbled path leads up to the **Monte Fort 7** (p345) and the **Macau Museum 8** (p344). Take the escalator down from the museum and walk westwards through the **ruins of the College of the Mother of God 9**, built by the Jesuits in the early 17th century, to the façade of the **Church of St Paul 10** (p345); there's a platform offering stunning views over the town on the north side leading to the former choir loft. Walk down the impressive stone steps in front of the façade and walk south along the Rua de São Paolo, which is lined with **antique shops 11** (p370). Turn right onto Rua das Estalagens, which is full of **traditional Chinese shops 12** (p370) and, once you reach Rua de Camilo Pessanha, turn left. At the western end of this street, turn left into Avenida de Almeida Ribeiro and immediately on your left you'll pass the **Pawnshop Museum 13** (p345) and **Cultural Club 14** (p344). Continue along Avenida de Almeida Ribeiro. After passing the **Leal Senado 15** (p344), turn right onto Rua Central, which changes names several times as it heads southwest for the Inner Harbour. If you're feeling peckish, you may want to stop for a bowl of *caldo verde* at **Afonso III 16** (opposite). Towering above this end of Rua Central is the **Church of St Augustine 17** (p343) and opposite that the **Dom Pedro V Theatre 18** (p344). Follow Rua Central's extensions, Rua de São Lourenço and Rua da Barra, passing the **Church of St Lawrence 19** (p343) and **Largo do Lilau 20**; according to local folklore, should you drink from the fountain in this romantic square, it's a given that you'll return to Macau one day. Further on are the enormous **Moorish Barracks 21**, completed in 1874 and now housing the offices of the maritime police. Rua do Peixe Salgado (Street of Salted Fish) debouches into Rua do Almirante Sérgio, where you should turn left. A short distance south is the ever-active **A-Ma Temple 22** (p355) and opposite, across Rua de São Tiago da Barra, is the **Maritime Museum 23** (p356). From here, you can follow Avenida da República to Avenida da Praia Grande and Avenida de Almeida Ribeiro or hop on bus 5 or 7.

EATING

MACAU PENINSULA

Like the Hong Kong Chinese, the people of Macau eat throughout the day – not just at specified meal times. Peninsular Macau's street stalls sell excellent stir-fried dishes; try any of the *daai-pàai-dawng* (open-air street stalls) along Rua do Almirante Sérgio and Rua da Caldeira near the Inner Harbour.

Yuk-gàwn, dried sweet strips of pork and other meats, are a tasty Macau speciality, as are *hang-yàn-béng*, delightful almond-flavoured biscuits sprinkled with powdery white sugar. The best places to find both of these are around Rua da Caldeira and Travessa do Matadouro, which are at the northern end of Avenida de Almeida Ribeiro near the Inner Harbour, and along Rua de São Paulo on the way to or from the ruins of the Church of St Paul.

Macau has about 10 *mercados* (markets) selling fresh fruit, vegetables, meat and fish from 6am to 8pm daily. Two of the largest are the **Almirante Lacerda City Market** (Mercado Municipal Almirante Lacerda; Map pp430–1; 130 Avenida do Almirante Lacerda), in northern Macau, which is known as the Red Market, and the **St Lawrence City Market** (Mercado Municipal de São Lourenço; Map p432; Rua de João Lecaros) in the south.

The largest supermarket in Macau is the **New Yaohan Supermarket** (Map pp430–1; ☎ 725 338; 2nd fl, New Yaohan Department Store, Avenida da Amizade; ⏰ 11am-10.30pm), opposite (and connected by walkway to) the ferry terminal.

Other supermarkets include **Park 'N' Shop** (Map pp430–1; ☎ 531 641; 44F Estrada da

TOP FIVE MACAU RESTAURANTS

- **A Lorcha** (opposite) – the 'quality benchmark' of Portuguese food on the Macau mainland
- **Antica Trattoria da Isa** (opposite) – fine Italian cuisine amid comfortable surrounds
- **Cozinha Pinocchio** (p366) – the place that launched the Taipa Village restaurant phenomenon
- **Espaço Lisboa** (p366) – gourmet Portuguese in a renovated Coloane Village house
- **Naam** (p364) – some of the finest (and most inventive) Thai food this side of Bangkok

Areia Preta; ☺ 8am-11pm), a huge branch of the Hong Kong supermarket chain in the northern section of peninsular Macau, and **Pavilions Supermercado** (Map p432; ☎ 333 636; 421 Avenida da Praia Grande; ☺ 10am-9pm Mon-Sat, 11am-8pm Sun), which is dead in the centre of the Macau Peninsula and has a wide selection of imported food and drinks, including an impressive Portuguese section in the basement.

A LORCHA Map pp430-1   Portuguese
☎ 313 193; 289A Rua do Almirante Sérgio; starters MOP$24-44, mains MOP$58-128; ☺ 12.30-3.30pm & 7-11pm Wed-Mon
'The Sailboat', hard by the A-Ma Temple, has some of the best Portuguese food in Macau. Among the fine dishes to try are *porco balichão tamarino*, spicy *piri-piri* (hot chilli sauce) prawns and clams with garlic, coriander and olive oil.

AFONSO III Map p432   Portuguese
☎ 586 272; 11A Rua Central; starters MOP$20-45, mains MOP$68-82; ☺ noon-3pm & 6.30-10.30pm Mon-Sat
This simple Portuguese restaurant, a short stroll southwest of the Leal Senado, has won a well-deserved reputation among the Portuguese community in Macau, especially for its *feijoada*, but tables can often be in short supply, so phone ahead.

ANTICA TRATTORIA DA ISA
Map pp430-1   Italian
☎ 755 102; 1st fl, Vista Magnífica Bldg, 40-46 Avenida Sir Anders Ljungstedt; starters MOP$38-70, mains MOP$65-110; ☺ noon-11pm
This excellent Italian restaurant in NAPE has an extensive menu of well-prepared dishes, lovely décor and warm, helpful service. Pizzas (MOP$50 to MOP$85) and pasta (MOP$65 to MOP$80) are popular.

CAFFÈ TOSCANA Map p432   Italian
☎ 370 354; 11 Travessa de São Domingos; mains MOP$50-68; ☺ noon-9pm Wed-Mon
You can have a full meal at this friendly Italian café, but it's especially recommended for its focaccias (MOP$16 to MOP$38) and excellent desserts (MOP$18 to MOP$26).

CARLOS Map pp430-1   Macanese, Portuguese
☎ 751 838; Ground fl, Vista Magnífica Bldg, Rua Cidade de Braga; mains MOP$50-80; ☺ noon-3pm & 6-11pm Tue-Sun
Carlos, which has some of the warmest service in town, serves very decent Macanese food (try the *minchi*) and Portuguese food that is more Med than Luso.

CLUBE MILITAR DE MACAU
Map pp430-1   Portuguese
☎ 714 000; 975 Avenida da Praia Grande; starters MOP$30-88, mains MOP$90-112, lunch buffet MOP$90; ☺ noon-3pm & 7-11pm
The Portuguese dishes may not be the best in town, but the Military Club is one of Macau's most distinguished colonial buildings and its restaurant is as atmospheric as you'll find in Macau. Be sure to dress smartly.

FOOK LAM MUN Map pp430-1   Cantonese
☎ 786 622; Kam Wah Kok Bldg, 259 Avenida da Amizade; meals per person from MOP$250; ☺ lunch & dim sum 11am-3pm Mon-Fri, 8.30am-3pm Sat & Sun, dinner 5.30-11pm daily
This place serves some of the finest Cantonese food in the territory. It is especially well known for its seafood dishes.

HENRI'S GALLEY Map pp430-1   Macanese
☎ 556 251; 4G-H Avenida da República; starters MOP$30-64, mains MOP$54-110; ☺ 11am-11pm
An institution on the Macau restaurant scene for three decades now, Henri's Gallery is on the waterfront at the southern end of the Macau Peninsula. Its specialities are African chicken (MOP$96) and Macau sole (MOP$92).

KO LUNG Map pp430-1   Thai
☎ 334 067; 23 Rua de Ferreira Amaral; dishes MOP$25-90; ☺ 11am-7am
This little place that *almost* never sleeps is one of the most authentic Thai restaurants north of Bangkok – down to the toilet roll encased in a plastic dispenser on the table. The picture menu will help the uninitiated.

LA BONNE HEURE Map p432   French
☎ 331 209; 12A-B Travessa de São Domingos; starters MOP$42-136, mains MOP$92-156, 1-/2-/3-course set lunch MOP$60/75/85; ☺ noon-3pm & 7-10.30pm
Macau's first affordable French restaurant has set up shop in a charming old building, just up from the Largo do Senado. The set lunches are particularly good value.

LITORAL Map pp430-1   Macanese, Portuguese

☎ 967 878; 261A Rua do Almirante Sérgio; starters MOP$30-50, mains MOP$60-120; ☉ noon-3pm & 6-10.30pm

This is arguably the best Macanese restaurant on the peninsula, with excellent duck and baked rice dishes.

LONG KEI Map p432   Cantonese

☎ 589 508; 7B Largo do Senado; dishes MOP$40-120; ☉ 11.30am-3pm & 6-11.30pm

This landmark place, below the neon sign of a cow on Largo do Senado, is a straightforward Cantonese restaurant with more than 300 dishes on offer.

MEZZALUNA Map pp430-1   Italian

☎ 791 3861; 2nd fl, Mandarin Oriental, 956-1110 Avenida da Amizade; starters MOP$65-100, mains MOP$170-280; ☉ 12.30-3pm & 6.30-11pm Tue-Sun

This restaurant serves *la cucina italiana* in classy surroundings that have been given a total makeover. The pasta (MOP$85 to MOP$190) is fresh and the pizzas (MOP$85 to MOP$120) come piping hot from wood-fired ovens. Try the lobster ravioli or the gnocchi made with spinach and ricotta.

NAAM Map pp430-1   Thai

☎ 793 4818; Mandarin Oriental, Ground fl, 956-1110 Avenida da Amizade; starters MOP$45-110, salads MOP$55-70, mains MOP$55-250; ☉ noon-3pm & 6.30-10.30pm

If you want to experience excellent Thai fare in sublime surrounds, head for Naam at the Mandarin. The Thai chefs obviously do not compromise for limp-tongued *farang* (foreigners).

PIZZERIA TOSCANA II Map pp430-1   Italian

☎ 963 015; Ground fl, Cheong Seng Bldg, Calçada da Barra; mains MOP$80-120; ☉ 11.30am-3pm & 6.30-11pm Tue-Sun

This Italian eatery near the inner Harbour – not to be confused with the pizzeria near the ferry terminal – has some fine pizzas and pastas (MOP$50 to MOP$80), but concentrates on the traditional dishes of Tuscany.

PLAZA Map pp430-1   Cantonese

☎ 706 623; 2nd fl, Xin Hua Bldg, 35 Rua da Nagasaki; starters MOP$35-100, mains MOP$55-130; ☉ 8am-11pm

This positively cavernous restaurant is among the most popular Chinese restaurants in Macau. Dim sum is served from 8am to 3pm daily. The clay pot dishes (MOP$48 to MOP$150) are especially good.

PORTO EXTERIOR

Map pp430-1   Macanese, Portuguese

☎ 703 276, 703 898; Shop L, Ground fl, Chong Yu Bldg, 779 Avenida da Amizade; starters MOP$15-63, mains MOP$38-120; ☉ noon-11pm

Just north of NAPE, in a forest of high-rise buildings, the 'Outer Harbour' has earned itself a loyal local following in a relatively short time with its mixture of Macanese and Portuguese dishes.

PRAIA GRANDE Map pp430-1   Portuguese

☎ 973 022; 10A Praça Lobo d'Avila; starters MOP$35-65, mains MOP$80-200; ☉ noon-11pm Mon-Fri, 11.45am-11pm Sat & Sun

This stylish place serves adequate Portuguese dishes on the historic Praia Grande. Try to get a table by the window upstairs.

ROBUCHON A GALERA

Map pp430-1   French

☎ 377 666; 3rd fl, New/West Wing, Lisboa Hotel, 2-4 Avenida de Lisboa; starters MOP$190-290, mains MOP$330-570; ☉ noon-2.30pm & 6.30-10.30pm

Should you hit the jackpot at any of Macau's gambling venues (and we're talking big time here), celebrate at this new restaurant opened by Joël Robuchon, Michelin-starred French chef and serious *bon vivant*. The wine cellar contains more than 2000 labels. There is a three-course set lunch for MOP$288 and a sublime 12-course tasting menu for MOP$1400.

SAI NAM Map p432   Chinese, Seafood

☎ 574 072; 36 Rua da Felicidade; abalone & shark's fin plate from MOP$350; ☉ 5.30-10.15pm

If you want to sample abalone at its freshest, try this small restaurant, which specialises in that shellfish and has quite a reputation in Macau.

SUSHI KING Map p432   Japanese

☎ 356 336; Basement, Lung Cheong Bldg, 20-22 Rua de São Domingos; sushi MOP$10-60, sashimi MOP$25-120; ☉ noon-10.30pm

This popular Japanese eatery, just down from the Macau Cathedral, attracts students from the nearby colleges.

Cheap Eats

A VENCEDORA Map pp430-1   Portuguese

☎ 355460; 264 Rua do Campo; mains MOP$20-53; ☼ 11.45am-10pm

If wealth is to be measured in years, 'The Winner' – established in 1918 – has won the jackpot. It's a very old-fashioned sort of place, with tried and tested Sino-Portuguese dishes and a warm welcome.

ARUNA Map pp430-1   Indian

☎ 701 850; Shop 0, Ground fl, Chong Yu Bldg, 779 Avenida da Amizade; curries MOP$30-38; ☼ 11.30am-midnight

Indian is not a cuisine easily found in Macau, so if you need a fix of *rogan josh* or dhal, this little curry house and café can oblige.

CAFFÉ CHOCOLÁ Map p432   Café

☎ 976 522; 10A Travessa de São Domingos; hot chocolate MOP$13-16, cakes & pastries MOP$12-16; ☼ 8am-8pm

Chocaholics will beat a path to the door of this place, which serves some 30 different types of hot chocolate. Light meals are available at lunch.

CARAVELA Map p432   Café

☎ 712 080; Ground fl, Kam Loi Bldg, 7 Pátio do Comandante Mata e Oliveira; cakes MOP$10-25, set lunch MOP$60; ☼ 8am-10.30pm

This excellent *pastelaria* (pastry shop), just north of Avenida de Dom João IV, is a bit tricky to find, but the delectable pastries and snacks make it worth the effort. It's the hangout of choice for Portuguese residents on the peninsula.

OU MUN CAFÉ Map p432   Café

☎ 372 207; 12 Travessa de São Domingos; sandwiches MOP$12-25, dishes MOP$50; ☼ 8am-8pm Tue-Sun

This rather flash little café with the imaginative name of 'Macau' has decent sandwiches, cakes and coffee and is a cut above the rest.

PAPA TUDO Map pp430-1   Snack Bar

☎ 703 117; Ground fl, Nam Yuen Bldg, 68G-F Rua de Luís Gonzaga Gomes; snacks & sandwiches MOP$7.50-25, starters MOP$22-42, mains MOP$57-95; ☼ 8am-midnight

Little Papa Tudo serves sandwiches, snacks and pastries (MOP$6 to MOP$15), as well

as more ambitious dishes such as *naco na pedra* (beef tenderloin cooked on a hot stone; MOP$95).

WONG CHI KEI Map p432   Cantonese

☎ 331 313; 17 Largo do Senado; rice & noodle dishes MOP$16-32; ☼ 8am-midnight

Visit this centrally located Chinese eatery for a fix of cheap late-night noodles.

YES BRAZIL Map p432   Brazilian

☎ 358 097; 6A Travessa Fortuna; mains MOP$38-78; ☼ 11.30am-7pm Mon-Fri, 11.30am-9pm Sat

This always welcoming hole-in-the-wall, close to the ruins of the Church of St Paul, serves an excellent *feijoada* (MOP$70) and other Luso-Brazilian specialities. Come here, too, for a late breakfast (MOP$7 to MOP$25).

TAIPA & COLOANE ISLANDS

The number of restaurants in Taipa, particularly in the village, has grown by leaps and bounds in just a few short years. While much of the choice is restricted to Portuguese and Macanese cuisine, you'll also find some excellent Cantonese eateries here. If you want to try street food, head for Rua de São João at lunch time on Sunday when food hawkers set up their stalls.

Coloane is not the treasure-trove of restaurants and other eateries that Taipa is, but there are a few decent options offering a variety of cuisines at various price levels.

Taipa Island

A PETISQUEIRA Map p433   Portuguese

☎ 825 354; 15A-B Rua de São João; starters MOP$25-78, mains MOP$65-150; ☼ noon-3pm & 7-10.30pm

'The Snackery', an excellent restaurant set in a little alley that is easy to overlook, gets some people's vote for having the best Portuguese food in Taipa. It has a decent wine list and serves its own *queijo fresca da casa* (homemade cheese; MOP$22). Try the spicy prawns (MOP$135), the *acorda de marisco* (MOP$75) or the *bife à portuguesa* (beef cooked in a clay pot; MOP$90).

CHUN CHUN KUN Map p433   Cantonese

☎ 827 168; Rua da Cunha; meals per person MOP$120-350; ☼ 11am-3pm & 6-11.30pm

This Chinese restaurant, arguably the best known on Taipa Island, serves a special kind of shark's fin soup prepared without chemicals, as well as its signature duck and tofu dishes.

COZINHA PINOCCHIO

Map p433   Macanese

☎ 827 128; 4 Rua do Sol; starters MOP$35-58, mains MOP$48-128; 🕑 11.45am-11.45pm

You should at least make a visit to pay your respects to 'Pinocchio Kitchen' (provided you can get in), a Taipa institution. Recommended dishes include grilled fresh sardines (MOP$10), quail (MOP$11), pigeon (MOP$52) and roast lamb (MOP$98).

GALO Map p433   Macanese, Portuguese

☎ 827 423; 45 Rua da Cunha; starters MOP$16-40, mains MOP$40-100; 🕑 11am-3pm & 6-10.30pm

This place, opposite the old covered market, can be easily recognised by the picture of a red-combed *galo* (rooster) above the door. The food is adequate and the service seamless.

O CAFÉ ESTALAGEM

Map p433   Portuguese

☎ 821 041; 410 Estrada Governador Albano de Oliveira; starters MOP$30-70, mains MOP$62-120; 🕑 noon-3.30pm & 7-10.30pm Tue-Sun

'The Inn Café' hasn't continued to make the same sort of splash as it did when it first opened in 2004, but the prawn and crab dishes are still to be recommended.

O CAPÍTULO Map p433   Portuguese

☎ 821 519; Ground fl, Nam San Bldg, Avenida de Kwong Tung; starters MOP$24-128, mains MOP$62-96; 🕑 noon-10pm

This superb eatery, north of Macau Stadium, serves scrumptious homemade Portuguese dishes made with the freshest of ingredients. 'There's not a frozen morsel in this kitchen,' is their boast. If you're here at the weekend, try the roast suckling pig, and don't miss sampling the *fatias de Tomar*, a rich dessert made with egg yolks and syrup that has to be tasted – and seen – to be believed.

O MANEL Map p433   Portuguese

☎ 827 571; 90 Rua de Fernão Mendes Pinto; starters MOP$25-30, mains MOP$60-135; 🕑 noon-3.30pm & 6-11pm Wed-Mon

This small and friendly place serves classic Portuguese dishes such as *caldo verde* and

bacalhau, be it baked, stewed, boiled or grilled over charcoal.

O SANTOS Map p433   Portuguese

☎ 827 508; 20 Rua da Cunha; mains MOP$62-120; 🕑 noon-3pm & 6.30-10.30pm

This tiny place is famous for its stuffed pork loin and its codfish dishes, especially *bacalhau à zé do pipo* (dried cod baked with mashed potatoes; MOP$72) and *sapateira recheada* (MOP$150 for two), a type of crab flown in fresh from Portugal.

CHEAP EATS

CAFÉ LISBOA Map p433   Portuguese

☎ 843 313; Ground fl, Mei Keng Bldg, 47D Rua Bragança; dishes MOP$36-75; 🕑 café 9.30am-11.30pm, restaurant 1-3pm & 7-10pm

A real find, this one, and a favourite (and very authentic) lunch spot serving homemade Portuguese dishes to jockeys from the nearby racecourse, academics from the university and workers from the airport.

DOCA DE ABRIGO Map p433   Cantonese

☎ 825 003; 33-35 Rua da Cunha; soups & hotpots from MOP$20; 🕑 noon-11pm

The 'Harbour Dock', which also goes by its Chinese name Bei Feng Tong, is a noodle shop specialising in soups and hotpots.

POU TAI TEMPLE RESTAURANT

Map p433   Chinese, Vegetarian

☎ 893 0321; 5 Estrada Lou Lim Ieok; dishes MOP$20-48; 🕑 9am-6pm Mon-Sat, 9am-9.30pm Sun

This restaurant, set in a Buddhist temple in northern Taipa, is strictly vegetarian. It's not *haute cuisine* but a boon for those looking for a meatless meal.

SENG CHEONG Map p433   Cantonese

☎ 825 323; 28-30 Rua da Cunha; meals per person under MOP$100; 🕑 noon-midnight

This simple Chinese restaurant is celebrated for its fried fish balls, steamed eel and *congee* (rice porridge with savoury titbits).

Coloane Island

ESPAÇO LISBOA Map p433   Portuguese

☎ 882 226; 8 Rua dos Gaivotas; starters MOP$45-150, soups MOP$28-65, mains MOP$88-240; 🕑 noon-3pm & 6.30-10pm Tue-Fri, noon-10.30pm Sat & Sun

The 'Lisbon Space' restaurant, located in a renovated village house over two floors, serves some of the most carefully prepared Portuguese dishes in Macau. Try the fish (swordfish, grouper etc) stewed in a *cataplana* (traditional copper pot) or the curried crab. Daily specials cost MOP$88 to MOP$99, and the wine list is superb (indulge with a slightly effervescent white Paço de Teixeiró).

FERNANDO Map p433   Portuguese
☎ 882 531; 9 Hác Sá Beach; starters MOP$22-26, mains MOP$50-148, rice dishes MOP$60-66; ☽ noon-9.30pm
Famed for its seafood, Fernando has a devoted clientele and a pleasantly relaxed atmosphere – though it can get pretty crowded in the evening. The bar stays open till midnight.

KWUN HOI HEEN Map p433   Cantonese
☎ 899 1320; 3rd fl, Westin Resort Macau, 1918 Estrada de Hác Sá; rice & noodle dishes MOP$24-70, mains MOP$55-150; ☽ lunch 11am-3pm Mon-Fri, 9.30am-4pm Sat & Sun, dinner 6.30-11pm daily
The Kwun Hoi Heen stands out among the hotel restaurants on Coloane Island for its superb Cantonese cuisine, alfresco dining and sumptuous views. Dim sum is MOP$18 to MOP$22. The Saturday buffet lunch (MOP$118 to MOP$158) and dinner (from MOP$198) are excellent value.

LA GONDOLA Map p433   Italian
☎ 880 156; Cheoc Van Beach; mains MOP$65-110; ☽ noon-midnight
Next to the swimming pool at Cheoc Van Beach, La Gondola offers some excellent pastas (MOP$55 to MOP$65), pizzas (MOP$45 to MOP$66) cooked in a wood-fired oven and outside seating on a terrace.

RESTAURANTE PARQUE HÁC SÁ
Map p433   Portuguese
☎ 882 297, Hác Sá Sports & Recreation Park, Estrada Nova de Hác Sá; snacks & sandwiches MOP$12-25, mains MOP$26-88; ☽ noon-11pm
This is a pleasant place for meals by the beach at Hác Sá, and barbecue figures prominently. Sit inside or out on the terrace.

CHEAP EATS
LORD STOW'S CAFÉ Map p433   Café
☎ 882 174; 9 Largo do Matadouro; sandwiches & quiches MOP$20-25, desserts MOP$6-14; ☽ 9am-6pm
This little café serves the baked items and other goodies prepared at **Lord Stow's Bakery** (☎ 882 534; 1 Rua da Tassara; ☽ 7am-10pm Thu-Tue, 7am-7pm Wed) around the corner, including its celebrated *pastéis de nata,* a warm egg-custard tart (MOP$6) and cheesecake (MOP$14) in unusual flavours, including chestnut, black sesame and green tea.

NGA TIM CAFÉ
Map p433   Cantonese, Portuguese
☎ 882 086; 1 Rua Caetano; meals per person about MOP$100; ☽ 11am-1am
The food at this small café, across from the Chapel of St Francis Xavier, is Sino-Portuguese, and while the restaurant is certainly no work of art, the view outside is. If it's a sunny day, take a seat on the square and savour the scenery and the hybrid food.

VILLAGE CAFÉ Map p433   Café
☎ 881 142; 115 Rua da Cordoaria; dishes MOP$6-10; ☽ 10am-10pm
The Village Café, next to the bus stop in Coloane Village, serves MSG-free sandwiches and simple dishes at knockdown prices. Set lunch is MOP$25.

ENTERTAINMENT
The **Macau Cultural Centre** (p355) is the territory's premier venue for classical music concerts, dance performances and studio film screenings. To book tickets ring ☎ 555 555 or, in Hong Kong, ☎ 7171 7171, or check the website www.macauticket.net.

Macau Travel Talk, a free bimonthly available at MGTO outlets and larger hotels, has some useful entertainment listings at the back.

DRINKING
There are plenty of pubs and bars – some with live music – to keep you occupied in Macau. The main place for a pub crawl on the Macau Peninsula is the southern end of the reclaimed NAPE area – what locals call Lan Kwai Fong – where theme bars line the waterfront.

On Taipa Island, the area within the **Nam San** (Map p433) complex of buildings, just north of the racetrack, has also become something of a nightlife area in recent years, with a handful of late-night pubs and bars opening their doors. They're usually open till 3am or 4am daily. Among the most popular are the **Irish Bar** (☎ 820 708; 116C Avenida de Kwong Tung) and **Hugo's Pub** (☎ 822 816; Ground fl, Nam San Garden Bldg, Estrada Governador Albano de Oliveira).

While Carlsberg and San Miguel from Hong Kong and China's Tsingtao dominate the market here, Macau Beer produces a couple of its own brews: the citrus-tasting Blond Ale and Amber Ale, which is quite hoppy. If you want something stronger, all sorts of 'ruby' ports are available in Macau – the Parador is particularly fine – but go for something different, such as the evocatively named Lágrima do Christo (Tears of Christ), an unusual white port. Some Portuguese *aguardentes* (brandies) are worth trying, including Adega Velha and Antqua VSOP Aliança.

A ROLHA Map p433
☎ 688 2525; 122 Rua de Fernão Mendes Pinto, Taipa Island; 8pm-2am
'The Cork' is a pretty basic cellar bar, with beer on tap and bottom-shelf spirits on display, but the enthusiasm of the karaoke aficionados may have you lingering (or even performing).

CASABLANCA CAFÉ Map pp430-1
☎ 751 281; Ground fl, Vista Magnífica Court Bldg, Avenida Doutor Sun Yat Sen, Macau Peninsula; 6pm-4am, happy hour 6-8pm
This somewhat elegant watering hole has photos of Hollywood and Hong Kong film icons decorating the walls, cool jazz playing and pool tables.

CHAMPAGNE LOUNGE BAR
Map pp430-1
☎ 751 306; Ground fl, Vista Magnífica Court Bldg, Avenida Doutor Sun Yat Sen, Macau Peninsula; 5pm-4am, happy hour 6-8pm
Arguably the most sophisticated of the south NAPE bars, this place sells Portuguese bubbly for MOP$35 a glass.

EMBASSY BAR Map pp430-1
☎ 567 888; Ground fl, Mandarin Oriental, 956-1110 Avenida da Amizade, Macau Peninsula; 5pm-2.30am Tue-Thu, 5pm-4am Fri & Sat, 5pm-3am Sun, happy hour 5-9pm
This very popular bar features a live band nightly at 10.30pm and has a small dance floor that sees a lot of action as the night wears on.

MOONWALKER BAR Map pp430-1
☎ 751 326; Ground fl, Vista Magnífica Court Bldg, Avenida Doutor Sun Yat Sen, Macau Peninsula; 4pm-4am, happy hour 4-8pm

Moonwalker features fun live entertainment on most nights (usually Filipina chanteuses).

OSKAR'S PUB Map pp430-1
☎ 783 333; Holiday Inn Macau, 82-86 Rua de Pequim, Macau Peninsula; noon-3am, happy hour 5-9pm
This pub, off the main lobby of the Holiday Inn, draws a large number of local expats. There's live music Monday to Saturday from 9.30pm to 2.15am.

SANSHIRO PUB Map pp430-1
☎ 751 238; Ground fl, Vista Magnífica Court, Avenida Doutor Sun Yat Sen, Macau Peninsula; 6pm-4am, happy hour 6-8pm
This is a much simpler pub, and attractive for that, with all sorts of beer slams ('buy three, get six' sort of thing) and outside tables.

CLUBBING
The club scene in Macau has yet to reach the level of sophistication that it has in Hong Kong, and nightlife here is for the most part limited to tacky nightclub floorshows and hostess clubs.

DD DISCO Map p432
☎ 711 800; cnr Avenida do Infante Dom Henrique & Avenida de Dom João IV, Macau Peninsula; 11pm-7am, happy hour 11pm-2am
This popular bar and dance club, opposite the landmark Escola Portuguesa de Macau, has a small hall with live music, a main hall with a big dance floor, and the **Lime Light Bar**, which features live music every night except Wednesday from 11pm.

THEATRE

There's very little in the way of legitimate theatre in Macau, though, as in Las Vegas, floorshows – including the following two – are popular.

Crazy Paris Show (Map pp430–1; ☎ 377 666, ext 3193; Portas do Sol restaurant, 2nd fl, Old/East Wing, Lisboa Hotel, 2-4 Avenida de Lisboa, Macau Peninsula; ✆ 10-10.30pm) sees lots of women strutting around in a couple of beads and a feather or two. Under-18s are not admitted. **Jai Alai Show Palace** (Map pp430–1; ☎ 726 126; 3rd fl, Jai Alai Complex, Travessa do Reservatório, Macau Peninsula; ✆ continuous shows 7pm-2am) has lots of women wannabes (it's a transvestite show) doing what the girls in the Crazy Paris Show do – only much better.

ACTIVITIES

CYCLING

You can rent bicycles (MOP$12 to MOP$20 per hour) in Taipa Village from **Bicicleta Iao Kei** (Map p433; ☎ 827 975; 36 Rua Governador Tamagini Barbosa). On Coloane you'll find them for hire from a shop called **Lin Kei** (Map p433; ☎ 882 683), next door to Fernando restaurant on Hác Sá Beach.

You're not allowed to cross the Macau-Taipa Bridge on a bike, but they're permitted on the Cotai road linking Taipa and Coloane.

GO-KARTING

The **Coloane Kartodrome** (Map p433; ☎ 882 126; Estrada de Seac Pai Van; ✆ 11.30am-7pm Mon-Fri, 11am-8.30pm Sat & Sun), run by the Macau Motorsports Club (MCC) and located on the southern end of Cotai on Coloane's northern shore, is the region's most popular venue for go-karting. It's floodlit and there's a choice of seven circuits. It costs MOP$100/MOP$180 for 10/20 minutes; a two-seater is MOP$150 for 10 minutes. Racing suit/shoes cost MOP$20/MOP$50 to hire. Races are held on Sunday.

GOLF

The 18-hole, par-71 course at **Macau Golf & Country Club** (Map p433; ☎ 871 188; 1918 Estrada de Hác Sá), which is connected to the Westin Resort Macau on Coloane by walkway on the 9th floor, is open to foreigners through the hotel. Green fees are MOP$750/MOP$1400 on weekdays/weekends, and you must have a handicap certificate to tee off. There's also a **driving range** (☎ 871 111; 40 balls for MOP$40), accessible from the 2nd floor of the hotel, from where you drive balls into the ocean.

Go-karting, Coloane Kartodrome (above), Coloane Island

HIKING

There are two trails on Guia Hill (Map pp430–1), in central Macau Peninsula, that are also good for jogging. The **Walk of 33 Curves** (1.7km) circles the hill; inside this loop is the shorter **Fitness Circuit Walk**, with 20 exercise stations.

The **Little Taipa Trail** (Trilho de Taipa Pequena; Map p433) is a 2km-long circuit around a hill (111m) of that name in the northwestern part of Taipa. Reach it via Estrada Lou Lim Ieok. The 2.2km-long **Big Taipa Trail** (Trilho de Taipa Grande) rings Taipa Grande, a 160m-high hill at the eastern end of the island. You can access the trail via a short paved road off Estrada Colonel Nicolau de Mesquita.

Coloane's longest trail, the **Coloane Trail** (Trilho de Coloane; Map p433), begins at Seac Pai Van Park and is just over 8km long; the main trailhead is called the Estrada do Alto de Coloane. The shorter **Northeast Coloane Trail** (Trilho Nordeste de Coloane), near Ká Hó, runs for about 3km. Other trails that offer good hiking include the 1.5km-long **Altinho de Ká Hó Trail** and the 1.5km-long **Hác Sá Reservoir Circuit** (Circuito da Barragem de Hác Sá), which both loop around the reservoir to the northwest of Hác Sá Beach.

WATER SPORTS

The **Hác Sá Sports & Recreation Park** (Map p433; ☎ 882 296, Estrada Nova de Hác Sá; ☺ 8am-9pm Sun-Fri, 8am-11pm Sat), by the beach, seems to have just about everything on offer, but its main draw is the **outdoor swimming pool** (adult/child/student MOP$15/5/7; ☺ 10am-9pm Mon, 8am-9pm Tue-Fri & Sun, 8am-11pm Sat). You'll also find three **tennis courts** (per hr MOP$30, after 7pm MOP$60; racquet & ball hire each MOP$5), a five-a-side **football ground** (per hr MOP$70, after 7pm MOP$100), a **mini-golf course** (per hr MOP$10), **table tennis tables** (per hr MOP$5) and **badminton courts** (per hr MOP$10).

The **Cheoc Van swimming pool** (Map p433; ☎ 870 277), which costs the same for entry and keeps the same hours as the Hác Sá pool, is at the southern end of the beach.

There are stands where you can hire windsurfing boards, jet skis and water scooters at either end of Hác Sá Beach.

SHOPPING

The main shopping areas in peninsular Macau are along Avenida do Infante Dom Henrique and Avenida de Almeida Ribeiro. Other shopping zones can be found along Rua da Palha, Rua do Campo and Rua Pedro Nolasco da Silva.

The largest department store in Macau is the Japanese-owned **New Yaohan** (Map pp430–1; Avenida da Amizade), opposite the ferry terminal. The **Landmark Macau** (Map pp430–1; Avenida da Amizade) has a number of upmarket boutiques selling high-quality clothing and accessories. The **Lisboa Hotel** (p372) has a good shopping arcade in the basement.

ANTIQUES & CURIOS

While exploring Macau's back lanes and streets you'll stumble across bustling markets and traditional Chinese shops. Rua de Madeira is a charming market street, with many shops selling carved Buddha heads and other religious items.

Rua dos Mercadores, which leads up to Rua da Tercena, will lead you past tailors, wok sellers, tiny jewellery shops, incense and mahjong shops and other traditional businesses (Map p432). At the far end of Rua da Tercena, where the road splits, is a **flea market** (Map p432), where you can pick up baskets and other rattan ware, jade pieces and old coins.

Great streets for antiques, ceramics and curios (eg traditional Chinese kites) are Rua de São Paulo, Rua das Estalagens and Rua de São António, and the lanes off them; most shops are open from 10.30am or 11am to 6pm or 7pm, with a one-hour lunch some time between 12.30pm and 2pm.

The backstreets of Coloane Village, especially Rua dos Negociantes, have a few shops selling bric-a-brac, traditional goods and antiques. One of the best and most reliable antique shops in Macau is **Asian Artefacts** (Map p433; ☎ 881 022; 9 Rua dos Negociantes; ☺ 10am-7pm).

CLOTHING

The **St Dominic Market** (Map p432), in an alley just north of Largo do Senado, is a good place to pick up T-shirts and other cheap clothing. The so-called **Three Lamps District**, especially around Rotunda de Carlos da Maia (Map pp430–1), near the Almirante Lacerda City Market in northern peninsular Macau, is also good for this type of thing.

STAMPS

Macau produces some wonderful postage stamps, real collector's items that include images of everything from key colonial landmarks to roulette tables and high-speed ferries. Mint sets and first-day covers are available from counter Nos 17 & 18 at the **main post office** (Map p432) facing Largo do Senado.

SLEEPING

Accommodation in Macau runs the gamut from glimmering five-star palaces to guesthouses, many of them no more than dosshouses, that go by such names as *vila*, *hospedaria* or *pensão*. There are two Hostelling International–affiliated hostels on Coloane Island.

In general Macau's hotels are cheaper than those in Hong Kong. On top of that, substantial discounts (30% or more) are available if you book through a travel agency, but this usually only applies to hotels of three stars and above. In Hong Kong you'll find a lot of these agents at the **Shun Tak Centre** (Map pp408–9; 200 Connaught Rd Central, Sheung Wan), from where the ferries to Macau depart. If you haven't booked your room before your arrival, you can do it at one of the many hotel desks in the ferry terminal pier in Macau.

Visiting Macau at the weekend, on public holidays or during the summer high season should be avoided at all costs, as rooms are scarce and hotel prices can double or even treble. 'Weekend' usually means just Saturday night in relation to accommodation; Friday night is generally not a problem unless it's a holiday, though it pays to check.

Most large hotels add a 10% service charge and 5% government tax to the bill. Prices listed here are the rack rates quoted to walk-in customers.

MACAU PENINSULA

Hotels in Macau are generally split geographically into price constituencies, with cheap hotels and guesthouses occupying the southwestern part of the peninsula, around Rua das Lorchas and Avenida de Almeida Ribeiro, and top-end hotels generally in the east and centre of town.

At the time of writing, the landmark **Pousada de São Tiago** (Map pp430–1; ☎ 378 111; www.saotiago.com.mo), built into the ruins of the 17th-century Barra Fort and one of the most romantic places to stay in Macau, was being gutted in order to double the number of guestrooms to 50. Ring or check the website for updates.

FORTUNA HOTEL Map pp430-1   Hotel
☎ 786 333; www.hotelfortuna.com.mo; 63 Rua da Cantão; s & d Sun-Thu MOP$720, Fri & Sat MOP$980-1120, ste from MOP$1888
This smart, 342-room hotel is in a very central location and now boasts its own

flashy casino. It's located in a useful position if you want to frequent the casino in the Lisboa Hotel but don't actually want to stay there.

GUIA HOTEL Map pp430-1   Hotel
☎ 513 888; guia@macau.ctm.net;
1-5 Estrada do Engenheiro Trigo; s & d MOP$730-1080, tr MOP$930, ste from MOP$1380
If you want something smaller and a bit 'isolated' (if there is such a thing in Macau), choose this recently renovated 90-room place at the foot of Guia Hill.

HOLIDAY INN MACAU Map pp430-1   Hotel
☎ 783 333; www.macau.holiday-inn.com;
82-86 Rua de Pequim; s & d MOP$1000-1480, ste from MOP$3300
The 410-room hotel, popular with groups from the mainland and run a little bit erratically, has an excellent location and a very popular late-night bar called Oskar's Pub (p368).

Macau

SLEEPING

371

LANDMARK MACAU Map pp430-1   Hotel
☎ 781 781; www.landmarkhotel.com.mo;
555 Avenida da Amizade; s & d MOP$1780-2280,
ste from MOP$3080

This new five-star kid on the block has 451 luxurious rooms and a slew of outlets and recreational facilities. Best of all, two casinos are just a lift ride away.

LISBOA HOTEL Map pp430-1   Hotel
☎ 377 666; www.hotellisboa.com; 2-4 Avenida de Lisboa; s & d MOP$1650-3000, ste from MOP$3800

Macau's most famous and unsightly landmark has both an old (east) and a new (west or tower) wing, close to 1000 rooms and 16 restaurants. The five-star Lisboa has probably the best shopping arcade in Macau, and for many punters its casino remains the only game in town.

MANDARIN ORIENTAL Map pp430-1   Hotel
☎ 567 888; www.mandarinoriental.com;
956-1110 Avenida da Amizade; s & d MOP$2000-2600, ste from MOP$5300

This five-star, 435-room hotel has a huge swimming pool and spa, lovely gardens, three stunning restaurants and a great bar. Unfortunately the nearby Sands Macau casino has robbed it of its waterfront location.

POUSADA DE MONG HÁ Map pp430-1   Inn
☎ 515 222; www.ift.edu.mo; Colina de Mong Há;
s/d Mon-Fri MOP$500/600, Sat & Sun MOP$600/800,
ste Mon-Fri/Sat & Sun MOP$1000/1200

This traditional-style Portuguese inn (20 rooms) sits atop Mong Há Hill, near the ruins of a fort built in 1849. It is run by students at the Instituto de Formação Turística (Institute for Tourism Studies), so service is more than eager. Rates include breakfast. The restaurant here is open from 12.30pm to 3pm for lunch on weekdays, from 7pm to 10.30pm on Friday for a Macanese buffet (MOP$150) and from noon to 2.30pm for Sunday brunch (MOP$120).

RITZ HOTEL Map pp430-1   Hotel
☎ 339 955; www.ritzhotel.com.mo; 11-13 Rua do Comendador Kou Ho Neng; s & d MOP$980-1380, ste from MOP$2080

This palace of a place, in a quiet street high above Avenida da República, is as close as you'll get to staying at the legendary Bela Vista across the road. The five-star hotel has 161 rooms and a wonderful recreation centre, with a huge heated pool. Good value.

ROYAL HOTEL Map pp430-1   Hotel
☎ 552 222; www.hotelroyal.com.mo;
2-4 Estrada da Vitória; s & d MOP$750-1100,
ste from MOP$2200

This hotel is a little removed from the action (but attractive for that reason). It offers some good-value weekday packages and is next to a stunning new Tap Seac sports centre.

SUN SUN MACAU HOTEL Map p432   Hotel
☎ 939 393; www.bestwestern.com;
14-16 Praça Ponte e Horta; s & d MOP$600-880,
ste from MOP$1680

The modern, 178-room Best Western property usually offers big discounts during the week. Rooms on the upper floors have views of the Inner Harbour.

Cheap Sleeps

CENTRAL HOTEL Map p432   Hotel
☎ 373 888; fax 332 275; 264 Avenida de Almeida Ribeiro; s Sun-Thu MOP$150-188, Fri & Sat MOP$173-210, d Sun-Thu MOP$160-198, Fri & Sat MOP$210-232

The tired old Central Hotel has seen better days, but it is just what its name suggests – a short hop northwest of Largo do Senado.

EAST ASIA HOTEL Map p432   Hotel
☎ 922 433; fax 922 431; 1A Rua da Madeira;
s MOP$298-391, d MOP$408-483, tr MOP$575,
ste from MOP$780

The East Asia is housed in a classic green and white colonial-style building and, though it's been remodelled, it has not lost all of its charm. The 98 rooms are spacious and have private bathrooms.

MACAU MASTERS HOTEL Map p432   Hotel
☎ 937 572; www.mastershotel-macau.com;
162 Rua das Lorchas; s/d MOP$440/550, ste from MOP$1000

This 75-room hotel, right on the Inner Harbour, has relatively modern rooms and facilities, and bargain-basement prices.

MONDIAL HOTEL Map pp430-1   Hotel
☎ 566 866; fax 514 083; 8-10 Rua de António Basto; s & d Mon-Thu MOP$300, Fri MOP$350, Sat & Sun MOP$400

The Mondial is on the east side of peaceful Lou Lim Ioc Garden. It offers very basic accommodation, but the price is right.

SAN VA HOSPEDARIA Map p432   Guesthouse
☎ 573 701; info@sanvahotel.com; 67 Rua de
Felicidade; s & d MOP$100-150
On the 'street of happiness', once the hub
of the red-light district, the traditional-style
guesthouse has character and a homy feel,
though the rooms are like cupboards and
separated by flimsy cardboard partitions.

TAIPA & COLOANE ISLANDS

Taipa has several excellent top-end hotels,
one of which is within easy walking distance
of the village. Coloane offers quite a diver-
sity when it comes to accommodation –
from a cosy 'inn' and the territory's most
exclusive resort to two budget hostels.

Taipa Island

GRANDVIEW HOTEL Map p433   Hotel
☎ 837 788; www.grandview-hotel.com;
142 Estrada Governador Albano de Oliveira;
s & d MOP$1180-1480, ste from MOP$2380
The rather tasteful 406-room Grandview is a
short gallop northeast of the Macau Jockey
Club racetrack and close to the Nam San
nightlife area (see p367). If you don't want
to watch the nags or bend your elbow, you
can take advantage of the hotel's swimming pool, sauna and gym.

POUSADA MARINA INFANTE
Map p433   Hotel
☎ 838 333; www.pousadamarinainfante.com;
Marina da Taipa Sul; s & d MOP$880-1180, ste from
MOP$1680
This hotel with the cosy-sounding name is
actually a huge 312-room structure built on
reclaimed land south of the racetrack. The
Pousada Marina's facilities include a popular
casino; the hotel is said to possess excellent
feng shui for gamblers. The hotel is very
convenient for those crossing the nearby
Lotus Flower Bridge to or from Zhuhai.

Coloane Island
POUSADA DE COLOANE
Map p433   Inn
☎ 882 143; fax 882 251; Estrada de Cheoc Van;
s & d MOP$680-750, tr MOP$880-950
This renovated 31-room inn overlooks Cheoc
Van Beach. With a relaxed atmosphere, its
own swimming pool, and a fantastic Sunday
lunch buffet, it's an excellent choice.

WESTIN RESORT MACAU
Map p433   Hotel
☎ 871 111; www.westin.com/macau;
1918 Estrada de Hác Sá; s & d MOP$2100-2600,
ste from MOP$5500
This 'island resort' complex is on the eastern side of Hác Sá Beach. Each of the 208
rooms in this five-star place is the same size
and has a large terrace. The overall atmosphere is that of a country club, with an
attached 18-hole golf course (p369), tennis
and squash courts, two swimming pools, an
outdoor spa, sauna and fitness centre on 60
hectares of land. The resort's **Panorama Lounge**
(☎ 899 1020; ☺ 11am-1am) is a delightful
spot for a sundowner.

Cheap Sleeps

To stay at either of the following hostels, you
must book through the **Education & Youth Services Department** (☎ 555 533, 397 2640; www
.dsej.gov.mo) and have a Hostelling International card or equivalent. Prices quoted
are per person. There are separate quarters
for men and women.

POUSADA DE JUVENTUDE DE CHEOC VAN
Map p433   Hostel
☎ 882 024; Rua de António Francisco;
dm/d Sun-Fri MOP$40/70, Sat MOP$50/100
This very clean 24-bed hostel is on the eastern side of Cheoc Van Bay, below – and not
to be confused with, please – the Pousada
de Coloane (left). During the low season
(basically winter) it's pretty easy to get in
here, but during the high season (summer
and holidays) competition for beds is keen
and it might be shut altogether in August.
Dorm rooms have 10 beds. The hostel has
a garden and a small kitchen for making
hot drinks.

POUSADA DE JUVENTUDE DE HÁC SÁ Map p433   Hostel
☎ 882 701; Rua de Hác-Sá Long Chao Kok;
dm/d/q Sun-Fri MOP$40/50/70, Sat MOP$50/70/100
This circular, grey-tiled building, at the
southern end of Hác Sá Beach, is more
modern than the Cheoc Van hostel though
it is sometimes reserved for groups only. It
has 100 beds in 19 rooms; the three dorm
rooms have 16 beds each but the rest are
quads and doubles.

TRANSPORT
MACAU TO HONG KONG
Air

The vast majority of people make their way from Macau to Hong Kong by ferry, but if you're in a small group a flight by helicopter is a viable alternative and becoming increasingly popular for residents and visitors alike.

East Asia Airlines (EAA; ☎ 727 288, in Hong Kong ☎ 2108 9898; www.helihongkong .com), in conjunction with Heli Hong Kong, runs a 16-minute helicopter shuttle service between Macau and Hong Kong (HK$1700 Monday to Thursday, HK$1800 Friday to Sunday) with up to 27 daily flights leaving between 9am and 10.30pm (9.30am to 11pm from Hong Kong). Flights arrive and depart in Macau from the roof of the **ferry terminal** (Map pp430–1; ☎ 790 7240). In Hong Kong departures are from the helipad atop the ferry pier which is linked to the **Shun Tak Centre** (Map pp408–9; ☎ 2859 3359; 200 Connaught Rd Central) in Sheung Wan.

Macau levies a MOP$130 (MOP$80 for children under 13 years of age) tax on all departures by air to Hong Kong, but it is usually included in the quoted fare.

Sea

Although Macau is separated from Hong Kong by 65km of water, the journey can be made in just an hour. Sometimes queues at customs and immigration can add another 30 minutes to the journey. There are frequent departures throughout the day. The schedule is somewhat reduced between midnight and 7am, but boats run virtually 24 hours.

Two ferry companies operate services to and from Macau, one from Hong Kong Island for the most part and the other usually from Tsim Sha Tsui.

TurboJet (☎ 790 7039, in Hong Kong information ☎ 2859 3333, bookings ☎ 2921 6688; www.turbojet.com.hk) operates three types of vessels, from the ferry terminal in Macau and the Shun Tak Centre in Hong Kong, that take between 55 and 65 minutes. You don't choose the type of vessel you take; just buy your ticket and board the vessel. Economy-/super-class tickets cost HK$142/HK$244 on weekdays, HK$154/HK$260 at the weekend and on public holidays, and HK$176/HK$275 at night (ie

from 5.45pm to 6.30am). They are HK$1 less when travelling from Hong Kong to Macau. Children under 12 and seniors over 60 pay HK$15 less.

New World First Ferry (NWFF; ☎ 727 676, in Hong Kong ☎ 2131 8181; www.nwff.com.hk) operates high-speed catamarans from the Macau ferry terminal bound for the **China ferry terminal** (Map pp420–1; Canton Rd, Tsim Sha Tsui) in Hong Kong 25 times a day on weekdays, with departures on the half-hour from 7am and 8.30pm. On Saturday and Sunday there are 33 daily departures, with the last leaving Macau at 12.30am. On weekdays they depart Tsim Sha Tsui every 30 minutes from 7am to 7pm, with additional sailings at 8pm and 9pm. At the weekend they go every half-hour from 7am to midnight. The trip takes between 65 and 75 minutes and tickets cost HK$140/HK$175 Monday to Friday during the day/night (night fares are from 6pm in both directions), and HK$155/HK$175 at weekends and on public holidays. Deluxe class costs HK$245/HK$275 during the day/night on weekdays, and HK$260/HK$275 at the weekend and on public holidays.

Tickets can be booked up to 28 days in advance and are available at the ferry terminals, all China Travel Service (CTS) branches and many travel agencies. There is a standby queue before each sailing for passengers wanting to travel before their ticketed sailing. On weekends and public holidays book your return ticket in advance as boats are often full. You need to arrive at the pier at least 15 minutes before departure, but you should allow 30 minutes because of occasional long queues at the immigration checkpoint, especially on the Hong Kong side.

Luggage space is limited; some boats have small overhead lockers while others have storage space at the bow and stern. You are limited to 10kg of carry-on luggage in economy class, but oversized or overweight bags can be taken on as checked luggage.

There's a departure tax of MOP$20 on anyone leaving Macau by sea, though it's normally included in the price of the ticket.

MACAU TO CHINA

Nationals of Australia, Canada, European Union, New Zealand, USA and most other countries will be able to purchase their visas at the border with Zhuhai, but it will ultimately save you time and some effort if you buy one in advance. These are available in Hong Kong (p306) or in Macau from **China Travel Service** (Map pp430–1; ☎ 700 888; 10th fl, Xin Hua Bldg, 35 Rua de Nagasaki; ⏰ 9am-5pm) for MOP$150 (plus photos), usually in one day.

Air

Air Macau (NX; Map pp430–1; ☎ 396 5555; www.airmacau.com.mo; Ground fl, Nam Ngan Garden Bldg, 398 Alameda Doutor Carlos d'Assumpção) and/or several carriers of the **China National Aviation Corporation** (CNAC; Map p432; ☎ 788 034; fax 788 036; 5th fl, Iat Teng Hou Bldg, Avenida de Dom João IV) group link **Macau International Airport** (Map p433; ☎ 861 111; www.macau-airport .gov.mo) with around 15 destinations in mainland China, with at least five flights a week to Beijing, Fuzhou, Guilin, Hangzhou, Kunming, Shanghai, Shenzhen, Xiamen and Xian. The departure tax for adults is MOP$80 and for children aged two to 12 MOP$50.

East Asia Airlines (EAA; ☎ 727 288, in Hong Kong ☎ 2108 9898; www.helihongkong .com) has a helicopter shuttle linking Macau with Shenzhen five times a day from 9.15am to 7.45pm (9.45am to 8.30pm from Shenzhen) for HK$1600 Monday to Thursday and HK$1700 Friday to Sunday. The trip takes 25 minutes.

Land

Macau is an easy gateway by land into China. Simply take bus 3, 5 or 9 to the **Portas do Cerco** (Border Gate; Off Map pp430–1; ⏰ 7am-midnight) and walk across. A second – and much less busy crossing – is the **Cotai Frontier Post** (⏰ 9am-8pm) on the causeway linking Taipa and Coloane, which allows visitors to cross over the Lotus Flower Bridge by shuttle bus (MOP$4) to the Zhuhai Special Economic Zone. Buses 15, 21 and 26 will drop you off at the crossing.

If you want to travel further afield in China, buses run by the **Kee Kwan Motor Road Co** (Map p432; ☎ 933 888) leave the bus station on Rua das Lorchas, 100m southwest of the end of Avenida de Almeida Ribeiro. Buses for Guangzhou (MOP$55, 2½ hours) depart about every 15 minutes and for Zhongshan (MOP$15, one hour) every 20 minutes between 8am and 6.30pm or so. There are many buses to Guangzhou (MOP$75) and

Dongguan (MOP$80) from Macau International Airport.

Sea

A daily ferry run by the **Yuet Tung Shipping Co** (☎ 574 478) connects Macau with the port of Shekou in the Shenzhen Special Economic Zone. The boat departs from Macau at 10am, 2pm and 6.30pm and takes 1½ hours; they return from Shekou at 8.15am, 11.45am and 4.45pm. Tickets (adult/child MOP$114/MOP$67) can be bought up to three days in advance from the point of departure, which is **pier 14** (Map p432) in the Inner Harbour, just off Rua das Lorchas and 100m southwest of the end of Avenida de Almeida Ribeiro. A departure tax of MOP$20 applies.

Sampans and ferries also leave from the same pier for Wanzai (MOP$12.50) across the Inner Harbour on the mainland. Departures are hourly between 8am and 4pm, returning a half-hour later.

CAR & MOTORCYCLE

The streets of peninsular Macau are a gridlock of cars and mopeds that will cut you off at every turn. While driving here may look like it could be fun, it's strictly for the locals. That said, a Moke (a brightly coloured Jeeplike convertible) can be a convenient way to explore the islands, as can a motorbike.

Hire

Happy Rent A Car (☎ 726 868; fax 726 888), in room 1025 of the ferry terminal arrivals hall, has four-person Mokes available for hire for MOP$300 a day; hiring from 9am to 5.30pm costs just MOP$250. Mokes seating six from **Avis Rent A Car** (Map pp430–1; ☎ 336 789; www.avis.com.mo; Room 1022, Ground fl, Macau ferry terminal; ⏰ 8am-7pm), which also has an office at the Mandarin Oriental hotel car park, cost MOP$500/MOP$600 on weekdays/weekends. Avis also hires out cheap Suzuki Vitaras for MOP$550 a day during the week and MOP$700 at the weekend.

New Spot Tourism Bike Rental (Map pp430–1; ☎ 750 880; www.yp.com.mo/newspotbike; Ground fl, Zhu Kuan Bldg, Rua de Londres; ⏰ 10am-10pm) in NAPE hires out motorbikes for MOP$250 a day, including petrol, helmet and insurance.

PUBLIC TRANSPORT

Public buses and minibuses run by TCM (☎ 850 060) and Transmac (☎ 271 122) operate on 40 routes from 6.45am till shortly after midnight. Fares – MOP$2.50 on the peninsula, MOP$3.30 to Taipa Village, MOP$4 to Coloane Village, MOP$5 to Hác Sá Beach – are dropped into a box upon entry; there's no change given.

The *Macau Tourist Map* (opposite) has a full list of both bus companies' routes. The two most useful buses on the peninsula are Nos 3 and 3A, which run between the ferry terminal and the city centre, near the post office. No 3 continues up to the border crossing with the mainland, as does No 5, which can be boarded along Avenida Almeida Ribeiro. Bus 12 runs from the ferry terminal, past the Lisboa Hotel and then up to the Lou Lim Ioc Garden and Kun Iam Temple.

The best buses to Taipa and Coloane are Nos 21, 21A, 25 and 26A. Bus 22 goes to Taipa, terminating at the Macau Jockey Club.

TAXI

Flag fall is MOP$10 for the first 1.5km and MOP$1 for each additional 200m. There is a MOP$5 surcharge to go to Coloane; travelling between Taipa and Coloane is MOP$2 extra. Journeys starting from the airport incur an extra charge of MOP$5. A taxi from the airport to the centre of town should cost about MOP$40. Large bags cost an extra MOP$3. Taxis can be dispatched by radio by ringing ☎ 519 519 or ☎ 939 939.

DIRECTORY

Much of the advice given for Hong Kong applies to Macau as well. If you find any sections missing here, refer to the ones in the Hong Kong Directory chapter (p308).

BOOKS

A Macao Narrative, by the late Hong Kong–based writer Austin Coates, is a slim but comprehensive history of the territory up until the mid-1970s. *Macau*, by César Guillén-Nuñez, is rather dry but can be read in one sitting. Novels set in Macau are rare but Austin Coates' *City of Broken Promises*, a fictionalised account 18th-century Macanese trader Martha Merop (p345) is a classic. *Lights and Shadows of a Macao Life: the Journal of Harriett Low, Travelling Spinster*, by

Harriett Low Hillard, is an American woman's account of Macau from 1829 to 1834. If you want to learn more about Macau's distinctive hybrid cuisine, try Annabel Jackson's *Taste of Macau: Portuguese Cuisine on the China Coast*. For short stories, you won't do better than *Visions of China: Stories from Macau*, edited by David Brookshaw, which includes works by four writers with strong Macau connections, including Henrique de Senna Fernandes (p335).

BUSINESS HOURS

Most government offices are open from 9am to 1pm and 2.30pm to 5.30pm or 5.45pm on weekdays. Banks normally open from 9am to 5pm weekdays and to 1pm on Saturday.

CLIMATE

Macau's climate is similar to Hong Kong's (p309), with one major difference: there is a delightfully cool sea breeze on warm summer evenings along the waterfront.

CUSTOMS

Customs formalities are virtually nonexistent here, but Hong Kong only allows you to import small amounts of duty-free tobacco and alcohol (see p311).

DISCOUNT CARDS

The Macau Museums Pass, a card allowing you entry to half a dozen museums (Grand Prix Museum, the Macau Wine Museum, the Maritime Museum, Lin Zexu Memorial Hall in Lin Fung Temple, the Macau Museum of Art and the Macau Museum) over a five-day period, is available for MOP$25/12 for adults/concessions, from the MGTO or any participating museum.

EMERGENCY

In the event of any emergency, phone the central SOS number (☎ 999) for the fire services, police or an ambulance. The Tourist Assistance Hotline is open from 9am to 6pm. Important numbers:

Ambulance (☎ 577 199)

Consumer Council (☎ 988 9315)

Fire service (☎ 572 222)

Police (☎ 573 333)

Tourist Assistance Hotline (☎ 340 390)

HOLIDAYS

In Macau half-days are allowed on the day before the start of Chinese New Year and on the day of New Year's Eve. For holidays celebrated in both Hong Kong and Macau, see p314. The following are public holidays in Macau only.

All Souls' Day 2 November

Feast of the Immaculate Conception 8 December

Macau SAR Establishment Day 20 December

Winter Solstice 22 December

INTERNET ACCESS

In NAPE, you can check email at the **Unesco Internet Café** (Map pp430–1; ☎ 727 066; Alameda Doutor Carlos d'Assumpção; per 30/60 min MOP$5/10; ☺ noon-8pm Wed-Mon), opposite the Landmark Macau, and for free in the library of the **Macau Museum of Art** (Map pp430–1; ☎ 791 9814, 791 9801; ☺ 2-7pm Tue-Fri, 11am-7pm Sat & Sun).

LEFT LUGGAGE

There are electronic lockers on both the arrivals and departure levels of the Macau ferry terminal. They cost MOP$20 or MOP$25, depending on the size, for the first two hours and MOP$25/30 for each additional 12-hour period. There is also a left-luggage office on the departures level that's open from 6.45am to midnight daily. It charges MOP$10 for the first six hours and another MOP$10 till midnight. Each additional day costs MOP$10.

MAPS

The MGTO distributes the excellent (and free) *Macau Tourist Map*, with major tourist sights and streets labelled in English, Portuguese and Chinese characters, small inset maps of Taipa and Coloane, and bus routes marked.

MEDICAL SERVICES

Macau's two hospitals both have 24-hour emergency services.

Conde São Januário Central Hospital (Map pp430–1; ☎ 313 731; Estrada do Visconde de São Januário) Southwest of the Guia Fort.

Kiang Wu Hospital (Map pp430–1; ☎ 371 333; Rua de Coelho do Amaral) Northeast of the ruins of the Church of St Paul.

MONEY

Macau's currency is the pataca (MOP$), which is divided up into 100 avos. Bills are issued in denominations of MOP$10, MOP$20, MOP$50, MOP$100, MOP$500 and MOP$1000. There are little copper coins worth 10, 20 and 50 avos and silver-coloured MOP$1, MOP$2, MOP$5 and MOP$10 coins.

The pataca is pegged to the Hong Kong dollar at the rate of MOP$103.20 to HK$100. As a result, exchange rates for the pataca are virtually the same as for the Hong Kong dollar, which is accepted everywhere in Macau. Usually when you spend Hong Kong dollars in big hotels, restaurants and department stores your change will be returned in that currency. Try to use up all your patacas before leaving Macau.

Most ATMs, which are everywhere but concentrated around the Lisboa Hotel, allow you to choose between patacas and Hong Kong dollars, and credit cards are readily accepted at Macau's hotels, larger restaurants and casinos. You can also change cash and travellers cheques at the banks lining Avenida da Praia Grande and Avenida de Almeida Ribeiro, as well as at major hotels.

POST

Correios de Macau, Macau's postal system, is efficient and inexpensive.

The **main post office** (Map p432; ☎ 323 666; 126 Avenida de Almeida Ribeiro; ☺ 9am-6pm Mon-Fri, 9am-1pm Sat) faces Largo do Senado; pick up poste restante from counter No 1 or 2. There are other post offices in peninsular Macau, including a **Macau ferry terminal branch** (Map pp430–1; ☎ 396 8526; ☺ 10am-7pm Mon-Sat), and some on the islands.

Domestic letters cost MOP$1/MOP$1.50 for up to 20g/50g while those to Hong Kong are MOP$1.50/MOP$3. For international mail, Macau divides the world into zones: zone 1 (MOP$3.50/MOP$4.50 for up to 10g/20g) is east and Southeast Asia; zone 2 (MOP$4.50/MOP$6) is everywhere else except for the mainland (MOP$2/MOP$3) and Portugal (MOP$3/MOP$4.50).

EMS Speedpost (☎ 596 688) is available at the main post office. Other companies that can arrange express forwarding are **DHL** (☎ 372 828), **Federal Express** (☎ 703 333) and **UPS** (☎ 751 616).

TELEPHONE

Macau's telephone service provider is **Companhia de Telecomunicações de Macau** (CTM; inquiry hotline ☎ 1000; www.ctm.net).

Local calls are free from private telephones, while at a public payphone they cost MOP$1 for five minutes. Most hotels will charge you at least MOP$3. All payphones permit International Direct Dialling (IDD) using a phonecard available from CTM for between MOP$50, MOP$100 and MOP$200. Rates are cheaper from 9pm to 8am during the week and all day Saturday and Sunday.

The international access code for every country *except* Hong Kong is ☎ 00. If you want to phone Hong Kong, dial ☎ 01 first, then the number you want; you do not need to dial Hong Kong's country code (☎ 852). To call Macau from abroad – including Hong Kong – the country code is ☎ 853.

Convenient CTM branches in Macau include the following:

CTM branch (Map p432; 22 Rua do Doutor Pedro José Lobo; ☒ 10.30am-7.30pm) South of Avenida da Praia Grande.

CTM main office (Map pp430–1; 25 Rua Pedro Coutinho; ☒ 10.30am-7.30pm) Two blocks northeast of the Lou Lim Ioc Garden.

Useful Numbers

The following is a list of some important telephone numbers. For numbers to call at more difficult times, see p376.

International directory assistance (☎ 101)

Local directory assistance (☎ 181)

Macau ferry terminal (☎ 790 7240)

New World First Ferry (☎ 726 301)

Time in English (☎ 140)

TurboJet (☎ 790 7039)

TOURIST INFORMATION

The **Macau Government Tourist Office** (MGTO; ☎ 315 566, hotline ☎ 333 000; www.macau tourism.gov.mo) is a well-organised and helpful source of information. It has a half-dozen outlets scattered around town, including ones in the **Largo do Senado** (Map p432; ☎ 397 1120; ☒ 9am-6pm), at the **Guia Lighthouse** (Map pp430–1; ☎ 569 808; ☒ 9am-1pm & 2.15-5.30pm), at the **ruins of the Church of St Paul** (Map pp430–1; ☎ 358 444; ☒ 9.15am-1pm & 2.30-6pm), and in the **Macau ferry terminal** (Map pp430–1; ☎ 726 416; ☒ 9am-10pm), which dispense information and a large selection of free literature, including pamphlets on everything from Chinese temples and Catholic churches to fortresses, gardens and walks. The MGTO also runs a **tourist assistance unit** (☎ 340 390; ☒ 9am-6pm) to help travellers who may have run into trouble.

MGTO's **Hong Kong branch** (Map pp408–9; ☎ 2857 2287; Room 336-337 Shun Tak Centre, 200 Connaught Rd Central, Sheung Wan; ☒ 9am-1pm & 2.15-5.30pm) is in the building above where the ferries depart and arrive.

VISAS

Most travellers, including citizens of the European Union (EU), Australia, New Zealand, the USA, Canada and South Africa, can enter Macau with just their passports for between 30 and 90 days.

Travellers who do require them can get visas valid for 30 days on arrival in Macau. They cost MOP$100/MOP$50/MOP$200 for adults/children under 12/families.

You can get a single one-month extension from the Macau **Immigration Department** (Map pp430–1; ☎ 725 488; Ground fl, Travessa da Amizade; ☒ 9am-12.30pm & 2.30-5pm Mon-Fri).

WEBSITES

Useful Macau websites:

Cityguide (www.cityguide.gov.mo) Strong practical information such as transport.

Government Statistics Department (www.dsec.gov.mo) All the data you need (or don't) need on Macau.

Macau Cultural Institute (www.icm.gov.mo) Macau's cultural offerings month by month.

Macau Government Information (www.macau.gov.mo) The No 1 source for non-tourism information about Macau.

Macau Government Tourist Office (www.macautourism .gov.mo) The best source of information for visiting Macau.

Macau Yellow Pages (www.yp.com.mo) Telephone directory – with maps.

Pronunciation   380
Vowels & Vowel Combinations 380
Consonants 380
Tones 380

Social   381
Meeting People 381
Going Out 381
Local Lingo 381

Practical   381
Accommodation 381
Banking 382
Days 382
Food & Drink 382
Internet 382
Numbers 382
Phones & Mobile Phones 382
Post 383
Shopping 383
Transport 383

Emergencies   384

Health   384
Symptoms 384

Glossary   385

Language

Language

It's true – anyone can speak another language. Don't worry if you haven't studied languages before or that you studied a language at school for years and can't remember any of it. It doesn't even matter if you failed English grammar. After all, that's never affected your ability to speak English! And this is the key to picking up a language in another country. You just need to start speaking.

Learn a few key phrases before you go. Write them on pieces of paper and stick them on the fridge, by the bed or even on the computer – anywhere that you'll see them often.

You'll find that locals appreciate travellers trying their language, no matter how muddled you may think you sound. So don't just stand there, say something! If you want to learn more Cantonese than we've included here, pick up a copy of Lonely Planet's comprehensive but user-friendly *Cantonese Phrasebook*.

PRONUNCIATION

Cantonese sounds aren't that different to English ones, although there are some unique vowel combinations. The biggest challenge for English speakers is the tonal system, but with a bit of practice you'll find Cantonese quite easy to pronounce.

Vowels & Vowel Combinations

a	as the 'u' in 'but'
eu	as the 'er' in 'fern'
ew	as in 'blew' (short with tightened lips)
i	as the 'ee' in 'deep'
o	as in 'go'
u	as in 'put'
ai	as in 'aisle' (short sound)
au	as the 'ou' in 'out'
ay	as in 'pay'
eui	as in French *feuille* (eu with i)
iu	as the 'yu' in 'yuletide'
oy	as in 'boy'
ui	as in French *oui*

Consonants

In Cantonese, the ng sound can appear at the start of the word. Practise by saying 'sing along' slowly and then do away with the 'si' at the beginning.

Note that words ending with the consonant sounds p, t, and k must be clipped in Cantonese. This happens in English as well – say 'pit' and 'tip' and listen to how much shorter the p sound is in 'tip'.

Many Cantonese speakers, particularly young people, replace an n sound with an l if it begins the word – náy (you), is often heard as láy. Where relevant, this change is reflected in the words and phrases in this language guide.

Tones

The use of tones in Cantonese can be quite tricky for an English speaker. The 'tone' is the pitch value of a syllable when you pronounce it. The same word, pronounced with different tones can have a very different meaning, eg gwat means 'dig up' and gwàt means 'bones'.

In our simplified pronunciation guide there are six tones: high, high rising, level, low falling, low rising and low. They can be divided into two groups: high and low pitch. High pitch tones involve tightening your vocal muscles to get a higher note, whereas lower pitch tones are made by relaxing the vocal chords to get a lower note. These tones are represented as accents and diacritics as shown in the list below; the low tones are all underlined in the Romanisations. Tones in Cantonese fall on vowels (a, e, i, o, u) and on n.

à	high
á	high rising
a	level
à̠	low falling
á̠	low rising
a̠	low

SOCIAL
Meeting People

Hello.
láy·hó 你好。

How are you?
láy gáy hó à maa 你幾好啊嗎？

Fine, and you?
gáy hó láy lè 幾好，你呢？

Good morning.
jó·sàn 早晨。

Goodbye/Bye.
joy·gin/bàai·baai 再見/拜拜。

What's your name?
láy giu màt·yé méng aa 你叫乜嘢名？

My name is …
ngáw giu … 我叫…

Please …
ǹg·gòy … 唔該…

Thank you.
ǹg·gòy 唔該。 (for a service)
dàw·je 多謝。 (for a gift)

You're welcome.
ǹg·sái haak·hay 唔駛客氣。

Yes.
hai 係。

No.
ǹg·hai 不係。

Excuse me. (to get attention)
deui·ǹg·jew 對唔住。

Excuse me. (to get past)
ǹg·gòy je·je 唔該借借。

I'm sorry.
deui·ǹg·jew 對唔住。

Do you speak (English)?
láy sìk·ǹg·sìk gáwng 你識唔識講
　(yìng·mán) aa 　(英文)啊？

Do you understand?
láy mìng·ǹg·mìng aa 你明唔明啊？

Yes, I do understand.
mìng·baak 明白。

No, I don't understand.
ngáw ǹg mìng 我唔明。

Could you please …?
ǹg·gòy láy … 唔該你…？
　repeat that
　joy gáwng yàt chi 再講一次
　write it down
　sé lawk lài 寫落嚟

Going Out

What's on …?
… yáu màt·yé wut·dung
…有乜嘢活動？

locally
lày·do fu·gan 呢度附近

this weekend
lày·gaw jàu·mut 呢個週末

today
gàm·yat 今日

tonight
gàm·máan 今晚

I feel like going to (a/the) …
ngáw séung heui …
我想去…

Where can I find …?
bìn·do yáu …
邊度有…？
　clubs
　ye·júng·wuí 夜總會
　gay venues
　tung·ji·bàa 同志吧
　places to eat
　sik·faan ge day·fawng 食飯嘅地方
　pubs
　jáu·bàa 酒吧

Is there a local entertainment guide?
yáu mó bún·day yèw·lawk jí·làam
有冇本地娛樂指南？

Local Lingo

Beautiful!	jeng aa	靚啊！
Excellent!	mó·dàk·díng	冇得頂！
Great!	mó·dàk·díng	冇得頂！
It's OK.	ò·kày	OK。
Maybe.	háw·làng	可能。
No way!	mó·dàk·kìng	無得傾！
No problem.	mó·man·tài	無問題。

PRACTICAL
Accommodation

Where's a …?
bìn·do yáu … 邊度有…？
　guesthouse
　bàn·gún 賓館
　hotel
　jáu·dim 酒店
　hostel
　jiù·doy·sáw 招待所

Do you have a … room?
yáu·mó … fáwng
有冇…房？
　double
　sèung·yàn (to) 雙人
　single
　dàan·yàn 單人

How much is it per …?
yàt … gáy·dàw chín
…幾多錢？
night
máan 晚
person
gaw yàn 個人

Banking
Where can I …?
ngáw hái bìn·do háw·yí …
我喺邊度可以…？
I'd like to …
ngáw yiu …
我要…
cash a cheque
deui yàt jèung jì·piu 兌一張支票
change money
wun chín 換錢

Where's the nearest …?
jeui kán ge … hái bìn·do
最近嘅…喺邊度？
automatic teller machine (ATM)
ji·dung tài·fún·gày
自動提款機
foreign exchange office
wun ngoy·bai ge day·fàwng
換外幣嘅地方

Days
Monday	sìng·kày·yàt	星期一
Tuesday	sìng·kày·yi	星期二
Wednesday	sìng·kày·sàam	星期三
Thursday	sìng·kày·say	星期四
Friday	sìng·kày·ńg	星期五
Saturday	sìng·kày·luk	星期六
Sunday	sìng·kày·yat	星期日

Food & Drink
See the Food chapter (p33) for information on food and dining out in Hong Kong, including loads more Cantonese words and phrases.

Internet
Where's the local Internet café?
fu·gan yáu·mó máwng·bàa
附近有冇網吧？

I'd like to …
ngáw séung …
我想…
check my email
tái háa ngáw ge din·jí yàu·sèung
睇下我嘅電子信箱

get Internet access
séung·máwng
上網

Numbers
0	lìng	零
1	yàt	一
2	yi	二
3	sàam	三
4	say	四
5	ńg	五
6	luk	六
7	chàt	七
8	baat	八
9	gáu	九
10	sap	十
11	sap·yàt	十一
12	sap·yi	十二
13	sap·sàam	十三
14	sap·say	十四
15	sap·ńg	十五
16	sap·luk	十六
17	sap·chàt	十七
18	sap·baat	十八
19	sap·gáu	十九
20	yi·sap	二十
21	yi·sap·yàt	二十一
22	yi·sap·yi	二十二
30	sàam·sap	三十
40	say·sap	四十
50	ńg·sap	五十
60	luk·sap	六十
70	chàt·sap	七十
80	baat·sap	八十
90	gáu·sap	九十
100	yàt·baak	一百
200	léung·baak	兩百
1,000	yàt·chìn	一千
10,000	yàt·maan	一萬

Phones & Mobile Phones
I want to …
ngáw séung …
我想…
buy a phonecard
máai jèung din·wáa·kàat
買張電話卡
call (Singapore)
dáa din·wáa heui (sàn·gaa·bàw)
打電話去(新加坡)

Where's the nearest public phone?
lày·do fu·gan yáu·mó gùng·jung din·wáa aa
呢度附近有冇公眾電話呀？

I'd like a …
ngáw séung máai gaw …
我想買個…
  charger for my phone
  sáu·gày chùng·dìn·hay
  手機充電器
  mobile/cell phone for hire
  chèut·jò sáu·gày
  出租手機
  prepaid mobile/cell phone
  yew·fu sáu·gày
  預付手機
  SIM card for your network
  láy·day máwng·làwk yung ge sím·kàat
  你地網絡用嘅SIM卡

Post

Where is the post office?	
yàu·gúk hái·bìn·do	郵局喺邊度？

I want to send a …
ngáw séung …
我想…
  parcel
  gay bàau·gwáw   寄包裹
  postcard
  gay ming·seun·pín   寄明信片

I want to buy a/an …
ngáw séung máai …
我想買…
  aerogram
  gaw hàwng·hùng   個航空
    yàu·gáan   郵柬
  envelope
  gaw seun·fùng   個信封
  stamp
  jèung yàu·piu   張郵票

Shopping

I'd like to buy …	
ngáw séung máai …	我想買…
I'm just looking.	
tái haa	睇下。
How much is it?	
gáy·dàw chín	幾多錢？

Can I pay by credit card?
háw·ǹg·háw·yí yung seun·yung·kàat máai·
dàan aa
可唔可以用信用卡埋單呀？

less	siú dì	少啲
more	dàw dì	多啲
bigger	gang daai	更大
smaller	sai dì	細啲

Transport

Where's …?	
… hái bìn·do	
…喺邊度？	
the airport	
gày·chèung	機場
bus stop	
bàa·sí·jaam	巴士站
China Ferry terminal	
jùng·gawk haak·wan	中國客運
máa·tàu	碼頭
subway station	
day·tit·jaam	地鐵站

Is this the … to (…)?
lày bàan … hai·ǹg·hai heui (…) gaa
呢班…係唔係去(…)㗎？
Which … goes to (…)?
heui (…) cháw bìn·bàan …
去(…)坐邊班…？
  bus
  bàa·sí   巴士
  ferry
  do·lèun   渡輪
  train
  fáw·chè   火車
  tram
  dìn·chè   電車

What time does it leave?
gáy·dím jùng chèut·faa
幾點鐘出發？
How much is a (soft-seat) fare to …?
heui … ge (yéwn·jaw fày) gáy·dàw chín
去…嘅(軟座飛)幾多錢？
I'd like to get off at (Panyu).
ngáw yiu hái (pùn·yèw) lawk·chè
我要喺(番禺)落車。
Please stop here. (taxi, minibus, etc)
ǹg·gòy lawk·chè
唔該落車。

Where is …?	
… hái·bìn·do	…喺邊度？
How far is it?	
yáu gáy yéwn	有幾遠？

By …	
… heui	…去。
bus	
cháw·chè	坐車
foot	
hàang·lo	行路
train	
cháw dai·tit	坐地鐵

USEFUL PORTUGUESE

A few words in Portuguese will come in handy when travelling in Macau. Portuguese is still common on signs (along with Cantonese script) and where opening and closing times are written.

Monday	*segunda-feira*
Tuesday	*terça-feira*
Wednesday	*quarta-feira*
Thursday	*quinta-feira*
Friday	*sexta-feira*
Saturday	*sábado*
Sunday	*domingo*

1	*um/uma*
2	*dois/duas*
3	*três*
4	*quatro*
5	*cinco*
6	*seis*
7	*sete*
8	*oito*
9	*nove*

10	*dez*
20	*vint*
21	*vint e um*
22	*vint e dois*
30	*trinta*
40	*quarenta*
50	*cinquenta*
60	*sessenta*
70	*setenta*
80	*oitenta*
90	*noventa*
100	*cem*
1000	*mil*

Entrance	*Entrada*
Exit	*Saída*
Open	*Aberto*
Closed	*Encerrado*
No Smoking	*Não Fumadores*
Prohibited	*Proíbido*
Toilets	*Lavabos/WC*
Men	*Homens (H)*
Women	*Senhoras (S)*

Can you show me (on the map)?
láy háw·n̄g·háw·yí (hái day·to do) jí báy ngáw tái ngáw hái bìn·do
你可唔可以(喺地圖度)指俾我睇我喺邊度？

EMERGENCIES

Help!
gau·meng 救命！
Could you please help?
n̄g·gòy bàwng bàwng màwng 唔該幫幫忙?
Call the police!
faai·dì giu gíng·chaat 快啲叫警察！
Call a doctor!
faai·dì giu yì·sàng 快啲叫醫生！
Call an ambulance!
faai·dì giu gau·sèung·chè 快啲叫救傷車！

HEALTH

Where's the nearest …?
jeui kán ge … hái bìn·do
最近嘅…喺邊度？
  dentist
  ngàa·yì 牙醫
  doctor
  yì·sàng 醫生
  hospital
  yì·yéwn 醫院

(night) pharmacist
(jau·ye) yeuk·fàwng （晝夜）藥房

I'm sick.
ngáw beng·jáw
我病咗。
I need a doctor (who speaks English).
ngáw yiu tái (sìk gáwng yìng·mán ge) yì·sàng
我要睇(識講英文嘅)醫生。

Symptoms

I have (a/an) …
ngáw yáu …
  我有…
  asthma
  hàau·chéwn 哮喘
  diarrhoea
  tó·ngàw 肚瀉
  fever
  faat·siù 發燒
  headache
  tàu·tung 頭痛
  sore throat
  hàu·lùng·tung 喉嚨疼

It hurts here.
làybo tung
呢度痛。

GLOSSARY

Refer to the Food chapter (p45) for a detailed glossary of items that you are likely to encounter on menus.

amah – literally 'mummy'; a servant, traditionally a woman, who cleans houses, sometimes cooks and looks after the children

arhats – Buddhist disciple freed from the cycle of birth and death

Bodhisattva – Buddhist striving toward enlightenment

chàu – Cantonese for 'island'

cheongsam – a fashionable, tight-fitting Chinese dress with a slit up the side (*qípáo* in Mandarin)

chìm – bamboo sticks shaken out of a cylindrical box usually at temples, and used to divine the future

chop – see *name chop*

daai-pàai-dawng – open-air eating stalls, especially popular at night, but fast disappearing in Hong Kong

dim sum – literally 'touch the heart'; a Cantonese meal of various titbits eaten as breakfast, brunch or lunch and offered from wheeled steam carts in restaurants; see also *yum cha*

dragon boat – long, narrow skiff in the shape of a dragon, used in races during the Dragon Boat Festival

feng shui – Mandarin spelling for the Cantonese *fung sui* meaning 'wind water'; the Chinese art of geomancy that manipulates or judges the environment to produce good fortune

gàwn-buì – literally 'dry glass'; 'cheers' or 'bottoms up'

godown – a warehouse, originally on or near the waterfront, but now anywhere

gùng-fù – Chinese for 'kung fu'

gwái-ló – literally 'ghost person'; a derogatory word for 'foreigner', especially a Caucasian Westerner, but now used jocularly

gwái-páw – female equivalent of *gwái-ló*

Hakka – a Chinese ethnic group who speak a different Chinese language from the Cantonese; some Hakka people still lead traditional lives as farmers in the New Territories

háwng – major trading house or company, often used to refer to Hong Kong's original trading houses, such as Jardine Matheson and Swire

hell money – fake-currency money burned as an offering to the spirits of the departed

HKTB – Hong Kong Tourism Board

Hoklo – boat dwellers who originated in the coastal regions of present-day Fujian province

II – illegal immigrant

joss – luck or fortune

joss sticks – incense

junk – originally Chinese fishing boats or war vessels with square sails; diesel-powered, wooden pleasure yachts that can be seen on Victoria Harbour

kaido – small to medium-sized ferry that makes short runs on the open sea, usually used for non-scheduled services between small islands and fishing villages; sometimes spelled *kaito*

KCR – Kowloon-Canton Railway

KMB – Kowloon Motor Bus Company

kung fu – the basis of many Asian martial arts

LRT – Light Rail Transit, former name for the KCR's Light Rail system

màai-dàan – bill (in a restaurant)

mahjong – popular Chinese game played among four persons using tiles engraved with Chinese characters

makee learnee – Anglo-Chinese pidgin for 'apprentice' or 'trainee'; rarely heard in Hong Kong today

name chop – carved seal; the stamp it produces when dipped into red ink paste often serves as a signature

nullah – uniquely Hong Kong word referring to a gutter or drain and occasionally used in place names

PLA – People's Liberation Army

PRC – People's Republic of China

Punti – the first Cantonese-speaking settlers in Hong Kong

sampan – motorised launch that can only accommodate a few people and is too small to go on the open sea; mainly used for inter-harbour transport

SAR – Special Administrative Region of China; both Hong Kong and Macau are now SARs

SARS – Severe Acute Respiratory Syndrome

SEZ – Special Economic Zone of China that allows more unbridled capitalism but not political autonomy; both Shenzhen and Zhuhai have SEZ status

shroff – Anglo-Indian word meaning 'cashier'

sitting-out area – Uniquely Hong Kong word meaning open space reserved for passive or active recreation

snakehead – a smuggler of *IIs*

t'ai chi – slow-motion shadow boxing and form of exercise; also spelled *tai chi*

tai tai – any married woman but especially the leisured wife of a businessman

taijiquan – Mandarin for *t'ai chi*; usually shortened to *taiji*

taipan – 'big boss' of a large company

Tanka – Chinese ethnic group that traditionally lives on boats

Triad – Chinese secret society originally founded as patriotic associations to protect Chinese culture from the influence of usurping Manchus, but today Hong Kong's equivalent of the Mafia

wàan – bay

walla walla – motorised launch used as a water taxi and capable of short runs on the open sea

wet market – local word for an outdoor market selling fruit, vegetables, fish and meat

yum cha – literally 'drink tea'; common Cantonese term for *dim sum*

Behind the Scenes

THE LONELY PLANET STORY

The story begins with a classic travel adventure: Tony and Maureen Wheeler's 1972 journey across Europe and Asia to Australia. There was no useful information about the overland trail then, so Tony and Maureen published the first Lonely Planet guidebook to meet a growing need.

From a kitchen table, Lonely Planet has grown to become the largest independent travel publisher in the world, with offices in Melbourne (Australia), Oakland (USA) and London (UK). Today Lonely Planet guidebooks cover the globe. There is an ever-growing list of books and information in a variety of media. Some things haven't changed. The main aim is still to make it possible for adventurous travellers to get out there – to explore and better understand the world.

At Lonely Planet we believe travellers can make a positive contribution to the countries they visit – if they respect their host communities and spend their money wisely. Every year 5% of company profit is donated to charities around the world.

THIS BOOK

This 12th edition was written by Steve Fallon. He wrote the 10th and 11th editions, too. This edition was commissioned in Lonely Planet's Melbourne office and produced by:

Commissioning Editor Rebecca Chau

Coordinating Editor Katie Lynch

Coordinating Cartographer Sarah Sloane

Coordinating Layout Designer Indra Kilfoyle

Managing Cartographer Corie Waddell

Assisting Editors Helen Christinis, Kate Whitfield

Proofreader Kate Majic

Cover Designer Pepi Bluck

Managing Editor Suzannah Shwer

Project Managers Rachel Imeson, Brigitte Ellemor

Language Content Coordinator Quentin Frayne

Thanks to Chiu-yee Cheung, David Connolly, Sally Darmody, Mark Germanchis, Rebecca Lalor, Stephanie Pearson, Lushan Charles Qin, Gabbi Wilson, Celia Wood

Cover photographs by Lonely Planet Images: Exchange Square, Central, Hong Kong Island, Dallas Stribley (top); Chinese opera star, Rick Browne, Photolibrary (bottom); burning incense sticks, Ray Laskowitz (back).

Internal photographs by Lonely Planet Images and Greg Elms except for the following: p351 (#4) Jon Davison; p351 (#3), p352 (#1, #3) Richard I'Anson; p351 (#2), p352 (#4), p353 (#1, 3, 4) Oliver Strewe; p277 Keren Su; p351 (#1), p352 (# 2) Michael Taylor; p353 (#2) Lawrence Worcester.

THANKS
STEVE FALLON

People who helped in the research of this book – on topics as diverse as Hong Kong politics, economy, transport, fashion, nightlife and art – included Diane Stormont, Rob Stewart of Bloomberg, Rocky Dang of Phoenix Services Agency, Patrick Chan of the Hong Kong Trade Development Council, Keir Blauuw of Get Smart, Ben Yuen and Ian Findlay-Brown of *Asian Art News*. Once again Miko Ismail was a lifesaver at the 11th hour. *M goi sai* to each and every one of you.

Thanks, too, to the inimitable Teresa Costa Gomes of the Macau Government Tourist Office for help and hospitality beyond the call of duty and to Brent Deverman of Shenzhen Party for showing me what's where after dark in the Shenzhen SEZ.

Margaret Leung and her team at Get Smart – Kaushikee 'Pia' Ghose, Keir Blauuw, Ethel del Fierro and James Lee – were, once again, extremely helpful, hospitable and excellent lunching and dining companions.

As always I'd like to dedicate my efforts to my partner, Michael Rothschild, who doesn't allow a day to slip by without giving our 'hometown' a passing thought.

OUR READERS

Many thanks to the travellers who used the last edition and wrote to us with helpful hints, useful advice and interesting anecdotes. Your names follow:

John Aitken, Raymond Ang, Steve Bailey, Jonathan Bromberg, Heather Bronson, Matt Bryce, Edward Channon, Laura Chant, J F Cheung, Nigel Clements, Emili Cowan, Trung Dung Nguyen, Peter Dwyer, Angela Faerber, Catherine Fan, Liliane Foederer, Carolin Gaven, Nicole Ghiotto, Stephen Gibbons, Kimberly Gibson, Joao Girao, Sawdra Griffin, Moritz Herrmann, Matthias Hess, Peter Hilton, Jonas Holl Epstein, Sara Jarman, Anja Johnson, Daniel Johnson, Jimmy Johnson, Marc P Jones, Ashley Kaar, Lisa Kaar, Lau Ka-kin, Ian Kershaw, Jorge Lascar, Gerry Leblanc, Clara Leigh-Wong, Luke Lethborg, Chris Lim, Chu Ling Lui, Stephen Maidment, Erika Malitzky, Miquel Martin, Melvin McClanahan, David Mccoy, Rowena Mccoy, F Mclean, Monica Mengoli, M Michaels, Kjell Mittag, Alejandro Moreno, Antoinette Nania, Ranjit Narula, Christoph Neumann, Angela Newnham, Alex Nikolic, Bonnie Nolen, Cindy Norum, Julien Pagliaroli, Jenny Palmer, Rick Peltz, Jens Quist, Nick Racanelli, Yvette Rogers, David Rosner, Evelyn Saal, Rick Scavetta, Suzanne Shum, Ellwyn Smith, Patrick Sperano, Nizza Stein, Yaron Stein, Jennifer Stephens, Tong-Khee Tan, Dianne Thomas, Debora & Laura Tydecks, Toshiko Ueda, Lilian Vyth, Shabnam Walji, Will Webster, Joanne Wen, Jonas Wernli, Lyndon Whaite, Andrew Whitby, Ann Yukha Wong, Heather Worthington, Linda Wotherspoon, Phil Wotherspoon, Allan York.

ACKNOWLEDGMENTS

Many thanks to the following for the use of their content: MTR system map © 2005 MTR Corporation.

Notes

Index

See also separate indexes for Eating (p397), Entertainment (p399), Shopping (p400) and Sleeping (p401).

10, 000 Buddhas Monastery 118

A
Aberdeen 87-9, **411**, **65**, **349**
food 175-6
Aberdeen Boat Club 225
Aberdeen Marina Club 225
Academy for the Performing Arts 78
accommodation 250-74, 308, see also Sleeping index 401, individual neighbourhoods
guesthouses 251
hiking 219
hostels 251
hotels 250-1
renting 252
reservations 250
activities 216-26, see also individual activities
information 217
venues 217
addresses 308
Admiralty 77-80, **408-10**
accommodation 254-6
bars & pubs 202-3
food 164-9
shopping 240-2
Afternoon Beach 128
air travel 288-91
air fares 288
airline offices 288
airport 289
helicopter 66
to/from airport 289-91
to/from China 304, 374-5
to/from Hong Kong 374
to/from Macau 374-5
Alliance Française 311
Altinho de Ká Hó Trail 370
Alto de Coloane 359
A-Ma 338
A-Ma Cultural Village 359
A-Ma Festival 329
A-Ma Statue 359
A-Ma Temple 355, **351**
Amah Rock 118-19
amahs 73

ambulance 312, 317, 376
animals 21, 126
antiques 230, 239, 370
Ap Lei Chau 88
Apliu Street Market 96
architecture 24-5, 335
books 25
colonial 24-5
contemporary 25, **25**
preservation 87
traditional Chinese 24-5
area codes, see inside front cover
arts 24-32, 334-5
Association for Democracy and People's Livelihood 19
ATMs 318, 377
Avenida da República 355
Avenue of the Stars 93, **106**, **349**
avian flu 50
aviary 79, 91

B
baby-sitting organisations 309
baccarat 332
Balanced Rock 123
Bank of China (BOC) building 69, 335
Bank of China Tower 69, **100**
bargaining 229
bars & pubs 199-207, see also Entertainment index 399, individual neighbourhoods
Basic Law 19-20, 50-1, 59
bathrooms 323
Bauhinia blakeana 21
beaches
Afternoon Beach 128
Cheoc Van Beach 359
Cheung Sha 134
Cheung Sha Wan 123
Clearwater Bay First Beach 123
Clearwater Bay Second Beach 123
Hác Sá Beach 360, **360**
Hung Shing Yeh Beach 125

Lo So Shing Beach 126
Nam Tam Wan 128
Pak Tso Wan 128
Silvermine Bay Beach 132
Silverstrand Beach 123
Tai Long Wan 131
Tung O Wan 126-7
Tung Wan Beach 127, 136
Biblia pauperum 346
bicycle travel, see cycling
Big Taipa Trail 370
Big Wave Bay 85
bird watching 217
birds 21, 221
Birthday of Lord Buddha 11, 329
Birthday of Tin Hau 11
Bishop's House 72
Bishop's Palace 356
blackjack 332
boat travel, see ferry travel
booking 150, 199, 250
books 376, see also literature
architecture 25
culture 9, 32, 145
Filipino amahs 73
hiking guides 221
history 62
natural history 221
Triads, the 94
bookshops 248
boule 332
Bowen Road Sports Ground 224
bowling 217-18
Bowring, Sir John 70
brand names 284
Bride's Pool 116
British Council 311
British rule
ceding of Hong Kong 55
colonialisation 54-62
handover 50, 58-62
Bronze Age habitations 52
Buddhism 13, 330
bus travel
night buses 297
schedules & routes 297
to/from China 304
within Hong Kong 296-7

business 308
business hours 308, 376, see also inside front cover
eating 150
shopping 228
Butterfly Hill Watchtower 132

C
California Fitness 225
Camões Grotto 357
Canidrome 331-2
canoeing 222, see also kayaking
Cantonese 18, 380-5
Cantonese Opera Heritage Hall 119
Cantopop 29-30, 210
car travel 297-8, 375
driving licence 297-8
permits 297-8
rental 298, 375
road rules 298
Casa Garden 356
Casa Real Casino 331
Casino Kingsway 331
casinos 331
Cat Street 74, **103**
Cat Street Galleries 74
Cattle Depot Artists Village 28
Causeway Bay 80-2, **414-416**
accommodation 256-9
bars & pubs 203-4
food 169-73, **150**
shopping 242-3
Causeway Bay Typhoon Shelter 81
cell phones 322
Cemetery of St Michael the Archangel 343, **352**
Cenotaph 73
Central 68-73, **408-10**, **20**, **105**, **347**
accommodation 253-4
bars & pubs 200-1
food 151-8, **2**, **347**
shopping 233-9
walking tour 141, **141**

Central District Police Station 69
central escalator 140
Central Library 81, 316
Central Market 72
Central Plaza 25, 78
Chai Wan 84
Chan, Jackie 26, 107
Chao Shao-an 27
Chao Shao-an Gallery 119
Chapel of Our Lady of Guia 356-7
Chapel of Our Lady of Penha 356
Chapel of St Francis Xavier 359, **352**
Chapel of St Joseph Seminary 335, 343
Chapel of St Michael 343
Chater Garden 71
Che Kung Temple 119
Chek Keng 121
Chek Lap Kok-up 50
chemists 318
Cheng, Barney 16
Cheoc Van Beach 359
cheongsam 17, **16**
Cheung Chau 127-9, **428**
    accommodation 272
    bars & pubs 206
    food 192-3
    walking tour 147-8, **148**
Cheung Chau Bun Festival 11, 128
Cheung Chau Typhoon Shelter 128
Cheung Chau Village 128-9
Cheung Chau Windsurfing Water Sports Centre 222, 224
Cheung Kong Garden 70
Cheung Po Tsai Cave 129
Cheung Sha 134
Cheung Sha Wan 123
Cheung Yeung 12
Chi Heng Foundation 313
Chi Lin Nunnery 98, 107
Chi Ma Wan 130-1
Chi Ma Wan Correctional Institution 131
children, travel with 124, 308-9
Children's Discovery Gallery 119

chìm 98
China Folk Culture Village 279, 280
China Gas lamps 72, **99**
China, relationship with 59
China Travel Services offices 306
Chinese Communist Party 60
Chinese Cuisine Training Institute 310
Chinese Garden 91
Chinese New Year 10, 11
Chinese opera 31, 214
Chinese Reading Room 343
Chinese Revolution 57
Chinese University of Hong Kong 117, 310, 323
Chinese University of Hong Kong Art Museum 117-18
Ching Chung Temple 111
Chinnery, George 334
Chopsticks Cooking Centre 310
Chuk Lam Sim Monastery 109
Chung On St 108
Church of St Augustine 343
Church of St Dominic 335, 343
Church of St Lawrence 343-4
Church of St Paul 345, **352**
Cia Ch'ing, Emperor 54-5
cinema 25-7
    Hong Kong Film Archive 83-4
    Hong Kong International Film Festival 10
cinemas 213-14, see also Entertainment index 399
City Hall Public Library 316
City University of Hong Kong 97
Clearwater Bay Country Park 124
Clearwater Bay Country Park Visitor Centre 124
Clearwater Bay First Beach 123
Clearwater Bay Golf & Country Club 218
Clearwater Bay Peninsula 123-5
Clearwater Bay Second Beach 123

climate 309, 376
climbing 218
clothing sizes 231
clubs 207-10, 368, see also Entertainment index 399
Coates, Austin 31-2
cohong 54, 339
Coloane Island 359-60, **433-4**
    accommodation 373
    food 366-7
Coloane Kartodrome 369, **369**
Coloane Trail 370
Coloane Village 359-60
colonial architecture 24-5
comedy 214
Chinese Communist Party 58-9
congee 40
consulates 310
Contemporary Hong Kong Art Gallery 90
costs 6, 18-19
    discount cards 303, 311-12
    food 150
    shopping 229
courses 310-11
    cooking 310
    cultural 310
    language 310-11
    visual arts 310
Court of Final Appeal 69
Coward, Noel 81
credit cards 318-19
cricket 216
Cross-Harbour Tunnel 58
Cuiheng 284
cuisines, see also food
    asian 43
    Cantonese 35
    Chiu Chow 41-2
    international 43
    Macanese 335-7
    Northern Chinese 42
    Portuguese 335-7
    Shanghainese 42
    Sichuanese 42-4
    vegetarian 43
cultural centres 311
Cultural Club 344
culture 12-18, 330-3
    books 9, 32, 145
    food 34-5
    traditional customs 14

customs regulations 311, 376
Cybernetic Fountains 344
cycling 218, 291, 369

D

daai-sai 332
Dairy Farm Building 72
Deep Bay 112
Deep Water Bay 87
Deep Water Bay Golf Club 218
Democratic Party 19
Deng Xiaoping 59
dengue fever 313
departure tax 289, 306
Diamond Casino 331
Diamond Hill 98, 107
dim sum 36-7, 176, **353**
disabled travellers 311
discount cards 376
Discovery Bay 131
    food 194-5
Discovery Bay Golf Club 219
Discovery Bay Plaza 131
Discovery Bay Tunnel 131
Disneyland 131
DK Aromatherapy 226
Dr Sun Yat Sen Residence Memorial Museum 284, 285
dog racing 331-2
Dog's Tooth Peak 134
Dom Pedro V Theatre 335, 344
Donghu Park 277
Dongmen Market 279, 280
Dragon Boat Festival 11, 329-30
Dragon Centre 96
Dragonfly 222
Dragonfly Pond 120-1
Dragon's Back 85
drinks 44-5
driving, see car travel
Duan Zong 53
Duk Ling junk 66, **350**

E

East India Company 54
Eastern Han dynasty 52
eating, see Eating index 397, food
economy 8, 18-19, 58, 333-4
education 15
Edward Youde Aviary 79, **79**

000 map pages
000 photographs

electricity 312
Elliot, Captain Charles 55
embassies 310
emergency services 312, 376, *see also inside front cover*
English language 18
entertainment 198-214, *see also* Entertainment index 399
environmental issues 8, 20-2, 126
environmental hazards 314
Essential Chinese Language Centre 311
etiquette 6, 13
food 15, 35-7
exchange rates, *see inside front cover*
Exchange Square 69, **100**

F
fàan-tàan 332
Fan Lau 131
Fan Lau Fort 131
Fanling 114
Far East Finance Centre 78
fashion 16-17, *see also* Shopping index 400
World Boutique Hong Kong Fair 10
fast food 151
Feast of the Drunken Dragon 329
feng shui 14
ferry travel 291-6, **2**
to/from China 305-6
to/from Hong Kong Island 291-2
to/from Macau 374-5
to/from New Territories 292
to/from Outlying Islands 292-6
Festival Walk Glacier 224, **224**
Festival Walk Shopping Centre 97
festivals
A-Ma Festival 329
Birthday of the Lord Buddha 11, 329
Birthday of Tin Hau 11
Cheung Chau Bun Festival 11, 128
Chinese New Year 10, 11
Ching Ming 10

Dragon Boat Festival 11, 329-30
Feast of the Drunken Dragon 329
Hong Kong Arts Festival 10
Hong Kong Artwalk 10
Hong Kong City Fringe Festival 10
Hong Kong International Arts Carnival 11
Hong Kong International Film Festival 10
Hong Kong Youth Arts Festival 12
Hungry Ghosts Festival 11
Macau Arts Festival 329
Macau International Fireworks Display Contest 330
Macau International Music Festival 330
Macau Lotus Flower Festival 330
Maidens' Festival 11
Man Hong Kong International Literary Festival 10
Mid-Autumn Festival 12
Procession of Our Lady of Fatima 329
Procession of the Passion of Our Lord 329
Spring Lantern Festival 10
Fightin' Fit 222
Filipino people 73
film & camera equipment 320
films, *see* cinema
Finger Hill 136
fire services 312, 376
Fire Services Museum 356
First Opium War 55
fishing 218
fitness 225-6
Fitness Circuit Walk 370
fitness clubs 225
FIVB Women's Volleyball Grand Prix 330
Flagstaff House Museum of Tea Ware 80
Flora Garden 357
Flower Market 95-6, **103**

food 6, 34-48, 150-96, 335-7, **347**, *see also* cuisines, Eating index 397, *individual neighbourhoods*
booking tables 150
business hours 150
Cantonese cuisine 35
dim sum 36-7, 176, **353**
etiquette 15, 35-7
fast food 151
fruit 38
history 34-5
menu decoder 45-8
regional variations 41-3
self-catering 151
snacks 36
specialities 37-41
staples 37-41
tipping 150
football 216
Foreign Correspondents' Club of Hong Kong 72
Former French Mission Building 69-70
Former KCR Clock Tower 89-90
Forsgate Conservatory 80
forts
Fan Lau Fort 131
Guia Fort 356-7
Monte Fort 345, **351**
Tung Chung Fort 135
Tung Lung Fort 138
Fortuna Casino 331
fortune telling 14
Foster, Sir Norman 25
Four Lanes Square 115
Four-Faced Buddha Shrine 358
Frontier Party 19
Fung Ping Pavilion 136
Fung Ying Sin Temple 114

G
Galaxy Casino 331, **333**
galleries
Cattle Depot Artists Village 28
Chao Shao-an Gallery 119
Chinese University of Hong Kong Art Museum 117-18
Contemporary Hong Kong Art Gallery 90
Grotto Fine Art 28

Hanart TZ Gallery 28
Historical Pictures Gallery 90
Hong Kong Artwalk 10
Hong Kong Museum of Art 90
Hong Kong Planning & Infrastructure Exhibition Gallery 70
Hong Kong Visual Arts Centre 80
IACM Gallery 344
John Batten Gallery 28
KS Lo Gallery 80
Macau Museum of Art 355
Pao Sui Loong & Pao Yue Kong Galleries 79
Para/Site Artspace 28
Plum Blossoms 28
Schoeni Art Gallery 28
Shanghai Street Artspace 28
Sin Sin Fine Art 28
Tap Seac Galleries 335
TT Tsui Gallery of Chinese Art 119
University Museum & Art Gallery 75
gambling 331-2
gay travellers 312-13
gay venues 208
gems 232
Gen Gen 279, 280
geography 20-1
giardia 313
godowns 80
gods & goddesses 12, **102**
Goethe-Institut 311
go-karting 369, **369**
Golden Bauhinia 78-80, **61**
Golden Dragon Casino 331
Golden Mile, the 91
golf 218-19, 369
Gongbei 282
Gongbei Port 282
Good Wish Gardens 98
government 8, 19-20, 334
Government House 70, 335, 344
Graham St Market 72, **39**, **103**, **348**
Grand Prix 333
Grand Prix Museum 346
Greek Mythology Casino 331
green minibuses 299

green turtles 126
Grotto Fine Art 28
Guia Cable Car 357
Guia Fort 356–7
Guia Lighthouse 357
gyms 225

H

Hác Sá Beach 360, **360**
Hác Sá Reservoir Circuit 370
Hác Sá Sports & Recreation
  Park 370
Haibin Park 283, 285
Han Chinese people 52
Hanart TZ Gallery 28
handover 50, 58–62, 341
Handover of Macau Gifts
  Museum 355
Happy Foot Reflexology
  Centre 226
happy hour 199
Happy Valley 82–3
  food 173
Happy Valley Racecourse 83
Happy Valley Sports
  Ground 216
Hau people 52
Hau Wong Temple 135
háwng 56, 80
Healing Plants 226
health 313–14
  local issues 8
  traditional medicine 15
  vaccinations 314
  websites 314
Hebe Haven 120–1
Hebe Haven Yacht Club 225
Hepatitis 313
Herboland 125
High Island Reservoir 122
High Junk Peak 124
High Junk Peak Country
  Trail 124
High Level Tramway 57, *see
  also* Peak Tram
hiking 17, 219–22, 370
  accommodation 219
  Altinho de Ká Hó Trail
    370
  Big Taipa Trail 370
  books 221
  Coloane Trail 370
  Dog's Tooth Peak 134
  Fitness Circuit Walk 370

---
000 map pages
000 photographs

Hác Sá Reservoir Circuit
  370
High Junk Peak Country
  Trail 124
Lantau Trail 220, **131**
Little Taipa Trail 370
MacLehose Trail 220–1
Northeast Coloane Trail
  370
Pak Tam Chung Nature
  Trail 121
Pat Sin Leng Nature
  Trail 116
Tai Po Kau Nature
  Reserve 117
tours 219–20
Tung Ping Chau 123
Walk of 33 Curves 370
Historical Pictures Gallery 90
history 8–10, 50–62, 337–41
  books 62
  food 34–5
HMS *Tamar* 72
Hoi Ha 121
Hoi Ha Wan Marine Park 121
holidays 314, 377
  Birthday of Lord Buddha
    11
  Cheung Yeung 12
  Chinese New Year 10, 11
  Ching Ming 10
Hollywood Road 73
Home Management Centre
  310
Hong Kong Arts Centre 79
Hong Kong Arts Festival 10
Hong Kong Artwalk 10
Hong Kong Baptist
  University 97
Hong Kong Chinese Martial
  Arts Association 222
Hong Kong City Fringe
  Festival 10
Hong Kong City Hall 70
Hong Kong Club Building 73
Hong Kong Coliseum
  92, 212
Hong Kong Convention &
  Exhibition Centre 25, 79
Hong Kong Correctional
  Services Museum 86
Hong Kong Cricket Club 216
Hong Kong Cultural Centre
  90, 212, **100**
Hong Kong Design Centre
  79, **99**
Hong Kong Disneyland 131

Hong Kong Film Archive
  83–4
Hong Kong Golf Club
  218
Hong Kong Heritage
  Museum 119
Hong Kong Identity Card
  314–15
Hong Kong Institute of
  Languages 311
Hong Kong International
  Arts Carnival 11
Hong Kong International
  Film Festival 10
Hong Kong Island 68–88,
  406–7
  accommodation 253–9
  bars & pubs 200–4
  food 151–76
  shopping 233–43
  walking tour 140–2,
    141, **142**
Hong Kong Jockey Club
  216–17
Hong Kong Jockey Club
  Giant Panda Habitat 88
Hong Kong Marathon 10
Hong Kong Monetary
  Authority Information
  Centre 72
Hong Kong Museum of Art
  90
Hong Kong Museum of
  Coastal Defence 84
Hong Kong Museum of
  History 92–3, **30**
Hong Kong Museum of
  Medical Sciences 76
Hong Kong Museums Pass
  311
Hong Kong Observatory
  90, 309
Hong Kong Park 79–80
Hong Kong Planning &
  Infrastructure Exhibition
  Gallery 70
Hong Kong Players 30
Hong Kong Polytechnic
  University 92, 323
Hong Kong Racing Museum
  83
Hong Kong Railway Museum
  115
Hong Kong Repertory
  Theatre 30
Hong Kong Rugby World
  Cup Sevens 10

Hong Kong Science Museum
  93
Hong Kong Space Museum
  & Theatre 90–1
Hong Kong Special
  Administrative Region
  (SAR) **404–5**
Hong Kong Squash Centre
  224
Hong Kong Stadium 217
Hong Kong Tai Chi
  Association 222
Hong Kong Tennis Centre
  224
Hong Kong Tourism Board
  323
Hong Kong Toy Story 119
Hong Kong Trail 220
Hong Kong University
  75, 323
Hong Kong University of
  Science & Technology
  323
Hong Kong Visual Arts
  Centre 80
Hong Kong Wetland Park
  111
Hong Kong Wushu Union
  222
Hong Kong Youth Arts
  Festival 12
Hong Kong Youth Hostels
  Association 311–12
Hong Kong Zoological &
  Botanical Gardens 70
Hong Kung Temple 344
Hongkong & Shanghai
  Bank building 25, 70–1
Hopewell Centre 80
Horizons 313
horse racing 216–17, 331
horse riding 222
hostel card 311–12
hostels 251
hostess clubs 210
hotels 250–1, *see also*
  Sleeping index 401
Hung Hing Ying 75
Hung Hom 92–3, **420–2**
  accommodation 266–7
Hung Shing shrine 88
Hung Shing Temple 80, 113,
  102
Hung Shing Yeh Beach 125
  food 191
Hung, William 30
Hungry Ghosts Festival 11

I

IACM Gallery 344
Ice House Street 72
ice skating 224
imperial China 53
Imperial Hot Springs 284, 285
influenza 313
International Finance Centre 72
Internet access 315, 377
Internet resources 324-5, 378
Island East 83-4
  bars & pubs 204
  food 173-4
Island South 84-8
  bars & pubs 204
  food 174-6
i.t group 16
itineraries 66
  Macau 330

J

Jade Market 94, **143**
Jai Alai Casino 331
Jamia Mosque 75
Jardine House 71, **100**
jewellery 232
Jian Fu Mei Health & Beauty Centre 279, 280
Jiang Zemin, Premier 62
Jida 282
Jiuzhou Harbour 282
Jockey Club Kau Sai Chau Public Golf Course 122, 218
John Batten Gallery 28

K

Kadoorie Farm & Botanic Garden 110
kaidos 122, 296
Kam Pek Casino 331
Kam Tin 113-14
kamikaze caves 126
Kat Hing Wai 52, 113
Kau Sai Chau 122
kayaking 134, 222
Kerfoot Hughes, William 76
King Hu 26
King's Park Tennis Courts 224
Kiu Tsui Chau 122
Kowloon 88-107, **418-19**, **99**
  accommodation 259-69
  bars & pubs 204-5

food 176-86
  shopping 243-8
  walking tour 143-5, **144**
Kowloon-Canton Railway 57, 301
Kowloon City 97-8
Kowloon Cricket Club 216
Kowloon Mosque & Islamic Centre 91
Kowloon Park 91, **106**
Kowloon Park Sports Centre 224
Kowloon Tong 97
Kowloon Walled City Park 97-8, **350**
KS Lo Gallery 80
Kun Iam Statue 355
Kun Iam Temple 357, 360
kung fu 223
Kwan Tai temple 135, **102**
Kwan Yu 12
Kwun Yam 12
Kwun Yam temple 74, 86, 128
Kyrie, Phineas 76

L

Lam Tsuen Wishing Tree 115-16
Lamma 125-7, **426**
  accommodation 271-2
  food 190-2
Lan Kwai Fong 71, 198, **412-13**, **71**, **198**
land-reclamation projects 341
language 18, 330, 380-5
  Cantonese 18, 380-5
  courses 310-11
  glossary 385
  Mandarin 18
  menu decoder 45-8
  Portuguese 384
Lantau 129-35, **427**
  accommodation 272-4
  bars & pubs 206-7
  food 193-5
Lantau Link Bridges 136, **137**
Lantau Link Visitors Centre 137
Lantau Peak 129, 132
Lantau Tea Garden 133
Lantau Trail 220, **131**
Largo do Senado 361, **328**, **351**
laundry 315

Law Uk Folk Museum 84
Leal Senado 335, 344
Lee, Bruce 27
Lee Lai-shan 128
left luggage 315-16, 377
legal matters 312, 316
Legend Club 331
Legislative Council Building 71
Lei Cheng Uk Han Tomb Museum 96-7, **53**
Lei Yue Mun 107
lesbian travellers 312-13
lesbian venues 208
Leung Shuen Wan 122
Li Yuen Street East 16, 71, **16**
Li Yuen Street West 71
libraries 316
Light Rail 301-2
Lin Fung Temple 357
Lin Zexu 55
Lingnan School of Painting 27
lion dance 31
Lion Rock Country Park 118
Lions Nature Education Centre 120-1
Lisboa Casino 331, **354**
Litchi Park 277
literature 31-2, 335, *see also* books
Little Taipa Trail 370
Liu people 52
Lo Hon Monastery 132
Lo So Shing Beach 126
Long Coast Seasports 134, 224
Longevity Bridge 87
Lost City 284, 285
Lotus Flower Bridge 341
Lou Lim Ioc Garden 357, **352**
Lou Lim Ioc Garden Pavilion 357
Lover's Rock 76-7
Lower Albert Road 72
Lower Cheung Sha 134
Luís de Camões Garden 357
Luk Tei Tong Watchtower 132
Lung Tsai Ng Garden 132
Lung Yeuk Tau Heritage Trail 146-7, **147**

M

Ma On Shan Country Park 120
Ma, Walter 16

Ma Wan 136
Macau 6, 328-78, **351**, **354**
  accommodation 371-3
  arts 334-5
  attractions 341-60
  bars & pubs 367-8
  economy 333-4
  food 335-7, 362-7
  history 337-41, **339**
  tours 342-3
  travel to/from 374-5
  travel within 375-6
Macau Arts Festival 329
Macau Cathedral 344
Macau Cultural Centre 355
Macau Dome 333
Macau Fisherman's Wharf 346
Macau Formula 3 Grand Prix 330
Macau International Fireworks Display Contest 330
Macau International Marathon 330
Macau International Music Festival 330
Macau Jockey Club 331
Macau Jockey Club Casino 331
Macau Lotus Flower Festival 330
Macau Museum 344-5, **345**
Macau Museum of Art 355
Macau Open Golf Tournament 329
Macau Palace Casino 331
Macau Peninsula 343-58, **430-1**, **432**
  accommodation 371-3
  food 362-5
  walking tour 361-2, **361**
Macau people 334
Macau Security Forces Museum 343
Macau Stadium 333
Macau Tower 335, 355-6
Macau Wine Museum 346
MacLehose Trail 220-1
Madame Tussaud's 77
magazines 17, 319-20
Mai Po Marsh 112-13
Mai Po Nature Reserve 112-13
Maidens' Festival 11
Main Building 75
Mak, Antonio 29

Man Cheung 12
Man Hong Kong International Literary Festival 10
Man Mo temple 74, 116, 132, **101**
Man people 52
Man Wa Lane 74
Mandarin Oriental Casino 331
Mang Bing Massage Centre 279
maps 316-17, 377
Marina Casino 331
Maritime Museum 356
markets 246
    Apliu Street Market 96
    Central Market 72
    Dongmen Market 279, 280
    Fanling 114
    Flower Market 95-6, **103**
    Graham St Market 72, **39**, **103**, **348**
    Jade Market 94, **143**
    Sheung Shui 114
    Stanley Market 86
    Tai Po Market 116
    Temple Street night market 94-5, **103**
    Tung Choi St market 95, **101**
    Wan Chai Market 80
    Western Market 75
martial arts 222-3
Mass Transit Railway 58, 299, **417**
Mau Ping Shan 123
measures 325
medical services 317-18, 377
menu decoder 45-8
metric conversions, see inside front cover
micro malls 232
Mid-Autumn Festival 12
Mid-Levels, the 75-6
    accommodation 253-4
    food 161-3
Ming dynasty 53, 339
minibuses 298-9
Minsk World 278, 280
Miu Fat Monastery 111

000 map pages
000 photographs

Mo Shan Country Park Visitor Centre 110
Mo Tat Wan 126
    food 192
mobile phones 322
Modern Literature & Art Association 28
money 318-19, 377, see also costs
    budget sightseeing 67
    discount cards 311-12
Mong Fu Shek 118
Mong Kok 95-6, **423**
    accommodation 267-9
    food 184-5, **348**
    shopping 247-8
    walking tour 143-5, **144**
Mong Kok Stadium 216
Monte Fort 345, **351**
Morrison Hill Public Swimming Pool 225
motorcycle travel 297-8, 375
Mui Wo 132, **429**
    food 193-4
Murray House 86
museum passes 311
museums
    Fire Services Museum 356
    Flagstaff House Museum of Tea Ware 80
    Grand Prix Museum 346
    Handover of Macau Gifts Museum 355
    Hong Kong Correctional Services Museum 86
    Hong Kong Heritage Museum 119
    Hong Kong Museum of Coastal Defence 86
    Hong Kong Museum of History 92-3, **30**
    Hong Kong Museum of Medical Sciences 76
    Hong Kong Racing Museum 83
    Hong Kong Railway Museum 115
    Hong Kong Science Museum 93
    Hong Kong Space Museum & Theatre 90-1
    Law Uk Folk Museum 84
    Lei Cheng Uk Han Tomb Museum 96-7, **53**
    Macau Museum 344-5, **345**

Macau Security Forces Museum 343
Macau Wine Museum 346
Maritime Museum 356
Museum of Ethnology 117
Museum of Sacred Art & Crypt 345
Museum of the Holy House of Mercy 345
Pawnshop Museum 345
Police Museum 77
Sam Tung Uk Museum 109
Sheung Yiu Folk Museum 121
Taipa House Museum 335, 359
University Museum & Art Gallery 75
music 29-30, 210-13

N
Nam Tam Wan 128
Nanking Street 93
NAPE 346, 355
Nathan Road 91
National People's Congress 50, 59
Natural Excursion Ideals 222
Neolithic period 52
New Kowloon 96-108
    food 185-6
    shopping 248
New Territories 108-24
    accommodation 269-71
    bars & pubs 205-6
    food 186-90
    walking tours 145-7, **146**, **147**
New Territories Heritage Hall 119
New Town Plaza 118
New Yuan Ming Palace 283-4, 285
newspapers 17, 319-20
Ng Tung Chai Waterfall 110
Ngong Ping 132-3
    food 195
Ngong Ping 360 133
Ngong Ping Village 133
Ning Po Street 93
Noonday Gun 81, **82**
North Point 83
    accommodation 259
Northeast Coloane Trail 370
numerology 14

O
Ocean Park 88, **349**
Ocean Park cable car 88
Ocean Terminal 92
Octopus card 303
OGC Golf City 219
Ohel Leah Synagogue 76
Old Protestant Cemetery 357
Old Stanley Police Station 86
Old Wan Chai Post Office 80
Omega Hong Kong Open Golf Championships 12
One International Finance Centre 72
opium 54-5
Orientation Theatre 119
Outlying Islands 124-38
    accommodation 271-4
    bars & pubs 206-7
    food 190-6
Ox Warehouse 335

P
pàai-gáu 332
Pak Sha Chau 122
Pak Tai Temple 129
Pak Tam Chung 121
Pak Tam Chung Nature Trail 121
Pak Tso Wan 128
pandas 88
Pang people 52
Pao Sui Loong & Pao Yue Kong Galleries 79
Para/Site Artspace 28
Paradise Hill 283
Paradise Hill Cable Car 283, 285
Paradise Park 283, 285
passport 320
Pat Sin Leng Nature Trail 116
Patten, Chris 61
Pawnshop Museum 345
Peak Galleria 77
Peak, the 76-7
    food 163-4
Peak Tower 77, **350**
Peak Tram 57, 76, 302-3, **2**
Peng Chau 135-6, **429**
    bars & pubs 207
    food 195-6
Penha Hill 356
Peninsula Hong Kong 92, **91**
People's Liberation Army 62, 340
Pharaoh's Palace Casino 331
pharmacies 318

philosophy 13
photography 320
Ping Kong 114
Ping Shan Heritage Trail 145, **146**
places of worship 320
Plover Cove 116-17
Plover Cove Country Park 123
Plover Cove Country Park Visitor Centre 116
Plover Cove Reservoir 117
Plum Blossoms 28
Po Lam Monastery 132
Po Lin 132-3
Po Toi 138
  food 196
police 312, 376
Police Museum 77
politics 19-20, 334
pollution 21-2
population 6, 12-13, 334
Portuguese colonialisation 6, 337-41
Portuguese culture 330
Portuguese traders 54, 337-8
Possession Street 74
postal services 320-1, 377
Pou Tai Temple 358
Procession of Our Lady of Fatima 329
Procession of the Passion of Our Lord 329
public holidays, *see* holidays
public transport 376
pubs, *see* bars & pubs
Pui O Beach 134, **273, 349**
Punti People 52-3
Pure Fitness 225

Q

Q Yoga 226
Qin dynasty 52
Qing dynasty 53, 57
Quarry Bay 83
Queen Elizabeth Stadium 224
Queer Sisters 313

R

radio 321
red minibuses 298
refugees 57, 339
refunds 321
religion 13, 330
renting 252-3

Repulse Bay 86-7
  food 175
Repulse Bay, the 87, **99**
restaurants, *see* food, Eating index 397
Revolutionary Martyrs' Memorial 283, 285
rickshaws 303
Ripley's Believe It or Not Odditorium 77
rock carvings 124, 127, 129, 134, 138
roulette 332
Royal Hong Kong Yacht Club 81, 225
rugby 217
Rugby World Cup Sevens 217
Ruins of the Church of St Paul 345-6, **352**
running 223, **349**

S

safety 14
Sai Kung Country Park Visitor Centre 121
Sai Kung Ho Chung Driving Range 219
Sai Kung Peninsula 120-1
  accommodation 271
Sai Kung Town 120-1, **425**
  bars & pubs 205-6
  food 188-90, **194**
Sai Wan Ho 83-4
Saigon Street 94
sailing 225
St Francis Barracks 343
St Francis Garden 343
St Stephen's Beach 86
St Stephen's Beach Water Sports Centre 222, 224
Salisbury Gardens 29, 90
Sam Ka Tsuen Typhoon Shelter 107
Sam Tung Uk Museum 109
sampans 296, **121**
  tours 88
Sands Macau 331
Sanxiang 284
SAR Government Headquarters 72
sauces 40
scams 229
Schoeni Art Gallery 28
School of Professional & Continuing Education 310
scuba diving 223
Sculpture Walk 91

Seac Pai Van Park 360
Second Convention of Peking 56
Second Opium War 56
Senate Library 344
seniors card 312
Severe Acute Respiratory Syndrome 51
Sha Tin 118-19, **425**
  accommodation 270-1
  food 188
Sha Tin Racecourse 83, 119
Sham Shui Po 96-7
Sham Shui Po Police Station 96
Sham Wan 126
Shanghai Street 94, **105, 140**
Shanghai Street Artspace 28
Shau Kei Wan 84
Shek O 85
  food 174
Shek O Beach 85
Shek O Golf & Country Club 85, 219
Shek Pik Prison 134
Shek Pik Reservoir 134
Shen Zong, Emperor 132
Shenzhen 6, 277-81, **278, 277**
  accommodation 281
  attractions 280
  food 281
  Internet access 279
  tourist informaton 279
  tours 279
  travel to/from 282
Shenzhen Art Gallery 277, 280
Shenzhen Museum 277, 280
Shenzhen Sea World 278, 280
Sheung Shui 114
Sheung Wan 73-5, **408-10**
  bars & pubs 201
  food 161-3
  shopping 240
  walking tour 142-3, **142**
Sheung Yiu Folk Museum 121
Shing Mun Country Park Visitor Centre 221
shopping 5, 228-48, 370-1, *see also* Shopping index 400, *individual neighbourhoods*
  antiques 230, 239, 370

bargaining 229
books 248
business hours 228
carpets 230-1
clothing 231, 371
computers 231
curios 245, 370
electronic goods 232, **228**
jewellery 232
leather goods 233
luggage 233
markets 246
micro malls 232
photographic equipment 233
refunds 230
scams 229
stamps 371
warranties 230
watches 233, **104**
shopping centres
  Beverley Commercial Centre 232
  Island Beverley 232
  New Town Plaza 118
  Rise Commercial Centre 232
  Times Square shopping mall 242, **104**
  Trendy Zone 232
  Up Date Mall 232
Shui Tau Tsuen 113-14
Sik Sik Yuen Wong Tai Sin Temple 98
Silvermine Bay Beach 132
Silvermine Cave 132
Silvermine Waterfall 132
Silverstrand Beach 123
Sin Sin Fine Art 28
Sing Ancestral Hall 74
Sino-Portuguese Pact 340
skating 223-4
Skyrink 224, **224**
soccer 216
Soho 71, **412-13**
  accommodation 253-4
  bars & pubs 201
  food 158-61
Sok Kwu Wan 126
  food 191-2
Song dynasty 53
South Lantau Rd 134
  food 195
Special Administrative Region 19, 59, 328, 340
Special Economic Zone 277, 282

Splendid China 279, 280
sport 216-17, 333, *see also individual sports*
sporting events
FIVB Women's Volleyball Grand Prix 330
Hong Kong Marathon 10
Hong Kong Rugby World Cup Sevens 10
Macau Formula 3 Grand Prix 330
Macau International Marathon 330
Macau Open Golf Tournament 329
Omega Hong Kong Open Golf Championships 12
Spring Lantern Festival 10
squash 224
Stanley 85-6, **411**
food 174-5
Stanley Market 86
Stanley Military Cemetery 86
Star Ferry 291
Statue Square 72-3
stilt houses 134
student cards 312
Sun Yat Sen, Dr 282, 285, 358
Sun Yat Sen Memorial Home 358
swimming 82, 217, 225, 370

T
Tai Au Mun 124
t'ai chi 222-3, **350**
Tai Long 121
Tai Long Wan 131
Tai Mei Tuk 116
accommodation 270
Tai Mei Tuk Fish Farm 218
Tai Mei Tuk Water Sports Centre 222
Tai Miu Temple 124
Tai Mo Shan 110
accommodation 270
Tai O 134-5
food 195, **348**
Tai Ping Shan Temples 74-5
Tai Po 115-16, **424**
food 187-8
Tai Po Kau 117
Tai Po Kau Interactive Nature Centre 117

000 map pages
000 photographs

Tai Po Kau Nature Reserve 117
Tai Po Market 116
tai tai 280
Tai Wan 138
Tai Wong shrine 86
Taipa House Museum 335, 359
Taipa Island 358-9, **433-4**
accommodation 373
food 365-6
walking tour 358
Taipa Village 359
Tak Wah Park 108
Tam Kong Temple 360
Tam, Vivienne 16
Tang Chi Ngong Buildings 75
Tang Ching Lok Ancestral Hall 113
Tang Kwong U Ancestral Hall 113
Tang people 52
Tanka people 52-3
Taoism 13, 330
Tap Mun Chau 121-3
food 190
Tap Seac Gallery 335
taxes 229, 321
taxis 300-1, 376
tea, Chinese 44, **104**
teacher cards 312
telephone services 321-2, 378
television 322
temple offerings **102**
Temple Street night market 94-5, **2**, **103**
temples, *see also* Tin Hau temples
A-Ma Temple 355, **351**
Che Kung Temple 119
Ching Chung Temple 111
Fung Ying Sin Temple 114
Hau Wong Temple 135
Hong Kung Temple 344
Hung Shing Temple 80, 113, **102**
Kun Iam Temple 357, 360
Kwan Tai temple 135, **102**
Kwun Yam temple 74, 86, 128
Lin Fung Temple 357
Man Mo temple 74, 116, 132, **101**
Pak Tai Temple 129
Po Lin 132-3
Pou Tai Temple 358

Sik Sik Yuen Wong Tai Sin Temple 98
Tai Miu Temple 124
Tai Ping Shan Temples 74-5
Tam Kong Temple 360
temple offerings **102**
Tian Hou Temple 359
10, 000 Buddhas Monastery 118
tennis 224
theatre 30-1, 214, *see also* Entertainment index 399
therapy clinics 226
Three Lamps District 371
Tian Hou Temple 359
Tian Tan Buddha 133, **2**
Tiananmen massacre 60
time 6, 322
Times Square shopping mall 242, **104**
Tin Ha Shan 124
Tin Hau 12
Tin Hau temples
Aberdeen 88
Causeway Bay 82
Largo Tin Hau Miu 360
Nam Tan Wan 129
Peng Chau 136
Ping Kong 114
Po Toi 138
Sai Wan 129
Shui Tau Tsuen 113
Sok Kwu Wan 126
Stanley 86
Tai Shek Hau 129
Tap Mun Chau 122
Tung Ping Chau 123
Yau Ma Tei 95
tipping 150, 322-3
toilets 323
Tong Fuk 134
Tou Tei 12
tourism 6, 333
tourist information 323, 378, 284
tourist passes 303
tours 66-8
hiking 219-20
kayaking 222
Macau 342-3
river boat tours 134
sailing 225
sampan 88
walking 68, 140-8, 361
Towngas Cooking Centre 310

traditional medicine 15, 318, **105**
train travel
to/from China 304-5
within Hong Kong 299-300, 301-2
trams 302-3
transport 288-306, 374-6
air 288-91
bicycle 291
boat 291-6
bus 296-7
car & motorcycle 297-8
taxi 300-1
to/from China 304-6
to/from Shenzhen 282
to/from Zhuhai 286
train 299-300, 301-2
trams 302-3
Trappist Monastery 135
travel passes 303
travellers cheques 319
travellers' diarrhoea 313-14
Treasury of Sacred Art 343
Treaty of Nanking 55, 339
Treaty of Tientsin 339-40
trekking, *see* hiking
Triads, the 53, 94
trivia 107
Tsang, Donald 19-22, 70
Tsim Sha Tsui 89-92, **420-2**, **9**, **140**
accommodation 260-6
bars & pubs 204-5
food 176-83
shopping 243-6
Tsim Sha Tsui East 92-3, **420-2**
accommodation 266-7
food 183-4
Tsim Sha Tsui East Promenade 93
Tsing Yi 136-7
Tsuen Wan 108-10, **424**
accommodation 270
food 186-7
TT Tsui Gallery of Chinese Art 119
Tuen Mun 110-11
food 187
Tuen Mun Public Riding School 222
Tung Chee Hwa 50-1, 70
Tung Choi St market 95, **101**
Tung Chung 135-6
Tung Chung Battery 135
Tung Chung Fort 135

Tung Chung Old Village 135
Tung Lung Chau 137-8
Tung Lung Fort 138
Tung O 126
Tung O Wan 126-7
Tung Ping Chau 123
Tung Wan Beach 127, 136
Two International Finance
    Centre 25, 72
typhoons 309

U
UN embargo 57
Unicorn Hall 98
United Democratic Party 60
universities 323
University Museum &
    Art Gallery 75
Upper Cheung Sha 134
urban planning 22

V
vegetarian food 43
Victoria Park 82, 224
Victoria Peak 77
visas 284, 306, 324, 378,
    see also passports
visual arts 27-9, 334-5,
    339

W
wakeboarding 224-5
Walk of 33 Curves 370
walking, *see* hiking,
    walking tours
walking tours 140-8
    books 145
    Central 141, **141**
    Cheung Chau 147-8, **148**
    Hong Kong Island 140-2,
        141, **142**
    Kowloon 143-5, **144**
    Lung Yeuk Tau Heritage
        Trail 146-7, **147**
    Macau Peninsula 361-2,
        361
    Mong Kok 143-5, **144**
    New Territories 145-7,
        146, **147**
    Outlying Islands 147-8,
        148
    Ping Shan Heritage Trail
        145, **146**
    Sheung Wan 142-3, **142**
    Taipa Island 358
    Yau Ma Tei 143-5, **144**
walla wallas 296

Wan Chai 77-88, **414-16**,
    106
    accommodation 254-6
    bars & pubs 202-3
    food 164-9
    shopping 240-2
Wan Chai Market 80-1
Wan Kei Ho International
    Martial Arts Association
    223
websites 324-5, 378
weights 325
Western Districts 75
Western Monastery 109
wetland 112
white dolphins 133
wholesale fruit market 95
Wilson Trail 222
Window of the World
    279, 280
windsurfing 224-5
    Cheung Chau
        Windsurfing Water
        Sports Centre 128
    Long Coast Seasports 134
    Sai Kung Peninsula 120
    Windsurfing Centre 224
Wing Chun Yip Man Martial
    Arts Athletic Association
    223
women travellers 325
Wonderful World of
    Whampoa 92
Wong Shek 121
Wong Shek Water Sports
    Centre 222
Wong, Suzie 17
Wong Tai Sin 98
Woo, John 26
Woo Sung St 95
work 14, 325-6
World Boutique Hong Kong
    10
World Wide Fund for
    Nature Hong Kong 113

X
Xavier, Francis 338
Xiangshan Park 283, 285
Xiangzhou 282

Y
yachting 225
Yan Yuen Sek 76
Yau Ma Tei 93-5, **423**
    accommodation 267-9
    food 184-5, **347**

shopping 247-8
    walking tour 143-5, **144**
Yeung Chau 122
Yi Tai Study Hall 113
Yim Tin Tsai 122
yoga 226
Yoga Central 226
Yoga Fitness 226
youth cards 312
Yuen Long 111-12
    food 187
Yuen Po Street Bird Garden
    95-6, **96**
Yuen Wo Ping 26
Yuen Yuen Institute 109-38
yum cha 36
Yung Shue Wan 127
    food 190-1

Z
Zhongshan Hot Springs
    284, 285
Zhuhai 6, 282-6, **283**
    accommodation 285-6
    attractions 285
    food 285
    tourist information 284
    tours 285
    travel to/from 286
Zhuhai City Museum 282,
    285
Zhuhai Fisher Girl 283, 285
zodiac 14
zoo 70
Zuni Icosahedron 30

EATING
2 Sardines 158
369 Shanghai Restaurant 164
A Lorcha 363
A Petisqueira 365
A Touch of Spice 176
A Vencedora 365
Adventist Vegetarian
    Cafeteria 173
Afonso III 363
Al Dente 158-9
Al's Diner 151
Ali-Oli 188
Almirante Lacerda City
    Market 362
Amaroni's Little Italy 185
American Restaurant 164
Amigo 173
Antica Trattoria da Isa 363
A-1 Restaurant 188
Aqua 176, **177**

Archie B's New York Deli 159
Arirang 169, 176
Aruna 365
Assaf 151
Avenue 176
Bagel Factory 161
Bahçe 193
Bali Restaurant 176-7
Banana Leaf Curry House 169
Bayside Brasserie 174
BBC Restaurant 281
Beijing Shui Jiao Wong 168
Beirut 151
Bhet Ghat Restaurant 164
Blowfish 159
Blue Bird 190
Bo Kung 169
Boathouse 174
Boca 159
Bombay Dreams 151
Bookworm Café 190
Branto 181
Brezza 194-5
Busan Korean Restaurant
    177-83
Café 151
Café des Artistes 152
Café E.S. Kimo 285
Café Lisboa 366
Café Siam 152
Café TOO 164
Caffé Chocolá 365
Caffè Toscana 363
Can.teen 156
Caramba! 159
Caravela 365
Carlos 363
Carriana Chiu Chow
    Restaurant 164
Casa Blanca 281
Causeway Bay 150
Chang Won Korean
    Restaurant 177
Chedi 159
Che's Cantonese Restaurant
    164
Chicken on the Run 161
Chili Chili 187
Chilli Fagara 159
Chilli N Spice 174
China Tee Club 152
Chippy 156
Chong Fat Chiu Chow
    Restaurant 185
Chow Phaya Thai Restaurant
    281
Chuen Cheung Kui 170, **170**

Chuen Kee Seafood Restaurant 188
Chun Chun Kun 365-6
Chung Chuk Lau Restaurant 170
Chung Shing Thai Restaurant 187
Chungking Mansions 182
Cine Città 164
Cinta-J 164-5
City Hall Maxim's Palace 152, **34**
city'super 156
Clube Militar de Macau 363
Concerto Inn 191
Cosmopolitan Curry House 187
Coyote Bar & Grill 165
Cozinha Pinocchio 366
Cul-de-Sac 156
Dai Pai Dong 182
Dan Ryan's Chicago Grill 165, 177
Delhi Club 182
Deli Lamma Café 191
Delicatessen Corner 182
Delicious Chow Noodle Restaurant 182
Délifrance 168, 175, 182
Deyue Fang 285
Dia 188
Doca de Abrigo 366
Dong 177
Dynasty 165, 177
East Lake 170, 192
East Ocean Seafood Restaurant 165
Eastern Palace Chiu Chow Restaurant 177
El Cid Caramar 174
El Taco Loco 159
Emperor Sushi 187
Espaço Lisboa 366-7
Everest Club 182
Fat Angelo's 159, 177
Federal Restaurant 185
Felix 178
Fernando 367
Finds 152
Firenze 189
First Cup Coffee 182
Fook Lam Moon 178
Fook Lam Mun 363
Fook Moon Lam 195

Forever Green Taiwanese Restaurant 170
Forum 170
Friday Cafe 281
Friendship Thai Food 186
Fringe Club 152
Fung Shing Restaurant 162
Gaddi's 178
Gaia Ristorante 162
Gallery 195
Galo 366
Gaylord 178
Genki Sushi 168, 183
Genroku Sushi 172
Gogo Café 173
Golden Bull 170, 178
Golden Myanmar 168
Golden Orchid Thai 186
Gomitori 183
Good Hope Noodle 184
Good Luck Thai 156-7
Good Satay 183
Graham St Market 157, **39**, **103**, **348**
Grand Buffet & Balcony 186
Grand Stage 162
Grappa's Peak Pizzeria 163
Grappa's Ristorante 165
Great 168
Greenlands India Club 152
Gunga Din's Club 152-3
Habibi 153
Han Lok Yuen 191
Happy Garden Noodle & Congee Kitchen 182
Hard Rock Café 178
Heichinrou 170
Henri's Galley 363
Higashiyama 170
Hing Lok 192
Hippo Bar Restaurant 193
Hometown Teahouse 192
Hong Kee 192
Hong Kong Old Restaurant 173
Hongdu Seafood City 285
Hot Basil Thai Cuisine 186
Hot Dog 157
Hunan Garden 153
Hung Kee Seafood Restaurant 189
Hyang Chon Korean Restaurant 165
India Today 159
Indian Curry Hut 189
Indian Restaurant 285
Indochine 1929 153

Indonesian Restaurant 1968 171
Islam Food 186
Islamabad Club 182
Island Seafood & Oyster Bar 178
Ivan the Kozak 153
Jade Garden 179
Jaks 194
Jaspa's 189
Jimmy's Kitchen 153, 179
Jo Jo Mess 166
Joyful Vegetarian 184
Jumbo Kingdom Floating Restaurant 175, **349**
June 173
Kaga Japanese Restaurant 188
Kar Shing Restaurant 187
Kath+Man+Du 160
King Elephant Restaurant 281
King Palace 179
Kiyotaki Japanese Restaurant 160
Ko Lung 363
Koh-i-Noor 153, 179, 188
Kokage 166
Korea House Restaurant 162
Korea Restaurant 171
Kowloon City Thai Restaurants 190
Kubrick Bookshop Café 184, **43**, **185**
Kung Shing 195
Kung Tak Lam 171
Kwun Hoi Heen 367
Kyozasa Restaurant 179
Kyushu-Ichiban 179
La Baguette 157
La Bonne Heure 363
La Comida 160
La Fontaine 157
La Gondola 367
La Kasbah 153
La Pizzeria 193
Lamma Bistro 191
Lamma Hilton Shum Kee Seafood Restaurant 192
Lancombe Seafood Restaurant 191
Laurel 281
Le Rendez-Vous 161
Leung Hing Chiu Chow Seafood Restaurant 162-3
Life 160

Lin Heung Tea House 162, **163**, **347**
Litoral 364
Little Egret Restaurant 188
Liu Yuan Restaurant 166
Lo Yu Vietnam Restaurant 176
Long Island Restaurant 192
Long Kei 364
Lord Stanley at the Curry Pot 174
Lord Stow's Café 367
Louis' Steak House 166
Lucy's 174
Luk Yeung Galleria 187
Luk Yu Tea House 153
Lung Moon Restaurant 166
M at the Fringe 154
Mak's Noodle 157
Mali-Bu 188
Man Fung Seafood Restaurant 191
Margaux 183
May Flower Restaurant 285
Merhaba 179
Mezzaluna 364
Ming Court 184
Ming Kee Seafood Restaurant 196
Miu Fat Monastery 187
Miu Gute Cheong Vegetarian Restaurant 184
Mix 157
Moon Garden Tea House 173
Mozart Stub'n 154
Mui Wo Cooked Food Market 194
Mui Wo Market 194
Mui Wo supermarkets 194
Muslim Hotel Restaurant 281
Naam 364
Nadaman 183
Nang Kee Goose Restaurant 187
Napa Valley Oyster Bar & Grill 173
Nepal 160
New Baccarat 192
New Hon Kee 190
New North Sea Fishing Village 183
New Yaohan Supermarket 362
Nga Tim Café 367
Nicholini's 166

000 map pages
000 photographs

Index

Ning Po Residents Association 154
Noodle King 281
O Café Estalagem 366
O Capítulo 366
O Manel 366
O Santos 366
Ocean King Restaurant 281
Olive 160
Oliver's 157
Oliver's Super Sandwiches 183
One Harbour Road 166
One One Pasta 188
Ooh La La! 195
Orange Tree 160
Orphée 171, 179
Ou Mun Café 365
Pak Bo Vegetarian Kitchen 184
Pak Loh Chiu Chow Restaurant 171
Palm Court 184
Papa Tudo 365
Park 'N' Shop 157, 163, 193, 362-3
Peak Cafe Bar 160
Peak Lookout 163-4
Pearl Vietnamese Restaurant 157
Peking Restaurant 179
Peng Chau Market 196
Pep 'n' Spices 180
Pepperoni's Pizza 168, 189
Petrus 166
Phoenix 162
Phuket's 162
Pizza Milano 191
Pizzeria Toscana II 364
Plaza 364
Po Lin Vegetarian Restaurant 195, **101**
Port Cafe 167
Porto Exterior 364
Post 97 154
Pou Tai Temple Restaurant 366
Praia Grande 364
Queen's Cafe 171
Rainbow Seafood Restaurant 192
Red Diamond Chinese Restaurant 175-6
Red Pepper 171
Restaurante Parque Hác Sá 367
Rico's 160

Robuchon a Galera 364
Rome Restaurant 194
Royal Garden Chinese Restaurant 183
R66 167
Ruby Tuesday 180
Rughetta 154
Ruth's Chris Steakhouse 167
Sabah 167
Sabatini 183
Sai Kung **190**, **194**
Sai Kung Supermarkets 190
Sai Nam 364
Sai Square 189
Saigon 167
Saigon Beach 168-9
St Lawrence City Market 362
Saint's Alp Teahouse 185
Sakurada 184
Salisbury Dining Room 180
Sampan Seafood Restaurant 191
San Marzano 154
Sauce 189
Schnurrbart 154, 180
Sea Dragon King 193
Secret Garden 154
Seng Cheong 366
Shabu Shabu 167
Shaffi's Malik 169
Shalimar 188
Shalom Grill 154
Sheung Wan Ho Choi Seafood Restaurant 162-3
Shougon 195
Shui Hu Ju 160-1
Silvermine Beach Hotel 193
Singapore Restaurant 180
Snake King 186
Soho Soho 155
Song 155
Sorabol Korean Restaurant 171
Spaghetti House 155
Spicy Island 191
Spoon by Alain Ducasse 180
Spring Deer 180
Spring Moon 180
Stanley's Italian 175
Steamers Bar & Restaurant 189
Stoep Restaurant 195
Stonegrill 161
Stormy Weather 155
street stalls 150, **353**
Sunny & Barbie 157-8

Super Star Seafood Restaurant 155
Sushi King 364
Swagat Restaurant 182
Sweet Dynasty 180
Tai Fung Lau Peking Restaurant 181
Tai Ping Koon 171
Tai Woo Seafood Restaurant 163, 172
Tai Yuen Restaurant 192
Taj Indian Restaurant 281
Taj Mahal Club 182
Tak Chai Kee Seafood Restaurant 194
Tan Ta Wan Restaurant 167
Tea Palace 285
Thai Basil 167
Thai Farm Restaurant 186
Thai Golden Elephant Restaurant 285
Thai Lemongrass 155
Three-Five Korean Restaurant 181
369 Shanghai Restaurant 164
Tim's Kitchen 169
Tokio Joe 155
Tomokazu 172
Tony Roma's 181
Towngas Avenue 172
Tsim Chai Kee Noodle 158, **158**
Tsui Wah 155
Tung Kee Restaurant 189
Tung Lok Hin 173-4
2 Sardines 158
Typhoon Shelter 196
Uncle Willie's Deli 155
Va Bene 156
Valentino 181
Veda 161
Vegetarian Court 167
Verandah Restaurant 175
Viceroy Restaurant & Bar 168
Victoria City 168
Village Café 367
Vong 156
Wan Loong Court 181
Weinstube 181
Wellcome 158, 175, 183, 193, 196
Wong Chi Kei 158, 365
Wong Chun Chun Thai Restaurant 186
Woodlands 184
W's Entrecôte 172

Wu Kong Shanghai Restaurant 181
Xiao Nan Guo 172
Xin Jin Shi 172
XTC on Ice 158
Yan Toh Heen 181
Y-by-the-Bay 175
Yè Shanghai 168
Yes Brazil 365
Yi Jiang Nan 161
Yin Ping Vietnamese Restaurant 172
Yorohachi 156
Yoshinoya Noodles 169
Yung Kee Restaurant 156, **348**
Zambra 169
Zen 186

ENTERTAINMENT

1/5 207
48th Street Chicago Blues 211
A Rolha 368
Agnès B Cinema 79, 213
AMC Festival Walk 214
Après 200
Aqua Spirit 204
Bahama Mama's 207
Bar 204
Bar George 200
Bar Leo 279, 280
Bar 1911 201
Biergarten 204
Bit Point 200
BJ'zz.com Bar 279, 280
Blue Door Jazz Club 211
Bohemian Lounge 211
Brecht's Bar 203
Bridge 202
Broadway Cinematheque 214
C Club 207
Café Einstein 204
Captain's Bar 200
Carnegie's 211
Casablanca Café 368
Causeway Lounge 211
Cavern 211
Champagne Bar 202
Champagne Lounge Bar 368
Chapter 3 200
Chasers 211
Chicago Club 279, 280
China Bear 206-7
Cine-Art House 213
Class Club 280

Club Bboss 210
Club de Millennium 210
Club 97 207
Club NU 207
Club 64 200
Courtney's 204
Crazy Paris Show 369, **354**
DD Disco 368
Delaney's 202, 204
Devil's Advocate 202
Dickens Bar 203
Diesel's Bar 206
Dragon-I 200
Drop 208, **105**
Dublin Jack 200
Duke of York Pub 205
Dusk till Dawn 211
East End Brewery 204
East End Brewery &
    Inn Side Out 204
Edge 211
Embassy Bar 368
Feather Boa 201
Felix 205
Fenwick the Dock 202
Forest Bar & Restaurant 207
48th Street Chicago Blues
    211
Fountainhead Drinking
    Bar 206
Fringe Gallery 211-12
Fringe Studio 214
Gecko Lounge 200
Globe 200-1
Grand Ocean Cinema 214
Groovy Mule 202
Hari's 212
Henry J Bean's Bar & Grill
    279, 280
HITEC Rotunda 212
Homebase 208
Hong Kong Academy for
    the Performing Arts 212
Hong Kong Arts Centre 212
Hong Kong City Hall 212
Hong Kong Coliseum 212
Hong Kong Cultural Centre
    212
Hong Kong Film Archive 213
Horse & Groom 202
Insomnia 208
Island Society Bar 206
Jai Alai Show Palace 369
Jewel 208

JK's Club 207
Joe Bananas 208
Kangaroo Downunder 202
Ko Shan Theatre 212
Kwai Tsing Theatre 212
La Dolce Vita 201
La Tasca 205
Lan Kwai Fong 198, **198**
Le Jardin 201
Les Visages 208
Mang Bing Massage Centre
    280
Manhattan Club Ing 209
McCawley's Irish Bar &
    Restaurant 279, 280
Mes Amis 203
Moonwalker Bar 368
Ned Kelly's Last Stand 212
Neptune Disco II 209, **209**
New Makati Pub & Disco 209
New Wally Matt Lounge 205
Old China Hand 203
Om Lounge 201
1/5 207
Organ Bar 205
Oskar's Pub 368
O² Theatre 214
Palace IFC Cinema 213
Patio Café 206
Poets 205-6
Propaganda 209
Punchline Comedy Club 214
Queen Elizabeth Stadium 212
Red Rock 209
Rennie Mac's Brasserie 203
Rice Bar 201
Rick's Café 209
Sanshiro Pub 368
Sha Tin Town Hall 212
Skitz 203
Sky Lounge 205
Smugglers Inn 204
Soho Restaurant &
    Night Club 279, 280
Staunton's Wine Bar & Cafe
    201, **202**
Sunbeam Theatre 214
Tango Martini 203
Today's Tonnochy Nightclub
    210
Tony's Bar 205
UA Pacific Place 213
V-13 201
Venue 209
Wally Matt Lounge 210
Wanch 212-13
Wasabisabi 210

Watering Hole 205
Whiskey Priest 201
White Stag 203
Windsor Cinema 214
Works 210-11
X-Ta-Sea 279, 280
Xtreme Bar & Restaurant
    206

SHOPPING

Alan Chan Creations 243-4
Al-Shahzadi Persian Carpet
    Gallery 240
Amours Antiques 233
Anglo-Chinese Florist 233
Arch Angel Antiques 233
Beverley Boutique 233
Blanc de Chine 233
Bloomsbury Books 234
Bookazine 234
Bunn's Divers 240
Camper 242
Caravan 234
Carpet Centre 234
Chamonix Alpine Equipment
    247
Chine Gallery 234
Chinese Arts & Crafts 240
Chinese Carpet Centre 244
Christie 234
Chung Yuen Electrical
    Co 242
Cigar Express Central 234
Cigarro 234
City Chain 234
Cityplaza 242
Curio Alley 244, **104**
Dada Cabaret Voltaire 243
David Chan Photo Shop 244
Design Gallery 240
D-Mop 242
Dymocks 234
Eu Yan Sang 235
Everbest Photo Supplies
    235
Festival Walk 248
Flow Organic Bookshop 235
Flying Ball Bicycle Co 247
Fook Ming Tong Tea Shop
    235
Giga Sports 244
Golden Computer Arcade
    248
Golf Creation 244
Government Publications
    Office 235
Harbour City 244

Hing Lee Camera Company
    235
HMV 235
Hobbs & Bishops Fine Art 235
Honeychurch Antiques 235
Hong Kong Book Centre 235
Hong Kong Records 240-1
IFC Mall 236
In Square 243
Indosiam 236
i.t 244
Joint Publishing 236
Joyce 236
Karin Weber Gallery 236
Kelly & Walsh 241
Kent & Curwen 241
King & Country 241
King Fook 236, **237**
King Sing Jewellery 244
KS Ahluwalia & Sons 244
Kung Fu Supplies 241
Landmark 236
Lane Crawford 236
Langham Place Mall 247
Lids 244
Linva Tailor 236-7, **106**
Little Misses & Mini
    Masters 237
Liuligongfang 237
Lock Cha Tea Shop 237
Luohu Commercial City
    279, 280
Mandarin Oriental Flower &
    Gift Shop 237
Minamoto Kitchoan 244
Ming's Sports Company 245
Mir Oriental Carpets 237
Mitsukoshi 243
Miu Miu 237
Mong Kok Computer Centre
    247
Monitor Records 245
Mountain Folkcraft 237
Mountaineer Supermarket
    247
Mountaineering Services 243
Museum Bookshop 90
New Capital Computer Plaza
    248
New Town Plaza 118
New Wing Hing Dispensary
    237
Ocean Optical 238
Ocean Sky Divers 245
Olympia Graeco-Egyptian
    Coffee 238
Om International 245

Onesto Photo Company 245
Opal Mine 245
Pacific Custom Tailors 241
Pacific Place 241
Page One 248
Photo Scientific 238
Po Kee Fishing Tackle 238
Ponti Food & Wine Cellar 245
Premier Jewellery 245
Prince's Building 238
Rag Brochure 247
Sam's Tailor 245
Seibu 241, **242**
Shanghai Tang 238
Sincere 240
Sister 243
Sogo 243
Soho Wines & Spirits 238
Sotheby 238
Spy 243
Star Computer City 246
Sunmark Camping Equipment 241
Swindon Books 246
Tai Sing Fine Antiques 238
Tai Yip Art Book Centre 238-9
Teresa Coleman Fine Arts 239
Tibetan Gallery 239
Times Square 243
Tom Lee Music Company 246
Toto 239
Toy Museum 239
Travellers' Home 246
Travelmax 246
Tse Sui Luen 239
Vivienne Tam 241
Wah Tung China Arts 242
Walter Ma 243
Wan Chai Computer Centre 242
Wanko 239
Watson's Wine Cellar 239
Wattis Fine Art 239
Wing On 240
Wing Shing Photo Supplies 247
Wise Kids 242
Wise Mount Sports 247
X Game Sporting Goods 239

Yue Hwa Chinese Products Emporium 247
Yuet Wah Music Company 248

SLEEPING

Ascension House 270
Alisan Guest House 258
Anne Black Guest House 268-9
Bali Holiday Resort 271-2
Bishop Lei International House 253
Booth Lodge 269
BP International Hotel 260
Bradbury Lodge 270
Caritas Bianchi Lodge 269
Caritas Lodge 269
Causeway Bay Guest House 258
Central Hotel 372
Century Plaza Hotel 281
Charterhouse Hotel 254-5
Cheung Chau Accommodation Kiosks 272
Chung Kiu Inn 258
Chungking House 263
Chungking Mansions 262-3
Concerto Inn 271
Conrad Hong Kong 255
Cosmic Guest House 263
Cosmopolitan Hotel 255
Dorsett Seaview Hotel 267
Dragon Inn 263
East Asia Hotel 372
Eaton Hotel 267
Eden 253
Empire Hotel Hong Kong 255
Empire Kowloon 260
Excelsior Hong Kong 256-7
Express by Holiday Inn 257
First-Class Guest House 264
Fortuna Hotel 371
Friendship Hotel 285-6
Garden Guest House 264
Garden Hostel 264
Garden View International House 253
Gold Hotel 281
Golden Crown Court 263
Golden Crown Guest House 264
Gongbei Palace Hotel 286
Good World Hotel 286
Grand Hyatt Hotel 255

Grand Stanford Inter-Continental 266-7
Grandview Hotel 373
Guangdong Hotel 281
Guangdong International Hotel 260
Guia Hotel 371
Hakka's Guest House 269
Hanlun Habitats 253
Harbour Plaza Metropolis 266
Harbour View Hotel 286
Harbour View International House 255
Holiday Inn Golden Mile 260
Holiday Inn Macau 371
Hong Kong Hostel 258-9
Hongkong Bank Foundation SG Davis Hostel 272
Hotel Inter-Continental Hong Kong 260
Hotel Miramar Hong Kong 260
Hotel Nikko Hongkong 266
Hung Kiu Guest House 264
Ice House 253-4
Imperial Hotel 260
Island Shangri-La Hong Kong 256
Jackson Property Agency 271
Jetvan Travellers' House 259
JIA 257, **257**
Jockey Club Mong Tung Wan Hostel 272-3
Jockey Club Mount Davis Hostel 254
Kimberley Hotel 260-1
Knutsford 261
Kowloon Hotel Hong Kong 261
Kowloon Shangri-La 266-7
Kyoto Guest House 264
Landmark Macau 372
Langham Hotel Hong Kong 261
Langham Place Hotel 267
Lily Garden Hostel 264
Lisboa Hotel 372, **354**
Long Coast Seasports 273
Lucky Guesthouse 264
Luk Kwok Hotel 256
Macau Masters Hotel 372
Majestic Hotel 267
Man Hing Lung Hotel 264
Man Lai Wah Hotel 271-2
Mandarin Oriental 254, 372, **250**

Marco Polo HongKong Hotel 261
Metropark Hotel 257
Metropole Hotel 267
Minden 261
Mirador Mansion 263
Mondial Hotel 372
Mui Wo Accommodation Kiosks 273
Mui Wo Inn 273
Nathan Hotel 268
New Kings Hotel 269
New Lucky House 268
New Shanghai Guest House 264
Newton Hotel Kowloon 268
Noble Hostel 259
Ocean Guest House 269
Overseas House 269-70
Pak Sha O Hostel 271
Park Guest House 265
Park Hotel 261
Park Lane Hong Kong 257-8
Peking Guest House 265
Peninsula Hong Kong 261-2, **92**
Petrel Hotel 281
Pinnacle Apartment 262
Pousada de Coloane 373
Pousada de Juventude de Cheoc Van 373
Pousada de Juventude de Hác Sá 373
Pousada de Mong Há 372
Pousada Marina Infante 373
Regal Airport Hotel 273-4
Regal Hongkong Hotel 258
Regal Kowloon Hotel 267
Regal Riverside Hotel 270
Renaissance Harbour View Hotel 256
Rent-a-Room Hong Kong 265
Ritz Hotel 372
Ritz-Carlton Hong Kong 254
Rosedale on the Park 258
Royal Garden Hotel 267
Royal Hotel 372
Royal Pacific Hotel & Towers 262
Royal Park Hotel 270-1
Royal Plaza Hotel 268
Salisbury 265, **265**
San Va Hospedaria 373
Sealand House 265
Seaview Holiday Resort 274
Shama 258

Shamrock Hotel 268
Shangri-La Hotel 281
Shenzhen Hotel 281
Sheraton Hong Kong Hotel &
    Towers 262
Silvermine Beach Hotel 274
South Pacific Hotel Hong
    Kong 256
Stanford Hillview Hotel 262

Stanford Hotel 268
Star Guest House 265
Sun Sun Macau Hotel 372
Tom's Guest House 266
Travellers Hostel 266
Treasure Island on Lantau
    274
Wah Chung International
    Hotel 281

Warwick Hotel 272
Welcome Guest House
    266
Wesley Hong Kong 256
Westin Resort Macau 373
Wharney Guangdong Hotel
    Hong Kong 256
Yan Yan Guest House 266
Yindo Hotel 286

YMCA International House
    268
YWCA Building 254
Zhongshan Hot Springs
    Hotel 284, 286
Zhuhai Holiday Resort
    286
Zhuhai Overseas Chinese
    Hotel 286

000 map pages
000 photographs

MAP LEGEND

ROUTES

Freeway	One-Way Street
Primary Road	Mall/Steps
Secondary Road	Tunnel
Tertiary Road	Walking Tour

TRANSPORT

Ferry	Rail
Bus Route	Rail (Underground)

HYDROGRAPHY

River, Creek	Canal
Intermittent River	Water

BOUNDARIES

International	Regional, Suburb
State, Provincial	Ancient Wall

AREA FEATURES

Airport	Cemetery, Other
Beach, Desert	Forest
Building, Information	Land
Building, Other	Park
Building, Transport	Sports
Cemetery, Christian	Urban

POPULATION

CAPITAL (NATIONAL)	CAPITAL (STATE)
Large City	Town, Village

SYMBOLS

Sights/Activities
- Beach
- Buddhist
- Castle, Fortress
- Christian
- Islamic
- Jewish
- Monument
- Museum, Gallery
- Other Site
- Ruin
- Zoo, Bird Sanctuary

Eating
- Eating

Drinking
- Drinking
- Café

Entertainment
- Entertainment

Shopping
- Shopping

Sleeping
- Sleeping
- Camping

Transport
- Airport, Airfield
- Border Crossing
- Bus Station
- General Transport
- Parking Area
- Petrol Station
- Taxi Rank

Information
- Bank, ATM
- Embassy/Consulate
- Hospital, Medical
- Information
- Internet Facilities
- Police Station
- Post Office, GPO
- Telephone
- Toilets

Geographic
- Lighthouse
- Lookout
- Mountain, Volcano
- National Park
- Waterfall

Hong Kong Special Administrative Region (SAR)	404
Hong Kong Island	406
Sheung Wan, Central & Admiralty	408
Aberdeen	411
Stanley	411
Lan Kwai Fong & Soho	412
Wan Chai & Causeway Bay	414
Hong Kong MTR System Map	417
Kowloon	418
Tsim Sha Tsui, Tsim Sha Tsui East & Hung Hom	420
Yau Ma Tei & Mong Kok	423
Tsuen Wan	424
Tai Po	424
Sha Tin	425
Sai Kung Town	425
Lamma	426
Lantau	427
Cheung Chau	428
Mui Wo (Lantau)	429
Peng Chau	429
Macau Peninsula	430
Central Macau Peninusla	432
Taipa & Coloane Islands	433

Maps

HONG KONG SPECIAL ADMINISTRATIVE REGION (SAR)

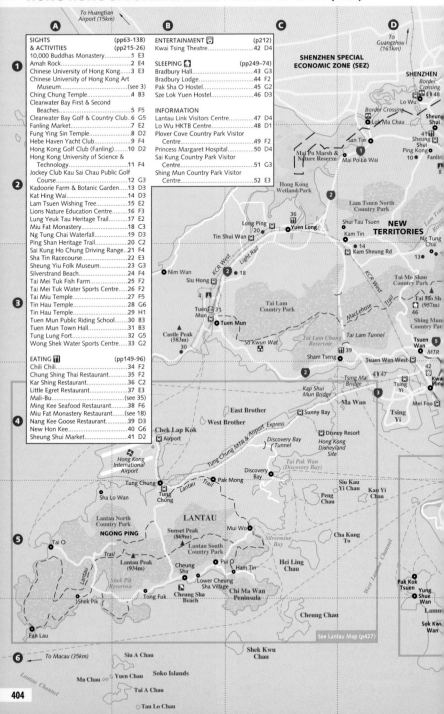

SIGHTS (pp63-138)
& ACTIVITIES (pp215-26)
10,000 Buddhas Monastery...............1 E3
Amah Rock.......................................2 E4
Chinese University of Hong Kong.....3 E3
Chinese University of Hong Kong Art
    Museum...................................(see 3)
Ching Chung Temple.........................4 B3
Clearwater Bay First & Second
    Beaches.......................................5 F5
Clearwater Bay Golf & Country Club..6 G5
Fanling Market..................................7 E2
Fung Ying Sin Temple........................8 D2
Hebe Haven Yacht Club.....................9 F4
Hong Kong Golf Club (Fanling).........10 D2
Hong Kong University of Science &
    Technology................................11 F4
Jockey Club Kau Sai Chau Public Golf
    Course.......................................12 G3
Kadoorie Farm & Botanic Garden.....13 D3
Kat Hing Wai...................................14 D3
Lam Tsuen Wishing Tree...................15 E2
Lions Nature Education Centre..........16 F3
Lung Yeuk Tau Heritage Trail............17 E2
Miu Fat Monastery...........................18 C3
Ng Tung Chai Waterfall.....................19 D3
Ping Shan Heritage Trail....................20 C2
Sai Kung Ho Chung Driving Range....21 F4
Sha Tin Racecourse...........................22 E3
Sheung Yiu Folk Museum..................23 G3
Silverstrand Beach............................24 F4
Tai Mei Tuk Fish Farm.......................25 F2
Tai Mei Tuk Water Sports Centre.......26 F2
Tai Miu Temple................................27 F5
Tin Hau Temple................................28 G6
Tin Hau Temple................................29 H1
Tuen Mun Public Riding School........30 B3
Tuen Mun Town Hall........................31 B3
Tung Lung Fort................................32 G5
Wong Shek Water Sports Centre.......33 G2

EATING (pp149-96)
Chili Chili..34 F2
Chung Shing Thai Restaurant.............35 F2
Kar Shing Restaurant........................36 C2
Little Egret Restaurant......................37 E3
Mali-Bu.......................................(see 35)
Ming Kee Seafood Restaurant...........38 F6
Miu Fat Monastery Restaurant.......(see 18)
Nang Kee Goose Restaurant.............39 D3
New Hon Kee...................................40 G6
Sheung Shui Market..........................41 D2

ENTERTAINMENT (p212)
Kwai Tsing Theatre...........................42 D4

SLEEPING (pp249-74)
Bradbury Hall...................................43 G3
Bradbury Lodge................................44 F2
Pak Sha O Hostel.............................45 G2
Sze Lok Yuen Hostel.........................46 D3

INFORMATION
Lantau Link Visitors Centre...............47 D4
Lo Wu HKTB Centre.........................48 D1
Plover Cove Country Park Visitor
    Centre.......................................49 F2
Princess Margaret Hospital...............50 D4
Sai Kung Country Park Visitor
    Centre.......................................51 G3
Shing Mun Country Park Visitor
    Centre.......................................52 E3

0   10 km
0   6 miles

E   F   G   H

SOUTH
CHINA
SEA

Sha Tau Kok
Border Crossing
Kat O & Port Island Country Parks
Crooked Island
Tung Ping Chau 29

Closed Area Boundary

**NEW
TERRITORIES**
Starling Inlet
Kat O Hoi

Nam Chung Reservoir
Luk Keng
Yan Chau Tong
Crescent Island
Double Island
Tai Pang Wan (Mirs Bay)

7 17
Fanling
Pat Sin Leng Country Park
Hok Tau Wai
Wong Leng Shan (639m)
Wilson Trail
Pat Sin Leng Nature Trail
Bride's Pool
Plover Cove Country Park
Port Island
Chek Chau Hau (Middle Channel)
See Enlargement

Hok Tau Reservoir
35
34   25
44   Tai Mei Tuk 49
26
Plover Cove Reservoir
Hoi Ha Wan Marine Park
Tap Mun Chau

15
KCR East
Tai Po
Ma Shi Chau Protected Area
Tolo Channel
Hoi Ha
Tai Tan Hoi Hap
Ko Lau Wan

Tai Po Market
Tai Po Kau
San Mun Tsai
Wu Kai Sha
Lai Chi Chong 45
Sham Chung
33
Wong Shek
43
Tai Long

37
Tai Po Kau Nature Reserve
Tsung Tsai Yuen
Ma Liu Shui
3
University
Ma On Shan Rail
Ma On Shan
Nai Chung
Sai Kung West Country Park
Pak Tam Au
Chek Keng
Ham Tin

Lead Mine Pass
22
Racecourse
Fo Tan
Ma On Shan (702m)
Sai Kung Peninsula
Tai Long Wan

Shing Mun Reservoir
52
Smuggler's Ridge
Shing Mun Tunnel
16
See Sha Tin Map (p425)
Sha Tin
Ma On Shan Country Park
MacLehose Trail
Pak Tam Chung
51
23
High Island Reservoir
Sai Wan

Sha Tin
Tai Wai
Cham Tau Chau
Pak Sha Chau
Kau Sai Chau
SOUTH CHINA SEA

Kam Shan Country Park
2
Tai's Cairn
Sai Kung
16
Buffalo Hill
Kin Tsui Chau
Leung Sheun Wan

Kowloon Reservoir
Lai Chi Kok
Eagle's Nest
Lion Rock
6
Lion Rock Country Park
Tate's Cairn Tunnel
9
21
Hebe Haven
Marina Cove
Tai Tau Chau
12

Kowloon Peak (602m)
Trio Beach
Port Shelter
Wong Nai Chau
Kong Tau Pai

Kowloon Tong
See Kowloon Map (pp418-19)
Wilson Trail
11
Tiu Chung Chau
See Chau
Bluff Island
Basalt Island

1
Nam Cheong KCR West Rail Terminal
YAU MA TEI
KOWLOON
HUNG HOM
KWUN TONG
Tseung Kwan O Tunnel
Kwun Tong
Po Lam
24
Shelter Island

Western Harbour Crossing
TSIM SHA TSUI
East Tsim Sha Tsui KCR East Rail Terminal
Hang Hau
Lung Ha Wan

Cross-Harbour Tunnel
MTR
Yau Tong
High Junk Peak (344m)
Tai Au Mun

CENTRAL
WAN CHAI
Victoria Harbour
Eastern Harbour Crossing
SHAU KEI WAN
Lei Yue Mun
27
Tin Ha Shan (273m)
Clearwater Bay Country Park
Clearwater Bay

CAUSEWAY BAY
Joss House Bay
5
6
32

Victoria Peak (552m)
HONG KONG
Aberdeen Tunnel
HONG KONG ISLAND
Big Wave Bay
Tung Lung Chau

Aberdeen
Ap Lei Chau
Shek O
Repulse Bay

Mo Tat Wan
East Lamma Channel
Stanley
Tai Tam Bay
Sung Kong

See Hong Kong Island Map (pp406-7)
Lo Chau
Po Toi
38

Sham Wan
Tung O Wan

Tap Mun Chau

Chek Chau Hau (Middle Channel)
Cham Pai (Channel Rock)

0   1 km

Pak Wan
Kung Chau

Hau Tsz Kok
Man Ping Shan (125m)
Che Wan

Hau Tsz Kok Pai
Lung Keng Kan

CHUNG MEI KOK
28
40
SHEUNG WAI

Chau Tsai Kok
Tap Mun
CHUNG WAI
Fish Farms
New Fishermens' Village
Balanced Rock

Tit Shue Pai

A **B** **C** **D**

KCR East Rail

2

1

Stonecutters
Island

**YAU MA
TEI**

To Discovery Bay

Kowloon

East Tsim
Sha Tsui
(KCR East Rail
Terminus)

Hung
Hom

Airport Express

MTR

Cross
Harbour
Tunnel

Western Harbour Crossing

**TSIM SHA
TSUI**

To Outlying Islands;
Macau

Victoria Harbour

2

Green
Island

See Sheung Wan, Central & Admiralty Map (pp408-9)

See Wan Chai & Causeway
Bay Map (pp414-15)

**SHEK TONG
TSUI**

**SAI YING
PUN**

Sheung
Wan

Hong Kong Airport
Express Station

7

**CAUSEWAY
BAY**

6

Mt Davis
(269m)

**KENNEDY
TOWN**

**SHEUNG
WAN**

MID-LEVELS

CENTRAL

Central

WAN CHAI

Causeway
Bay

**SO KO
PO**

Victoria Rd

20

Victoria Peak
(552m)

Admiralty

ADMIRALTY

Wan Chai

**HAPPY
VALLEY**

27

Pok Fu Lam
Country Park

THE PEAK

Peak
Tram

10

Bowen Rd

Stubbs Rd

Stubbs Rd

22

3

Pok Fu Lam
Reservoir

Peak Rd

Mt
Cameron
(439m)

Mt
Nicholson
(430m)

Pok Fu Lam Rd

Saudy Bay

9

23

26

Aberdeen
Country
Park

Aberdeen
Reservoir

Aberdeen Tunnel

Wah Fu
Estate

Shek Pai Wan Rd

See Aberdeen Map (p411)

**SHOUSON
HILL**

Magazine
Island

ABERDEEN

1

**WONG CHUK
HANG**

Wong Chuk Hang Rd

Ocean
Park

Island Rd

West Lamma Channel

See Lamma Map (p426)

Ap Lei
Chau

Brick Hill
(284m)

Deep Water
Bay

4

Ocean
Park

Cable Car

Middle
Island

Pak Kok
Tsuen

Pak Kok
Shan
(138m)

East Lamma Channel

Ap Lei Pai

Aberdeen Channel

Luk Chau Wan

Ngan Chau

Luk Chau

Yung Shue Wan

5

Lamma

Ha Mei Wan

Tit Sha Long

Sok Kwu Wan
(Picnic Bay)

Sok Kwu Wan

Mo Tat Wan

6

Tung O Wan

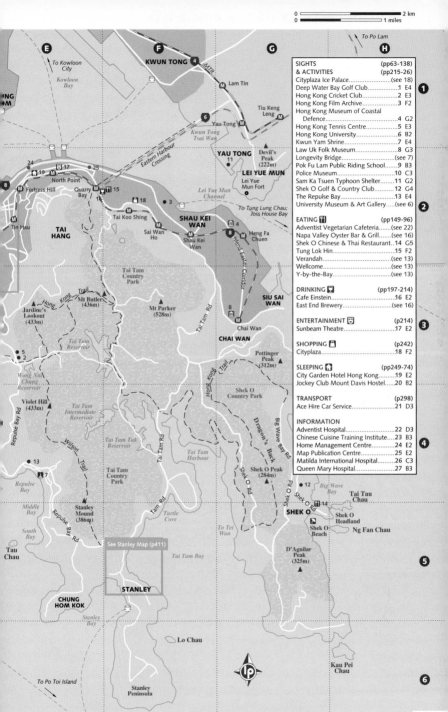

SIGHTS	(pp63-138)
& ACTIVITIES	**(pp215-26)**
Cityplaza Ice Palace	(see 18)
Deep Water Bay Golf Club	1 E4
Hong Kong Cricket Club	2 E3
Hong Kong Film Archive	3 F2
Hong Kong Museum of Coastal	
Defence	4 G2
Hong Kong Tennis Centre	5 E3
Hong Kong University	6 B2
Kwun Yam Shrine	7 E4
Law Uk Folk Museum	8 G3
Longevity Bridge	(see 7)
Pok Fu Lam Public Riding School	9 B3
Police Museum	10 C3
Sam Ka Tsuen Typhoon Shelter	11 G2
Shek O Golf & Country Club	12 G4
The Repulse Bay	13 E4
University Museum & Art Gallery	(see 6)

EATING	(pp149-96)
Adventist Vegetarian Cafeteria	(see 22)
Napa Valley Oyster Bar & Grill	(see 16)
Shek O Chinese & Thai Restaurant	14 G5
Tung Lok Hin	15 F2
Verandah	(see 13)
Wellcome	(see 13)
Y-by-the-Bay	(see 13)

DRINKING	(pp197-214)
Cafe Einstein	16 E2
East End Brewery	(see 16)

ENTERTAINMENT	(p214)
Sunbeam Theatre	17 E2

SHOPPING	(p242)
Cityplaza	18 F2

SLEEPING	(pp249-74)
City Garden Hotel Hong Kong	19 E2
Jockey Club Mount Davis Hostel	20 B2

TRANSPORT	(p298)
Ace Hire Car Service	21 D3

INFORMATION	
Adventist Hospital	22 D3
Chinese Cuisine Training Institute	23 B3
Home Management Centre	24 E2
Map Publication Centre	25 E2
Matilda International Hospital	26 C3
Queen Mary Hospital	27 B3

To Macau (65km)

Victoria Harbour

Macau Ferry Pier

To Shek Tong Tsui (1km);
Kennedy Town (3.5km);
Aberdeen (10km)

Western Harbour Crossing

West Fire Service St

Chung Kong Rd

Connaught Rd West

Des Voeux Rd West

Tramway

Sutherland St

Queen St

Wing Lok St

New Market St

SHEUNG WAN

Governm Pier

SAI YING PUN

Ko Shing St

Wilmer St

Bonham Strand West

Strand

Queen St

Wing Lok St

Cleverly Strand

Bonham

Morrison St

Hillier St

Main St

Connaught Rd Central

Rumsey St

Pier St

Des Voeux Rd Central

Centre St

Eastern St

New St

Hollywood Road Park

Hospital Rd

Queen's Rd West

Burd St

Jervois St

Mercer St

Gilman's Bazaar

Wing Wo St

Wing Kut St

The Center

King George V Memorial Park

High St

Possession St

Ta Ping Shan St

Po Yan St

Upper Lascar Row (Cat St)

Lok Ku Rd

Hollywood Square

Gough St

Queen's Rd Central

Wing Lok St

U Fong

Cage St

Jubilee St

To Hong Kong University (250m)

Bonham Rd

Blake Garden

Pound La

Po Hing Fong

Kui In Fong

Tank La

Tung St

Sai St

Wa La

Shing St

Wong St

Hollywood Rd

Park Rd

Caine La

Ladder St

Ludlum St

Bridges St

Wing Lee St

See Lan Kwai Fong & Soho Map (p412)

Lyttelton Rd

Kotewall Rd

Breezy Path

Seymour Rd

Aberdeen St

Peel St

Graham St

Elgin St

Lyndhurst Tce

Wellington St

SOHO

Conduit Rd

Castle Rd

Robinson Rd

Shelley St

Pedestrian Escalator

Old Bailey St

Chancery La

Arbuthnot Rd

Wyndham St

D'Aguilar St

LAN KWAI FO

Po Shan Rd

MID-LEVELS

Mosque St

Mosque Jct

Leung Fai Terr

Caine Rd

Glenealy

Hong Kong Trail

Conduit Rd

Glenealy

Lugard Rd

Po Shan Rd

Victoria Peak (552m)

Pok Fu Lam Country Park

Tregunter Path

Hornsey Rd

Old Peak Rd

Albany Rd

Robinson Rd

Mt Austin Rd

Mt Austin Rd

May Rd

Old Peak Rd

Brewin

Tregunter Path

Victoria Peak Garden

The Governor's Walk

Lugard Rd

Old Peak Rd

THE PEAK

Peak Tramway

Mt Austine Rd

Harlech Rd

Old Peak Rd

Finlay Rd

Barker Rd

Pok Fu Lam Country Park

Peak Rd

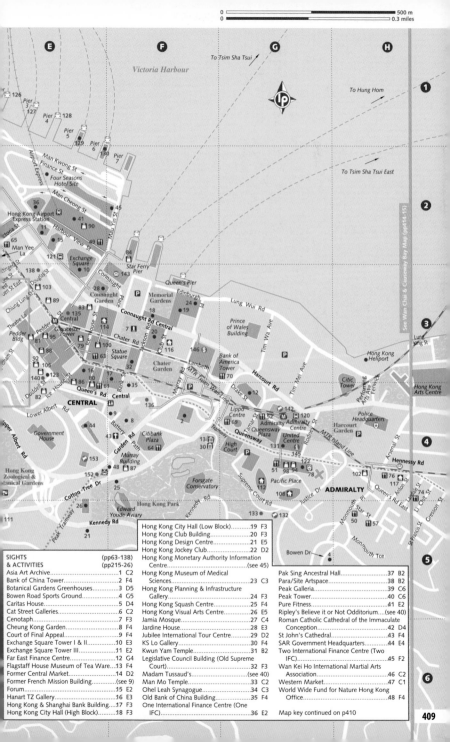

0 _____ 500 m
0 _____ 0.3 miles

E   **F**   To Tsim Sha Tsui   **G**   **H**

Victoria Harbour

To Hung Hom

To Tsim Sha Tsui East

See Wan Chai & Causeway Bay Map (pp414-15)

To Tsim Sha Tsui East

1

2

3

4

5

6

Pier 3
Pier 4
Pier 5
Pier 6
Pier 7
Pier 128
Pier 129
Pier 130

Airport Express
Man Kwong St
Finance St
Four Seasons Hotel Site
Man Cheong St
Hong Kong Airport Express Station
Harbour View St
Man Yee La
Exchange Square
Connaught Place
Star Ferry Pier
Queen's Pier
Memorial Gardens
Edinburgh Pl
Connaught Garden
Connaught Rd Central
Lung Wui Rd
Prince of Wales Building
Tim Wa Ave
Hong Kong Heliport
Lung King St
Hong Kong Arts Centre
Chater Rd
Statue Square
Chater Garden
Bank of America Tower
Harcourt Rd
Tim Mei Ave
Citic Tower
Police Headquarters
Harcourt Garden
CENTRAL
Queen's Rd Central
Lower Albert Rd
Lippo Centre
Admiralty Centre
Queensway Plaza
United Centre
Performing Arts Ave
Arsenal St
Hennessy Rd
Government House
Citibank Plaza
Queensway
High Court
Pacific Place
ADMIRALTY
Queen's Rd East
Monmouth Pl
Star St
Li Chit St
St Francis St
Cresson St
Hong Kong Zoological & Botanical Gardens
Cotton Tree Dr
Murray Building
Hong Kong Park
Forsgate Conservatory
Supreme Court Rd
Kennedy Rd
Justice Dr
Monmouth Tce
Bowen Dr
Edward Youde Aviary
Kennedy Rd

SIGHTS & ACTIVITIES (pp63-138) (pp215-26)

Asia Art Archive..................................1 C2
Bank of China Tower...........................2 F4
Botanical Gardens Greenhouses..........3 D5
Bowen Road Sports Ground................4 G5
Caritas House.....................................5 D4
Cat Street Galleries.............................6 C2
Cenotaph...7 F3
Cheung Kong Garden..........................8 F3
Court of Final Appeal..........................9 E3
Exchange Square Tower I & II.............10 E3
Exchange Square Tower III.................11 E2
Far East Finance Centre......................12 G4
Flagstaff House Museum of Tea Ware..13 F4
Former Central Market........................14 D2
Former French Mission Building.....(see 9)
Forum...15 E2
Hanart TZ Gallery..............................16 E3
Hong Kong & Shanghai Bank Building..17 F3
Hong Kong City Hall (High Block).......18 F3
Hong Kong City Hall (Low Block)........19 F3
Hong Kong Club Building....................20 F3
Hong Kong Design Centre..................21 E5
Hong Kong Jockey Club......................22 D2
Hong Kong Monetary Authority Information Centre......................(see 45)
Hong Kong Museum of Medical Sciences..23 C3
Hong Kong Planning & Infrastructure Gallery..24 F3
Hong Kong Squash Centre.................25 F4
Hong Kong Visual Arts Centre............26 E5
Jamia Mosque...................................27 C4
Jardine House....................................28 E3
Jubilee International Tour Centre........29 D2
KS Lo Gallery.....................................30 F4
Kwun Yam Temple.............................31 B2
Legislative Council Building (Old Supreme Court)..32 F3
Madam Tussaud's......................(see 40)
Man Mo Temple................................33 C2
Ohel Leah Synagogue........................34 C3
Old Bank of China Building................35 F3
One International Finance Centre (One IFC)...36 E2
Pak Sing Ancestral Hall......................37 B2
Para/Site Artspace.............................38 B2
Peak Galleria.....................................39 C6
Peak Tower..40 C6
Pure Fitness......................................41 E2
Ripley's Believe it or Not Odditorium....(see 40)
Roman Catholic Cathedral of the Immaculate Conception.......................................42 D4
St John's Cathedral............................43 F4
SAR Government Headquarters...........44 E4
Two International Finance Centre (Two IFC)..45 F2
Wan Kei Ho International Martial Arts Association...................................46 C2
Western Market.................................47 C1
World Wide Fund for Nature Hong Kong Office...48 F4

Map key continued on p410

409

SHEUNG WAN, CENTRAL & ADMIRALTY

Map key continued from p409

EATING 🍴   (pp149-96)
Cafe Deco..(see 39)
Café...(see 114)
Café TOO...(see 112)
Can.teen...49 E2
Cine Città..50 H5
City Hall Maxim's Palace.......................(see 19)
city'super...(see 49)
Dan Ryan's Chicago Grill..........................51 G4
Délifrance...52 G4
Fung Shing Restaurant.............................53 C1
Gaia Ristorante..54 D2
Genki Sushi..(see 12)
Graham St Market....................................55 D3
Grand Stage..(see 47)
Grappa's Peak Pizzeria............................(see 40)
Grappa's Ristorante.................................(see 51)
Great...56 D3
Habibi..(see 10)
Hunan Garden..(see 10)
Jo Jo Mess Branch.................................(see 70)
Kokage..57 H5
Korea House Restaurant............................58 D2
La Fontaine..(see 10)
Leung Hing Chiu Chow Seafood
  Restaurant..59 B2
Lin Heung Tea House................................60 D2
Mix..61 E4
Mix...(see 49)
Mozart Stub'n...62 D4
Nicholini's...(see 108)
Oliver's..63 E3
Oliver's Super Sandwiches........................64 F4
Park 'N' Shop (Des Voeux Rd)....................65 E2
Park 'N' Shop Supermarket (Peak
  Galleria)..(see 39)
Peak Lookout...66 C6
Petrus..(see 112)
Phoenix..67 C3
Phuket's...68 C4
Ruth's Chris Steakhouse...........................69 G4
Secret Garden..70 G3
Shalom Grill..71 D2
Sheung Wan Ho Choi Seafood
  Restaurant..72 C2
Tai Woo Seafood Restaurant......................73 C3
Tan Ta Wan Restaurant.............................74 H4
Thai Basil..(see 51)
Tsim Chai Kee Noodle...............................75 D2
Vong..(see 114)
Wellcome...(see 10)
Yè Shanghai...(see 51)
Yoshinoya Noodles...................................76 H4
Zen...(see 51)

DRINKING 🍷   (pp197-206)
Captain's Bar...(see 114)
Rice Bar...77 C2

ENTERTAINMENT 🎭   (pp197-214)
1/5...(see 57)
Palace IFC Cinema..................................(see 90)
UA Pacific Place......................................78 G4

SHOPPING 🛍   (pp227-48)
Alexandra House......................................79 E3
Beverley Boutique....................................80 E4

Blanc de Chine...81 E3
Bloomsbury Books.....................................82 E4
Bookazine..(see 12)
Bookazine...(see 100)
China Tee Club..(see 81)
Chinese Arts & Crafts..............................(see 98)
Christie..(see 79)
Cigarro...83 E3
City Chain..(see 98)
Dymocks..84 F2
Dymocks..(see 41)
Eu Yan Sang...85 D2
Fook Ming Tong Tea Shop.........................(see 49)
Galleria Shopping Centre...........................86 E3
Government Publications Office....................87 F4
HMV...88 E3
Hong Kong Book Centre.............................89 E3
Hong Kong Records.................................(see 98)
IFC Mall..90 D2
Joint Publishing.......................................91 D2
Joyce..92 E3
Joyce...(see 94)
Karin Weber Gallery..................................93 D3
Kelly & Walsh Branch...............................(see 10)
Kelly & Walsh...(see 94)
Kent & Curwen..94 G4
King & Country..(see 94)
Landmark..95 E3
Lane Crawford...(see 94)
Lane Crawford...(see 90)
Little Misses & Mini Masters.....................(see 100)
Liuligongfang..(see 88)
Liuligongfang..(see 90)
Lock Cha Tea Shop....................................96 C2
Mandarin Oriental Flower &
  Gift Shop...(see 114)
Miu Miu..(see 95)
New Wing Hing Dispensary........................97 D3
Ocean Optical...(see 80)
Pacific Custom Tailors.............................(see 98)
Pacific Place..98 G4
Po Kee Fishing Tackle................................99 C2
Ponti Food & Wine Cellar.........................(see 63)
Prince's Building.....................................100 E3
Seibu...(see 98)
Shanghai Tang..(see 81)
Shun Tak Centre.....................................(see 148)
Sincere..101 D2
Sotheby...(see 80)
Toto..(see 100)
Toy Museum..(see 100)
Vivienne Tam..(see 98)
Wah Tung China Arts...............................102 H4
Wanko...103 E3
Wing On...104 D2
Wise Kids...(see 100)
Wise Kids...(see 98)
www.izzue.com.......................................105 E3

SLEEPING 🛏   (pp249-74)
Bauhinia Furnished Suites.........................106 D2
Bishop Lei International House....................107 D4
Conrad Hong Kong...................................108 G4
Daisy Court...109 C3
Eden...110 D2
Garden View International House.................111 E5
Island Shangri-La Hotel.............................112 G4
Lily Court..113 C4
Mandarin Oriental....................................114 E3

Peach Blossom..115 C4
Ritz-Carlton Hong Kong............................116 F3
Wesley Hong Kong...................................117 H4
YWCA Building..118 B2

TRANSPORT   (pp287-306)
Aero International.....................................119 D2
Air New Zealand.....................................(see 28)
British Airways..(see 28)
Bus Station (Admiralty).............................120 G4
Central Bus Terminus................................121 E2
China Airlines..122 G4
China Eastern/China Southern Airlines.......123 F2
Dragon Air..124 D2
HKKF Customer Service Centre.................(see 128)
Licensing Division of the Transport
  Department..(see 131)
Macau Ferry Bus Terminus.........................125 C1
Northwest Airlines..................................(see 124)
NWFF Customer Service Centre.................(see 130)
Peak Tram Lower Terminus.......................(see 152)
Pier 2 (Ferries to Ma Wan)........................126 E1
Pier 3 (Ferries to Discovery Bay).................127 E1
Pier 4 (Ferries to Lamma).........................128 E1
Pier 5 (Ferries to Cheung Chau)..................129 E1
Pier 6 (Ferries to Lantau & Peng Chau).......130 E1
Qantas Airways......................................(see 28)
Singapore Airlines...................................131 G4
United Airlines..(see 95)
Virgin Atlantic Airways.............................(see 79)

INFORMATION
American Chamber of Commerce................(see 70)
British Consulate.....................................132 G5
British Council...133 G5
Canadian Consulate................................(see 10)
Canossa Hospital.....................................134 D4
Chater House..135 E3
Cheung Kong Centre.................................136 F4
China Travel Service (Main Branch).............137 D2
Chinese General Chamber of
  Commerce..138 E3
Chinese Manufacturers' Association
  of Hong Kong.......................................(see 22)
City Hall Public Library............................(see 18)
Community Advice Bureau..........................139 D2
Drake International...................................140 E3
Dutch Consulate.....................................(see 136)
Essential Chinese Language Centre.............141 D2
French Consulate.....................................142 G4
General Post Office...................................143 F3
German Consulate..................................(see 145)
Hong Kong Consumer Council....................144 D2
Hong Kong General Chamber of
  Commerce..145 G4
Hong Kong Labour Department.................(see 144)
HSBC...146 F3
IT Fans...147 D2
Japanese Consulate.................................(see 10)
Macau Government Tourist Office................148 C1
Martinizing...149 D4
New Furama Dry-Cleaning........................(see 70)
Pacific Coffee Company...........................(see 49)
PCCW i Shop...150 D2
Post Office..151 D2
St John's Building....................................152 E4
US Consulate..153 E4

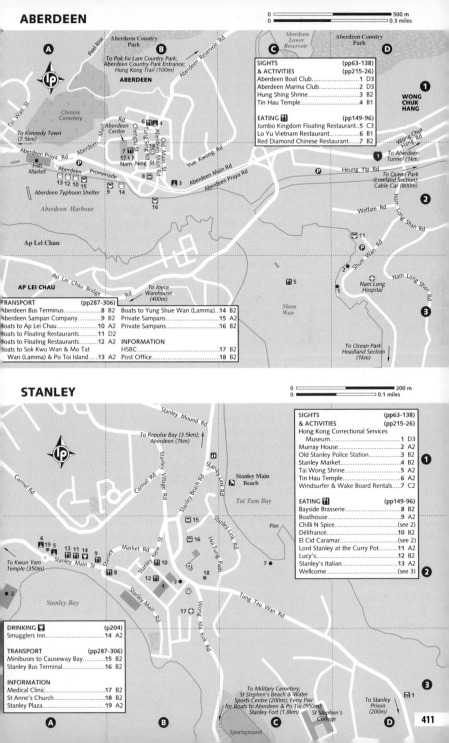

ABERDEEN

0 — 500 m
0 — 0.3 miles

SIGHTS	(pp63-138)
& ACTIVITIES	(pp215-26)
Aberdeen Boat Club	1 D3
Aberdeen Marina Club	2 D3
Hung Shing Shrine	3 B2
Tin Hau Temple	4 B1

EATING	(pp149-96)
Jumbo Kingdom Floating Restaurant	5 C3
Lo Yu Vietnam Restaurant	6 B1
Red Diamond Chinese Restaurant	7 B2

TRANSPORT	(pp287-306)
Aberdeen Bus Terminus	8 B2
Aberdeen Sampan Company	9 B2
Boats to Ap Lei Chau	10 A2
Boats to Floating Restaurants	11 D2
Boats to Floating Restaurants	12 A2
Boats to Sok Kwu Wan & Mo Tat	
Wan (Lamma) & Po Toi Island	13 A2
Boats to Yung Shue Wan (Lamma)	14 B2
Private Sampans	15 A2
Private Sampans	16 B2

INFORMATION	
HSBC	17 B2
Post Office	18 B2

WONG CHUK HANG

To Pok Fu Lam Country Park;
Aberdeen Country Park Entrance;
Hong Kong Trail (100m)

To Kennedy Town
(7.5km)

To Ocean Park
(lowland Section);
Cable Car (800m)

To Aberdeen
Tunnel (1km)

To Joyce
Warehouse
(400m)

To Ocean Park
Headland Section
(1km)

Chinese Cemetery
Aberdeen Centre
Fish Market
Aberdeen Promenade
Aberdeen Typhoon Shelter
Aberdeen Harbour
Ap Lei Chau
AP LEI CHAU
Ap Lei Chau Bridge
Sham Wan
Nam Long Hospital

STANLEY

0 — 200 m
0 — 0.1 miles

SIGHTS	(pp63-138)
& ACTIVITIES	(pp215-26)
Hong Kong Correctional Services	
Museum	1 D3
Murray House	2 A2
Old Stanley Police Station	3 B2
Stanley Market	4 B2
Tai Wong Shrine	5 A2
Tin Hau Temple	6 A2
Windsurfer & Wake Board Rentals	7 C2

EATING	(pp149-96)
Bayside Brasserie	8 B2
Boathouse	9 A2
Chilli N Spice	(see 2)
Délifrance	10 B2
El Cid Caramar	(see 2)
Lord Stanley at the Curry Pot	11 A2
Lucy's	12 B2
Stanley's Italian	13 A2
Wellcome	(see 3)

DRINKING	(p204)
Smugglers Inn	14 A2

TRANSPORT	(pp287-306)
Minibuses to Causeway Bay	15 B2
Stanley Bus Terminal	16 B2

INFORMATION	
Medical Clinic	17 B2
St Anne's Church	18 B2
Stanley Plaza	19 A2

To Repulse Bay (3.5km);
Aberdeen (7km)

Stanley Main Beach
Tai Tam Bay
Pier

To Kwun Yam
Temple (350m)

Stanley Bay

To Military Cemetery;
St Stephen's Beach & Water
Sports Centre (200m); Ferry Pier
for Boats to Aberdeen & Po Toi (550m);
Stanley Fort (1.8km)
St Stephen's College

To Stanley
Prison
(200m)

Sportsground

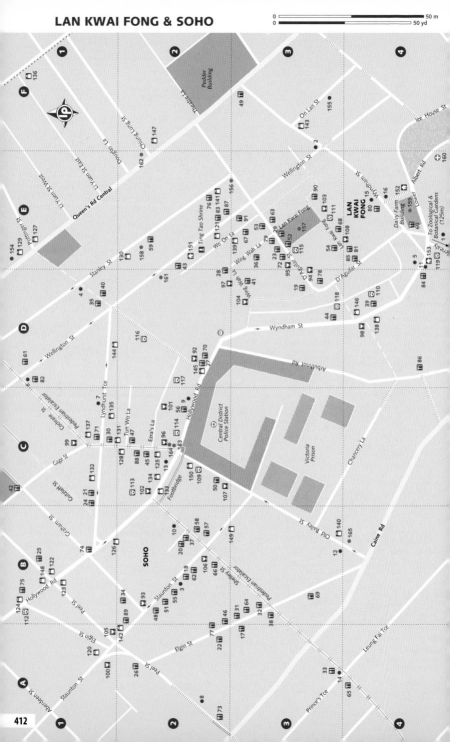

LAN KWAI FONG & SOHO

0 —————— 50 m
0 —————— 50 yd

412

LAN KWAI FONG & SOHO

SIGHTS
& ACTIVITIES (pp63–138)
Bishop's House......................................1 E4
California Fitness...................................2 F3
DK Aromatherapy.................................3 B2
Fightin' Fit...4 D1
Grotto Fine Art.....................................5 E4
Happy Foot Reflexology........................6 D1
Healing Plants.......................................7 C1
John Batten Gallery...............................8 A2
Plum Blossoms......................................9 C2
Pure Fitness..10 B2
Q Yoga...11 B4
Schoeni Art Gallery.............................12 B3
Schoeni Art Gallery Branch..................13 C2
Sin Sin Fine Art...................................14 A3
Yoga Central.......................................15 E4
Yoga Fitness..16 E4

EATING (pp149–96)
2 Sardines...17 A3
Al Dente...18 B2
Al's Diner..19 D3
Archie B's New York Deli......................20 B2
Assaf..21 C1
Bagel Factory......................................22 A2
Beirut...23 E3
Beyrouth Café Central..........................24 C1
Blowfish...25 B1
Boca..26 A2
Bombay Dreams...........................(see 22)
Bon Appétit..27 D2
Café des Artistes.................................28 D2
Café Siam...29 E3
Carambal..30 C1
Ched..31 B3
Chicken on the Run.............................32 B3
Chilli Fagara..33 A3
Chippy...34 B2
Cul-de-Sac...35 D1
El Taco Loco.......................................36 E3
Fat Angelo's..37 B2
Finds..38 B3
Fringe Club2.................................39 D4
Golden Fruit Juice........................(see 159)
Good Luck Thai...................................40 D1
Graham St Market...............................41 D3
Greenlands India Club..........................42 C1
Gunga Din's Club................................43 D3

Hot Dog...44 D3
India Today...45 C2
Indochine 1929...................................46 B2
Ivan the Kozak...........................(see 157)
Jaspa's...47 C2
Jimmy's Kitchen..................................48 F3
Kath+Man+Du....................................49 F3
Kiyotaki Japanese Restaurant...............50 C2
Kohi-i-Noor..51 B2
Kyoto Joe...52 E3
La Baguette..53 E3
La Comida..54 E1
La Kasbah...55 D2
Le Rendez-Vous..................................56 C2
Life..57 B2
Luk Yu Tea House................................58 B2
M at the Fringe....................................59 E2
Mak's Noodle......................................60 E4
Nepal...61 D1
Ning Po Residents' Association..............62 B3
Olive..63 B3
Orange Tree..64 B3
Peak Cafe Bar.....................................65 A4
Pearl Vietnamese Restaurant................66 B2
Post 97...67 E3
Rico's...68 A2
Rughetta..69 B3
San Marzano.......................................70 D2
Schnurrbart..71 C1
Shui Hu Ju..72 B1
Soho Bakery.......................................73 A2
SoHo SoHo..74 B1
Song..75 B1
Spaghetti House..................................76 E2
Stone Grill..77 A2
Stormy Weather..................................78 D3
Sunny & Barbie...................................79 E3
Super Star Seafood Restaurant.............80 E4
Thai Lemongrass.........................(see 157)
Tokio Joe..81 E4
Tsim Chai Kee....................................82 D1
Tsui Wah..83 B2
Uncle Willie's Deli...............................84 D4
Va Bene...85 E4
Veda..86 D4
Wong Chi Kei.....................................87 E2
XTC on Ice..88 C2
Yi Jiang Nan..89 B2

Yorohachi..90 E3
Yung Kee Restaurant............................91 E2

DRINKING (pp197–206)
Après..92 D2
Bar 1911...93 B2
Bar George..................................(see 99)
Bit Point...94 D3
Club 64..95 C1
Dragon–1..96 C2
Dublin Jack...97 D2
Feather Boa..98 D4
Gecko Lounge.....................................99 A1
Globe...100 C1
La Dolce Vita.....................................101 C2
Le Jardin..102 C2
Om Lounge.......................................103 E3
Staunton's Wine Bar & Cafe................104 D3
V-13...105 A1
Whiskey Priest...................................106 D2
....107 D2
....108 E4

ENTERTAINMENT (pp197–206)
Blue Door Jazz Club...........................109 C2
Bohemian Lounge..............................110 D4
C Club..(see 157)
Cavern...111 E3
Club 97...112 B1
Club NU..113 C2
Drop...(see 98)
Edge...(see 22)
Fringe Gallery............................(see 159)
Fringe Studio & O2 Theatre.........(see 159)
Homebase...114 C2
Insomnia...115 B1
Jewel..116 D2
Propaganda.......................................117 D2
Red Rock..118 D3
Works...119 E4

SHOPPING (pp227–48)
Amours Antiques................................120 A1
Anglo-Chinese Florist.........................121 E2
Arch Angel Antiques..........................122 D1
Arch Angel Fine Art...........................123 B1
Caravan..124 D1
Carpet Centre....................................125 C2
Chine Gallery.....................................126 B1

Chinese Arts & Crafts.........................127 E1
Cigar Express Central..........................128 C2
City Chain..129 E1
Everbest Photo Supplies.....................130 E2
Flow Organic Bookshop......................131 C1
Hing Lee Camera Company..................132 C1
Hobbs & Bishops Fine Art...................133 C1
Honeychurch Antiques........................134 C2
Indosiam..135 C1
King Fook...136 F1
Linva Tailor..137 C1
Mir Oriental Carpets...........................138 D4
Mountain Folkcraft..............................139 E3
Olympia Graeco-Egyptian Coffee.........140 B3
Photo Scientific..................................141 E2
Soho Wines & Spirits..........................142 A2
Tai Sing Fine Antiques........................143 F3
Tai Yip Art Book Centre.......................144 D1
Teresa Coleman Fine Arts....................145 D2
Tibetan Gallery...................................146 D4
Tse Sui Luen.......................................147 F2
Wah Tung China Arts..........................148 B1
Watson's Wine Cellar..........................149 B3
Wattis Fine Art...................................150 C2
X Game Sporting Goods..............(see 80)

SLEEPING (pp249–74)
Hanlun Habitats (Main Office)..............151 E2
Ice House..152 E4
Shama Main Office..............................153 E4

TRANSPORT (pp287–306)
China Travel Service............................154 E1
Concorde Travel.................................155 F3
Natori Travels.............................(see 162)

INFORMATION
1010 CSL Outlet.................................156 E2
California Tower..................................157 E2
Color Six..158 E2
Fringe Club..159 E4
Hong Kong Central Hospital................160 E4
Hong Kong Institute of Languages.......161 D2
Melbourne Plaza.................................162 E2
Pacific Coffee Company.......................163 C2
Rent-A-Mum......................................164 C2
Wei Wei Dry Cleaner & Laundry...........165 B4

WAN CHAI & CAUSEWAY BAY

A   B   C   D

1

To
Tsim Sha Tsui
(1.5km)

Enlargement (inset)

Gloucester Rd

52   135   1

34   96   24   O'Brien Rd
56   88   Jaffe Rd   79
Fenwick St   94   97   60   28   68
83   82   145   100   36 78   84
91   89   85
Lockhart Rd   80 31 62   98 86 35
127   Hennessy Rd   151   Wan Chai
0 — 200 m   147   119   111

To Hung Hom
(2.3km)

2

3

3   57
Expo Dr
7   Expo Dr East
149
158
Convention Ave   141   Hung Hing Rd   Wan Shing St
150   Marsh Rd
6   130   Harbour Rd   159   168   Harbour Centre   Wan Chai
Shui on Centre   114   Wan Chai Tower   165   Great Eagle Centre   Sports Ground
95   90   131   105   China Resources Building   61   Causeway Sun Hung Kai Centre   Tonnochy Rd
5   Revenue Tower   156 Immigration Tower   148   93   43   Jaffe Rd
Harbour Dr   8   30   45   15   Lockhart Rd
See Enlargement   Central Plaza   Wan Chai Police Station   76   99   63   Marsh Rd
Gloucester Rd   29   Stewart Rd   51   Hennessy Rd   MTR Island Line
Jaffe St   Luard Rd   Jaffe Rd   Fleming Rd   Lockhart Rd   Tonnochy Rd   Tramway

4

101   161   Fenwick St   Lockhart Rd   Lockhart Rd Market   Heard St   Tak Yan Rd   Wan Chai   44
87   Jaffe St   Hennessy Rd   Wan Chai   WAN CHAI   64   124   Sharp St
25   162   O'Brien Rd   Johnston Rd   Burrows St   Wan Chai Rd   144
Anton St   Thomson Rd   Southorn Playground   Thomson Rd   Mallory St   Cross La   Morrison Hill   126
Landale St   Tramway   Johnston Rd   117   103   Wood St   Salvation Army St   15
Li Chit St   Cresson St   106   47   53   Bullock La   Ruttonjee Hospital   Oi Kwan Rd   18   Shiu Kin La
Queen's Rd East   Ship St   Tai Wing St West   Swatow St   Amoy St   Stone Nullah La   Wan Chai Park   Queen's Rd East   163   Sung Tak La
13   Tai Wong St East   Lee Tung St   Spring Garden La   Cross St   MORRISON HILL   Stubbs Rd   Hau Tak La   Wong Nai Chung Rd

5

Bowen Rd
12   MORRISON HILL   23   Muslim Cemetery   9
152   17   Queen's Rd East   102   St Margaret's College   Catholic Cemetery
Fung Wong Terr   Kennedy Rd   Wan Chai Gap Rd   Stone Nullah La   Kennedy Rd
Bowen Rd

6

14   Aberdeen (6km)
Hong Kong Cemetery
1
Aberdeen Tunnel

See Sheung Wan, Central & Admiralty Map (pp108-9)

MTR Tsuen Wan Line

Lung King St

414

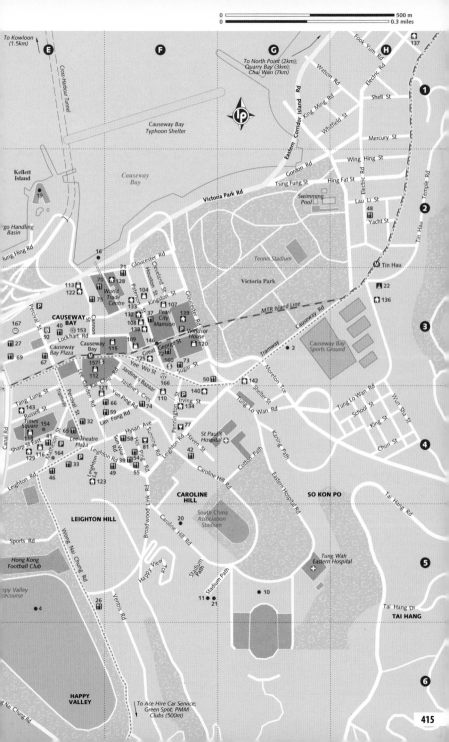

SIGHTS & ACTIVITIES (pp63-138) (pp215-26)
California Fitness 1 D1
Central Library 2 G3
Golden Bauhinia 3 B2
Happy Valley Sports Ground 4 E5
Hong Kong Amateur Athletic Association (see 21)
Hong Kong Arts Centre 5 A3
Hong Kong Chinese Martial Arts Association (see 21)
Hong Kong Convention & Exhibition Centre 6 B3
Hong Kong Convention & Exhibition Centre (New Wing) 7 B2
Hong Kong Cricket Association (see 21)
Hong Kong Cycling Association (see 21)
Hong Kong Federation of Roller Sports (see 11)
Hong Kong Golf Association (see 21)
Hong Kong Jockey Club 8 C3
Hong Kong Mountaineering Union (see 21)
Hong Kong Racing Museum 9 D5
Hong Kong Rugby Football Union (see 21)
Hong Kong Sailing Federation (see 11)
Hong Kong Stadium 10 G5
Hong Kong Wakebording Association (see 11)
Hong Kong Water Ski Association (see 11)
Hong Kong Wushu Union 11 F5
Hopewell Centre 12 B5
Hung Shing Temple 13 A5
Lover's Rock 14 C6
Morrison Hill Public Swimming Pool 15 D5
Noonday Gun 16 E2
Old Wan Chai Post Office 17 B5
Pao Sui Loong & Pao Yue Kong Galleries (see 90)
Queen Elizabeth Stadium 18 D5
Royal Hong Kong Yacht Club 19 E2
South China Athletic Association 20 F5
Sports House 21 F5
Tin Hau Temple 22 H3
Wan Chai Market 23 C5
Windsurfing Association of Hong Kong (see 11)

EATING (pp149-96)
369 Shanghai Restaurant 24 D1
American Restaurant 25 A4
Amigo 26 E5
Arirang (see 154)
Banana Leaf Curry House 27 E3
Beijing Shui Jiao Wong 28 D1
Bhet Ghat Restaurant 29 C4
Bo Kung (see 154)
Carriana Chiu Chow Restaurant 30 D3
Che's Cantonese Restaurant 31 C1
Chuen Cheung Kui 32 E4
Chung Chuk Lau Restaurant 33 E4
Cinta-J 34 C1
Coyote Bar & Grill 35 D2
Cul-d-Sac 36 C1
Dynasty (see 141)
East Lake 37 F3
East Ocean Seafood Restaurant 38 C3
Forever Green Taiwanese Restaurant 39 F4
Forum 40 E3
Genroku Sushi 41 E4
Gogo Café 42 F4
Golden Bull (see 154)
Golden Myanmar 43 D3
Heichinrou (see 154)
Higashiyama 44 D4
Hong Kong Old Restaurant (see 137)
Hyang Chon Korean Restaurant 45 D3
Indonesian Restaurant 1968 46 E4
Jo Jo Mess 47 B4
June 48 H2
Korea Restaurant 49 F4
Kung Tak Lam 50 F3
Liu Yuan Restaurant 51 D4
Louis' Steak House 52 C1
Lung Moon Restaurant 53 B4
Moon Garden Tea House 54 F4
One Harbour Road (see 130)
Orphée 55 F4
Pak Loh Chiu Chow Restaurant (see 65)
Pepperoni's Pizza 56 C1
Port Cafe 57 B2
Queen's Cafe 58 F4
R66 (see 12)
Red Pepper 59 F4
Sabah 60 D1
Saigon 61 C3
Saigon Beach 62 C2
Shabu Shabu 63 D4
Shaffi's Malik 64 D4
Sorabol Korean Restaurant 65 E4
Tai Ping Koon 66 F4
Tai Woo Seafood Restaurant 67 E3
Tim's Kitchen 68 D1
Tomokazu 69 E3
Tony Roma's 70 E3
Towngas Avenue 71 F3
Vegetarian Court (see 51)
Viceroy Restaurant & Bar (see 61)
Victoria City (see 61)
Wellcome 72 F3
W's Entrecôte (see 129)
Xian Nan Guo 73 F3
Xin Jin Shi 74 F4
Yin Ping Vietnamese Restaurant 75 E3
Zambra 76 C4

DRINKING (pp197-206)
Brecht's Bar 77 F4
Bridge 78 C1
Champagne Bar (see 130)
Delaney's 79 C1
Devil's Advocate 80 C1
Dickens Bar (see 128)
East End Brewery & Inn Side Out 81 F4
Fenwick the Dock 82 C1
Groovy Mule 83 C1
Horse & Groom 84 D1
Kangaroo Downunder (see 31)
Mes Amis 85 C1
Old China Hand 86 D2
Rennie Mac's Brasserie 87 A4
Skitz 88 C1
Tango Martini 89 C1
White Stag (see 31)

ENTERTAINMENT (pp197-214)
Agnés b Cinema 90 A3
Carnegie's 91 C1
Causeway Lounge 92 E3
Cine-Art House 93 C3
Dusk till Dawn 94 C1
Hong Kong Academy for the Performing Arts 95 A3
Joe Bananas 96 C1
Les Visages (see 88)
Manhattan Club Ing (see 141)
Neptune Disco II 97 D1
New Makati Pub & Disco 98 D2
Punchline Comedy Club (see 61)
Shouson Theatre (see 90)
Sister (see 109)
Today's Tonnochy Nightclub 99 D4
Venue 100 C1
Wanch 101 A4
Wasabisabi (see 154)
Windsor Cinema (see 120)

SHOPPING (pp227-48)
Al-Shahzadi Persian Carpet Gallery 102 C5
Bunn's Divers 103 C4
Camper 104 F3
Chinese Arts & Crafts 105 C3
Chung Yuen Electrical Co (see 118)
Cosmos Books 106 A4
D-Mop 107 F3
Dada Cabaret Voltaire 108 F3
Design Gallery (see 7)
HMV (see 120)
i.t (see 118)
In Square (see 120)
Island Beverley 109 F3
Jardine's Bazaar 110 F4
Joint Publishing 111 D2
Kung Fu Supplies (see 103)
Lane Crawford (see 118)
Mitsukoshi 112 E3
Mountaineering Services 113 E3
Small Claims Tribunal 114 B3
Sogo 115 F3
Spy 116 E4
Sunmark Camping Equipment 117 C4
Times Square 118 E4
Walter Ma (see 129)
Wan Chai Computer Centre 119 D2
Watson's Wine Cellar (see 120)
Windsor House 120 F3
X Game Sorting Goods 121 E4

SLEEPING (pp249-74)
Alisan Guest House 122 E3
Asia Hostel (see 132)
Causeway Bay Guest House 123 E4
Charterhouse Hotel 124 D4
Chung Kiu Inn 125 F3
Cosmopolitan Hotel 126 D5
Empire Hotel Hong Kong 127 C2
Excelsior Hong Kong 128 F3
Express by Holiday Inn 129 E4
Grand Hyatt Hotel 130 B3
Harbour View International House 131 B3
Hong Kong Hostel 132 F3
Jetvan Travellers' House 133 F3
JIA 134 F4
Luk Kwok Hotel 135 D1
Metropark Hotel 136 H3
Newton Hotel Hong Kong 137 H1
Noble Hostel 138 F3
Park Lane Hong Kong 139 F3
Regal Hongkong Hotel 140 F4
Renaissance Harbour View 141 B3
Rosedale on the Park 142 G3
Shama 143 E4
South Pacific Hotel Hong Kong 144 D4
Wharney Guangdong Hotel Hong Kong 145 C1
Wung Fat Hostel (see 132)

TRANSPORT (pp287-306)
China Travel Service 146 F3
China Travel Service (see 147a)
Southorn Centre 147 D2
Visa Office of the People's Republic of China 148 C3
Wan Chai Ferry Pier 149 C2
Wan Chai Ferry Pier Bus Terminus 150 C3

INFORMATION
Alliance Française 151 D2
Australian Consulate (see 38)
Chinese Medicine Council of Hong Kong 152 B5
Cyber Pro Internet 153 E3
Food Forum 154 E4
Goethe-Institut (see 90)
Hong Kong Federation of Women 155 D3
Hong Kong Immigration Department 156 B3
Hong Kong Island HKTB Centre 157 E3
Hong Kong TDC Business Info Centre 158 B3
Hong Kong Trade Development Council (Head Office) 159 B3
HSBC 160 F3
Irish Consulate 161 A4
Joint Council for the Physically and Mentally Disabled 162 A4
Khalsa Diwan Sikh Temple 163 D5
Leighton Centre 164 E4
New Zealand Consulate 165 B3
PCCW iShop 166 F3
Post Office 167 E3
South African Consulate 168 C3
Towngas Cooking Centre (see 164)
Water Supplies Department (see 156)

HONG KONG MTR SYSTEM MAP

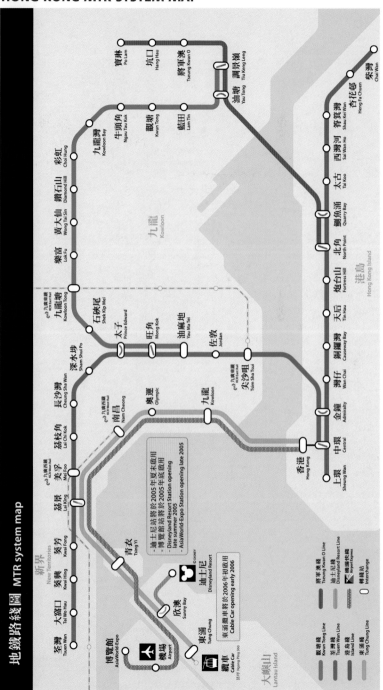

地鐵路綫圖 MTR system map

寶琳 Po Lam
坑口 Hang Hau
將軍澳 Tseung Kwan O
調景嶺 Tiu Keng Leng
柴灣 Chai Wan
油塘 Yau Tong
杏花邨 Heng Fa Chuen
筲箕灣 Shau Kei Wan
西灣河 Sai Wan Ho
太古 Tai Koo
鰂魚涌 Quarry Bay
北角 North Point
炮台山 Fortress Hill
天后 Tin Hau
銅鑼灣 Causeway Bay
灣仔 Wan Chai
金鐘 Admiralty
中環 Central
上環 Sheung Wan
香港 Hong Kong

華頭角 Ngau Tau Kok
觀塘 Kwun Tong
藍田 Lam Tin
九龍灣 Kowloon Bay
彩虹 Choi Hung
鑽石山 Diamond Hill
黃大仙 Wong Tai Sin
樂富 Lok Fu
九龍塘 Kowloon Tong
石硤尾 Shek Kip Mei
太子 Prince Edward
旺角 Mong Kok
油麻地 Yau Ma Tei
佐敦 Jordan
尖沙咀 Tsim Sha Tsui
九龍 Kowloon

九鐵西鐵 KCR West Rail
深水埗 Sham Shui Po
長沙灣 Cheung Sha Wan
荔枝角 Lai Chi Kok
美孚 Mei Foo
荔景 Lai King
葵芳 Kwai Fong
葵興 Kwai Hing
大窩口 Tai Wo Hau
荃灣 Tsuen Wan

九鐵東鐵 KCR East Rail

九龍 Kowloon

港島 Hong Kong Island

九鐵西鐵 KCR West Rail

奧運 Olympic
南昌 Nam Cheong
青衣 Tsing Yi
欣澳 Sunny Bay
東涌 Tung Chung
博覽館 AsiaWorld-Expo
機場 Airport
纜車 Cable Car
昂坪 Ngong Ping 360

迪士尼 Disneyland Resort

新界 New Territories

大嶼山 Lantau Island

- 迪士尼站將於2005年夏末啟用
- 博覽館站將於2005年底啟用
  Disneyland Resort Station opening late summer 2005
  AsiaWorld-Expo Station opening late 2005

東涌纜車將於2006年初啟用
Cable Car opening early 2006

將軍澳綫 Tseung Kwan O Line
迪士尼綫 Disneyland Resort Line
機場快綫 Airport Express
轉車站 Interchange

觀塘綫 Kwun Tong Line
荃灣綫 Tsuen Wan Line
港島綫 Island Line
東涌綫 Tung Chung Line

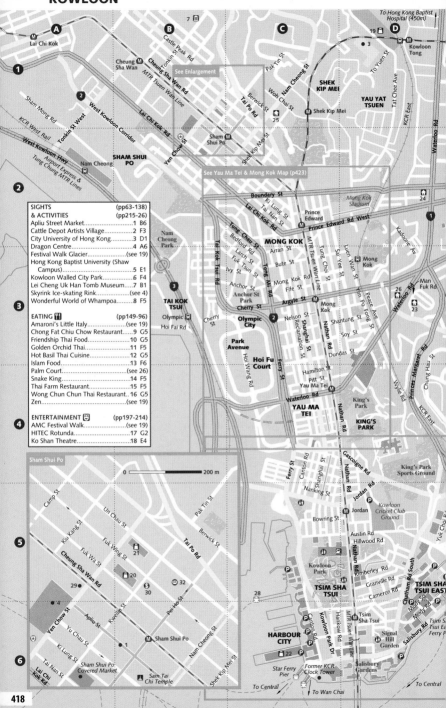

To Hong Kong Baptist
Hospital (450m)

Lai Chi Kok

Castle Peak Rd

See Enlargement

To Yuen Long

Kowloon
Tong

SHEK
KIP MEI

YAU YAT
TSUEN

Cheung
Sha Wan

Cheung Sha Wan Rd

MTR Tsuen Wan Line

Tonkin St

Tai Po Rd

Woh Chai St

Nam Cheong St

Shek Kip Mei

Berwick St

Pak Tin St

Tat Chee Ave

KCR East

Waterloo Rd

Sham Mong Rd

West Kowloon Corridor

Lai Chi Kok Rd

Tonkin St West

KCR West Rail

West Kowloon Hwy

Airport Express &
Tung Chung MTR Lines

Nam Cheong

SHAM SHUI
PO

Yen Chow St

Sham
Shui Po

Shek Kip Mei St

See Yau Ma Tei & Mong Kok Map (p423)

Boundary St

Mong Kok
Stadium

Nam
Cheong
Park

Ki Lung St

Tai Nan St

Lai Chi Kok Rd

Prince
Edward

Prince Edward Rd West

Kadoorie Av

Tung Chau St

Tung Choi St

Sai Yee St

Luen Wan St

Yim Po Fong St

Peace Ave

Man
Fuk Rd

Bedford
Larch St
Fuk Tsun St
Ivy St

Arran St
Bute St

Mong Kok Rd

MONG KOK

Mong
Kok

Anchor St

Fife St

Anchor St
Park

Argyle St

Mong
Kok

TAI KOK
TSUI

Cherry St

Cherry St

Olympic

Hoi Fai Rd

Olympic
City

Nelson St

Shanghai St
Reclamation St

Shantung St

Soy St

Dundas St

Park
Avenue

Hoi Fu
Court

Hoi Wang Rd

Hamilton St

Pitt St
Yau Ma Tei

Wylie Rd

Ferry St

Nathan Rd

Princess Margaret Rd

Chung Hau St

KCR East

Waterloo Rd

YAU MA
TEI

King's
Park

Nathan Rd

KING'S
PARK

SIGHTS
& ACTIVITIES (pp63–138)
(pp215–26)
Apliu Street Market.....................1 B6
Cattle Depot Artists Village...........2 F3
City University of Hong Kong.........3 D1
Dragon Centre..........................4 A6
Festival Walk Glacier..............(see 19)
Hong Kong Baptist University (Shaw
    Campus)..............................5 E1
Kowloon Walled City Park.............6 F4
Lei Cheng Uk Han Tomb Museum....7 B1
Skyrink Ice-skating Rink.............(see 4)
Wonderful World of Whampoa........8 F5

EATING (pp149–96)
Amaroni's Little Italy...............(see 19)
Chong Fat Chiu Chow Restaurant....9 G5
Friendship Thai Food.................10 G5
Golden Orchid Thai..................11 F5
Hot Basil Thai Cuisine...............12 G5
Islam Food............................13 F6
Palm Court.........................(see 26)
Snake King...........................14 F5
Thai Farm Restaurant...............15 F5
Wong Chun Chun Thai Restaurant..16 G5
Zen................................(see 19)

ENTERTAINMENT (pp197–214)
AMC Festival Walk.................(see 19)
HITEC Rotunda.......................17 G2
Ko Shan Theatre......................18 E4

Gascoigne Rd

King's Park
Sports Ground

Ferry St

Canton Rd

Shanghai St

Nathan Rd

Jordan Rd

Kowloon
Cricket Club
Ground

Nanking St

Jordan

Bowring St

Austin Rd

Hillwood Rd

Yuk Choi Rd

Sham Shui Po

0   200 m

Camp St

Un Chau St

Pak Tin St

Tai Po Rd

Kowloon
Park

Nathan Rd

Kimberley Rd

TSIM SHA
TSUI EAST

Kiu Kiang St

Fuk Wing St

Berwick St

Granville Rd

Cameron Rd

Chatham Rd South

Mody Rd

Fuk Wa St

Cheung Sha Wan Rd

21

20

29

30

32

Pei Ho St

Kweilin St

TSIM SHA
TSUI

Kowloon Park Dr

Hankow Rd

Tsim
Sha Tsui

MTR Tsuen Wan Line

Signal
Hill
Garden

Tsim S.
Tsui Ea.
Ferry Pi.

Tsim S.
Tsui Ea.
Ferry P.

Yen Chow St

Yu Chau St

Apliu St

Nam Cheong St

Shek Kip Mei St

Sham Shui Po

HARBOUR
CITY

Canton Rd

Salisbury Rd

Tai Nan St

Ki Lung St

Lai Chi
Kok Rd

Sham Shui Po
Covered Market

Sam Tai
Chi Temple

Star Ferry
Pier

Former KCR
Clock Tower

Salisbury
Gardens

22

28

To Central

To Wan Chai

To Central

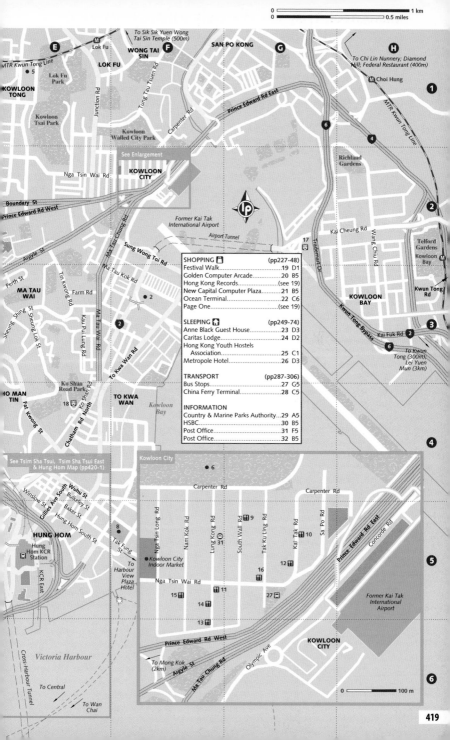

TSIM SHA TSUI, TSIM SHA TSUI EAST & HUNG HOM

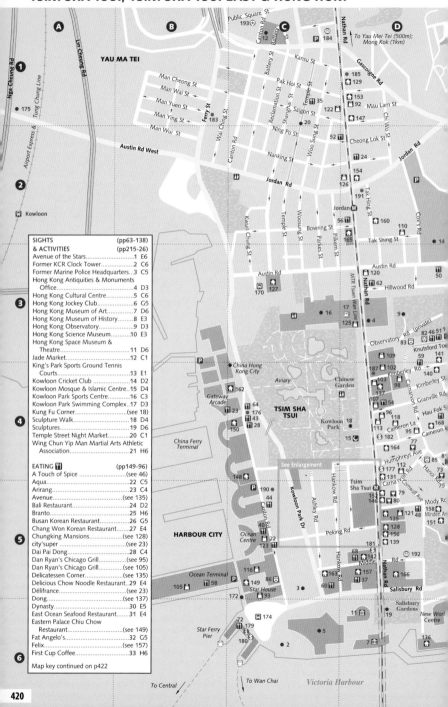

SIGHTS	(pp63–138)
& ACTIVITIES	(pp215–26)
Avenue of the Stars	1 E6
Former KCR Clock Tower	2 C6
Former Marine Police Headquarters	3 C5
Hong Kong Antiquities & Monuments Office	4 D3
Hong Kong Cultural Centre	5 C6
Hong Kong Jockey Club	6 G5
Hong Kong Museum of Art	7 D6
Hong Kong Museum of History	8 E3
Hong Kong Observatory	9 D3
Hong Kong Science Museum	10 E3
Hong Kong Space Museum & Theatre	11 D6
Jade Market	12 C1
King's Park Sports Ground Tennis Courts	13 E1
Kowloon Cricket Club	14 D2
Kowloon Mosque & Islamic Centre	15 D4
Kowloon Park Sports Centre	16 C3
Kowloon Park Swimming Complex	17 D3
Kung Fu Corner	(see 18)
Sculpture Walk	18 D4
Sculptures	19 D6
Temple Street Night Market	20 C1
Wing Chun Yip Man Martial Arts Athletic Association	21 H6

EATING	(pp149–96)
A Touch of Spice	(see 46)
Aqua	22 C5
Arirang	23 C4
Avenue	(see 135)
Bali Restaurant	24 D2
Branto	25 H6
Busan Korean Restaurant	26 G5
Chang Won Korean Restaurant	27 E4
Chungking Mansions	(see 128)
city'super	(see 23)
Dai Pai Dong	28 C4
Dan Ryan's Chicago Grill	(see 95)
Dan Ryan's Chicago Grill	(see 105)
Delicatessen Corner	(see 135)
Delicious Chow Noodle Restaurant	29 E4
Délifrance	(see 23)
Dong	(see 137)
Dynasty	30 E5
East Ocean Seafood Restaurant	31 E4
Eastern Palace Chiu Chow Restaurant	(see 149)
Fat Angelo's	32 G5
Felix	(see 157)
First Cup Coffee	33 H6

Map key continued on p422

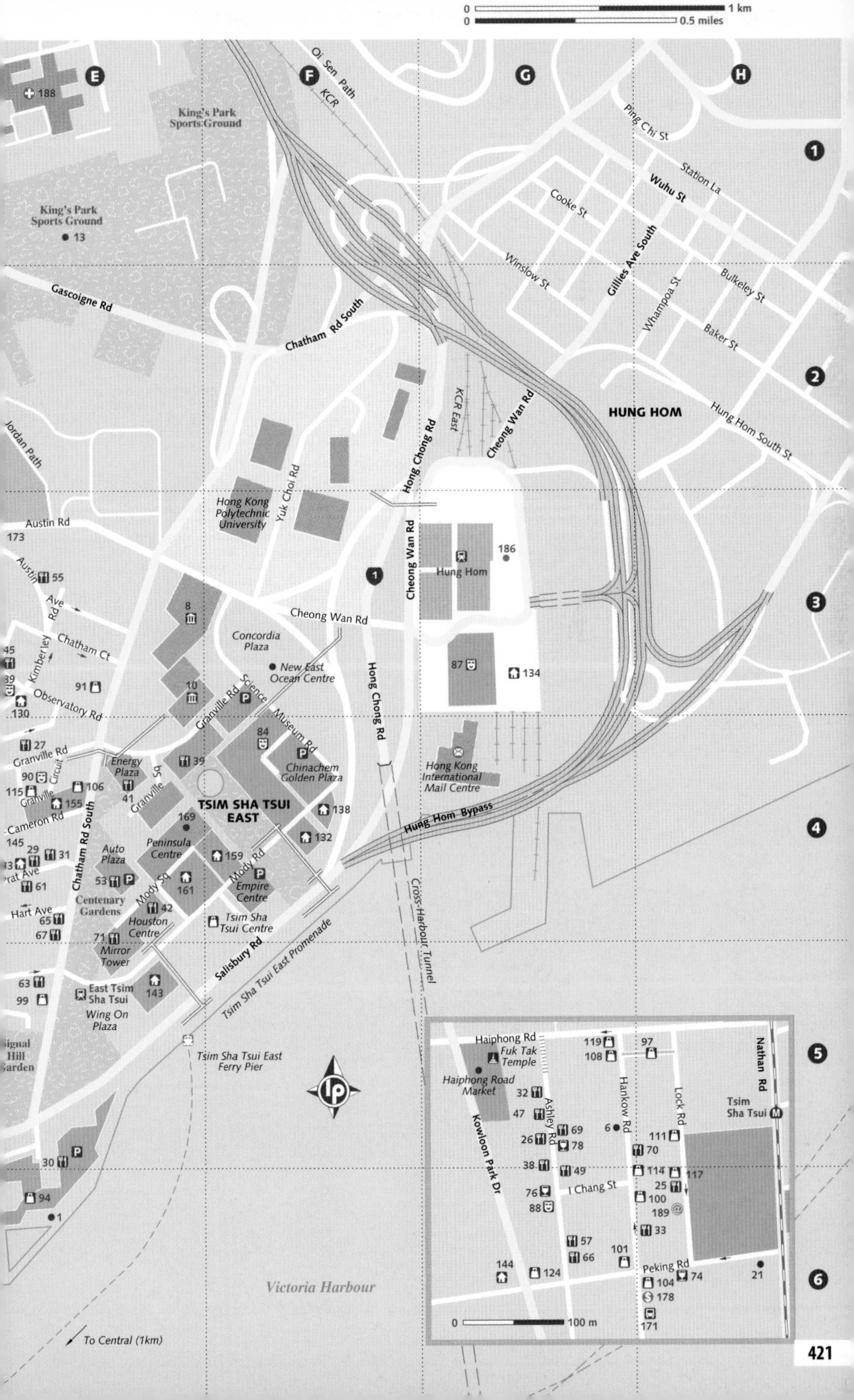

0 1 km
0 0.5 miles
E
F
G
H
1
2
3
4
5
6
188
King's Park Sports Ground
King's Park Sports Ground
13
Oi Sen Path
KCR
Ping Chi St
Station La
Wuhu St
Cooke St
Winslow St
Gillies Ave South
Bulkeley St
Whampoa St
Baker St
Gascoigne Rd
Chatham Rd South
KCR East
Cheong Wan Rd
HUNG HOM
Hung Hom South St
Jordan Path
Hong Chong Rd
Yuk Choi Rd
Hong Kong Polytechnic University
Austin Rd
173
Austin
55
Ave Rd
Cheong Wan Rd
186
Hung Hom
Cheong Wan Rd
Chatham Ct
Kimberley
45
39
130
Observatory Rd
91
8
10
Concordia Plaza
New East Ocean Centre
Hong Chong Rd
87
134
Granville Rd
Science Museum Rd
84
27
Granville Rd
Circuit
90
115
Granville
106
155
Energy Plaza
41
Granville Sq
39
Chinachem Golden Plaza
Hong Kong International Mail Centre
TSIM SHA TSUI EAST
138
132
169
Cameron Rd
145
29
31
Prat Ave
61
Chatham Rd South
Auto Plaza
53
Peninsula Centre
159
Mody Rd
161
Empire Centre
Hung Hom Bypass
Cross-Harbour Tunnel
Hart Ave
65
67
Centenary Gardens
Mody Sq
42
Houston Centre
Tsim Sha Tsui Centre
71
Mirror Tower
Salisbury Rd
Tsim Sha Tsui East Promenade
63
99
East Tsim Sha Tsui
143
Wing On Plaza
Signal Hill Garden
Tsim Sha Tsui East Ferry Pier
30
94
1
Victoria Harbour
To Central (1km)
Haiphong Rd
119
108
97
Fuk Tak Temple
Haiphong Road Market
Nathan Rd
32
47
Ashley Rd
Hankow Rd
Lock Rd
Tsim Sha Tsui
Kowloon Park Dr
69
26
78
6
111
70
38
49
114
117
25
I Chang St
76
100
88
189
33
57
66
101
144
124
Peking Rd
104
74
21
178
171
0 100 m

Map key continued from p420

Food Stalls 34 D4
Food Stalls 35 C1
Fook Lam Moon 36 E3
Gaddi's 37 D5
Gaylord 38 G6
Genki Sushi 39 E4
Golden Bull 40 C5
Gomitori 41 E4
Good Satay 42 E4
Happy Garden Noodle & Congee Kitchen 43 C4
Hard Rock Café 44 C5
Hong Kong Old Restaurant (see 102)
Indonesian Restaurant 1968 45 E3
Island Seafood & Oyster Bar 46 D3
Jade Garden (see 93)
Jimmy's Kitchen 47 G5
King Palace (see 133)
Koh-I-Noor 48 D5
Kyozasa 49 G6
Kyushu-Ichiban 50 D3
Margaux (see 143)
Merhaba 51 D3
Miu Gute Cheong Vegetarian Restaurant 52 D2
Nadaman (see 143)
New North Sea Fishing Village 53 E4
Oliver's Super Sandwiches (Canton Rd) (see 40)
Oliver's Super Sandwiches (Nathan Rd) 54 D4
Orphée 55 E3
Peking Restaurant 56 D2
Pep 'n' Spices 57 G6
Royal Garden Chinese Restaurant (see 161)
Ruby Tuesday 58 B5
Sabatini (see 161)
Saint's Alp Teahouse 59 D3
Salisbury Dining Room 60 C5
Schnurrbart 61 E4
Shabu Shabu 62 D3
Singapore Restaurant (see 38)
Spoon By Alain Ducasse (see 136)
Spring Deer 63 E5
Spring Moon (see 37)
Sweet Dynasty 64 C4
Tai Fung Lau Peking Restaurant 65 E4
Three-Five Korean Restaurant 66 G6
Tony Roma's (see 102)
Valentino 67 E4
Wan Loong Court 68 D5
Weinstube 69 G5
Wellcome 70 H5
Woodlands 71 E4
Wu Kong Shanghai Restaurant (see 21)
Xi (see 137)
XTC on Ice 72 C6
Yan Toh Heen (see 136)

DRINKING (pp197-206)
Aqua Spirit (see 22)
Bar (see 157)
Biergarten 73 D4
Courtney's (see 151)
Delaney's 74 H6
La Tasca 75 D5
Mes Amis 76 G6
New Wally Matt Lounge 77 D4
Organ Bar 78 G5
Sky Lounge (see 166)
Tony's Bar 79 D5
Watering Hole 80 D5

ENTERTAINMENT (pp197-206)
48th Street Chicago Blues 81 D4
Bahama Mama's 82 D3
Chasers 83 D3
Club Bboss 84 F4
Club de Millennium 85 D4
Grand Ocean Cinema 86 C5
Hari's (see 135)
Hong Kong Coliseum 87 G3
Ned Kelly's Last Stand 88 G6
Rick's Café 89 E3
Wally Matt Lounge 90 E4

SHOPPING (pp227-48)
Alan Chan Creations (see 157)
Beverley Commercial Centre 91 E3
Burlington Arcade & Milton Mansion (see 113)
Burlington Arcade (see 152)
Chinese Arts & Crafts 92 D1
Chinese Arts & Crafts 93 C5
Chinese Carpet Centre 94 E6
Chinese Carpet Centre (see 42)
Chung Yuen Electrical Co (see 123)
City Chain 95 D4
Cosmos Books 96 D4
Curio Alley 97 H5
David Chan Photo Shop 98 D4
Eu Yan Sang 99 E5
Fook Ming Tong Tea Shop (see 23)
Giga Sports (see 105)
Golf Creation 100 H6
HMV 101 G6
i.t 102 D4
King Fook 103 D4
King Sing Jewellery (see 93)
KS Ahluwalia & Sons 104 H6
Lane Crawford 105 B5
Lids 106 E4
Minamoto Kitchoan 107 D4
Ming's Sports Company 108 G5
Miramar Shopping Centre 109 D3
Monitor Records 110 D2
Museum Bookshop (see 7)
Ocean Optical (see 123)
Ocean Sky Divers 111 H5
Om International 112 D4
Onesto Photo Company (see 98)
Opal Mine 113 D4
Page One (see 123)
Ponti Food & Wine Cellar 114 H6
Premier Jewellery (see 135)
Rise Commercial Centre 115 E4
Sam's Tailor (see 113)
Shopping Arcade 116 C5
Spy (see 115)
Star Computer City (see 93)
Swindon Books 117 H6
Swindon Books (see 123)
Tom Lee Music Company 118 D4
Travellers' Home 119 G5
Travelmax (see 105)
Tse Sui Luen 120 D3
Up Date Mall 121 D5
Wing On 122 C1
wwwizzuecom 123 C5
Yue Hwa Chinese Products Emporium 124 G6
Yue Hwa Chinese Products Emporium 125 D3
Yue Hwa Chinese Products Emporium 126 D2

SLEEPING (pp249-74)
BP International Hotel 127 C3
Chungking House (see 128)
Chungking Mansions 128 D5
Cosmic Guest House (see 152)
Dragon Inn (see 128)
Eaton Hotel 129 D1
Empire Kowloon 130 E3
First-Class Guest House (see 152)
Garden Guest House (see 128)
Garden Hostel (see 152)
Golden Crown Court 131 D4
Golden Crown Guest House (see 131)
Grand Stanford Inter-Continental 132 F4
Guangdong International Hotel 133 E4
Hakka's Guest House (see 154)
Harbour Plaza Metropolis 134 G3
Holiday Inn Golden Mile 135 D5
Hong Kong Hotels Association (see 190)
Hotel Inter-Continental Hong Kong 136 D6
Hotel Miramar Hong Kong 137 D4
Hotel Nikko Hongkong 138 F4
Hung Kiu Guest House (see 152)
Imperial Hotel 139 D5
Kimberley Hotel 140 D4
Knutsford 141 D3
Kowloon Hotel Hong Kong 142 D5
Kowloon Shangri-La 143 E5
Kyoto Guest House (see 128)
Langham Hotel Hong Kong 144 G6
Lee Garden Guest House 145 E4
Lily Garden Hostel 146 D5
Lucky Guesthouse (see 146)
Majestic Hotel 147 D1
Man Hing Lung Hotel (see 146)
Marco Polo Gateway 148 C4
Marco Polo Hongkong Hotel 149 C5
Marco Polo Prince 150 C4
Minden 151 D5
Mirador Mansion 152 D5
Nathan Hotel 153 D1
New Lucky House 154 D2
New Shanghai Guest House (see 128)
Ocean Guest House (see 154)
Overseas House (see 154)
Park Guest House (see 128)
Park Hotel 155 E4
Peking Guest House 156 D5
Peninsula Hong Kong 157 D5
Pinnacle Apartment 158 D5
Regal Kowloon Hotel 159 F4
Rent-a-Room Hong Kong 160 D2
Royal Garden Hotel 161 E4
Royal Pacific Hotel & Towers 162 C4
Salisbury 163 C5
Sealand House 164 D4
Shamrock Hotel 165 D2
Sheraton Hong Kong Hotel & Towers 166 D5
Stanford Hillview Hotel 167 D3
Star Guest House 168 D4
Tom's Guest House (see 156)
Travellers Hostel (see 156)
Welcome Guest House (see 156)
Yan Yan Guest House (see 156)

TRANSPORT (pp287-306)
Avis 169 E4
Cross-Border Coach Terminus (Buses to China) 170 C3
Eternal East Cross Border Coach (Buses to China) 171 H6
Harbour Sighseeing Cruise Pier 172 C5
Phoenix Services Agency 173 E3
Star Ferry Bus Terminal 174 C6
Traveller Services (see 190)
West Kowloon Heliport 175 A1

INFORMATION
1010 CSL Outlet 176 C4
Citibank 177 D4
Cyber Clan (see 131)
Hang Seng Bank 178 H6
HKTB Centre 179 C6
Hong Kong Dolphinwatch (see 93)
HSBC 180 C6
HSBC 181 D5
HSBC 182 D4
International Women's League 183 B1
Kowloon Central Post Office 184 C1
Map Publications Centre 185 D1
Metropolis Mall 186 G3
Pacific Coffee Company (see 102)
PCCW i Shop 187 D4
Queen Elizabeth Hospital 188 E1
Shadowman Cyber Cafe 189 H6
Silvercord Towers & Shopping Centre 190 C5
Sincerity Travel/Hong Kong Student Travel (see 93)
Sunshine Laundry 191 D2
Towngas Cooking Centre (see 94)
Tsim Sha Tsui Post Office 192 D5
Watertours (see 93)
Wing Hoi Money Exchange (see 152)
Yau Ma Tei Police Station 193 C1

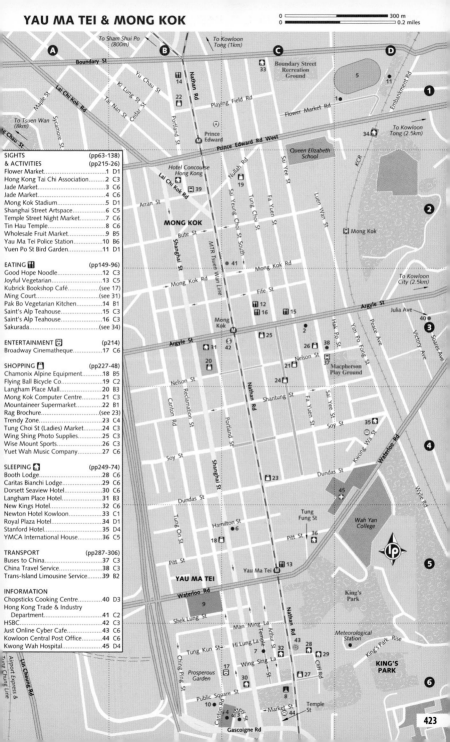

TSUEN WAN

0 — 500 m
0 — 0.3 miles

SIGHTS & ACTIVITIES (pp63-138) (pp215-26)
Chuk Lam Sim Monastery...................1 B2
Sam Tung Uk Museum......................2 C3
Tin Hau Temple..................................3 C3
Western Monastery...........................4 C1

EATING (pp149-96)
Grand Buffet & Balcony Restaurants..(see 6)
Park 'N' Shop..................................(see 13)

ENTERTAINMENT (p213)
Tsuen Wan Town Hall........................5 A3

SLEEPING (p270)
Panda Hotel.....................................6 C3

To Tsuen Kam Au (5km)
Tai Mo Shan Country Park
To Yuen Yuen Institute (1km)
Hilltop Rd
Lo Wai Rd
To Sam Tung Uk Rd (4km)
Cheung Pei Shan Rd
To Tuen Mun (18km)
Fu Yung Shan Rd
Ma Sim Pai Rd
Shek Wai Kok Rd
Route Twisk
Discovery Park
Castle Peak Rd -Tsuen Wan
Tai Ho Rd North
Wai Tsuen Rd
Texaco Rd North
Tam Path
Tai Chung Rd
Hoi Pa St
Tso Kung St
Sha Tsui Rd
Tsuen Wan
Heung Wo St
Tai Pa St
Yuen Tun Cir
Tai Ho Rd
Chuen Lung St
Tsuen Wan Market/Food Stalls
Shiu Wo St
Castle Peak Rd
Kwu Uk La
Sam Tung Uk Gardens
Sai Lau Kok Rd
Shing Mun Rd
Tai Wo Hau
Castle Peak Rd
Tai Pei Square
Chung On St
Ham Tin St
Tak Wah Park
Tak Hoi St
Tsuen Wan Market St
Tak Wah St
Yan Chai St
Kwan Mun Hau St
To Sam Pei Square

TRANSPORT (pp287-306)
Bus 43X...7 B3
Bus 51 (on Overpass).......................8 B2
Bus 53...9 B3
Bus 930..10 B3
Bus Station.....................................11 B3
Minibuses 81, 82 & 85....................12 B3

INFORMATION
Luk Yeung Galleria..........................13 B3
Yan Chai Hospital...........................14 B3

TAI PO

0 — 500 m
0 — 0.3 miles

To San Mun Tsai (4.5km)
On Chee Rd
On Cheung Rd
Tai Po Plaza
On Pong Rd
Tai Po Tai Wo Rd
KCR Railway
Tai Po Centre
To Lam Tsuen Wishing Tree (3km)
Tai Wo
Tai Wo Bridge
Po Nga Rd
Lam Tsuen River
Tai Po Tai Wo Rd
To San Mun Tsai (5.5km); Tai Mei Tuk (8.5km)
Pak Shing St
Po Yick St
TAI PO HUI
Sui On St
Yan Hing St
Fu Shin St
Tsing Yuen St
Wai Yan St
Plover Cove Rd
Clothing Market
Luk Heung La
Kwong Fuk Rd
Hong Ka Rd
On Fu Rd
Wai Yi St
Four Lanes Square
Tai Wing La
Tai Kwong La
Tai Ming La
Wan Tai St
Shung Tak St
Po Heung St
Po Heung Sze Wui St
Covered Tai Po Market
Wan Tau Kok La
Park & Sports Ground
To Bus Terminal; Uptown Plaza; Minibus/Maxicab Terminal (400m)

SIGHTS & ACTIVITIES (pp63-138) (pp215-26)
Hong Kong Railway Museum...........1 B3
Man Mo Temple................................2 B2
Old Tai Po District Office..................3 D3
Tai Po Market..................................4 C2

EATING (pp149-96)
Cosmopolitan Curry House...............5 C2
Emperor Sushi...................................6 C3
Shalimar..7 D2

TRANSPORT (pp287-306)
Bus & Minibus Stop..........................8 C3
Bus & Minibus Stop..........................9 C1
Bus Stop 70,72,72A & 74................10 C2
Minibus 25K...................................11 C2

A   B   C   D

SHA TIN

0 ———————————— 500 m
0 ———————————— 0.3 miles

SIGHTS	(pp63-138)
& ACTIVITIES	(pp215-26)
Bicycle Rentals	1 B2
Che Kung Temple	2 A3
Hong Kong Heritage Museum	3 B3
Sha Tin Super Bowl	(see 6)
Swimming Pool	4 C2

EATING	(pp149-96)
A-1 Bakery	(see 7)
A-1 Restaurant	(see 7)
Kaga Japanese Restaurant	(see 7)
Koh-I-Noor	(see 7)
One One Pasta	(see 7)
Saints Alp Teahouse	(see 7)

ENTERTAINMENT	(p212)
Sha Tin Town Hall	5 B2

SHOPPING	(pp227-48)
City One Plaza Sha Tin	6 D1
New Town Plaza	7 B2

SLEEPING	(pp249-74)
Regal Riverside Hotel	8 C2
Royal Park Hotel	9 B2

TRANSPORT	(p306)
China Travel Service	(see 7)

INFORMATION	
Prince of Wales Hospital	10 D2

To Hong Kong Jockey Club;
Sha Tin Racecourse (500m);
Tai Po (10km)

Fo Tan Rd

Banyan
Bridge

Sui Lek
Yuen Rd

City One

Yuen Wo Rd

Shing Mun River

Tai Chung Kiu Rd

Pai Tau St
To 10,000
Buddhas
Monastery
(500m)

KCR East Rail

Sha Tin Rural Committee Rd

YUEN CHAU
KOK

Yuen Chau Kok Rd

Sha Tin Rd

Ngan Shing St

Sha Tin

Centre St

Tai Po Rd

To Ascension
House (200m)

Tung Lo
Wan Hill Rd

Tao Fong

Lion Rock

Pak Hok
Ting St

Sha Tin
Park

Lek Yuen
Bridge

Sha Lek Hwy

Ma On
Shan Rail

SHA TIN
WAI

Sha Tin Wai

TO SHEK

Shing Mun Tunnel Rd

TAI
WAI

Shing Chuen Rd

Man Lam
Rd

Tunnel Rd

Tai Chung Kiu Rd

Sha Kok St

Che Kung
Temple

Che Kung Miu Rd

To Amah Rock (3.5km);
Kowloon (6km)

Sha Tin Rd

Tai Wai

SAI KUNG TOWN

0 ———————————— 200 m
0 ———————————— 0.1 miles

To Sai
Kung Park Entrance (100m);
Sha Ha (750m);
Windsurfing Centre (750m)

Tang Shiu Kin
Sports Ground

Swimming
Pool

Po Tung Rd

Sai Kung
Town Hall

Fuk Man Rd

Sai Kung
Sports Centre

Wai Man Rd

Chan Man St

Man Nin St

Sha Tsui Path:
Children's
Playground

Hoi Pong
Square

Pier

Fruit
Stands

Tin Hau
Temple

Wan King Path

Nin Chun St

Sai Kung
Market

Yi Chun St

Old
Town

See Cheung St

Sai Kung Hoi
(Inner Port
Shelter)

EATING	(pp149-96)
Ali-Oli	4 B2
Chuen Kee Seafood Restaurant	5 B2
Dia	6 B1
Firenze	7 A2
Hung Kee Seafood Restaurant	8 B2
Indian Curry Hut	9 A2
Jaspa's	10 B2
Park 'N' Shop	11 B1
Pepperoni's Pizza	12 A2
Sai Square	13 C2
Sauce	14 B2
Steamers Bar & Restaurant	15 A1
Tung Kee Restaurant	16 B3
Tung Kee Restaurant Branch	17 B3
Wellcome	18 A1

DRINKING	(pp197-206)
Duke of York Pub	19 B2
Poets	20 A2
Xtreme Bar & Restaurant	21 A2

TRANSPORT	(pp287-306)
Bus Terminus	22 B2
Hong Kong & Kowloon Taxis	23 B2
Maxicab/Minibus Terminus	24 B2
New Territories Taxis	25 B2

INFORMATION	
HSBC	26 A2
Post Office	27 B2

SIGHTS	(pp63-138)
& ACTIVITIES	(pp215-26)
High Island Reservoir Doloose	1 B3
Jockey Club Kau Sai Chau Public	
Golf Course Pier	2 C1
Sampan Hire	3 B2

LAMMA

SIGHTS (pp63-138)
& ACTIVITIES (pp215-26)
Herboland..1 B4
Hoi Nam Gift & Bicycle Shop...........2 A3
Tin Hau Temple..............................3 C5
Tin Hau Temple..............................4 A3

EATING 🍴 (pp149-96)
Blue Bird.......................................5 B6
Bookworm Café.............................6 B6
Cococabana...................................7 C4
Concerto Inn.................................8 B4
Deli Lamma Café............................9 B6
Han Lok Yuen................................10 B3
Lamma Bistro................................11 B6

Lamma Hilton Shum Kee Seafood
   Restaurant.................................12 C4
Lancombe Seafood Restaurant........13 B6
Man Fung Seafood Restaurant........14 B5
Pizza Milano.................................15 B6
Rainbow Seafood Restaurant.......(see 12)
Sampan Seafood Restaurant..........16 B5
Spicy Island..................................17 B6
Tai Yuen Restaurant....................(see 12)

DRINKING 🍷 (pp197-206)
Diesel's Bar...................................18 B6
Fountainhead Drinking Bar.............19 B5
Island Society Bar..........................20 B5

SLEEPING 🛏 (pp249-74)
Bali Holiday Resort.........................21 B5
Concerto Inn1............................(see 8)
Jackson Property Agency................22 B5
Man Lai Wah Hotel........................23 B5

INFORMATION
HSBC..24 B5
Post Office....................................25 B5

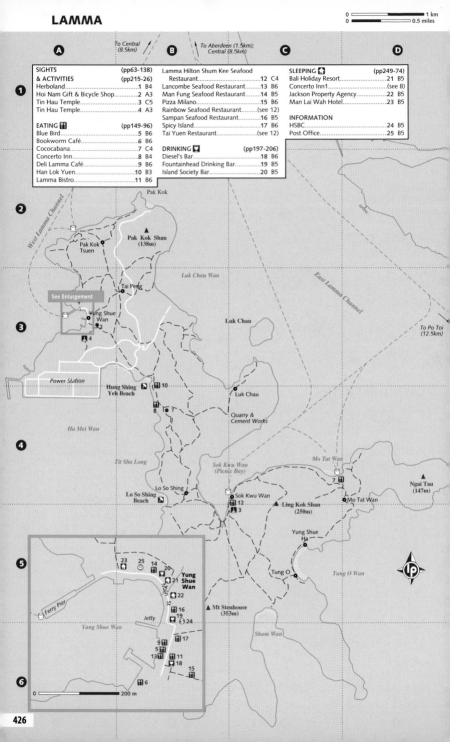

LANTAU

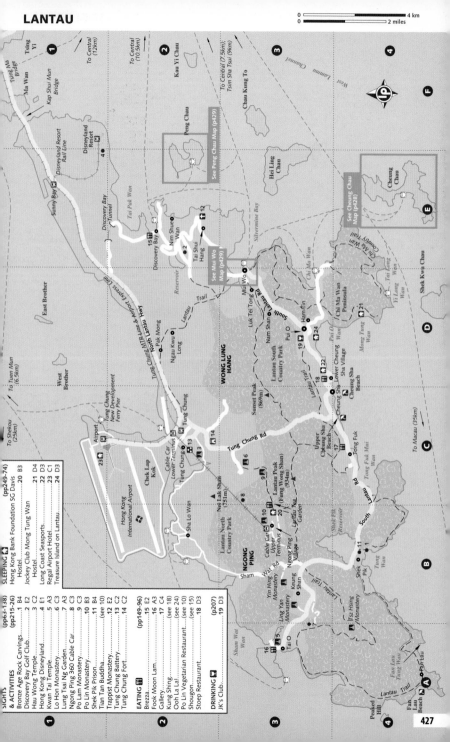

0 ——————— 4 km
0 ——————— 2 miles

SIGHTS (pp63-188)
& ACTIVITIES
Bronze Age Rock Carvings..........1 B4
Discovery Bay Golf Club.............2 C2
Hau Wong Temple......................3 C2
Hong Kong Disneyland...............4 E1
Kwan Tai Temple........................5 A3
Lo Hon Monastery......................6 C3
Lung Tsai Ng Garden..................7 B3
Ngong Ping 360 Cable Car.........8 C3
Po Lam Monastery......................9 C3
Po Lin Monastery.....................10 B3
Shek Pik Prison.......................11 B4
Tian Tan Buddha.................(see 10)
Trappist Monastery.................12 E2
Tung Chung Battery.................13 C2
Tung Chung Fort.....................14 C2

EATING (pp149-96)
Brezza....................................15 E2
Fook Moon Lam.......................16 A3
Gallery..................................17 C4
Kung Shing..........................(see 18)
Ooh La La!...........................(see 24)
Po Lin Vegetarian Restaurant...(see 10)
Shougon..............................(see 15)
Stoep Restaurant.....................18 D3

DRINKING (p207)
JK's Club.................................19 D3

SLEEPING (pp249-74)
Hong Kong Bank Foundation SG Davis
Hostel.....................................20 B3
Jockey Club Mong Tung Wan
Hostel.....................................21 D4
Long Coast Seasports..............22 D3
Regal Airport Hotel..................23 C1
Treasure Island on Lantau........24 D3

See Peng Chau Map (p429)
See Cheung Chau Map (p428)
See Mui Wo Map (p429)

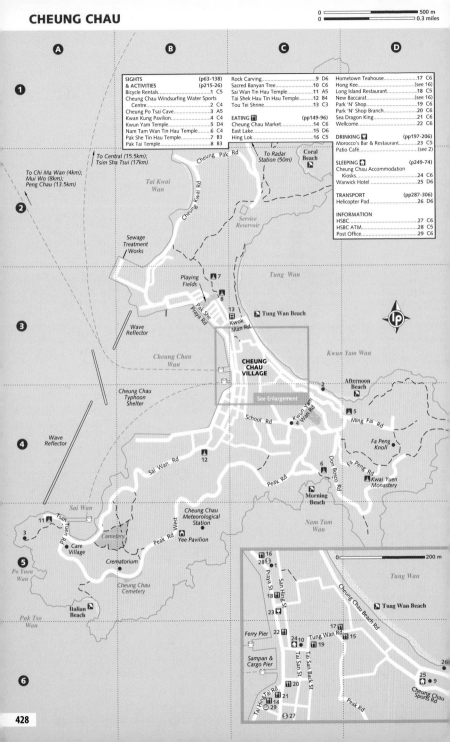

0 — 500 m
0 — 0.3 miles

SIGHTS & ACTIVITIES (p63-138) (p215-26)
Bicycle Rentals..................................1 C5
Cheung Chau Windsurfing Water Sports
   Centre...2 C4
Cheung Po Tsai Cave........................3 A5
Kwan Kung Pavilion..........................4 C4
Kwun Yam Temple.............................5 D4
Nam Tam Wan Tin Hau Temple.........6 C4
Pak She Tin Hau Temple....................7 B3
Pak Tai Temple.................................8 B3

Rock Carving...................................9 D6
Sacred Banyan Tree.........................10 C6
Sai Wan Tin Hau Temple..................11 A5
Tai Shek Hau Tin Hau Temple..........12 B4
Tou Tei Shrine.................................13 C3

EATING (pp149-96)
Cheung Chau Market........................14 C6
East Lake.......................................15 D6
Hing Lok..16 C5

Hometown Teahouse........................17 C6
Hong Kee.................................(see 16)
Long Island Restaurant....................18 C6
New Baccarat...........................(see 16)
Park 'N' Shop................................19 C6
Park 'N' Shop Branch.......................20 C6
Sea Dragon King.............................21 C6
Wellcome.......................................22 C6

DRINKING (pp197-206)
Morocco's Bar & Restaurant...........23 C5
Patio Café..................................(see 2)

SLEEPING (p249-74)
Cheung Chau Accommodation
   Kiosks.......................................24 C6
Warwick Hotel................................25 D6

TRANSPORT (pp287-306)
Helicopter Pad...............................26 D6

INFORMATION
HSBC...27 C6
HSBC ATM......................................28 C5
Post Office.....................................29 C6

To Central (15.5km);
Tsim Sha Tsui (17km)

To Chi Ma Wan (4km);
Mui Wo (8km);
Peng Chau (13.5km)

To Radar
Station (50m)

Coral
Beach

Cheung Pak Rd

Tai Kwai
Wan

Cheung Kwai Rd

Service
Reservoir

Sewage
Treatment
Works

Playing
Fields

Pak She Praya Rd

Kwok Man Rd

Tung Wan Beach

Tung Wan

Wave
Reflector

Cheung Chau
Wan

CHEUNG
CHAU
VILLAGE

Kwun Yam Wan

Cheung Chau
Typhoon
Shelter

See Enlargement

Afternoon
Beach

Wave
Reflector

School Rd

Kwun Yam Wan Rd

Ming Fai Rd

Fa Peng
Knoll

Sai Wan Rd

Fa Peng Rd

Kwai Yuen
Monastery

Don Bosco Rd

Peak Rd

Morning
Beach

Nam Tam
Wan

Po Yuen
Wan

Tsan Tuen Pak

Cheung Chau
Meteorological
Station

Yee Pavilion

Care
Village

Cemetery

Crematorium

Cheung Chau
Cemetery

Peak Rd West

Italian
Beach

Pak Tso
Wan

0 — 200 m

Praya St

San Hing St

Ferry Pier

Cheung Chau Beach Rd

Tung Wan

Tung Wan Beach

Tung Wan Rd

Tai San St

Tai San Back St

Sampan &
Cargo Pier

Tai Hing Tai Rd

Peak Rd

Cheung Chau
Sports Rd

MUI WO (LANTAU)

0 _____ 200 m
0 _____ 0.1 miles

WANG TONG

To Trappist Monastery (2.5km)

To Silvermine Cave, Waterfall & Garden (3km)

Barbecue Pits & Picnic Tables

Silvermine Bay Beach

Butterfly Hill (67m)

Silvermine Bay

Mui Wo Rural Committee Rd

Silver River

Ngan Kwong Wan Rd

NGAN WAN ESTATE

To Peng Chau (5.5km)

To Tsim Sha Tsui (15km); Central (15.5km)

To Chi Ma Wan (5km); Cheung Chau (8km)

South Lantau Rd

Ferry Pier Rd

Mui Wo

Ngan Wan Rd

Ferry Pier

SIGHTS & ACTIVITIES	(pp63-138) (pp215-26)
Bike Shop	1 D3
Butterfly Hill Watchtower	2 B1
Friendly Bicycle Shop	3 D3
Luk Tei Tong Watchtower	4 B3
Man Mo Temple	5 A1
Mui Wo Swimming Pool	6 B3
Rental Bicycles	7 C2
Rental Bicycles	8 C2

EATING	(pp149-96)
Bahçe	9 D3
Hippo Bar Restaurant	10 D3
Jaks	11 D3
La Pizzeria	12 D3
Mui Wo Cooked Food Market	13 D3
Mui Wo Market	14 B2
Park 'N' Shop	15 D3
Rome Restaurant	16 D3
Silvermine Beach Hotel Restaurant	(see 24)
Tak Chai Kee Seafood Restaurant	17 C3
Wellcome	18 D3

DRINKING	(pp197-206)
China Beach Club	19 C1
China Bear	20 D3

SLEEPING	(pp249-74)
Mui Wo Accommodation Kiosks	21 D3
Mui Wo Inn	22 C1
Seaview Holiday Resort	23 C1
Silvermine Beach Hotel	24 C1

TRANSPORT	(pp287-306)
Bus Terminal & Taxi Rank	25 D3
Ferries to Discovery Bay	26 D3

INFORMATION	
Country & Marine Parks Authority Information Kiosk	27 D3
HSBC	28 D3
Mui Wo Clinic	29 C3
Post Office	30 C3

PENG CHAU

0 _____ 200 m
0 _____ 0.1 miles

To Transmitting Radio Station (300m)

Transmitting Radio Station

Tung Wan

To Tai Lei Island (100m)

Tung Wan

BBQ Area

Kam Fa Temple

Tung Wan Beach

To Trappist Monastery (1.8km); Discovery Bay (3km)

Park

Lo Peng

Po Peng St

Wing On St

Lung Mo Temple

Ferry Pier

Pier

Wing Hing St

Shing Ka Rd

Finger Hill (95m)

Wave Reflector

Nam Shan Rd

Yuen Tong Monastery

To Mui Wo (5.5km); Cheung Chau (13.5km)

To Central (13km)

SIGHTS & ACTIVITIES	(pp63-138) (pp215-26)
Peng Chau Market	1 B2
Tin Hau Temple	2 B2

EATING	(pp149-96)
Typhoon Shelter	3 B2
Wellcome	4 A2

DRINKING	(p207)
Forest Bar & Restaurant	5 B2

INFORMATION	
HSBC	6 B2
Post Office	7 B2

SIGHTS & ACTIVITIES (pp341-60)

A-Ma Temple.....................................1 A6
Bank of China Building........................2 C5
Bishop's Palace................................(see 5)
Casa Garden....................................3 B3
Cemetery of St Michael the
    Archangel...................................4 C3
Chapel of Our Lady of Guia..................(see 13)
Chapel of Our Lady of Penha.................5 A5
Chapel of St Michael..........................(see 4)
Cybernetic Fountains...........................6 B5
Cybernetic Fountains...........................7 B5
Fire Services Museum...........................8 C3
Government House...............................9 B5
Grand Prix Museum.............................(see 36)
Grand Prix Viewing Stand.....................10 D4
Guia Cable Car Lower Terminus..............11 D3
Guia Cable Car Upper Terminus..............12 D3
Guia Fort.......................................13 D3
Guia Lighthouse...............................(see 13)
Handover of Macau Gifts Museum.............14 E5
Kun Iam Statue & Ecumenical
    Centre.......................................15 D6
Kun Iam Temple................................16 D2
Lin Fung Temple................................17 D1
Lin Zexu Memorial Hall........................18 D1
Lou Lim Ioc Pavilion...........................19 D3
Macau Convention & Entertainment
    Centre.......................................(see 23)
Macau Cultural Centre..........................20 E5
Macau Fisherman's Wharf.......................21 E4
Macau Forum....................................22 D4
Macau Museum...................................(see 26)
Macau Museum of Art............................(see 20)
Macau Security Forces Museum.................(see 32)
Macau Tower.....................................23 B7
Maritime Museum................................24 A6
Macau Wine Museum..............................25 D2
Mong Há Fort Ruins.............................26 C4
Monte Fort.....................................(see 30)
Museum of Sacred Art & Crypt...............27 B3
Old Protestant Cemetery.......................28 C2
Oriental Foundation............................(see 3)
Ox Warehouse...................................29 B6
Residence of the Portuguese Consul
    General......................................30 B4
Ruins of the Church of St Paul...............31 C4
Ruins of the College of the Mother
    of God.......................................32 C4
St Francis Barracks.............................33 A6
Santa Sancha Palace.............................34 D3
Sun Yat Sen Memorial Home.....................35 D3
Tap Seac Gallery................................36 D4
Tourist Activities Centre.....................(see 13)

EATING (pp362-7)

A Lorcha.......................................37 A6
A Vencedora....................................38 D4
Almirante Lacerda City Market................39 C2
Antica Trattoria da Isa........................40 D5
Aruna..41 D5
Carlos...42 D5
Clube Militar de Macau........................43 C5
Fook Lam Mun Restaurant......................44 C4
Henri's Gallery...............................45 A6
Ko Lung..46 C4
Litoral..47 A5
Mezzaluna.....................................(see 75)
Naam...(see 69)
New Yaohan Supermarket........................48 D4
Papa Tudo......................................49 D2
Park 'N' Shop.................................(see 75)
Pizzeria Toscana..............................50 A5
Plaza..(see 83)
Porto Exterior.................................51 D5
Praia Grande...................................52 C6
Robuchon a Galera.............................53 C5
Serradura......................................54 D2

DRINKING (pp367-8)

Casablanca Café................................55 D5
Champagne Lounge Bar..........................56 D6
Embassy Bar...................................(see 72)
Moonwalker Bar.................................57 D5
Oskar's Pub...................................(see 72)
Sanshiro Pub..................................58 D5

ENTERTAINMENT (pp367-9)

Canidrome......................................59 C1
Casa Real Casino..............................60 B4
Casino Kingsway................................61 D4
Crazy Paris Show.............................(see 74)
Diamond Casino...............................(see 72)
Fortuna Casino.................................62 D4
Galaxy Casino.................................63 E4
Golden Dragon Casino..........................64 E4
Jai Alai Casino..............................(see 64)
Jai Alai Show Palace..........................65 C5
Kam Pek Casino................................(see 73)
Legend Club....................................66 C5
Lisboa Casino.................................67 E4
Macau Palace Casino............................68 E4

Macau Sports Institute.......................(see 22)
Mandarin Oriental Casino.....................(see 75)
Pharaoh's Palace Casino......................(see 73)
Sands Macau....................................69 E4

SHOPPING (p362)

New Yaohan.....................................(see 48)

SLEEPING (pp371-3)

Fortuna Hotel..................................70 D5
Guia Hotel.....................................71 D4
Holiday Inn Macau.............................72 D5
Landmark Macau................................73 C5
Lisboa Hotel...................................74 C5
Mandarin Oriental.............................75 D5
Mondial Hotel..................................76 D3
Pousada de Mong Há............................77 D2
Pousada de Saõ Tiago..........................78 A6
Ritz Hotel.....................................79 B6
Royal Hotel....................................80 D4

TRANSPORT (pp374-6)

Air Macau......................................81 D5
Avis Rent A Car................................82 E4
Avis Rent A Car...............................(see 84)
China Travel Service..........................83 D4
Ferry Terminal.................................84 E4
Gray Line....................................(see 84)
Happy Rent A Car..............................85 C5
Heliport......................................(see 84)
New Spot Tourism Bike Rental................86 F3
                                              87 E5

INFORMATION

Central People's Government Macau
    SAR Liaison Office..........................88 D4
Conde Saõ Januário Central Hospital.........89 C4
CTM Main Office................................90 D3
Immigration Department........................91 E4
Kiang Wu Hospital..............................92 C3
Macau Government Tourist
    Office Branch..............................(see 13)
Macau Government Tourist
    Office Branch...............................93 B6
Macau Government Tourist
    Office Branch...............................94 D5
Macau Legislative Assembly Building..........(see 84)
Unesco Internet Café...........................(see 73)

Ponte da Amizade: Friendship Bridge

To Taipa (2.5km);
Airport (4km);
Coloane (7km)

Baía da Praia
Lagos de Nam Van

Ponte Governador Nobre de
Carvalho
(Macau-Taipa
Bridge)

To Taipa (2.5km);
Coloane (7km)

NAPE

Lago Sai
Van

To Taipa
(2km)

Sai Van Bridge

Grand Prix Circuit

0   500 m
0   0.3 miles

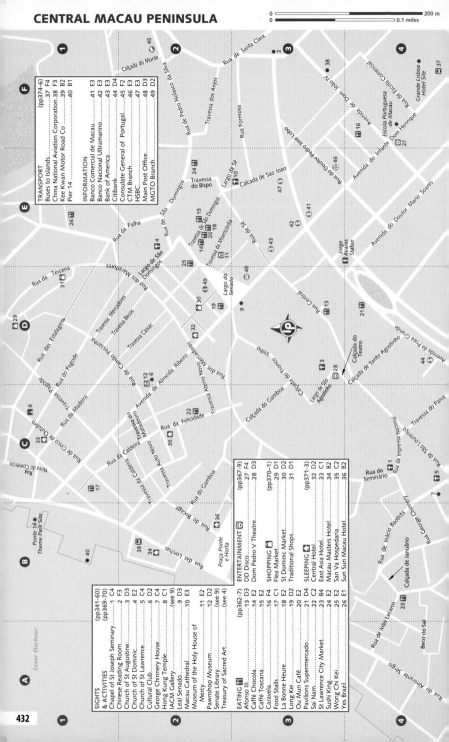

0 _____ 200 m
0 _____ 0.1 miles

TRANSPORT (pp374-6)
Buses to Islands....................37 F4
China National Aviation Corporation..38 F3
Kee Kwan Motor Road Co..........39 B2
Pier 14...................................40 B1

INFORMATION
Banco Comercial de Macau........41 E3
Banco Nacional Ultramarino.......42 E3
Bank of America.......................43 D4
Citibank..................................44 D4
Consulate General of Portugal....45 F2
CTM Branch.............................46 E3
HSBC......................................47 E3
Main Post Office.......................48 D3
MGTO Branch...........................49 D2

SIGHTS & ACTIVITIES (pp341-60) (pp869-70)
Chapel of St Joseph Seminary.......1 C4
Chinese Reading Room...................2 F3
Church of St Augustine...................3 D3
Church of St Dominic.....................4 C4
Church of St Lawrence....................5 C4
Cultural Club................................6 D2
George Chinnery House...................7 C4
Hong Kung Temple........................8 C1
IACM Gallery................................9 D2
Leal Senado...............................10 E3
Macau Cathedral.........................11 E2
Museum of the Holy House of
  Mercy....................................12 D2
Pawnshop Museum................(see 9)
Senate Library.....................(see 9)
Treasury of Sacred Art..........(see 4)

EATING (pp362-7)
Afonso III.................................13 D3
Caffé Chocola...........................14 E2
Caffé Toscana...........................15 E2
Caravela...................................16 F4
Food Stalls................................17 C1
La Bonne Heure.........................18 E2
Long Kei...................................19 D2
Ou Mun Café.............................20 D2
Pavilions Supermercado..............21 D4
Sai Nam....................................22 C2
St Lawrence City Market.............23 B4
Sushi King.................................24 E2
Wong Chi Kei............................25 E2
Yes Brazil..................................26 E1

ENTERTAINMENT (pp367-9)
DD Disco...................................27 F4
Dom Pedro V Theatre..................28 D3

SHOPPING (pp370-1)
Flea Market...............................29 D1
St Dominic Market......................30 D2
Traditional Shops.......................31 D1

SLEEPING (pp371-3)
Central Hotel.............................32 D2
East Asia Hotel..........................33 C1
Macau Masters Hotel..................34 E2
San Va Hospedaria.....................35 C2
Sun Sun Macau Hotel.................36 B2